The United States Government Internet Directory

The United States Government Internet Directory

Edited by Shana Hertz Hattis

Bernan Press

Lanham • Boulder • New York • London

Published by Bernan Press
An imprint of The Rowman & Littlefield Publishing Group, Inc.
4501 Forbes Boulevard, Suite 200, Lanham, Maryland 20706
www.rowman.com
800-865-3457; info@bernan.com

Unit A, Whitacre Mews, 26-34 Stannary Street, London SE11 4AB

ISBN: 978-1-59888-772-3

eISBN: 978-1-59888-773-0

ISSN: 1547-2892

∞™ The paper used in this publication meets the minimum requirements of American National Standard for Information Sciences Permanence of Paper for Printed Library Materials, ANSI/NISO Z39.48-1992.

Printed in the United States of America

Contents

Quick Guide to Primary Government Web Sites and Finding Aids

U.S. Congress

House of Representatives   http://www.house.gov/

Senate   http://www.senate.gov/

THOMAS   https://www.congress.gov/

U.S. Judiciary

Supreme Court of the United States   http://www.supremecourt.gov/

Administrative Office of the U.S. Courts   http://www.uscourts.gov/

U.S. President   http://www.whitehouse.gov/administration/president-obama

U.S. Vice President   http://www.whitehouse.gov/vicepresident/

Cabinet and Cabinet-Level Offices

Agriculture   http://www.usda.gov/

Commerce   http://www.commerce.gov/

Council of Economic Advisers   http://www.whitehouse.gov/administration/eop/cea

Defense   http://www.defense.gov/

Education   http://www.ed.gov/

Energy   http://www.energy.gov/

Environmental Protection Agency   http://www.epa.gov/

Health and Human Services	http://www.hhs.gov/
Homeland Security	http://www.dhs.gov/
Housing and Urban Development	http://www.hud.gov/
Interior	http://www.doi.gov/
Justice	http://www.justice.gov/
Labor	http://www.dol.gov/
Office of Management and Budget	http://www.whitehouse.gov/omb/
State	http://www.state.gov/
Transportation	http://www.dot.gov/
Treasury	http://www.treasury.gov/
U.S. Mission to the UN/New York	http://usun.state.gov/
U.S. Trade Representative	http://www.ustr.gov/
Veterans Affairs	http://www.va.gov/

Major Libraries, Catalogs, and Data Sources

Bureau of Labor Statistics	http://www.bls.gov/
Census Bureau	http://www.census.gov/
Data.gov	http://www.data.gov/
FedStats	http://fedstats.sites.usa.gov/
Government Printing Office	http://www.gpo.gov/
Library of Congress	http://www.loc.gov/
National Agricultural Library	http://www.nal.usda.gov/
National Archives and Records Administration	http://www.archives.gov/
National Institutes of Health	http://www.nih.gov/
National Library of Medicine	http://www.nlm.nih.gov/
National Technical Information Service	http://www.ntis.gov/

U.S. Government Finding Aids

FDsys   http://www.gpo.gov/fdsys/

USA.gov   http://www.usa.gov/

Preface

Due to its massive online presence, federal government–related information can be difficult to find, even with an Internet search engine. *The United States Government Internet Directory* is intended to lead its users to valuable government information that could otherwise be overlooked. The *Directory* organizes selected government and nongovernment Web sites into subject-themed chapters, covering topics such as Transportation and Energy, with an additional chapter for organizations and agencies that are either privately funded or funded significantly by entities beyond the U.S. government. This subject-based approach allows users to narrow their searches to solely encompass their fields of interest; this type of directed and specifically aimed method streamlines and tailors results for quick and efficient use. This book has been designed in order to help meet the research needs of businesses, teachers, students, and citizens in the United States and around the world. It also provides a resource that more casual users can employ to discover the breadth and depth of government-related information and services available online.

The *Directory* features entries for approximately 1,800 government and nongovernment Web sites. Each site was chosen for its value individually and as a part of the whole publication. Each site is described to help users define its role and its value as a resource. Web site descriptions can include information about the sponsoring agency, useful or unique aspects of the site, and when pertinent, lists of some of the publications hosted on the site. Appendixes provide Internet addresses for individual members of Congress, standing and joint committees, and embassies of the United States abroad and foreign countries within the United States.

Special features in the directory include a "Quick Guide" to the Web sites of major federal agencies, libraries, and data sources, as well as organizational charts for federal, congressional, and Cabinet-level agencies.

The staff of Rowman & Littlefield provided invaluable support in the creation of the 2015 edition.

The authors and site maintainers of the Web sites listed in this book provide a valuable service for writers, editors, students, and researchers alike—without them, this book would not be possible.

About the Editor

Shana Hertz Hattis, writer-editor of *The United States Government Internet Directory*, has worked as an editor and writer for nearly a decade. Her work has spanned the fields of hospitality, health, business, and popular culture. She earned her bachelor's degree in journalism and master's degree in education from Northwestern University. Hattis's other titles for Bernan include *Housing Statistics of the United States*, *Vital Statistics of the United States, 2014: Births, Life Expectancy, Deaths, and Selected Health Data*, and *State Profiles 2013: The Population and Economy of Each U.S. State*.

Introduction

The United States Government Internet Directory is a guide to the multitude of Web sites from the executive, judicial, and legislative branches of the U.S. federal government. As the federal Internet evolves slowly, the new entries and revised descriptions in the book reflect general trends. These trends are shaped by both changes in federal policies and in how people use the Internet.

The Obama presidential administration also encourages agency publication of data in open formats. "Open data" has been defined in various ways, but it generally refers to machine-readable data that can be downloaded in full and is free of charge or other restrictions. Many of the agencies have put open data sets on their Open Government Web pages, and these are available at Data.gov. Publishing open data enables citizens to use this data in their own analyses instead of relying on the government's statistical summaries.

The *Directory* does not make a separate entry for every agency blog but does often mention them in the site descriptions. Separate entries are provided for blogs that exceed the scope of the related Web site. RSS feeds are specially formatted current awareness news feeds, and their prevalence warrants mention throughout the book. USA.gov provides lists of government blogs and RSS feeds along with an explanation of these items. The online presence of agencies on popular social media sites like Facebook, Flickr, and Twitter has become common. Mobile sites and applications are not listed individually in the *Directory*; USA.gov provides a list at http://apps.usa.gov.

USING *THE UNITED STATES GOVERNMENT INTERNET DIRECTORY*

Web-based government information can be difficult to find, as the offerings are diverse, decentralized, and not uniformly indexed by search engines. The *Directory* presents some key advantages to sifting through this massive amount of information. It provides the context that is rarely found in an alphabetical list of agency links or in the nebulous results of a search engine query. It offers Web sites of value and identifies noteworthy resources, such as online publications and databases, within large sites.

Search engines are most helpful when a researcher is confident that certain information exists somewhere on the Web and can construct a search that produces the desired Web site within the first few pages of the search results. Even then, information may be missed because search engines cannot and do not find everything on the Web. The *Directory* offers complementary and overlapping approaches to browsing for government information, as it helps users discover new resources and quickly locate established resources that cannot be described via keyword search.

SCOPE

The *Directory* focuses on United States federal government information and services accessible via the Web. The majority of the Web sites described in this book are the products of federal government agencies. The book also includes sites from some interagency groups, international organizations, federal advisory boards and commissions, private organizations established by congressional legislation, and quasi-governmental organizations, as well as Web sites produced by outside organizations with federal agency sponsorship or partnerships. In addition, the *Directory* covers selected sites created by nongovernmental organizations to help researchers find federal government information; an excellent example of this type of site is the CyberCemetery, an online archive maintained by the University of North Texas Libraries to preserve the Web sites of defunct federal agencies and commissions. Specific CyberCemetery URLs are provided where appropriate. Also included are a number of Web sites either nominally or not at all funded by the government; these organizations have been included in order to supplement the governmental sites with those that provide related, yet additional, information.

The sites included in the *Directory* span a broad range of subjects and serve an equally broad range of audiences. The government Web sites selected for this publication are designed to meet the information needs of citizens, consumers, businesses, librarians, teachers, scientists, students, and others. For the most part, only sites that do not require payment or registration, or otherwise limit public access, are included. Exceptions to this policy are noted. Some sites are publicly accessible but block portions of their content; when significant, this is also noted.

Each entry typically represents one Web site or a distinct section of a site. In some cases, complementary or companion sites are described in the same entry. Due to the networked nature of the Web, it is sometimes difficult to define where one Web site ends and another begins. Some component databases, publications, or services considered to be of high value for researchers have been given their own entries.

ORGANIZATION

The *Directory*'s table of contents provides a start for browsing Web sites by topic. The table of contents shows the starting page numbers for the subject-oriented chapters and the sub-topic breakdown within those chapters.

Featured in the *Directory* is a "Quick Guide" to major federal Web sites, which can be found just after the table of contents. The Quick Guide includes URLs for frequently used government Web sites. Chapter 1 of the book, Finding Aids, is also a good starting point for researching information.

The book's introductory pages include organization charts for U.S. government agencies. Charts are provided for each Cabinet-level department and agency and for an overview of the United States government. The charts are based on similar organization charts from the departments' Web sites, when available. The charts include Web addresses for each organizational component, also when available. These organization charts are not intended to represent the complete or formal organization of government entities, but instead to provide a strong overview of their structure and a tool for locating government Web sources.

Other material in this introduction consists of an overview of government agencies' use of social media Web sites, a list of the types of information typically found on an agency Web site, and information on the Freedom of Information Act (FOIA)—a tool for obtaining government information not publicly accessible—with a list of agency FOIA offices.

Arranged alphabetically, the chapters are further divided by sub-topic. The Finding Aids chapter includes sites that encompass many subject areas. The book sections covering libraries and kids' pages also include many subject areas.

Individual entries are organized in the following manner:

Site Name: Leading each entry is a site name or title for the resource. For the purposes of this work, several sources are used to identify the site name: agency press releases referring to the site, the name given to the site in the HTML tag, or the name in initial heading or graphic. Because names of Web sites are subject to ambiguity and change and do not always uniquely identify a site, names are just one way to refer to a resource. The Uniform Resource Locator, or URL, is the best way to uniquely identify a resource, although even this is subject to change.

Primary URL: The Web address or URL indicates the location that should be entered in to retrieve the Web site.

Alternate URL (when necessary): For Web sites with several valid addresses or significant complementary Web sites, additional

URLs are listed in the "Alternate URL" field. The site description often explains the content connected to by the alternate URL.

Sponsors: This section identifies the lead organization or organizations that produce the site. Sponsors are typically federal government agencies, although commercial, educational, and nonprofit organizations are also listed when they host or sponsor a specific resource. Most of the government agencies listed are United States federal agencies; thus, "United States" has usually been dropped from the start of the sponsoring agency names in order to streamline the entries. For government agencies, the sponsor name in the entries usually includes a full or partial organizational hierarchy, such as "Agriculture Department—Economic Research Service." In some cases, the full hierarchy has been collapsed. Consult *The United States Government Internet Directory*, the agency's Web site, or other resources for official organizational information.

Description: The resource description explains a site's organization, principal features, menu items, and significant links. When pertinent, a brief description of the agency's mission is included to help delineate the site's subject coverage.

Subjects: The subject terms describe the primary focus or focuses of the entry. Some of the subject terms contain subheadings to more accurately represent the topic.

Publications: This section lists selected publications that are available from the Web site. The types of publications listed include important titles, series, and/or periodicals, but not every available publication is listed. Information for publications may also be incomplete. The Superintendent of Documents (SuDoc) number is used by the Federal Depository Library Program to identify and often to shelve print publications from the Government Printing Office. The root SuDoc number is most often used rather than the full SuDoc for each individual item, when available. Publications without SuDoc numbers are also included in this field.

Two appendixes at the end of the book list Web addresses for members of the House and Senate and for congressional committees.

At the back of the book, an index lists every Web site referenced.

HOW TO USE THIS BOOK

If You Want . . .	Consult . . .
Major department or agency Web site	U.S. government organization charts
Web sites on a specific topic	Table of contents, with chapters and chapter subtopics, or the index
Web site for which the name, but not the URL, is known	Index
Specific congressional contact information	Congressional appendixes
Embassy and ambassador information	Ambassadorial appendixes

What Can You Find at Agency Web Sites?

Executive Branch departments and agencies and related organizations vary widely in the amount and type of information they provide online, but some standard content can typically be found at these sites. A list of the type of content or features one might find at federal agency sites is provided here.

- Advisory council information
- Agency history
- Agency leadership biographies
- Agency leadership speeches and congressional testimony
- Budgets, annual reports, and strategic plans
- Business opportunities in the areas of agency acquisitions, contracting, and technology transfer programs
- Databases related to the regulatory, research, education, or outreach mission of the agency
- Education resources, career information, and pages designed for kids
- E-mail forms for submitting comments or questions
- Employment, fellowships, and/or internship opportunities
- Forms for program applications, regulatory requirements, and/or other purposes (many agencies have automated their program application or regulatory filing processes)
- Freedom of Information Act (FOIA) information and copies of popular documents previously requested via FOIA
- Frequently asked questions (FAQs) sections on programs or services
- Granting and funding information
- Information and reports from the agency's Office of the Inspector General
- Laws and regulations under which the agency operates or that they are responsible for enforcing
- Legal or administrative decisions, rulings, or guidance issued by the agency
- Links to nongovernmental Web sites on topics relevant to the agency's work
- Links to related federal, state, and tribal agencies

- Links to the agency's presence on social media sites such as Facebook or YouTube
- Links to the Web pages for the agency's departments, divisions, or regional offices
- Mobile applications that allow smartphone users access to the sites' contents
- Official documents, publications, and publication catalogs
- Press releases, media kits, fact sheets, and digital photos related to agency operations
- Program descriptions and mission statements
- Program information or publications in Spanish and/or additional languages
- Site search features and site indexes
- Statistics on programs or populations served
- User services including e-mail alerts, RSS news feeds, blogs, online video, and webcasts

Required Information for Executive Branch Agency Web Sites:

Agencies are required to provide certain Web content, such as information on their organizational structure and their Freedom of Information Act procedures. The list above includes, but is not limited to, required content.

Under President Obama, Cabinet-level departments and agencies have been required to provide information on their Recovery Act spending; sites usually have a */recovery* subdirectory for this information. Departments have also been directed to show their progress toward open government practices; the sites usually have a */open* subdirectory for this information. For examples, see these Department of Justice Web sites: http://www.justice.gov/open/ and http://www.justice.gov/recovery/ .

What to Watch for in 2015

Some key information for the use of government Web sites in 2015 and beyond is listed here.

- The government, led by the Office of Management and Budget, is continuing to trim its online offerings in order to reduce expense, streamline content, and unify redundant entities in the wake of the budget sequestration and subsequent shutdown
- The Census Bureau will continue to release data from the annual American Community Survey
- Redistricting from the 2010 Census took effect for the 2012 national elections. More information on the redistricting, which was critical to the outcomes of the midterm elections in 2014, can be found at this URL: http://www.census.gov/rdo/. Redistricting will also come into play for the 2016 presidential election
- The White House will continue to refine Performance.gov to track how well federal agencies are meeting performance goals
- FOIAOnline, the central FOIA request area of the U.S. government, as of early 2015, has incorporated the General Services Administration, the Small Business Administration, and the U.S. Citizenship and Immigration Services
- This year marks the end of the Civil War sesquicentennial remembrances. Information can be found at this URL: http://www.civilwar.org/150th-anniversary/

Freedom of Information Act (FOIA) Web Pages

The Freedom of Information Act (FOIA) grants public access to U.S. federal executive agency records, unless the records requested meet specific FOIA exemption criteria. Under FOIA, federal executive agency Web sites are required to include information about how to request records from the agency. Many agency Web sites also contain "Electronic Reading Rooms," or similar features, to fulfill FOIA requirements. These types of pages contain copies of frequently requested documents. Before submitting a FOIA request to an agency, be sure to check for current information and instructions, which are usually available on the agency's FOIA page.

The central unit responsible for guiding agency compliance with FOIA is the Department of Justice's Office of Information Policy (OIP), http://www.justice.gov/oip/oip.html. The OIP Web site includes guidance for citizens using FOIA and has a full list of links to other federal agency FOIA Web pages at http://www.justice.gov/oip/other_age.htm. A partial list of FOIA contacts for major agencies, along with links to the main agencies' online request forms, follows this introduction.

In late 2012, the FOIAOnline Web site was formed to serve as a device for making multiagency requests. At the time this book went to print, the following agencies and offices were participating: the Environmental Protection Agency, Department of Commerce (except the US Patent and Trademark Office), U.S. Customs and Border Protection, Office of General Counsel of the National Archives and Records Administration, Merit Systems Protection Board, Federal Labor Relations Authority, Federal Communications Commission, Pension Benefit Guaranty Corporation, Department of the Navy, General Services Administration, Small Business Administration, and U.S. Citizenship and Immigration Services. The site can be found at https://foiaonline.regulations.gov/foia/action/public/home.

Please note that the contact information will vary from agency to agency.

CABINET-LEVEL DEPARTMENTS AND AGENCIES

Department of Agriculture

Main FOIA site: http://www.dm.usda.gov/foia/
Individual agencies: http://www.dm.usda.gov/foia_agency_pocs.htm

Alexis Graves
1400 Independence Avenue SW
Room 428-W, Whitten Building
Washington, DC 20250-0706
Email: USDAFOIA@ocio.usda.gov
Online: https://efoia-pal.usda.gov/palMain.aspx

Department of Commerce

Main site: http://www.osec.doc.gov/omo/FOIA/FOIAWebsite.htm
Individual agencies: http://www.osec.doc.gov/omo/FOIA/contactfoia
.htm#bureaus

Brenda Dolan
Departmental Freedom of Information Officer
Office of Privacy and Open Government
14th and Constitution Avenue NW
Mail Stop A300
Washington, DC 20230
Phone: (202) 482-3258
E-mail: EFoia@doc.gov
Online: https://foiaonline.regulations.gov/foia/action/public/home

Department of Defense

Main site: http://www.dod.mil/pubs/foi/dfoipo/
Military services: http://www.dod.mil/pubs/foi/dfoipo/mil_services
.html
Defense agencies: http://www.dod.mil/pubs/foi/dfoipo/def_agencies
.html
Combatant Commands: http://www.dod.mil/pubs/foi/combatcomm
.html

Department of Defense
Defense Freedom of Information Division
1155 Defense Pentagon
Washington, DC 20301-1155
Phone: (866) 574-4970
Online: http://www.dod.mil/pubs/foi/

Department of Education

Main site: http://www2.ed.gov/policy/gen/leg/foia/foiatoc.html

U.S. Department of Education
Attn: FOIA Public Liaison
Office of Management
Office of the Chief Privacy Officer
400 Maryland Avenue, SW, LBJ 2E321
Washington, DC 20202-4536
Fax: (202) 401- 8365
E-mail: EDFOIAManager@ed.gov
   Online: http://www2.ed.gov/policy/gen/leg/foia/foia_request_form_1
.html

Department of Energy

Main site: http://www.management.energy.gov/foia_pa.htm

FOIA Requester Service Center
1000 Independence Avenue, SW
Mail Stop MA-90
Washington, DC 20585
Phone: (202) 586-5955
Online: http://energy.gov/doe-headquarters-foia-request-form

Environmental Protection Agency

Main site: http://www.epa.gov/foia/
Headquarters and regional: http://www.epa.gov/foia/contacts.html

National Freedom of Information Officer
U.S. Environmental Protection Agency
1200 Pennsylvania Avenue NW (2822T)
Washington, DC 20460
Phone: (202) 566-1667
   Online: http://www.epa.gov/foia/make_a_request.html and https://
foiaonline.regulations.gov/foia/action/public/home

Department of Health and Human Services

Main site: http://www.hhs.gov/foia/

Freedom of Information Officer
Mary E. Switzer Building, Room 2221
330 C Street, S.W.
Washington, DC 20201
Phone: (202) 690-7453
Online: http://wcdapps.hhs.gov/FoiaRequest/

Department of Homeland Security

Main site: http://www.dhs.gov/freedom-information-act-and-privacy
-act

xxx The United States Government Internet Directory

Individual agencies: http://www.dhs.gov/foia-contact-information

Dr. James V.M.L. Holzer, CIPP/G
Sr. Director, FOIA Operations
The Privacy Office
U.S. Department of Homeland Security
245 Murray Lane SW
STOP-0655
Washington, DC 20528-0655
Phone: (202) 343-1743 or (866) 431-0486
E-mail: foia@hq.dhs.gov
Online: http://www.dhs.gov/make-foia-request

Department of Housing and Urban Development
Main site: http://www.hud.gov/offices/adm/foia/

U.S. Department of Housing and Urban Development
Freedom of Information Act Office
451 7th Street, SW, Room 10139
Washington, DC 20410-3000
Fax: (202) 619-8365
Online: http://portal.hud.gov/hudportal/HUD?src=/program_offices/administration/foia/requests

Department of the Interior
Main site: http://www.doi.gov/foia/
Individual agencies: http://www.doi.gov/foia/contacts.cfm

Cindy Cafaro
Departmental FOIA Officer
MS-7328, MIB
1849 C Street NW
Washington, DC 20240
Phone: (202) 208-5342
Online: http://www.doi.gov/foia/foia-request-form.cfm

Department of Justice
Main site: http://www.justice.gov/oip/
Individual agencies: http://www.justice.gov/oip/make-foia-request-doj

FOIA/PA Mail Referral Unit
Department of Justice
Room 115
LOC Building
Washington, DC 20530-0001
Phone: (301) 583-7354

E-mail: MRUFOIA.Requests@usdoj.gov
Online: http://www.justice.gov/oip/make-foia-request-doj

Department of Labor

Main site and agencies: http://www.dol.gov/dol/foia/

Office of the Solicitor
Division of Management and Administrative Legal Services
200 Constitution Avenue NW, Room N-2420
Washington, DC 20210
Phone: (202) 693-5389

Department of State

Main site: http://foia.state.gov/

Office of Information Programs and Services
A/GIS/IPS/RL
Department of State, SA-2
U. S. Department of State
Washington, DC 20522-8100
Online: http://foia.state.gov/#3

Department of Transportation

Main site: http://www.dot.gov/foia/
Individual agencies: http://www.dot.gov/individuals/foia/dot
-foia-service-centers-and-liasions

Departmental FOIA Office
1200 New Jersey Ave SE
Washington, DC 20590
Phone: (202) 366-4542

Department of the Treasury

Main site: http://www.treasury.gov/foia/
Individual agencies: http://www.treasury.gov/FOIA/pages/bureaus
.aspx

FOIA Request
Department of the Treasury
Washington, DC 20220
Phone: (202) 622-0930
Online: https://www.treasury.gov/foia/pages/gofoia.aspx

Department of Veterans Affairs

Main site: http://www.foia.va.gov/
Individual offices: http://www.foia.va.gov/FOIA_Offices.asp

James P. Horan, CIPP/G
Director, FOIA Service/FOIA Public Liaison/E-Discovery
(005R1C) VACO
810 Vermont Avenue NW
Washington, DC 20420
Phone: (877) 750-3642
E-mail: vacofoiaservice@va.gov

Organization Charts

THE GOVERNMENT OF THE UNITED STATES

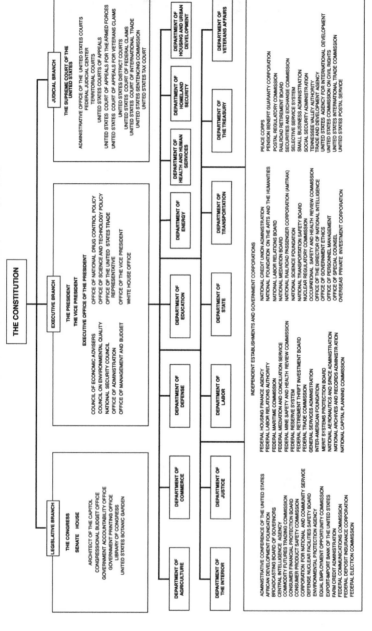

THE CONSTITUTION

LEGISLATIVE BRANCH

THE CONGRESS

SENATE   HOUSE

ARCHITECT OF THE CAPITOL
CONGRESSIONAL BUDGET OFFICE
GOVERNMENT ACCOUNTABILITY OFFICE
GOVERNMENT PRINTING OFFICE
LIBRARY OF CONGRESS
UNITED STATES BOTANIC GARDEN

EXECUTIVE BRANCH

THE PRESIDENT
THE VICE PRESIDENT

EXECUTIVE OFFICE OF THE PRESIDENT

COUNCIL OF ECONOMIC ADVISERS
COUNCIL ON ENVIRONMENTAL QUALITY
NATIONAL SECURITY COUNCIL
OFFICE OF ADMINISTRATION
OFFICE OF MANAGEMENT AND BUDGET

OFFICE OF NATIONAL DRUG CONTROL POLICY
OFFICE OF SCIENCE AND TECHNOLOGY POLICY
OFFICE OF THE UNITED STATES TRADE
   REPRESENTATIVE
OFFICE OF THE VICE PRESIDENT
WHITE HOUSE OFFICE

JUDICIAL BRANCH

THE SUPREME COURT OF THE
UNITED STATES

ADMINISTRATIVE OFFICE OF THE UNITED STATES COURTS
FEDERAL JUDICIAL CENTER
TERRITORIAL COURTS
UNITED STATES COURTS OF APPEALS
UNITED STATES COURT OF APPEALS FOR THE ARMED FORCES
UNITED STATES COURT OF APPEALS FOR VETERANS CLAIMS
UNITED STATES DISTRICT COURTS
UNITED STATES COURT OF FEDERAL CLAIMS
UNITED STATES COURT OF INTERNATIONAL TRADE
UNITED STATES SENTENCING COMMISSION
UNITED STATES TAX COURT

DEPARTMENT OF
AGRICULTURE

DEPARTMENT OF
COMMERCE

DEPARTMENT OF
DEFENSE

DEPARTMENT OF
EDUCATION

DEPARTMENT OF
ENERGY

DEPARTMENT OF
HEALTH AND HUMAN
SERVICES

DEPARTMENT OF
HOUSING AND URBAN
DEVELOPMENT

DEPARTMENT OF
THE INTERIOR

DEPARTMENT OF
JUSTICE

DEPARTMENT OF
LABOR

DEPARTMENT OF
STATE

DEPARTMENT OF
TRANSPORTATION

DEPARTMENT OF
THE TREASURY

DEPARTMENT OF
HOMELAND
SECURITY

DEPARTMENT OF
VETERANS AFFAIRS

INDEPENDENT ESTABLISHMENTS AND GOVERNMENT CORPORATIONS

ADMINISTRATIVE CONFERENCE OF THE UNITED STATES
AFRICAN DEVELOPMENT FOUNDATION
BROADCASTING BOARD OF GOVERNORS
CENTRAL INTELLIGENCE AGENCY
COMMODITY FUTURES TRADING COMMISSION
CONSUMER FINANCIAL PROTECTION BOARD
CONSUMER PRODUCT SAFETY COMMISSION
CORPORATION FOR NATIONAL AND COMMUNITY SERVICE
DEFENSE NUCLEAR FACILITIES SAFETY BOARD
ENVIRONMENTAL PROTECTION AGENCY
EQUAL EMPLOYMENT OPPORTUNITY COMMISSION
EXPORT-IMPORT BANK OF THE UNITED STATES
FARM CREDIT ADMINISTRATION
FEDERAL COMMUNICATIONS COMMISSION
FEDERAL DEPOSIT INSURANCE CORPORATION
FEDERAL ELECTION COMMISSION

FEDERAL HOUSING FINANCE AGENCY
FEDERAL LABOR RELATIONS AUTHORITY
FEDERAL MARITIME COMMISSION
FEDERAL MEDIATION AND CONCILIATION SERVICE
FEDERAL MINE SAFETY AND HEALTH REVIEW COMMISSION
FEDERAL RESERVE SYSTEM
FEDERAL RETIREMENT THRIFT INVESTMENT BOARD
FEDERAL TRADE COMMISSION
GENERAL SERVICES ADMINISTRATION
INTER-AMERICAN FOUNDATION
MERIT SYSTEMS PROTECTION BOARD
NATIONAL AERONAUTICS AND SPACE ADMINISTRATION
NATIONAL ARCHIVES AND RECORDS ADMINISTRATION
NATIONAL CAPITAL PLANNING COMMISSION

NATIONAL CREDIT UNION ADMINISTRATION
NATIONAL FOUNDATION ON THE ARTS AND THE HUMANITIES
NATIONAL LABOR RELATIONS BOARD
NATIONAL MEDIATION BOARD
NATIONAL RAILROAD PASSENGER CORPORATION (AMTRAK)
NATIONAL SCIENCE FOUNDATION
NATIONAL TRANSPORTATION SAFETY BOARD
NUCLEAR REGULATORY COMMISSION
OCCUPATIONAL SAFETY AND HEALTH REVIEW COMMISSION
OFFICE OF THE DIRECTOR OF NATIONAL INTELLIGENCE
OFFICE OF GOVERNMENT ETHICS
OFFICE OF PERSONNEL MANAGEMENT
OFFICE OF SPECIAL COUNSEL
OVERSEAS PRIVATE INVESTMENT CORPORATION

PEACE CORPS
PENSION BENEFIT GUARANTY CORPORATION
POSTAL REGULATORY COMMISSION
RAILROAD RETIREMENT BOARD
SECURITIES AND EXCHANGE COMMISSION
SELECTIVE SERVICE SYSTEM
SMALL BUSINESS ADMINISTRATION
SOCIAL SECURITY ADMINISTRATION
TENNESSEE VALLEY AUTHORITY
TRADE AND DEVELOPMENT AGENCY
UNITED STATES AGENCY FOR INTERNATIONAL DEVELOPMENT
UNITED STATES COMMISSION ON CIVIL RIGHTS
UNITED STATES INTERNATIONAL TRADE COMMISSION
UNITED STATES POSTAL SERVICE

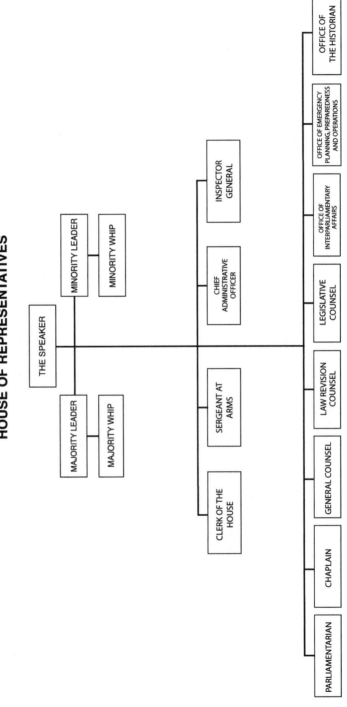

HOUSE OF REPRESENTATIVES

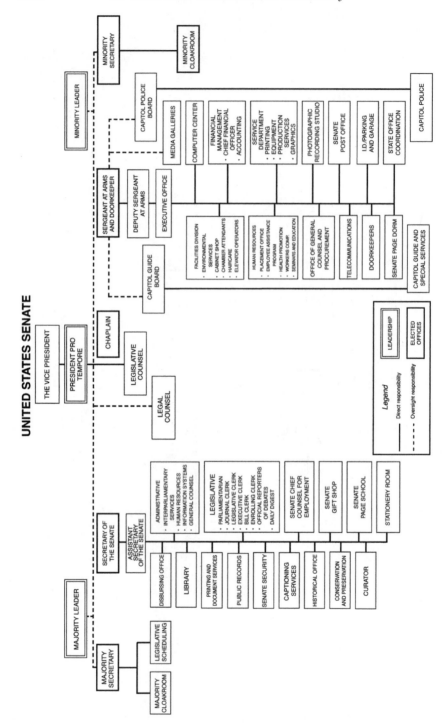

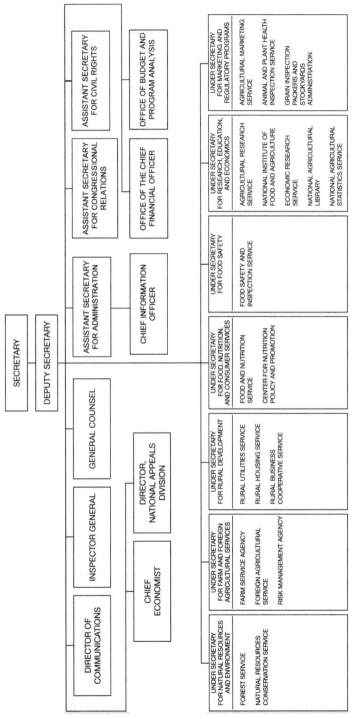

DEPARTMENT OF AGRICULTURE

SECRETARY

DEPUTY SECRETARY

DIRECTOR OF COMMUNICATIONS

INSPECTOR GENERAL

GENERAL COUNSEL

CHIEF ECONOMIST

DIRECTOR, NATIONAL APPEALS DIVISION

ASSISTANT SECRETARY FOR ADMINISTRATION

CHIEF INFORMATION OFFICER

ASSISTANT SECRETARY FOR CONGRESSIONAL RELATIONS

OFFICE OF THE CHIEF FINANCIAL OFFICER

ASSISTANT SECRETARY FOR CIVIL RIGHTS

OFFICE OF BUDGET AND PROGRAM ANALYSIS

UNDER SECRETARY FOR NATURAL RESOURCES AND ENVIRONMENT
- FOREST SERVICE
- NATURAL RESOURCES CONSERVATION SERVICE

UNDER SECRETARY FOR FARM AND FOREIGN AGRICULTURAL SERVICES
- FARM SERVICE AGENCY
- FOREIGN AGRICULTURAL SERVICE
- RISK MANAGEMENT AGENCY

UNDER SECRETARY FOR RURAL DEVELOPMENT
- RURAL UTILITIES SERVICE
- RURAL HOUSING SERVICE
- RURAL BUSINESS COOPERATIVE SERVICE

UNDER SECRETARY FOR FOOD, NUTRITION, AND CONSUMER SERVICES
- FOOD AND NUTRITION SERVICE
- CENTER FOR NUTRITION POLICY AND PROMOTION

UNDER SECRETARY FOR FOOD SAFETY
- FOOD SAFETY AND INSPECTION SERVICE

UNDER SECRETARY FOR RESEARCH, EDUCATION, AND ECONOMICS
- AGRICULTURAL RESEARCH SERVICE
- NATIONAL INSTITUTE OF FOOD AND AGRICULTURE
- ECONOMIC RESEARCH SERVICE
- NATIONAL AGRICULTURAL LIBRARY
- NATIONAL AGRICULTURAL STATISTICS SERVICE

UNDER SECRETARY FOR MARKETING AND REGULATORY PROGRAMS
- AGRICULTURAL MARKETING SERVICE
- ANIMAL AND PLANT HEALTH INSPECTION SERVICE
- GRAIN INSPECTION PACKERS AND STOCKYARDS ADMINISTRATION

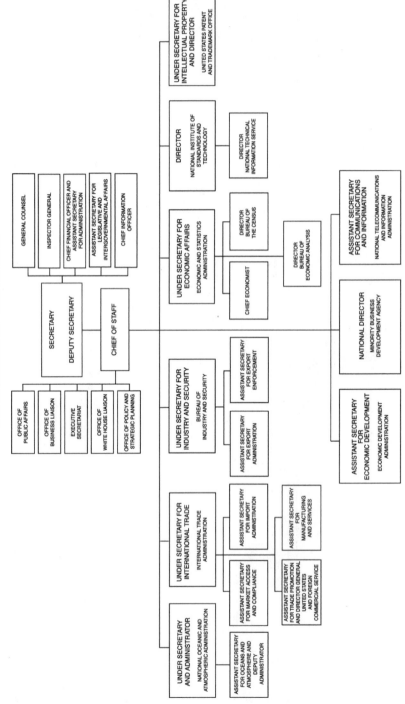

DEPARTMENT OF COMMERCE

DEPARTMENT OF DEFENSE

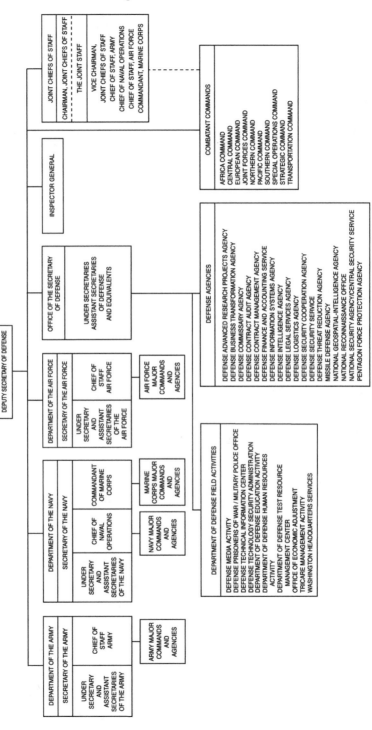

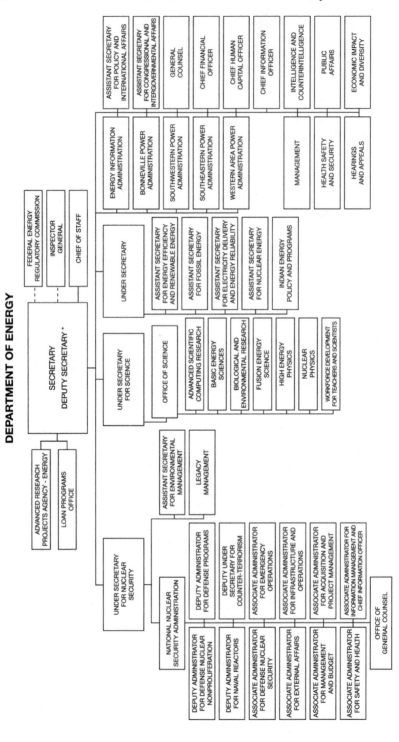

DEPARTMENT OF ENERGY

* The Deputy Secretary also serves as the Chief Operating Officer.

DEPARTMENT OF EDUCATION

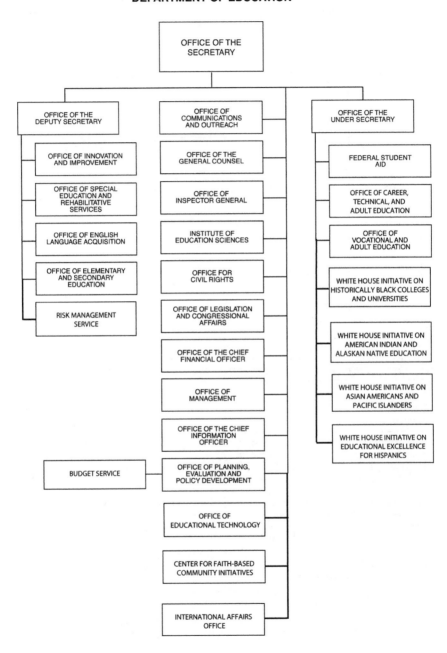

ENVIRONMENTAL PROTECTION AGENCY

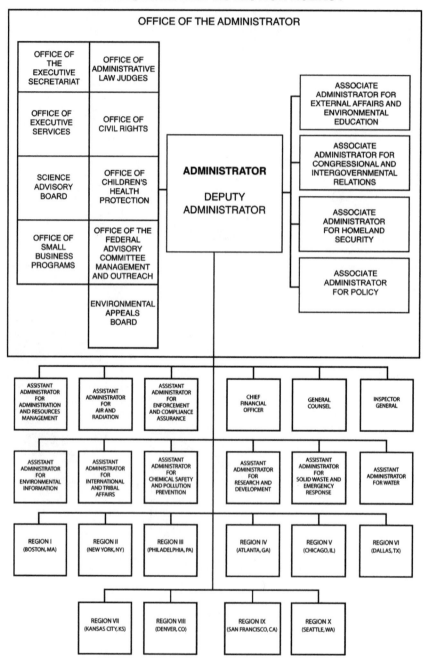

DEPARTMENT OF HEALTH AND HUMAN SERVICES

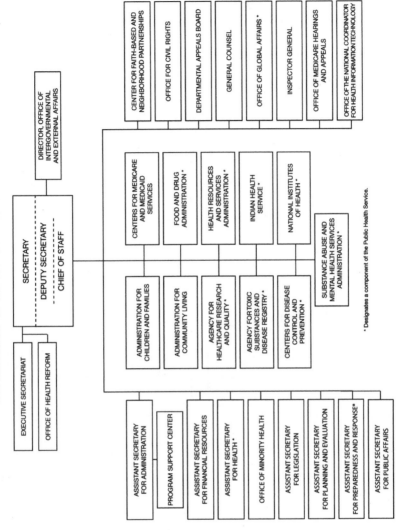

* Designates a component of the Public Health Service.

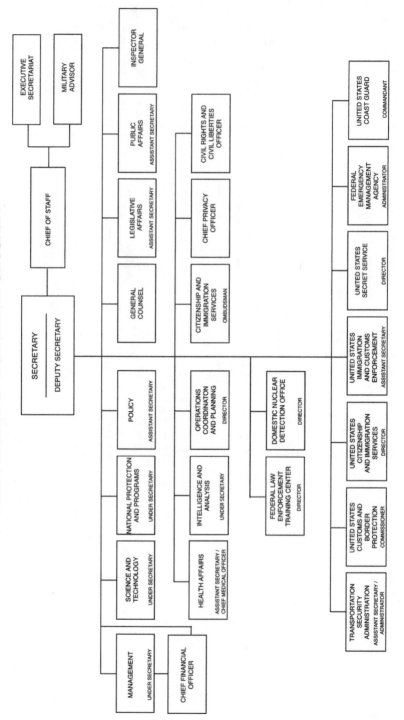

DEPARTMENT OF HOMELAND SECURITY

DEPARTMENT OF HOUSING AND URBAN DEVELOPMENT

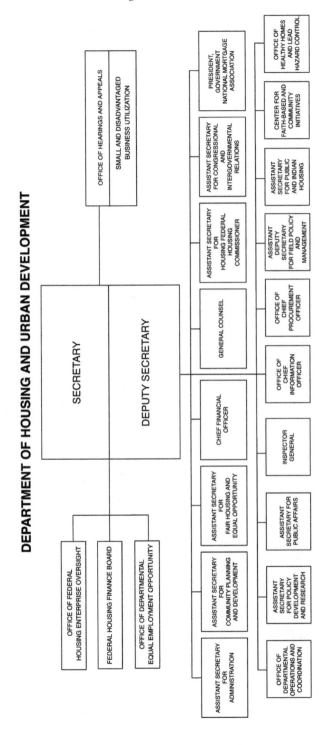

DEPARTMENT OF THE INTERIOR

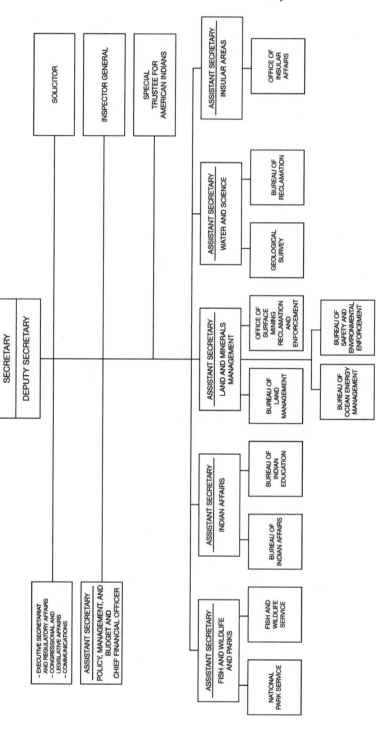

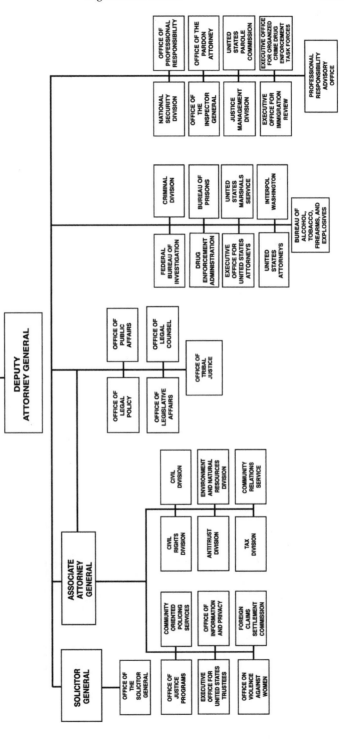

DEPARTMENT OF JUSTICE

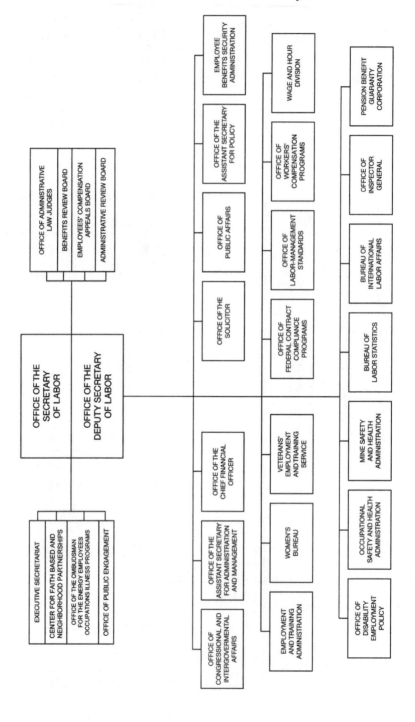

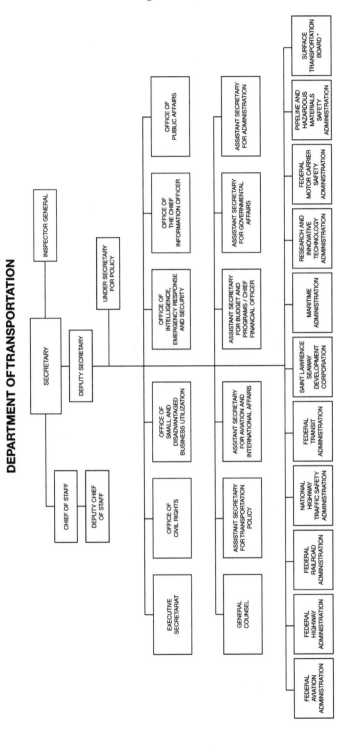

DEPARTMENT OF TRANSPORTATION

*The Surface Transportation Board is administratively affiliated with the Department of Transportation.

DEPARTMENT OF THE TREASURY

SECRETARY

DEPUTY SECRETARY

OFFICE OF THE CHIEF OF STAFF

INSPECTOR GENERAL

TREASURY INSPECTOR GENERAL FOR TAX ADMINISTRATION

SPECIAL INSPECTOR GENERAL FOR THE TROUBLED ASSET RELIEF PROGRAM

UNDER SECRETARY INTERNATIONAL AFFAIRS

- ASSISTANT SECRETARY INTERNATIONAL FINANCE
- ASSISTANT SECRETARY INTERNATIONAL MARKETS AND DEVELOPMENT

UNDER SECRETARY TERRORISM AND FINANCIAL INTELLIGENCE

- ASSISTANT SECRETARY TERRORIST FINANCING
- ASSISTANT SECRETARY INTELLIGENCE AND ANALYSIS
- FINANCIAL CRIMES ENFORCEMENT NETWORK
- OFFICE OF FINANCIAL ASSETS CONTROL

UNDER SECRETARY DOMESTIC FINANCE

- ASSISTANT SECRETARY FINANCIAL MARKETS
- ASSISTANT SECRETARY FINANCIAL STABILITY
- ASSISTANT SECRETARY FINANCIAL INSTITUTIONS
- COMMUNITY DEVELOPMENT FINANCIAL INSTITUTIONS FUND
- FEDERAL INSURANCE OFFICE
- ASSISTANT SECRETARY FISCAL
  - BUREAU OF THE FISCAL SERVICE
  - OFFICE OF FINANCIAL RESEARCH

INTERNAL REVENUE SERVICE

OFFICE OF THE COMPTROLLER OF THE CURRENCY

ASSISTANT SECRETARY TAX POLICY

ALCOHOL AND TOBACCO TAX AND TRADE BUREAU

ASSISTANT SECRETARY ECONOMIC POLICY

ASSISTANT SECRETARY PUBLIC AFFAIRS

ASSISTANT SECRETARY LEGISLATIVE AFFAIRS

ASSISTANT SECRETARY MANAGEMENT / CHIEF FINANCIAL OFFICER

GENERAL COUNSEL

LEGAL DIVISION

TREASURER

UNITED STATES MINT

BUREAU OF ENGRAVING AND PRINTING

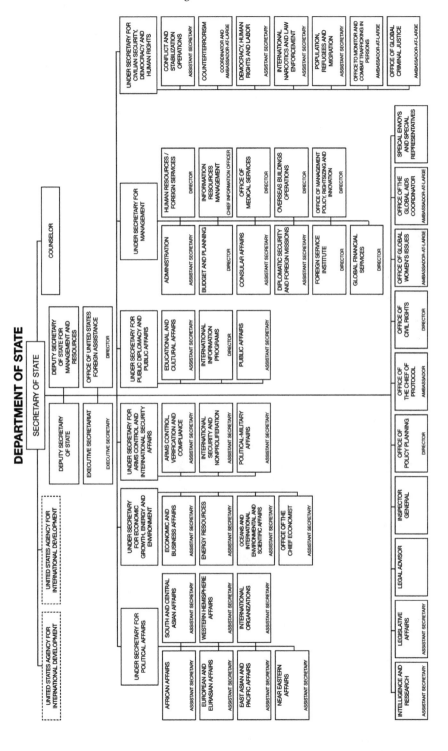

DEPARTMENT OF STATE

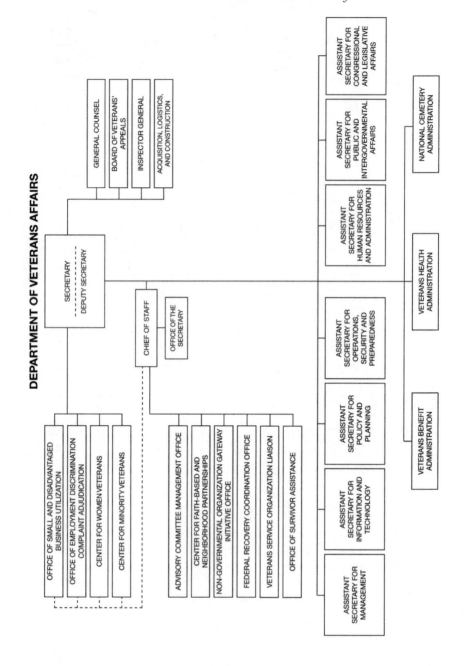

DEPARTMENT OF VETERANS AFFAIRS

ONE

Finding Aids

The Web sites described in this chapter are designed specifically to help people find United States federal government information. These sites organize access to government grants, forms, press releases, publications, statistics, and more. When searching for government information, they can be much more effective tools than general search engines.

The two subsections of this chapter describe, first, finding aids developed by the U.S. government and, second, those developed by non-government organizations.

GOVERNMENT SOURCES

Catalog of U.S. Government Publications (CGP)
http://catalog.gpo.gov/
Sponsor(s): Government Printing Office (GPO)—Superintendent of Documents
Description: CGP is a catalog of both print and electronic government publications from the legislative, executive, and judicial branches of the U.S. government. The records provide bibliographic information and link to a copy of the cited publication if one is available online. Use the advanced search option to take full advantage of the CGP's features, such as limiting searches by year or format.

The CGP is the online version of the *Monthly Catalog of United States Government Publications* printed catalog and constitutes the National Bibliography of U.S. Government Publications. The CGP is not a sales catalog. Sales publications can be found in the online GPO U.S. Government Bookstore at http://bookstore.gpo.gov

Contact Your Government

http://www.usa.gov/Contact.shtml

Sponsor(s): General Services Administration (GSA)

Description: This section of the USA.gov site features contact information for many federal and state government offices and legislators and toll-free hotline numbers. Links are organized by elected official, topic, and agency.

FedWorld

http://fedworld.ntis.gov/

Sponsor(s): Department of Commerce—National Technical Information Service (NTIS)

Description: As stated on the Web site, FedWorld serves as "the online locator service for a comprehensive inventory of information disseminated by the federal government." The site links to information troves such as Science.gov, as well as governmental reports and publications.

Subject(s): Finding Aids

Find Government Forms

http://www.usa.gov/Topics/Reference-Shelf/forms.shtml

Sponsor(s): General Services Administration (GSA)

Description: This portal site provides "one-stop shopping" for forms commonly needed for federal government services. Locate forms by agency or by quick links to frequently used forms. Links lead to the page at the agency Web site where the forms are available.

GobiernoUSA.gov

http://www.usa.gov/gobiernousa/

Sponsor(s): General Services Administration (GSA)

Description: This Spanish-language Web site is not a word-for-word translation of the English-language USA.gov site; instead, it is customized for those more likely to use it, with features such as a section for recent immigrants. The search engine allows users to search for words in Spanish and retrieve federal and state government Web results that are in Spanish. Users can also complete some government transactions online in Spanish.

Government News

http://www.usa.gov/Topics/Reference_Shelf/News.shtml

Sponsor(s): General Services Administration (GSA)

Description: This section of the USA.gov Web site offers several useful compilations, including links to agency press releases, e-mail newsletters, blogs, and RSS news feeds.

Each compilation is not necessarily complete. Researchers interested in news from specific agencies should check the agency Web sites directly to find any additional news sources they may provide.

Grants.gov

http://www.grants.gov/

Sponsor(s): Health and Human Services Department

Description: Grants.gov is the federal government portal for finding and applying for competitive grant opportunities from federal grant-making agencies, including grants available under the Recovery Act. Users can search the full text of grants and refine searches by limiting to certain agencies, topics, dates, or types of grants. Applications can be downloaded and completed offline. Completed grant application packages can then be submitted online. In addition to using the grants search feature, researchers can subscribe to receive e-mail notification of grant opportunities in their areas of interest.

Subject(s): Grants; Finding Aids

Registry of U.S. Government Publication Digitization Projects

http://registry.fdlp.gov/

Sponsor(s): Government Printing Office (GPO)

Description: The Registry of U.S. Government Publication Digitization Projects describes and links to online collections of digitized U.S. government publications. The collections are from government agencies, universities, and other institutions.

U.S. Government Photos and Multimedia

http://www.usa.gov/Topics/Graphics.shtml

Sponsor(s): General Services Administration (GSA)

Description: Part of the USA.gov Web site, this resource links to collections of graphics and photos on federal agency Web sites. The images are arranged by agency or photo collection name. Many but not all of these graphics are freely available for use in the public domain; check the specific disclaimers posted at each source.

U.S. Government YouTube Channel

http://www.youtube.com/USGovernment

Sponsor(s): General Services Administration (GSA)—Citizen Services and Communications Office

Description: The official YouTube channel of the U.S. federal government, launched in May 2009, provides a single point of access for videos from numerous government agencies.

Subject(s): Government information; Movies

USA.gov

http://www.usa.gov/

Sponsor(s): General Services Administration (GSA)

Description: Labeled "Government Made Easy," USA.gov is an Executive Branch initiative that offers multiple routes to government information on the Internet. USA.gov links are most prominently organized by audience: citizens, businesses, seniors, kids, government employees, and visitors to the United States. Topics for citizens include consumer guides, federal benefits and grants, health research, and jobs and education information. A Reference and General Government subsection, under Citizens, links to sites with federal forms, data and statistics, and laws and regulations.

USA.gov also has quick links to federal agency Web sites and to the main Web sites for state and tribal governments. A special USA.gov Web search engine searches federal, state, and local government Web sites.

A Spanish-language version of USA.gov, GobiernoUSA.gov, is described earlier in this chapter.

USA.gov does an excellent job of serving multiple audiences and helping users find basic government information faster. The design is particularly well suited for browsing and finding information and services when the responsible agency is unknown.

Subject(s): Government information; Finding aids

OTHER SOURCES

CyberCemetery

http://govinfo.library.unt.edu/

Sponsor(s): University of North Texas Libraries

Description: As described on the site, the CyberCemetery is "an archive of government websites that have ceased operation (usually websites of defunct government agencies and commissions that have issued a final report)." Links to the archived sites are organized by branch of government, by date of the office's expiration, and by name; the sites can also be searched by keyword. Archived sites include those of the Citizens' Heath Care Working Group, Coalition Provisional Authority for Iraq, and the National Commission on Terrorist Attacks Upon the United States. The CyberCemetery is operated under a partnership with the U.S. Government Printing Office and is an Affiliated Archives of the National Archives and Records Administration.

The policies, processes, and technologies for systematic archiving of electronic government information—and for providing access to and preservation of that information—are being actively developed by federal agencies. In the meantime, the CyberCemetery is providing a commendable service to researchers with straightforward access to resources that might otherwise be lost.

Subject(s): Digital Libraries; Government Information

TWO

Agriculture, Fishing, and Forestry

This chapter describes Web sites covering agricultural practices, science, marketing, statistics, and related areas. Web sites concerning food and nutrition can be found in the Health and Safety chapter. This chapter also includes Web sites about fishing (or aquaculture) and forestry; additional resources on fish and forests can be found in the Environment and Nature chapter.

Subsections in this chapter are Agriculture, Fishing, and Forestry.

AGRICULTURE

AGRICOLA

http://agricola.nal.usda.gov/

Sponsor(s): Agriculture Department (USDA)—National Agricultural Library (NAL)

Description: AGRICOLA, also called the NAL Catalog, is a large bibliographic database covering literature from all areas of agriculture and related fields. It indexes journal articles, short reports, book chapters, and other materials. The database was created in 1970 but also contains content from prior years. Users of AGRICOLA on the Web can search the book collection of the National Agricultural Library (NAL) separately or in combination with AGRICOLA. Cited materials are not available online through AGRICOLA in full-text format. The site describes document delivery options; most remote users will need to find the materials through their local libraries.

Due to its quality, size, scope, and historical coverage, AGRICOLA is a key resource for conducting literature searches on topics related to agriculture.

Subject(s): Agriculture Information

Agricultural Marketing Service (AMS)

http://www.ams.usda.gov/

Sponsor(s): Agriculture Department (USDA)—Agricultural Marketing Service (AMS)

Description: The Agricultural Marketing Service (AMS) supports the marketing, testing, regulation, and efficient transportation of agricultural commodities and issues marketing orders that establish basic minimum prices for commodities. The agency also runs the National Organic Program, and the site links to information about how to get a product certified as organic.

AMS programs described on the site concern cotton, dairy, poultry, fruits and vegetables, livestock and seed, tobacco, commodity purchasing, grading and certification, and agricultural transportation interests. Additional sections cover farmers markets and local food marketing, the National Organic Program, science and research, federal rulemaking developments, and AMS services in the global marketplace. The About AMS section has information on the agency's civil rights program.

Subject(s): Agricultural Commodities; Food Safety

Publication(s): *Daily Cattle Summary Reports*
Daily Spot Cotton Quotations, A 88.11/4
Dairy Market News Weekly
Grain Transportation Report, A 88.68
Market News Reports, A 88.66
National Farmers Market Directory, A 88.69/2
National Fruit and Vegetable Organic Summary
National Weekly Pricing Report, A 88.71
Pesticide Data Program Annual Summary, A 88.60
Plant Variety Protection Database, A 88.52/2
Poultry and Egg Market Reports

Agricultural Research Service (ARS)

http://www.ars.usda.gov/

Sponsor(s): Agriculture Department (USDA)—Agricultural Research Service (ARS)

ARS leads the Department of Agriculture's research projects in agriculture, nutrition, technology, and the environment. The ARS Web site presents information about its national research programs. The Research section of the site includes a database of ARS research projects and detailed information on the agency's national and international research programs.

In the Newsroom section, the ARS Web site links to educational resources, ARS publications (including *Agricultural Research* magazine issues back to January 1995). The TEKTRAN database of pre-publication notices of recent ARS research results can be found in the Research section. This section also provides software and datasets of interest to scientists working in agricultural research areas.

The ARS Web site will primarily be of interest to agricultural researchers and research institutions

Subject(s): Agricultural Research

Publication(s): *Agricultural Research, A 77.12*

Food & Nutrition Research Briefs, A 77.518

Healthy Animals, A 77.519

Agriculture Network Information Center (AgNIC)

http://www.agnic.org/

Sponsor(s): Agriculture Department (USDA)—National Agricultural Library (NAL)

Description: AgNIC links to agricultural information on the Internet as selected by the National Agricultural Library, land grant universities, and other institutions. AgNIC is a distributed network that provides access to agriculture-related information, subject area experts, and other resources. From the AgNIC Web site's home page, users can perform a simple search of the information database or browse its contents by subject. A calendar of events lists conferences, meetings, and seminars in various agricultural fields.

AgNIC is not a government organization but is supported in part by the National Agricultural Library.

Agriculture, US EPA

http://www.epa.gov/agriculture/

Sponsor: Environmental Protection Agency (EPA)

Description: The EPA's Agriculture site is a portal to information about regulatory compliance and environmental stewardship for the agricultural community. Information is organized by agricultural sector, such as crops, forestry, and food safety. The site has an A to Z Subject Index that features specific topics, such as animal feeding operations, nutrient management and fertilizer, pesticides, and water.

Alternative Farming Systems Information Center (AFSIC)

http://afsic.nal.usda.gov/

Sponsor(s): Agriculture Department (USDA)—National Agricultural Library (NAL)

Description: AFSIC is a portal to information on sustainable and alternative agricultural systems, crops, and livestock. Topics include alternative crops and plants, farm energy options, organic production, aquaculture, ecological pest management, and sustainability in agriculture.

Amber Waves

http://www.ers.usda.gov/Amberwaves/

Sponsor(s): Agriculture Department (USDA)—Economic Research Service (ERS)

Description: *Amber Waves*, a Department of Agriculture magazine published between four and six times a year (although generally on a quarterly basis), features information and economic analysis about food, farms, natural resources, and rural community issues. The magazine is exclusively electronic. *Amber Waves* began publication in February 2003, replacing *Agricultural Outlook*, *Food Review*, and *Rural America*.

Subject(s): Agricultural Economics

Animal & Veterinary

http://www.fda.gov/AnimalVeterinary/

Sponsor(s): Health and Human Services Department—Food and Drug Administration (FDA)—Center for Veterinary Medicine (CVM)

Description: CVM regulates the manufacture and distribution of drugs and feed additives intended for animals. Their Web site provides information on the drug approval process, approved drugs, and recalls. For consumers, it has information on feeding and caring for pets. Resources on the site include the *Green Book* (FDA Approved Animal Drug Products).

Subject(s): Veterinary Medicine

Publication(s): *FDA Approved Animal Drug Products*, HE 20.4411
FDA Veterinarian, HE 20.4410

Animal and Plant Health Inspection Service (APHIS)

http://www.aphis.usda.gov/

Sponsor(s): Agriculture Department (USDA)—Animal and Plant Health Inspection Service (APHIS)

Description: APHIS's mission is to protect the animal and plant resources of the United States from agricultural pests and diseases. Major sections of its Web site cover animal health, plant health, biotechnology, emergency preparedness and response, wildlife damage management, animal welfare, and importing and exporting concerns. The Animal Health section includes a wealth of information from major animal health monitoring and surveillance programs. The site also has information about reporting a pest or disease, veterinarian accreditation information, and tips on traveling with a pet.

Subject(s): Animals—Regulations; Plants—Regulations; Veterinary Medicine

Publication(s): *Animal Health Report*, A 1.75/5

APHIS Fact Sheets, A 101.31

Animal Disease Traceability

http://www.aphis.usda.gov/traceability/

Sponsor(s): Agriculture Department (USDA)—Animal and Plant Health Inspection Service (APHIS)

Description: This APHIS Web site explains the agency's new approach to animal disease traceability, which was announced in February 2010. The most current modification was proposed in January 2013.

Subject(s): Animals—Regulations

Beltsville Agricultural Research Center (BARC)

http://www.ba.ars.usda.gov/

Sponsor(s): Agriculture Department (USDA)—Agricultural Research Service (ARS)

Description: BARC performs research in a variety of agricultural science disciplines, working on such topics as plant diversity, bioenergy, and food safety. The BARC site describes research coming out of the center's many laboratories. Major sections include information about nutrition and research projects.

Subject(s): Agricultural Research; Nutrition—Research; Plants —Research

Carl Hayden Bee Research Center

http://gears.tucson.ars.ag.gov/

Sponsor(s): Agriculture Department (USDA)—Agricultural Research Service (ARS)

Description: The mission of the Carl Hayden Bee Research Center is "to conduct research to optimize the health of honey bee colonies, through improved nutrition and control of Varroa mites in order to maximize production of honey bee pollinated crops." (from the Web site) The site's Research section describes current and future research. The Products and Services section includes peer reviewed research articles, research and beekeeping software, such as the peer-reviewed journal *Comparison of Productivity Between Honey Bee Colonies Supplemented with Sucrose or High Fructose Corn Syrup (HFCS)*.

Subject(s): Beekeeping; Entomology

Crop Explorer

http://www.pecad.fas.usda.gov/cropexplorer/

Sponsor(s): Agriculture Department (USDA)—Foreign Agricultural Service (FAS)

Description: Crop Explorer is an interactive Web tool for mapping global crop condition information, based on satellite imagery and weather data. For major crop-growing areas around the world, Crop Explorer displays thematic maps of conditions such as precipitation, temperature, and soil moisture. The site also provides frequently updated satellite data and imagery, regional growing season profiles, and narrative reports. Crop Explorer has its own mapping view and a Google Maps view.

Crop Explorer is designed to assist in forecasting production, supply, demand, and food assistance needs. The site has a well-designed interface and a rich library of current data.

Subject(s): Agriculture — International

Department of Agriculture (USDA)

http://www.usda.gov/

Sponsor: Agriculture Department (USDA)

Description: The main Department of Agriculture Web site provides efficient and uncluttered access to department information. The front page of the site contains current news, event announcements, quick task-based links (such as "Know Your Farmer, Know Your Food" and "Civil Rights"), information about administration initiatives, and a link for emergency preparedness and response. Major topical sections include Topics, Programs and Services, Newsroom, and Blog. The Newsroom section provides speech transcripts, radio and television broadcasts, e-mail and RSS news alerts, and agency publications.

As the umbrella site for a large department, the Department of Agriculture site provides a page of links to the Web sites for its agencies, services, and programs. It also reports on the department's activities related to the Open Government Initiative and the Recovery Act. The site features a Spanish-language version, which contains news, program information, and educational material.

This is a well-organized site with a simple, consistent interface. It serves as a gateway to the organization of the department and its major programs and publication.

Subject(s): Agriculture

Economic Research Service (ERS)

http://www.ers.usda.gov/

Sponsor(s): Agriculture Department (USDA) — Economic Research Service (ERS)

Description: ERS produces key economic indicators and detailed data on the economics of food, farming, natural resources, and rural development. The ERS Web site provides multiple ways of accessing its information by topic. The Topics section includes a breakdown of information into multiple topical and subtopical sections. Popular topics are prominently linked on the home page. The New Releases & Events calendar on the home page includes a dated list of ERS releases, as well as a link to the ERS Twitter feed.

The Data section includes statistics on food pricing, farm economics, international food trade, and other topics. Many data sets can be downloaded in spreadsheet format or output into a tailored report.

Subject(s): Agricultural Economics; Agriculture—Statistics; Rural Development—Statistics

Publication(s): *Amber Waves*, A 93.62

Cotton and Wool Outlook, A 93.24/2

Feed Outlook, A 93.11/2

Foreign Agricultural Trade of the United States, A 93.17/7

Fruit and Tree Nuts Outlook, A 93.12/3

Livestock, Dairy, and Poultry Outlook, A 93.46/3

Oil Crops Outlook, A 93.23/2

Retail Scanner Prices for Meat, A 93.2

Rice Outlook, A 93.11/3

Sugar and Sweeteners Outlook, A 93.31/3

Vegetables and Melons Outlook, A 93.12/2

Farm Credit Administration (FCA)

http://www.fca.gov/

Sponsor: Farm Credit Administration (FCA)

Description: As stated on the Web site, "FCA's mission is to ensure a safe, sound, and dependable source of credit and related services for agriculture and rural America. Our agency was created by a 1933 Executive order of President Franklin D. Roosevelt. Today the Agency derives its authority from the Farm Credit Act of 1971, as amended." The Farm Credit System (FCS) includes the Federal Agricultural Mortgage Corporation (Farmer Mac). The Reports & Publications section of the FCA Web site has financial reports on the FCS. The Law & Regulations section includes rules and regulatory guidance. The FCS Information section includes details on FCS institutions and Farmer Mac programs.

Farm Service Agency (FSA)

http://www.fsa.usda.gov/

Sponsor(s): Agriculture Department (USDA)—Farm Service Agency (FSA)

Description: FSA assists farmers in income stabilization, resource conservation, credit services, and disaster recovery. The Web site links to state FSA offices and information about their services and provides online services and forms for FSA customers. Specific programs and topics covered by the Web site include aerial photography (with over 10 million aerial images), commodity operations, disaster assistance, farm loan programs, price support, and the Tobacco Transition Payment Program.

FAS Online
http://www.fas.usda.gov/
Sponsor(s): Agriculture Department (USDA)—Foreign Agricultural Service (FAS)
Description: FAS represents U.S. interests in foreign markets. Its Web site includes information about commodities, trade policy and negotiations, export assistance programs, and buying U.S. products. News releases, reports, an RSS feed, congressional testimony, *Federal Register* notices, and featured reports are available in the Newsroom section. The Data & Analysis section has helpful information for constructing FAS searches.
    Subject(s): Agricultural Trade; International Trade—Statistics
    Publication(s): *Citrus: World Markets and Trade*
    Coffee: World Markets and Trade, A 67.18:FTROP
    Cotton: World Markets and Trade, A 67.18:FC
    Dairy: World Markets and Trade, A 67.18:FD
    Grain: World Markets and Trade, A 67.18:FG
    Livestock & Poultry: World Markets and Trade, A 67.18:FL&P
    Monthly Summary of Export Credit Guarantee Program Activity, A 67.47
    Oilseeds: World Markets and Trade, A 67.18:FOP
    Sugar: World Markets and Trade, A 67.18:FS
    U.S. Export Sales Report, A 67.40
    U.S. Planting Seed Trade, A 67.18/3
    Wine: World Markets and Trade

Food Safety and Health Service
http://www.fsis.usda.gov/wps/portal/informational/about-fsis/key-contacts/ophs/ophs
Sponsor(s): Agriculture Department (USDA)—Food Safety and Inspection Service (FSIS)
Description: OPHS provides scientific analysis and recommendations on public health and science topics of concern to FSIS. The OPHS Web site describes the agency's major departments and programs, including the Food Emergency Response Network, the Human Health Sciences Division, and the Microbiology Division. It also links to a directory of the FSIS Regulatory Field Services Laboratories.
    Subject(s): Food Safety—Research

Grain Inspection, Packers, and Stockyards Administration (GIPSA)
http://www.gipsa.usda.gov/
Sponsor(s): Agriculture Department (USDA)—Grain Inspection, Packers, and Stockyards Administration (GIPSA)
Description: GIPSA facilitates the marketing of grains, livestock, poultry, and meat for the overall benefit of consumers and U.S. agriculture. GIPSA also investigates fraud, unfair competition, and deceptive

practices under the Packers and Stockyards (P&S) Act. Target audiences for the agency's Web site include grain inspectors, livestock producers, poultry growers, and international governments and customers. The Newsroom section includes news about P&S Act investigations and links to GIPSA publications.

Subject(s): Grains—Regulations; Livestock—Regulations

Publication(s): *Annual Report of the Grain Inspection, Packers and Stockyards Administration,* A 113.1

Grain Inspection Handbook, A 113.8

Official United States Standards for Beans, A 113.10/3

Official United States Standards for Grain, A 113.10

Official United States Standards for Rice, A 113.10/2

Official United States Standards for Whole Dry Peas, Split Peas, and Lentils, A 113.10/4

GrainGenes

http://wheat.pw.usda.gov/

Sponsor(s): Agriculture Department (USDA)—Agricultural Research Service (ARS)

Description: GrainGenes is a genetic database for Triticeae, oats, and sugarcane. Access to the data is available through an alphabetical browse feature (by category and name) and by a variety of keyword searches. The site also has information about related news, projects, data, publications, and other resources.

The GrainGenes database contains a substantial amount of genetic information and many links to other genome databases. The interactive and collaborative capabilities of the Internet are used to good advantage, as researchers can submit data for entry into the database and browse through data that has already been included.

Green Book

http://www.fda.gov/AnimalVeterinary/Products/

Sponsor(s): Health and Human Services Department—Food and Drug Administration (FDA)—Center for Veterinary Medicine (CVM)

Description: *FDA Approved Animal Drug Products,* known as the *Green Book,* is available online in searchable form. The printed publication is issued annually, with monthly updates. The online book includes FDA Approved Animal Drug Database files that support production of the book, all chapters of the printed book itself, and a searchable archive of monthly updates.

Subject(s): Veterinary Medicine

Publication(s): *FDA Approved Animal Drug Products (Green Book),* HE 20.4411

GRIN—Germplasm Resources Information Network (National Genetic Resources Program)

http://www.ars-grin.gov/

Sponsor(s): Agriculture Department (USDA)—Agricultural Research Service (ARS)

Description: The National Genetic Resources Program is responsible for acquiring, characterizing, preserving, documenting, and distributing scientific information about germplasms of all life forms important for food and agricultural production. Its Web site features the Germplasm Resources Information Network (GRIN), which has germplasm information for plants, animals, microbes, and invertebrates within the National Genetic Resources Program. Information from the National Genetic Resources Advisory Council (NGRAC) is also available.

This site will primarily be of interest to users researching the germplasm of plants and animals.

Subject(s): Germplasms; Plant Genetics

Journal of Extension (JOE)

http://www.joe.org/

Sponsor(s): Agriculture Department (USDA)—National Institute of Food and Agriculture (NIFA)

Description: The *Journal of Extension* (JOE), a peer-reviewed journal for U.S. Extension personnel, is published six times a year and only in electronic format. The print version ceased publication in 1994. Issues from 1963 through the present are available on the site.

JOE is an easy-to-use online journal, with supplemental material about the journal, its peer review procedures, and usage statistics.

Subject(s): Extension Services

Publications(s): Journal of Extension

National Ag Safety Database (NASD)

http://nasdonline.org/

Sponsor(s): Health and Human Services Department—Centers for Disease Control and Prevention—National Institute of Occupational Safety and Health (NIOSH)

Description: NASD is an online clearinghouse for a diverse array of materials related to agricultural health, safety, and injury prevention. Its long list of topics includes chemicals/pesticides, hearing conservation, lightning, personal protective equipment (PPE), and supervising for safety. Safety videos and interactive training are available for online use. Many brochures are also available in Spanish.

NASD provides easy access to practical guides that may also be of use to nonfarm industries. Due to the diversity of these materials, users may want to check the source and date provided at the bottom of each document.

Subject(s): Farms and Farming; Safety

National Agricultural Library Digital Collections (NALDC)

http://naldr.nal.usda.gov/

Sponsor(s): Agriculture Department (USDA)—National Agricultural Library (NAL)

Description: NALDC is a collection of digitized agriculture documents from past years. The collection can be browsed or searched by keyword.

Subject(s): Agriculture Information

National Agricultural Statistics Service (NASS)

http://www.nass.usda.gov/

Sponsor(s): Agriculture Department (USDA)—National Agricultural Statistics Service (NASS)

Description: NASS publishes a broad range of state and national statistics on crops, livestock, and farming. The Web site's sidebar allows users to browse NASS data by the following topics: Crops and Plants; Demographics; Economics and Prices; Environmental; Livestock and Animals; Charts and Maps; Research, Science and Technology; and Education and Outreach. The site has searchable data from the Census of Agriculture, which is conducted every five years. The Data and Statistics section features the Quick Stats database for searching national, state, and local data by commodity, state, and year. The Newsroom section provides NASS statistical reports and news releases, available as an RSS feed.

Subject(s): Crop Production—Statistics; Farms and Farming—Statistics; Livestock—Statistics

Publication(s): *Agricultural Prices*, A 92.16
Agricultural Statistics, A 1.47
Census of Agriculture, A 92.53
Farm Labor, A 92.12

National Arboretum

http://www.usna.usda.gov/

Sponsor(s): Agriculture Department (USDA)—Agricultural Research Service (ARS)

Description: The National Arboretum's Web site is more than an online brochure for those planning to visit its gardens in Washington, D.C. The site has information of interest to the general gardening public, including horticultural facts, pest management, new hybrid plant releases, lists of state trees and flowers, and a plant hardiness map depicting the lowest expected temperatures in the United States. Information for researchers includes a directory of National Arboretum scientists and their specialties.

Subject(s): Gardening and Landscaping; Trees

Publication(s): *Arboretum Plant Introduction and Winners* (fact sheets), A 77.38/2:

National Center for Agricultural Law

http://www.nationalaglawcenter.org/

Sponsor: University of Arkansas School of Law

Description: The National Center for Agricultural Law is funded by the Department of Agriculture and operated by the University of Arkansas School of Law. The center conducts original research into areas of food and agricultural law. Its Web site presents this research alongside research material from other sources. A Reading Rooms section organizes information by topic, including biotechnology, country of origin labeling, marketing orders, and international law and organization. Each Reading Room category links to related major laws, regulations, case law, legal research, and government publications. Other highlights on the site include an agricultural policy glossary, legislative histories for past Farm Bills, general reference links, and digests of federal regulations and court cases concerning agricultural law.

The National Center for Agricultural Law site is an excellent starting point for legal, legislative, and government documents research on agricultural policy topics.

Subject(s): Agriculture—Laws

National Institute of Food and Agriculture (NIFA)

http://nifa.usda.gov/

Sponsor(s): Agriculture Department (USDA)—National Institute of Food and Agriculture (NIFA)

Description: NIFA was established in 2009 and replaced the former Cooperative State Research, Education, and Extension Service (CSREES). The agency helps fund research at the state and local level in a variety of areas, such as farm economics, wildlife and fish, animal and plant breeding, pest management, nutrition, and food safety. Its Web site has information for research grant seekers and recipients.

Subject(s): Agricultural Research—Grants; Extension Services; Food Safety—Research

Publication(s): *NIFA Update,* A 94.20

National Organic Program

http://www.ams.usda.gov/nop/

Sponsor(s): Agriculture Department (USDA)—Agricultural Marketing Service (AMS)

Description: This Web site presents Department of Agriculture regulations and policies concerning growing, labeling, and marketing farm produce as organic. It includes the National List of Allowed and Prohibited Substances, identifying synthetic substances that may be used and the non-synthetic substances that cannot be used, in organic production and handling operations. It also has a section on the National Organic Standards Board.

This informative site should be of practical benefit to producers, retailers, and consumers of organic food.

Subject(s): Food—Regulations

NRCS Soils

http://soils.usda.gov/

Sponsor(s): Agriculture Department (USDA)—Natural Resources Conservation Service (NRCS)

Description: The NRCS Soils Web site is part of the National Cooperative Soil Survey, a cooperative federal-state-academic project. The site has a broad range of scientific, applied, and educational information about soils. The centerpiece of the site is the Soil Survey, which has survey maps, soil characterization data, and soil climate data. The Soil Data Mart enables the downloading of tabular and spatial soil data. Other major sections provide images of soil, information about soil use, classification standards, current research topics, and resources for teachers and students.

Subject(s): Soil Surveys

Publication(s): *Field Book for Describing and Sampling Soils*, A 57.2
Keys to Soil Taxonomy, A 57.2
National Soil Survey Handbook, A 57.6/2
Soil Taxonomy, A 1.76

Plants and Animals

http://www.nrcs.usda.gov/wps/portal/nrcs/main/national/
plantsanimals

Sponsor(s): Agriculture Department (USDA)—Natural Resources Conservation Service (NRCS)

Description: This site focuses its resources on the acquisition, development, integration, quality control, dissemination, and access of plant and animal information. Its Web site features the fully searchable PLANTS Database and detailed fact sheets on selected trees and plants. Its areas of focus are fish and wildlife, insects and pollinators, invasive species and pests, livestock, and plants.

PLANTS National Database

http://plants.usda.gov/

Sponsor(s): Agriculture Department (USDA)—Natural Resources Conservation Service (NRCS)

Description: The PLANTS National Database features standardized information about the plants found in the United States and its territories. It includes names of plants, checklists, automated tools, identification information, species abstracts, distributional data, crop information, plant symbols, plant growth data, plant materials information, plant links, and references. The database can generate reports such as lists of endangered and threatened plants, invasive and noxious plants, wetlands plants, and state-specific lists of plants. The PLANTS Web site includes a gallery of over 50,000 plant images.

This database is an excellent source for verifying plant names and other plant information.

Subject(s): Plants

Publication(s): *PLANTS Database*, A 57.80

PS&D Online

http://www.fas.usda.gov/psdonline/

Sponsor(s): Agriculture Department (USDA)—Foreign Agricultural Service (FAS)

Description: The Production, Supply and Distribution (PS&D) online database has current and historical Department of Agriculture data on production, supply, and distribution of agricultural commodities for the United States and selected producing and consuming countries. The site offers predefined tables and the opportunity to download the raw data in comma-separated value format. Users can also perform custom queries by searching for a specific commodity, type of statistic, country, and year.

Subject(s): Agricultural Commodities—Statistics

Risk Management Agency (RMA)

http://www.rma.usda.gov/

Sponsor(s): Agriculture Department (USDA)—Risk Management Agency (RMA)

Description: RMA manages the Federal Crop Insurance Corporation (FCIC) and other risk management programs for agricultural producers. The site features extensive information and data to support farm risk planning. It also has a directory of insurance agent and company locators, an annual list of insurable crops, and other program information.

Subject(s): Crop Insurance—Disaster Assistance

State Fact Sheets from USDA/ERS

http://www.ers.usda.gov/data-products/state-fact-sheets.aspx#.
U1HJFcev-lY

Sponsor(s): Agriculture Department (USDA)—Economic Research Service (ERS)

Description: The State Fact Sheets Web site contains basic demographic and farm statistics for each state. These statistics are also available for the United States as a whole and include population, employment, income, farm characteristics, top agriculture commodities, top agriculture exports, and farm financial indicators. Data are updated as new information becomes available.

This is a simple service for basic demographic and agricultural profiles of the states. Researchers looking for more detailed data can click on the links provided throughout each fact sheet to consult more extensive data tables. Agency contacts are also provided.

USDA Economics, Statistics and Market Information System (ESMIS)

http://usda.mannlib.cornell.edu/MannUsda/homepage.do

Sponsor(s): Cornell University—Mann Library

Description: Hosted by Cornell University, this Web site features a collection of nearly 2,500 reports and data sets from Department of Agriculture economics agencies, including the Agricultural Marketing Service, Economic Research Service, the National Agricultural Statistics Service, and the World Agricultural Outlook Board. It includes current and historical data and reports on national food and agricultural developments; it also forecasts the effects of changing conditions and policies on domestic and international agriculture.

Users may search the entire database or a combination of its components for reports or datasets. They may also browse by topic, with available topics including agricultural baseline projections; commodities; economics and management; livestock, dairy, and poultry; specialty agriculture; trade and international; weather; and market news. In addition, information may be browsed alphabetically by agency through the links toward the top of the home page.

Materials cover both U.S. and international agricultural topics. Most reports are presented as PDF or ASCII text files. Most datasets are in spreadsheet format and include time-series data that are updated annually.

While some of these reports are available in full from Department of Agriculture Web sites, the value of this Cornell University Web site lies in its standard interface, centralized access, and historical back files.

Subject(s): Agriculture—Statistics

Weather and Climate

http://www.usda.gov/oce/weather/

Sponsor(s): Commerce Department—National Oceanic and Atmospheric Administration (NOAA)Agriculture Department (USDA)—World Agricultural Outlook Board

Description: The Joint Agricultural Weather Facility (JAWF) collects global weather and agricultural information to determine the impact of growing season weather conditions on international crops and livestock production prospects. This JAWF Web site features U.S. Agricultural Weather Highlights, Major World Crop Areas and Climatic Profiles, and the Weekly Weather and Crop Bulletin.

Subject(s): Agriculture—International; Weather

Publication(s): *Weekly Weather and Crop Bulletin*, C 55.209

World Agricultural Outlook Board (WAOB)

http://www.usda.gov/oce/commodity/

Sponsor(s): Agriculture Department (USDA)—World Agricultural Outlook Board

Description: WAOB coordinates analysis from many Department of Agriculture agencies to produce a monthly World Agricultural Supply and Demand Estimates report, and it houses the Joint Agricultural Weather Facility. This Web page, part of the larger Department of Agriculture Office of the Chief Economist Web site, provides information about the WAOB and copies of publications.

Subject(s): Agricultural Economics—International

Publication(s): *USDA Agricultural Baseline Projections to . . .* , A 93.44

FISHING

Atlantic States Marine Fisheries Commission (ASMFC)

http://www.asmfc.org/

Sponsor: Atlantic States Marine Fisheries Commission

Description: The ASMFC, a group made up of the 15 Atlantic coastal states, was formed by an interstate compact approved by Congress. These states work together through ASMFC to manage the Atlantic fisheries. The ASMFC Web site includes news, research and statistics, law enforcement compliance reports, links to other fisheries organizations, and information about pending actions open for public input.

Subject(s): Fisheries

Fisheries and Habitat Conservation

http://www.fws.gov/fisheries/

Sponsor(s): Interior Department—Fish and Wildlife Service (FWS)

Description: FWS maintains this Web site as a portal to FWS division and program Web sites concerned with fisheries and habitat conservation. Topics include invasive species, pollution, restoration, and climate change. Program links lead to the Web sites for Fish and Wildlife Conservation Offices, the National Fish Hatchery System, and related sites.

Subject(s): Conservation (Natural Resources); Fisheries

FishWatch—U.S. Seafood Facts

http://www.nmfs.noaa.gov/fishwatch/

Sponsor(s): Commerce Department—National Oceanic and Atmospheric Administration (NOAA)—National Marine Fisheries

Description: FishWatch provides consumers with information on the health and sustainability of U.S. seafood fisheries. The site explains what is meant by "sustainable" and supplies detailed sustainability, management, and nutrition profiles for over 30 types of fish. Other information details fisheries management, fishing vessels, U.S. seafood trade, and health and nutrition information.

FishWatch is an excellent consumer-oriented site that provides quick access to information written for the general public, as well as significant detail for those who wish to learn more.

Gulf States Marine Fisheries Commission (GSMFC)

http://www.gsmfc.org/

Sponsor: Gulf States Marine Fisheries Commission (GSMFC)

Description: GSMFC is a Congress-authorized organization made up of the five Gulf of Mexico states (Texas, Louisiana, Mississippi, Alabama, and Florida). Its Web site includes sections with information on programs, publications, databases, and regulations.

Subject(s): Fisheries

NOAA Aquaculture Program

http://aquaculture.noaa.gov/

Sponsor(s): Commerce Department—National Oceanic and Atmospheric Administration (NOAA)

Description: The aquaculture program at NOAA seeks to support an economically sound industry, provide safe seafood, and promote a healthy marine ecology. The Web site provides an overview of aquaculture in the United States. It also identifies competitive grant programs and financial assistance available from NOAA and other federal agencies.

NOAA Fisheries—National Marine Fisheries Service

http://www.nmfs.noaa.gov/

Sponsor(s): Commerce Department—National Oceanic and Atmospheric Administration (NOAA)—National Marine Fisheries

Description: The National Marine Fisheries Service is the component of NOAA charged with conserving, protecting, and managing living marine resources. The Web site covers issues related to overfishing, domestic fisheries, highly migratory species, seafood inspection, and laws such as the Magnuson-Stevens Fishery Conservation and Management Reauthorization Act. The Regions and Science Centers sections of the site group content into local and regional areas. The Science and Technology section, under Programs, includes fisheries statistics and economic information, along with reports on the work of NOAA Fisheries science centers and research vessels; science publications, such as the NOAA Fisheries Glossary, can be found here. The Law Enforcement subsection describes the work of NOAA Fisheries special agents and enforcement officers. The Web site also has information on aquaculture and on the NOAA Seafood Inspection Program.

Although it sports an uncluttered and fun look, the NOAA Fisheries site contains broad and deep coverage of its topics. Users can easily navigate the NOAA divisions to find science, research, statistics, regulations, and other information related to NOAA's marine resources activities.

Subject(s): Fisheries; Marine Mammals

Publication(s): *Fisheries of the United States,* C 55.309/2-2

Fishery Bulletin, C 55.313

Fishery Market News, C 55.318

Imports and Exports of Fishery Products, Annual Summary, C 55.309/2-10

NOAA Fisheries Glossary, C 55.13/2

Our Living Oceans, Annual Report on the Status of U.S. Living Marine Resources, C 55.1/2

Northwest Fisheries Science Center (NWFSC)

http://www.nwfsc.noaa.gov/

Sponsor(s): Commerce Department—National Oceanic and Atmospheric Administration (NOAA)—National Marine Fisheries

Description: NWFSC is a NOAA Fisheries research center. Its Web site describes the center's research and includes publications and image libraries for marine life, marine mammals, and killer whales. This site has a wide variety of research information, primarily in the Publications and Resources sections.

Subject(s): Fisheries

Pacific States Marine Fisheries Commission (PSMFC)

http://www.psmfc.org/

Sponsor(s): Pacific States Marine Fisheries Commission (PSMFC)

Description: PSMFC, authorized by Congress in 1947, is one of three interstate commissions dedicated to resolving fishery issues. It serves as a forum for discussion of fishery issues in California, Oregon, Washington, Idaho, and Alaska. Its Web site has information about current projects, events, grants and contracts, workshop proceedings, and links to fisheries data projects.

FORESTRY

Ecosystem Management Coordination (EMC)

http://www.fs.fed.us/emc/

Sponsor(s): Agriculture Department (USDA)—Forest Service (USFS)

Description: The EMC Office is concerned with information and analysis to support Forest Service planning. Its Web site includes information about the Forest Service's environmental appeals and litigation, information related to the National Environmental Protection Act and Environmental Impact Statements, and planning documents related to the National Forest Management Act.

Forest Service

http://www.fs.fed.us/

Sponsor(s): Agriculture Department (USDA)—Forest Service (USFS)

Description: The Forest Service manages public lands in national forests and grasslands. The Web site's home page features a forest and grassland locator tool and coverage of topical issues such as water use and climate change. The site also has sections for Employment, Fire & Aviation, Maps & Brochures, Passes & Permits, Recreational Activities, Safety & Occupational Health, Research & Development, and State & Private Forestry. The Pubs, Regs, & Manuals section includes the full-text versions of USFS directives, manuals, handbooks, and other publications. The Projects & Policies section highlights proposed regulatory and policy initiatives and links to the Schedule of Proposed Actions "that will soon begin or are currently undergoing environmental analysis and documentation." (From the Web site)

The State & Private Forestry section concerns Forest Service assistance to landowners, state governments, and other communities and institutions. Topics covered include tribal relations, sustainable development, conservation education, and urban forestry.

Subject(s): Forestry

Publication(s): *Fire Management Today,* A 13.32

Global Leaflet, A 13.153

Land Areas of the National Forest System, A 13.10

U.S. Forest Facts and Historical Trends, A 13.2:F 76/

Forestry Technical Resources

http://www.nrcs.usda.gov/technical/forestry.html

Sponsor(s): Agriculture Department (USDA)—Natural Resources Conservation Service (NRCS)

Description: This Web page serves as a central point for links to the Department of Agriculture and other federal agencies that provide information about forestry. Web links cover topics from silvopasture to windbreaks.

Subject(s): Forestry

Forests and Rangelands

http://www.forestsandrangelands.gov/

Sponsor(s): Interior Department

Description: The Forests and Rangelands Web site is a portal to information about the Federal Wildland Emergency Plan and related initiatives. The site provides reports, news, and documents relating to wildfires. The resources section includes a wildland firefighting glossary (under Resources).

Subject(s): Forest Fires; Forests—Policy

USDA National Agroforestry Center (NAC)

http://www.unl.edu/nac/

Sponsor(s): Agriculture Department (USDA)

Description: Agroforestry combines forestry, agriculture, land conservation, and sustainable development practices. NAC is a partnership of the Department of Agriculture's Forest Service and National Resource Conservation Service. The NAC Web site provides research publications, analytical tools, guides, and other material related to agroforestry practices. Special topics include riparian forest buffers, silvopasture, and forest farming. The site also provides a collection of images and videos and a blog with conservation news.

Subject(s): Forestry—Research

Publication(s): *Agroforestry Notes*, A 13.164/2

Inside Agroforestry, A 13.164

Working Trees, A 13.2

THREE

Business and Economics

The federal government both regulates and supports U.S. businesses, and it monitors and influences the national economy. These roles drive much of the business and economic information published by the government, which has long been an important, authoritative source of industry and finance data. While this chapter has broad coverage, it does not feature labor-related information (see the Employment chapter) or government finance and taxation (see the Government and Politics chapter).

Subsections in this chapter are Business and Industry, Consumer Information, Economics, Federal Reserve System, Finance, International Trade, and Money.

BUSINESS AND INDUSTRY

Alcohol and Tobacco Tax and Trade Bureau (TTB)
http://www.ttb.gov/
Sponsor(s): Treasury Department—Alcohol and Tobacco Tax and Trade Bureau (TTB)
Description: TTB was created by the Homeland Security Act of 2002, which moved the law enforcement functions of the Bureau of Alcohol, Tobacco, and Firearms (ATF) from the Department of the Treasury to the Department of Justice. The act established TTB as manager of the ATF functions that remained at Treasury Department. TTB administers and enforces the federal laws and tax code provisions related to the production and taxation of alcohol and tobacco products. The bureau also collects all excise tax on the manufacture of firearms and ammunition.

The TTB Web site is divided into industry sections covering beer, wine, distilled spirits, other alcohol, tobacco, and firearms and ammunition. Information is also organized by topic, including labeling, permits, taxes/filings, imports/exports, and forms/publications. Information for industry about the TTB and compliance is available in Spanish, French, and Chinese. The site has a search engine and A to Z index to help researchers locate specific information.

Subject(s): Guns—Regulations; Taxation; Tobacco—Regulations; Alcohol—Regulations

Publication(s): *Statistical Release. Tobacco Products.*, T 70.9/2
Statistical Report. Distilled Spirits, T 70.9/3
Statistical Report. Wine, T 70.9/5
TTB Newsletter

Baldrige National Quality Program (BNQP)

http://www.nist.gov/baldrige/

Sponsor(s): Commerce Department—Technology Administration (TA)—National Institute of Standards and Technology (NIST)

Description: The Malcolm Baldrige National Quality Award, sponsored by the Department of Commerce, is the centerpiece of the BNQP. This award recognizes performance excellence and focuses on an organization's overall performance management system. The award may be presented to several types of organizations: manufacturers, service companies, small businesses, nonprofit/government, education, or health care organizations. The BNQP Web site presents detailed information about the award, the award process, performance criteria, and past winners.

Business USA

http://business.usa.gov/

Sponsor(s): Agriculture Department (USDA)—Commerce Department—Labor Department—Treasury Department—Veterans Affairs Department (VA)

Description: Business USA provides plentiful resources for businesses and entrepreneurs, including help with starting and growing a business, exporting goods, and finding funding opportunities. The home page provides a clickable list of topics to help users navigate the site's offerings, including Start a Business, Grow Your Business, Find Opportunities, and Explore Exporting.

Census Bureau Business & Industry

http://www.census.gov/econ/

Sponsor(s): Commerce Department—Economics and Statistics Administration (ESA)—Census Bureau

Description: This Web page provides a central access point for business and industry data from a variety of Census Bureau programs. It provides an overview of the survey programs and finding aids. The site's sidebar organizes links to Census Bureau data by sector (such as construction) and by topic (such as business dynamics, small business, and historical data).

Center for Veterans Enterprise
http://www.vetbiz.gov/
Sponsor(s): Veterans Affairs Department (VA)
Description: The Center for Veterans Enterprise works to promote veteran-owned businesses. Its Web site includes the VA VOSB Verification Program Document Submission Web Portal and the Vendor Information Pages (VIP).

Committee on Foreign Investments in the United States (CFIUS)
http://www.treasury.gov/resource-center/international/Pages/
Committee-on-Foreign-Investment-in-US.aspx
Sponsor(s): Committee on Foreign Investments in the United States (CFIUS)
Description: CFIUS, an interagency committee chaired by the Secretary of the Treasury, reviews notices of foreign acquisitions of U.S. companies and may investigate on behalf of the president if such acquisitions could threaten national security. This Department of the Treasury Web page links to regulations, guidance, and legislation.

Competition and Real Estate
http://www.usdoj.gov/atr/public/real_estate/
Sponsor(s): Justice Department—Antitrust Division
Description: This special Web site from the Antitrust Division of the Justice Department focuses on the real estate brokerage industry. The site examines laws and practices that increase prices and suggests alternative models. Information about additional sites is also provided, as is contact information.

Department of Commerce
http://www.commerce.gov/
Sponsor(s): Commerce Department
Description: The Department of Commerce Web site is an excellent starting point for finding government information related to the world of business. It links to the sites for the department's bureaus dealing with different aspects of commerce and the information that supports it; these include the Bureau of Economic Analysis (BEA), the International Trade Administration (ITA), the U.S. Patent and Trademark Office (USPTO), and the National Oceanic and Atmospheric Administration (NOAA). The Commerce home page links to current news and the department's blog. As a Cabinet-level department, Commerce also provides reports on its Recovery Act and Open Government activities on the site.

Most substantive program information can be found at the individual Web sites for the Commerce Department's bureaus.

E-Stats: Measuring the Electronic Economy
http://www.census.gov/eos/www/ebusiness614.htm

Sponsor(s): Commerce Department—Economics and Statistics Administration (ESA)—Census Bureau

Description: E-Stats is a central clearinghouse for reports and data from the Census Bureau that define and measure electronic commerce across multiple economic sectors. The E-Stats Web site has quarterly reports on online retail sales and annual reports comparing e-commerce sales to total sales. In May 2012, the 2010 e-commerce multi-sector "E-Stats" report was released.

Federal Trade Commission (FTC)
http://www.ftc.gov/

Sponsor(s): Federal Trade Commission (FTC)

Description: The FTC enforces federal antitrust and consumer protection laws. Its Web site provides tabbed pages for each of the FTC's roles. The For Consumers section includes guides for businesses and individual consumers dealing with unfair or fraudulent business practices. The Commissions Actions tab provides documents such as FTC advisory opinions, adjudicative opinions of the commission, advocacy filings, public comments on proposed regulations, and commission and staff reports. Other tabbed sections provide FTC news, economic reports, congressional testimony, and information on the FTC's international efforts. The site also provides several RSS news feeds.

On the consumer side, the FTC site offers many fact sheets and guides, an online complaint form, and links to federal consumer Web sites on specific topics such as identity theft, Internet scams, and the National Do Not Call Registry. The FTC also has a version of the site available in Spanish, with an emphasis on providing news and consumer protection information.

This Web site serves a valuable public function by presenting clear, fresh, and timely information. The multiple ways to access information ensure that both consumers and antitrust researchers will be able to find what they need.

Subject(s): Business—Regulations; Consumer Information

Publication(s): *Federal Trade Commission Decisions*, FT 1.11

FTC Bureau of Consumer Protection—Business Center
http://business.ftc.gov/

Sponsor(s): Federal Trade Commission (FTC)—Bureau of Consumer Protection

Description: This section of the FTC Web site is a central point for finding compliance information for businesses and fraud protection advice for businesses. Topics include credit, identity theft, information security, and telemarketing.

Manufacturing, Mining, and Construction Statistics

http://www.census.gov/mcd/

Sponsor(s): Commerce Department—Economics and Statistics Administration (ESA)—Census Bureau

Description: This Census Bureau gateway Web site compiles all census-related information about manufacturing, mining, and construction into one page. Data primarily come from the Annual Survey of Manufactures, Current Industrial Reports, and the Economic Census, although information from other programs is also available. Construction statistics include new residential construction, sales, and building permits. The Manufacturing section includes the latest releases on manufacturers' shipments, inventories, and orders. The site also links to a service for tailoring your own statistical reports, called Just The Facts and offered by the Census Bureau's Manufacturing and Construction Division.

Subject(s): Construction Industry—Statistics; Manufacturing—Statistics; Mining—Statistics

Publication(s): *Annual Survey of Manufactures*, C 3.24/9
Current Industrial Reports, Manufacturing Profiles, C 3.158/4

Manufacturing.gov

http://www.manufacturing.gov/

Sponsor(s): Commerce Department—National Institute of Standards and Technology (NIST)

Description: Manufacturing.gov links to information about U.S. manufacturing policy and support initiatives and to resources for manufacturers. It spotlights programs from NIST and the International Trade Administration. It also serves as a home site for the Manufacturing Council, a board with industry and government representation. Resources on the site include a directory of manufacturing and trade associations, U.S. Web sites and publications, and analyses of the manufacturing industry.

MBDA Web Portal

http://www.mbda.gov/

Sponsor(s): Commerce Department—Minority Business Development Agency (MBDA)

Description: MBDA's mission is to promote the growth and competitiveness of American minority business enterprises of all sizes. The agency funds business development centers throughout the United States. The MBDA Web site has agency news and announcements, a directory of regional offices, contract opportunity announcements, and background information about federal contracting, business development, and finance. The Business Tools section of the site offers a variety of online business tools, such as an interactive business plan writer. These can be used after setting up a free account.

NAICS—North American Industry Classification System

http://www.census.gov/epcd/www/naics.html

Sponsor(s): Commerce Department—Economics and Statistics Administration (ESA)—Census Bureau

Description: NAICS is the official industry classification system used by U.S. statistical agencies. Adopted in 1997, NAICS replaced the Standard Industrial Classification (SIC) codes that had been used in government reports since the 1930s. This Web site is the central location for NAICS news and documentation. It includes information about the current, 2012 edition of the *NAICS Manual* and previous editions. A NAICS Search section allows keyword and NAICS code number searching of the 2012, 2007, and 2002 editions of the *NAICS Manual*, with links to display the code's hierarchy and description.

The official 2012 manual is available from the National Technical Information Service and Bernan Press.

Subject(s): Industries

National Women's Business Council

http://www.nwbc.gov/

Sponsor(s): National Women's Business Council

Description: The National Women's Business Council is a federal advisory council that provides advice and policy recommendations to the president, Congress, and the Small Business Administration on issues relevant to female business owners. Its Web site features reports, an events calendar, and referrals to counseling and training programs. The Issues & Research section includes reports pertaining to women and entrepreneurship. Fact sheets are also available on the site.

Office of Women's Business Ownership

http://www.sba.gov/about-offices-content/1/2895

Sponsor(s): Small Business Administration (SBA)

Description: According to the Web site, "The Office of Women's Business Ownership's mission is to establish and oversee a network of Women's Business Centers (WBCs) throughout the United States and its territories." The Resources section provides a directory of SBA offices. Funding and financial assistance information is available in the Loans & Grants section.

Patent and Trademark Office (PTO)

http://www.uspto.gov/

Sponsor(s): Commerce Department—Patent and Trademark Office (PTO)

Description: Major sections of the PTO Web site include Patents, Trademarks, and Learning and Resources. The first two sections include the relevant guides, legal information, and agency contacts. PTO publications are listed in the Products and Services section, along with a directory of Patent and Trademark Depository Libraries (PTDLs). The *Official Gazette for Patents*, the *Official Gazette for Trademarks*, and Federal Register notices are in the News and Notices section.

The site also has searchable patent and trademark databases and electronic filing. TESS, a database of pending, registered, and dead federal trademarks, is also available on the site.

Patent law and trademark law are complex fields, and the PTO site is a complex interface to resources on the topic. The overall site could be organized to serve specific audiences, from the novice to the patent professional.

Subject(s): Intellectual Property; Patent Law; Trademarks

Publication(s): *Basic Facts About Registering a Trademark*, C 21.2:R 26/
Electronic Official Gazette: Patents, C 21.5
General Information Concerning Patents, C 21.26/2
Index to the U.S. Patent Classification, C 21.12/2
List of Patent Classification Definitions (database), C 21.3/2
Manual of Patent Classification, C 21.12
Manual of Patent Examining Procedure, C 21.15
Patent Public Advisory Committee Annual Report, C 21.1/4
Products and Services Catalog, C 21.30
Trademark Official Gazette, C 21.5/4
Trademark Public Advisory Committee Annual Report, C 21.1/3
U.S. Patent Applications Database, C 21.31/17

Small Business Administration (SBA)

http://www.sba.gov/

Sponsor(s): Small Business Administration (SBA)

Description: The mission of the SBA is to assist and protect the interests of small business. Its Web site defines the parameters of a small business in the Getting Started, under Contracting. The Starting & Managing section links to information about writing a business plan, business counseling, and growing a business. Forms can also be found in this section. Financial information is contained in the Loans and Grants section.

As of 2011, Business.gov's content moved to the SBA Web site. Business.gov provided one-stop access to practical business resources and services from state and federal agencies and other organizations.

This one-stop shop for small businesses has information in over 50 languages to meet the needs of entrepreneurs engaging in any type of small business practice.

Subject(s): Small Business

StopFakes.gov / Small Business
http://www.uspto.gov/smallbusiness/
Alternate URL(s)
http://www.stopfakes.gov/smallbusiness/
Sponsor(s): Commerce Department—Patent and Trademark Office (PTO)
Description: This Web site is part of the PTO campaign to educate small businesses about the effects of piracy, counterfeiting, and theft of intellectual property. It includes basic information about patents, trademarks, copyright, and the government's anti-piracy campaign.

Subject(s): Intellectual Property; Small Business

CONSUMER INFORMATION

Aviation Consumer Protection Division
http://www.dot.gov/airconsumer
Sponsor(s): Transportation Department
Description: The Aviation Consumer Protection Division of the Department of Transportation receives the general public's complaints about airline consumer issues and works with the aviation industry to improve compliance with consumer protection requirements. Complaints about air travel safety, security, airline service, and disability or discrimination claims can be made through the site. The Most Popular Services sections includes the following links: File an Aviation Consumer Complaint, Air Travel Consumer Reports, Aviation Enforcement Orders, Guidance on Aviation Rules and Statute, and Air Travel Tips.

Subject(s): Airlines; Consumer Information

Consumer Product Safety Commission (CPSC)
http://cpsc.gov/
Sponsor(s): Consumer Product Safety Commission (CPSC)
Description: CPSC develops and enforces standards to reduce the risk of injury or death from consumer products. The CPSC Web site highlights recent product recall news; these highlights are available as an RSS feed, e-mail, or Android app. The site has a database of previous recall announcements organized by date, product category, and company. The Newsroom section of the site includes links to CPSC publications, CPSC *Federal Register* notices, and statistics related to consumer product safety. The Research & Statistics section features the National Electronic Injury

Surveillance System (NEISS) database of emergency hospital visits involving an injury associated with consumer products.

The Business & Manufacturing section of the site includes regulatory guidance, information on how to report a potentially hazardous product, and a directory of testing labs by product. Some portions of the CPSC Web site, consumer guides and alerts in particular, are available in Spanish, Chinese, and Vietnamese.

This is a useful site for consumers, who can use it to report defective consumer products and check to see which products have been recalled. Consumers may also wish to visit the federal government's Recalls.gov Web site.

Subject(s): Product Recalls; Product Safety

EConsumer.gov

http://www.econsumer.gov/

Sponsor(s): Federal Trade Commission (FTC)

Description: The EConsumer.gov Web site is a collaborative effort of 26 nations; the FTC is primarily in charge of United States participation. The site was developed in response to the international nature of Internet fraud. It provides general information about consumer protection in all of the countries that belong to the International Consumer Protection Enforcement Network (ICPEN), contact information for consumer protection authorities in those countries, and an online complaint form. The site can be viewed in English, Spanish, German, French, Korean, Chinese, Turkish, and Polish.

FCC Consumer and Governmental Affairs Bureau (CGB)

http://www.fcc.gov/cgb/

Sponsor(s): Federal Communications Commission (FCC)—Consumer and Governmental Affairs Bureau

Description: CGB informs consumers on telecommunications issues and works with other government agencies to formulate telecommunications policy. The CGB Web site policy and regulatory information along with consumer fact sheets and alerts on topics such as charges on phone bills, broadband Internet access, disability access, and the regulation of indecency and obscenity on broadcasts. The Inquiries and Complaints Division section features a quarterly press release with statistics on the types of consumer inquiries and complaints received by the bureau. The site also provides a wealth of consumer information in Spanish.

FTC Consumer Information

http://www.consumer.ftc.gov/

Sponsor(s): Federal Trade Commission (FTC)—Bureau of Consumer Protection

Description: This Web site features a blog with FTC consumer information. Also featured are informational sections for Money & Credit; Homes & Mortgages; Health & Fitness; Jobs & Making Money; and Privacy & Identity. A Spanish-language version of the site is available.

HelpWithMyBank.gov

http://www.helpwithmybank.gov/

Sponsor(s): Treasury Department—Comptroller of the Currency (OCC)

Description: HelpWithMyBank.gov is designed for customers of national banks. It addresses common consumer questions about bank accounts, credit cards, insurance, loans and credits, mortgages, and other banking topics. The site's "Need More Help?" section discusses how to determine if a financial institution is a national bank and how to file a banking complaint. The site's top menu links to a dictionary of financial terms. Some information is available in Spanish.

Mymoney.gov

http://www.mymoney.gov/

Sponsor(s): Financial Literacy and Education Commission

Description: Aimed at the individual consumer, this Web site provides tips on financial planning, credit, saving, home ownership, retirement, and other personal finance topics. A Spanish-language version is also available. The U.S. Financial Literacy and Education Commission, an interagency organization, sponsors the site.

Subject(s): Personal Finance

National Consumer Protection Week

http://www.ncpw.gov/

Sponsor(s): Federal Trade Commission (FTC)

Description: This one-stop government Web site provides links to information about National Consumer Protection Week, which took place from March 1 through 7 in 2015. Some content is available in Spanish.

National Do Not Call Registry

http://www.donotcall.gov/

Sponsor(s): Federal Trade Commission (FTC)

Description: The National Do Not Call Registry is managed by FTC and allows individuals to block most telemarketing calls to their phones. Consumers can use this Web site to register their phone numbers or file complaints about violations of the "do not call" rules or scammers posing as members of the registry. A Spanish-language version of the site is available. The site also links to compliance information for telemarketers.

This site is clearly written and easy to use.

OnGuard Online

http://onguardonline.gov/

Sponsor(s): Federal Trade Commission (FTC)

Description: OnGuard Online presents tips for securing personal computers and personal information. Topics covered on its Web site include wireless security, laptop security, computer disposal, online scams, and kids' online safety. The File a Complaint link at the bottom of the page directs users to appropriate agencies. A Spanish-language version is also available.

SaferProducts.gov

http://www.saferproducts.gov/

Sponsor(s): Consumer Product Safety Commission (CPSC)

Description: According to the Web site, "The U.S. Consumer Product Safety Commission is charged with protecting the public from unreasonable risks of injury or death from thousands of types of consumer products under the agency's jurisdiction." SaferProducts.gov allows users to search recalls and reports and to file reports about unsafe products. Registered businesses can respond to the complaints. The Web site, in the About section, also provides information about the Consumer Product Safety Improvement Act (CPSIA) of 2008.

Subject(s): Product Safety

ECONOMICS

ALFRED: Archival Federal Reserve Economic Data

http://alfred.stlouisfed.org/

Sponsor(s): Federal Reserve—Federal Reserve Bank of St. Louis

Description: ALFRED is an economic database that allows researchers to analyze historical decisions made based on the data that were available at the time (prior to revisions and updates). "Vintage" data sets, as they are called on ALFRED, can be downloaded as compressed spreadsheets or as tab-delimited text files. Data is available for 54,700 series in 9 categories, including Academic Data; Money, Banking, & Finance; National Accounts; Population, Employment, & Labor Markets; Production & Business Activity; Prices; International Data; Greenbook Projections; and U.S. Regional Data. The Regional Data category has vintage data sets for such areas as states, Census regions, and Freddie Mac regions.

ALFRED is intended for academic professionals and other advanced economics researchers.

Annual and Quarterly Services

http://www.census.gov/services/index.html

Sponsor(s): Commerce Department—Economics and Statistics Administration (ESA)—Census Bureau

Description: According to the Web site, "The Quarterly Services Survey (QSS) and the Service Annual Survey (SAS) work together to produce the most comprehensive data available on service activity in the United States." Sectors covered include information sector services; professional, scientific, and technical services; administrative and support, and waste management and remediation services; and health care and social assistance.

Bureau of Economic Analysis (BEA)

http://www.bea.gov/

Sponsor(s): Commerce Department—Economics and Statistics Administration (ESA)—Bureau of Economic Analysis (BEA)

Description: BEA produces the data for the U.S. national income and product accounts (NIPAs), including gross domestic product (GDP) and related measures of the national economy. The BEA home page features the latest economic releases, an annual schedule for all BEA releases, and an RSS feed of BEA news releases. BEA also has the online *Survey of Current Business.* (Issues from 1921 to 2002 are available on the Web site of the Federal Reserve Bank of St. Louis at http://fraser.stlouisfed.org/publications/SCB/.)

BEA organizes links to its data under National, International, Regional, Integrated Accounts, and Industry sections. National data includes GDP, Personal Income and Outlays, and Corporate Profits. International data includes Balance of Payments and Trade in Goods and Services. Regional data includes GDP by State and Metropolitan Area. Industry data includes GDP by Industry and Travel and Tourism Satellite Accounts. Integrated Accounts includes Integrated Income, Product, and Federal Reserve Financial Accounts and Integrated BEA GDP-BLS Productivity Accounts. Bureau of Economic Analysis Regional Fact Sheets (BEARFACTS) are available by state, county, metropolitan statistical area (MSA), and BEA economic area.

The BEA Web site presents important national economic statistics, with multiple access points and several convenient downloading options. The site design makes it easy to access current or historical data.

Subject(s): Economic Statistics; National Accounts—Statistics

Publication(s): *National Income and Product Accounts*, C 59.11/5-3

State BEARFACTS . . . , C 59.29/

Economic Census

http://www.census.gov/econ/census07/

Alternate URL(s)

http://www.census.gov/econ/census/index.html

Sponsor(s): Commerce Department—Economics and Statistics Administration (ESA)—Census Bureau

Every five years, the Economic Census profiles the U.S. economy from the national to the local level. This census tabulates the number of business establishments (or companies), number of employees, payroll, and measures of output (such as sales and receipts); data are reported by industry sector and by geography. The Economic Census also surveys business owner characteristics such as race, age, and education. Data and reports from the Economic Census are available from this Web site and via the Census Bureau's American FactFinder (described elsewhere in this book). The Web site also supplies a number of guides for using the data.

The release of the 2012 Economic Census began in early 2014 and will continue through mid-2016. The 2007 Economic Census releases occurred from 2009 through 2011.

Subject(s): Economic Statistics; Industries—Statistics

Economic Indicators (CEA)

http://www.gpo.gov/fdsys/browse/collection.action?collectionCode= ECONI

Sponsor(s): Council of Economic Advisers (CEA)

Description: The monthly publication Economic Indicators is prepared by the CEA for Congress's Joint Economic Committee. Economic Indicators is hosted online by the Government Printing Office FDsys system. Analyzed indicators include gross domestic product (GDP), sources of personal income, unemployment rates, productivity, producer prices, consumer prices, federal receipts and outlays, and more. Economic Indicators issues from 1995 forward are available at this site.

Economic Indicators is a convenient compilation for reference use. However, as it is a monthly publication, researchers should check elsewhere to see if an indicator has recently been updated. Economic Indicators notes the source of each indicator and makes it easy for users to check the Web site of the issuing agency, such as the Bureau of Labor Statistics. Researchers will also want to consult the Economic Indicators.gov site, which is described elsewhere in this chapter. The Federal Reserve's FRASER® Web site has Economic Indicators back to 1948. FRASER® is described on the following page.

Subject(s): Economic Statistics

Economics and Statistics Administration (ESA)

http://www.esa.doc.gov/

Sponsor(s): Commerce Department—Economics and Statistics Administration (ESA)

Description: ESA delivers economic data, analyses, and forecasts. Its Web site links to information from its better-known component agencies, including the Census Bureau and the Bureau of Economic Analysis. ESA periodically conducts its own studies, and these are available in the Reports section.

FRASER®—Federal Reserve Archival System for Economic Research

http://fraser.stlouisfed.org/

Sponsor(s): Federal Reserve—Federal Reserve Bank of St. Louis

Description: FRASER® provides copies of historical economic statistical publications and releases in PDF format. Key documents include *All Bank Statistics, United States, 1896–1955*, which was published by the Federal Reserve Board of Governors in 1959, and the Fed's *Banking and Monetary Statistics* for the periods 1914–1941 and 1941–1970. Other statistical series include the *Annual Statistical Digest* (1976–2000), *Productivity and Costs* (1971–2004), and the *Business Statistics* supplement to the Survey of Current Business. The site also carries digitized documents reflecting the Fed's history, such as excerpts from the Open Market Investment Committee and its successor for the 1923–1931 period.

By providing resources that were previously only available in printed form, FRASER® helps researchers compile uninterrupted historical data series. FRASER® also allows researchers to obtain data as they were reported in preliminary, revised, and final releases.

FRED®—Economic Data

http://research.stlouisfed.org/fred2/

Sponsor(s): Federal Reserve—Federal Reserve Bank of St. Louis

Description: FRED®—Federal Reserve Economic Data—is a database of U.S. economic data available as time series. FRED® data can be downloaded in spreadsheet or text formats or viewed as charts. Data series are grouped by source and under categorical headings such as Money, Banking, & Finance; National Accounts; Population, Employment, & Labor Markets; Production & Business Activity; Prices; International Data; and U.S. Regional Data. The site offers RSS alerts to announce new data.

GeoFRED™

http://geofred.stlouisfed.org/

Sponsor(s): Federal Reserve—Federal Reserve Bank of St. Louis

Description: GeoFRED™ can be used to create thematic maps of U.S. economic data for states, counties, metropolitan statistical areas (MSAs), and other geographic areas. The data available to be mapped depends upon the geographic area selected. Custom maps can be printed or saved as PDF files, GeoFRED™ can build a Web link for the map, and the data can be downloaded. The site also offers tutorials and lessons plans for educators based on GeoFRED™.

GeoFRED puts simple thematic mapping of economic data into the hands of the general public. For important background information and instructions, see the Help link.

Office of Economic Policy

http://www.treasury.gov/about/organizational-structure/offices/Pages/Economic-Policy.aspx

Sponsor(s): Treasury Department—Office of Economic Policy

Description: The Department of the Treasury's Office of Economic Policy analyzes domestic and international economic issues and the financial markets. The office's Web site includes economic policy reports, reports on key economic indicators, and annual reports of Total Taxable Resources (TTR). It also contains the *Social Security Trustees Report and the Medicare Trust Funds Trustees Report*, which the office prepares for the secretary of the treasury.

Subject(s): Economic Policy

Publication(s): *Annual Report of the Board of Trustees of the Federal Old-Age and Survivors Insurance and Disability Insurance Trust Funds*, SSA 1.1/4:

Page One Economics

http://liber8.stlouisfed.org/

Sponsor(s): Federal Reserve—Federal Reserve Bank of St. Louis

Description: The full subtitle of the Page One Economics Web site is "The Back Story on Front Page Economics." The site links to the latest economic indicators, featured data series, and other useful economics-oriented information. The site includes practice information and graphing tutorials for the FRED database, as well as an economic newsletter.

This site provides an uncluttered interface that links to a carefully selected and organized set of Web resources. It should be of assistance to anyone unsure of where to begin researching economic conditions.

Regional Economic Conditions (RECON)

http://www2.fdic.gov/recon/

Sponsor(s): Federal Deposit Insurance Corporation (FDIC)

Description: RECON provides standard reports, graphs, and maps depicting economic conditions and their changes over time at the state, county, and metropolitan statistical area (MSA) levels. Data cover employment and job growth, housing and construction, commercial real estate activity, and banking conditions. A tutorial is available at the site. Selected charts and data can be added to the user's "shopping cart" and then downloaded.

FEDERAL RESERVE SYSTEM

Board of Governors of the Federal Reserve System
http://www.federalreserve.gov/
Sponsor(s): Federal Reserve—Board of Governors
Description: The Federal Reserve, the central bank of the United States, hosts this Web site with sections on About the Fed, Monetary Policy, Banking Information & Regulation, Payment Systems, Economic Research & Data, Consumer Information, and Community Development. The site offers RSS feeds of news and data. Some consumer-level information is also available in Spanish.

The Economic Research & Data section has a special Data Download option for custom downloads of the Fed's statistical releases. In the Monetary Policy section, the site has information on the Federal Open Market Committee, which announces targets for the federal funds rate. The Monetary Policy section also links to the Fed's Summary of Commentary on Current Economic Conditions by Federal Reserve District, commonly known as the Beige Book. The Publications section includes articles from the Federal Reserve Bulletin (no longer available in print), bank supervision manuals, and news releases and historical data for interest rates, foreign exchange rates, consumer credit, and other related topics.

This Web site offers a substantial body of information and statistics from the Board of Governors of the Federal Reserve System. It serves as a good starting point for users seeking information about the system as a whole. However, valuable data are also available from the individual Federal Reserve Banks. One limitation of this main site is that its links to the member bank Web sites are several clicks away; they can be found in the About the Fed section.
Subject(s): Banking Regulation; Monetary Policy
Publication(s): *Annual Report of the Board of Governors of the Federal Reserve System*, FR 1.1
Federal Reserve Bulletin, FR 1.3
Monetary Policy Report to the Congress, Y 4.B 22/3

CASSIDI
http://cassidi.stlouisfed.org/
Sponsor(s): Federal Reserve—Federal Reserve Bank of St. Louis
Description: The CASSIDI database has geographic and deposit information for all U.S. bank holding companies, banks, thrifts, and their branches. It also has tools to compare market concentrations across banking markets. The site is intended to help those in the banking and finance industry examine how potential mergers or acquisitions could affect market structures and competition.
Subject(s): Federal Reserve

Fed in Print

http://www.fedinprint.org

Sponsor(s): Federal Reserve—Federal Reserve Bank of San Francisco

Description: Fed in Print is an index to Federal Reserve economic research. Sponsored by the Federal Reserve Bank of San Francisco, it covers Federal Reserve publications from all of the system's banks. The search form supports searches by keyword, title, author, bank, publication year, and publication name.

Fed in Print focuses on economic research. The Federal Reserve System has a comprehensive online catalog on the New York Fed's Web site at http://www.newyorkfed.org/publications/.

Subject(s): Federal Reserve

Federal Reserve Bank of Atlanta

http://www.frbatlanta.org/

Sponsor(s): Federal Reserve—Federal Reserve Bank of Atlanta

Description: The Federal Reserve Bank of Atlanta encompasses banking institutions in the Sixth Federal Reserve District, which is made up of Alabama, Florida, and Georgia, and portions of Louisiana, Mississippi, and Tennessee. The main sections of the Atlanta Fed's Web site are About the Fed (including information about the Atlanta Fed and the Federal Reserve System), Banking, Community Development, Consumer Information, Research & Data, Regional Economy, and News & Events. The Publications section includes the quarterly magazine *EconSouth*, which focuses on the economy of the Southeast region. The Web site also features blogs and podcasts with regional economic commentary.

Subject(s): Banking Regulation; Monetary Policy

Federal Reserve Bank of Boston

http://www.bostonfed.org/

Sponsor(s): Federal Reserve—Federal Reserve Bank of Boston

Description: The Federal Reserve Bank of Boston serves the First Federal Reserve District, which includes the six New England states: Connecticut (excluding Fairfield County), Massachusetts, Maine, New Hampshire, Rhode Island, and Vermont. Along with full information from the Federal Reserve System, local information includes the Web site for the Federal Reserve Banks' New England Public Policy Center; the monthly *New England Economic Indicators* publication; and banking, economic, and government finance profiles for the region. Online publications include *Communities & Banking*.

Subject(s): Banking Regulation; Monetary Policy

Federal Reserve Bank of Chicago

http://www.chicagofed.org/

Sponsor(s): Federal Reserve—Federal Reserve Bank of Chicago

Description: The Federal Reserve Bank of Chicago's Web site features a wide range of banking information for the Seventh Federal Reserve District, which comprises all of Iowa and most of Illinois, Indiana, Michigan, and Wisconsin. The main sections of the site include Research, Banking, Markets, and Education. Online periodicals include *AgLetter, Chicago Fed Letter,* and *Economic Perspectives.* Regional information for the Midwest economy includes the Chicago Fed Midwest Manufacturing Index and National Activity Index.

Subject(s): Banking Regulation; Monetary Policy

Publication(s): *AgLetter*

Chicago Fed Letter

Federal Reserve Bank of Cleveland

http://www.clevelandfed.org/

Sponsor(s): Federal Reserve—Federal Reserve Bank of Cleveland

Description: This Web site serves the Fourth Federal Reserve District, which is made up of Ohio, western Pennsylvania, eastern Kentucky, and the northern panhandle of West Virginia. The Our Region section provides local demographic, business, and economic statistics. The Cleveland Fed has set up a special Foreclosure Resource Center in the Community Development section of their site.

Subject(s): Banking Regulation; Monetary Policy

Federal Reserve Bank of Dallas

http://www.dallasfed.org/

Sponsor(s): Federal Reserve—Federal Reserve Bank of Dallas

Description: The Federal Reserve Bank of Dallas covers the 11th Federal Reserve District, which includes Texas, northern Louisiana, and southern New Mexico. It has branches in El Paso, San Antonio, and Houston. Regional economic data is available in the Research & Data sections, including the DataBasics introduction to Texas economic indicators. The Dallas Fed houses the Globalization and Monetary Policy Institute and links to the Institute site. The site also offers e-mail alerts and RSS news feeds.

The Dallas Fed Web site is a good resource for information on economic factors affecting the 11th District, such as the impacts of the oil industry and trade with Mexico.

Subject(s): Banking Regulation; Monetary Policy

Publication(s): *Banking and Community Perspectives*

Federal Reserve Bank of Kansas City

http://www.kc.frb.org/

Sponsor(s): Federal Reserve—Federal Reserve Bank of Kansas City

Description: This Web site serves the 10th Federal Reserve District, which comprises Colorado, Kansas, Nebraska, Oklahoma, Wyoming, northern New Mexico, and western Missouri. The Kansas City Fed's site includes sections that cover financial services, banking, community development, consumer help, and education. Regional economy information under Research & Data includes regional economic indicators and the Kansas City Financial Stress Index, and the online newsletter Main Street Economist can be found under Publications.

Subject(s): Banking Regulation; Monetary Policy

Publication(s): *Main Street Economist*

Federal Reserve Bank of Minneapolis

http://www.minneapolisfed.org/

Sponsor(s): Federal Reserve—Federal Reserve Bank of Minneapolis

Description: This Web site features a variety of resources for the Ninth Federal Reserve District, which includes Montana, North Dakota, South Dakota, Minnesota, the Upper Peninsula of Michigan, and northwestern Wisconsin. Publications online include the *Fedgazette*, *The Region*, and *Community Dividend*. Data on the site include regional economic data and forecasts, agricultural credit conditions, and manufacturing surveys.

Subject(s): Banking Regulation; Monetary Policy

Publication(s): *Community Dividend*
Fedgazette

Federal Reserve Bank of New York

http://www.newyorkfed.org/

Sponsor(s): Federal Reserve—Federal Reserve Bank of New York

Description: The New York Federal Reserve Bank is responsible for the Second District: New York State, the 12 northern counties of New Jersey, Fairfield County in Connecticut, Puerto Rico, and the U.S. Virgin Islands. Research and data on the geographical region can be found throughout the site but are most readily available in the Research and Regional Outreach sections. Second District publications include *Current Issues in Economics and Finance*, *Second District Highlights*, and *Upstate New York Regional Review*. In addition to the regional economic research and data, the site has a rich Education section with information for all levels of learners. The site also hosts the publications section for the Federal Reserve System.

Subject(s): Banking Regulation; Monetary Policy
Publication(s): *Current Issues in Economics and Finance*
Economic Policy Review
Second District Highlights

Federal Reserve Bank of Philadelphia

http://www.philadelphiafed.org/
Sponsor(s): Federal Reserve—Federal Reserve Bank of Philadelphia
Description: The Federal Reserve Bank of Philadelphia is responsible for eastern Pennsylvania, southern New Jersey, and the state of Delaware. It features a special Payment Cards Center (PCC) that "provides meaningful insights into developments in consumer credit and payments that are of interest not only to the Federal Reserve but also to the industry, other businesses, academia, policymakers, and the public at large." (from the Web site) The PCC includes pertinent studies, legislative information, and consumer information. Other sections of the site include Research & Data, Bank Resources, Community Development, and Education. The Publications page includes the Annual Report, Circular Letters, Consumer Publications, and Financial Institutions subsections.

The PCC provides information useful at a national level. The current and diverse resources from the PCC should be of interest to consumers, policymakers, academics, and others.

Subject(s): Banking Regulation; Consumer Credit—Research; Monetary Policy

Federal Reserve Bank of Richmond

http://www.richmondfed.org/
Sponsor(s): Federal Reserve—Federal Reserve Bank of Richmond
Description: The Federal Reserve Bank of Richmond serves the Fifth Federal Reserve District, which includes the District of Columbia, Maryland, Virginia, North Carolina, South Carolina, and most of West Virginia. Its Web site features Research, Banking, Publications, Community Development, and Education sections. Regional data can be found in both the Research section and in the online magazine *Region Focus*.

Subject(s): Banking Regulation; Monetary Policy
Publication(s): *Region Focus*

Federal Reserve Bank of San Francisco

http://www.frbsf.org/
Sponsor(s): Federal Reserve—Federal Reserve Bank of San Francisco
Description: This Web site serves the 12th Federal Reserve District, which comprises the states of Alaska, Arizona, California, Hawaii, Idaho, Nevada, Oregon, Utah, and Washington, as well as the territories of American Samoa, Guam, and the Northern Mariana Islands. The Web site features information on the recent financial crisis and on mortgage

foreclosures. The site hosts the Fed In Print index of Federal Reserve research publications, which can be found at www.fedinprint.org/ and is described earlier in this chapter.

Subject(s): Banking Regulation; Monetary Policy

Federal Reserve Bank of St. Louis

http://www.stlouisfed.org/

Sponsor(s): Federal Reserve—Federal Reserve Bank of St. Louis

Description: The Federal Reserve Bank of St. Louis represents the Eighth Federal Reserve District, which comprises all of Arkansas and portions of Illinois, Indiana, Kentucky, Mississippi, Missouri, and Tennessee. The site hosts a Financial Crisis Timeline at http://timeline.stlouisfed.org/. The Research and Data/Economic Research section of their Web site provides numerous research resources not available on other Fed sites. For example, the site's FRED® database provides easy access to U.S. economic time series. Another database, FRASER®, provides historical economic statistical publications. The ALFRED® database has archival economic data. These resources from the St. Louis Fed are also described in separate entries in this book.

The innovative resources in the Research and Data/Economic Research section make the St. Louis Fed Web site one of the more interesting regional sites for national-level research.

Subject(s): Banking Regulation; Monetary Policy

Publication(s): *Central Banker*
Federal Reserve Bank of St. Louis Review
Regional Economist

Federal Reserve Education

http://www.federalreserveeducation.org/

Sponsor(s): Federal Reserve

Description: This Web site organizes links to the many educational resources made available by the Federal Reserve Banks. Sections provide both classroom resources (lesson plans, activities) and resources on personal finance relevant to the general public. A Multimedia section includes education videos, games, and simulations.

Subject(s): Economics; Educational Resources

Federal Reserve System Online

http://www.federalreserveonline.org/

Sponsor(s): Federal Reserve—Board of Governors

Description: This Web directory site provides links to the Web sites of the individual Reserve Banks and to system-wide sites such as the Reserve System's online publication catalog and consumer help page.

Subject(s): Federal Reserve System

National Information Center—Federal Reserve System
   http://www.ffiec.gov/nicpubweb/nicweb/nichome.aspx
   Sponsor(s): Federal Reserve—Board of Governors
   Description: This Web site describes the National Information Center
   (NIC) database as a "central repository of data about banks and other
   institutions for which the Federal Reserve has a supervisory, regulatory,
   or research interest, including both domestic and foreign banking organ-
   izations operating in the United States." The Institution Search and USBA
   Search enable searches by institution name, location, or type. In addition,
   NIC has lists and information on the nation's top 50 bank holding companies.
   Subject(s): Banking; Databases

FINANCE

Commodity Futures Trading Commission (CFTC)
   http://www.cftc.gov/
   Sponsor(s): Commodity Futures Trading Commission (CFTC)
   Description: CFTC is an independent agency regulating commodity
   futures and options markets in the United States. The Market Reports
   section of the Web site includes Commitments of Traders reports in short
   and long formats, *Bank Participation Reports,* and other reports. The Consumer Protection section includes reparations programs and fraud case
   status reports.
      The About the CFTC section includes commissioner biographies, the
   CFTC organization chart, advisory committee information, and CFTC
   history. The Industry Oversight section links to the exchanges designated
   by the CFTC as contract markets and derivatives clearing organizations
   registered with the CFTC. The site also features an Education Center with
   basic information on how futures markets work and consumer protection
   advice for those investing in futures markets.
   Subject(s): Securities and Investments—Regulations
   Publication(s): *Commitments of Traders in Futures,* Y 3.C 73/5:9-3/

Community Development Financial Institutions (CDFI) Fund
   http://www.cdfifund.gov/
   Sponsor(s): Treasury Department—Office of Domestic Finance
   Description: The CDFI Fund assists community development financial institutions to promote economic revitalization in underserved and
   low-income areas. The site has information for applicants and for recipients of CDFI Fund awards. Under the Impact We Make heading, the site
   has a database of awards made from 1996 to the present.
   Subject(s): Economic Development

EDGAR—SEC Filings and Forms

http://www.sec.gov/edgar.shtml

Sponsor(s): Securities and Exchange Commission (SEC)

Description: The EDGAR database holds reports and documents submitted by publicly traded companies and others required by law to file forms with the SEC. The filings provide information on company finances, management, legal proceedings, and more. The EDGAR search page includes options for finding companies and their current associated filings and searching archived EDGAR documents. In 2006, the SEC added the capability to search the full texts of filings. The About EDGAR section provides essential information about the database scope and coverage. The EDGAR Web site also has a tutorial, a guide to SEC filings, and file transfer capability.

The SEC has launched an interactive system built on the XBRL, or eXtensible Business Report Language, format. See http://xbrl.sec.gov/, listed elsewhere in this book, for more information.

The filings available through EDGAR are a standard source of information about publicly traded companies. Many researchers supplement EDGAR with commercial, for-fee database subscriptions that provide the same data but with enhanced search and report features. There are also free commercial Web sites for EDGAR filings, such as SEC Info at http://www.secinfo.com/.

Subject(s): Companies and Enterprises

FDIC and Financial Regulatory Reform

http://www.fdic.gov/regulations/reform/

Sponsor(s): Federal Deposit Insurance Corporation (FDIC)

Description: This section of the FDIC Web site explains the FDIC's work in implementing financial regulatory reform measures. The site also links to speeches, press releases, and related FDIC documents.

Federal Deposit Insurance Corporation (FDIC)

http://www.fdic.gov/

Sponsor(s): Federal Deposit Insurance Corporation (FDIC)

Description: The FDIC was created during the Great Depression to insure deposits in banks and thrift institutions in the United States. Major topical sections of the FDIC Web site are Deposit Insurance, Consumer Protection, Industry Analysis (bank statistics, a directory of FDIC-insured institutions, and a failed banks list), Regulations & Examinations, and Institution & Asset Sales (from failed banks). The site organizes content by audience, with separate pages for bankers, consumers & communities, analysts, and regulators.

The FDIC Web site's offerings will be appealing to both professionals and consumers. For professionals, the detailed statistics and various full-text reports provide opportunities for research into banking trends and specific institutions. For consumers, the site offers advice, referrals to rating services, and statistics on individual institutions.

Subject(s): Banking Regulation

Publication(s): *FDIC Consumer News*, Y 3.F 31/8:24/

FDIC Quarterly, Y 3.F 31/8:38/

FDIC Quarterly Banking Profile, Y 3.F 31/8:29/

FDIC Statistics on Banking, Y 3.F 31/8:1-4/

Financial Institution Letters, Y 3.F 31/8:34

Historical Statistics on Banking, Y 3.F 31/8:26/

Federal Financial Institutions Examination Council (FFIEC)

http://www.ffiec.gov/

Sponsor(s): Federal Financial Institutions Examination Council (FFIEC)

Description: The FFIEC is "a formal interagency body empowered to prescribe uniform principles, standards, and report forms for the federal examination of financial institutions by the Board of Governors of the Federal Reserve System (FRB), the Federal Deposit Insurance Corporation (FDIC), the National Credit Union Administration (NCUA), the Office of the Comptroller of the Currency (OCC), and the Consumer Financial Protection Bureau (CFPB), and to make recommendations to promote uniformity in the supervision of financial institutions," according to the Web site. Financial institutions and examiners are primary audiences for the site, which provides reporting forms and data to facilitate regulatory compliance. The Enforcement Actions section links to enforcement and orders pages at council members' Web sites.

The FFIEC's Uniform Bank Performance Reports (UBPRs), technical reports intended for use by banks and bank supervisors, have been made available through a modernized Central Data Repository's Public Data Distribution (CDR) Web site. CDR makes FFIEC data available for searching and for bulk download.

Subject(s): Banking Regulation

Publication(s): *Bank Secrecy Act/Anti-Money Laundering Examination Manual*, Y 3.F 49

HMDA Aggregate Reports, FR 1.63/54

HMDA Disclosure Statements, FR 1.63/55

Financial Crisis Inquiry Commission

http://fcic.law.stanford.edu/

Alternate URL(s)

http://www.fcic.gov/

Sponsor(s): Financial Crisis Inquiry Commission (FCIC)

Description: The FCIC was created by the Fraud Enforcement and Recovery Act of 2009 (Public Law 111-21). The commission investigated 22 areas of potential fraud, risk, and enforcement problems including the mortgage industry, lending practices, the credit rating system, derivatives and unregulated financial products, corporate governance, and the performance of federal and state financial regulators. The Web site includes commission reports and testimony before the commission.

Financial Crisis Timeline

http://timeline.stlouisfed.org/

Sponsor(s): Federal Reserve—Federal Reserve Bank of St. Louis

Description: This site provides news, data, and government reports related to the 2008-2009 financial crisis. The site is organized around a timeline starting in February 2007. Each event on the timeline links to the related source document

Subject(s): Banking; Economic Conditions

FinancialStability.gov

http://financialstability.gov/

Sponsor(s): Treasury Department

Description: This site provides news and information on the administration's Financial Stability Plan. It describes the Troubled Assets Relief Program (TARP) established under the Emergency Economic Stabilization Act of 2008 (Public Law 110-343). TARP includes the Capital Assistance Program, Consumer and Business Lending Initiative, Making Home Affordable Program, Public-Private Investment Program, Capital Purchase Program, Asset Guarantee Program, Targeted Investment Program, and Automotive Industry Financing Program. The site provides TARP Transaction Reports, the Tranche Reports, and other reports to Congress. The Impact section has a searchable database of contracts and agreements related to the Financial Stability Plan, copies of the monthly bank lending surveys, and a map showing locations where the Department of the Treasury has funded transactions through the Capital Purchase Program.

Investor.gov

http://investor.gov/

Sponsor(s): Securities and Exchange Commission (SEC)

Description: Investor.gov has information on saving, investing, and protecting money. The site covers managing investments, transitioning into retirement, and fraud prevention, and provides SEC investor alerts and bulletins.

Joint Board for the Enrollment of Actuaries

http://www.irs.gov/Tax-Professionals/Enrolled-Actuaries

Sponsor(s): Treasury Department—Internal Revenue Service (IRS)

Description: The Joint Board for the Enrollment of Actuaries sets the qualification standards and certification process for individuals who perform actuarial services as required under the Employee Retirement Income Security Act of 1974 (ERISA). Its Web site provides information on the board and its qualification and renewal processes.

Money Services Businesses

http://www.fincen.gov/financial_institutions/msb/

Sponsor(s): Treasury Department

Description: MSBs are nonbank financial institutions defined as such for purposes of the Bank Secrecy Act. The MSB Web site includes a list of the conditions that define an MSB. The site also has regulatory guidance, forms, news, and background information.

National Credit Union Administration (NCUA)

http://www.ncua.gov/

Sponsor(s): National Credit Union Administration (NCUA)

Description: NCUA is an independent federal agency that supervises and insures credit unions. Information for credit unions includes regulatory information and credit union financial data. Information for consumers includes educational information about credit unions and a list of recently closed credit unions. Documents available from the NCUA Web site include relevant laws, rules, and regulations; statistical reports; and NCUA Letters to Credit Unions. The Credit Union Data and Applications section has a searchable credit union directory.

    Subject(s): Credit Unions—Regulations

    Publication(s): *Accounting Manual for Federal Credit Unions*, NCU 1.8:

    NCUA Credit Union Directory, NCU 1.16:

    NCUA Letters to Credit Unions, NCU 1.19:

Office of Domestic Finance

http://www.treasury.gov/about/organizational-structure/offices/Pages/Domestic-Finance.aspx

Sponsor(s): Treasury Department—Office of Domestic Finance

Description: The Office of Domestic Finance has broad policy and oversight roles in areas relating to financial institutions, financial markets, and government finance. The office's Web site provides detailed descriptions of their programs and links to offices, commissions, bureaus, and resources.

    Subject(s): Finance—Policy

Office of the Comptroller of the Currency (OCC)

http://www.occ.treas.gov/

Sponsor(s): Treasury Department—Comptroller of the Currency (OCC)

Description: An independent bureau of the Department of the Treasury, OCC charters, regulates, and supervises all national banks and supervises the federal branches and agencies of foreign banks. The OCC Web site features information about banking regulations, banker education, community development investments of national banks, consumer rights, and electronic banking, and other topics. The Corporate Activities subsection features the *Weekly Bulletin*, a record of the actions by the OCC on all applications involving national banks (nationwide) for new banks, branches, mergers, conversions, changes in bank control, fiduciary powers, domestic subsidiaries, relocations of main offices and branches, and information on notices such as changes in corporate titles and branch closings. The News and Issuances section consists of news releases, consumer advisories, alerts, and OCC Bulletins. The OCC Web site has both a site map and a Subjects(s) index to help users find specific information.

In late July 2011, OCC took over supervisory responsibility for federal savings associations, formerly in the Office of Thrift Supervision.

Subject(s): Banking Regulation
Publication(s): *Comptroller's Licensing Manual*, T 12.17/4
Economic Working Papers, T 12.22
OCC Alerts, T 12.21
OCC Bulletins, T 12.20
Survey of Credit Underwriting Practices, T 12.27
Weekly Bulletin, Office of the Comptroller of the Currency

Securities and Exchange Commission (SEC)

http://www.sec.gov/
Sponsor(s): Securities and Exchange Commission (SEC)
Description: The SEC, which is led by five presidentially appointed commissioners, regulates the securities markets. The SEC Web site features both financial information for investors and information for the securities industry that it oversees. A major offering is the EDGAR database of corporate filings, described elsewhere in this chapter. Information is arranged toward the bottom of the home page by audience groups such as accountants, funds and advisers, international, and small businesses.

The Investor Information (or Information for Investors) section contains the bulk of the online publications, with some consumer education publications available in Spanish. Under News, the SEC provides webcasts of its open meetings, forums, and other public events. The daily *SEC News Digest* in the same section is available as an RSS feed and is online back to 1956.

Subject(s): Securities and Investments—Regulations
Publication(s): *SEC Special Studies*, SE 1.38

SIGTARP

http://www.sigtarp.gov/

Sponsor(s): Treasury Department

Description: The Office of the Special Inspector General for the Troubled Asset Relief Program (SIGTARP) coordinates audits and investigations of the purchase, management, and sale of assets under the Troubled Asset Relief Program (TARP). The Web site includes SIGTARP organizational information, press releases, updates on audits and investigations, and quarterly reports to Congress. Citizens can report suspected TARP waste, fraud, or abuse via the Web site or through a toll-free number.

Subject(s): Financial Crimes; Inspectors General

StopFraud.gov

http://www.stopfraud.gov/

Sponsor(s): Financial Fraud Enforcement Task Force

Description: The StopFraud.gov Web site explains the work of the Financial Fraud Enforcement Task Force, established in 2009. The Task Force is a coalition of federal and state fraud enforcement agencies. The Web site has a page for reporting fraud by type, such as identity theft, mass marketing/telemarketing scams, tax fraud, Medicare fraud, and mortgage fraud and loan scams. It also has news of financial fraud convictions and information on how to protect oneself from fraud.

Subject(s): Financial Crimes

Treasury International Capital System

http://www.treas.gov/tic/

Sponsor(s): Treasury Department

Description: The Treasury International Capital (TIC) System tracks the flow of investment funds between U.S. residents and foreign residents. Data are released on a monthly, quarterly, and annual basis, and are available from this site.

Subject(s): International Finance—Statistics

XBRL.SEC.Gov

http://xbrl.sec.gov/

Sponsor(s): Securities and Exchange Commission (SEC)

Description: This site will be most useful to publicly traded companies and other entities that file reports with the SEC. It provides extensive information on the SEC's planned migration to the eXtensible Business Reporting Language (XBRL) standard for their data.

Subject(s): Companies and Enterprises; Securities and Investments

INTERNATIONAL TRADE

AESDirect

https://aesdirect.census.gov/

Sponsor(s): Commerce Department—Economics and Statistics Administration (ESA)—Census Bureau

Description: AESDirect (Automated Export System Direct) allows shippers to electronically file Electronic Export Information (EEI). Its Web site offers user guides, registration information, and online training. It also offers links to related sites.

Subject(s): Exports—Regulations; Shipper's Export Declarations

African Growth and Opportunity Act (AGOA)

http://www.agoa.gov/

Sponsor(s): Commerce Department—International Trade Administration (ITA)

Description: AGOA implementation is designed to offer incentives for African nations to maintain open economies and free market practices. Under the act, eligible sub-Saharan African countries may export certain products to the United States with no import duty. The AGOA Web site describes the original legislation, Public Law 106-200, and its subsequent amendments. The site includes AGOA reports to Congress, lists of eligible countries and products, African trade statistics, and information from the AGOA trade forums.

Subject(s): Trade Agreements; Africa

Bureau of Industry and Security (BIS)

http://www.bis.doc.gov/

Sponsor(s): Commerce Department—Bureau of Industry and Security (BIS)

BIS regulates the export of sensitive goods, such as weapons technologies and encryption software and regulates exports to certain countries in accordance with U.S. policy. BIS also enforces U.S. antiboycott laws, the Fastener Quality Act, and the reporting provisions of the Chemical Weapons Convention. The BIS Web site links to major regulations, export licensing guidelines, news, and training courses on export restrictions. The primary audience for the site is the U.S. exporter community.

The site links to the online Freedom of Information Act Reading Room with selected documents available in full. The Policy Guidance section provides general and specific information about export control. Other sections discuss enforcement (with a list of major cases) and the Defense Industrial Base programs.

While geared toward the practical needs of exporters, the BIS Web site is also a good source for general research on U.S. export controls.

Subject(s): Exports—Regulations

Publication(s): *Export Administration Regulations*, C 63.23

China Business Information Center

http://www.export.gov/china/

Sponsor(s): Commerce Department—International Trade Administration (ITA)

Description: This Web site provides information for U.S. companies seeking to do business with China. It provides information on trade policy initiatives and China's business laws and regulations. The site also has sections on trade leads, trade events, and links to other useful sites.

Subject(s): Exports; China

Committee for the Implementation of Textile Agreements (CITA)

http://otexa.ita.doc.gov/cita.htm

Sponsor(s): Committee for the Implementation of Textile Agreements (CITA)

Description: CITA is an interagency committee responsible for taking actions to comply with and ensure compliance with the international textile agreements to which the United States is a party. CITA is chaired by the Department of Commerce and receives staff assistance from the Office of Textiles and Apparel. The CITA Web site consists, among other things, of a description of the committee's role, trade data, foreign tariffs, and sections for publications and archives.

Subject(s): Textile Industry; Trade Agreements

Defense Technology Security Administration

http://www.dtsa.mil/

Sponsor(s): Defense Department—Defense Technology Security Administration (DTSA)

Description: DTSA's primary mission is to preserve critical U.S. military technological advantages through control of technology exports and technical exchanges. The Web site has sections describing the work of DTSA's Licensing, Policy, Space, and Technology Directorates.

Subject(s): Arms Control; Exports—Regulations; Military Technology

Directorate of Defense Trade Controls (DDTC)

http://pmddtc.state.gov/

Sponsor(s): State Department—Defense Trade Controls Directorate

Description: The DDTC Web site provides information about the rules governing U.S. exports of defense materials and services. For manufacturers, exporters, and brokers of defense articles, the site has information on registration and compliance. The site also has a chart of new country policies and embargoes as announced in the Federal Register and meeting records for the Defense Technology Advisory Group.

Subject(s): Exports—Regulations

Doing Business in International Markets

http://www.state.gov/e/eb/cba/

Sponsor(s): State Department—Economic and Business Affairs Bureau

Description: The Office of Commercial and Business Affairs (CBA) within the Department of State's Economic and Business Affairs Bureau sponsors this page of links to State Department international business information.

Subject(s): International Business

Export Administration Regulations

http://www.access.gpo.gov/bis/

Alternate URL(s)

http://www.fdsys.gov

Sponsor(s): Commerce Department—Bureau of Industry and Security (BIS)

Description: This is the online version of the loose-leaf subscription service for *Export Administration Regulations*, which features a compilation of official regulations and policies governing the export licensing of commodities and technical data.

Subject(s): Exports—Regulations

Export USA

http://www.thinkglobal.us/

Sponsor(s): Commerce Department—International Trade Administration (ITA)

Description: This Web site is the online version of *Commercial News USA*, an official export magazine of the Department of Commerce. The magazine and Web site are designed to assist importers around the world in their efforts to locate the desired American products and services and to help American sellers find buyers and distributors for the services and products.

Although an official publication of the Commerce Department, this magazine is managed by a private company and accepts advertising

Subject(s): Exports

Publication(s): *Export USA*

Export.gov

http://www.export.gov/

Sponsor(s): Commerce Department—International Trade Administration (ITA)

Description: Export.Gov is a portal for information relevant to U.S. exporters. The site covers export basics, trade leads, trade events, export finance, market research, trade data, and trade problems (such as trade barriers and unfair practices). Under Opportunities, the Market Research section includes a step-by-step guide for researching markets using government Web sites and other resources.

As with other subject-oriented government Web portals, this Web site provides one-stop access to resources available from a variety of government agencies. While it is intended for those in the export business, it also serves as a useful entry point and reference resource for international trade researchers.

Subject(s): Exports

ExportControl.org
   http://www.exportcontrol.org/
   Alternate URL(s)
   http://www.state.gov/t/isn/ecc/
   Sponsor(s): State Department—Nonproliferation Bureau
   Description: ExportControl.org is sponsored by the Export Control and Related Border Security Assistance program (EXBS), a U.S. government interagency program designed to help other countries improve their export control systems. The site has an overview of the U.S. export control program and describes its best practices. The Resources section directs users to information from the European Union, nongovernmental organizations, and other sources. The Department of State's Bureau of International Security and Nonproliferation manages the program. Information about the program is also available at the alternate URL listed above.
   Subject(s): Arms Control; Exports—Regulations

Export-Import Bank of the United States
   http://www.exim.gov/
   Sponsor(s): Export-Import Bank of the United States
   Description: The Export-Import Bank offers export financing for U.S. businesses. The Products section of its Web site provides information about the bank's working capital financing, export credit insurance, loan guarantees, and direct loans. Application forms and instructions on applying are included with the information. Users should also look in the How to Apply subsection, under Products, where more services are listed. The How to Apply section contains reference material, and the site also features sections for specific audiences, including small businesses and green businesses.
   Subject(s): Finance; International Trade

Foreign Trade Statistics

http://www.census.gov/foreign-trade/

Sponsor(s): Commerce Department—Economics and Statistics Administration (ESA)—Census Bureau

Description: The Foreign Trade Division (FTD) of the Census Bureau manages two major statistical programs: the Automated Export System (AES), which captures shipping data, and the compilation and reporting of trade statistics. The AES portion of the Web site will primarily be of interest to exporters participating in the program. Foreign trade data, which appears in the Data section, appeals to a much broader range of interests. The Data section also features reports on individual country balance of trade and products traded with the United States, a monthly list of the top trading partners with the United States, state export data, and historic trade balance data going back to 1960. Current and past issues of the FT900—the major monthly update of U.S. trade in goods and services—are available. Exhibits, or data announced in the FT900 release, are available in PDF, text, or spreadsheet formats.

Subject(s): Trade Statistics

Publication(s): *Imports of Steel Products*, C 3.164:900-A/

U.S. International Trade in Goods and Services, FT900, C 3.164:900/

Import Administration (IA)

http://www.trade.gov/ia/

Sponsor(s): Commerce Department—International Trade Administration (ITA)—Import Administration

Description: IA enforces laws and agreements to prevent unfairly traded imports. Its Web site provides IA documents on anti-dumping and countervailing duties reviews and determinations. The Highlights and News section provides notice of IA actions with links to related documents. The site provides guidance for U.S. businesses encountering unfair trade practices and information on IA programs such as the Foreign Trade Zones program and the Steel Import Monitoring and Analysis licensing system.

Subject(s): Trade Laws and Regulations

International Trade Commission (ITC)

http://www.usitc.gov/

Sponsor(s): International Trade Commission (ITC)

Description: ITC is an independent federal agency that examines unfair trade practices and the impact of imports on U.S. industries. The ITC Web site's Investigations section, under Popular Topics, includes major case news and documents regarding antidumping and countervailing duty investigations, intellectual property investigations (called "Section 337" investigations), and recent petitions and complaints. The site features DataWeb, ITC's international trade statistics and U.S. tariff database. The Tariff Affairs section includes the *Official Harmonized Tariff Schedule of the United States (HTS)*, which describes all goods in trade for duty, quota, and statistical purposes. *HTS* is available online in PDF and database formats. The Industry/Economic Analysis section contains detailed reports on products, services, and regions.

The availability of the tariff schedules and the DataWeb statistical tool makes this a core resource for international trade information.

Subject(s): International Trade

Publication(s): *Harmonized Tariff Schedule of the United States, Annotated for Statistical Reporting Purposes*, ITC 1.10:

Journal of International Commerce and Economics, ITC 1.29:

Manufacturing and Services

http://www.trade.gov/mas/

Sponsor(s): Commerce Department—International Trade Administration (ITA)

Description: Manufacturing and Services, a division of ITA, offers services to promote U.S. exports and has special expertise in U.S. industry and service sectors. Content on the sector pages varies, but most provide links to industry reports and information on industry-specific export programs. The site also has a directory of industry experts on staff.

Subject(s): Exports

Market Research Library

http://www.buyusainfo.net/

Sponsor(s): Commerce Department—International Trade Administration (ITA)—Commercial Service

Description: The Market Research Library is a full-text database of reports from the U.S. Commercial Service about foreign markets. The database can be searched by industry sector, country, and other criteria. It includes the *Country Commercial Guides* series prepared by U.S. Commercial Service trade specialists working in over 80 countries. The site also has customizable e-mail alerts for notices of new market research in an industry sector and region.

Subject(s): Market Research—International; Country Information

Publication(s): *Country Commercial Guides*, S 1.40/7:

Middle East and North Africa Business Information Center (MENABIC)

http://www.export.gov/middleeast/

Sponsor(s): Commerce Department—International Trade Administration (ITA)

Description: The MENABIC Web site provides information to assist U.S. companies doing business in that region. Sections include country-specific information.

Subject(s): Exports; Middle East

Notify U.S.

http://www.nist.gov/notifyus

Alternate URL(s)

http://tsapps.nist.gov/notifyus/data/index/index.cfm

Sponsor(s): Commerce Department—Technology Administration (TA)—National Institute of Standards and Technology (NIST)

Description: This free e-mail subscription service offers U.S. entities (citizens, industries, and organizations) an opportunity to review and comment on proposed foreign technical regulations that may affect their businesses and their business' access to international markets. The United States receives notice of these proposed regulations as a member of the World Trade Organization.

Subject(s): Exports—Regulations

Office of Industry Analysis

http://www.ita.doc.gov/td/industry/otea/

Sponsor(s): Commerce Department—International Trade Administration (ITA)

Description: The Office of Industry Analysis develops trade and economic data products and provides analysis on issues affecting the competitiveness of U.S. manufacturing and services. The Web site features links to the Trade Stats Express database (including state-level export data), U.S. metropolitan area export information, and profiles of the effects of exports and foreign investment in each of the 50 states. Offices within Industry Analysis are the Office of Trade and Industry Information, the Office of Trade Policy Analysis, and the Office of Competition and Economic Analysis. The section for the Office of Trade and Industry Information provides trade data and reference information, as well as the Exporter Database.

Subject(s): Trade Statistics

Office of Textiles and Apparel (OTEXA)

http://otexa.ita.doc.gov/

Sponsor(s): Commerce Department—International Trade Administration (ITA)

Description: The OTEXA Web site provides information on exporting U.S.-made textiles and apparel products. The site provides detailed trade data, information on trade agreements and trade preferences, Federal Register notices, and export requirements. It also has country-specific information on textile import tariffs with links to the Web site of the foreign government office responsible for tariff administration.

Subject(s): Exports; Textile Industry

Publication(s): *Major Shippers Report*, C 61.53

U.S. Exports of Textile and Apparel Products, C 61.50

U.S. Imports of Textile and Apparel Products, C 61.52

U.S. Textile and Apparel Category System, C 61.54

Office of the United States Trade Representative (USTR)

http://www.ustr.gov/

Sponsor(s): Trade Representative (USTR)

Description: USTR is responsible for developing and coordinating U.S. international trade, commodity, and direct investment policy and for overseeing trade negotiations with other countries. This Web site presents information on negotiations, treaties, and issues in sections organized by trade agreement and by world region. Under About Us, the Press Office section includes the agency blog, press releases, and reports. As a Cabinet-level office, USTR maintains an open government site at http://ustr.gov/open.

Subject(s): International Trade—Policy; Trade Agreements

Publication(s): *National Trade Estimate Report on Foreign Trade Barriers*, PREX 9.10

Technical Barriers to Trade Report

Trade Policy Agenda and Annual Report of the President of the United States on the Trade Agreements Program, PREX 9.11

Overseas Private Investment Corporation (OPIC)

http://www.opic.gov/

Sponsor(s): Overseas Private Investment Corporation

Description: OPIC is an independent U.S. government agency that assists U.S. companies investing in emerging economies around the world. For these companies, OPIC provides financing, political risk insurance, and investment funds. Its Web site has sections describing each of these services. The Media & Events section contains links to annual reports, press releases, and the OPIC blog.

Subject(s): International Business; International Economic Development

Publication(s): *OPIC Handbook*, OP 1.8

Special American Business Internship Training Program (SABIT)

http://www.mac.doc.gov/sabit/

Sponsor(s): Commerce Department—International Trade Administration (ITA)—Market Access and Compliance

Description: The SABIT program assists U.S. companies and organizations working in Eurasian countries by funding training programs for managers in that region. The program is intended to facilitate U.S.-Eurasian business partnerships. Its Web site describes the program and links to a Russian-language SABIT Web site.

Subject(s): Emerging Markets; Eurasia

StopFakes.gov

http://www.stopfakes.gov/

Sponsor(s): Commerce Department

Description: StopFakes.Gov is a multiagency product of the government's campaign against the piracy and counterfeiting of U.S. goods. Its Web site describes the campaign, provides resources for assistance, and includes links to relevant information at the Web sites of the U.S. Patent and Trademark Office and U.S. Customs and Border Protection.

This Web site is particularly helpful, as it brings together intellectual property information distributed across the Web sites of many agencies.

Subject(s): Intellectual Property; International Trade—Laws

Trade Compliance Center (TCC)

http://tcc.export.gov/

Sponsor(s): Commerce Department—International Trade Administration (ITA)

Description: TCC monitors foreign compliance with trade agreements and helps U.S. businesses overcome unfair trade practices. The TCC Web site features the following sections: Report a Trade Barrier, Defining a Trade Barrier, Removing Barriers, and Our Office.

The Trade Agreements section links leads to the TCC's Trade and Related Agreements Database (TARA). TARA covers active, binding agreements between the United States and its trading partners concerning manufactured products and services (excluding agriculture). TCC's Exporter's Guides, available on the same page as TARA, have concise explanations for a variety of trade agreements.

Subject(s): Trade Agreements; Trade Laws and Regulations

Trade.gov

http://trade.gov/

Alternate URL(s)

http://www.ita.doc.gov/

Sponsor(s): Commerce Department—International Trade Administration (ITA)

Description: Trade.gov is the Web site of the International Trade Administration. ITA promotes U.S. exports and U.S. companies seeking to export. Most information about the agency is included in the About ITA and Press sections of its Web site. The site integrates information from ITA's component agencies: the U.S. Commercial Service, Manufacturing and Services, Market Access and Compliance, and the Import Administration. The site features information on the President's Export Council, a Frequently Asked Questions section about importing and exporting, and the ITA Tradeology blog.

Subject(s): Exports; International Trade
Publication(s): *Basic Guide to Exporting*, C 61.8
Export Programs Guide, C 61.8
International Trade Update, C 61.46/2
Trade Finance Guide, C 61.8

TradeStats Express™
http://tse.export.gov/
Sponsor(s): Commerce Department — International Trade Administration (ITA)
Description: TradeStats Express™ delivers annual U.S. trade data in the form of basic world maps, pie charts, and data tables. Its Web site is divided into sections for National Trade Data and State Export Data. For national trade, researchers can find U.S. exports, imports, and trade balances for all countries for a given commodity, or they can find data on all products traded between the United States and another country. For state exports, researchers can find data on a state's or U.S. region's exports to one or all countries or world regions, or they can view a state-by-state profile of U.S. exports to a given country.

TradeStats™ meets its goal of being easy to use. However, the trade data are complex enough that researchers should review the manual available via the Help link.

Subject(s): International Trade — Statistics

U.S. Commercial Service
http://trade.gov/cs/
Sponsor(s): Commerce Department — International Trade Administration (ITA) — Commercial Service
Description: The U.S. Commercial Service promotes U.S. exports to global markets. This Web site provides basic information on the organization's leadership, structure, and mission. The Commercial Service uses another Web site to promote its services; that site, Export.gov, is described in a separate entry in this book.

Subject(s): Exports

United States Trade and Development Agency (USTDA)
http://www.ustda.gov/
Sponsor(s): U.S. Trade and Development Agency (USTDA)
Description: USTDA is an independent federal agency that provides assistance to developing countries for economic and infrastructure improvements and promotes opportunities for U.S. businesses abroad. This Web site has information on USTDA projects by world region and by

industry sector. Tools for businesses wishing to pursue USTDA contracts include a database of consultants, and in the USTDA Library Holdings section, under Publications & Resources, feasibility studies to support large infrastructure projects in developing markets abroad.

Subject(s): International Business; International Economic Development

USITC Interactive Tariff and Trade Dataweb

http://dataweb.usitc.gov/

Sponsor(s): International Trade Commission (ITC)

Description: DataWeb is a tariff and trade database designed by the U.S. International Trade Commission (USITC). The data comes from the Census Bureau, the Customs Service, and the ITC itself. The system is free of charge but requires registration. DataWeb offers a number of options for specifying commodity level and country or country groupings. The site has online sort capabilities with report options that include downloading to a spreadsheet format. DataWeb also generates prepared summary tables for commonly requested information, such as U.S. trade by geographic regions and by partner country. A separate tariff database presents tariff treatment information and links to trade data.

DataWeb is a flexible and relatively sophisticated system for U.S. trade data. For regular trade and tariff data users, it can be a very useful tool; new users may first wish to see if the site's prepared trade data tables can answer their questions.

Subject(s): Trade Statistics

MONEY

Advanced Counterfeit Deterrence (ACD)

http://www.treasury.gov/about/organizational-structure/offices/Pages/-Advanced-Counterfeit-Deterrence.aspx

Sponsor(s): Treasury Department—Office of Domestic Finance

Description: The Advanced Counterfeit Deterrence (ACD) program was established by the Department of Treasury to monitor counterfeit deterrence concerns. Its Web site provides information on the program and on counterfeit detection and links to the Bureau of Engraving and Printing for details on current currency design and security features.

Subject(s): Counterfeiting

Bureau of Engraving and Printing (BEP)

http://www.moneyfactory.gov/

Alternate URL(s)

http://www.bep.treas.gov/

Sponsor(s): Treasury Department—Bureau of Engraving and Printing

Description: BEP's Web site features information about the bureau, tours, U.S. currency production, and anti-counterfeiting measures. It also has a BEP Store section selling collectible products and souvenirs and a Youth Education section that links to educational quizzes and lesson plans.

This Web site is particularly strong in its education and outreach efforts.

Subject(s): Money

Foreign Exchange Rates

http://www.federalreserve.gov/releases/g5/current/

Alternate URL(s)

http://www.federalreserve.gov/releases/h10/Current/

Sponsor(s): Federal Reserve—Board of Governors

Description: The first URL listed above links to the Federal Reserve Statistical Release G.5, a monthly report of the average exchange rates for the previous month and comparable figures for earlier months. The alternate URL links to the Federal Reserve Statistical Release H.10 for weekly data on foreign exchange rates.

Subject(s): Exchange Rates

Publication(s): *Foreign Exchange Rates*, FR 1.32/2

United States Mint

http://www.usmint.gov/

Sponsor(s): Treasury Department—United States Mint

Description: The United States Mint produces and distributes United States coins, protects national gold and silver assets, and produces and sells platinum, gold, and silver bullion coins. In the About section, the Mint's Web site has coin production specifications, images of commemorative coins, information on the Mint Police, and biographies of its sculptor-engravers. An online store sells commemoratives, medals, and other Mint products. The Mint Web site also has general information about coin collecting and a section for children and their teachers.

Subject(s): Coins; Money

Publication(s): *Annual Report of the Director of the United States Mint*, T 28.1

FOUR

Culture and Recreation

Culture, for the purposes of this chapter, can be broadly defined to include the arts, humanities, and preservation of human heritage. The federal government has various roles in each of these areas, and in the promotion of recreational opportunities on federal lands. Many of the Web sites in this chapter are designed for the general public; others, particularly some of the federal libraries listed in the Libraries section, are for a far more limited and specialized audience. The federal library listings cover all subject areas, from the humanities to the sciences and engineering.

Subsections in this chapter are Arts, Culture, History, Libraries, Museums, Recreation, and Reference.

ARTS

Indian Arts and Crafts Board
http://www.doi.gov/iacb/
Sponsor(s): Interior Department
Description: The Indian Arts and Crafts Board enforces the legal requirement that products advertised as "Indian made" must indeed be made by American Indians. The board also promotes American Indian and Alaska Native arts and crafts and operates three regional museums. Its Web site includes an online version of the *Source Directory of American Indian and Alaska Native Owned and Operated Arts and Crafts Businesses*.
Subject(s): Arts; American Indians
Publication(s): *Source Directory of American Indian and Alaska Native Owned and Operated Arts and Crafts Businesses*, I 1.84/3

National Endowment for the Arts (NEA)
  http://www.arts.gov
  Sponsor(s): National Endowment for the Arts (NEA)
  Description: NEA is an independent federal agency that promotes and provides funding for the arts and arts education. Its Web site has information on how to apply for a grant and lists recent grant recipients. It also highlights winners of NEA's national awards: the Jazz Master Fellowships, NEA Opera Honors, National Heritage Fellowships, and National Medal of Arts honors program. A Partnerships section lists state and regional arts organizations. The About section includes NEA's bimonthly magazine, *NEA ARTS*, and information on the advisory National Council on the Arts. NEA offers a wide range of publications on its site, covering such topics as arts education, accessibility in museums, and city design.
  Subject(s): Arts—Grants
  Publication(s): *Before and After Disasters: Federal Funding for Cultural Institutions*, HS 5.102:
  NEA ARTS, NF 2.18:

National Film Preservation Board
  http://www.loc.gov/film/
  Sponsor(s): Library of Congress
  Description: The National Film Preservation Board serves as a public advisory group to the librarian of Congress on matters related to motion picture preservation. According to its Web site, the board assists the librarian each year in selecting up to 25 "culturally, historically or aesthetically significant films" to add to the National Film Registry. The Library of Congress then works to ensure that these films are preserved. The board's Web site includes title lists of selections dating back to 1989. The site also links to the National Film Preservation Foundation (with which it is associated) and to international film archive Web sites.
  Subject(s): Movies—History

Poetry and Literature Center of the Library of Congress
  http://www.loc.gov/poetry/
  Sponsor(s): Library of Congress
  Description: The Poetry and Literature Center is the home of the Poet Laureate Consultant in Poetry, who is named by the librarian of Congress. As of press time, Charles Wright has been appointed to follow Natasha Trethewey. The center also administers the Rebekah Johnson Bobbitt National Prize for Poetry and the Witter Bynner fellowships for poets. This Web site offers webcasts of poetry readings at the Library of Congress and further information about the center.

President's Committee on the Arts and the Humanities (PCAH)

http://www.pcah.gov/

Sponsor(s): President's Committee on the Arts and the Humanities

Description: PCAH works to demonstrate the value of the arts and humanities and to stimulate increased private investment in these fields. The Web site has information on PCAH's areas of focus: arts and humanities education, cultural exchange, and creative economy.

U.S. Commission of Fine Arts

http://www.cfa.gov/

Sponsor(s): U.S. Commission of Fine Arts

Description: The U.S. Commission of Fine Arts is an independent agency that advises the federal government and the District of Columbia governments on matters of art and architecture that affect the appearance of the nation's capital. Its Web site includes the legislative and regulatory history of the commission, public meeting agendas and minutes, and information about the National Capital Arts and Cultural Affairs program.

Subject(s): Architecture, public buildings

CULTURE

American Folklife Center

http://www.loc.gov/folklife/

Sponsor(s): Library of Congress—American Folklife Center

Description: The Library of Congress's American Folklife Center is charged with preserving and presenting American folklife. The center is responsible for the library's Archive of Folk Culture, a repository for American folk music and other materials. Its Web site offers a number of online collections, and featured projects include the Veterans History Project, the Civil Rights History Project, and StoryCorps, an oral history project. Many of the center's publications, guides to researching the collections, and resources for teachers are available on the site.

The A to Z Index is particularly useful for discovering the full scope of this site.

Subject(s): Folklife Studies; Music

Publication(s): *Folklife and Fieldwork*, LC 39.9

Archeology Program

http://www.cr.nps.gov/archeology/

Sponsor(s): Interior Department—National Park Service (NPS)

Description: The NPS Archeology Program Web site provides information about archeological investigations at national parks. It links to NPS regional archeological centers and offices. The site also carries the

NPS Archeology Guide, which details responsible management of archeological resources under the stewardship of NPS. Other sections cover the Federal Archeology Program, National Historic Landmarks, and topics such as preventing looting and vandalism and caring for collections.

Subject(s): Archeology

Center for the Book in the Library of Congress

http://www.read.gov/cfb/

Sponsor(s): Library of Congress

Description: The Center for the Book promotes books, reading, libraries, and literacy. It is affiliated with the state book centers that conduct local activities for the same purpose. Its Web site has information about and links to the center's themes and projects, literary events (including the National Book Festival), publications, and affiliate programs.

Corporation for Public Broadcasting (CPB)

http://www.cpb.org/

Sponsor(s): Corporation for Public Broadcasting (CPB)

Description: CPB is a private, nonprofit corporation that was created by Congress in 1967. It receives partial funding through annual congressional appropriations and, in turn, funds public television and radio programming. The About CPB section of this Web site includes leadership profiles, CPB's annual reports, and financial information. The Programs & Projects section has a directory of CPB-funded programs for television, radio, and the Web.

Cultural Heritage Center

http://eca.state.gov/cultural-heritage-center

Sponsor(s): State Department—Educational and Cultural Affairs Bureau

Description: The Cultural Heritage Center serves as the State Department's center of expertise on global cultural heritage protection issues. The Center includes the International Cultural Property Protection program, which supports U.S. compliance with laws and agreements on the import, export, and transfer of ownership of cultural property. The Web site also provides information from the Ambassadors Fund for Cultural Preservation and the Iraq Cultural Heritage Initiative.

State's Cultural Heritage Center Web site is an essential resource for those interested in the international sale, transfer, or repatriation of antiquities and other cultural artifacts.

Heritage Resources

http://www.blm.gov/wo/st/en/prog/more/CRM.html

Sponsor(s): Interior Department—Bureau of Land Management (BLM)

Description: This Web page links to BLM cultural resources program information. Linked pages cover historic preservation, tribal consultation, paleontology, BLM cultural policy, and heritage education.

Institute of Museum and Library Services (IMLS)

http://www.imls.gov/

Sponsor(s): Institute of Museum and Library Services (IMLS)

Description: IMLS is an independent federal agency that provides funding in support of all types of museums, libraries, and archives. The IMLS Web site has separate sections for grant applicants, grant reviewers, and grant recipients. Other sections cover IMLS programs for state library administrative agencies and the statistical reports from the IMLS surveys of public libraries and state library agencies.

Subject(s): Libraries—Grants; Museums—Grants

John W. Kluge Center at the Library of Congress

http://www.loc.gov/loc/kluge/

Sponsor(s): Library of Congress

Description: The Kluge Center hosts humanities scholars at the Library of Congress and presents the international John W. Kluge Prize in the Human Sciences. The center offers Kluge Chairs to selected accomplished scholars in such areas as world cultures, American law and governance, and modern culture. The Web site has information on the Kluge Chairs, fellowships, the Kluge Prize, resident scholars, and the Scholars Council.

National Archeological Database (NADB)

http://www.nps.gov/archeology/tools/nadb.htm

Sponsor(s): Interior Department—National Park Service (NPS); University of Arkansas. Center for Advanced Spatial Technologies

Description: The NADB online system is maintained through a cooperative agreement between the National Parks Service and the Center for Advanced Spatial Technologies (CAST) at the University of Arkansas. NADB has three components. The Archeological Reports section includes references to over 350,000 reports on archeological planning and investigation. The Permits section contains a database of permits issued by the Department of the Interior under the Antiquities Act of 1906 and the Archaeological Resource Protection Act (ARPA) of 1979. The MAPS (Multiple Attribute Presentation System) section is a graphical application that contains a variety of maps in GIS format. These maps show the national distribution of cultural and environmental resources across the United States at the state and county levels.

National Capital Planning Commission (NCPC)

http://www.ncpc.gov/

Sponsor(s): National Capital Planning Commission (NCPC)

Description: NCPC coordinates all planning activities for federal land and buildings in the National Capital Region, which includes Washington, D.C., and surrounding communities in Maryland and Virginia. The NCPC Web site provides information on current planning and public opportunities to comment.

National Center for Preservation Technology and Training (NCPTT)

http://www.ncptt.nps.gov/

Sponsor(s): Interior Department—National Park Service (NPS)

Description: As part of the National Park Service, NCPTT is concerned with the art and science of preservation in areas such as archeology and historic architecture. The center's grants program focuses on the training, technology, and basic research aspects of preservation and conservation. The site provides information on the grants and its programs in the areas of archeology, architecture and engineering, historic landscapes, materials research, and heritage education. It also covers cemetery conservation and disaster recovery projects.

National Endowment for the Humanities (NEH)

http://www.neh.gov/

Sponsor(s): National Endowment for the Humanities (NEH)

Description: According to its Web site, "The National Endowment for the Humanities (NEH) is an independent federal agency created in 1965. It is one of the largest funders of humanities programs in the United States." The site provides guidance on applying for and managing NEH grants. The Grants section has information about the awards process. The About NEH section includes a staff directory, links to the State Humanities Councils, and information on the Jefferson Lecture in the Humanities and the National Humanities Medals.

Subject(s): Grants; Humanities

Publication(s): *Humanities*, NF 3.11:

National NAGPRA

http://www.nps.gov/nagpra/

Sponsor(s): Interior Department—National Park Service (NPS)

Description: As part of the NPS National Center for Cultural Resources, National NAGPRA develops regulations and guidance for implementing the Native American Graves Protection and Repatriation Act (NAGPRA). National NAGPRA also provides training and grants. Its Web site is a resource for information on the act, which delineates a process for museums and federal agencies to return certain Native American cultural items. The Online Databases section includes the Native American Consultation Database of consultation contacts for Indian tribes, Alaska Native villages and corporations, and Native Hawaiian organizations.

National Recording Preservation Board

http://www.loc.gov/rr/record/nrpb/

Sponsor(s): Library of Congress

Description: According to its Web site, National Recording Preservation Board advises the Librarian of Congress on the selection of culturally, historically, or aesthetically important sound recordings to be added to the National Recording Registry. These selections may include music, non-music, spoken word, or broadcast sound. The Web site includes information about the registry, the nomination process, and the board's preservation planning work. It also links to the Web sites for other sound archives.

Preserve America

http://www.preserveamerica.gov/

Description: Preserve America is a White House initiative carried out in cooperation with multiple federal agencies. The initiative is intended to encourage federal agencies to integrate heritage preservation and economic development, bolster local heritage preservation efforts, and promote intergovernmental and public-private partnerships to help accomplish these goals. The Web site includes information on Preserve America grants and the Preserve America Presidential Awards. It also has a list of designated Preserve America communities and neighborhoods, and in the Clearinghouse section, links to related information from federal agencies and state governments.

Public Moving Image Archives and Research Centers

http://www.loc.gov/film/arch.html

Sponsor(s): Library of Congress

Description: This Web site provides an archive of moving images from the Library of Congress and other collections around the world. The site links to the National Film Registry and the National Film Preservation Foundation.

Subject(s): Movies

Read.gov

http://read.gov/

Sponsor(s): Library of Congress

Description: The Library of Congress Center for the Book uses this Web site to encourage reading at all levels. The site has sections for kids, teens, adults, and parents and educators. Read.gov has a wide variety of information, including booklists, online versions of children's classics, an online children's story in episodes, webcasts featuring prominent authors, and a directory of local book projects.

Subject(s): Reading

Smithsonian Center for Folklife and Cultural Heritage

http://www.folklife.si.edu/

Sponsor(s): Smithsonian Institution

Description: On its Web site, the Smithsonian Center for Folklife and Cultural Heritage describes itself as "dedicated to the collaborative research, presentation, conservation, and continuity of traditional knowledge and artistry with diverse contemporary cultural communities in the United States and around the world." The site has information about the center's major endeavors, including the annual Folklife Festival. The Web site also features online exhibits, educational resources, and *Smithsonian Folkways Magazine*.

Subject(s): Folklife Studies

Publication(s): *Smithsonian Folkways Magazine*

Smithsonian Institution

http://www.si.edu/

Sponsor(s): Smithsonian Institution

Description: The main Smithsonian Institution Web site links to all other Smithsonian museum sites and to information about the Smithsonian's research facilities, archives, and other centers. The site includes information about the history of the Smithsonian, hours and locations of the Smithsonian museums, and links to Smithsonian affiliate museums across the United States. Information can be obtained in German, Spanish, Japanese, French, and other languages. The Smithsonian also has a number of blogs available via the Connect section on the home page. See the Explore section to link to the Encyclopedia Smithsonian page; it provides site search engines and an index of Smithsonian Web content. These index sections help in exploring the remarkable amount of high quality content on the wide range of topics covered by the network of Smithsonian Web sites.

Subject(s): Museums

Publication(s): *Inside Smithsonian Research*, SI 1.50
Smithsonian (Web magazine), SI 1.45
Smithsonian Opportunities for Research and Study, SI 1.44

Smithsonian Institution Research Information System (SIRIS)

http://www.siris.si.edu

Sponsor(s): Smithsonian Institution

Description: SIRIS consolidates links and finding aids for the many specialized databases and image collections on the network of Smithsonian Institution Web sites. It links to searchable library, archives, and research catalogs and to collections that can be browsed online. SIRIS also links to the combined search engine for all collections.

Subject(s): Arts—Research; Museums

Smithsonian Magazine

http://www.smithsonianmag.com/

Sponsor(s): Smithsonian Institution

Description: This online version of the *Smithsonian* magazine includes articles and images from the print version, plus Web-only features. The archive section has issues back to 2001.

Subject(s): Culture and Recreation

Publication(s): *Smithsonian* (Web magazine), SI 1.45

HISTORY

A Guide to the War of 1812

http://www.loc.gov/rr/program/bib/1812/

Sponsor(s): Library of Congress

Description: This Library of Congress Web site presents an online compilation of material on the War of 1812. Material includes presidential papers, online exhibitions, information from the Prints and Photographs Online Catalog, external Web sites, and relevant days in history. Bibliographies for adults and children are also present.

Subject(s): War of 1812

Access to Archival Databases (AAD)

http://www.archives.gov/aad/

Sponsor(s): National Archives and Records Administration (NARA)

Description: AAD provides the public with access to a selection of historic databases and other electronic records maintained by the National Archives. This site includes nearly 85 million historic electronic records created by more than 30 federal agencies. The electronic records vary widely in subject matter, but all of them identify specific persons, geographic areas, organizations, or dates—making them useful as finding aids. Information includes several files on war casualties and prisoners of war, the Japanese-American Internee File for 1942–1946, the Work Stoppages Historical File for 1953–1981, and the Central Foreign Policy Files for 1973–1975.

First-time users should consult the Getting Started Guide for instructions on how to search AAD and for an explanation of what records are included on the site. The records in AAD represent only a small fraction of the electronic records holdings of the National Archives. For the most part, AAD does not include digitally scanned images of paper records and other non-electronic records.

Subject(s): Archives; Databases

Advisory Council on Historic Preservation (ACHP)

http://www.achp.gov/

Sponsor(s): Advisory Council on Historic Preservation

Description: ACHP is an independent federal agency and the major policy adviser to the federal government in the field of historic preservation. The Web site contains an overview of the National Historic Preservation Program, including directories of federal, state, and tribal preservation officers and preservation-related Web sites. The site also has the full text of the Code of Federal Regulations Section 106 regulations concerning the protection of historic properties and Section 106 compliance guidance.

Subject(s): Historic Preservation

Publication(s): *Federal Historic Preservation Case Law, 1966–2000,* Y 3.H 62

Protecting Historic Properties: A Citizen's Guide to Section 106 Review, Y 3.H 62:8/

Section 106 Primer: Preserving America's Heritage

American Memory

http://memory.loc.gov/

Sponsor(s): Library of Congress

Description: The Library of Congress's American Memory Web site provides online versions of distinctive, historical Americana materials from the library's collections. These include digitized photographs, manuscripts, rare books, maps, recorded sound, and moving pictures. The diverse collections include Civil War photographs, the papers of Thomas Jefferson, nineteenth-century American sheet music, and late eighteenth-century maps of North America. The collections can be accessed in a number of ways, such as browsing by topic, historical time period, or the material's original format type. A popular "Today in History" feature links information on event anniversaries to items from the American Memory collection. The site also provides a section for teachers with guides to using primary source materials in the classroom.

Subject(s): Digital Libraries; History

America's Historical Documents

http://www.archives.gov/historical-docs/index.html

Sponsor(s): National Archives and Records Administration (NARA)

Description: This Web site is an online exhibit of documents selected from the National Archives collections. Document images in the exhibit include the Declaration of Independence, the Louisiana Purchase Treaty, the check written for purchase of Alaska, Edison's patent for the light bulb, and the Apollo 11 flight plan. The site links to similar exhibits, such as the Charters of Freedom, and to material on teaching with primary documents.

Subject(s): Government Publications—History

BLM General Land Office Records

http://www.glorecords.blm.gov/

Sponsor(s): Interior Department—Bureau of Land Management (BLM)

Description: This site provides information on historical federal lands conveyance records and the initial transfer of land titles from the federal government to individuals for certain states and in certain time periods. It can be of use to genealogists tracking the location of individuals in the past.

According to the Web site, "Due to organization of documents in the GLO collection, this site does not currently contain every Federal title record issued for the Public Land States."

Subject(s): Genealogy; Public Lands—History

Heritage Documentation Programs

http://www.cr.nps.gov/hdp/

Alternate URL(s)

http://lcweb2.loc.gov/ammem/hhhtml/

Sponsor(s): Interior Department—National Park Service (NPS)

Description: Heritage Documentation Programs administers HABS (Historic American Buildings Survey) and companion programs HAER (Historic American Engineering Record), HALS (Historic American Landscapes Survey), and CRGIS (Cultural Resources Geographic Information Systems). The site also carries the standards and guidelines for its historical documentation drawings.

This Web site links to the database of the program's architectural, engineering, and landscape documentation at the Library of Congress, which can be found at the alternate URL provided above. Information is provided about a wide range of structures, including the Pueblo of Acoma, windmills, one-room schools, and the Golden Gate Bridge.

Subject(s): Architecture—History; Civil Engineering—History

History & Culture

http://www.nps.gov/history/

Sponsor(s): Interior Department—National Park Service (NPS)

Description: The History & Culture Web site is a portal to the cultural information available from NPS Web sites and publications. Dropdown menus on the home page allow users to find a program or a grant by topic. The site also has extensive information on tax credits and other programs to encourage preservation of cultural resources.

This Web site is a useful and well-designed portal for exploring the wide range of resources available through the National Parks Service. Several of its resources are described in separate entries.

Subject(s): Historic Sites; National Parks and Reserves—History

History of Social Security

http://www.ssa.gov/history/

Sponsor(s): Social Security Administration (SSA)

Description: The History of Social Security Web site provides extensive information and documentation on both the SSA and the Social Security Program. It includes transcripts and audio files of presidential statements and conversations, oral history interviews, and legislative history documents, as well as a photo gallery, chronology, and other resources.

Subject(s): Social Security—History

JFK Assassination Records

http://www.archives.gov/research/jfk/

Sponsor(s): National Archives and Records Administration (NARA)

Description: The President John F. Kennedy Assassination Records Collection Act (Public Law 102-526) requires that all records related to his 1963 assassination be housed in a single NARA collection. This Web site provides descriptions and finding aids for the physical collection of records, which can be viewed in NARA's College Park, Maryland, research rooms. Online finding aids include the JFK Collection Register, which lists all of the records in the collection at the general series level, and the JFK Database Search, which is an index of many of the documents in the collection.

Subject(s): Archives; President—History

Military Resources: War of 1812

http://www.archives.gov/research/military/war-of-1812/index.html

Sponsor(s): National Archives and Records Administration (NARA)

Description: The bicentennial commemoration of the War of 1812 began in 2012. NARA has provided this Web site of relevant military records information; sections include Genealogical Records of the War of 1812, War of 1812 Discharge Certificates, Genealogical Fallout from the War of 1812, and Records About Impressed Seamen, 1793-1814. Each section contains relevant information about the records listed. The site also links to outside pages, which discuss such topics as "The Star-Spangled Banner" and its role in the war.

Subject(s): Military History; War of 1812

MINERVA

http://www.loc.gov/minerva/

Sponsor(s): Library of Congress

Description: MINERVA is an acronym for Mapping the Internet Electronic Resources Virtual Archive. For the MINERVA project, the Library of Congress selected, saved, and cataloged historical information that had previously appeared exclusively on Web sites and might otherwise have been lost to future researchers. The collections are built around events such as the September 11, 2001, terrorist attacks and the national elections of 2000. The site also includes reports and presentations on the project.

For current and continuing information on web capture activities, the MINERVA site directs researchers to http://www.loc.gov/webarchiving/.

Subject(s): Digital Libraries; World Wide Web—History

National Historical Publication(s) and Records Commission (NHPRC)

http://www.archives.gov/nhprc/

Sponsor(s): National Archives and Records Administration (NARA)—National Historical Publications and Records Commission (NHPRC)

Description: NHPRC is a NARA grant-making affiliate whose purpose is to help identify, preserve, and provide public access to records, photographs, and other materials that document American history. Its Web site has directories of commission members, staff, and state coordinators along with information about the projects funded by the commission and how to apply for and administer a grant.

Subject(s): Archives—Grants

National Register of Historic Places

http://www.nps.gov/history/nr/

Sponsor(s): Interior Department—National Park Service (NPS)

Description: On its Web site, the National Register of Historic Places describes itself as "the official list of the Nation's historic places worthy of preservation." The site provides information about how to get a property listed on the National Register and what a listing means for the property owner. It features a weekly list of new properties on the register and a database of places listed in or determined eligible for the National Register of Historic Places. The Publications section has bulletins and brochures about the National Register process, including a basic brochure about the program available in English and Spanish.

Subject(s): Historic Sites

Publication(s): *How to Complete the National Register Registration Form,* I 29.76/3

Naval History and Heritage Command (NHHC)
http://www.history.navy.mil/
Sponsor(s): Navy—Naval History and Heritage Command (NHHC)
Description: The Naval Historical Center was renamed the Naval History and Heritage Command (NHHC) in 2008. The NHHC collects, preserves, and makes available artifacts, documents, and art related to U.S. Navy history. The NHHC Web site links to information from Navy libraries, Navy museums, art collections, archives, and underwater archaeology program under its management. Its Web site contains numerous online collections, exhibits, publications, and guides to information on U.S. Navy history and traditions.
Subject(s): Military History
Publication(s): *Cruise Books of the United States Navy in World War II: A Bibliography*, D 221.17:2
Historical Manuscripts in the Navy Department Library: A Catalog, D 221.17:3
The Reestablishment of the Navy, 1787-1801: Historical Overview and Select Bibliography, D 221.17:4
The Spanish-American War: Historical Overview and Select Bibliography, D 221.17:5
United States Naval History: A Bibliography, D 221.17:1

State-Level Lists of Fatal Casualties of Korea and Vietnam Wars
http://www.archives.gov/research/military/vietnam-war/casualty-lists/index.html
Sponsor(s): National Archives and Records Administration (NARA)
Description: The National Archives Center for Electronic Records has indexed the records for U.S. military casualties from the Korean War and the Vietnam War. For the Korean War, the database includes records for persons who died as a result of hostilities during the 1950–1954 period, including those who died while missing or captured. For Vietnam, the database includes records for persons who died during the 1956–2006 period as a result of hostile or nonhostile occurrences in the Southeast Asian Combat Area, including those who died while missing or captured. Full casualty records may be retrieved online through the Access to Archival Databases system at http://aad.archives.gov/aad/.
Subject(s): Korean War; Vietnam War

The Civil War: 150 Years
http://www.nps.gov/civilwar150/
Sponsor(s): Interior Department—National Park Service (NPS)
Description: The NPS has designed this Web site for the sesquicentennial anniversary of the American Civil War, which was observed from 2011–2015. It covers the 70-plus parks with resources related to Civil War history, programs related to protection of historic battlefields, and the

role of African Americans in the Civil War. The site also links to the NPS Civil War Soldiers and Sailors System, a database of servicemen from both sides during the Civil War.

As of early 2015, the home page features information about American Indians and the Civil War.

Subject(s): Civil War (United States); National Parks and Reserves—History

U.S. Army Center of Military History (CMH)

http://www.history.army.mil/

Sponsor(s): Army—Center of Military History (CMH)

Description: The CMH site offers full-text military history books, documents, and a museum display of army art. The majority of the collection can be found in the Bookshelves section. The Unit History section features the Army Lineage Series. The FAQ section addresses questions such as finding official unit records and the origin of the 21-gun salute. The site has a Medal of Honor citations list and a directory of Army museums. It also features a series of guides about researching military history, including information on oral history techniques, and a separate section about the history of military history.

Subject(s): Military History

Publication(s): *Army History*, D 114.20

Army Lineage Series

U.S. Army Heritage and Education Center (USAHEC)

http://www.carlisle.army.mil/AHEC/

Alternate URL(s)

http://www.usahec.org/

Sponsor(s): Army—Carlisle Barracks

Description: USAHEC encompasses the Military History Institute, the Army Heritage Museum, and a visitor and education center. The site has a catalog of the USAHEC collections, digitized photographs and documents, and research guides including numerous Civil War bibliographies. The site also presents multimedia exhibitions on several topics, including a profile of General Omar Bradley.

Subject(s): Military History

Veterans History Project

http://www.loc.gov/vets/

Sponsor(s): Library of Congress—American Folklife Center

Description: The Veterans History Project collects, presents, and preserves firsthand accounts from veterans of World War I, World War II, the Korean War, the Vietnam War, the Persian Gulf War, and the current conflicts in Afghanistan and Iraq. The accounts include letters, photographs, and oral histories in audio and video formats. Records describing the collections can be searched in a database, and digitized collections can be viewed or listened to online. The site also includes information on how to submit veterans' stories to the collection.

Subject(s): Veterans—History

Vietnam-Era Prisoner-of-War / Missing-in-Action Database
http://lcweb2.loc.gov/pow/powhome.html
Sponsor(s): Library of Congress—Federal Research Division (FRD)
Description: This database indexes government documents related to U.S. military personnel who were listed as unaccounted for in Southeast Asia during American involvement in Vietnam. Most of the documents are available to view online. The formal title of the collection is "Correlated and Uncorrelated Information Relating to Missing Americans in Southeast Asia."

Subject(s): Prisoners of War

LIBRARIES

Air University Library Index to Military Periodicals
http://www.dtic.mil/dtic/aulimp/
Sponsor(s): Air Force—Air University
Description: *Air University Library Index to Military Periodicals* is a Web site database of citations to journal, magazine, and trade paper articles on the topics of defense and aeronautics. The index goes back to 1988 and can be searched by author, subject, article title, journal title, and date range. Search results do not link to the full-text versions of the articles, but the Air University Library provides a list of indexed periodicals with online editions.

Subject(s): Defense Research

Publication(s): *Air University Library Index to Military Periodicals*, D 301.26/2

ALIC Archives Library Information Center
http://www.archives.gov/research/alic/
Sponsor(s): National Archives and Records Administration (NARA)
Description: ALIC serves National Archives staff and researchers, both on site and online. The ALIC Web site links to the center's collection catalog, full-text versions of NARA publications, and finding guides for NARA records. The Reference at Your Desk section organizes Web links for researching such topics as records management, genealogy, Congress, presidents, diplomacy, and military history. Some commercial databases linked on the ALIC page are only available to staff or on-site researchers.

Subject(s): Archives—Research; Genealogy

Publication(s): *Quarterly Compilation of Periodical Literature Reflecting the Use of Records in the National Archives*, AE 1.128

Bureau of Land Management Library

http://www.blm.gov/wo/st/en/info/blm-library.html

Sponsor(s): Interior Department—Bureau of Land Management (BLM)

Description: The BLM Library Web site links to current and archival BLM publications and to a page of links to Web resources on such topics as forests, plants, and weeds.

Subject(s): Public Lands—Research

Combined Arms Research Library (CARL)

http://usacac.army.mil/cac2/CGSC/carl/index.asp

Sponsor(s): Army—Command and General Staff College (CGSC)

Description: CARL, according to its Web site, "is the research center for the CGSC and the CAC. It also serves other TRADOC installations as well as military scholars and researchers throughout the United States and overseas." Its Digital Library section has several digitized and indexed collections, such as the World War II Operational Documents and School of Advanced Military Studies Monographs.

Subject(s): Military Information

Conservation Library

http://library.fws.gov/

Sponsor(s): Interior Department—Fish and Wildlife Service (FWS)

Description: The Conservation Library primarily serves the staff and students of the National Conservation Training Center, where it is located. The library Web site links to a number of conservation-related periodicals online.

Subject(s): Conservation (Natural Resources)

D'Azzo Research Library

http://www.afit.edu/library/

Sponsor(s): Air Force—Air Force Institute of Technology (AFIT)

Description: The D'Azzo Research Library supports the Air Force Institute of Technology and the Air Force Research Laboratory. The library's Web site offers public access to its online library catalog, but many of the resources are available for use only by the authorized researchers that the library supports.

Subject(s): Scientific and Technical Information

Department of the Interior Library

http://library.doi.gov/

Sponsor(s): Interior Department

Description: The Department of the Interior (DOI) Library Web site is primarily intended for the use of DOI staff and library visitors. It offers some publicly accessible resources, particularly on the Internet Resources section, including subject guides about wildlife, plants, science, Native Americans, and other topics.

Subject(s): Public Lands—Research

EPA National Library Network

http://www.epa.gov/libraries/

Sponsor(s): Environmental Protection Agency (EPA)

Description: This site links to EPA regional library Web sites and provides access to the Online Library System (OLS) catalog and links to the National Service Center for Environmental Publications (NSCEP). The site also links to the Web sites for each of the headquarters, regional, and research laboratory libraries in the EPA library network.

Subject(s): Environmental Protection—Research

ERDC: Professional Library Services

http://www.erdc.usace.army.mil/Library.aspx

Sponsor(s): Army—Army Corps of Engineers—Engineer Research and Development Center (ERDC)

Description: The ERDC Library Web site provides access to its online catalog and ERDC online publications.

Subject(s): Civil Engineering—Research

FBI Library

http://fbilibrary.fbiacademy.edu/

Sponsor(s): Justice Department—Federal Bureau of Investigation (FBI)

Description: The FBI Library at the FBI Academy has a Web site that includes the online library catalog, bibliographies on over 60 law enforcement topics, and links to sources of crime and criminal justice statistics.

Subject(s): Law Enforcement—Research

Federal Bureau of Prisons Library

http://bop.library.net/

Sponsor(s): Justice Department—Federal Bureau of Prisons

Description: This Web site is primarily a Web interface for the library catalog. The site also includes a description of the library, a periodicals list, and a video list.

Subject(s): Prisons—Research

Federal Depository Library Program (FDLP)

http://www.gpo.gov/libraries/

Sponsor(s): Government Printing Office (GPO)—Superintendent of Documents

Description: To facilitate public access to federal government information, FDLP provides print and electronic government publications to over 1,000 designated depository libraries open to the public throughout the country. This Web page provides an explanation of the program and a searchable directory of the federal depository libraries.

Subject(s): Federal Depository Library Program

Publication(s): *Federal Depository Library Directory*, GP 3.36/2-2

Federal Library and Information Center Committee (FLICC)

http://www.loc.gov/flicc/

Sponsor(s): Library of Congress—Federal Library and Information Center Committee (FLICC)

Description: FLICC and FEDLINK provide service and guidance to federal libraries and information centers. The Web site's resources will be of interest primarily to librarians, particularly federal librarians, and to vendors specializing in the federal library market.

Subject(s): Libraries

Publication(s): *Handbook of Federal Librarianship*, LC 1.32/6-2

Fermilab Library

http://bss.fnal.gov/library/

Sponsor(s): Energy Department—Fermi National Accelerator Laboratory

Description: The Fermilab Library Web site features access to its online catalog, journal list, and documents and preprints from the lab. Some databases on the site are only available to Fermilab staff.

Subject(s): Physics—Research; Preprints

Goddard Library

http://library.gsfc.nasa.gov/public/

Sponsor(s): National Aeronautics and Space Administration (NASA)—Goddard Space Flight Center (GSFC)

Description: The Goddard Space Flight Center Library's Extranet is the public version of the library's Web site. It features links to publicly available Web resources, such as technical reports, its Facebook page, and the library's online catalog.

Subject(s): Scientific and Technical Information

GOVDOC-L [e-mail list]

http://govdoc-l.org/

Sponsor(s): Duke University. Perkins Library

Description: This is the oldest (and still the primary) e-mail list for government documents librarians. While it is neither hosted nor sponsored by the federal government, the discussions, questions, and announcements relate directly to government information and the practice of government documents librarianship.

Previously, the Government Printing Office used GOVDOC-L for its official announcements to depository libraries. GPO now has its own announcements list, called GPO-FDLP-L.

Subject(s): Federal Depository Library Program; Email Lists

Library of Congress

http://www.loc.gov/

Sponsor(s): Library of Congress

Description: As the largest library in the world, it is only fitting that the Library of Congress Web site should be one of the most extensive and information-packed governmental library Web sites. Its American Memory section, with scanned images, movies, audio files, and other reproductions of historic documents, is a leading example of the how the Internet is being used to make rare collections available to the public. The site's Currently on Exhibit section has digital versions of major library exhibitions, past and present. A section called "Especially For..." organizes information by audience, including researchers, librarians, teachers, publishers, and kids and families. The section for researchers includes links to the Web sites for the library's special reading rooms, such as the Hispanic Area Studies, Science and Technology, and the Recorded Sound Reference Center. The library also provides links to its blogs, podcasts, webcasts, and presence on third-party sites such as Facebook and Twitter.

The main Library of Congress online catalog contains approximately 14 million records representing books, serials, computer files, manuscripts, cartographic materials, music, sound recordings, and visual materials. The library also has an online catalog for its special Prints and Photographs and Sound Recordings collections.

The library site links to the legislative information service THOMAS, the Copyright Office, the National Library Service for the Blind and Physically Handicapped, and more. The Web sites for some of the specialized collections and services are described in more detail elsewhere in this publication.

While the Web site offers only a small fraction of the material available at the library itself, it does provide a significant collection of free online material as well as detailed information about the library's collections and services. This is a large and well-structured Web site that offers substantial resources of interest to librarians, teachers, researchers, publishers, lawyers, Congress, and the general public.

Subject(s): Digital Libraries; Libraries; United States — History
Publication(s): *American Memory Digital Collections*, LC 1.54/3
Bibliographic Products and Services, LC 30.27/2
Country Studies Series
Global Legal Monitor, LC 42.16
LC Science Tracer Bullet, LC 33.10
Library of Congress Information Bulletin, LC 1.18
Thomas: Legislative Information on the Internet, LC 1.54/2
Veterans History Project Field Kit, LC 39.2

Library of Congress Blog

http://www.loc.gov/blog/
Sponsor(s): Library of Congress
Description: Managed by the public affairs office, the Library of Congress blog covers news about the institution's collections, events, and policies. Comments are permitted.
Subject(s): Blogs

Library of Congress Online Catalog

http://catalog.loc.gov/
Sponsor(s): Library of Congress
Description: The Library of Congress Online Catalog is a database of over 14 million records representing books, serials, computer files, manuscripts, cartographic materials, music, sound recordings, and visual materials in the collections. The Online Catalog also provides cross-references, notes, and circulation status as well as information about materials still in the acquisitions stage. Additional information on the catalog is provided in the Frequently Asked Questions and Help Contents sections. The Online Catalog page also links to online catalogs maintained for the Library of Congress Prints and Photographs Division and the Recorded Sound Reference Center.
Subject(s): Library Catalogs

Library Statistics Program

http://nces.ed.gov/surveys/libraries/
Sponsor(s): Education Department — Institute of Education Sciences — National Center for Education Statistics (NCES)
Description: NCES publishes survey data on academic libraries and school media centers. In addition to reading the survey reports, researchers can download the data at this site.
Subject(s): Libraries — Statistics

Los Alamos National Laboratory Research Library
http://www.lanl.gov/library/
Sponsor(s): Energy Department—Los Alamos National Laboratory (LANL)
Description: The general public can search the LANL Library catalog, but most resources on this Web site are restricted to authorized LANL users.
Subject(s): Scientific and Technical Information

Marine Corps Library Research Guides Portal
http://guides.grc.usmcu.edu/library
Sponsor(s): Marine Corps
Description: This Web site includes descriptions and some publicly available resources, such as research links and reading lists.
Subject(s): Marine Corps—Research

MERLN (Military Educational Research Library Network)
http://ndu.libguides.com/merln
Sponsor(s): Defense Department—National Defense University (NDU)
Description: MERLN is a resource-rich Web site maintained by a consortium of military education research libraries. The site's Digital Collections section features military education research materials digitized by MERLN participants. The site also has digitized White Papers from foreign ministries of defense. Military Policy Awareness Links (MiPALS) are MERLN Web bibliographies on such topics as Afghanistan, North Korea, and Terrorism; they are particularly helpful for reference and research. The Publications section provides a convenient collection of annotated links to journals and publications available from MERLN member sites. An RSS feed is available.
Subject(s): Military Information

MSHA Library Information
http://www.msha.gov/TRAINING/LIBRARY/library.htm
Sponsor(s): Labor Department—Mine Safety and Health Administration (MSHA)
Description: The Technical Information Center and Library of the National Mine Health and Safety Academy is located in West Virginia. The physical collection includes current publications, the Accident Investigation File Archives, historic photographs, archival material from the former Bureau of Mines, and materials relating to major mine disasters in the U.S. from 1840 to the present. Online, the library site provides access to its catalog and the MSHA Digital Materials Collection (also called the

Digital Library). The MSHA Digital Library is divided into sections for accident reports, research material, photographs, and moving images.
Subject(s): Mining—Research

Muir S. Fairchild Research Information Center
http://www.au.af.mil/au/aul/lane.htm
Sponsor(s): Air Force—Air University
Description: Many of the resources available through this Air University (AU) library Web site are restricted to AU users. However, the site provides public access to Web-linked bibliographies compiled by the library staff about topics such as leadership, unmanned systems, and terrorism.
Subject(s): Military Information; Bibliographies
Publication(s): *Air University Library Index to Military Periodicals*, D 301.26/2

NARA Locations Nationwide
http://www.archives.gov/locations/
Sponsor(s): National Archives and Records Administration (NARA)
Description: The National Archives operates research facilities across the United States, including NARA regional facilities and presidential libraries. This Web site provides collections and location information for each facility. The NARA regional facilities typically offer genealogy resources, archived federal agency records from the region, and federal courts records including bankruptcy cases. NARA Presidential Library Web sites, linked from this site, are described in a separate entry in this section.
Subject(s): Archives; Genealogy—Research

NASA Headquarters Library
http://www.hq.nasa.gov/office/hqlibrary/
Sponsor(s): National Aeronautics and Space Administration (NASA)
Description: The NASA Headquarters Library serves NASA staff and provides information online for the public. The library catalog and selected other resources on the library Web site are only available to staff. For the public, the library site provides online bibliographies, links to NASA documents databases, and links to NASA video and imagery sites. The Browse Topics section of the library site organizes bibliographies and Web links under such topics as aerospace, engineering, science, and NASA itself.
Subject(s): Space—Research

National Agricultural Library (NAL)
http://www.nal.usda.gov/

Sponsor(s): Agriculture Department (USDA)—National Agricultural Library (NAL)

Description: NAL is a major source for national and international agricultural information. The NAL Web site acts as a gateway to the library's resources and associated institutions. The NAL Catalog, also known as AGRICOLA, is an extensive database of published agriculture information. NAL Collections include the National Agricultural Library Digital Collections (NALDC). The Web site also links to the *NAL Agricultural Thesaurus*, an online vocabulary look-up tool for agricultural and biological terms, and a glossary of over 2,000 terms related to agriculture. The thesaurus and the glossary are available in both English and Spanish. The site can be browsed by audience, with sections for USDA employees, librarians, and kids and teens.

This site can be used as an excellent starting point for finding agricultural information. NAL helpfully organizes its many resources by topic, such as Animals and Livestock, Food and Nutrition, and Rural and Community Development.

Subject(s): Agriculture Information; Libraries

Publication(s): *List of Journals Indexed in AGRICOLA*, A 17.18/5

NAL Agricultural Thesaurus

National Defense University Library

http://www.ndu.edu/Research/Library.aspx

Sponsor(s): Defense Department—National Defense University (NDU)

Description: The NDU Library resources available online include the library catalog, professional military reading lists, and digitized collections focusing on Fort McNair history, special commission reports on national defense, and related topics. The site also hosts the Military Education Research Library Network (MERLN).

Subject(s): Military Information

National Institute of Corrections Robert J. Kutak Memorial Library

http://nicic.gov/Kutak

Sponsor(s): Justice Department—Federal Bureau of Prisons

Description: The NIC Robert J. Kutak Memorial Library collects published and unpublished material on the topics of correctional operations and policies, offender programs, and special offender issues. The library staff provides research assistance, giving priority for custom research to corrections professionals. The library Web site organizes and links to a wealth of studies, documents, statistical reports, online videos and other content covering corrections topics.

Subject(s): Prisons—Research

National Library of Education (NLE)
http://ies.ed.gov/ncee/projects/nle/
Sponsor(s): Department of Education—Institute of Education Science
Description: NLE, though established in 1994, has roots going back to the 19th century. Its collections are intended for use by the general public, the education community, and government agencies. The site links to the library's catalog, as well as the Education Resources Information Center (ERIC) and The What Works Clearinghouse (WWC).
Subject(s): Libraries

National Library of Medicine (NLM)
http://www.nlm.nih.gov/
Sponsor(s): National Institutes of Health (NIH)—National Library of Medicine (NLM)
Description: As a leading center for health sciences information, NLM offers a wealth of resources through its Web site. The site's home page provides quick links to major NLM databases—such as PubMed and MedlinePlus—and to information for NLM client groups: the general public, health care professionals, researchers, librarians, and publishers. Links to NLM's social media pages are provided.

The site map helps to show the full scope of the Web site's content. It organizes links under Explore NLM, Research at NLM, and NLM for You: Health Information, Library Catalog and Services (includes NLM publications), History of Medicine, Online Exhibitions and Digital Projects, Human Genome Resources, Biomedical Research and Informatics (which includes the UMLS/Unified Medical Language System), Environmental Health and Toxicology, About NLM, Grants and Funding, Training and Outreach, Network of Medical Libraries, and Health Services Research and Public Health.

The NLM Web site is a gateway to the various programs and information resources offered by the library. Many of the specific Web resources created by NLM are described elsewhere in this publication.
Subject(s): Libraries; Medical Information
Publication(s): *List of Serials Indexed for Online Users* , HE 20.3618/2
Medical Subject Headings, HE 20.3612/3-8
National Library of Medicine Classification, HE 20.3602
National Library of Medicine Fact Sheet, HE 20.3621
National Library of Medicine Programs and Services, HE 20.3601
NLM LOCATORplus, HE 20.3626
NLM Technical Bulletin, HE 20.3603/2

National Library Services for the Blind and Physically Handicapped (NLS)

http://www.loc.gov/nls/

Sponsor(s): Library of Congress—National Library Services for the Blind and Physically Handicapped (NLS)

Description: NLS administers a free library program that circulates Braille and recorded materials to eligible borrowers through a network of cooperating libraries. The Learn section of its Web site has information on how NLS works, how to sign up, and where NLS network libraries are located. The Web site provides access to the online catalog of Braille and audio books, the *Braille Book Review*, and other bibliographies. The NLS/BPH Publications section of the site includes NLS fact sheets, bibliographies, circulars, and directories of libraries and resources related to reading material for the blind and physically handicapped. It also includes information on digital talking books and Web-Braille.

The NLS site is designed for text-based browsers, such as Lynx, that are frequently used by blind readers. See the About This Site section for more information.

Subject(s): Libraries; Vision Disorders

Publication(s): *Braille Book Review*, LC 19.9

For Younger Readers, Braille and Talking Books, LC 19.11/2

Magazines in Special Media, LC 19.11/2-2

News (NLS), LC 19.13

Talking Book Topics, LC 19.10

Update (NLS), LC 19.13/2

National Network of Libraries of Medicine (NN/LM)

http://nnlm.gov/

Sponsor(s): National Institutes of Health (NIH)—National Library of Medicine (NLM)

Description: NN/LM is coordinated by NLM with the goal of improving access to medical information for both health professionals and the public. The Web site has a directory of member libraries, information on each regional component of NN/LM, training schedules and modules, and funding opportunities. The site also has a section about finding and using health information on the Web.

Librarians and health educators are the intended audiences for much of the information on this site. General public users interested in medical libraries and information systems may also find helpful material.

Subject(s): Libraries; Medical Information

National Radio Astronomy Observatory Library

http://library.nrao.edu/index.shtml

Sponsor(s): National Science Foundation (NSF)—National Radio Astronomy Observatory (NRAO)

Description: This Web site features the library's catalog and the NRAOPapers database of published papers and preprints for staff and visitor works. Some sections of the site are restricted to NRAO staff.

Subject(s): Astronomy—Research; Preprints

National Transportation Library (NTL)

http://ntl.bts.gov/

Sponsor(s): Transportation Department—Bureau of Transportation Statistics (BTS)

Description: NTL serves federal, state, and local governments. NTL's Web site also links to transportation information and reference services for the general public. Publicly available databases include the NTL catalog, the *Transportation Research Thesaurus*, and the cooperatively produced TRIS Online database of published transportation literature. The Research/Tools section links to numerous reference sources, such as transportation statistics, directories of transportation-related organizations, and transportation glossaries.

Subject(s): Transportation—Research

NIEHS Library

http://www.niehs.nih.gov/research/resources/library/

Sponsor(s): National Institutes of Health (NIH)—National Institute of Environmental Health Sciences (NIEHS)

Description: The NIEHS Library serves the scientific and administrative staff of NIEHS but also provides limited services to the public.

Subject(s): Health and Safety—Research

NIH Library Online

http://nihlibrary.nih.gov/

Sponsor(s): National Institutes of Health (NIH)

Description: The NIH Library Online Web site features information about the library and services. Most information is restricted to authorized users; however, some information and social media links are available to the public.

Subject(s) Medical Information

Nimitz Library, U.S. Naval Academy

http://www.usna.edu/Library/

Sponsor(s): Navy—United States Naval Academy (USNA)

Description: The Nimitz Library Web site features information about the library and its services. Most resources are accessible to Naval Academy faculty and students only. Several online historical exhibitions can be accessed by the public, including one on the Army-Navy football game going back to 1890, under Digital Collections.

Subject(s): Engineering Research

NIST Virtual Library

http://nvl.nist.gov/nvl2.cfm?doc_id=127

Alternate URL(s)

http://nvl.nist.gov/

Sponsor(s): Commerce Department—Technology Administration (TA)—National Institute of Standards and Technology (NIST)

Description: Beyond general information about the library and its services, the NIST Virtual Library Web site offers its online catalog, standards and patent information, and publications. Many of the resources on the site are restricted to NIST staff.

Subject(s): Scientific and Technical Information

Publication(s): *Journal of Research of the National Institute of Standards and Technology*, C 13.22

NOAA Central Library

http://www.lib.noaa.gov/

Sponsor(s): Commerce Department—National Oceanic and Atmospheric Administration (NOAA)

Description: The NOAA Central Library and regional libraries provide information and research support to NOAA staff and the public on topics such as atmospheric sciences, oceanography, and cartography. The NOAA Library Web site links to their many digital collections, including the NOAA Photo Library, digitized historical documents on U.S. fisheries and the old Weather Bureau. The Quick Links section of the Web site points to the WINDandSEA Internet Guide of over 1,000 links to Web sites concerned with oceanic and atmospheric issues. The site also has a number of other specialized web bibliographies and subject guides for researchers.

The NOAA Central Library is one of over 30 specialized NOAA libraries across the nation; the Web site links to all NOAA Libraries sites. Disciplines covered by the libraries include weather and atmospheric sciences, oceanography, ocean engineering, nautical charting, marine ecology, marine resources, ecosystems, coastal studies, aeronomy, geodesy, cartography, and mathematics and statistics.

Subject(s): Atmospheric Sciences—Research; Oceanography—Research

NOAA Seattle Regional Library

http://www.wrclib.noaa.gov/

Sponsor(s): Commerce Department—National Oceanic and Atmospheric Administration (NOAA)

Description: This regional NOAA library serves NOAA agencies in the West. The site's Environmental Data Sources section is particularly useful. It provides a portal to data sets from the government and educational institutions, organized by subject, region, and provider.

Subject(s): Atmospheric Sciences—Research

Northwest and Alaska Fisheries Science Centers Library

http://lib.nwfsc.noaa.gov/

Sponsor(s): Commerce Department—National Oceanic and Atmospheric Administration (NOAA)—National Marine Fisheries

Description: This library supports the centers and field stations located in the Pacific Northwest and Alaska that serve NOAA's National Marine Fisheries Service (NMFS). Its Web site links to information on fisheries, maps, and charts, with an emphasis on the Pacific region.

Subject(s): Fisheries—Research

Patent and Trademark Depository Library Program

http://www.uspto.gov/go/ptdl/

Sponsor(s): Commerce Department—Patent and Trademark Office (PTO)

Description: The PTO designates qualified libraries throughout the country to act as Patent and Trademark Depository Libraries. These libraries receive printed materials and electronic access from the PTO to assist the general public researching patent and trademark information. The Web site provides links to depository and partner library Web sites, and lists the core publications and databases available through these libraries.

Subject(s): Libraries; Patent Law; Trademarks

Pentagon Library

http://www.whs.mil/library/

Sponsor(s): Defense Department

Description: The Pentagon Library Web site provides access to numerous resources, including bibliographies, digitized historic materials, and military documents.

Subject(s): Libraries; Military Information

Presidential Libraries

http://www.archives.gov/presidential-libraries/

Sponsor(s): National Archives and Records Administration (NARA)—Presidential Libraries Office

Description: This National Archives Web page provides general information about the presidential libraries system and guides for doing research in presidential materials. Links to each of the presidential librar-

ies Web sites are provided. The presidential library system currently includes 13 libraries, for Presidents Herbert Hoover to George W. Bush.
Subject(s): Presidential Documents

Ralph J. Bunche Library
http://www.state.gov/m/a/ls/
Sponsor(s): State Department
Description: This Web site offers a description of the main Department of State library. The library's mission is to support the research needs of State Department personnel, and it offers few services to the public. The site calls the State Department's library "the oldest Federal Government library . . . founded by the first Secretary of State, Thomas Jefferson, in 1789."
Subject(s): Foreign Policy—Research

Ruth H. Hooker Research Library InfoWeb
http://library.nrl.navy.mil/
Sponsor(s): Navy—Naval Research Laboratory (NRL)
Description: In support of the Naval Research Laboratory staff, the library focuses on such topics as chemistry, meteorology, oceanography, physics, and space sciences. While some sections of its Web site are restricted to staff, the online catalog is publicly available. The catalog covers the library's books, journals, and unclassified reports.
Subject(s): Engineering Research

SCAMPI—Staff College Automated Military Periodicals Index
http://www.dtic.mil/dtic/scampi/
Sponsor(s): Defense Department—National Defense University (NDU)
Description: SCAMPI indexes defense-related magazines and journals, such as the Military Review and the Armed Forces Journal, from 1985 to the present.
Subject(s): Military Information

Scientific Library, National Cancer Institute—Frederick
http://www-library.ncifcrf.gov/
Sponsor(s): National Institutes of Health (NIH)—National Cancer Institute (NCI)
Description: The NCI Scientific Library's Web site offers public access to its online catalog and links to publications of its researchers. The site also links to PubMed@FNLCR.
Subject(s): Medical Information

Smithsonian Institution Libraries

http://www.sil.si.edu/

Sponsor(s): Smithsonian Institution

Description: The 20 Smithsonian Institution libraries support research in such wide-ranging areas as space exploration, art and design, tropical biology, and American history. Major resources on the site include the SIRIS combined catalog of the library collections, a database of images from books and manuscripts in the collections, and information on the Smithsonian special collections.

Subject(s): Libraries

U.S. Geological Survey Library

http://library.usgs.gov/

Sponsor(s): Interior Department—U.S. Geological Survey (USGS)

Description: Established in 1879, the USGS Library maintains a Web site with access to its catalog and an extensive set of Web links on map topics. An RSS feed for new USGS publications is available.

Subject(s): Geology—Research; Maps and Mapping

USAID Knowledge Management

http://www.usaid.gov/results-and-data/information-resources/knowledge-management-support

Sponsor(s): Agency for International Development (USAID)

Description: According to the Web site, "The focus of USAID's Knowledge Management Program is to connect people to the processes and technology that will help them to work effectively with partners to accomplish USAID's mission." Its Web site offers the library catalog and economic and social data related to USAID and development.

Subject(s): International Economic Development—Research

USDOJ Library Staff

http://www.usdoj.gov/jmd/ls/

Sponsor(s): Justice Department—Justice Management Division

Description: The libraries of the Justice Department primarily serve Justice employees. The libraries are open to the public by appointment only for access to government depository items or unique titles.

Subject(s): Law Libraries

USNO James Melville Gilliss Library

http://www.usno.navy.mil/USNO/library/

Sponsor(s): Navy—Naval Observatory (USNO)

Description: This site provides access to the United States Naval Observatory Library's online catalog and collection of historical photos of the observatory, astronomers, telescopes, and astronomy texts.

Subject(s): Astronomy—Research

Wirtz Labor Library
http://www.dol.gov/oasam/library/
Sponsor(s): Labor Department
Description: The Department of Labor's Wirtz Labor Library has a Web site with the library's online catalog and links to online labor research resources. The site also has a digital library of historical labor publications and an archive of past Labor Department Web sites.
Subject(s): Libraries; Employment Law

MUSEUMS

Anacostia Community Museum
http://anacostia.si.edu/
Sponsor(s): Smithsonian Institution
Description: The Smithsonian Institution's Anacostia Community Museum focuses on the history and culture of the African American community and family. It is located in the historic Washington, D.C., neighborhood of Anacostia, the former home of abolitionist Frederick Douglass. The museum's Web site has information on the collection, exhibits, visiting, and education resources.
Subject(s): History; Museums

Cooper-Hewitt, National Design Museum
http://cooperhewitt.org/
Sponsor(s): Smithsonian Institution
Description: The Cooper-Hewitt, in New York City, concentrates on historic and contemporary design. Its Web site has information on the museum, its education programs, and the annual National Design Awards. The site also provides links to Cooper-Hewitt's Facebook page, Twitter feed, YouTube channel, and Pinterest page.
Subject(s): Arts — Awards and Honors; Museums

Hill Aerospace Museum
http://www.hill.af.mil/library/museum/
Sponsor(s): Air Force — Hill Aerospace Museum
Description: Located at Hill Air Force Base in Utah, the Hill Aerospace Museum collection includes a wide variety of military aircraft and missiles, munitions and weapons, ground vehicles associated with aircraft and missiles, and thousands of other historical artifacts. Its Web site provides information about visiting, museum activities and exhibits, and base history.
Subject(s): Aviation — History

Museum Management Program

http://www.nps.gov/history/museum/

Sponsor(s): Interior Department—National Park Service (NPS)

Description: The Museum Management Program supports policy and technical standards for the management of NPS museum collections, including natural, cultural, archival, and manuscript materials. The Web site has NPS museum collection profiles and information on current exhibits. For museum professionals, it features a calendar of professional events and a listing of laws and regulations relevant to NPS museum administration, archeology, records, and archives. The site also has a section that covers teaching with museum collections. The Virtual Museum Exhibits section is of general interest, with digitized images of objects from the NPS collections.

Subject(s): Museums

Publication(s): *Conserve O Grams*

Museum Handbook

National Air and Space Museum

http://www.nasm.si.edu/

Sponsor(s): Smithsonian Institution

Description: The National Air and Space Museum offers information about the museum and its programs, including the Steven F. Udvar-Hazy Center in Virginia, which provides an exhibition hangar, theater, and classrooms. In addition to visitor information, the Web site has digital images of objects in its collection, an extensive research section, and educational resources.

Subject(s): Aviation; Museums

National Gallery of Art (NGA)

http://www.nga.gov/

Sponsor(s): National Gallery of Art (NGA)

Description: On the NGA Web site, the Plan a Visit section includes information about the gallery's location and hours, as well as maps and information about how the NGA is organized and funded. The Collection section offers searches of the collections by artist, title, or subject; searches can also be limited to items for which online images are available.

Subject(s): Museums; Visual Arts

National Museum of African American History and Culture (NMAAHC)

http://www.nmaahc.si.edu/

Sponsor(s): Smithsonian Institution

Description: Authorized by law in 2003, the National Museum of African American History is currently organizing traveling exhibitions. The museum building in Washington, D.C., is scheduled to be completed in 2016. In the meantime, the Web site provides a wealth of online images and information from its collection, as well as information about the gallery at the American History Museum.

Subject(s): African Americans—History; Museums

National Museum of African Art

http://www.nmafa.si.edu/

Sponsor(s): Smithsonian Institution

Description: The National Museum of African Art Web site has information about its exhibits, programs, collections, library, and archives. The Research section has a collections catalog that can be browsed visually or searched by a variety of criteria. The Radio Africa section has African music from the Smithsonian Institution. The site also has a section of activities for children.

This is a colorful, multimedia-providing site that makes use of high-quality photographs, sound, and images.

Subject(s): Museums; Visual Arts; Africa

National Museum of American History

http://americanhistory.si.edu/

Sponsor(s): Smithsonian Institution

Description: The National Museum of American History Web site provides images, online exhibits, and research information related to American history. Educational resources are available in the Kids and Educators sections, including "Ripped Apart," a game for the iPad based in the Civil War era.

Subject(s): Museums; United States—History

National Museum of Health and Medicine

http://www.medicalmuseum.mil/

Sponsor(s): Defense Department—Armed Forces Institute of Pathology (AFIP)

Description: The National Museum of Health and Medicine's main focus is on American military medicine. Its collections include anatomical specimens and medical devices, many of which are from the Civil War era, when the museum was established. This Web site has online guides to the museum's collections and photographs of many of its exhibits.

Subject(s): Medicine and Medical Devices—History; Museums

National Museum of Natural History

http://www.mnh.si.edu/

Sponsor(s): Smithsonian Institution

Description: This Web site presents information about the National Museum of Natural History's exhibits, collections, programs, and research. The Research & Collections section features a collections database, bibliographies, and links to Department of Science Web sites for anthropology, botany, entomology, invertebrate zoology, mineral sciences, paleobiology, and vertebrate zoology. The Explore a Topic section presents material from the museum organized into broad themes, such as "The Evolving Earth" and "The Diversity of Life."

Subject(s): Museums; Natural History

National Museum of the American Indian (NMAI)
http://www.nmai.si.edu/
Sponsor(s): Smithsonian Institution
Description: This Web site describes the Smithsonian NMAI facilities in New York City and Washington, D.C. Major sections include Visit, Explore, Support, Connect, and Shop.

Subject(s): Museums; American Indians

National Postal Museum
http://postalmuseum.si.edu/
Sponsor(s): Smithsonian Institution
Description: The National Postal Museum is funded by the U.S. Postal Service, the Smithsonian Institution's federal appropriation, and private gifts. The museum's collections include stamps, vehicles used to transport the mail, mailboxes, postage meters, and greeting cards. Major sections of its Web site include Exhibits, Collection, Educators, Stamp Collecting, Research, Museum Library, Getting Involved, and the Activity Zone (for both kids and adults).

Subject(s): Postage Stamps; Postal Service—History

Naval Undersea Museum
http://www.navalunderseamuseum.org/
Sponsor(s): Navy—Naval Sea Systems Command (NAVSEA)
Description: The Naval Undersea Museum in Washington State presents submarines, torpedoes, diving equipment, and other artifacts related to naval undersea history, science, and operations. This Web site includes information about exhibits, volunteer information, and information about visiting the museum.

Subject(s): Museums; Underwater Warfare—History

Smithsonian American Art Museum (SAAM)
http://americanart.si.edu/
Sponsor(s): Smithsonian Institution
Description: This Web site features an illustrated narrative overview of the museum's collections, and information about its current exhibits and events. The Luce Center on the site (under Collections) provides images of more than 3,500 items in the American art collections. The

SAAM site also has information about the Renwick Gallery, which specializes in American crafts and decorative arts.

Subject(s): Arts; Museums

United States Botanic Garden (USBG)

http://www.usbg.gov/

Sponsor(s): Congress—Architect of the Capitol

Description: The USBG Web site has information about its gardens, production facility, and conservatory on the National Mall. The site offers visitor information, a virtual tour, and a description of the Botanic Garden's plant collections and work in plant conservation. Under the Grow heading, USBG provides gardening tips and a Plant Hotline.

Subject(s): Botany

United States Holocaust Memorial Museum (USHMM)

http://www.ushmm.org/

Sponsor(s): United States Holocaust Memorial Council

Description: The United States Holocaust Memorial Museum became an independent establishment of the U.S. government under Public Law 106-292. The museum's Web site provides information about the museum and extensive resources on Holocaust education, research, and history. It features a multimedia "Introduction to the Holocaust" and an online Holocaust encyclopedia in 13 languages beyond English. The site includes numerous online exhibitions, a section on Days of Remembrance, and information on contemporary genocide.

Subject(s): Museums; War Crimes—History

RECREATION

America's Byways®: National Scenic Byways Online

http://www.byways.org/

Sponsor(s): Transportation Department—Federal Highway Administration (FHWA)

Description: The Department of Transportation has designated certain roads as National Scenic Byways, or All American Roads, based on their archaeological, cultural, historic, natural, recreational, and scenic qualities. This Web site provides information about the designated roads or byways. It offers maps and descriptions of noteworthy sites along the routes.

Subject(s): Highways and Roads

Publication(s): *America's Byways Bulletin*, TD 2.88

Corps Lakes Gateway

http://www.corpslakes.us/

Alternate URL(s)

http://corpslakes.usace.army.mil/visitors/

Sponsor(s): Army—Army Corps of Engineers

Description: Corps Lakes Gateway describes outdoor recreation opportunities at lakes managed by the Army Corps of Engineers. The site has a clickable U.S. map for finding Corps lakes and related information.

Subject(s): Lakes; Outdoor Recreation

Fishing

http://www.fws.gov/fishing/

Sponsor(s): Interior Department—Fish and Wildlife Service (FWS)

Description: This FWS Web site focuses on recreational fishing. The site describes the agency's work to improve fisheries and links to other organizations that provide information for recreational fishers. It features national and state fishing statistics from the National Survey of Fishing, Hunting, and Wildlife-Associated Recreation and hunting and fishing license statistics back to 1975.

Subject(s): Fishing

Publication(s): *National Survey of Fishing, Hunting, and Wildlife-Associated Recreation*, I 49.98

Your Guide to Fishing on National Wildlife Refuges, I 49.6/2

Forest Service National Avalanche Center

http://www.fsavalanche.org/

Sponsor(s): Agriculture Department (USDA)—Forest Service (USFS)

Description: This Forest Service site provides detailed avalanche awareness information and interactive guides for snowmobilers, skiers, snowboarders, snowshoers, and others exploring the steep and snowy backcountry.

Subject(s): Outdoor Recreation; Avalanches

National Park Service (NPS)

http://www.nps.gov/

Sponsor(s): Interior Department—National Park Service (NPS)

Description: The official NPS Web site is the primary source for information about America's national parks. It includes information about national memorials, national battlefields, national seashores, national historic sites, and other related sites. The Find a Park section links to information on each of the NPS locations by name, state, or topic (such as Civil War, fossils/dinosaurs, or geysers/hot springs). Individual parks have their own Web pages, which contain printable travel guides, maps, and background information. The Discover History section of the site describes significant people, places, and events associated with the national parks. It offers learning programs and information about historic preservation grants. The Explore Nature section organizes a wealth of information related to science and environmental practices in the parks, under the Air Resources, Biological Resources, Geologic Resources, Natural Sounds & Night Skies, and Water Resources categories. The About Us section has information on laws, regulations, policy, budget, and publications. *Morning Report*, in the site's News section, compiles daily news from a number of NPS sources and replaces the *NPS Digest*. Elsewhere on the site, there is a section for kids and teachers, information on volunteering at the parks, links to social media and iTunes pages, and video features about the parks and NPS.

With its broad approach to the resources and heritage of the national parks system, the NPS Web site is relevant for many audiences, including travelers, scientists, history buffs, and teachers.

Subject(s): Historic Preservation; National Parks and Reserves
Publication(s): *National Park Statistical Abstract*, I 29.114
Park Science, I 29.3/4

National Trails System

http://www.nps.gov/ncrc/programs/nts/
Sponsor(s): Interior Department—National Park Service (NPS)
Description: The National Trails System is a network of scenic, historic, and recreational trails administered by the Department of the Interior and the Department of Agriculture in partnership with other agencies and organizations. Its Web site includes a trail system map, information about designating national scenic and national historic trails, and a link to the nonprofit Partnership for the National Trails System organization's Web site.

Subject(s): Outdoor Recreation

National Zoological Park

http://nationalzoo.si.edu/
Sponsor(s): Smithsonian Institution
Description: The National Zoo's Web site features information and photos for visitors and researchers. The Giant Pandas section (under the Animals heading) has PandaCams, a panda photo gallery, and giant panda facts. Live cams are available for other animals as well. The Education section includes field trip guides, classroom resources, and information on further education and training opportunities. The Science section covers zoological medicine, land and aquatic ecosystems, biodiversity, and endangered species science. It links to information from the specialized research centers of the Smithsonian Conservation Biology Institute.

Subject(s): Animals; Conservation Biology; Zoos

Presidio Trust

http://www.presidio.gov/

Sponsor(s): Presidio Trust

Description: The Presidio, a former U.S. Army installation in San Francisco, is now a National Historic Landmark District. The Presidio Trust, a federal agency established by Congress in 1996, manages it. This Web site provides information about the management of the Presidio and visiting the park.

Subject(s): Historic Sites

Recreation.gov

http://www.recreation.gov/

Sponsor(s): Agriculture Department (USDA)—Forest Service (USFS)

Description: Recreation.gov is designed to be a one-stop portal for learning about and getting permits and reservations for activities on public lands. The Web site is an interagency project, with information about recreation opportunities on land managed by the Army Corps of Engineers, the Bureau of Land Management, the Bureau of Reclamation, the Forest Service, and the National Park Service. Users can find recreation locations by state or activity (such as boating, camping, fishing, or hiking) or by a clickable U.S. map. For locations requiring a reservation, Recreation.gov has an online reservation system.

Subject(s): Outdoor Recreation

USDA Forest Service Recreational Activities

http://www.fs.fed.us/recreation/

Sponsor(s): Agriculture Department (USDA)—Forest Service (USFS)

Description: The Forest Service offers this Web site as an overview of the recreational opportunities and the guidelines for the use of national forests and grasslands. The forests and grasslands can be found by using a clickable map or by browsing by state or site name. Other sections provide information about passes, permits, and travel advisories.

Subject(s): National Forests

Your Guide to Fishing on National Wildlife Refuges

http://www.fws.gov/refuges/FishingGuide/

Sponsor(s): Interior Department—Fish and Wildlife Service (FWS)

Description: This interactive online guide displays wildlife refuge information by state and by type of fish available. The Special Features section includes tips about catch and release, and invasive aquatic species.

Subject(s): Fishing

Publication(s): *Your Guide to Fishing on National Wildlife Refuges*, I 49.6/2

REFERENCE

Official U.S. Time

http://www.time.gov/

Sponsor(s): Commerce Department—Technology Administration (TA)—National Institute of Standards and Technology (NIST); Navy—Naval Observatory (USNO)

Description: This Web site provides the current time in all U.S. time zones, including the time zones for the U.S. Pacific territories.

Subject(s): Time

Plain Language

http://www.plainlanguage.gov/

Sponsor(s): Plain Language Action and Information Network (PLAIN)

Description: The Plain Language Web site focuses on improving communications from the federal government to the public. The idea is to use "plain language" that can be understood at first reading. The intended audience is government agencies. The site includes relevant examples, guidelines, and resources. The site is managed by the federal employees group Plain Language Action and Information Network (PLAIN).

While this site is intended for government writers, other writers will also find it to be a useful reference as well.

Subject(s): Writing

Popular Baby Names

http://www.socialsecurity.gov/OACT/babynames/

Sponsor(s): Social Security Administration (SSA)

Description: This database of trends in baby names is compiled from names listed on Social Security card applications. Users can search for the most popular baby names by year and by state, track the popularity of a name over time, or look up popular names for twins.

Subject(s): Families

FIVE

Defense and Intelligence

The national defense, homeland security, and intelligence operations of the United States are all represented to varying degrees on the Web. The Department of Defense (DoD) and the nation's armed forces, in particular, maintain numerous publicly accessible Web sites. These sites cover topics ranging from current military operations, to advanced research, to administrative and acquisitions matters. This chapter concludes with a Military Morale and Welfare section covering many of the services available for veterans, service members, and their families that are described on the Web.

Researchers may also wish to check the International Relations chapter for information on arms treaties, the Education chapter for information on the educational activities managed by the DoD and the armed forces, and the Business and Economics chapter for sites on defense trade controls.

Subsections in this chapter are Armed Forces, Defense Operations, Defense Research, Homeland Security, Intelligence, and Military Morale and Welfare.

ARMED FORCES

AF.mil—Official Web Site of the U.S. Air Force
http://www.af.mil/
Sponsor(s): Air Force
Description: The emphasis of this central Air Force Web site is on current news. Along with a wealth of articles, the site provides Air Force TV and has links to related social media sites. In addition to current news, the site has information about and from Air Force senior leadership.

The site has convenient links for headquarters, major commands, field operating agencies, bases, and deployed locations

Subject(s): Air Force; News Services
Publication(s): *Air Force News*, D 301.122
Airman, D 301.60
United States Air Force Posture Statement, D 301.1/3

Air Education and Training Command (AETC)

http://www.aetc.af.mil/
Sponsor(s): Air Force—Air Education and Training Command (AETC)
Description: AETC is responsible for Air Force programs in military, technical, and flight training, as well as education programs at many levels. This Web site provides information on Air Force career opportunities, basic military training, and technical training. It also links to the Air Force Academy, Air Force ROTC, and Officer Training School.
Subject(s): Military Training and Education

Air Force Personnel Center (AFPC)

http://www.afpc.af.mil/
Sponsor(s): Air Force—Air Force Personnel Center (AFPC)
Description: This public Web site from the Air Force Personnel Center has information for and about military and civilian Air Force personnel. The Library section includes demographic profiles of military and civilian personnel. The site also has personnel news and career information.
Subject(s): Air Force; Civilian Defense Employees

Air Force Reserve Command

http://www.afrc.af.mil/
Sponsor(s): Air Force—Air Force Reserve (AFRES)
Description: The Air Force Reserve Command Web site features news, pay information, leadership biographies, fact sheets, and photos. The Join the Air Reserve section links to the official recruiting page.
Subject(s): Military Reserves
Publication(s): *Air Force Reserve Handbook*
Citizen Airman, D 301.8

Air Force Space Command

http://www.afspc.af.mil/
Sponsor(s): Air Force—Air Force Space Command
Description: The Air Force Space Command leads the Air Force space and cyberspace missions. The Web site has current news, photos, fact sheets, and a directory of unit Web sites. The Library section has biographies and fact sheets.
Subject(s): Air Force; Military Computing; Rockets

Publication(s): *High Frontier*, D 301.130

Air Mobility Command (AMC)
http://www.amc.af.mil/
Sponsor(s): Air Force—Air Mobility Command (AMC)
Description: AMC's mission is to provide airlift, air refueling, special air mission, and aeromedical evacuation for U.S. forces. Its public Web site provides current news, unit information, fact sheets, and biographies of AMC leadership.
Subject(s): Airlifts; Military Logistics

Airforce.com
http://www.airforce.com/
Sponsor(s): Air Force
Description: This Air Force recruitment Web site offers information for prospective recruits at all levels. The site also has a Spanish-language version and a live chat feature.
Subject(s): Military Recruiting

Army Live
http://armylive.dodlive.mil/
Sponsor(s): Army
Description: According to the Web site, Army Live is "the official blog of the United States Army." Comments meeting the posted guidelines are accepted. The blog provides links to its social media pages, as well as its YouTube channel.
Subject(s): Army; Blogs

Army Publishing Directorate
http://www.apd.army.mil/
Sponsor(s): Army—Army Publishing Agency (USAPA)
Description: The Publishing Directorate is the Army's agency for publishing and distributing information products. The Products Map, which can be accessed by the direct link to "all Army publications and forms" on the home page, links to publications by source and type. The Order/Subscriptions section links to information for users with and without accounts. The Search section allows for text and proponent searches.

ASA (ALT)
https://www.alt.army.mil/
Sponsor(s): Army
Description: The Office of the Assistant Secretary of the Army for Acquisition, Logistics, and Technology, or ASA(ALT), leads Army acquisitions and research and development to support military readiness. The Web site provides organizational information and links to related sites.

Subject(s): Military Procurement

Bureau of Naval Personnel
http://www.npc.navy.mil/Channels/
Sponsor(s): Navy—Naval Personnel Bureau
Description: The Bureau of Naval Personnel Web site serves current officers and enlisted personnel by providing information about pay, benefits, career progression, and quality of life services. It also includes information for retirees. The Reference Library section provides Navy personnel forms, manuals, and regulations, as well as links to various publications, such as *Shift Colors* (for retirees).

The site will primarily be of interest to people in the Navy. Some sections are only open to authorized, registered users.
Subject(s): Defense Administration
Publication(s): *Shift Colors, The Newsletter for Navy Retirees,* D 208.12/3-2

Center for Army Lessons Learned (CALL)
http://call.army.mil/
Sponsor(s): Army—Center for Army Lessons Learned (CALL)
Description: According to its Web site, "The Center for Army Lessons Learned facilitates the Army's lessons learned program by identifying, collecting, analyzing, disseminating, and archiving issues and best practices; and by maintaining situational awareness in order to share knowledge throughout the Army as well as our unified action partners utilizing tools like networks, workshops, and interviews." Many sections of the site are restricted to authorized users. CALL provides some information for the public, including a custom search feature and the CALL Thesaurus.
Subject(s): Military Information
Publication(s): *Center for Army Lessons Learned,* D 101.22/25

GoArmy.com
http://www.goarmy.com/
Sponsor(s): Army—Army Reserves (USAR)
Description: Established as a recruitment site for both the Army and the Army Reserves, this Web site features information likely to be of interest to prospective members. It includes sections on careers, benefits, and soldier life, and also provides an extra section for parents.
Subject(s): Military Recruiting

Headquarters—Air Force Materiel Command (AFMC)
http://www.afmc.af.mil/
Sponsor(s): Air Force—Air Force Materiel Command (AFMC)
Description: AFMC equips and supplies the Air Force through supply management, depot maintenance, systems testing and evaluation, information services, and combat support. The AFMC Web site has current news and background on the command's organization and programs. The Units section links to AFMC field operating agencies, test centers, laboratories, and other establishments.
Subject(s): Military Logistics; Military Supplies

Headquarters—Air Reserve Personnel Center (AFRES)
http://www.arpc.afrc.af.mil/
Sponsor(s): Air Force—Air Force Reserve (AFRES)
Description: The AFRES Personnel Center Web site has information about assignments, mobilization, training and education, retirement, separations and discharges, re-enlistments, and other related topics.
Subject(s): Military Reserves

Joint Chiefs of Staff (JCS)
http://www.jcs.mil/
Sponsor(s): Defense Department—Joint Chiefs of Staff
Description: The JCS Web site provides information about the chairman of the Joint Chiefs of Staff, the Joint Chiefs, Joint Staff, and the combatant commands. It also provides links to news, speeches, interviews, and photos.
Subject(s): Military Leadership
Publication(s): *Joint Electronic Library*, D 5.21

Los Angeles Air Force Base
http://www.losangeles.af.mil/
Sponsor(s): Air Force—Air Force Space and Missile Systems Center
Description: The Los Angeles Air Force Base hosts the Space and Missile Systems Center (SMC), part of the Air Force Space Command. SMC manages the acquisitions programs for military satellites and space systems. Organizations at the base are described in the Units section; they include the Military Satellite Communications (MILSATCOM) Systems Wing and the 61st Air Base Wing. The Library section has leadership biographies and fact sheets on satellite programs and space-based systems.
Subject(s): Air Force Bases; Space Technology

Marine Forces Reserve (MFR)
http://www.marforres.marines.mil/
Sponsor(s): Marine Corps—Marine Forces Reserves (MFR)

Description: The MFR Web site has a directory of Reserve units with links to the unit Web sites. It also has news, photos, and information about joining the Reserves and staying in the Reserves.

Publication(s): *Continental Marine*, D 214.23

Marines

http://www.marines.com/

Sponsor(s): Marine Corps

Description: This Web site is the Marine Corps recruiting site. The site includes background information on service in the Marine Corps, recruiting contacts, and a companion section for parents and mentors. For general information about the Marines, see the official Marine Corps Web site at http://www.marines.mil.

Subject(s): Marine Corps; Military Recruiting

Marines Manpower and Reserve Affairs

https://www.manpower.usmc.mil/

Sponsor(s): Marine Corps

Description: The Marines Manpower Web site is organized into sections for the Active Marine, Reserve Marine, Veteran Marine, Civilian Marine, and Family. Frequently used sections of the site deal with the Wounded Warrior Regiment, awards, promotions, and assignments. Some online systems are limited to eligible, registered users who must log in to receive access.

Subject(s): Marine Corps

National Guard

http://www.nationalguard.mil/

Sponsor(s): National Guard Bureau

Description: The National Guard Web site provides news and information about the National Guard Bureau, its leadership, and Joint Staff organization. The Resources section includes links to each state's Web sites for the National Guard.

Subject(s): National Guard

Publication(s): *On Guard*

Naval Network Warfare Command (NETWARCOM)

http://www.netwarcom.navy.mil/

Sponsor(s): Navy—Naval Network Warfare Command

Description: NETWARCOM is concerned with network and information technology, intelligence and information operations, and space systems. The Web site provides basic information on the command, its leadership, and its core functions.

Subject(s): Military Computing; Military Intelligence

Naval Surface Warfare Center

http://www.navsea.navy.mil/nswc/

Sponsor(s): Navy—Naval Sea Systems Command (NAVSEA)

Description: The Naval Surface Warfare Center performs research, development, and testing and evaluation for the Navy's surface ships. The Web site provides basic information from each of its 10 locations.

Subject(s): Navy

Naval Undersea Warfare Center (NUWC)

http://www.navsea.navy.mil/nuwc/

Sponsor(s): Navy

Description: NUWC is the Navy's research, development, testing, engineering, and fleet support center for submarines, weapons associated with undersea warfare, and other underwater systems. Its Web site features links to the sites for its divisions in Keyport, Washington, and Newport, Rhode Island; these sites provide more information on the center's activities. Other sections include Leadership, History, Acquisition Support, and Development.

Subject(s): Submarines; Underwater Warfare

NAVSEA HQ

http://www.navsea.navy.mil/

Sponsor(s): Navy—Naval Sea Systems Command (NAVSEA)

Description: The Naval Sea Systems Command develops, acquires, modernizes, and maintains affordable ships, ordnance, and systems for the Navy. The NAVSEA Web site has information on headquarters and leadership, and it links to the Web sites for NAVSEA field activities. Other sections of the site include News, Resources (with NAVSEA Instruction documents), and Business Partnerships.

Subject(s): Military Ships; Military Technology

Navy Blue Angels

http://www.blueangels.navy.mil/

Sponsor(s): Navy

Description: This Web site provides information about the choreographed flying of the Navy's Blue Angels squadron, including biographies of the squadron's officers and enlisted team. The site also features information about the show schedule and an RSS news feed.

Subject(s): Military Aircraft; Navy

Navy Reserve

https://www.navyreserve.navy.mil/Pages/default.aspx

Sponsor(s): Navy—Naval Reserve Forces

Description: The Web site for the Commander of the Navy Reserve Force includes current news, leadership information, and career information for reservists. The site also provides back issues of *The Navy Reservist* magazine and links to pertinent social media pages. As with other secured military sites, your Web browser may issue a warning that this is a suspicious site; provided you are using the correct URL, you can proceed to access the site. The Navy Reserve recruiting site is online at http://www.navyreserve.com/.

Subject(s): Military Reserves

Publication(s): *TNR: The Navy Reservist*

Navy.com

http://www.navy.com/

Alternate URL(s)

http://www.navy.com/advisors/en-espanol.html

Sponsor(s): Navy

Description: This is the primary Navy recruiting site. The Careers & Jobs section covers the many fields of specialty for officers or the enlisted. The site also has a Spanish-language version.

Subject(s): Military Recruiting

OACSIM (Installation Management)

http://www.acsim.army.mil/

Sponsor(s): Army

Description: The Army's Office of the Assistant Chief of Staff for Installation Management (OACSIM) is the Army's proponent for military bases and the soldiers, civilians, and families who live on them. The Web site has information on leadership, staff, and OACSIM division operations. The site also links to statistics from the *Real Property Green Book* on changes to the Army's Federal Real Property Inventory.

Redstone Arsenal

http://www.garrison.redstone.army.mil/default.aspx

Sponsor(s): Army—Redstone Arsenal

Description: The Redstone Arsenal in Alabama is the home of the U.S. Army Aviation and Missile Command (AMCOM) and the Space and Missile Defense Command. The Web site has news and information about these and other units at Redstone. Redstone played an early role in U.S. rocket research and Cold War activities.

Subject(s): Army Bases; Missile Defense; Rockets—History

Soldiers **Magazine**
http://www.army.mil/soldiers/
Alternate URL(s)
http://soldiers.dodlive.mil/
Sponsor(s): Army—Army Publishing Agency (USAPA)
Description: This is the Web site for the well-known print publication, *Soldiers*, the official magazine of the Army. The site features the most recent issue in PDF format and maintains an archive of issues back to 2011.
Subject(s): Army
Publication(s): *Soldiers*, D 101.12

Space and Naval Warfare Systems Command (SPAWAR)
http://www.spawar.navy.mil/
Sponsor(s): Navy—Space and Naval Warfare Systems Command (SPAWAR)
Description: SPAWAR's mission is to acquire, develop, and maintain integrated command, control, communications, computer, intelligence, and surveillance systems. Major sections of this Web site include Careers, Products & Services, and Support.
Subject(s): Military Technology

Today's Military
http://www.todaysmilitary.com/
Sponsor(s): Defense Department
Description: Today's Military is an overall guide to the benefits of joining the U.S. armed forces, with information from each military service branch. A special section is tailored to parents.
Subject(s): Military Recruiting

U.S. Air Force Live
http://airforcelive.dodlive.mil/
Sponsor(s): Air Force
Description: This official blog of the United States Air Force is maintained by the Air Force Public Affairs Agency. The blog carries news and stories by those serving in the Air Force. Comments meeting the posted guidelines are accepted. Links to the blog's Facebook and Twitter pages are provided.
Subject(s): Air Force; Blogs

United States Africa Command (AFRICOM)
http://www.africom.mil/
Sponsor(s): Defense Department
Description: The U.S. Africa Command, or AFRICOM, was created in 2007. The Web site includes the command's posture statement, leader-

ship biographies, news, speech transcripts, and links to component commands Web sites. The site is also available in French, Portuguese, and Arabic.

Subject(s): Unified Combatant Commands

United States Air Force

http://www.af.mil/

Sponsor(s): Air Force

Description: This Web site is the central point for information about the United States Air Force. The home pages includes links to featured news stories, topics of interest, and information about its senior leadership. The News section links to commentaries, photos, art, and Air Force TV. The About Us section includes a CSAF Reading List, biographies, and an events schedule.

Subject(s): Air Force

United States Army

http://www.army.mil/

Sponsor(s): Army

Description: This is the central Web site for the Army. The site links to Army news services, video and images, publications, and the Army Live blog. Under the Info heading, the Organization section connects users to major commands and units; it also links to installations and facilities, including airfields, barracks, camps, libraries, medical centers, institutes, museums, and more. Also listed under Info, the References section links to official Army strategic documents, other Army publications, and libraries. Other sections cover Army history and heritage, career management, veterans' service organizations, and community outreach. The A-Z section provides a helpful alphabetical listing of Army Web sites.

This well-designed and well-organized site should be one of the first stopping points for anyone seeking information about the Army, its bases, or related news. It is also a good resource for active servicemembers, reservists, and those who have retired from the Army.

Subject(s): Army
Publication(s): *Soldiers*, D 101.12

United States Central Command (USCENTCOM)

http://www.centcom.mil/

Sponsor(s): Defense Department—Central Command

Description: USCENTCOM is one of the Unified Combatant Commands assigned operational control of U.S. combat forces. Its area of responsibility spans a region from the Horn of Africa to Central Asia and includes Iraq and Afghanistan. Its Web site has extensive information about the Iraq and Afghanistan operations. The site also provides news, photos, leadership information, command history, and links to related military Web sites and social media pages. Information is available in Arabic, Russian, Farsi, and Urdu.

Subject(s): Unified Combatant Commands; Iraq

United States Coast Guard (USCG)

http://www.uscg.mil/

Alternate URL(s)

http://homeport.uscg.mil/

Sponsor(s): Homeland Security Department—Coast Guard

Description: USCG is part of the Department of Homeland Security, but in wartime or when directed by the president, it operates under the Secretary of the Navy. The breadth of information on the Coast Guard's Web site reflects its multiple roles. Its mission includes national defense and homeland security, as well as maritime search and rescue, International Ice Patrol operations, polar and domestic waterway icebreaking, bridge administration, aids to navigation, recreational boating safety, vessel traffic management, at-sea enforcement of living marine resource laws and treaty obligations, and at-sea drug and illegal migrant interdiction.

In the About Us section, the USCG has fact sheets on Coast Guard aircraft, cutters, and boats. It also contains a History subsection with information on lighthouses, the Coast Guard Museum, historic photographs, and more. The Our Organization section links to each of the regional Coast Guard districts. The Coast Guard maintains a separate site about boating safety at http://www.uscgboating.org/.

The Coast Guard also has a major Web site called Homeport at the alternate URL listed above. It provides more technical and much more in-depth coverage.

Subject(s): Coast Guard; Homeland Security

Publication(s): *Coast Guard Directives System*, TD 5.8:D 62

Coast Guard Magazine, TD 5.3/11

Navigation and Vessel Inspection Circulars, TD 5.4/2

United States Cyber Command (USCYBERCOM)

http://www.arcyber.army.mil/org-uscc.html

Sponsor(s): Defense Department—Strategic Command

Description: USCYBERCOM, a sub-unit of the United States Strategic Command (USSTRATCOM), "plans, coordinates, integrates, synchronizes, and conducts activities to: direct the operations and defense of specified Department of Defense information networks and; prepare to, and when directed, conduct full-spectrum military cyberspace operations in order to enable actions in all domains, ensure US/Allied freedom of action in cyberspace and deny the same to our adversaries." (from the Web site) The Cyber Awareness section provides information and cybersecurity tips for consumers. The Vendors section offers guidance for those looking to contract with USCYBERCOM.

Subject(s): Electronic warfare, Unified Combatant Commands

United States European Command (EUCOM)

http://www.eucom.mil/

Sponsor(s): Defense Department—European Command

Description: EUCOM is a unified combatant command headquartered in Stuttgart, Germany. EUCOM's area of responsibility includes 51 nations and territories extending from Greenland east to include all of Europe, Turkey, Israel, and Russia. The Web site carries current news about EUCOM, leadership biographies, an organizational directory, a recommended reading list, and links to the sites for U.S. armed forces in Europe and the George C. Marshall European Center for Security Studies. The site also has a blog and links to the EUCOM presence on social media Web sites. Information is available in many European languages, including Spanish, French, German, Hungarian, and Czech.

Subject(s): Unified Combatant Commands

United States Marine Corps (USMC)

http://www.marines.mil/

Sponsor(s): Marine Corps

Description: The official USMC Web site focuses on current news, featuring articles written by Marines. Major sections provide information about the USMC Headquarters and links to individual units' Web pages. The site connects to other USMC sites of interest on recruiting, careers, community relations, and quality of life issues.

Subject(s): Marine Corps

Publication(s): *Marine Corps Orders and Directives*
Marines Magazine

United States Navy

http://www.navy.mil/

Sponsor(s): Navy

Description: The official Web site of the Navy features Navy news, leadership biographies, photos, videos, and policy documents such as the Secretary of the Navy's Posture Statement. Under the About heading, the site provides Status of the Navy statistics and links to fun facts and a command directory. This section also has organizational information, profiles of current and past Navy ships, and fact sheets on Navy aircraft, weapons systems, submarines, missiles, ships, and other topics. Under Media, the site has archived, digitized copies of all issues of the Navy magazine *All Hands* going back to its start in 1922.

Subject(s): Navy

Publication(s): *All Hands* (monthly), D 207.17
Posture Statement, Department of the Navy, D 214.2

United States Northern Command (USNORTHCOM)

http://www.northcom.mil/

Sponsor(s): Defense Department—Northern Command

Description: USNORTHCOM was established in 2002 to counter threats and aggression aimed at the United States and its territories. The command's geographic area of responsibility includes North America, Puerto Rico, the U.S. Virgin Islands, and their respective air, land, and sea approaches. The command's Web site provides news and leadership information. The Educational section includes information about homeland defense for students.

Subject(s): Homeland Security; Unified Combatant Commands

United States Pacific Command (USPACCOM)

http://www.pacom.mil/

Sponsor(s): Defense Department—Pacific Command

Description: USPACCOM is one of the Unified Combatant Commands assigned to oversee operational control of U.S. combat forces. Headquartered in Hawaii, the command's geographic area of responsibility is the Asia-Pacific region, including China, Japan, India, Indonesia, and Australia. The Web site includes command news, leadership information, and the Pacific Command blog and Flickr pages.

Subject(s): Unified Combatant Commands; Asia

United States Southern Command (USSOUTHCOM)

http://www.southcom.mil/

Sponsor(s): Defense Department—Southern Command

Description: USSOUTHCOM, one of the Unified Combatant Commands, is headquartered in Miami. According to the Web site, "US-SOUTHCOM is responsible for providing contingency planning, operations, and security cooperation in its assigned Area of Responsibility, which includes Central America, South America, and the Caribbean (except U.S. commonwealths, territories, and possessions). The command is also responsible for the force protection of U.S. military resources at these locations. SOUTHCOM is also responsible for ensuring the defense of the Panama Canal." The command's Web site includes information about its mission, activities, and components. The News section includes Fact Files, topical one-page websites with links to related news.

Subject(s): Unified Combatant Commands

United States Strategic Command (USSTRATCOM)

http://www.stratcom.mil/

Sponsor(s): Defense Department—Strategic Command

Description: USSTRATCOM is one of the Unified Combatant Commands. USSTRATCOM has responsibility for missions in the areas of space operations; information operations; integrated missile defense; global command and control; intelligence, surveillance, and reconnaissance; global strike; and strategic deterrence. Its Web site has information about the command's organization and leadership. The Organization section has links to the command's functional and service components, information on USSTRATCOM's history, and fact sheets on missile systems, military space forces, and strategic computer and communications networks.

A new United States Cyber Command (USCYBERCOM) has been established as a sub-unit of STRATCOM. USCYBERCOM centralizes command of cyberspace operations. The command's responsibilities include protection of Defense Department information networks and the military cyberspace infrastructure.

Subject(s): Electronic Warfare; Unified Combatant Commands; Missile Defense

United States Transportation Command (USTRANSCOM)
http://www.transcom.mil/

Sponsor(s): Defense Department—Transportation Command

Description: USTRANSCOM provides strategic mobility support for the Defense Department and the combatant commands. The site has information on USTRANSCOM's organization, component units, leadership, news, and history.

Subject(s): Airlifts; Military Logistics; Unified Combatant Commands

Wright-Patterson Air Force Base
http://www.wpafb.af.mil/

Sponsor(s): Air Force—Wright-Patterson Air Force Base (WPAFB)

Description: This is the main public Web site for Wright-Patterson, where missions include logistics management, research and development, and flight operations. The site has information on the base history, the 88th Air Base Wing, Air Force research laboratories, and other units hosted at the base.

Subject(s): Air Force Bases

DEFENSE OPERATIONS

ACQWeb
http://www.acq.osd.mil/

Sponsor(s): Defense Department—Office of the Under Secretary of Defense for Acquisition, Technology, and Logistics

Description: ACQWeb is the official Web site for the Office of the Under Secretary of Defense for Acquisition, Technology, and Logistics

(AT&L). The AT&L Offices section of the site presents a large menu of AT&L component offices and directorates, with links to their sites as well as to other Defense components.

Subject(s): Defense Administration; Military Procurement

Army Civilian Personnel Online

http://cpol.army.mil/

Sponsor(s): Army

Description: Army Civilian Personnel Online provides employment, training, compensation, and career information for the Army's civilian employees. Some sections intended only for current Army employees may require an employee account to access.

Subject(s): Civilian Defense Employees; Job Openings

Publication(s): *Civilian Personnel Bulletin*, D 101.138

Army Financial Management

http://www.asafm.army.mil/

Sponsor(s): Army

Description: Manuals, documents, and other information about Army accounting and financial management practice make up the bulk of this site. Sections include Army Budget, Financial Information Management, and Cost and Economics. The Army Budget section contains detailed materials on the current fiscal year.

The primary target audience for this fairly technical site is Army's budget and resource management staff.

Subject(s): Army; Defense Administration

Civilian Personnel Management Service (CPMS)

http://www.cpms.osd.mil/

Sponsor(s): Defense Department—Civilian Personnel Management Service

Description: CPMS provides centralized management and policy support for the department's civilian personnel programs. The home page links directly to the monthly DoD Civilian Workforce Demographics report and to DoD hiring reform information.

Subject(s): Civilian Defense Employees; Defense Administration

Combating Terrorism Technology Support Office (CTTSO)

http://www.cttso.gov/

Sponsor(s): Defense Department

Description: CTTSO facilitates the development and acquisition of counterterrorism technology to support the Defense Department, State Department, other federal agencies, and domestic law enforcement organizations. Major sections of the site are Business Opportunities, Technology Transition, Contract Awards, and International Partners. The site also describes the CTTSO programs: Technical Support Working Group, Explosive Ordnance Disposal/Low-Intensity Conflict, and Irregular Warfare Support. The CTTSO operates as a program office under the Assistant Secretary of Defense for Special Operations and Low-Intensity Conflict.

Subject(s): Defense Contracting; Military Technology

Defense Energy Support Center (DESC)

http://www.desc.dla.mil/

Sponsor(s): Defense Department—Defense Energy Support Center

Description: Defense Energy Support Center (DESC) acquires, stores, and distributes fuel for the military. The Vendor Resources section includes information on contracts and Small Business Office support. The Policies/Publications section includes a PDF version of the DESC Fact Book, with detailed statistical information on the business operations of DESC. The Links section links to the petroleum agencies within the armed services and to DESC's own Alternative Fuels Information Station.

Subject(s): Military Logistics

Publication(s): *DESC Fact Book*, D 7.1/6-2

Fuel Line, D 7.24

Defense Finance and Accounting Service (DFAS)

http://www.dfas.mil/

Sponsor(s): Defense Department—Defense Finance and Accounting Service (DFAS)

Description: DFAS handles pay for the military, Department of Defense civilian employees, retirees, and annuitants. They also make travel payments, process contractor invoices, manage military retirement trust funds, and manage other aspects of military accounting. Major sections on the home page are Military Members, Retired Military & Annuitants, and Civilian Employees.

Subject(s): Accounting; Defense Administration

Defense Information Systems Agency (DISA)

http://www.disa.mil/

Sponsor(s): Defense Department—Defense Information Systems Agency (DISA)

Description: DISA develops information technology systems and provides communications solutions for the military. Some information on the site can be accessed only by authorized users. The site's About section covers the agency's mission, history, and organization. The site also has information on contracting opportunities and the full text of the DSN Telephone Directory. (Defense Switched Network, or DSN, is used for voice communications between Department of Defense offices.)

Subject(s): Military Computing; Communications Technology

Defense Logistics Agency (DLA)

http://www.dla.mil/

Sponsor(s): Defense Department—Defense Logistics Agency (DLA)

Description: DLA is the central supply and distribution agency for the military; it provides goods such as weapons parts, fuel, uniforms, food rations, and medical supplies. The Team DLA section links to the Web sites of major DLA offices. A DLA Web portal links to DLA information by topic. The site also has a section on business operations and an 89-page guide to DLA acronyms.

Subject(s): Military Logistics

Publication(s): *DLAPS Publications*, D 7.41

Loglines, D 7.43

Defense Media Activity (DMA)

http://www.dma.mil/

Sponsor(s): Defense Department

Description: DMA creates and distributes news and information products for military and civilian audiences. DMA consolidates the Soldiers Media Center, Naval Media Center, Marine Corps News, Air Force News Service, and American Forces Information Service into a single field activity; it also includes *Stars and Stripes* newspaper and the Defense Information School. The Web site describes DMA's work and links to related services.

Subject(s): Military Information

Defense Prisoner of War/Missing in Action Accounting Agency

http://www.dpaa.mil/

Sponsor(s): Defense Department–Defense Prisoner of War/Missing in Action Accounting Agency

Description: This Web site covers the federal government's efforts to account for missing persons from all wars. The site includes Defense Department policies and procedures, DNA identification, information on archival research, and information specifically for families of POW/MIAs. The site also features lists from missing personnel databases from Iraq and Other Conflicts, the Cold War, the Vietnam War, the Korean War, and World War II.

Subject(s): Prisoners of War

Defense Procurement and Acquisition Policy (DPAP)

http://www.acq.osd.mil/dpap/

Sponsor(s): Defense Department—Office of the Under Secretary of Defense for Acquisition, Technology, and Logistics

Description: DPAP is responsible for all acquisition and procurement policy matters in the Department of Defense. The Defense Acquisition

Regulations System section of the site includes the Defense Federal Acquisition Regulations Supplement and any new Defense Acquisition Regulations rules open for public comments. Other content on the site includes the Contract Pricing Reference Guides, e-business and purchase card program information, and sections on contract policy, international contracting, and strategic sourcing. The Policy Vault section has acquisition policy documents available for dissemination to the public.

Subject(s): Defense Contracting—Policy; Government Procurement—Policy

Defense Security Service (DSS)

http://www.dss.mil/

Sponsor(s): Defense Department—Defense Security Service (DSS)

Description: DSS conducts personnel security investigations and operates programs in industrial security and security training. The DSS Web site describes its programs, including National Industrial Security Program (Facility Security Clearance), Personnel Security, and the Defense Security Service Academy (DSSA).

Much of the information at this site is for DSS customers, who are federal agencies and private industry and universities carrying out government contracts or conducting research and development.

Subject(s): Military Intelligence; National Security

Department of Defense

http://www.defense.gov/

Sponsor(s): Defense Department

Description: The official Department of Defense Web site features armed forces news, RSS news feeds, leadership biographies and speeches, defense-related reports of current interest, a searchable knowledgebase (FAQ), and links to the many Defense social media sites. The Web site serves the media at large with photos, videos, transcripts, and blogs.

The DoD Sites section organizes links to the numerous DoD sites alphabetically and by category, and it has a search engine specifically for Defense Department sites. As with other cabinet-level departments, the Defense Web site features an Open Government section and a Recovery Act section.

This site is an excellent starting point for users looking for U.S. military Web sites or current DoD news.

Subject(s): Military Information; Finding Aids

Publication(s): *Ballistic Missile Defense Review*
Nuclear Posture Review, D 1.2
Quadrennial Defense Review, D 1.2
Space Posture Review

DoD Dictionary of Military Terms

http://www.dtic.mil/doctrine/dod_dictionary/index.html

Sponsor(s): Defense Department—Joint Chiefs of Staff

Description: This is the online version of the DOD Dictionary of Military and Associated Terms. It provides brief explanations of terms such as "unconventional assisted recovery" and "reserved obstacles." The dictionary may be used online or downloaded in PDF or XML format.

Subject(s): Military Information; Reference

Joint Electronic Library (JEL)

http://www.dtic.mil/doctrine/

Sponsor(s): Defense Department—Joint Chiefs of Staff

Description: JEL is the source for joint doctrine and training information for the U.S. military forces. The site provides access to Joint Publications, Future Joint Warfare documents, and information on training and education. The Doctrine section includes the Joint Doctrine Hierarchy Chart, history publications, and research publications. Some sections of the site are restricted to military users.

Subject(s): Military Doctrine

Publication(s): *Joint Force Quarterly*, D 5.20

Office of the Under Secretary of Defense (Comptroller)

http://comptroller.defense.gov/

Sponsor(s): Defense Department—Office of the Under Secretary of Defense (Comptroller)

Description: The comptroller's page provides an extensive set of Department of Defense budget documents. The site also has the Defense Department's Agency Financial Report (AFR) and Performance and Accountability Report (PAR).

Subject(s): Defense Administration

Overseas Basing Commission

http://govinfo.library.unt.edu/osbc/

Sponsor(s): Overseas Basing Commission

Description: The full name of the Overseas Basing Commission was the United States Congress Commission on Review of Overseas Military Facility Structure of the United States. The commission was charged with making recommendations to Congress and to the president regarding overseas military facilities. The commission closed after having made its final report in 2005. The Web site has been archived by the University of North Texas Libraries CyberCemetery Web site project.

Subject(s): Military Bases and Installations

Pentagon Force Protection Agency (PFPA)

http://www.pfpa.mil/

Sponsor(s): Defense Department—Police Force Protection Agency (PFPA)

Description: PFPA is responsible for security at the Pentagon and other Department of Defense facilities and activities in the Washington, D.C., area. It performs standard police work and criminal investigations and is also concerned with terrorist, chemical, biological, and nuclear threats. The PFPA Web site has basic information about the agency, its component organizations, and employment opportunities.

Subject(s): Homeland Security; Police

Selective Service System (SSS)

http://www.sss.gov/

Sponsor(s): Selective Service System (SSS)

Description: The SSS Web site features information about the agency and the military draft and can be used to register online or check a registration. The site includes sections About the Agency, the History/Records section, Publications, Registration Info, What Happens in a Draft, and Fast Facts. History/Records includes historical draft statistics, a guide to requesting archival records of draft registrants, and a general history of the draft in the United States. The Publications section contains current and past editions of the agency's *Annual Report to Congress, Selective Service System* and back issues of the newsletter *The Register*.

Subject(s): Military Draft

Publication(s): *Annual Report to Congress, Selective Service System*
The Register, Y 3.SE 4:27/

DEFENSE RESEARCH

Air Force Office of Scientific Research (AFOSR)—Wright-Patterson Air Force Base

http://www.wpafb.af.mil/AFRL/afosr/

Sponsor(s): Air Force

Description: AFOSR directs the Air Force's basic research program, with research concerning aerospace and materials sciences, chemistry and life sciences, mathematics and information sciences, and physics and electronics. Its Web site includes current news, research opportunity announcements, and information about its technology directorates. The site also has information about AFOSR educational, outreach, and special programs.

Subject(s): Military Research Laboratories

Air Force Research Laboratory (AFRL)—Wright-Patterson Air Force Base

http://www.wpafb.af.mil/AFRL/

Sponsor(s): Air Force—Air Force Research Laboratory

Description: AFRL conducts basic and applied research to improve the Air Force fighting capabilities. AFRL is headquartered at Wright-Patterson Air Force Base in Ohio, and its Web site is part of the base's site. The site has fact sheets on the Small Business Innovation Research Program, technology transfer, and partnership opportunities with AFRL.

Subjects(s): Military Research Laboratories

Army Research Laboratory (ARL)

http://www.arl.army.mil/

Sponsor(s): Army—Army Materiel Command

Description: ARL's Web site provides information about its organization, research, and collaborative alliances. ARL's research directorates include computational and information science, sensors and electron devices, survivability/lethality analysis, weapons and materials research, human research and engineering, and vehicle technology. Research and analysis programs include robotics, precision guided missiles, tactical communications, and battlefield weather research. Each is described in more detail at the Web site. A separate section provides information about doing business with ARL.

Subject(s): Military Computing; Military Research Laboratories; Weapons Research

Biometrics Identity Management Agency

http://www.biometrics.dod.mil

Sponsor(s): Army—Biometrics Identity Management Agency (BIMA)

Description: The Biometrics Identity Management Agency was established as a permanent organization within the Army in March 2010. BIMA maintains the Defense Department's authoritative biometric database in support of the National Security Strategy. Biometrics consists of the tools to verify the identity of an individual based on distinct and measurable physiological characteristics, such as fingerprints. This Web site has information about the program and about biometrics, including a basic tutorial, glossary, and news stories on the topic.

Subject(s): Biometrics—Research

Publication(s): *The Biometric Scan*

Combating Terrorism Center at West Point (CTC)

http://www.ctc.usma.edu/

Sponsor(s): Army—United States Military Academy (USMA)

Description: CTC conducts education, research, and policy analysis on such topics as terrorism, counterterrorism, homeland security, and weapons of mass destruction. Along with information about the study program, the CTC Web site has current news, publications, and information about the Downing Scholars and the Harmony Program. Also featured is *The CTC Sentinel,* a monthly publication that reflects the center's mission.

Subject(s): Terrorism—Research

Publication(s): *The CTC Sentinel*

Defense Advanced Research Projects Agency (DARPA)

http://www.darpa.mil/

Sponsor(s): Defense Department—Defense Advanced Research Projects Agency (DARPA)

Description: DARPA, founded in 1958 as the Advanced Research Projects Agency (ARPA), manages research and development to promote the technological superiority of the U.S. military. The DARPA Web site features an overview and history of the agency, with links to the Web sites of its component offices. Each DARPA office section has extensive information about current and completed projects. The Opportunities section has information on DARPA solicitations and small business funding opportunities.

Subject(s): Military Technology—Research

Defense Science Board (DSB)

http://www.acq.osd.mil/dsb/

Sponsor(s): Defense Department—Office of the Under Secretary of Defense for Acquisition, Technology, and Logistics

Description: DSB advises the Department of Defense leadership on matters relating to science, technology, research, engineering, manufacturing, and the acquisition process. DSB accomplishes much of its work through special task forces. The DSB Web site lists current task forces and their missions; it also has PDF copies of past task force reports.

Subject(s): Military Technology; Defense Research

Publication(s): *DSB Newsletter,* D 1.107/2

DoD High Performance Computing Modernization Program (HPCMP)

http://www.hpcmo.hpc.mil/

Sponsor(s): Defense Department—High Performance Computing Modernization Program (HPCMP)

Description: HPCMP provides supercomputer services, high-speed network communications, and computational science expertise for the research, development, and test activities of the Department of Defense laboratories and test centers. Its Web site provides information about the program and related high-performance computing activities.

While focusing on military high-performance computing, this site will be of interest to others in the high-performance computing community.

Subject(s): High Performance Computing; Military Computing

Publication(s): *High Performance Computing Modernization Program Annual Report*

DTIC Online

http://www.dtic.mil/dtic/

Alternate URL(s)

http://www.dtic.mil/dtic/search/tr/

Sponsor(s): Defense Department—Defense Technical Information Center (DTIC)

Description: DTIC is a Department of Defense (DoD) Field Activity for scientific, research, and engineering information services. It offers the Defense community, including contractors and DoD-funded researchers, a broad range of services for locating and delivering technical reports, research summaries, summaries of independent research and development, and other relevant publications. DTIC also offers publicly accessible databases on this Web site.

In the search drop-down menu, the Technical Reports menu option searches technical reports generated for and by the Department of Defense; this database was formerly known as Public STINET and its direct Web address is listed above as the alternate URL.

Subject(s): Scientific and Technical Information; Databases

Foreign Military Studies Office

http://fmso.leavenworth.army.mil/

Sponsor(s): Army—Foreign Military Studies Office (FMSO)

Description: According to its Web site, FMSO "provides translated selections and analysis from a diverse range of foreign articles and other media that our analysts believe will give military and security experts an added dimension to their critical thinking about the Operational Environment." Many of the FMSO analytical products are available online, organized by world region and by topic. Topics include border security, energy security, and terrorism.

Subject(s): Military Intelligence; Defense Research

Information Analysis Centers (IACs)

http://iac.dtic.mil/

Sponsor(s): Defense Department—Defense Technical Information Center (DTIC)

Description: This site provides a central directory for home pages of the Department of Defense and other military Information Analysis Centers (IACs). The IACs establish databases of historical, technical, scientific, and other data and information on a variety of technical topics. Information collections include unclassified, limited distribution, and classified information. The IACs also provide analytical tools such as models and simulations. Most of the home pages of the IACs describe the databases that they maintain, although they rarely provide public access.

The Defense Department IACs include AMMTIAC (Advanced Materials, Manufacturing, and Testing Information Analysis Center), CBRNIAC (Chemical, Biological, Radiological, and Nuclear Defense Information Analysis Center), CPIAC (Chemical Propulsion Information Analysis Center), DACS (Data and Analysis Center for Software), IATAC (Information Assurance Technology Analysis Center), MSIAC (Modeling and Simulation Information Analysis Center), RIAC (Reliability Information Analysis Center), SENSIAC (Military Sensing Information Analysis Center), and WSTIAC (Weapons Systems Technology Information Analysis Center). The armed services, or military, IACs include APMIAC (Airfields Pavement & Mobility Information Analysis Center), CEIAC (Coastal Engineering Information Analysis Center), CRSTIAC (Cold Regions Science and Technology Information Analysis Center), CTIAC (Concrete Technology Information Analysis Center), DTRIAC (Defense Threat Reduction Information Analysis Center), EIAC (Environmental Information Analysis Center), HEIAC (Hydraulic Engineering Information Analysis Center), SAVIAC (Shock and Vibration Information Analysis Center), and SMIAC (Soil Mechanics Information Analysis Center).

Many of the resources from the IACs will only be of interest to the defense community due to the access restrictions. However, there are a few databases that have unclassified material available.

Subject(s): Information Analysis Centers; Military Information; Scientific and Technical Information

Institute for National Strategic Studies (INSS)

http://inss.ndu.edu/

Sponsor(s): Defense Department—National Defense University (NDU)

Description: INSS conducts policy research and analysis for senior U.S. military decision-makers and for decision-makers in the Executive Branch and in Congress. This Web site has information on the INSS, its centers, research programs, reports, symposia, and the INSS blog. See the NDU library digital collections for access to INSS publications prior to 2009 (under the Publications section on the INSS Web site).

Subject(s): Defense Research

Publication(s): *INSS Special Reports,* D 5.417

McNair Papers, D 5.416

Strategic Forum, Institute for National Strategic Studies, D 5.417

Naval Research Laboratory (NRL)

http://www.nrl.navy.mil/

Sponsor(s): Navy—Naval Research Laboratory (NRL)

Description: This is the main page for the many directorates and divisions of NRL. The laboratory's research focus is broad, including specialties within the areas of materials science, ocean and atmospheric science, and space technology. NRL also has a Nanoscience Institute. The site provides information on NRL accomplishments in these areas, business opportunity news, and information on career and student opportunities.

Subject(s): Navy—Research; Research Laboratories
Publication(s): *NRL Fact Book*, D 201.17/3
NRL Review, D 210.17/2

SENSIAC: Military Sensing Information Analysis Center
http://www.sensiac.gatech.edu/
Sponsor(s): Defense Department—Defense Technical Information Center (DTIC)
Description: SENSIAC focuses on sensing technologies for military use, such as infrared sensors, laser systems, radar, underwater acoustics, and seismic sensors. Only the most general information is available free of charge on this Web site.

U.S. Army Combined Arms Center (CAC) and Fort Leavenworth
http://www.leavenworth.army.mil/
Sponsor(s): Army
Description: CAC is the largest organization at the Fort Leavenworth Army Garrison. The Web site covers each of the many organizations, functions, centers, schools, and special activities of the CAC. These include the Center for Army Leadership, the Command and General Staff College, and the Combat Studies Institute, among others. Some links on the site may only be accessible to military users.

Subject(s): Military Training and Education
Publication(s): *Military Review*, D 110.7

U.S. Army Medical Research Institute of Infectious Diseases (USAMRIID)
http://www.usamriid.army.mil/
Sponsor(s): Army—Army Medical Command
Description: USAMRIID researches and develops medical solutions to protect troops from biological threats. Its Web site has information about the institute's achievements, current news, and technology transfer opportunities. The Scientific Publications section provides a bibliography of staff-authored journal articles. The Reference Materials section includes downloadable copies of textbooks and manuals.

Subject(s): Bioterrorism; Military Medicine

Publication(s): *Defense Against Toxin Weapons*, D 101.2

Medical Management of Biological Casualties Handbook (Blue Book), D 101.6/5

Weapons Systems Technology Information Analysis Center (WSTIAC)
http://www.dtic.mil/dtic/iac/wstiac.html

Sponsor(s): Defense Department—Weapons Systems Technology Information Analysis Center (WSTIAC)

Description: WSTIAC is the defense community's central information service for advanced technologies research relevant to weapons systems. Many other sections of the site are restricted to authorized users.

Subject(s): Information Analysis Centers; Weapons Research

Publication(s): *WSTIAC Quarterly*

HOMELAND SECURITY

Center for Homeland Defense and Security (CHDS)
http://www.chds.us/

Sponsor(s): Navy—Naval Postgraduate School (NPS)

Description: NPS's Center for Homeland Defense and Security (CHDS) provides educational programs for government and military leaders. Its Web site has information on the program, an index of faculty published papers, and the full text of master's theses from the program. The center's online Homeland Security Digital Library section is open to federal, state, tribal, and local government officials; homeland security researchers and academics, and the U.S. military, but is not available to the general public. Eligible users must register for access. The center's *Homeland Security Affairs* journal is publicly available on the site.

Subject(s): Homeland Security—Research; Military Training and Education

Publication(s): *Homeland Security Affairs*, D 201.48

Civil Air Patrol (CAP)
http://www.gocivilairpatrol.com/

Sponsor(s): Air Force—Civil Air Patrol (CAP)

Description: CAP is a nonprofit corporation that operates as the all-volunteer civilian auxiliary of the U.S. Air Force when performing services for the federal government and files an annual report to Congress. CAP assists assist federal, state, and local authorities in performing various reconnaissance, emergency services, disaster relief, and homeland security missions. Its Web site describes these core operations, CAP aerospace education and cadet programs, and joining CAP.

Subject(s): Civil Air Patrol

Defense Nuclear Facilities Safety Board (DNFSB)
http://www.dnfsb.gov/

Sponsor(s): Defense Nuclear Facilities Safety Board

Description: DNFSB is responsible for independent, external safety oversight of the Department of Energy (DOE) nuclear weapons complex. Its Web site offers information about the board's members and organizational structure. The Board Activities section organizes DNFSB documents by type, with links including Recommendations and Reports; an interactive map on the site's home page provides access to the same documents by DOE nuclear site name. The Board Activities section also includes annual reports to Congress and public hearings information.

Subject(s): Nuclear Weapons

Publication(s): *DNFSB Site Representatives Weekly Activities Report*, Y 3.D 36/3:11

DNFSB Staff Issue Reports, Y 3.D 36/3:12

DNFSB Technical Reports, Y 3.D 36/3:9

Recommendations of the DNFSB, Y 3.D 36/3:10

Defense Threat Reduction Agency (DTRA)

http://www.dtra.mil/

Sponsor(s): Defense Department—Defense Threat Reduction Agency (DTRA)

Description: The full name of this Web site is Defense Threat Reduction Agency & USSTRATCOM Center for Combating WMD. These entities' names are abbreviated DTRA and SSC-WMD, respectively, and they work closely together. DTRA addresses the threat of weapons of mass destruction (chemical, biological, radiological, nuclear, and high explosives) with combat support, technology development, threat control, and threat reduction. SSC-WMD coordinates counter-WMD activities at U.S. military locations around the world. Each mission link on the home page provides further information on DTRA's work. The Web site includes current information on DTRA research grants and business opportunities. The site also has information on the Nuclear Test Personnel Review to assist veterans who received doses of radiation while participating in U.S. atmospheric nuclear tests during the Cold War era.

Subject(s): National Defense; Radiation Exposure

Department of Homeland Security (DHS)

http://www.dhs.gov/

Sponsor(s): Homeland Security Department

Description: DHS was formed in January 2003 by consolidating many existing agencies and agency divisions whose missions relate to domestic defense. The DHS Web site organizes information into major sections under the Topics link, including Preventing Terrorism, Border Security, Cybersecurity, Civil Rights and Civil Liberties, and Immigration Enforcement. Each of these sections has publications, grants, laws, program links, and background information as appropriate. A complete list of links to component agencies and offices is provided in the About DHS section along with budget information, an organization chart, and guidance on major laws and regulations.

Information is also organized on the home page (under "How Do I?"), with links to frequently asked questions, including "Find Overseas Travel Alerts" and "Report Cyber Incidents." As Cabinet departments are required to do, DHS maintains an Open Government page.

Researchers may also want to check the Web sites of DHS component agencies for detailed information. Many DHS component agencies are described elsewhere in this publication.

Subjects(s): Homeland Security

Department of Homeland Security SBIR Program
http://www.dhs.gov/st-sbir

Sponsor(s): Homeland Security Department

Description: DHS participates in the federal government's Small Business Innovation Research (SBIR) grant program. This official Web site presents information about solicitations, proposal review, and awards. (The Small Business Administration has additional information about the SBIR program on its Web site. SBA is described elsewhere in this book.)

Subject(s): Grants; Homeland Security—Research; Small Business— Grants

FBI National Security Branch (NSB)
http://www.fbi.gov/hq/nsb/nsb.htm

Sponsor(s): Justice Department—Federal Bureau of Investigation (FBI)

Description: NSB was established in 2005 to combine the bureau's counterterrorism, counterintelligence, and intelligence resources; a consolidated Weapons of Mass Destruction Directorate was added in 2006. The NSB Web site has news and background information about the branch, a member of the U.S. Intelligence Community. The Counterterrorism Division page has a most wanted list and a form for reporting tips. It also provides information on the National Counterterrorism Center and the Terrorism Screening Center.

Subject(s): Homeland Security; Terrorism

Homeland Security Advisory Council
http://www.dhs.gov/files/committees/editorial_0331.shtm

Sponsor(s): Homeland Security Department

Description: The Homeland Security Advisory Council provides advice and recommendations to the secretary of the Department of Homeland Security. The council includes members from state and local government, academia, and the private sector. Its Web site contains member information, meeting minutes, and completed task force reports on topics such as the Southwest border and community resilience.

Subject(s): Homeland Security

Homeland Security Digital Library

http://www.hsdl.org/

Sponsor(s): Navy—Naval Postgraduate School (NPS)

Description: HSDL provides access to open source resources on homeland security policy, strategy, and organizational management. The extensive database of full text resources can be searched or browsed by topic. The site's On The Homefront blog announces significant new reports and documents on homeland security issues.

HSDL is maintained to support the information needs of homeland security officials in the government and military, academic researchers, and qualified homeland security researchers. This primary audience can request an ID to access the full HSDL collection. The general public has immediate access to what is called HSDL Collection (limited). This smaller collection includes federal government documents and papers written at federal academic institutions, such as the Naval Postgraduate School and the Army War College. The Homeland Security Blog Search, a search engine for multiple homeland security blogs, and a guide to sources of homeland security grants are among the other resources available without a login ID. Some Federal Depository Libraries provide public access to the full collection; to find the depository library nearest to you, see http://www.gpo.gov/libraries/.

Subject(s): Homeland Security—Research

Homeland Security Research

http://www.epa.gov/nhsrc/

Sponsor(s): Environmental Protection Agency (EPA)—National Homeland Security Research Center (NHSRC)

Description: EPA's Homeland Security Research develops expertise and technology to counter public health and environmental emergencies arising from terrorist incidents. The Web site has publications and background information on the center's research in such areas as water infrastructure protection and indoor and outdoor decontamination.

Subject(s): Public Health—Research; Terrorism

Information Sharing Environment (ISE)

http://www.ise.gov

Sponsor(s): Office of the Director of National Intelligence

Description: ISE was established by the Intelligence Reform and Terrorism Prevention Act of 2004. ISE works to promote information sharing between all levels of government and with the private sector and foreign partners. The Web site links to documents relevant to the establishment and operation of ISE and describes ISE privacy guidelines. The site also describes work with state, local, and tribal governments including information fusion centers and the Interagency Threat Assessment Coordination Group.

Subject(s): Law Enforcement Policy; Terrorism

Missile Defense Agency (MDA)

http://www.mda.mil/

Sponsor(s): Defense Department—Missile Defense Agency (MDA)

Description: MDA is charged with developing an integrated missile defense system. The Ballistic Missile Defense Organization (BMDO) became the MDA in 2002, elevating the organization to agency status. The agency's Web site explains the basics of missile defense, budget information, and a guide to doing business with MDA. The News & Resources section includes images and videos of missile defense systems, fact sheets, environmental impact documents, and congressional testimony.

Subject(s): Missile Defense

National Commission on Terrorist Attacks Upon the United States

http://www.9-11commission.gov/

Sponsor(s): National Commission on Terrorist Attacks Upon the United States

Description: The National Commission on Terrorist Attacks Upon the United States—also known as the 9-11 Commission—was an independent, bipartisan commission charged with investigating the September 11, 2001, terrorist attacks. The 9-11 Commission issued its final public report in July 2004 and closed in August 2004.

Documents at the site include the final report, video and transcript archives of the 12 public hearings, and staff monographs on terrorist financing and terrorist travel. The Press section includes photos and press releases.

This site is archived and will not be updated further. It has been kept online in its archived state by the University of North Texas Libraries' CyberCemetery Web site. Transcripts of hearings can be accessed at http://govinfo.library.unt.edu/911/hearings/index.htm

Subject(s): Homeland Security; Terrorism

Publication(s):

27/2/FINAL/EXEC.SUM The 9/11 Commission Report. Executive Summary, Y 3.2:T

49 Monograph on Terrorist Financing: Staff Report to the Commission, Y 3.2:T 27/2/F

9/11 and Terrorist Travel: Staff Report of the National Commission on Terrorist Attacks, Y 3.2:T 27/2/T 69

Eighth Public Hearing of the National Commission on Terrorist Attacks Upon the United States (March 23–24, 2004), Y 3.2

Eleventh Public Hearing of the National Commission on Terrorist Attacks Upon the United States (May 18–19, 2004), Y 3.2

Hearing of the National Commission on Terrorist Attacks Upon the United States (May 22–23, 2003), Y 3.2

Hearing of the National Commission on Terrorist Attacks Upon the United States: Fourth Public Hearing, Intelligence and the War on Terrorism (October 14, 2003), Y 3.2

Hearing of the National Commission on Terrorist Attacks Upon the United States: Subject, Private-Public Sector Partnerships for Emergency Preparedness (November 19, 2003), Y 3.2

Hearing of the National Commission on Terrorist Attacks Upon the United States: Subject, Sixth Public Hearing (December 8, 2003), Y 3.2

Hearing of the National Commission on Terrorist Attacks Upon the United States: Terrorism, Al Qaeda, and the Muslim World (July 9, 2003), Y 3.2

Hearing of the National Commission on Terrorist Attacks Upon the United States: Witness, Dr. Condoleezza Rice (April 8, 2004), Y 3.2

National Commission on Terrorist Attacks Upon the United States: Public Hearing (April 1, 2003), Y 3.2

National Commission on Terrorist Attacks Upon the United States: Public Hearing (March 31, 2003), Y 3.2

Seventh Public Hearing of the National Commission on Terrorist Attacks Upon the United States: Subject—Borders, Transportation and Managing Risks (January 26–27, 2004), Y 3.2

Tenth Public Hearing of the National Commission on Terrorist Attacks Upon the United States (April 13–14, 2004), Y 3.2

The 9/11 Commission Report: Final Report of the National Commission on Terrorist Attacks, Y 3.2:T 27/2/FINAL

Twelfth Public Hearing of the National Commission on Terrorist Attacks Upon the United States (June 16–17, 2004), Y 3.2

National Nuclear Security Administration (NNSA)

http://www.nnsa.doe.gov/

Sponsor(s): Energy Department—National Nuclear Security Administration

Description: NNSA, a semi-autonomous agency within the Department of Energy, officially began operations on March 1, 2000. Its mission is to carry out the national security responsibilities of the Department of Energy, including maintenance of nuclear weapons, promotion of international nuclear safety and nonproliferation, and management of the naval nuclear propulsion program. The Web sites section Our Programs, under About, describes the activities of NNSA. The Defense Programs subsection (under Our Programs) covers the Stockpile Stewardship Program. Other sections focus on nuclear nonproliferation, naval reactors, and nuclear security. The About section includes information about the agency's leadership, locations, and budget.

Subject(s): Nuclear Weapons

Publication(s): *NNSA News*

NIAID Biodefense Research
http://www.niaid.nih.gov/biodefense/
Sponsor(s): National Institutes of Health (NIH)—National Institute of Allergy and Infectious Diseases (NIAID)
Description: NIAID, in cooperation with other agencies, academic, and industry, is studying medical countermeasures against radiological and nuclear threats. The site has information on its work in the areas of biodefense, radiation countermeasures, and chemical countermeasures.
Subject(s): Biological Warfare—Research

Ready.gov
http://www.ready.gov
Alternate URL(s)
http://www.listo.gov/
Sponsor(s): Homeland Security Department
Description: The Ready.gov Web site provides advice on preparing for potential terrorist attacks or other emergencies. Advice is also given for businesses and kids. Information includes advice for military families, people with disabilities and special needs, and people with pets. Checklists and brochures can be downloaded in PDF format.
A Spanish-language version of the site is available at the alternate URL listed above. Ready.gov also has pages translated into Chinese, French, Korean, Tagalog, Vietnamese, and more.
Subject(s): Disaster Preparedness; Homeland Security

SAFETY Act
http://www.safetyact.gov
Sponsor(s): Homeland Security Department
Description: The SAFETY Act, part of the Homeland Security Act of 2002 (Public Law 107-296), provides liability protections for sellers of qualified anti-terrorism products. This Web site provides information about the legislation and applications for the SAFETY Act Designation or Certification for products.
Subject(s): Business—Regulations

Transportation Security Administration (TSA)
http://www.tsa.gov/
Sponsor(s): Homeland Security Department—Transportation Security Administration (TSA)
Description: TSA was established within the Department of Transportation in response to the terrorist attacks of September 11, 2001; it has since been transferred to the Department of Homeland Security. The agency has responsibility for transportation security nationwide. The TSA Web site provides current news about travel security and information on the agency's mission, organization, and operations. The Traveler

Information portion of the site includes lists of items prohibited in carry-on or checked luggage, tips for travelers with special needs, and information about privacy and risk-based security. The Press Room section has news, press releases, speeches, and testimony. TSA also maintains an active blog for travelers at http://blog.tsa.gov and has a mobile app for smartphone users.

Subject(s): Aviation Safety; Transportation Security

United States Secret Service

http://www.secretservice.gov/

Sponsor(s): Homeland Security Department—Secret Service

Description: The United States Secret Service was transferred in 2003 from the Department of the Treasury, where it was founded in 1865, to the Department of Homeland Security. The Secret Service has a role in protecting the president, vice president, former U.S. presidents, visiting foreign dignitaries, and other leaders, as well as investigating counterfeiting and other financial crimes. On the Web site, the Protection section covers the high-profile presidential security role. Under Investigations, the Know Your Money subsection provides details on how to detect counterfeit currency and guard against forgery loss. Other sections cover Secret Service history, most wanted fugitives, and employment opportunities.

Although the Secret Service does not discuss details of its security operations, its Web site is designed to give clear answers to many of the questions the public might have. The Frequently Asked Questions section answers such questions as "Who is the Secret Service authorized to protect?" and "How long do former presidents receive Secret Service protection after they leave office?"

Subject(s): Counterfeiting; Homeland Security; Law Enforcement

USDOJ National Security Division (NSD)

http://www.justice.gov/nsd/

Sponsor(s): Justice Department—National Security Division (NSD)

Description: NSD was created within the Justice Department in 2006 to combat terrorism and other threats to national security. It manages the administration and enforcement of the Foreign Agents Registration Act (FARA), and the Web site links to FARA registration and the FARA document database. The Electronic Reading Room, within the NSD FOIA section, provides the *Annual Foreign Intelligence Surveillance Act (FISA) Report to Congress*. This annual document reports applications made by the government for authority to conduct electronic surveillance and physical search for foreign intelligence purposes under FISA.

Subject(s): National Security; Terrorism

Y12 National Security Complex
http://www.y12.doe.gov
Sponsor(s): Energy Department; Consolidated Nuclear Security, LLC
Description: "The Y-12 National Security Complex is a premier manufacturing facility dedicated to making our nation and the world a safer place and plays a vital role in the Department of Energy's Nuclear Security Enterprise . . . developing innovative solutions in manufacturing technologies, prototyping, safeguards and security, technical computing and environmental stewardship." (from the Web site) The program's focal points are delineated in the Nuclear Deterrence, Global Security, and Naval Reactors sections. A news feed is available in the News section.
Subject(s): Security; Nuclear Weapons

INTELLIGENCE

Air Force Intelligence, Surveillance and Reconnaissance (ISR) Agency
http://www.afisr.af.mil/
Sponsor(s): Air Force—Air Force Intelligence, Surveillance and Reconnaissance Agency (AFISR)
Description: The Air Force ISR Agency, formerly known as the Air Intelligence Agency, is headquartered at Lackland Air Force Base in Texas. The Web site features news, leadership biographies, and unit information.
Subject(s): Intelligence Agencies; Military Intelligence

Bureau of Intelligence and Research (INR)
http://www.state.gov/s/inr/
Sponsor(s): State Department
Description: The Department of State's Bureau of Intelligence and Research (INR) analyzes intelligence to support U.S. diplomacy. INR is a member of the U.S. intelligence community. Its Web site provides information about the Title VIII Grant Program, which supports advanced research, language, and graduate training programs conducted by U.S.-based organizations. The site also has INR's Independent States and Dependencies lists, which give the department's official short and long names and standard country codes for independent countries and dependencies of the world.
Subject(s): Intelligence; Language Education—Grants

Central Intelligence Agency (CIA)
http://www.cia.gov/
Sponsor(s): Central Intelligence Agency (CIA)
Description: The CIA Web site has news, links to offices within the CIA, information on CIA careers, and information on CIA tours and the

CIA Museum. Full-text, bibliographic, and order information for CIA maps and publications are in the Library section. The full-text versions of two major reference publications, *The World Factbook* and *Chiefs of State and Cabinet Members of Foreign Governments*, are regularly updated on the site.

The Offices of CIA section includes information on the Directorate of Intelligence, the National Clandestine Service, the Directorate of Support, and the Directorate of Science and Technology. The Library section includes information on the Center for the Study of Intelligence and the Kent Center, along with their publications. The Library section also contains the CIA's FOIA Electronic Reading Room.

The availability of *The World Factbook* and Chiefs of State and Cabinet Members of Foreign Governments makes the CIA Web site an important reference source.

Subject(s): Foreign Countries; Intelligence Agencies

Publication(s): *Center for the Study of Intelligence (General Publications)*, PREX 3.17

Center for the Study of Intelligence (Monographs), PREX 3.18

Chiefs of State and Cabinet Members of Foreign Governments, PREX 3.11/2

Studies in Intelligence, PREX 3.19

The World Factbook, PREX 3.15/2

CIA Electronic Reading Room

http://www.foia.cia.gov/

Sponsor(s): Central Intelligence Agency (CIA)

Description: This is the CIA's public gateway for access to agency documents through the Freedom of Information Act (FOIA) and the Electronic Freedom of Information Act. The centerpiece is a searchable database called the "25 Year Program Archive Search," a searchable database ("CREST") of declassified documents. The Frequently Requested Records section of the Web site has the full text of a small set of frequently requested documents such as the Bay of Pigs report and Vietnam POW/MIA documents. The Special Collections sections includes documents related to former CIA director Richard Helms, documents from the National Intelligence Council Collection, and other themed collections. The Your Rights section identifies the laws governing the release of documents.

The CIA Electronic Reading Room will answer the basic questions a researcher may have about FOIA and other access to declassified documents from the CIA. Researchers may also want to check the Web site of the private National Security Archive group (http://www.gwu.edu/~nsarchiv/), which maintains a repository of declassified documents obtained through FOIA.

Subject(s): Declassified Documents; Freedom of Information Act; Intelligence

Commission on the Intelligence Capabilities of the United States Regarding Weapons of Mass Destruction (WMD Commission)

http://govinfo.library.unt.edu/wmd/

Sponsor(s): Commission on the Intelligence Capabilities of the United States Regarding Weapons of Mass Destruction

Description: The WMD Commission closed its offices in May 2005 after making its final report. The Web site has been archived at the University of North Texas Libraries' CyberCemetery. The site includes the final report and information about the WMD Commission and its members.

Subject(s): Intelligence Agencies

Publication(s): *The Commission on the Intelligence Capabilities of the United States Regarding Weapons of Mass Destruction Report to the President of the United States*, PREX 1.19

CREST Finding Aid

http://www.foia.cia.gov/collection/crest-25-year-program-archive

Sponsor(s): Central Intelligence Agency (CIA)

Description: This CIA site provides searchable access to the index of the CIA CREST (CIA Records Search Tool) database. The CREST full text collection of declassified CIA documents can only be used in person at the main Maryland campus of the National Archives. The CIA refers to the index as the "25 Year Program Archive" because it is designed to include historically valuable records 25 years old or older. This index has citations to the full text documents but does not include the documents themselves. Citations include the ESDN tracking number to be used when submitting a FOIA request to the CIA.

Subject(s): Declassified Documents; Intelligence

Defense Intelligence Agency (DIA)

http://www.dia.mil/

Sponsor(s): Defense Department—Defense Intelligence Agency (DIA)

Description: DIA provides military intelligence to warfighters, defense planners, and defense and national security policymakers. Its Web site has information about DIA's organization and history, and employment and contracting opportunities with the agency. The site has an organization chart, but does not provide much information on its centers and directorates. The National Intelligence University has its own section on the site.

Subject(s): Intelligence Agencies; Military Intelligence

IARPA

http://www.iarpa.gov/

Sponsor(s): Office of the Director of National Intelligence

Description: The Intelligence Advanced Research Projects Activity (IARPA) invests in cutting-edge research to advance U.S. intelligence capabilities. The Web site provides information about the organization, its programs, news, and events.

Subject(s): Intelligence—Research

In-Q-Tel

https://www.iqt.org/

Sponsor(s): In-Q-Tel

Description: In-Q-Tel is a private, nonprofit enterprise originally associated with the CIA. It was established to help apply new commercial information technologies to intelligence and analysis. In-Q-Tel's clients are the CIA and other members of the intelligence community. The In-Q-Tel Web site has information about the organization's history, partners, and leadership. The Technology Portfolio section gives an overview of In-Q-Tel's focus in such areas as advanced analytics and digital identity.

Subject(s): Information Technology; Intelligence

Marine Corps Intelligence Department

http://www.hqmc.marines.mil/intelligence/UnitHome.aspx

Sponsor(s): Marine Corps

Description: The Marine Corps Intelligence Department is part of the U.S. intelligence community. The department's Web site has basic information about its mission, functions, and organization. Organizational acronyms link to further information from each of the department's branches.

Subject(s): Military Intelligence

National Clandestine Service (NCS)

https://www.cia.gov/offices-of-cia/clandestine-service

Sponsor(s): Central Intelligence Agency (CIA)

Description: As stated on the Web site, the mission of the National Clandestine Service (NCS) is "to strengthen national security and foreign policy objectives through the clandestine collection of human intelligence (HUMINT) and Covert Action." The site describes career and internship opportunities at NCS and has answers to frequently asked questions.

Subject(s): Intelligence

National Counterterrorism Center (NCTC)

http://www.nctc.gov/

Sponsor(s): Office of the Director of National Intelligence

Description: NCTC serves as the nation's central point for integrating and analyzing intelligence pertaining to terrorism and counterterrorism. The NCTC site provides background information about the agency and its role. According to the Web site, "Through the Terrorist Identities Datamart Environment (TIDE), NCTC maintains a consolidated repository of information on international terrorist identities and provides the authoritative database supporting the Terrorist Screening Center and the USG's watchlisting system." The site also features a Counterterrorism Calendar each year, which can be printed from a PDF file or used online in an interactive fashion. The calendar includes anniversaries of terrorist incidents and profiles of terrorist groups and individuals.

Subject(s): Terrorism

National Geospatial-Intelligence Agency (NGA)

http://www.nga.mil/

Sponsor(s): Defense Department—National Geospatial-Intelligence Agency (NGA)

Description: NGA is an intelligence and combat support agency with expertise in geospatial intelligence, imagery analysis, geodesy, cartography, and related disciplines. A section on how to get NGA products explains what is available and provides contact information. The Products & Services section also features NGA's GEOnet Names Server (GNS), a database of standard names for places and geographic features around the world, excluding the United States and Antarctica. The NGA Web site also has information on careers with the agency.

Subject(s): Maps and Mapping; Military Intelligence

Publication(s): *GEOnet Names Server (database)*, D 5.319/2

Pathfinder: The Geospatial Intelligence Magazine, D 5.362

National Reconnaissance Office (NRO)

http://www.nro.gov/

Sponsor(s): Defense Department—National Reconnaissance Office (NRO)

Description: As part of the U.S. intelligence community, the NRO designs, builds, and operates the nation's reconnaissance satellites. The Web site provides an agency overview, press releases, and contracting information. One section of History and Studies is dedicated to information, photos, and videos about Corona, the first photoreconnaissance satellite system.

Subject(s): Intelligence Agencies

National Security Agency—Central Security Service (NSA)

http://www.nsa.gov/

Sponsor(s): Defense Department—National Security Agency (NSA)

Description: Specializing in cryptology, NSA works to protect U.S. information systems security and to produce foreign intelligence. The Central Security Service coordinates with the U.S. armed forces. The Web site's About NSA section includes leadership biographies, answers to frequently asked questions, and an overview of the Information Assurance and Signal Intelligence fields. A Cryptologic Heritage subsection has information on NSA history, the National Cryptologic Museum, and the Center for Cryptologic History. The Research section includes published staff work, technology transfer information, and a feature on security-enhanced Linux. The Public Information section links to press releases, congressional testimony, Freedom of Information Act (FOIA) releases, and information from NSA's own declassification initiatives.

Subject(s): Cryptography and Encryption; Intelligence Agencies

National Security Archive

http://www.gwu.edu/~nsarchiv/

Sponsor(s): National Security Archive

Description: The National Security Archive is a private, independent research institute and library located at George Washington University in Washington, D.C. Despite the official-sounding name, it is not a government agency. The archive collects and publishes declassified documents acquired through the Freedom of Information Act (FOIA). Only a fraction of the archive's holdings are online; nevertheless, the online offerings are significant.

The documents section of the site includes "electronic briefing books," collections of scanned declassified documents along with National Security Archive analysis. The collections are grouped by topic, such as nuclear history. These online briefing books are free; other formal collections and analysis are available for purchase. The FOIA (Freedom of Information) section of the site includes the downloadable guide "Effective FOIA Requesting for Everyone" and information on document classification.

The National Security Archive provides a valuable research service offline, with its archive of declassified U.S. documents obtained through FOIA and its own print and microform publications. The online collections meet some popular information needs and present documents with contextual commentary identifying the people and events related to the documents.

Subject(s): Declassified Documents; Foreign Policy—Research; Freedom of Information Act

Publication(s): *Effective FOIA Requesting for Everyone*

National Virtual Translation Center (NVTC)

http://www.nvtc.gov/

Sponsor(s): National Virtual Translation Center

Description: NVTC is an interagency enterprise supported by agencies in the defense and intelligence communities. NVTC acts as a clearinghouse for facilitating interagency use of translators, and it partners with government, academia, and private industry to identify translator resources and engage their services. The NVTC Web site discusses its mission and employment with NVTC. The Customers section offers an explanation of the services provided and a FAQ area.

Subject(s): Foreign Languages; Language Education

Office of Naval Intelligence (ONI)
http://www.oni.navy.mil/
Sponsor(s): Navy—Naval Intelligence Office
Description: This Web site has basic information about ONI, its leadership, news, and employment opportunities. The Proud History section, under the This Is ONI heading, provides a brief illustrated history of ONI since its founding in 1882.

Subject(s): Intelligence Agencies; Military Intelligence

Office of the Director of National Intelligence (ODNI)
http://www.dni.gov/
Sponsor(s): Office of the Director of National Intelligence
Description: The Office of the Director of National Intelligence (ODNI) was established by the Intelligence Reform and Terrorism Prevention Act of 2004 (Public Law 108-458), following a recommendation of the 9-11 Commission. The director is the principal adviser to the president on intelligence, separate from the CIA. The Web site includes an interactive organization chart and sections on major ODNI organizations, including the Information Sharing Environment, the National Counterterrorism Center, the National Intelligence Council, and the National Counterintelligence Executive.

Subject(s): Intelligence Agencies
Publication(s): *Intelligence Community Legal Reference Book*, PREX 28.2
National Intelligence Strategy of the United States of America, PREX 28.2

Office of the National Counterintelligence Executive
http://www.ncix.gov/
Sponsor(s): Office of the National Counterintelligence Executive
Description: The National Counterintelligence Executive is charged with improving the performance of U.S. counterintelligence efforts. This Web site has information about the office, its mission, and organization. Under the Publications heading, the site provides the text of counterintelligence laws and booklets with advice about economic espionage and protecting oneself while traveling abroad.

Subject(s): Intelligence Agencies
Publication(s): *Annual Report to Congress on Foreign Economic Collection and Industrial Espionage*, Y 3.C 83/2
National Counterintelligence Strategy of the United States, Y 3.C 83/2:15/

Open Source Center
http://www.opensource.gov/

Sponsor(s): Central Intelligence Agency (CIA)—Open Source Center (OSC)

Description: The Open Source Center Web site is only available to registered, qualified government and military employees and government contractors. It provides English translations of news and information from a wide array of unclassified international sources. The Open Source Center was established as part of the CIA in late 2005; it absorbed the Foreign Broadcast Information Service (FBIS), which previously published English-language translations of foreign broadcasts and printed news.

Subject(s): Intelligence—International; News Services

OpenNet

http://www.osti.gov/opennet/

Sponsor(s): Energy Department—Nuclear and National Security Information Office

Description: According to the Web site, "OpenNet is a web site supported by the Department of Energy's Office of Classification to provide easy, timely access to recently declassified documents and other related information, in support of the national Openness Initiative. In addition to DOE documents declassified and determined to be publicly available after October 1, 1994, citations to older agency document collections are included." The documents concern nuclear weapons testing, studies of the effects of radiation, and related activities of the United States and other governments. The site's Advanced Search function includes the ability to search full-text documents, as well as limit searches by declassification status, document location, and other factors. The main page of the Web site links to the Department's *Reports to Congress on the Inadvertent Releases of Restricted Data and Formerly Restricted Data Under Executive Order 12958* (as presented to Congress) and other Department of Energy Openness Initiative products.

Subject(s): Declassified Documents; Nuclear Weapons—History

Publication(s): *Reports to Congress on the Inadvertent Releases of Restricted Data and Formerly Restricted Data Under Executive Order 12958*, E 1.143

U.S. Army Intelligence and Security Command (INSCOM)

http://www.inscom.army.mil/

Sponsor(s): Army—Army Intelligence and Security Command

Description: INSCOM conducts intelligence, security, and information operations for military commanders and national decision makers. The central INSCOM Web site links to its major subordinate commands (MSCs). The site also has information on business opportunities with INSCOM.

Subject(s): Military Intelligence

Publication(s): *INSCOM Journal*, D 101.85/2

MILITARY MORALE AND WELFARE

Air Force Bands Program

http://www.bands.af.mil/

Sponsor(s): Air Force—Air Force Bands

Description: This site provides extensive background information on the Air Force Bands and Air National Guard Bands, including performance schedules, song recordings, requests for performances, and position openings in the bands.

Subject(s): Military Bands; Music

Air Force Crossroads

http://www.afcrossroads.com/

Sponsor(s): Air Force

Description: Air Force Crossroads is the official community Web site of the U.S. Air Force. The site offers a multitude of links to information important for Air Force family members on topics such as casualty and loss, Department of Defense installations, education, employment, deployment, financial information, and relocation.

Subject(s): Military Morale and Welfare

Air Force Surgeon General

http://www.afms.af.mil/

Sponsor(s): Air Force—Air Force Medical Service

Description: The Air Force Surgeon General Web site provides information on the Air Force Medical Service, news, photos, and history.

Subject(s): Air Force; Military Medicine

America's Heroes at Work

http://www.americasheroesatwork.gov/

Sponsor(s): Labor Department

Description: The America's Heroes at Work project is designed to provide support for employers of returning service members living with traumatic brain injury (TBI) or post-traumatic stress disorder (PTSD). The site includes answers to frequently asked questions, fact sheets, and training presentations to inform audiences about TBI and PTSD. The site also includes success stories for veterans and employers.

Subject(s): Veterans

Arlington National Cemetery

http://www.arlingtoncemetery.org

Sponsor(s): Arlington National Cemetery

Description: The official Web site for Arlington National Cemetery is organized into the following sections: Plan Your Visit, Funeral Information, Explore the Cemetery, Events, and News. The site is rich in historical information on such topics as famous memorials, lists of famous individuals buried at Arlington, the origins of "Taps" and the 21-gun salute, and the history of the Tomb of the Unknowns. The Photo Gallery section includes photographs of military burial ceremonies. The Funeral Information section provides information about eligibility requirements for interment or inurnment at Arlington.

The simple and uncluttered home page leads users to sections rich in information.

Subject(s): Military History; Veterans' Cemeteries

Armed Forces Retirement Home

http://www.afrh.gov/

Sponsor(s): Armed Forces Retirement Home (AFRH)

Description: The Armed Forces Retirement Home consists of two campuses, one in Washington, D.C., and one in Gulfport, MS. The Gulfport campus was damaged by Hurricane Katrina; it was renovated and has reopened. The site has information about both facilities.

Subject(s): Veterans

Army and Air Force Exchange Service (AAFES)

http://www.aafes.com/

Sponsor(s): Defense Department—Army and Air Force Exchange Service (AAFES)

Description: AAFES serves active duty military members, retirees, reservists, and their dependents by providing goods and services through a corporation and central store with a wide range of consumer products. While AAFES's physical facilities are located on military bases, its online presence provides access to its services to any eligible person with Internet access. The AAFES Web site includes online shopping, store locations, business opportunities, and information about AAFES, with some sections open only to authorized users. It also has an option for sending gift certificates or prepaid phone cards to deployed troops. The site also offers social media pages on Facebook and Twitter.

This site caters to the active and retired military community authorized to shop at Army and Air Force Exchanges. Others may find useful information in the About Exchange section, which explains the history and operations of the military base exchanges and provides information for suppliers or manufacturers wanting to do business with AAFES.

Subject(s): Military Morale and Welfare

Department of Defense Education Activity (DoDEA)

http://www.dodea.edu/

Sponsor(s): Defense Department—Department of Defense Education Activity

Description: This is the official Internet presence of the K–12 schools operated by the Department of Defense. The schools are located overseas and in the United States. The Data Center section of the Web site (under DoDEA HQ) features school contact information, school enrollment data, and standardized achievement test scores. Employment information can be found in the Human Resources subsection (also under DoDEA HQ).

Subject(s): Elementary and Secondary Education; Military Morale and Welfare

Department of Veterans Affairs (VA)

http://www.va.gov/

Sponsor(s): Veterans Affairs Department (VA)

Description: Major sections of the VA Web site in the Veterans Services section include Health, Benefits, and Burials & Memorials. The site has direct links to topics in demand, such as prescriptions, VA forms, and federal jobs for veterans. The site also has a directory of VA locations and a link to online services. The About VA section has organization information, congressional testimony, and budget information.

More institutional information is provided in the News Room sections. Because it is a Cabinet-level department, the VA also has an Open Government section on its Web site.

This site should prove useful to veterans and people involved in assisting them. Using the site map will help to uncover all of the available information.

Subject(s): Veterans

Publication(s): *Federal Benefits for Veterans, Dependents and Survivors,* VA 1.19

Geographic Distribution of VA Expenditures, VA 1.2/11

DU Library (Depleted Uranium Information)

http://fhp.osd.mil/du/

Sponsor(s): Defense Department—Office of the Secretary of Defense

Description: Depleted uranium (DU) is a dense metal used by the Defense Department in tank armor and some munitions. The DU Library Web site provides information on the health, chemical, radiation, and environmental effects of DU. For members of the armed services, the site has information on DU policy and medical follow-ups. The site also provides fact sheets and research reports.

Subject(s): Military Technology; Radiation Exposure—Research; Environmental Health

Employer Support of the Guard and Reserve (ESGR)

http://www.esgr.mil/

Sponsor(s): Defense Department—Office of the Secretary of Defense

Description: The National Committee for Employer Support of the Guard and Reserve (ESGR) works to facilitate the relationship between Reserve component members and their civilian employers. The Reserve is defined as all National Guard members and Reserve forces from all branches of the military. This Web site has information about the Uniformed Services Employment and Reemployment Rights Act (USERRA), ESGR incentive programs for employers, and local employer support volunteers. It also provides tips and facts sheets for employers and for members of the Reserve forces.

Subject(s): Labor-Management Relations; Military Reserves; National Guard

eVetRecs

http://vetrecs.archives.gov

Alternate URL(s)

http://www.archives.gov/veterans/military-service-records/

Sponsor(s): National Archives and Records Administration (NARA)

Description: This site provides instructions on requesting information from a military record and is intended for veterans or the next of kin of a deceased former member of the military. The site also links to guidance on requests from the general public, which requires a different procedure. The eVetRecs site includes information on how the National Archives protects the privacy and security of veterans' and military personnel's records.

Subject(s): Veterans

Force Health Protection and Readiness

http://fhp.osd.mil/

Sponsor(s): Defense Department

Description: This is the Web site for the Deputy Assistant Secretary of Defense for Force Health Protection and Readiness Policy and Programs. The target audience consists of service members, military leadership, and health care planners and providers. Military health researchers will also be interested in the site.

Most of the information on the site is organized by FHP&R division. For example, the Force Readiness & Health Assurance division links to information on Global Health Surveillance and to the Deployment Health and Family Readiness Library. The Civil-Military Medicine division links to information on the National Disaster Medical System and to the DoD Pandemic Influenza Watchboard site. Reference material on the site includes *FHP&R Health Topics*, an online encyclopedia covering anthrax, land mines, malaria, stress, and other issues.

Subject(s): Military Medicine

Publication(s): *FHP&R Magazine*

National Resource Directory
https://www.nrd.gov/
Sponsor(s): Defense Department
Description: The subtitle of the National Resource Directory Web site is "Connecting Wounded Warriors, Service Members, Veterans, Their Families and Caregivers with Those Who Support Them." The Departments of Defense, Labor, and Veterans Affairs maintain the site. It links to information on benefits and compensation, education and training, employment, health care, family and caregiver support, and other topics. The linked information is from federal, state and local government agencies, veterans' service and benefit organizations, non-profit community-based and faith-based organizations, academic institutions, professional associations, and philanthropic organizations.
Subject(s): Veterans; Military Medicine

Nationwide Gravesite Locator
http://gravelocator.cem.va.gov/
Sponsor(s): Veterans Affairs Department (VA)
Description: The Nationwide Gravesite Locator has burial records from many sources. It includes burial locations of veterans and their family members in VA National Cemeteries, state veterans cemeteries, other military and Department of Interior cemeteries, and for veterans buried in private cemeteries (1997 to present) when the grave is marked with a government grave marker. Researchers can search the database by name, birth or death date, and cemetery name.
Subject(s): Veterans' Cemeteries

Navy and Marine Corps Public Health Center
http://www.med.navy.mil/sites/nmcphc/Pages/Home.aspx
Sponsor(s): Navy—Navy Environmental Health Center
Description: The Navy Environmental Health Center aims to ensure Navy and Marine Corps readiness through leadership in the prevention of disease and the promotion of health. The site covers such topics as deployment health, environmental and occupational health, and preventive medicine. Sections also link to the center's field activities and leadership information. An alphabetical index assists in finding information on this large site. Some sections may be closed to all but registered users.
Subject(s): Preventive Health Care; Military Medicine

Navy Medicine
http://www.med.navy.mil/
Sponsor(s): Navy—Medicine and Surgery Bureau
Description: The Navy Bureau of Medicine and Surgery provides health care to active duty Navy and Marine Corps members, retired ser-

vice members, and their families. This site primarily provides information and services for those working in the Navy medical system and for the sailors they serve. The site carries the texts of Navy Medicine Policies and Navy Medicine Directives. It also has a list of links to the Web sites of Navy medical facilities around the world.

Subject(s): Military Medicine
Publication(s): *Navy Medicine Magazine*

Returning Service Members (OEF/OIF)

http://www.oefoif.va.gov/
Sponsor(s): Veterans Affairs Department (VA)
Description: This VA Web site provides information on benefits and transition assistance available for service members returning from Operation Iraqi Freedom and Operation Enduring Freedom. The site has special sections for returning members of the Guard and Reserve and for families of returning service members.

Subject(s): Veterans; Military Medicine

Servicemembers.gov

http://www.justice.gov/crt/spec_topics/military/
Sponsor(s): Justice Department—Civil Rights Division
Description: This Web site explains the major laws that support the rights of veterans and military service members: the Uniformed Services Employment and Reemployment Rights Act (USERRA), the Uniformed and Overseas Citizen Absentee Voting Act (UOCAVA), and the Servicemembers Civil Relief Act (SCRA). The site has brochures about protecting servicemember rights and returning servicemembers with disabilities.

Subject(s): Military Forces—Laws; Veterans—Laws

U.S. Army Bands

http://bands.army.mil/
Sponsor(s): Army—Army Bands
Description: The Army Bands Web site has links to the various bands, news, and performance schedules. The Music section includes the lyrics of the official Army song and music for the Army bugle calls.

Subject(s): Military Bands; Music

United States Navy Band

http://www.navyband.navy.mil/
Sponsor(s): Navy—Navy Band
Description: The Navy Band's Web site has information about each of the Navy's bands and ensembles. The site includes concert schedules, a discography, history, resources for music educators, and the Fanfare

newsletter. The site also has information on the Navy Hymn and the Navy Service Song, "Anchors Aweigh."
   Subject(s): Military Bands; Music
   Publication(s): *Fanfare*

USA4MilitaryFamilies
   http://www.usa4militaryfamilies.dod.mil/
   Sponsor(s): Defense Department
   Description: USA4Military Families is a Defense Department initiative to educate and encourage state policymakers, non-profits, business, and others to adopt policies that have a positive effect on military families. It outlines and provides the status of ten quality of life issues, such as improving absentee voting processes for military family members overseas.
   Subject(s): Armed Forces—Policy

Veterans Benefits Administration (VBA)
   http://www.vba.va.gov/
   Sponsor(s): Veterans Affairs Department (VA)—Veterans Benefits Administration (VBA)
   Description: The VBA Web site is part of the larger Department of Veterans Affairs (VA) Web site. Major sections of the site cover education benefits, home loans, compensation and pensions, survivors' benefits, vocational rehabilitation, employment, and life insurance. The site links to forms, manuals, publications, and benefits fact sheets.
   Subject(s): Veterans

Wounded Warrior Regiment
   http://www.woundedwarriorregiment.org/
   Sponsor(s): Marine Corps
   Description: Established in 2006, the Wounded Warrior Regiment "serves Marines who are wounded in combat, fall ill, or are injured in the line of duty. This includes active duty, reserve and veteran Marines." (from the Web site) The site has information for both Marines and their families.
   Subject(s): Marine Corps; Veterans

SIX

Demographics and Sociology

Much of the statistical information about the U.S. population comes from the Commerce Department's Bureau of the Census. This chapter includes Census Web sites presenting demographic data, Web sites from other agencies producing demographic data, and sites from academic institutions that play a role in making Census data available on the Web. Information on other types of federal government statistics, such as education statistics, can be found in the relevant subject chapter, such as the Education chapter.

Subsections in this chapter are Census and Statistics, and Demographic Groups.

CENSUS AND STATISTICS

American Community Survey (ACS)

http://www.census.gov/acs/www/

Sponsor(s): Commerce Department—Economics and Statistics Administration (ESA)—Census Bureau

Description: The Census Bureau's American Community Survey (ACS) is an ongoing survey sent to a small sample of the U.S. population. The goal of the program is to provide governments with data more current than the data from the decennial census in order to help administer federal programs, distribute funding, and plan future projects. The ongoing ACS sampling replaces the census long-form sample data collected in 2010 (but not the short form distributed to all U.S. households). ACS data supplements data collected from the short-form respondents.

The Web site describes how to access, use, and understand ACS data, which is integrated into the Census Bureau's American FactFinder interface and available for downloading. Basic information about ACS is provided in Spanish, Vietnamese, and other languages.

This site provides a wealth of background information about the relatively new ACS and about the transition from the long-form data.

Subject(s): Census Techniques

Publication(s): *American Community Survey*, C 3.297

American FactFinder

http://factfinder2.census.gov/

Sponsor(s): Commerce Department—Economics and Statistics Administration (ESA)—Census Bureau

Description: American FactFinder allows researchers to create simple reports, custom tables, and reference maps using Census Bureau data. The main search box retrieves quick fact sheets for a single geographic area or topic.

The Guided Search section of American FactFinder is straightforward and menu driven. Users can refine queries by topics, geographies, and racial and ethnic groups. Each data set page offers a detailed description of the offering.

The Reference Maps section provides direct access to tools for reference.

American FactFinder accesses enough data and has enough functionality to make it the first and last stop for many users, especially those looking for population and housing statistics. Consult the What We Provide section for guides to using American FactFinder.

Subject(s): Census; Economic Statistics; Population Statistics

Census 2000 Gateway

http://www.census.gov/main/www/cen2000.html

Sponsor(s): Commerce Department—Economics and Statistics Administration (ESA)—Census Bureau

Description: This site provides information from the 2000 census. The Census 2000 Gateway Web site is a starting point for finding products, data sets, news, documentation, and other information relating to the 2000 decennial census of population and housing. There are three main approaches to the data itself. The American FactFinder section provides tables and maps of Census 2000 data for all geographies, from the nation as a whole to the block level. The State and County Quick Facts section has summaries of the most requested data for states and counties. The Data Highlights section links to a variety of information at the state, county, and place level, including American FactFinder tables and maps, FTP access to data sets, technical documentation, news releases, state data center contacts, redistricting data, and other related statistics. Other data reports include rankings and comparisons, briefs and special reports, and selected historical census data. A Census in Schools section includes teaching resources and lesson plans.

For access to current Census Bureau data on multiple topics, see the bureau's American FactFinder database at http://factfinder.census.gov.

Subject(s): Census; Population Statistics

Census 2010

http://www.census.gov/2010census/

Sponsor(s): Commerce Department—Economics and Statistics Administration (ESA)—Census Bureau

Description: The Census 2010 site contains the most relevant information from the most recent Census. Items under the Data heading include 2010 Census Summary Files 1 and 2, 2010 Census Demographic Profiles, and briefs on such topics as the American Indian and Alaska Native population and population distribution and change.

Subject(s): Census

Census Bureau

http://www.census.gov/

Sponsor(s): Commerce Department—Economics and Statistics Administration (ESA)—Census Bureau

Description: The Census Bureau home page offers multiple routes to the wide variety of information from and about the bureau. Major categories include Topics, Library, Data, Geography, Newsroom, and About the Bureau. The Publications link (under Library) and the Subjects A to Z link provide other avenues to the data. The Data Tools section (under Data) links to Internet data tools, software, and databases. The American FactFinder is described elsewhere in this chapter. Information about the Census Bureau itself is provided in the About the Bureau section. Important resources within the Census Bureau Web site are described separately in this and other chapters in the book.

Overall, the Census Bureau Web site offers one of the largest collections of readily accessible statistical data and recent statistical press releases on the Internet. This should be one of the first sites checked by users for demographic and economic statistics.

Subject(s): Census; Economic Statistics; Population Statistics; Databases

Publication(s): *American FactFinder*, C 3.300
American Housing Survey, H-150, C 3.215/19
America's Families and Living Arrangements, C 3.186/17-2
Annual Benchmark Report for Retail Trade, C 3.138/3-8
Annual Benchmark Report for Wholesale Trade, C 3.133/5
Annual Survey of Manufactures, C 3.24/9
Census Brief, C 3.205/8
Census of Governments, C 3.145/4

Census Product Update, C 3.163/7-2

Construction Reports: Housing Units Authorized by Building Permits, C 3.215/4

Construction Reports: New One-Family Homes Sold and For Sale, C 3.215/9

Construction Reports: Value of Construction Put in Place, C 3.215/3

County Business Patterns, United States, C 3.204/3-1

Current Business Reports: Monthly Retail Trade Report, C 3.138/3

Current Business Reports: Monthly Wholesale Trade, C 3.133

Current Housing Reports, C 3.215

Current Industrial Reports, C 3.158

Current Population Reports, Consumer Income, C 3.186:P-60/

Current Population Reports, Population Characteristics, C 3.186:P-20/

Current Population Reports, Special Studies, C 3.186:P-23/

Economic Census, C 3.277/3

Government Finance and Employment Classification Manual, C 3.6/2:F 49/6/

Guide to Foreign Trade Statistics, C 3.6/2:F 76

Housing Vacancies and Homeownership Survey, C 3.294

Measuring America: the Decennial Censuses from 1790 to 2000, C 3.2

News Releases, Census Bureau, C 3.295

Population Profile of the United States, C 3.186/8

Public Elementary-Secondary Education Finances, C 3.191/2-10

Quarterly Financial Report for Manufacturing, Mining, and Trade Corporations, C 3.267

Quarterly Tax Survey, C 3.145/6

School Enrollment Social and Economic Characteristics, C 3.186/12

State Government Tax Collection Data by State, C 3.191/2-8

Survey of Business Owners, C 3.277/3

Telephone Contacts for Data Users, C 3.238/5

The Hispanic Population in the United States, C 3.186/14-2

U.S. Trade with Puerto Rico and U.S. Possessions, FT-895, C 3.164:895/

Voting and Registration in the Election of . . . , C 3.186/3-2

Census Bureau Regional Offices

http://www.census.gov/field/www/

Sponsor(s): Commerce Department—Economics and Statistics Administration (ESA)—Census Bureau

Description: This Web site uses a clickable image map and alternative text list to link to the Web sites of the Census Bureau's six regional offices. Each office's page provides local contact information and information about regional resources.

Subject(s): Census

Census State Data Center Program

http://www.census.gov/sdc/www/

Sponsor(s): Commerce Department—Economics and Statistics Administration (ESA)—Census Bureau

Description: This Web site provides basic contact information for the Census Data Center in each state, along with an overview of services available at each center. It also links to related sites, such as the Census Information Centers and Census Depository Library Web sites.

Subject(s): Census

DataFerrett

http://dataferrett.census.gov/

Sponsor(s): Commerce Department—Economics and Statistics Administration (ESA)—Census Bureau

Description: DataFerrett is a software tool that allows enhanced viewing and manipulation of selected government data sets. The Web site includes a users' guide and tutorial, as well as a section on frequently asked questions.

Subject(s): Statistics

Fast Facts for Congress

http://fastfacts.census.gov/

Sponsor(s): Commerce Department—Economics and Statistics Administration (ESA)—Census Bureau

Description: This Web site was designed for use by members of Congress and their staff, but it is available to the general public. The site's emphasis is on access to Census Bureau data by congressional district, state, and other local geographies. Searches by congressional district locate basic population, housing, and economic statistics with the data mapped to the district boundaries. The home page also links to congressional district maps and other popular Census Bureau products.

Subject(s): Congressional Districts—Statistics

Historical Census Browser

http://mapserver.lib.virginia.edu/

Sponsor: Inter-University Consortium for Political and Social Research (ICPSR); University of Virginia Library

Description: The Historical Census Data Browser has statistics from each of the decennial census reports from 1790 to 1960. The data on this Web site come from data sets created by ICPSR and taken from the U.S. decennial censuses and other sources. Coverage is available for all existing counties and states during the 1790–1960 period. Subject coverage includes population and a variety of other criteria, depending on which date is chosen. Researchers may also want to consult the Census Bureau's Selected Historical Decennial Census Population and Housing Counts Web page.

Subject(s): Census

International Programs Center (IPC)

http://www.census.gov/ipc/www/

Sponsor(s): Commerce Department—Economics and Statistics Administration (ESA)—Census Bureau

Description: IPC, part of the Census Bureau's Population Division, offers a variety of international population statistics at its Web site, including the World POPClock with a second-by-second simulation of the world's population growth. IPC's International Data Base has much more extensive information on world demographics. IPC also produces the HIV/AIDS Surveillance Database, a compilation of information from small-scale surveys of developing countries. The IPC Web site has information and software products related to its work in assisting developing countries with census administration.

Subject(s): Vital Statistics—International

IPUMS USA

http://usa.ipums.org/usa/

Sponsor: University of Minnesota—Minnesota Population Center

Description: The Integrated Public Use Microdata Series (IPUMS) consists of census microdata for social and economic research. It is a project of the University of Minnesota that is partially funded by federal grants. IPUMS USA offers population and household data samples from the U.S. decennial censuses from 1850 forward and data from the American Community Survey starting in 2000. Variables have been given consistent names across time, and other data fields have been harmonized across data sets. Users can download the IPUMS USA data by either extracting custom files or downloading entire data sets. IPUMS is free but registration is required before extracting data.

The IPUMS tools are intended for expert researchers running statistical studies using sample data. The data itself cannot be browsed online, and extracted files are very large. IPUMS does, however, offer an online data analysis system.

Subject(s): Census

POPClocks

http://www.census.gov/main/www/popclock.html

Sponsor(s): Commerce Department—Economics and Statistics Administration (ESA)—Census Bureau

Description: Two population clocks, or POPClocks, give up-to-the-minute estimates of the population in the nation and in the world. New features show population data by day and year, regional population by year, age and sex, and most populous and high density. The United States POPClock estimates the resident population of the United States at the current minute and gives the criteria for how the estimate is derived;

historical estimates and documentation are also available. The World POPClock estimates the world's population at the current minute and lists monthly estimates. The Census Bureau also provides an RSS feed for daily updates on the United States and world populations. New features on the site allow users to search population data by age and gender, most populous and high density areas, day and year, and regional population by year.

The POPClocks are useful for demonstrating the rate of change in the U.S. and world populations. However, before citing the estimates, users should read the documentation on how those estimates are reached and revised.

Subject(s): Population Statistics

Selected Historical Decennial Census Counts

http://www.census.gov/population/www/censusdata/hiscendata.html

Sponsor(s): Commerce Department—Economics and Statistics Administration (ESA)—Census Bureau

Description: The full title of this Web page is "Selected Historical Decennial Census Population and Housing Counts." It compiles links to past census reports. The actual decennial reports are online in PDF format for every decade from 1790 through 2000, along with corresponding historical notes. The page also links to tabulations of data items across the years. For example, it links to a table comparing urban and rural populations for 1790 through 1990 and to historical census statistics on the foreign-born population for 1850 through 1990. Histories and questionnaires from past censuses are also provided.

Subject(s): Census—History; Population Statistics

Publication(s): *Historical Census Statistics on the Foreign-Born Population of the United States: 1850-1900*, C 3.223/27

Historical Statistics of the United States: Colonial Times to 1970, C 3.2

Measuring America: the Decennial Censuses from 1790 to 2000, C 3.2

State and County QuickFacts

http://www.census.gov/quickfacts/

Sponsor(s): Commerce Department—Economics and Statistics Administration (ESA)—Census Bureau

Description: State and County QuickFacts offers simple access to frequently requested national, state, and county data from various Census Bureau programs, as well as data for cities and towns with more than 5,000 residents. In 2015, a revamped version of the Web site was made available. Users can choose a state from a list or from the clickable U.S. map and then select a county or city. Information at each geographic level is presented for three topics: people, business, and geography. At the state level, statistics are given for the state versus the country as a whole; at the county and city levels, county and city statistics are compared to the statewide numbers. Each state and county data table also has a link to more data sets for that location. The additional data sets include historical population counts, congressional district statistics, and tables from the American Community Survey, Economic Census, County Business Patterns, and the Consolidated Federal Funds Reports, among other resources.

This site serves as both a quick reference tool and a resource locator. By clicking on the information icon next to each data heading, users link to a page that presents the source, definition, scope, and methodology for that heading, along with a list of relevant links.

Subject(s): Census; Population Statistics

TIGER Page
http://www.census.gov/geo/www/tiger/
Sponsor(s): Commerce Department—Economics and Statistics Administration (ESA)—Census Bureau
Description: TIGER (Topologically Integrated Geographic Encoding and Referencing system) is the name given to the Census Bureau's digital mapping system for decennial census and other data. The TIGER home page offers TIGER-based digital geographic products, documentation and metadata, and information about the system. The TIGER/Line files are the primary public product created from the data in the TIGER database. The files comprise a database of geographic features, such as roads, railroads, and rivers. They can be used with the mapping or geographic information system (GIS) software that can import TIGER/Line files.

The TIGER Page is the central place to check for updates to the TIGER/Line files and related products. Explanatory material is available for both the newcomer and the experienced community of digital geographic data users.

Subject(s): Census Mapping; Geographic Information Systems (GIS)

DEMOGRAPHIC GROUPS

AgingStats.Gov
http://www.agingstats.gov
Sponsor: Federal Interagency Forum on Aging-Related Statistics
Description: The Federal Interagency Forum on Aging-Related Statistics is made up of 15 federal agencies that produce or use statistics on aging. Their Web site, AgingStats.gov, is a finding aid for these statistics. The site links directly to aging-related statistics on its members' Web sites, including relevant data at the Census Bureau, the Department of Veterans Affairs, the National Center for Health Statistics, and the Social Security Administration. The Contacts section provides the names, area of expertise, and contact information for federal agency experts. The site

also carries the full text of Older Americans: Key Indicators of Well-Being and Data Sources on Older Americans.

Subject(s): Senior Citizens—Statistics
Publication(s): *Data Sources on Older Americans*
Older Americans 2012: Key Indicators of Well-Being

American Indian and Alaska Native Data and Links

http://factfinder.census.gov/home/aian/

Sponsor(s): Commerce Department—Economics and Statistics Administration (ESA)—Census Bureau

Description: This Census Bureau Web page serves as a portal to Census information on American Indian and Alaska Native communities. In addition to the population data, maps, and tribal information, the site includes statistical policy background and a link to the Web site for the Census Advisory Committee on the American Indian and Alaska Native (AIAN) Populations. The site links to available information from the 2010 census.

Subject(s): American Indians—Statistics; Alaska Natives—Statistics

ChildStats.gov

http://www.childstats.gov/

Sponsor(s): Federal Interagency Forum on Child and Family Statistics

Description: This Web site provides access to federal and state statistics and reports on children and their families, including population and family characteristics, economic security, health, behavior and social environment, and education. The Federal Interagency Forum on Child and Family Statistics offers several reports on the site, the most prominent of which is the annual *America's Children: Key National Indicators of Well-Being*.

Subject(s): Child Welfare—Statistics
Publication(s): *America's Children: Key National Indicators of Well-Being*, PR 43.8
America's Young Adults: Special Issue, 2014

National Center for Veterans Analysis and Statistics

http://www.va.gov/vetdata/

Sponsor(s): Veterans Affairs Department (VA)

Description: This site provides current and projected veterans demographics at the national, state, county, and congressional district level. It also provides data on Veterans Administration expenditures by geographic area and links to other surveys and statistics on the veteran population.

   Subject(s): Veterans—Statistics

SEVEN

Education

The Education Department is, naturally, the leader in publishing federal government education information on the Internet. This chapter includes many of the Web resources made available by the Education Department, but it also includes information on military education activities, federally sponsored scholarships, and some education-related social service programs. The Kids' Pages section of this chapter includes over 50 Web sites designed for a younger audience and covering a wide variety of subject areas.

Subsections of this chapter are Adult Education, Curriculum, Early Childhood Education, Education Funding, Education Policy, Education Research and Statistics, Elementary and Secondary Education, Higher Education, International Education, Kids' Pages, and Teaching.

ADULT EDUCATION

DANTES—Defense Activity for Non-Traditional Education Support
http://www.dantes.doded.mil/index.html
Sponsor(s): Defense Department
Description: DANTES provides support for the Department of Defense's off-duty, voluntary education programs. Its Web site has information about counselor support, distance learning, and tuition assistance. It also has a section about the Troops to Teachers program, which assists military personnel interested in beginning a second career as a public school teacher.

Office of Vocational and Adult Education, Department of Education
http://www.ed.gov/about/offices/list/ovae/index.html

Sponsor(s): Education Department—Vocational and Adult Education Office

Description: This site provides information about the Office of Vocational and Adult Education programs, grants, events, legislation, and resources concerning the fields of adult education and vocational education. Key sections are Adult Ed and Literacy, Career and Technical Ed, and Community Colleges.

Subject(s): Adult Education; Literacy; Vocational Education

Opportunity.gov

http://federalstudentaid.ed.gov/opportunity/

Sponsor(s): Education Department; Labor Department

Description: Opportunity.gov is a guide to education and training resources for workers considering going back to school. The site links to information on student financial assistance, question and answer guides, and other resources.

Subject(s): Financial Aid to Students; Job Training

U.S.A. Learns

http://www.usalearns.org/

Sponsor(s): California. Sacramento County Education Department—Vocational and Adult Education Office

Description: U.S.A. Learns provides free, online lessons to help adults learn English and improve basic reading, writing, and speaking skills. The Web site was developed with funding from the U.S. Department of Education and the California Department of Education. Currently, the Sacramento County Office of Education retains full ownership rights for the U.S.A. Learns Web site. See the About Us section for further details.

Subject(s): Language Education

CURRICULUM

Agriculture in the Classroom

http://www.agclassroom.org/

Sponsor(s): Agriculture Department (USDA)—National Institute of Food and Agriculture (NIFA)

Description: The USDA's Agriculture in the Classroom program coordinates state education programs designed to teach children about the role of agriculture in the economy and in society. The site includes a directory of state programs, a directory of educational materials about agriculture, information on the national Agriculture in the Classroom conference, and the online magazine *AgroWorld* for high school educators and students.

Subject(s): Agricultural Education; Educational Resources

ArtsEdge: The National Arts and Education Information Network

http://artsedge.kennedy-center.org/educators.aspx

Sponsor(s): Kennedy Center for the Performing Arts; National Endowment for the Arts (NEA)

Description: ArtsEdge, from the Kennedy Center, is a major arts resource for educators and students. The site includes lesson plans and content standards for grades K–12. It also provides MyArtsEdge, where lessons can be stored and shared.

This well-designed site should be a primary starting point for users involved in arts education. The Kennedy Center is a federal government building, but its programs are privately funded. ArtsEdge and the John F. Kennedy Center for the Performing Arts hold the copyright to all of the content on the site.

Subject(s): Arts Education; Lesson Plans

BLM Learning Landscapes

http://www.blm.gov/wo/st/en/res/Education_in_BLM/Learning_Landscapes.html

Sponsor(s): Interior Department—Bureau of Land Management (BLM)

Description: This BLM Web site has information and activities for students and teachers. The Teachers section has information about field programs (mostly in the Western states), Web sites, resources, and classroom activities. Online resources for teachers and learners cover such areas as archeology, fire ecology, and energy on public lands.

Subject(s): Environmental Education; Science Education

DocsTeach.org

http://docsteach.org/

Sponsor(s): National Archives and Records Administration (NARA)

Description: The tagline of DocsTeach.org is "Bring history to life for your students." The site provides resources for using documents in the classroom, with links to thousands of primary source documents, such as illustrated family records from the 18th and 19th centuries and photos of the inauguration of John F. Kennedy.

Subject(s): Education; History

EDSITEment

http://edsitement.neh.gov/

Sponsor(s): National Endowment for the Humanities (NEH)

Description: The EDSITEment Web site's tag line is "the best of the humanities on the Web." It provides a cataloged selection of lesson plans built around high-quality, freely accessible material available on the Internet. The lesson plans are organized into sections including Art and

Culture, Literature & Language Arts, Foreign Language, and History & Social Studies. Lessons are sortable by grade range. Each detailed lesson plan is labeled with the subject area, time required, and skills taught. The site is sponsored by a partnership between the National Endowment for the Humanities, Thinkfinity.org, and the Verizon Foundation.

Subject(s): Lesson Plans; Humanities

Energy Education and Workforce Development

http://www.eere.energy.gov/education/

Sponsor(s): Energy Department—Energy Efficiency and Renewable Energy Office

Description: The Energy Education and Workforce Development Web site links to numerous resources for students, teachers, and adults pursuing energy or green energy jobs. For teachers, the site has a database of lesson plans and activities on energy efficiency and renewable energy for grades K–12. It also has information on internships and fellowships for teachers and students and a section called "Green Your School." For others, the site has a sections on clean energy jobs and education and training for these jobs.

Subject(s): Science Education; Jobs

Environmental Health Science Education: Teachers

http://www.niehs.nih.gov/health/scied/teachers/

Sponsor(s): National Institutes of Health (NIH)—National Institute of Environmental Health Sciences (NIEHS)

Description: The NIEHS Web page provides curricular material and lesson resources on environmental health topics. The lessons are aligned with the National Science Education Standards and designed for the grade 9–12 level.

Subject(s): Environmental Education

GLOBE Program

http://www.globe.gov/

Sponsor(s): National Aeronautics and Space Administration (NASA)

Description: The GLOBE (Global Learning and Observations to Benefit the Environment) program is designed to promote science education at the primary and secondary school levels. GLOBE is funded by NASA, the National Oceanic and Atmospheric Administration (NOAA), and the National Science Foundation, supported by the Department of State, and implemented through a cooperative agreement between NASA and the University Corporation for Atmospheric Research in Boulder, Colorado. The International Division is at University of Texas at Tyler (UT Tyler). The GLOBE program's primary objective is to involve students in taking environmental measurements. More than 24,000 schools in 112 countries are participating. The data they collect is accessible to anyone and there is information on how new schools can register to be included in the program. The site also has a teacher's guide and schedule of teacher workshops. Much of the content is available in Spanish and other non-English languages.

With participating schools from all over the world, this kind of collaborative project demonstrates how the Internet can be used in a K–12 environment.

Subject(s): Environmental Protection; Science Education

Learning Registry

http://www.learningregistry.org/

Sponsor(s): Defense Department; Education Department—Educational Technology Office

Description: The Learning Registry's goal is to assist educators and education administrators in finding digital learning resources and integrating them into their classrooms. The registry is a multi-agency initiative headed by the Department of Defense and the Department of Education. The site includes information about news and events, and also features a link to its Twitter feed.

Subject(s): Digital Libraries

NASA Education

http://www.nasa.gov/offices/education/about/index.html

Alternate URL(s)

http://www.nasa.gov/offices/education/about/

Sponsor(s): National Aeronautics and Space Administration (NASA)—Education Office

Description: The NASA Education Web site provides information about the education programs that NASA offers to K–12 educators and students, as well as those offered to undergraduate and graduate students and faculty at universities.

Subject(s): Science Education

National Marine Sanctuaries Education

http://sanctuaries.noaa.gov/education/

Sponsor(s): Commerce Department—National Oceanic and Atmospheric Administration (NOAA)

Description: The National Marine Sanctuaries Education Web site features lesson plans, free materials, information on workshops, and other items of interest to science or environment teachers. The section specifically for teachers includes information on the NOAA Ocean Data Education (NODE) Project, which is developing curriculum for grades 5–8 designed to help teachers and students use real scientific data.

Subject(s): Lesson Plans; Science Education

NOAA Education Resources

http://www.education.noaa.gov/

Sponsor(s): Commerce Department—National Oceanic and Atmospheric Administration (NOAA)

Description: The NOAA Education site has teacher training opportunity announcements and materials for teachers that cover weather, climate change, oceans and coasts, weather satellites, and space environments. The Student Opportunities section, under Special Topics, lists scholarships, internships, and fellowships. Featured resources include materials on marine mammals, weather systems and patterns, water cycle, ocean pollution, and carbon cycle.

Subject(s): Environmental Education

NSF Classroom Resources

http://www.nsf.gov/news/classroom/

Sponsor(s): National Science Foundation (NSF)

Description: This Web site provides organized links to classroom resources on the Internet. The site describes its intended audience as students, their families, and teachers. Links are organized into science topics such as biology, computing, Earth and environment, mathematics, and physics. The linked sites are from a variety of educational organizations and institutions.

Subject(s): Science Education

Office of English Language Acquisition (OELA)

http://www.ed.gov/about/offices/list/oela/

Sponsor(s): Education Department—English Language Acquisition Office

Description: The full title of this office is the Office of English Language Acquisition, Language Enhancement, and Academic Achievement for Limited English Proficient Students (OELA). OELA administers Title III of the No Child Left Behind Act (Public Law 107-110) on Language Instruction for Limited English Proficient and Immigrant Students. It also administers a state formula grant program. The site has program information and technical assistance for those applying for Title III grants, and it also links to the National Clearinghouse for English Language Acquisition and Language Instruction Educational Programs (NCELA), which is funded by the Department of Education.

Subject(s): Language Education—Grants

Picturing America

http://picturingamerica.neh.gov/

Sponsor(s): National Endowment for the Humanities (NEH)

Description: The Picturing America project provides schools with American art images and educational resources to facilitate teaching

American history and culture. The Web site has information about the program, a gallery of Picturing America images, and downloadable materials such as a guide to using the images in a preschool curriculum.

Subject(s): Arts Education

Statistics in Schools

http://www.census.gov/schools/

Sponsor(s): Commerce Department—Economics and Statistics Administration (ESA)—Census Bureau

Description: The Statistics in Schools program's Web site has materials for teachers (lesson plans, teaching ideas) and sections for kids and teens. It also has a section specifically for Census 2010 materials.

Subject(s): Census; Social Studies Education

Teachers' Resources

http://www.archives.gov/education/

Sponsor(s): National Archives and Records Administration (NARA)

Description: This National Archives site features history lesson plans and teaching activities correlated to the National History Standards and the National Standards for Civics and Government. It focuses on teaching with the primary documents available on the Archives site. The site links to information on teacher training, videoconferences, workshops, and other educational services from the National Archives. The site also links to education programs at the presidential libraries and resources for National History Day.

Subject(s): Lesson Plans; Social Studies Education

USGS and Science Education

http://education.usgs.gov/

Sponsor(s): Interior Department—U.S. Geological Survey (USGS)

Description: The USGS education Web site covers topics of concern to USGS scientists, including geography, geology, biology, and water resources. Educational resources are organized for grades K–6, grades 7–12, and undergraduate education. Resources include online lectures, science videos, satellite imagery, guides to teaching with maps, and educational products from the USGS online store. The site also covers USGS careers, internships, and postdoctoral fellowships.

Subject(s): Science Education; Kids' Pages

EARLY CHILDHOOD EDUCATION

Early Childhood Learning and Knowledge Center (ECLKC)

http://eclkc.ohs.acf.hhs.gov/hslc/

Sponsor(s): Health and Human Services Department—Administration for Children and Families (ACF)—Office of Head Start (OHS)

Description: The Early Childhood Learning and Knowledge Center (ECLKC) Web site states that Head Start is designed to provide services to enrolled children and their families. The site has extensive information on the Head Start Program and Early Head Start and on topics such as early childhood development, dual language learners, parenting, and professional development for program grantees. It includes an online directory of Head Start programs. ECLKC also provides information on Head Start regulations and policy, performance standards, and program monitoring. Some information is provided in Spanish

Head Start

http://www.acf.hhs.gov/programs/ohs

Sponsor(s): Health and Human Services Department—Administration for Children and Families (ACF)—Office of Head Start (OHS)

Description: The Office of Head Start administers grants for local public and private non-profit and for-profit agencies that provide child development services for low-income children and their families. The Web site has information on the program and relevant laws and regulations. The site also links to research on outcomes for the Head Start (preschool) and Early Head Start (infant to three years) programs.

Subject(s): Early Childhood Education

EDUCATION FUNDING

Bureau of Indian Education (BIE)

http://www.bie.edu/

Sponsor(s): Interior Department—Bureau of Indian Affairs (BIA)

Description: BIE oversees 183 elementary and secondary schools and two post-secondary schools for American Indian tribes and Alaska Native Villages. The BIE Web site has a directory of the schools, annual ratings of the schools, and performance reports on special education programs (the latter two in the Reports section). The site also has resources for teachers at the schools.

Subject(s): American Indians

Education Finance Statistics Center (EDFIN)

http://nces.ed.gov/edfin/

Sponsor(s): Education Department—Institute of Education Sciences—National Center for Education Statistics (NCES)

Description: The EDFIN Web site provides finance information on public elementary and secondary education. The site provides charts and data on per-pupil expenditures for public elementary and secondary education, distribution of expenditures for public elementary and secondary education by function, and similar measures.

Subject(s): Education Funding—Statistics

FAFSA4caster

http://www.fafsa4caster.ed.gov/

Sponsor(s): Education Department—Federal Student Aid Office

Description: The FAFSA4caster Web site is for those planning for higher education but not yet ready to apply for financial aid. The site provides an orientation to the financial aid process and an estimate of eligibility for aid.

Subject(s): Financial Aid to Students

Federal Cyber Service: Scholarship for Service

http://www.sfs.opm.gov/

Sponsor(s): Office of Personnel Management (OPM)

Description: OPM's Scholarship for Service program funds the education expenses of graduate and undergraduate students in information assurance fields in exchange for an obligation to work for the federal government for an agreed-upon term. The program is designed to strengthen the federal government's expertise in information assurance (the security of computer and communication networks and the information they carry). This Web site has further details about the program and a list of participating higher education institutions.

Subject(s): Computer Science; Scholarships

Federal Student Aid Gateway

http://federalstudentaid.ed.gov/

Sponsor(s): Education Department—Federal Student Aid Office

Description: This site provides information, referrals, and links for students, parents, financial aid professionals, and those doing business with the Federal Student Aid Office. It also provides program data, such as loan default rates.

The Federal Student Aid Gateway serves a broad audience. Other financial aid Web sites listed in this section are more specialized.

Subject(s): Financial Aid to Students

Free Application for Federal Student Aid (FAFSA)

http://www.fafsa.ed.gov/

Sponsor(s): Education Department—Federal Student Aid Office

Description: FAFSA on the Web makes it possible to apply online for federal financial aid for college. The site provides guidance on applying for aid, the application process, and deadlines.

Subject(s): Financial Aid to Students

GI Bill Website
http://www.gibill.va.gov/

Sponsor(s): Veterans Affairs Department (VA)

Description: The GI Bill Web site provides information on the range of education benefits for active duty and reserve servicemembers, veterans, survivors, and dependents. The site outlines the steps for applying and provides tools, such as benefits comparison tools, to encourage informed planning. The site has a history of the original GI Bill, the Servicemembers' Readjustment Act of 1944, which preceded the current program.

Subject(s): Military Training and Education; Veterans

Information for Financial Aid Professionals (IFAP)
http://ifap.ed.gov/ifap/

Sponsor(s): Education Department—Federal Student Aid Office

Description: IFAP is an extensive electronic library for financial aid professionals. The site provides publications, regulations, and guidance regarding the administration of the Title IV Federal Student Aid (FSA) Programs. It also features online tools, worksheets, and schedules related to the programs. The site has an RSS feed of program news.

Subject(s): Financial Aid to Students

Publication(s): *Counselors and Mentors Handbook*, ED 1.45
Federal School Code List, ED 1.92/2
Federal Student Aid Handbook, ED 1.45/4

Student Aid on the Web
http://studentaid.ed.gov/

Sponsor(s): Education Department—Federal Student Aid Office

Description: This Web site is a portal and service center for federal student aid information and programs, designed for students and their parents or advisers. It begins with information about preparing for, choosing, applying to, and attending a college. Other sections contain facts about funding a college education and repaying student loans. The site links to the Free Application for Federal Student Aid (FAFSA) online. The site is available in English and Spanish.

Subject(s): Education Funding; Student Loans

EDUCATION POLICY

Department of Education
http://www.ed.gov/

Sponsor(s): Education Department

Description: The Department of Education Web site features current news, the department's blog, and links to high-profile initiatives. Major sections of the site include Student Loans, Grants, Laws, and Data. Links to news and the department's social media pages are available on the home page. As a Cabinet-level department, Education also provides Recovery Act and Open Government Initiative information on its site.

Subject(s): Education—Policy; Educational Resources; Financial Aid to Students

Publication(s): *ED Review*, ED 1.2/18

Helping Your Child Succeed in School, ED 1.302:C 43/

Helping Your Child with Homework, ED 1.302:C 43/

U.S. Department of Education Strategic Plan, 2007-2012, ED 1.2

Directorate for Education and Human Resources—NSF (EHR)

http://www.nsf.gov/dir/index.jsp?org=ehr

Sponsor(s): National Science Foundation (NSF)

Description: The Directorate for Education and Human Resources (EHR) provides leadership in the effort to improve science, mathematics, engineering, and technology education in the United States. Its Web site includes links to descriptions of the EHR divisions—the Division of Graduate Education (DGE), the Division of Undergraduate Education (DUE), Research on Learning in Formal and Informal Settings (DRL), and the Human Resource Development (HRD)—and the types of projects they sponsor. The site provides directorate reports and notices of funding opportunities.

This site will be of assistance to science and engineering students and educators at all levels who are interested in pursuing grants or scholarships.

Subject(s): Science Education—Grants

No Child Left Behind / Elementary and Secondary Education Act

http://www.ed.gov/esea

Sponsor(s): Education Department

Description: The No Child Left Behind program established in 2001 concerns improvement and accountability in elementary and secondary public schools. The site has NCLB resources, a blueprint for reauthorization of the Elementary and Secondary Education Act (ESEA), and news.

Office of Innovation and Improvement (OII)

http://www.ed.gov/about/offices/list/oii/

Sponsor(s): Education Department—Innovation and Improvement Office

Description: OII administers discretionary grant programs, coordinates public school choice and supplemental educational efforts, works with the nonpublic education community, and develops guidance for the No Child Left Behind initiative. The Web site's link to the Office of Non-

Public Education section includes a private school locator and statistics on private education in the United States.

Subject(s): Elementary and Secondary Education—Education Policy

White House Initiative on Educational Excellence for Hispanic Americans

http://www2.ed.gov/about/inits/list/hispanic-initiative/

Sponsor(s): President's Advisory Commission on Educational Excellence for Hispanic Americans

Description: The Web site for the White House Initiative on Educational Excellence for Hispanic Americans provides a history of the initiative first established in 1990. The site has information on current activities and staff for the initiative.

Subject(s): Educational Resources; Hispanic Americans

EDUCATION RESEARCH AND STATISTICS

Ed Data Express

http://www.eddataexpress.ed.gov/

Sponsor(s): Education Department

Description: Ed Data Express provides access to data collected by the Department of Education from U.S. states and territories. Data included on the site comes from EDFacts, Consolidated State Performance Reports (CSPR), State Accountability Workbooks, the National Center for Education Statistics (NCES), the National Assessment of Education Progress (NAEP), the College Board, and the Department's Budget Service office. The State Snapshots section provides profiles for each state, and in the Data Element section, data can be narrowed down by category and group.

Subject(s): Education Research and Statistics

ERIC—Educational Resources Information Center

http://www.eric.ed.gov/

Sponsor(s): Education Department—Institute of Education Sciences

Description: ERIC is a database and information system funded by the Department of Education to provide organized access to a wide array of published and unpublished material about education. It generally references education literature from 1966 to the present, although some earlier sources are available, and is a standard resource for educational research. Many of the indexed documents are available in full text.

The ERIC search interface has basic and advanced versions. Searchable fields include title, author, ERIC number, identifier, ISBN, ISSN, publisher, sponsoring agency, thesaurus descriptor, and date range. Searches can be limited by type of material cited (e.g., journal article, nonprint media, or dissertation) and full-text availability. The ERIC Thesaurus is linked to the search interface; users can also browse and search the thesaurus separately.

Subject(s): Educational Resources; ERIC

Institute of Education Sciences (IES)

http://www.ed.gov/about/offices/list/ies/

Sponsor(s): Education Department—Institute of Education Sciences

Description: IES was established in 2002 to focus on education research. It includes the National Center for Education Research (NCER), the National Center for Education Statistics (NCES), the National Center for Education Evaluation and Regional Assistance (NCEE), and the National Center for Special Education Research (NCSER). The Web site has information on IES and its grants and component programs.

National Center for Education Statistics (NCES)

http://nces.ed.gov/

Sponsor(s): Education Department—Institute of Education Sciences—National Center for Education Statistics (NCES)

Description: NCES collects and analyzes data concerning education in the United States and other nations. NCES is a primary source for education statistics for all educational levels and for data on educational assessment, libraries, and international educational outcomes. The Web site describes NCES surveys and programs and provides advanced data tools for accessing them. The center's major annual reports are available in PDF and Web versions; the reports are *The Condition of Education, Digest of Education Statistics, Trends in High School Dropout and Completion Rates in the United States: 1972–2008, Indicators of School Crime and Safety,* and *Projections of Education Statistics to 2019.* Use the Publications & Products section and its subject index to locate other NCES reports. The Fast Facts section highlights frequently requested information on a range of topics from assessments to postsecondary education. The site also includes a searchable directory of private and public schools, colleges, and public libraries.

For users searching for statistics related to any form of education, this site should be the first place to visit.

Subject(s): Education Statistics

Publication(s): *Digest of Education Statistics,* ED 1.326
Directory of Postsecondary Institutions, ED 1.111/4
Dropout Rates in the United States, ED 1.329
Indicators of School Crime and Safety, ED 1.347
Projections of Education Statistics to 2019, ED 1.120
The Condition of Education, ED 1.109

Research on Learning in Formal and Informal Settings (DRL)

http://www.nsf.gov/div/index.jsp?div=DRL

Sponsor(s): National Science Foundation (NSF)

Description: DRL is concerned with teaching and learning in science, technology, engineering, and mathematics at all age levels. The division's Web site has information on funding opportunities for research in this area, along with division news and events.

Subject(s): Science Education—Grants

ELEMENTARY AND SECONDARY EDUCATION

Computers for Learning

http://computersforlearning.gov/

Sponsor(s): General Services Administration (GSA)

Description: The Computers for Learning Web site is designed for public, private, parochial, and home schools serving the K–12 student population, as well as other nonprofit educational organizations. The service allows these groups of students and nonprofit organizations to request donations of surplus federal computer equipment. The site includes program and eligibility information and sections on how to give and receive computers.

Subject(s): Educational Technology; Surplus Government Property

Education Resource Organizations Directory (EROD)

http://wdcrobcolp01.ed.gov/Programs/EROD/

Sponsor(s): Education Department—Elementary and Secondary Education Office

Description: EROD is a database of state and regional organizations that provide education-related information. This information is updated annually. It includes organizations such as state literary resource centers, state directors of adult education, curriculum materials centers, and education libraries. Each organization's entry has complete contact information and a description of its services.

Subject(s): Educational Resources

Emergency Planning

http://www2.ed.gov/admins/lead/safety/emergencyplan/index.html

Alternate URL(s)

http://www.ed.gov/admins/lead/safety/emergencyplan/

Sponsor(s): Education Department—Office of Safe and Drug-Free Schools

Description: The Emergency Planning Web site provides school leaders with information to plan for emergencies such as natural disasters or violent incidents. The site includes instructional webcasts, a crisis planning guide, information on pandemic flu preparedness, and links to related assistance programs from the Education Department.

Subject(s): Disaster Preparedness; School Buildings

NAEP Data Explorer

http://nces.ed.gov/nationsreportcard/naepdata/

Sponsor(s): Education Department—Institute of Education Sciences

Description: The NAEP Data Explorer allows researchers to analyze data from the National Assessment of Education Progress, the testing program administered to fourth, eighth, and twelfth graders that measures skills in reading, math, science, and other subjects. The Data Explorer includes assessment results in 10 subject areas for the nation and participating states. It enables state and school district comparisons and also has trend data on national mathematics and reading results dating from the 1970s. Users can create custom tables and charts and export data in several formats including spreadsheet format. The site provides a tutorial and quick reference guide.

Subject(s): Educational Assessment—Statistics

Nation's Report Card

http://nces.ed.gov/nationsreportcard/

Sponsor(s): Education Department—Institute of Education Sciences—National Center for Education Statistics (NCES)

Description: This is the online home of the National Assessment of Educational Progress (NAEP), an ongoing national assessment for student achievement in grades 4, 8, and 12. It provides background information on the history and current operations of the NAEP. Current results are available in the form of state profiles. Users can also construct custom data tables and get reports at the national level or by state, region, or major urban district. The Other Studies section links to information about special studies, such as Student Achievement in Private Schools and the Charter School Pilot Study.

Subject(s): Educational Assessment; Elementary and Secondary Education

Office of Elementary and Secondary Education (OESE)

http://www.ed.gov/about/offices/list/oese/

Sponsor(s): Education Department—Elementary and Secondary Education Office

Description: The OESE Web site has information on its programs, office contacts, and reports. The Laws, Regs & Guidance section is largely concerned with the No Child Left Behind Act. The Standards/Accountability and the Flexibility sections also cover areas of No Child Left Behind. The Consolidated State Info section has information on the No Child Left Behind Consolidated State Performance Report for states reporting accomplishments and data. The site is searchable through the Topics A–Z index, useful in uncovering all of the information at this site.

Much of the information on the site is intended for elementary and secondary education professionals and officials who need to comply with the No Child Left Behind Act or who are interested in its documents.

Subject(s): Education Standards; Educational Assessment; Elementary and Secondary Education

Office of Safe and Healthy Students (OSHS)

http://www2.ed.gov/about/offices/list/oese/oshs/index.html

Sponsor(s): Education Department—Office of Safe and Drug-Free Schools

Description: OSHS's major programs come under the categories of Safe and Supportive Schools; Health, Mental Health, Environmental Health, and Physical Education; Drug-Violence Prevention; Character and Civic Education; and Homeland Security, Emergency Management. Many of the programs are for the elementary and secondary level, although some programs also apply to higher education. Under Reports & Resources, links can be found to OSHS's webcasts, annual reports, and other publications.

Subject(s): Drug Control; School Safety

Office of Special Education Programs (OSEP)

http://www.ed.gov/about/offices/list/osers/osep/

Sponsor(s): Education Department—Special Education and Rehabilitative Services Office—Office of Special Education Programs (OSEP)

Description: OSEP has the primary responsibility of administering programs and projects relating to the education of all children, youth, and adults with disabilities, from birth through age 21. The Web site covers OSEP's programs and initiatives, reports, news, and office contacts. The site also includes offices within OSEP, the National Institute on Disability and Rehabilitation Research (NIDRR) and the Rehabilitation Services Administration (RSA). The site has extensive information on the Individuals with Disabilities Education Act (IDEA), which authorizes OSEP programs.

Subject(s): Special Education—Grants

Publication(s): *Annual Report to Congress on the Implementation of the Individuals with Disabilities Education Act*, ED 1.32

Presidential Scholars Program

http://www.ed.gov/programs/psp/

Sponsor(s): Education Department—Commission on Presidential Scholars

Description: The Presidential Scholars Program was established to recognize and honor some of the nation's most distinguished graduating high school seniors. This Web site includes information on the program, the application process, and frequently asked questions.

Subject(s): High Schools—Awards and Honors

School District Demographics System

http://nces.ed.gov/surveys/sdds/

Sponsor(s): Education Department—Institute of Education Sciences—National Center for Education Statistics (NCES)

Description: This site presents demographic and geographic data for school districts from the decennial census and American Community Survey. The Map Viewer application allows users to view state or individual school district maps. Users can also download school district data from the American Community Survey in spreadsheet file format.

Subject(s): Census; Elementary and Secondary Education—Statistics

USA Science and Engineering Festival

http://www.usasciencefestival.org/

Sponsor(s): USA Science and Engineering Festival

Description: The mission of the USA Science and Engineering Festival, which will take place in April 2016 in Washington, D.C., is "to stimulate and sustain the interest of our nation's youth in science, technology, engineering and math (STEM) by producing and presenting the most compelling, exciting, and educational Festival in the world." (from the Web site) The festival is sponsored by a variety of companies, organizations, and educational establishments. About section includes information about the congressional host committee, as well as links to the festival's social media pages. A science blog, press releases, and newsletters are available in the Newsroom section.

Subject(s): Science Education

HIGHER EDUCATION

Air Force Institute of Technology (AFIT)

http://www.afit.edu/

Sponsor(s): Air Force—Air Force Institute of Technology (AFIT)

Description: A component of Air University, AFIT is the Air Force's graduate school of engineering and management and its institute for technical professional continuing education. The Web site provides information on each of AFIT's schools and centers.

Subject(s): Air Force; Military Training and Education

Air University (AU)

http://www.au.af.mil/au/

Sponsor(s): Air Force—Air University

Description: Air University (AU), located at Maxwell Air Force Base, conducts professional military education, graduate education, and professional continuing education for officers, enlisted personnel, and civilians. This site links to each of the component schools that make up AU and to its research centers, including the Air Force Institute of Technology, Air Force Research Institute, and School of Advanced Air and Space Studies. The site also provides information on the university's history and mission.

Subject(s): Air Force; Military Training and Education
Publication(s): *Strategic Studies Quarterly*, D 301.133

Army Logistics University

http://www.alu.army.mil/

Sponsor(s): Army—Army Logistics Management College (ALMC)
Description: The Army Logistics Management College became the Army Logistics University (ALU) in 2009. ALU is the center for military and Defense Department logistics leader education. The Web site links to a course catalog, the Army Logistics Library, and an online version of *Army Sustainment* magazine (formerly *Logistician*).

Subject(s): Army; Military Training and Education
Publication(s): *Army Sustainment*, D 101.69

Barry M. Goldwater Scholarships

http://www.act.org/goldwater/

Sponsor(s): Goldwater Scholarship and Excellence in Education Foundation
Description: Goldwater Scholarships are awarded for undergraduate education in the fields of mathematics, science, and engineering. The Goldwater Foundation was established by Congress to encourage study in these fields. The Web site has scholarship application information and lists of past award recipients.

Subject(s): Higher Education; Scholarships

College Navigator

http://nces.ed.gov/collegenavigator/

Sponsor(s): Education Department—Institute of Education Sciences—National Center for Education Statistics (NCES)
Description: College Navigator is a database of information on colleges, universities, community colleges, technical colleges, and similar institutions. The database can be searched by institution name, location, type of school, programs offered, tuition and enrollment ranges, and other criteria. For each institution, the database typically supplies phone numbers, a URL, average costs, and basic background information. Colleges can also be compared for such factors as estimated student expenses and graduation rates.

College Navigator is a useful reference for college-bound students as well as for those simply looking for a college's phone number or URL. Note that the site states that an institution's inclusion in the database does not constitute a recommendation by the Department of Education.

Subject(s): Higher Education

Defense Language Institute Foreign Language Center (DLIFLC)

http://www.dliflc.edu/

Sponsor(s): Defense Department—Defense Language Institute (DLI)

Description: DLIFLC is the primary foreign-language training institution within the Department of Defense. Programs are for U.S. military personnel and select agency staff. The Web site has information on the history of the center and its current language programs. Some resources on the site are available only to authorized users, but many online cultural and language tutorials are open to the public.

Subject(s): Language Education; Military Training and Education

Harry S. Truman Scholarship Foundation

http://www.truman.gov/

Sponsor(s): Truman Scholarship Foundation

Description: Truman Scholarships are awarded to outstanding undergraduate students who wish to pursue graduate study and careers in government or public service. This Web site has information about the Truman Foundation and its scholarship program, with sections for candidates, faculty, and current Truman scholars.

Subject(s): Public Policy; Scholarships

Marine Corps University

http://www.mcu.usmc.mil/

Sponsor(s): Marine Corps—Training and Education Command

Description: The Marine Corps University's Web site provides information about its programs, history, and faculty.

Subject(s): Military Training and Education

Publication(s): *Marine Corps University Journal*

National Defense University (NDU)

http://www.ndu.edu/

Sponsor(s): Defense Department—National Defense University (NDU)

Description: The NDU Web site provides an online course catalog and links to the university's component colleges and schools: the Joint Forces Staff College, the National War College, the Dwight D. Eisenhower School for National Security and Resource Strategy (The Eisenhower School), the Information Resources Management College (iCollege), and the College of International Security Affairs. NDU Research Centers online include the NDU Research Council and the Institute for National Strategic Studies. The site also links to NDU's regional centers, such as the Asia-Pacific Center for Security Studies, and special components, such as the Center for Joint and Strategic Logistics.

Subject(s): Military Training and Education; National Defense— Research

Publication(s): *Defense Horizons*, D 5.420
Joint Force Quarterly, D 5.20
Prism Journal, D 5.426

Naval Postgraduate School (NPS)

http://www.nps.edu/

Sponsor(s): Navy—Naval Postgraduate School (NPS)

Description: NPS emphasizes education and research programs relevant to the Navy, defense, and national and international security interests. The Web site links to information from each of the NPS component schools: Business and Public Policy, Engineering and Applied Sciences, Operations and Information Sciences, and International Graduate Studies. The Research section includes archives of technical reports and abstracts from theses.

Subject(s): Military Training and Education

NSF Division of Graduate Education

http://www.nsf.gov/div/index.jsp?div=DGE

Sponsor(s): National Science Foundation (NSF)

Description: The programs of the NSF's Division of Graduate Education promote the early career development of scientists and engineers by offering support at critical junctures of their careers. This Web site describes the division's research and teaching fellowships for graduate students in the sciences. Major programs described on the site include the Graduate Research Fellowship Program (GRFP), Integrative Graduate Education and Research Traineeship Program (IGERT), and the Building Community and Capacity for Data-Intensive Research in the Social, Behavioral, and Economic Sciences and in Education and Human Resources (BCC-SBE/EHR).

Subject(s): Fellowships; Science Education

NSF Division of Undergraduate Education

http://www.nsf.gov/div/index.jsp?div=DUE

Sponsor(s): National Science Foundation (NSF)

Description: The NSF's Division of Undergraduate Education focuses on improving undergraduate education in science, technology, mathematics, and engineering. The division awards funds to scholarship programs at educational institutions; they do not award scholarships directly to students. The division also funds programs for teacher education and curriculum development. The Web site has information on the programs, deadlines, and awards.

Subject(s): Science Education

Office of Postsecondary Education (OPE)

http://www.ed.gov/about/offices/list/ope/

Sponsor(s): Education Department—Postsecondary Education Office

Description: In the Programs/Initiatives section, this Web site provides a guide to the postsecondary-related education programs administered by the OPE. Initiatives include programs for improving educational institutions, supporting international education, funding teacher training, and reaching out to students from disadvantaged backgrounds. The Reports & Resources section of the site includes the *Federal Campus-Based Programs Data Book* and other statistical reports on the programs including the Federal Pell Grant Program and the Federal Student Loan Program. The Accreditation section of the site explains the accreditation of educational institutions and has a directory of the numerous accrediting agencies. The OPE Web site has an A–Z subject index for finding information on specific topics.

This is a useful site with a substantial body of information sources of interest to students, educators, and financial aid offices.

Subject(s): Financial Aid to Students; Higher Education; International Education

Publication(s): *Fund for the Improvement of Postsecondary Education Program Book*, ED 1.23/2

Grant Application for the Undergraduate International Studies and Foreign Language Program, ED 1.94/2

Smithsonian Office of Fellowships

http://www.si.edu/ofg/

Sponsor(s): Smithsonian Institution

Description: The Office of Fellowships has applications, lists of fellowship and internship opportunities, and announcements of recipients.

Subject(s): Fellowships

Publication(s): *Smithsonian Opportunities for Research and Study*

U.S. Army Command and General Staff College (CGSC)

http://usacac.army.mil/organizations/cace/cgsc/

Sponsor(s): Army—Army Command and General Staff College

Description: The U.S. Army Command and General Staff College is focused on leadership development within the Army. This site offers information on the college, its training programs, and its organizations.

Subject(s): Army; Military Leadership; Military Training and Education
Publication(s): *Military Review*, D 110.7

U.S. Army War College

http://www.carlisle.army.mil/
Sponsor(s): Army—Carlisle Barracks
Description: The U.S. Army War College Web site provides information on the college, its library, and publications. The site includes information on affiliated centers, including the Center for Strategic Leadership, the Strategic Studies Institute, the U.S. Army Peacekeeping and Stability Operations Institute, the Army Physical Fitness Research Institute, and the Army Heritage and Education Center. The site's home page features news and summaries of timely studies in national defense. The site also carries the quarterly *Parameters*, the Army's senior professional journal; articles are available from 1971 onward.
Subject(s): Army; Military Training and Education
Publication(s): *Parameters: U.S. Army War College Quarterly*, D 101.72
Strategic Studies Institute (General Publications), D 101.146

U.S. Merchant Marine Academy

http://www.usmma.edu/
Sponsor(s): Transportation Department—Maritime Administration (MARAD)
Description: The Merchant Marine Academy Web site has information about admissions, academics, and other activities. In the Academics section, the site links to information about the academy's curriculum and majors.
Subject(s): Military Training and Education; Shipping

United States Air Force Academy

http://www.usafa.af.mil/
Sponsor(s): Air Force—Air Force Academy
Description: The United States Air Force Academy Web site provides information for cadets, staff, and faculty. It includes visitor information and sections on admissions, academics, and athletics. Information about the academy's libraries and research centers is also included.
Subject(s): Air Force; Military Training and Education

United States Military Academy at West Point

http://www.usma.edu/
Sponsor(s): Army—United States Military Academy (USMA)
Description: The West Point Web site has information for prospective and current students, alumni, visitors, and the West Point community. Sections include Admissions, Academics, Military, Athletics, Leadership,

Community, and News. A brief section on USMA history, found in the About Us section, includes a timeline and list of notable graduates.

Subject(s): Army; Military Training and Education

United States Naval Academy

http://www.usna.edu/homepage.php

Sponsor(s): Navy—United States Naval Academy (USNA)

Description: This site contains information on the Naval Academy, mainly for students, prospective students, and midshipmen. The About USNA section links to information about the academy's history and notable graduates.

White House Initiative on Historically Black Colleges and Universities

http://www.ed.gov/edblogs/whhbcu/

Sponsor(s): Education Department—White House Initiative on Historically Black Colleges and Universities

Description: The White House Initiative on Historically Black Colleges and Universities was established by executive order in 1981 and has since been renewed. This Web site has information on the initiative's work, conferences, scholarships, fellowships, and grants. It also has a list of Historically Black Colleges and Universities by state and type of institution, with Web addresses provided for each institution.

Subject(s): African Americans, Higher Education

INTERNATIONAL EDUCATION

Bureau of Educational and Cultural Affairs

http://exchanges.state.gov/

Sponsor(s): State Department—Educational and Cultural Affairs Bureau

Description: The Bureau of Educational and Cultural Affairs Web site has information about its many international exchange and education programs. For U.S. citizens, the site has information on English-language teaching abroad, hosting a study abroad student, and other opportunities. For the audience abroad, the site has information about studying in the United States and a range of programs and exchanges from the high school level up to the academic scholar and professional level. Use the exchange program search feature to look through a database of international exchange programs.

Subject(s): Cultural Exchanges; International Education

EducationUSA

http://www.educationusa.state.gov/

Alternate URL(s)

http://www.educationusa.info/

Sponsor(s): State Department—Educational and Cultural Affairs Bureau

Description: The State Department's central EducationUSA.gov Web site provides basic information on the EducationUSA program. The Web site links to a separate site for U.S. students who would like to study abroad and a site for international students who would like to study in the United States. For international students, the State Department's EducationUSA program maintains a global network of more than 400 advising centers in more than 170 countries.

Subject(s): International Education

International Affairs Office

http://www.ed.gov/about/inits/ed/internationaled/

Sponsor(s): Education Department

Description: The International Affairs Office coordinates the Education Department's international programs and works with international agencies such as the United Nations Educational, Scientific, Cultural Organization (UNESCO). The Web site provides a directory of Education Department programs that have an international aspect. It also describes the office's activities, such as the United States Network for Education Information (USNEI) program.

International Comparisons in Education

http://nces.ed.gov/surveys/international/

Sponsor(s): Education Department–National Center for Education Statistics (NCES)

Description: NCES provides a central page for linking to the international education statistics that the agency collects. The site links to information on the Trends in International Mathematics and Science Study (TIMSS), Program for International Student Assessment (PISA) assessments, Progress in International Reading Literacy Study (PIRLS), and other studies. The site offers prepared statistical tables and reports on the data. The site's International Data Explorer allows researchers to create their own custom tables and reports.

Subject(s): Educational Assessment–International

National Committee on Foreign Medical Education and Accreditation (NCFMEA)

http://www.ed.gov/about/bdscomm/list/ncfmea.html

Sponsor(s): Education Department

Description: NCFMEA reviews the standards used by foreign countries to accredit medical schools and determines whether those standards are comparable to standards used to accredit medical schools in the United States. The Web site provides information on the review process and lists countries the NCFMEA has found to have comparable standards.

Subject(s): Medical Schools—International

STEM at State

http://www.state.gov/e/oes/stc/stem/index.htm

Sponsor(s): State Department—Oceans and International Environmental and Scientific Affairs Bureau

Description: STEM (Science, technology, engineering, and mathematics) is the focus of this State Department Web site, which works to forward the cause of science diplomacy. According to the site, science diplomacy is key to issues such as ocean mapping, nuclear disarmament, passport safety, and cybersecurity. The Web site provides links to information about STEM careers in the department, the Virtual Student Foreign Service, and the Networks of Diasporas in Engineering and Science (NODES), which is an effort between the U.S. Department of State, the American Association for the Advancement of Science (AAAS), the National Academy of Sciences (NAS), and the National Academy of Engineering (NAE).

Subjects(s): Education; Science

U.S. Network for Education Information (USNEI)

http://www.ed.gov/about/offices/list/ous/international/usnei/edlite-index.html

Sponsor(s): Education Department

Description: USNEI is an interagency and public-private partnership set up to provide official information for anyone researching U.S. education. It also provides U.S. citizens with authoritative information about education in other countries. The site covers all levels of education, with topics including visas, accreditation, professional licensure, and teaching abroad (or in the United States).

Subject(s): International Education

Youth and Education

http://www.state.gov/youthandeducation/

Sponsor(s): State Department

Description: Designed as the student Web site for the Department of State, this Web site is largely written for students at the secondary school level. The site explains the work of the department, international exchange opportunities available to students, and the nature of careers within the Department of State.

The site also includes a substantial amount of information relating to diplomacy, U.S. diplomatic history, country information, international exchange programs, and educational outreach activities.

Subject(s): Career Information; Diplomacy

KIDS' PAGES

Admongo.gov

http://www.admongo.gov/

Sponsor(s): Federal Trade Commission (FTC)

Description: Admongo is a game designed to teach kids ages 8 to 12 to be savvy about advertisers' claims. The main site, which includes a section for parents and one for teachers with lesson plans and sample ads, also has a text version available.

Subject(s): Consumer Information; Kids' Pages

America's Story from America's Library

http://www.americaslibrary.gov/

Sponsor(s): Library of Congress

Description: This Library of Congress Web site is designed for children and their families. It uses digitized images from the library's collection, accompanied by text and graphics, to create educational pages about American history and culture. Sections include Explore the States, Jump Back in Time, and Meet Amazing Americans.

Subject(s): History; Kids' Pages

ATF Kids' Page

http://www.atf.gov/kids/

Sponsor(s): Justice Department—Bureau of Alcohol, Tobacco, Firearms, and Explosives

Description: Several sections of the site are designed specifically for children, such as those about Eliot Ness and ATF canines (in Stories). Other menu items link to content on the main ATF Web site, such as those about ATF history. Coloring pages and a word search are in the Games & Activities section.

Subject(s): Law Enforcement; Kids' Pages

Ben's Guide to U.S. Government for Kids

http://bensguide.gpo.gov/

Sponsor(s): Government Printing Office (GPO)—Superintendent of Documents

Description: With a cartoon version of Benjamin Franklin as a guide, this GPO site for children covers topics such as the U.S. Constitution, how laws are made, the branches of the federal government, and citizenship. It features sections for specific grade groups, plus a special section for parents and educators. The major sections are About Ben, K–2, 3–5, 6–8, 9–12, and Parents & Teachers.

BLS Career Information

http://www.bls.gov/k12/

Sponsor(s): Labor Department—Bureau of Labor Statistics (BLS)

Description: This BLS Career Information page for youth uses a graphical interface to match kids' interests with potential careers. A Teacher's Guide refers teachers to additional information available from BLS. The site is most appropriate for upper elementary grades and high school students.

Subject(s): Career Information; Kids' Pages

CIA Kids' Zone

https://www.cia.gov/kids-page

Sponsor(s): Central Intelligence Agency (CIA)

Description: The CIA Kids' Page has section for students in grades K–5 and 6–12 and for parents and teachers. It also has a separate games section and links to the kids' pages at other intelligence agency Web sites. Kids' activities include learning about the CIA seal, CIA history, and working for the CIA. Parent and teacher materials include lesson plans and guidance on topics such as Internet safety and helping children avoid drug abuse.

Subject(s): Intelligence Agencies; Kids' Pages

CryptoKids®

http://www.nsa.gov/kids/

Sponsor(s): Defense Department—National Security Agency (NSA)

Description: This site has games, activities, and background information about NSA's specialty, cryptography. The Student Resources section has NSA career information for high school and college students. The site has both a Flash and a text version.

Subject(s): Kids' Pages

EIA Energy Kids Page

http://www.eia.doe.gov/kids/

Sponsor(s): Energy Department—Energy Information Administration (EIA)

Description: The Department of Energy's Information Administration provides this educational page. Sections include What is Energy?; History of Energy; Energy Sources; Using & Saving Energy; and Games & Activities. The section for teachers has lesson plans and guides for teachers.

Subject(s): Energy; Kids' Pages

Endangered Species Homework Help

http://www.fws.gov/endangered/education/

Sponsor(s): Interior Department—Fish and Wildlife Service (FWS)

Description: The Fish and Wildlife Service Endangered Species Program maintains this site with a few tools for older students to use. The species information and image links lead to pages on the main program Web site, rather than special pages for kids; a third link leads to a more age-appropriate game. The Homework Help page also links to a Fish and Wildlife Service site for kids, parents, and educators called "Let's Go Outside."

Subject(s): Endangered Species; Kids' Pages

EPA Climate Change Kids Site

http://www.epa.gov/climatechange/kids/

Sponsor(s): Environmental Protection Agency (EPA)

Description: This site provides explanations of climate, weather, and the greenhouse effect. It also has games and a section for teachers. Due to the amount of text and the complicated nature of the subject, this site is best for students in the upper elementary grades.

Subject(s): Environmental Education; Kids' Pages

FBI Kids' Page

http://www.fbi.gov/fbikids.htm

Sponsor(s): Justice Department—Federal Bureau of Investigation (FBI)

Description: The FBI Web site provides pages for kids in kindergarten through fifth grade, such as the About Our Dogs section, and pages for those in grades 6–12, such as the How We Investigate section.

Subject(s): Crime Detection; Kids' Pages

FCC Kids Zone

http://www.fcc.gov/cgb/kidszone/

Sponsor(s): Federal Communications Commission (FCC)—Consumer and Governmental Affairs Bureau

Description: The FCC Kids Zone has information on the history of communications technology, online games, and a section about satellites. It also has special sections about communications technology designed for grades K–3, 4–8, and 9–12. The site links to an FCC Web page for parents, Parents' Place (described in a separate entry), covering such issues as children's television programming.

Subject(s): Telecommunications; Kids' Pages

FDA Kids' Site

http://www.fda.gov/oc/opacom/kids/

Sponsor(s): Health and Human Services Department—Food and Drug Administration (FDA)

Description: This Web page links to FDA or related kids' Web sites, including sites on health and nutrition and the kids site from the FDA's Center for Veterinary Medicine.

Subject(s): Adolescents; Health Promotion; Kids' Pages

FSA Kids

http://www.fsa.usda.gov/FSA/kidsapp?area=home&subject=landing&topic=landing

Sponsor(s): Agriculture Department (USDA) — Farm Service Agency (FSA)

Description: To avoid entering the long web address above, look for the FSA Kids link in the Outreach and Education section of the Farm Service Agency Web site, http://www.fsa.usda.gov. The kids' page provides coloring books and games with an agricultural theme.

Subject(s): Agricultural Education; Kids' Pages

GirlsHealth.gov

http://girlshealth.gov/

Sponsor(s): Health and Human Services Department

Description: GirlsHealth.gov is designed to help adolescent girls (ages 10 to 16) learn about the health issues and social situations that they will encounter during the teen years. Sections provide information about fitness, nutrition, bullying, relationships, and other related topics. The site also has sections for parents, caregivers, and teachers.

Subject(s): Health Promotion; Kids' Pages

Inside the White House

http://www.whitehouse.gov/about/inside-white-house

Alternate URL(s)

http://www.whitehouse.gov/about/white-house-101/

Sponsor(s): White House

Description: This Web site features sections on past presidents and presidential trivia. An Interactive Tour feature shows floor plans of the White House, allowing users a peek inside the famous structure. The West Wing Tour section provides additional information about the White House. A section on art and decor is also available.

Subject(s): White House (Mansion); Kids' Pages

Kids and Families—Social Security

http://www.ssa.gov/kids/

Sponsor(s): Social Security Administration (SSA)

Description: This SSA Web site includes a Kids' Place and a Parents' Place. The Kids' Place offers tales about saving for the future and an introduction to the Social Security card. On the main page, there is also a link to information for the families of youth with disabilities.

Subject(s): Social Security; Kids' Pages

Kids in the House

http://kids.clerk.house.gov/

Sponsor(s): Congress—House of Representatives—Office of the Clerk

Description: The House Clerk's Web site is divided into parallel sections for young learners, grade school, middle school, and high school. Each section provides age-appropriate information on Congress, how bills are made into law, and the art and architecture of the U.S. Capitol. The site also has a For Teachers section with resources and lesson plans.

Subject(s): Legislative Procedure; Kids' Pages; Civics Education

Kids' Resources

http://www.doi.gov/public/teachandlearn_kids.cfm

Sponsor(s): Interior Department

Description: This Department of the Interior site is a portal to the various kids' pages hosted by the department's agencies and bureaus. Linked sites include Zot the Frog, Web Rangers, and Otto Otter Water Safety Program. The target audience age varies between the sites. Many sites include sections for teachers and field trip information.

Subject(s): Environmental Education; Kids' Pages

Kids.gov

http://www.kids.gov/

Sponsor(s): General Services Administration (GSA)

Description: Kids.gov is a portal to U.S. federal and state government Web pages designed for children. The site groups Web links in sections for grades K–5 and grades 6–8. Links are then organized by topic, such as online safety, science, and government. A section for educators provides links organized in the same categories.

Kids.gov provides an easy way for children (as well as teachers and parents) to find kid-friendly information on the Web.

Subject(s): Government Information; Finding Aids; Kids' Pages

MyPlate for Kids

http://www.choosemyplate.gov/children-over-five.html

Sponsor(s): Agriculture Department (USDA)

Description: The Choose My Plate kids' page, designed for elementary school children, contains the "Blast Off" game and coloring pages that allow kids to show the items on their plates.

Subject(s): Nutrition; Kids' Pages

NASA for Students

http://www.nasa.gov/audience/forstudents/

Sponsor(s): National Aeronautics and Space Administration (NASA)—Education Office

Description: The NASA For Students page has sections for students in grades K–4, 5–8, 9–12, and postsecondary levels. It also features a NASA Kids' Club site with games and graphics. The NASA Education Web site at http://www.nasa.gov/offices/education/about/ provides comprehensive information for educators about the many NASA educational initiatives and opportunities.

Subject(s): Space; Kids' Pages

NCEH Kids' Page

http://www.cdc.gov/nceh/kids/

Sponsor(s): Health and Human Services Department—Centers for Disease Control and Prevention (CDC)—National Center for Environmental Health (NCEH)

Description: This site discusses how the environment can affect health and how the agency researches those environmental effects. It includes brief sections on asthma, emergency response, global health, lead poisoning, and other topics. The site's Fun Activities section features word games and puzzles.

Subject(s): Health Promotion; Kids' Pages

NGAkids

http://www.nga.gov/kids/

Sponsor(s): National Gallery of Art (NGA)

Description: This National Gallery of Art kids' page includes plenty of interactive activities, such as the Art Zone, where interactive art can be created.

Subject(s): Arts Education; Kids' Pages

NIEHS Kids' Pages

http://kids.niehs.nih.gov/

Sponsor(s): National Institutes of Health (NIH)—National Institute of Environmental Health Sciences (NIEHS)

Description: This Kids Page offering from the NIEHS has sections such as Discover and Explore, What's That Word?, Scientific Kids, and Fun and Games.

Subject(s): Environmental Education; Health Promotion; Kids' Pages

NLS Kids Zone

http://www.loc.gov/nls/children/

Sponsor(s): Library of Congress—National Library Services for the Blind and Physically Handicapped (NLS)

Description: This Web site for kids is designed to be used with text-based browsers, such as Lynx, frequently used by blind readers. It recommends audio, Braille, and print/Braille books for children. It also links to the kids' pages on the Web sites of NLS network libraries.

Subject(s): Kids' Pages

NRC: Students' Corner

http://www.nrc.gov/reading-rm/basic-ref/students.html

Sponsor(s): Nuclear Regulatory Commission (NRC)

Description: The NRC student's Web site explains everything from what nuclear energy is to emergency planning to radioactive waste. It also has a section for teachers' lesson plans.

Subject(s): Science Education; Kids' Pages

NROjr.GOV

http://www.nrojr.gov/

Sponsor(s): Defense Department—National Reconnaissance Office (NRO)

Description: The NRO kids' page features information and activities with a satellite and space theme. The site has sections for grades K–5, grades 6–12, teachers, and parents.

Subject(s): Space; Kids' Pages

Peace Corps Challenge Online Game

http://www.peacecorps.gov/kids/

Sponsor(s): Peace Corps

Description: The Peace Corps kids' page is a "Peace Corps Challenge" game simulating a volunteer experience in the fictional village of Wanzu-zu.

Subject(s): Geography; Kids' Pages

Sci4Kids

http://www.ars.usda.gov/is/kids/

Sponsor(s): Agriculture Department (USDA)—Agricultural Research Service (ARS)

Description: With a colorful all-graphics menu, Sci4Kids shows how scientific research affects many areas of life. The site includes information about careers in science, as well as a section for science projects.

Subject(s): Science Education; Kids' Pages

Science Education

http://energy.gov/science-innovation/science-education

Sponsor(s): Energy Department

Description: Science Education provides information about education-related science topics, such as the National Science Bowl. The home page features relevant news and announcements. The Science & Innovation section links to information about energy sources, uses, and efficiency.

Subject(s): Education; Science Education

Smithsonian Education

http://www.smithsonianeducation.org/students/

Sponsor(s): Smithsonian Institution

Description: The Smithsonian Web site for kids and students features themed IdeaLabs called Sizing Up the Universe, Walking on the Moon, and Digging for Answers. The At the Smithsonian section links to pages of interest to kids from many Smithsonian Web sites. More activities are organized under the topics of everything art, science and nature, history and culture, and people and places. Links in the upper right corner lead to Smithsonian content for educators, students, and families.

Subject(s): Kids' Pages

Space Place

http://spaceplace.nasa.gov/spacepl.htm

Alternate URL(s)

http://spaceplace.jpl.nasa.gov/sp/kids/

Sponsor(s): National Aeronautics and Space Administration (NASA)—Jet Propulsion Laboratory (JPL)

Description: Space Place is full of games, projects, and animations relating to earth and space science. The site has a Spanish-language version available; it can be linked from the top of the home page or directly accessed at the alternate URL listed above.

Subject(s): Space; Kids' Pages

State Facts for Students

http://www.census.gov/schools/facts/

Sponsor(s): Commerce Department—Economics and Statistics Administration (ESA)—Census Bureau

Description: A map of the United States serves as a menu for basic Census statistics, history, and trivia concerning each of the states, Puerto Rico, and the District of Columbia. It includes a lesson plan for teachers.

Subject(s): Geography; Kids' Pages

Stop Bullying Now

http://www.stopbullying.gov/

Sponsor(s): Health and Human Services Department—Health Resources and Services Administration (HRSA)

Description: This site has extensive information and a variety of activities for kids about dealing with bullying behavior. There is also information for parents and educators about bullying, responses, and interventions.

Subject(s): Children; Kids' Pages

Students for the Environment

http://www.epa.gov/students/index.html

Sponsor(s): Environmental Protection Agency (EPA)

Description: This EPA Web site serves as a portal to information at a variety of educational levels and has special sections for students and for educators and parents. The site also provides news, homework resources, and deadlines for contests.

Subject(s): Environmental Education; Kids' Pages

ToxMystery

http://toxmystery.nlm.nih.gov/

Sponsor(s): National Institutes of Health (NIH)—National Library of Medicine (NLM)

Description: ToxMystery is an interactive game designed to teach kids about dangerous household substances. The site includes sections for parents and teachers, and has a version in Spanish.

Subject(s): Kids' Pages; Environmental Health

United States Mint's Site for Kids—H.I.P. Pocket Change™

http://www.usmint.gov/kids/

Sponsor(s): Treasury Department—United States Mint

Description: This site features games and activities to teach children about the history of coins, coins around the world, and coin collecting. The site links to information for teachers, including activities and lesson plans.

Subject(s): Coins; Kids' Pages

USPTO for Kids

http://www.uspto.gov/kids/

Sponsor(s): Commerce Department—Patent and Trademark Office (PTO)

Description: The Patent and Trademark Office's main page for kids links to PTO's own kids' site. Sections are aimed at kids, parents, and educators.

TEACHING

Ames Educator Resource Center

http://www.nasa.gov/centers/ames/education/ERC/

Sponsor(s): National Aeronautics and Space Administration (NASA)—Ames Research Center (ARC)

Description: The page is almost exclusively descriptive of ARC, which is located at the National Aeronautic and Space Administration Ames Research Center at Moffett Field, California. It serves educators in the Western states (Alaska, Northern California, Hawaii, Idaho, Montana, Nevada, Oregon, Utah, Washington, and Wyoming). This page provides contact information, hours, and a listing of the kinds of educational materials available—only a few of which are available online.

The Ames Educator Resource Center Web site is most useful for those who want to visit or contact the center.

Subject(s): Educational Resources; Science Education

Federal Resources for Educational Excellence (FREE)

http://www.free.ed.gov/

Sponsor(s): Education Department

Description: FREE is a central finding aid for over 1,500 Web-based teaching and learning resources on government and government-supported sites; a new version was being trialed as this book went to press. Resources are organized by broad topics, such as Visual and Performing Arts, English Language Arts, Science, and Math. They include primary documents, photographs, animation, and video.

This is one of the most comprehensive finding aids for education-related U.S. government Web sites. Its primary focus is on K–12 resources.

Subject(s): Educational Resources; Finding Aids; Kids' Pages

For Teachers

http://www.loc.gov/teachers/

Sponsor(s): Library of Congress

Description: This Web site serves as an entry point for Library of Congress Web resources relevant to teachers, with an emphasis on teaching with the primary sources available in the Library of Congress online collections. The site has information on classroom materials and information on professional development opportunities for teachers. Classroom materials include lesson plans, activities, and themed sets of primary sources to use. For educators, the site has presentations that can be used to lead others in professional development and online training modules for individual use.

Subject(s): Educational Technology; Lesson Plans; Social Studies Education

James Madison Graduate Fellowships

http://www.jamesmadison.com/

Sponsor(s): James Madison Memorial Fellowship Foundation

Description: James Madison Graduate Fellowships are for teachers at the secondary school level who wish to enhance their knowledge of the U.S. Constitution. The fellowships are for graduate study leading to a master's degree. This Web site has more about the program and about the James Madison Memorial Fellowship Foundation, an independent agency within the Executive Branch.

Subject(s): Constitution of the United States; Fellowships; Civics Education

NCELA—National Clearinghouse for English Language Acquisition
http://www.ncela.us/
Sponsor(s): Education Department—English Language Acquisition Office
Description: NCELA, known in full as the National Clearinghouse for English Language Acquisition and Language Instruction Educational Programs and funded by the Department of Education, is concerned with the effective education of linguistically and culturally diverse learners in the United States. The NCELA Web site provides direct access to a wealth of information on research, resources, statistics, funding, and programs to assist those working with English-language learners.
Subject(s): Language Education

Teach.org
http://www.teach.org/
Sponsor(s): Education Department; Microsoft Corporation
Description: This site provides information and encouragement to those considering a career in teaching. The site's sections include Why Teach, Become a Teacher, and Community, which includes portfolio tips and interview hints. The site also includes a blog and links to the organization's social media pages.
Subject(s): Teachers; Teaching

What Works Clearinghouse (WWC)
http://ies.ed.gov/ncee/wwc/
Sponsor(s): Education Department—Institute of Education Sciences
Description: WWC collects and reviews studies of the effectiveness of educational programs and practices. It is intended to be a "central and trusted source of scientific evidence for what works in education." (from the Web site) In addition to the reports and guides, the site provides a database of education program evaluators and technical information on evaluating education programs.
Subject(s): Educational Assessment

EIGHT

Employment

The federal government has a role in employment law, in regulating workplace conditions, in measuring employment and promoting jobs growth, and also—to a degree—in labor-management relations. All of these areas are reflected in the following Web sites. Many of the sites covering government's role as an employer, however, are in the Government and Politics chapter.

Subsections in this chapter are Employment Law, Employment Statistics, Jobs, Labor-Management Relations, and Workplace Conditions.

EMPLOYMENT LAW

Benefits Review Board (BRB)
http://www.dol.gov/brb/welcome.html
Sponsor(s): Labor Department—Benefits Review Board (BRB)
Description: The BRB rules on appeals of worker's compensation claims that arise under the Longshore and Harbor Worker's Compensation Act and the Black Lung Benefits amendments to the Federal Coal Mine Health and Safety Act of 1969. Its Web site has the text of BRB published and unpublished opinions and lists of case citations for Longshore and Black Lung cases.

Davis-Bacon and Related Acts Home Page
http://www.dol.gov/whd/programs/dbra/Survey/surveys.htm
Sponsor(s): Labor Department—Wage and Hour Division (WHD)
Description: This Web site provides guidance for construction contractors complying with the Davis-Bacon Act. (The Davis-Bacon Act concerns wage rates for laborers working on public buildings or public works projects.) The site has fact sheets, forms, All Agencies Memoranda

(AAMs), and the Davis-Bacon work site poster. It also has information, in Spanish and English, on requirements for Recovery Act contracts and links to the online Prevailing Wage Resource Book used in training conferences.

Subject(s): Construction Industry—Regulations; Wages—Regulations

Department of Labor (DOL)
http://www.dol.gov/
Sponsor(s): Labor Department
Description: The Department of Labor home page provides one-click access to news, hot topics and features, frequently asked questions, Labor agencies and offices on the Web, and economic indicators. The home page browse menu helps researchers find information by topic (work hours, statistics, unemployment insurance) and has a feature for finding Labor services by state and ZIP code. The top menu links to social media pages, an RSS feed option, and a search feature.

The department's blog highlights programs, services, and legislative and regulatory news. As a Cabinet Department, the Labor Department also features information on their Recovery Act contracts and funding and on their Open Government Initiative plans. A Spanish-language version of the site is available.

This Web site provides effective access to Department of Labor information and to related Web sites by providing multiple paths for accessing information and by highlighting the most frequently consulted topics.

Subject(s): Employment; Labor Law; Labor Statistics; Labor-Management Relations

Department of Labor Enforcement Data
http://ogesdw.dol.gov/
Sponsor(s): Labor Department
Description: The Enforcement Data Web site provides a central location for searching and using data from the Labor Department's major enforcement agencies, such as the Mine Safety and Health Administration (MSHA), the Occupational Safety & Health Administration (OSHA), and the Wage & Hour Division (WHD).

Subjects: Employment Law

Elaws—Employment Laws Assistance for Workers and Small Businesses
http://www.dol.gov/elaws/
Sponsor(s): Labor Department
Description: The Elaws Advisors are interactive tools designed to help employees and employers understand their respective rights and responsibilities under the laws and regulations administered by the De-

partment of Labor. Each Elaws Advisor provides information about a specific law or regulation. The Advisor imitates the interaction that an individual might have with an employment law expert. It asks questions, provides information, and directs the user to the appropriate resolutions based on the user's responses. Featured expertise includes the Fair Labor Standards Act, Family and Medical Leave Act, Veterans' Preference, and Worker Adjustment and Retraining Notification (WARN) Act.

Subject(s): Labor Law

Employee Benefits Security Administration (EBSA)

http://www.dol.gov/ebsa/

Sponsor(s): Labor Department

Description: EBSA is concerned with private retirement plans and private health and welfare plans. Its Web site explains pension rights and employer compliance programs. Major sections include COBRA Assistance, the Affordable Care Act, the Pension Protection Act, Information for Reservists, ERISA (Employee Retirement Income Security Act) Enforcement, Technical Guidance, Compliance Assistance, and Consumer Information. The main page highlights news, upcoming compliance assistance seminars, and frequently asked questions. The site also has forms, criminal enforcement news releases, EBSA publications (some available in Spanish), and links to relevant laws, regulations, and proposed regulations. Consumer information covers health plans, retirement plans, and retirement savings.

The EBSA Web site has material for both employee benefit specialists and consumers. The site design makes it easy for both audiences to find relevant content.

Subject(s): Health Insurance; Pensions

E-Verify

http://www.uscis.gov/e-verify/

Sponsor(s): Homeland Security Department—Citizenship and Immigration Service (USCIS)

Description: E-Verify allows participating employers to electronically verify the employment eligibility of their newly hired employees and the validity of their Social Security Numbers. The program is run by USCIS in partnership with the Social Security Administration. The Web site has information for employees, employers, and federal contractors. It includes text and videos guides to the E-Verify system. The site also has information on the Systematic Alien Verification for Entitlements (SAVE) program. USCIS has a Spanish version of its Web site, and the E-Verify information is available there as well.

Subject(s): Employment—Regulations; Immigrant Workers

Foreign Labor Certification
http://www.foreignlaborcert.doleta.gov/
Sponsor(s): Labor Department—Employment and Training Administration (ETA)
Description: The Office of Foreign Labor Certification in the Department of Labor provides labor certifications to employers seeking to bring foreign workers into the United States. The site provides program news, employment verification information, and applications. The FAQs section covers questions about permanent, H1-B, H2-A, and other classifications, and about prevailing wages.
Subject(s): Immigrant Workers—Regulations; Wages—Regulations

Job Accommodation Network (JAN)
http://www.jan.wvu.edu/
Sponsor(s): Labor Department—Office of Disability Employment Policy
Description: JAN is an Americans with Disabilities Act (ADA) information service sponsored by the Department of Labor and operated by West Virginia University. This Web site provides information on JAN's free consulting service for employers and on the employability of people with disabilities. The Web site has numerous fact sheets on accommodations for disabilities and on the ADA law, information about JAN training webcasts and podcasts, and contacts for learning about JAN's offline information and training services. The site will be relevant to employers, employees, and other professionals concerned with accommodation of disabilities in the workplace.

Office of Disability Employment Policy (ODEP)
http://www.dol.gov/odep/
Sponsor(s): Labor Department—Office of Disability Employment Policy
Description: ODEP manages programs, policies, and grants to further its mission to increase employment opportunities for people with disabilities. The Web site links to further information on the programs and technical assistance centers that ODEP funds, sponsors, or otherwise participates in. The site's Newsroom section contains press releases and policy resources by topic.

Office of Special Counsel for Immigration-Related Unfair Trade Practices
http://www.usdoj.gov/crt/osc/
Sponsor(s): Justice Department—Civil Rights Division
Description: The Office of Special Counsel for Immigration-Related Unfair Trade Practices investigates employers charged with national origin and citizenship status discrimination under the antidiscrimination

provision of the Immigration and Nationality Act. This Web site provides guidance for both employers and employees and links to relevant laws and regulations. The site also has news of enforcement actions, updates on eligibility for Temporary Protected status, and information on the public education grant program.

Subject(s): Employment Discrimination—immigrant workers

Pension Benefit Guaranty Corporation (PBGC)

http://www.pbgc.gov/

Sponsor(s): Pension Benefit Guaranty Corporation (PBGC)

Description: PBGC is a federal corporation created by the Employee Retirement Income Security Act of 1974. It insures and protects pension benefits in certain pension plans. The Web site explains what PBGC does and does not guarantee, as well as the legal limits on their guarantees. PBGC offers online transactions for tasks such as applying for pension benefits and designating a beneficiary; instructions for doing these tasks by phone are also provided. Information is categorized for Workers & Retirees and for Practitioners (pension plan professionals). In the Workers section, the Find Unclaimed Pensions section is a searchable directory of people known to be entitled to a pension from a company that went out of business or ended its defined benefit pension plan, but who have not yet claimed their pension. The Practitioners section includes interest rates, mortality tables, premium filing instructions, laws, regulations, appeals board decisions, and opinion letters.

This Web site offers well-organized content and online services. It should prove useful to anyone seeking information on one of the PBGC-insured pension plans.

Subject(s): Pensions; Retirement

Publication(s): *Finding a Lost Pension,* Y 3.P 38/2

Pension Insurance Data Books, Y 3.P 38/2:2 P 38/7

Your Guaranteed Pension, Y 3.P 38/2:2 P 38/5/

Railroad Retirement Board (RRB)

http://www.rrb.gov/

Sponsor(s): Railroad Retirement Board (RRB)

Description: RRB is an independent agency that administers retirement-survivor and unemployment-sickness benefit programs for railroad workers and their families. The Web site provides benefits information, forms, and online services for railroad employees and beneficiaries as well as for employers. The section for the general public serves as a central location for RRB legal opinions and decisions, financial statistics, and organizational information. Due to frequent requests, this section also has useful information for people seeking former railroad employee records for genealogical research. The RRB site also has a collection of videos for online briefings, a listing of railroad job vacancies, and a ZIP code locator for finding the nearest RRB office.

Subject(s): Railroads; Retirement

Publication(s): *Annual Report on the Financial Status of the Railroad Unemployment Insurance System*

Annual Report on the Railroad Retirement System

U.S. Equal Employment Opportunity Commission (EEOC)

http://www.eeoc.gov/

Sponsor(s): Equal Employment Opportunity Commission (EEOC)

Description: EEOC coordinates federal equal employment opportunity regulations and investigates charges of employment discrimination. Its Web site provides information for employees, employers, small businesses, attorneys, and the public. The Discrimination by Type section has clear descriptions of laws related to age, disability, race/color, religion, and other areas. Statistics and additional information sources are provided for each area. A Laws, Regulations, Guidance, and MOUs section serves as a library for relevant legal documents. Other topics include enforcement and employment statistics, special information for federal agencies and employees, reports on litigation settlements, how to file a discrimination charge, training and outreach programs, publications and posters, news, and an RSS newsfeed. The Other Languages section has translations of fact sheets and basic information in Spanish, Chinese, Arabic, Russian, Vietnamese, Korean, and Haitian Creole. A Spanish-language version of the Web site is also available.

The EEOC Web site provides a straightforward presentation of important content. The home page has a clean table-of-contents style that makes the lack of a site map much less critical. The site offers adjustable font size and a plain text version, making it even more accessible for users.

Subject(s): Employment Discrimination—Laws

Publication(s): *Digest of Equal Opportunity Law*, Y 3.EQ 2:22

Enforcement Guidances, Y 3.EQ 2:2

Veterans' Employment and Training Service (VETS)

http://www.dol.gov/vets/welcome.html

Sponsor(s): Labor Department—Veterans Employment and Training Service (VETS)

Description: VETS advocates for veterans in the employment marketplace. Materials on the VETS Web site include the text of laws and regulations concerning veterans' employment, information about the Veterans Preference for federal jobs, grants announcements, and information about the Uniformed Services Employment and Reemployment Rights Act (USERRA).

Subject(s): Veterans

Wage and Hour Division (WHD)

http://www.dol.gov/whd/

Sponsor(s): Labor Department—Wage and Hour Division (WHD)

Description: The Department of Labor's Wage and Hour Division administers some of the best-known labor laws in the United States. These include Fair Labor Standards Act (which concerns minimum wage and overtime), the Family and Medical Leave Act, the Migrant and Seasonal Agricultural Worker Protection Act, worker protections provided in several temporary visa programs, and the prevailing wage requirements of the Davis-Bacon Act. Its Web site provides fact sheets, posters, opinion letters, and compliance information for these laws.

Subject(s): Wages—Laws; Employment Law

Wage Determinations Online.gov

http://www.wdol.gov/

Sponsor(s): Labor Department

Description: This Web site, intended for federal contracting officials, provides Service Contract Act (SCA) and Davis-Bacon Act (DBA) wage determinations. It is also open to labor organizations, contractor associations, employees, and the general public. SCA determinations can be searched by state and county. Archived SCA wage determinations can be retrieved by number. Users can also browse a list of determinations due to be revised. DBA wage determinations can be browsed by state, searched by number, or searched by a combination of state, county, and construction type. Archived DBA wage determinations and a list of determinations due to be revised are also online. The Library section links to the Federal Acquisition Regulations and other Web sites related to federal contracting.

Wage Determinations Online.gov is a collaborative effort of the Office of Management and Budget, the Department of Labor, the Department of Defense, the General Services Administration, the Department of Energy, and the Department of Commerce.

Subject(s): Construction   Industry—Regulations;   Government Contracts; Wages—Regulations

Publication(s): *Davis-Bacon Wage Determinations*, L 36.211/2

Service Contract Act Directory of Occupations, L 36.202

Youth at Work

http://www.eeoc.gov/youth/

Sponsor(s): Equal Employment Opportunity Commission (EEOC)

Description: Youth at Work is targeted at working teens. It provides straightforward information on employment discrimination, employee rights, and employee responsibilities. The site is available in English and Spanish.

Subject(s): Adolescents; Employment Discrimination

YouthRules!

http://www.youthrules.dol.gov/
Sponsor(s): Labor Department
Description: The Department of Labor's YouthRules! Program promotes safe work experiences for young workers. The Web site has information on federal and state laws and regulations governing child labor, including the "Final Rule," which is designed to protect working children from workplace hazards while also recognizing the value of safe work for children and their families. The main sections are centered on information pertaining to teens, parents, educators, and employers. The site includes some information in Spanish and other languages.
Subject(s): Adolescents—Regulations; Labor Law

EMPLOYMENT STATISTICS

Bureau of Labor Statistics (BLS)

http://www.bls.gov/
Sponsor(s): Labor Department—Bureau of Labor Statistics (BLS)
Description: The BLS Web site is a major source for employment, economic, and labor statistics. The home page features the latest key economic indicators from BLS, including the Consumer Price Index, unemployment rate, payroll employment, average hourly earnings, the Producer Price Index, the Employment Cost Index, productivity, and the U.S. Import Price Index.

BLS data and products are organized under the Subject Areas tab; subtopics include Inflation & Prices, Unemployment, and Pay & Benefits. For each subtopic, the site links to BLS news releases, databases, prepared tables, publications, and related documentation for its subsections. Online tutorials are available for the databases, along with tools and calculators to work with the data. The home page links to "At a Glance" tables for the U.S., regions, states, and specific industries.

BLS helps researchers by providing multiple approaches to their data. The database tutorials are a welcome feature on the site.
Subject(s): Labor Statistics; Wages—Statistics; Employment Statistics
Publications: *BLS Handbook of Methods*, L 2.3
BLS News Releases, L 2.120
Career Guide to Industries, L 2.3/4-3
Compensation and Working Conditions , L 2.44/4
Consumer Expenditure Survey, L 2.3/18
CPI Detailed Report, L 2.38/3
Employee Benefit Survey Data, L 2.46/6: to L 2.46/9
Employer Costs for Employee Compensation, L 2.120/2-13

Employment Characteristics of Families, L 2.118/2
Employment Cost Index, L 2.117
Extended Mass Layoffs, L 2.120/2-14
Geographic Profile of Employment and Unemployment, L 2.3/12
Local Area Unemployment Statistics
Major Work Stoppages, L 2.45/3
Monthly Labor Review, L 2.6
Monthly Series on Mass Layoffs, L 2.120/2-15
National Compensation Survey, L 2.121
News, Consumer Price Index, L 2.38/3-2
News, International Comparisons of Hourly Compensation Costs in Manufacturing, L 2.130
News, International Comparisons of Manufacturing Productivity and Unit Labor Cost Trends, L 2.120/2-6
News, Occupational Injuries and Illnesses , L 2.120/2-11
News, Producer Price Indexes, L 2.61/10
News, Productivity and Costs
News, Real Earnings, L 2.115
News, State and Regional Unemployment
News, The Employment Situation, L 2.53/2
News, Work Experience of the Population, L 2.120/2-18
NLS Handbook, L 2.46/3:N 21
Occupational Injuries and Illnesses by Selected Characteristics, L 2.3/11
Occupational Outlook Handbook, L 2.3/4
Occupational Outlook Quarterly, L 2.70/4
PPI Detailed Report, L 2.61
Producer Price Indexes Data, L 2.61
Summary Data from the Consumer Price Index, L 2.38/10
U.S. Import and Export Prices, L 2.60/3
Union Membership
Usual Weekly Earnings of Wage and Salary Workers, L 2.126

Current Population Survey (CPS)

http://www.bls.gov/cps/

Sponsor(s): Labor Department—Bureau of Labor Statistics (BLS)—Commerce Department—Economics and Statistics Administration (ESA)—Census Bureau

Description: CPS is the primary source of information on the labor force characteristics of the U.S. population. The Census Bureau surveys a sample of households to get the data for BLS. Estimates obtained from the CPS include employment, unemployment, earnings, hours of work, multiple jobholders, union membership and other statistics. The monthly CPS news release, The Employment Situation, is widely quoted for details on the current national unemployment rate.

The CPS home page links to CPS data in news releases, publications, databases, and prepared tables. Researchers can also download the entire database or subsets.

Subject(s): Employment Statistics
Publication(s): *Characteristics of Minimum Wage Workers*, L 2.140
The Employment Situation, L 2.53/2
Women in the Labor Force: A Databook, L 2.71

Income

http://www.census.gov/hhes/www/income/income.html
Sponsor(s): Commerce Department—Economics and Statistics Administration (ESA)—Census Bureau
Description: The Census Bureau's Web page for income data provides reports, briefs, and research in addition to aggregated data and microdata. It links to the income data from the Current Population Survey, American Community Survey, Decennial Census, Small Area Income and Poverty Estimates, Survey of Income and Program Participation, and other Census programs. Data tables include median state income and historic income inequality. The site provides detailed information on the data sources and links to other income data programs online.

Subject(s): Wages—Statistics
Publication(s): *Income, Poverty, and Health Insurance Coverage in the United States*, C 3.186/32

Longitudinal Employer-Household Dynamics (LEHD)

http://lehd.did.census.gov/
Sponsor(s): Commerce Department—Economics and Statistics Administration (ESA)—Census Bureau
Description: This Web site describes the LEHD project and provides access to the data. LEHD involves a Census Bureau partnership with the states, combining federal and state administrative data on employers and employees while ensuring confidentiality. Most of the site is concerned with Local Employment Dynamics (LED), which provide data on local labor market conditions. LED's Quality Workforce Indicators (QWI) include data for employment, job creation, wages, worker turnover, and other factors at state, county, and city levels. The site includes the QWI Explorer, OnTheMap (which maps work and home locations with other workforce data), and the LED Extraction Tool.

LEHD provides an extensive library of information, documentation, and research for social scientists, economic development specialists, and those familiar with the data; other users will face a learning curve. Most, but not all, states participate—the site has a list of participating states.

Subject(s): Employment Statistics

JOBS

Employment and Training Administration (ETA)
   http://www.doleta.gov/
   Sponsor(s): Labor Department—Employment and Training Administration (ETA)
   Description: ETA supports workforce training programs and job placement through employment services. The ETA Web site offers information about its services for businesses and industry, job seekers, and workforce professionals. The site has a Grants & Contracts section and links to regional and state resources. Grants information is also displayed on the home page. Other information on the site includes a research publications database, relevant laws and regulations, ETA advisories, and links to information on ETA programs. Major programs include Foreign Labor Certification, Migrant and Seasonal Farmworkers Program, and the Dislocated Worker Program.
   Many employment and training programs operate at the state level. The ETA Web site provides information and links to find state information in addition to federal guides and programs.
   Subject(s): Job Training
   Publication(s): *ETA Occasional Paper Series*, L 37.27:

Intelligence.Gov (Jobs)
   http://www.intelligence.gov/
   Sponsor(s): Director of National Intelligence
   Description: This Web site is dedicated to describing the Intelligence community to the general public and to job seekers. Its Careers section allows users to explore different positions and find jobs within the Intelligence Community.
   Subject(s): Jobs; Intelligence

O*NET—The Occupational Information Network
   http://online.onetcenter.org/
   Sponsors: Labor Department—Employment and Training Administration (ETA)
   Description: O*NET, the Occupational Information Network, is a database system with comprehensive information on job requirements and worker competencies. It is aligned with the Standard Occupational Classification (SOC) system. The Web site has a Find Occupations section to browse or search the database by keyword and other criteria, and a Skills search tool, under Advanced Search, that allows users to select from a list of skills and match them to occupations. It also has a crosswalk search between the O*NET classifications and other classifications, such as the Military Occupation Classification. O*NET has also added a section highlighting green occupations.

Subject(s): Job Skills; Occupations

Occupational Outlook Handbook

http://www.bls.gov/ooh/

Sponsors: Labor Department—Bureau of Labor Statistics (BLS)

Description: The *Occupational Outlook Handbook* profiles job and career options and describes the work involved and the training or education needed for each career. It is updated every two years. Each entry is available in HTML or PDF format. The *Handbook* is also available for purchase in print. BLS also offers Spanish-language descriptions for 100 occupations.

Occupation profiles can be found with a keyword search or through an A to Z index. Occupations can also be browsed by category, such as median pay and on-the-job training. The Web site links to supporting material, including a teacher's guide, the *Occupational Outlook Quarterly Online* magazine, and an overview of trends in job opportunities for the future.

This Web site contains an excellent online implementation of a standard reference source. The links to definitions and related occupations make the Handbook easy to browse online.

Subjects: Career Information; Occupations; Workforce

Publications: *Occupational Outlook Handbook*, L 2.3/4

Occupational Outlook Quarterly Online, L 2.70/4

Standard Occupational Classification (SOC) System

http://stats.bls.gov/soc/

Sponsor(s): Labor Department—Bureau of Labor Statistics (BLS)

Description: The SOC system is used by federal statistical agencies to classify workers into occupational categories for the purpose of collecting, calculating, and disseminating data. This Web site allows users to browse or search the classification system, or to order a copy of the printed edition of the *Standard Occupational Classification Manual*. Related reference material is provided, including the *Standard Occupational Classification (SOC) User Guide*. The SOC was updated in 2010. The 2000 version and related materials are archived at this site.

Subject(s): Occupations

Publications: *Standard Occupational Classification Manual*, PREX 2.6/3

Studentjobs.gov

https://www.usajobs.gov/StudentsAndGrads

Alternate URL(s)

http://www.studentjobs.gov/

Sponsor(s): Education Department—Federal Student Aid Office—Office of Personnel Management (OPM)

Description: Studentjobs.gov is a clearinghouse of information about the Pathways Program, which matches students with federal internships and career development opportunities. A Federal Jobs by College Major page lists degrees matched to occupations found in the federal government. In the summer of 2012, a streamlined version of the Pathways Program debuted.

Subject(s): Internships; Job Openings; Students

USAJOBS

http://www.usajobs.gov/

Sponsor(s): Office of Personnel Management (OPM)

Description: The core of the USAJOBS Web site is a database of current federal government employment opportunities. These openings can be searched by keyword or by other criteria, including by agency, occupational grouping, salary, or state. Users can create and store a resume online for applying for federal jobs and set up a profile to receive automated job alerts. The site has special sections for veterans, students, senior executives, and individuals with disabilities.

Subject(s): Government Employees; Job Openings

Women's Bureau

http://www.dol.gov/wb/welcome.html

Sponsor(s): Labor Department—Women's Bureau

Description: The Department of Labor's Women's Bureau was created in 1920 to promote profitable employment opportunities for women. Its Web site describes the bureau's current and past programs. The Data & Statistics section contains information from the Department of Labor, the Department of Commerce, and Congress's Joint Economic Committee.

Subject(s): Occupations—Statistics; Women—Policy

LABOR-MANAGEMENT RELATIONS

Federal Mediation & Conciliation Service (FMCS)

http://www.fmcs.gov/internet/

Sponsor(s): Federal Mediation & Conciliation Service (FMCS)

Description: FMCS is an independent agency set up by Congress to promote sound and stable labor-management relations. One of the agency's major responsibilities is to mediate collective bargaining negotiations. The What We Do section on its Web site provides information about collective bargaining, alternative bargaining processes, arbitration, the FMCS grants program, and other topics. The site also describes the FMCS e-service, which is called Technology Assisted Group Solutions (TAGS); TAGS includes capabilities for online meetings, online voting,

and other services. The Resources section has relevant forms and applications.
Subjects: Labor-Management Relations; Mediation

Key Workplace Documents
http://digitalcommons.ilr.cornell.edu/keydocs/
Sponsor(s): Cornell University. Catherwood Library
Description: Cornell University's Catherwood Library, while not a government institution, offers an online archive of historical government reports, statistics, and public policy papers from various agencies and commissions. The subject focus is on the workforce and employer-employee relationships. Federal publications in the collection include many reports from the Congressional Research Service.

This collection is small but focused. It is a nongovernmental information source but provides an excellent service in maintaining access to government reports that might not otherwise be available on the Internet.
Subject(s): Child Labor; Labor-Management Relations—Policy; Workforce—Policy

National Labor Relations Board (NLRB)
http://www.nlrb.gov/
Sponsor(s): National Labor Relations Board (NLRB)
Description: NLRB conducts secret-ballot elections to determine whether employees want union representation; it also investigates unfair labor practices by employers and unions. The Rights We Protect section explains the National Labor Relations Act. The site also has NLRB decisions and memos, the weekly summary of new documents, and the Cite-Net database for the Classified Index of NLRB Board Decisions and Related Court Decisions. The Reports & Guidance section includes NLRB manuals, regulations, annual reports, and some publications in Spanish.
Subject(s): Labor Unions
Publication(s): *Decisions and Orders*, NLRB, LR 1.8
Weekly Summary of NLRB Cases, LR 1.15/2

National Mediation Board (NMB)
http://www.nmb.gov/
Sponsor(s): National Mediation Board (NMB)
Description: NMB is an independent U.S. government agency whose principal role is to foster harmonious labor-management relations in the rail and air transport industries in order to minimize disruptions to the flow of interstate commerce. The NMB Web site's Mediation section includes information on Presidential Emergency Boards. The What's New section contains a weekly report on mediation, representation, and arbitration activity, as well as Freedom of Information Act links.
Subject(s): Airlines; Labor Mediation; Railroads

Publication(s): *Determinations of the National Mediation Board,* NMB 1.9

Office of Labor-Management Standards (OLMS)

http://www.dol.gov/olms/

Sponsor(s): Labor Department—Labor-Management Standards Office

Description: OLMS administers and enforces certain reporting, disclosure, and operational requirements for labor unions and union officers. The Web site has financial disclosure reports for labor unions, union officers, and union employees, as well as reports for employers and labor relations consultants. The scanned reports can be viewed in PDF format and are generally available from 2000 to the present. Data from the annual financial reports submitted by unions can also be searched by criteria, such as type of union, state or ZIP code, and the dollar range of assets, liabilities, receipts, and disbursements. The site also has compliance assistance information and notification of civil and criminal enforcement actions.

Subject(s): Labor Unions—Regulations

WORKPLACE CONDITIONS

Federal Occupational Health (FOH)

http://www.foh.dhhs.gov/

Sponsors: Health and Human Services Department—Health Resources and Services Administration (HRSA)

Description: FOH provides occupational health services to federal government managers and their employees. It is a quasi-governmental organization that must cover its operating costs with funds collected through the service provision. The FOH Web site includes information on topics such as worksite health centers, environmental health, safety, and health promotion.

Subject(s): Government Employees; Health Promotion

Mine Safety and Health Administration (MSHA)

http://www.msha.gov/

Sponsor(s): Labor Department—Mine Safety and Health Administration (MSHA)

Description: MSHA is charged with enforcing mine safety and health standards to prevent accidents and minimize health hazards. The MSHA Web site makes a wealth of current information on mine safety available for multiple audiences. The site has extensive information about mine safety laws and regulations and guidance on compliance with the laws. It has statistics on mining accidents, injuries, and fatalities. MSHA also provides the Mine Data Retrieval System, a database with mine overviews, accident histories, violation histories, inspection histories, inspector dust samplings, and operator dust samplings and employment/production data. Use the A–Z index to locate specific information on the extensive MSHA site. A version of the site is available in Spanish.

Subject(s): Mining; Workplace Safety—Regulations
Publication(s): *Fatalgrams*, L 38.15
Holmes Safety Association Bulletin (monthly), L 38.12
MSHA Program Information Bulletin, L 38.17/2

Nanotechnology at NIOSH

http://www.cdc.gov/niosh/topics/nanotech/

Sponsor(s): Health and Human Services Department—Centers for Disease Control and Prevention (CDC)—National Institute of Occupational Safety and Health (NIOSH)

Description: This site is concerned with the occupational safety and health implications related to applications of nanotechnology. It describes NIOSH research and published scientific research from other institutions. The Guidance & Publications section provides fact sheets and links to other resources.

Subject(s): Nanotechnology; Workplace Safety

National Institute of Occupational Safety and Health (NIOSH)

http://www.cdc.gov/niosh/

Sponsor(s): Health and Human Services Department—Centers for Disease Control and Prevention (CDC)—National Institute of Occupational Safety and Health (NIOSH)

Description: NIOSH is responsible for conducting research and making recommendations for the prevention of work-related injuries and illnesses. Its Web site offers multiple points of access to the agency's publications, databases, program information, and other resources. Information is organized into major sections, including Industries and Occupations, Hazards and Exposures, Diseases and Injuries, Chemicals, Safety & Prevention, and Emergency Preparedness & Response. NIOSH databases on the site include the NIOSHTIC-2 bibliographic database, the Power Tools Sound Level Database, National Occupational Respiratory Mortality System (NORMS), the Work-Related Injury Statistics Query System, and the Work-Related Lung Disease Surveillance System. It also links to the grant-supported Electronic Library of Construction Safety and Health. The Web site includes a NIOSH Science Blog. The site has an A to Z subject index and a search engine. A smaller version of the site is available in Spanish.

Subject(s): Workplace Safety
Publication(s): *Criteria for a Recommended Standard . . .*, HE 20.7110
Health Hazard Evaluation Summaries, HE 20.7125
NIOSH Certified Equipment List, HE 20.7124
NIOSH Current Intelligence Bulletins, HE 20.7155

NIOSH Manual of Analytical Methods, HE 20.7108:994/
NIOSH Pocket Guide to Chemical Hazards, HE 20.7108

Occupational Safety and Health Administration (OSHA)

http://www.osha.gov/

Sponsor(s): Labor Department—Occupational Safety and Health Administration (OSHA)

Description: OSHA's mission is to prevent work-related injuries, illnesses, and deaths. The OSHA Web site provides information on the agency and its regulations and educational and enforcement activities. The home page links to sections covering worker rights, how to file a complaint, compliance assistance/outreach, record keeping, resources for small businesses, the OSHA workplace poster, and other popular topics. The Data & Statistics section provides multiple ways of searching OSHA inspection data. OSHA links to the Bureau of Labor Statistics for workplace injury, illness, and fatality statistics. OSHA also offers RSS feeds for its news releases, OSHA interpretations, Federal Register notices, and the QuickTakes newsletter.

This Web site includes a Spanish-language section designed for employers and employees.

Subjects: Workplace Safety—Regulations

Publications: *Quick Takes*

NINE
Energy

The federal government is both a regulator and producer of energy. The government sets energy policy, and it plays a role in the development of energy-related technologies. This chapter covers the varied federal Web sites that describe energy use and production, consumer energy issues, and energy statistics. Information on the work of the Energy Department's research laboratories can be found in the Science and Space chapter. Information on some aspects of Energy's defense work can be found in the Defense and Intelligence chapter. The topic of transportation is covered in the Transportation chapter.

Subsections in this chapter are Alternative and Renewable Fuels, Energy Policy and Information, Fossil and Nuclear Fuels, and Utilities.

ALTERNATIVE AND RENEWABLE FUELS

Alternative Fuels and Advanced Vehicles Data Center
http://www.eere.energy.gov/afdc/
Sponsor(s): Energy Department—Energy Efficiency and Renewable Energy Office
Description: Alternative fuels for vehicles is the singular theme of this Department of Energy Web site. The site describes fuels such as biodiesel, electricity, ethanol, hydrogen, natural gas, and propane. The Fuels & Vehicles section includes buying guides and explanatory material. The Locate Stations section includes an alternative fuel station locator for finding CNG, ethanol/E85, propane, biodiesel, LNG, hydrogen, and electric refueling stations. Another section details state and federal incentives for alternative fuel use.
Subject(s): Fuels
Publication(s): *Alternative Fuels Price Report*

219

Bioenergies Technology Office

http://www.energy.gov/eere/bioenergy/bioenergy-technologies-office

Sponsor(s): Energy Department—Bioenergies Technology Office

Description: The Energy Department's Bioenergies Technology Office "is focused on forming cost-share partnerships with key stakeholders to develop, demonstrate, and deploy technologies for advanced biofuels production from lignocellulosic and algal biomas." (from the Web site) The Research & Development section provides resources for students and educators, as well as information about fellowships and the BioenergizeME Infographic Challenge. The Information Resources section includes publications, state and regional program information, and audience-specific pages for industry, researchers, policymakers, consumers, and students. The site also has information about funding for basic and applied research for converting biomass resources to biofuels.

Subject(s): Biomass Fuels—Research

Biomass Research

http://www.nrel.gov/biomass/

Sponsor(s): Energy Department—National Renewable Energy Laboratory (NREL)

Description: This Web site describes the biomass research activities of the National Renewable Energy Laboratory. Capabilities and projects discussed include biochemical conversion, thermochemical conversion, and microalgal biofuels. NREL also makes energy analysis information and tools available for researchers on the site.

Subject(s): Biomass Fuels—Research

Clean Cities

http://www.eere.energy.gov/cleancities/

Sponsor(s): Energy Department—Energy Efficiency and Renewable Energy Office

Description: The Clean Cities Program promotes alternative fuels and vehicles, fuel blends, fuel economy, hybrid vehicles, and a reduction in engine idle time for diesel vehicles. Clean Cities is a voluntary program that involves government, industry, and professional associations. Its Web site provides information about these coalitions and the program's accomplishments. The site also carries RSS feeds and the quarterly *Clean Cities Now* newsletter.

Subject(s): Alternative Fuel Vehicles

Publication(s): *Clean Cities Now*

Energy Efficiency and Renewable Energy (EERE)

http://www.eere.energy.gov/

Sponsor(s): Energy Department—Energy Efficiency and Renewable Energy Office

Description: EERE's mission is to enhance energy efficiency and productivity and bring clean, reliable, and affordable energy technologies to the marketplace. The EERE Web site describes their programs in energy efficiency (for homes, buildings, vehicles, industry, and government) and renewable energy sources (solar, wind, geothermal, and other sources). The site provides information on EERE technology commercialization, contract solicitations, and Recovery Act projects.

Subject(s): Energy Conservation; Renewable Energies

Publication(s): *Renewable Energy Data Book*

Hydrogen and Fuel Cells Interagency Working Group

http://www.hydrogen.gov/

Sponsor(s): Energy Department; White House

Description: The Hydrogen and Fuel Cells Interagency Working Group comprises a consortium of federal agencies that exchange information related to research and developments in hydrogen and fuel cell issues. The site provides an interagency action plan and a list of participating agencies, which include the Department of Agriculture, the Department of Homeland Security, the Office of Management and Budget, and the Environmental Protection Agency. Information about funding opportunities is also provided.

Subject(s): Alternative and Renewable Fuels—Research

National Renewable Energy Laboratory (NREL)

http://www.nrel.gov/

Sponsor(s): Energy Department—National Renewable Energy Laboratory (NREL)

Description: NREL focuses on renewable energy and energy efficiency research and development. This Web site presents detailed information about each of NREL's major research areas. The Technology Transfer and Technology Development sections cover the laboratory's commercialization programs, technology licensing, technical assistance to state and local governments, and programs for universities. The Resources section of the site, in the right sidebar, includes educational resources, photographs, and renewable resource maps and data.

NREL also provides information and reports on their energy data analysis, market analysis and policy impact analysis, technological and sustainability analysis, and energy forecasting and modeling.

Subject(s): Renewable Energies—Research; Research Laboratories

Publication(s): *Renewable Energy Data Book*, E 1.177

ENERGY POLICY AND INFORMATION

Building Energy Codes Program
http://www.energycodes.gov/
Sponsor(s): Energy Department—Energy Efficiency and Renewable Energy Office
Description: The Building Energy Codes Program develops model commercial and residential energy codes and compliance assistance. This Web site provides information on federal rules and on state adoption of model codes. The content will be of most interest to state and local governments, builders, and suppliers to the construction industry.
Subject(s): Construction Industry—Regulations; Energy Conservation—Regulations

Building Technologies Program: Building America
http://www.eere.energy.gov/buildings/building_america/
Alternate URL(s)
http://www.buildingamerica.gov/
Sponsor(s): Energy Department—Energy Efficiency and Renewable Energy Office
Description: Building America is a partnership program between the Department of Energy and industry to research new solutions for more energy-efficient homes. Its Web site features a national, interactive map/database of homes constructed as a result of participation in Building America research projects.

Much of the research conducted by the Building Technologies Program is funded through competitive solicitations, and the site provides information in the Financial Opportunities section.
Subject(s): Energy Conservation; Home Construction

Clean Energy
http://www.epa.gov/cleanenergy/
Sponsor(s): Environmental Protection Agency (EPA)
Description: This portal to EPA clean energy programs and information describes clean energy as including "energy efficiency and clean energy supply options like highly efficient combined heat and power as well as renewable energy sources." The site links to information on federal, state, and local programs and policy and links to specific programs such as the National Action Plan for Energy Efficiency and Green Power Partnership. It features a Power Profiler tool that shows what types of power are used in any ZIP code and how the emissions compare to a national average. The site links to other online tools, including a Greenhouse Gas Equivalencies Calculator and the eGRID database of plant-specific emissions data for all U.S. electricity-generating plants.
Subject(s): Air Quality; Energy Conservation

Department of Energy

http://www.energy.gov/

Sponsor(s): Energy Department

Description: The Department of Energy Web site's home page presents news and headlines, with links to popular topics such as Tax Credits, Rebates, and Savings; Heating & Cooling; and Appliances and Electronics. Each of these sections provides topical access to news and programs. The Offices section links directly to component organizations, laboratories, and technology centers. The Science & Innovation tab links to information on the department's Science & Technology, Science Education, Innovation, Energy Sources, Energy Usages, and Energy Efficiency focuses. As with other Cabinet departments, Energy has a section on its Web site devoted to tracking its Recovery Act work and a section on Open Government.

Subject(s): Energy Policy

Publication(s): *Office of Inspector General Public Reports*, E 1.136

U.S. Department of Energy National Telephone Directory, E 1.12/3

Energy Information Administration (EIA)

http://www.eia.doe.gov/

Sponsor(s): Energy Department—Energy Information Administration (EIA)

Description: EIA provides data, forecasts, and analyses regarding energy and its interaction with the economy and the environment. The EIA Web site is divided into major topical areas under Sources and Uses, including Petroleum & Other Liquids, Natural Gas, Electricity, Coal, Nuclear & Uranium, and Electricity. Each section has data, reports, analyses, and forecasts. Other major sections focus on environment, markets and finance, and projections and analyses.

EIA produces an extensive line of statistical publications and datasets. The home page links to a catalog of EIA reports and products and to the EIA e-mail update services and RSS feeds. The Press Room section lists new and upcoming reports and testimony. For highly specialized information beyond the scope of the site, EIA provides a directory of its subject experts on a wide range of topics, including statistical methods, environmental, and electric power emissions; this directory is available under Contact Us link at the bottom of the page. The site also includes an energy glossary.

With its broad scope and multiple access points, the EIA Web site is the place to start when looking for energy-related data. Much of the data are at the national level, but state, regional, and international data are also available. An A-Z Index helps in locating specific information on this large site.

Subject(s): Energy—Statistics; Energy Prices and Costs; Databases

Publication(s): *Annual Coal Report*, E 3.11/7-3
Annual Energy Outlook, E 3.1/4
Annual Energy Review, E 3.1/2
Country Analysis Briefs
Current EIA Publications, E 3.27/8
EIA Publications Directory, E 3.27
Electric Power Annual, E 3.11/17-10
Electric Power Monthly, E 3.11/17-8
Energy Education Resources, Kindergarten through 12th Grade, E 3.27/6
Fuel Oil and Kerosene Sales, E 3.11/11-3
International Energy Annual, E 3.11/20
International Energy Outlook, E 3.11/20
International Petroleum Monthly, E 3.11/5-6
Monthly Energy Review, E 3.9
Natural Gas Annual, E 3.11/2-2
Natural Gas Monthly, E 3.11
Natural Gas Weekly Update, E 3.11/2-12
Oil and Gas Field Code Master List, E 3.34/2
On-Highway Diesel Prices, E 3.13/8
Petroleum Marketing Annual, E 3.13/4-2
Petroleum Marketing Monthly, E 3.13/4
Petroleum Supply Annual, E 3.11/5-5:(year)/V.1 and V.2
Petroleum Supply Monthly, E 3.11/5
Quarterly Coal Report, E 3.11/9
Renewable Energy Annual, E 3.19/2
Retail Gasoline Prices, E 3.13/9
Short Term Energy Outlook, E 3.31
State Electricity Profiles, E 3.2:ST 2/5
State Energy Data Reports, E 3.42
State Energy Price and Expenditure Reports, E 3.42/3
This Week in Petroleum, E 3.32/5
U.S. Crude Oil, Natural Gas, and Natural Gas Liquids Reserves, E 3.34
Uranium Marketing Annual Report, E 3.46/5
Weekly Natural Gas Storage Report
Weekly Petroleum Status Report, E 3.32

Energy Savers
http://www.energysavers.gov/
Sponsor(s): Energy Department—Energy Efficiency and Renewable Energy Office
Description: This Energy Savers Web site includes tips for consumers on saving energy and reducing energy costs in house cooling and heating, water heating, lighting, windows, insulation, and other areas. The site also has information on tax credits and other financial incentives to save energy.

Subject(s): Energy Conservation

Energy Savers Blog

http://www.eereblogs.energy.gov/energysavers/

Sponsor(s): Energy Department—Energy Efficiency and Renewable Energy Office

Description: This blog focuses on energy-saving tips for consumers, covering topics such as energy-efficient appliances and weatherization.

Subject(s): Energy Conservation; Blogs

ENERGY STAR

http://www.energystar.gov/

Sponsor(s): Energy Department; Environmental Protection Agency (EPA)

Description: ENERGY STAR is a voluntary labeling program de-signed to identify and promote energy-efficient products. The core of this Web site is its extensive and detailed directory of qualified projects. Oth-er sections cover energy-efficient home improvement projects, finding new homes that qualify for ENERGY STAR, and guidelines for energy-efficient commercial buildings.

Subject(s): Energy Conservation

Federal Energy Regulatory Commission (FERC)

http://www.ferc.gov/

Sponsor(s): Federal Energy Regulatory Commission (FERC)

Description: FERC is an independent regulatory commission, orga-nized under the Department of Energy, with responsibilities in the areas of electricity, natural gas, oil, and hydroelectric power businesses. The About section of its Web site enumerates the responsibilities that are inside and outside FERC's jurisdiction. The site has extensive data and analysis of the electricity, gas, and other markets in the Market Oversight section. The site's eLibrary section (under the Practitioners heading) serves as a central point for parties filing documents with FERC and for researchers seeking FERC documents. The Legal Resources section has current information about administrative litigation, court cases involving FERC, and the FERC Alternative Dispute Resolution process. Special sec-tions provide guidance to regulated parties and other users on such top-ics as the Energy Policy Act of 2005 and open access transmission tariff reform. FERC has RSS feeds for its news releases, Market Oversight up-dates, and Technical Conference notices.

Subject(s): Energy—Regulations

Publication(s): *State of the Markets*

Saving Starts at Home

http://www.ftc.gov/energysavings

Sponsor(s): Federal Trade Commission (FTC)
Description: This consumer-oriented Web site provides tips on reducing energy costs through the use of energy-saving appliances, compact fluorescent bulbs, better gas mileage in cars, and other household strategies. The site is also available in Spanish.
Subject(s): Energy Conservation

Weatherization and Intergovernmental Program
http://www.eere.energy.gov/wip/
Sponsor(s): Energy Department—Energy Efficiency and Renewable Energy Office
Description: The Weatherization and Intergovernmental Program works with regional and state energy offices to promote energy-efficient technologies and policies. This Web site outlines its major program areas and funding opportunities. Major programs include Energy Efficiency and Conservation Block Grants, the Weatherization Assistance Program, the State Energy Program, the Tribal Energy Program, the Weatherization Innovation Pilot Program, and the Renewable Energy Production Incentive.
Subject(s): Energy Conservation—Grants

FOSSIL AND NUCLEAR FUELS

Blue Ribbon Commission on America's Nuclear Future
http://cybercemetery.unt.edu/archive/brc/20120620211605/http:/brc.gov//
Sponsor(s): Blue Ribbon Commission on America's Nuclear Future—University of North Texas Libraries
Description: The Blue Ribbon Commission was established to review the processing, storage, and disposal of used nuclear fuel. The commission's Web site has information about its membership, videos of its meetings, and copies of relevant documents. The final commission report was released in January 2012, and the site has been archived by the University of North Texas.
Subject(s): Nuclear Fuels

Depleted UF6 Management Information Network
http://web.ead.anl.gov/uranium/
Sponsor(s): Energy Department—Argonne National Laboratory (ANL)
Description: The Depleted UF6 Management Information Network is a public information Web site about the Department of Energy's management of its depleted uranium hexafluoride inventory. The material is a product of the uranium enrichment process and must be managed to

protect the environment and the safety of workers and the public. This Web site provides information about the material, its uses and risks, and the status of the management program. It includes environmental impact statements, program documents, and answers to frequently asked questions.

Subject(s): Nuclear Waste

Energy Resources Program

http://energy.usgs.gov/

Sponsor(s): Interior Department—U.S. Geological Survey (USGS)

Description: The USGS Energy Resources Program conducts research and provides scientific information and supply assessments for geologically based energy resources, such as oil, natural gas, and coal. Information, including maps and images, is organized by energy source. Other sections cover environmental and health issues, such as acid mine drainage and mercury emissions from coal, and USGS research in geochemistry and geophysics.

Subject(s): Fossil Fuels

Fuel Economy

http://www.fueleconomy.gov/

Sponsor(s): Energy Department; Environmental Protection Agency (EPA)

Description: The Department of Energy and the Environmental Protection Agency co-sponsors this Web site, which is also known as Fueleconomy.gov. The site features a database that can be used to find and compare gas mileage, greenhouse gas emissions, and air pollution ratings for various car and truck models. The site also has tips for improving gas mileage and explains why miles per gallon (MPG) rates can vary. The Gasoline Prices section, under Save Money and Fuel, links to gas price data from other sources and has information about related topics, such as gasoline taxes and regional variations in retail price. Other sections cover hybrid and alternative fuel vehicles. The annual *Fuel Economy Guide* compiles fuel economy values for the model year for gasoline and alternative fuel cars, as well as light trucks, minivans, and sport utility vehicles. Versions of the fuel economy comparison tool and an alternative fuel station locator are available for mobile Internet devices; the mobile versions are linked from this site. A Spanish-language version of the site is also available.

Subject(s): Gasoline; Motor Vehicles—Statistics

Publication(s): *Fuel Economy Guide*, E 1.8/5

Idaho National Laboratory (INL)

http://www.inl.gov/

Sponsor(s): Energy Department—Idaho National Laboratory (INL)

228   *The United States Government Internet Directory*

Description: The Idaho National Engineering and Environmental Laboratory (INEEL) and the Argonne National Laboratory-West became the Idaho National Laboratory (INL) in February 2005. This Web site describes INL's research and development work in the nuclear energy, national security, and energy science and technology areas. It includes information about the Center for Advanced Energy Studies and the Next Generation Nuclear Plant projects.

Subject(s): Nuclear Energy—Research; Scientific Research

National Energy Technology Laboratory (NETL)
http://www.netl.doe.gov/
Sponsor(s): Energy Department—Fossil Energy Office
Description: NETL conducts research related to coal, natural gas, and oil. The Web site's Research section describes NETL's research capabilities in basic sciences, energy system dynamics, geological and environmental systems, and materials science. The Technologies section covers topics including oil and natural gas supply, carbon sequestration, and hydrogen as an energy source. Information about research grants and technology transfer is available in the Business section. The Newsroom section of the site links to numerous news articles, papers, presentations, reports, and other publications in NETL's areas of expertise; they are grouped into categories including carbon sequestration, coal and power systems, hydrogen and clean fuels, and oil and natural gas supply.

Subject(s): Fossil Fuels—Research

Nuclear Regulatory Commission (NRC)
http://www.nrc.gov/
Sponsor(s): Nuclear Regulatory Commission (NRC)
Description: NRC is an independent agency charged with regulating civilian use of nuclear materials. Its Web site highlights current news, public meetings schedules, and current rulemakings. Much of the material explaining NRC regulations and responsibilities can be found under the Nuclear Reactors, Nuclear Materials, Radioactive Waste, and Nuclear Security headings. Of interest to the general public, the site has a section on public involvement in NRC regulatory activities, information about reporting a safety or security concern, a directory of operating nuclear facilities, a section on radiation protection, and the option to receive e-mail news notices. The Event Reports section gives a daily status of nuclear power reactors, and the For the Record section provides NRC responses to "information on controversial issues or to significant media reports that could be misleading." (from the Web site)

The NRC Library section organizes access to NRC public documents. It features the Agencywide Documents Access and Management System (ADAMS), a database that provides access to all image and text documents that the NRC has made public since November 1999, as well as bibliographic records made public by the NRC before that date. Other online document collections include NRC regulations, commission paper and orders, significant enforcement actions, NUREG-Series Publications, and Regulatory Guides.

Subject(s): Nuclear Energy—Regulations

Publication(s): *Brochure Reports (NUREG-BR) Series*, Y 3.N 88:31/
Contractor Reports (NUREG/CR) Series, Y 3.N 88:25/
FSME Quarterly Newsletter, Y 3.N 88:57/
Information Digest, Y 3.N 88:10/1350/
NRC News Releases, Y 3.N 88:7/
NRC Staff Reports (NUREGs) Series, Y 3.N 88:10
NUREG/CP Series, Y 3.N 88:27/
Weekly Information Report, Y 3.N 88:50/

Office of Fossil Energy

http://fossil.energy.gov/

Sponsor(s): Energy Department—Fossil Energy Office

Description: The Department of Energy's Office of Fossil Energy organizes its Web site content into major sections, including Services, Science & Innovation, Mission, and About Us. Topical sections in Science & Innovation include Clean Coal, Carbon Capture and Storage, and Oil & Gas. News, a link to the office's blog, and social media page links are also included on the home page.

Subject(s): Fossil Fuels

Publication(s): *Coal and Power Systems: Strategic Plan and Multi-Year Program Plans*, E 1.84
Fossil Energy R&D Project Database, E 1.90/9
Natural Gas Import and Export Regulations, E 1.84/8

Office of Nuclear Energy

http://www.energy.gov/ne/office-nuclear-energy

Alternate URL(s)

http://www.nuclear.gov/

Sponsor(s): Energy Department—Nuclear Energy Office

Description: The Office of Nuclear Energy is concerned with developing new nuclear energy generation technologies, managing the national nuclear infrastructure, and working to support university nuclear engineering programs. Programs include Fuel Cycle Research and Development, Generation IV Nuclear Energy Systems (Gen-IV), and International Nuclear Energy Policy and Cooperation (INEPC). The Document Library section includes budget information, reports to Congress, a Price-Anderson Indemnification section regarding insuring the public for damages from nuclear accidents, and a link to more publications.

Subject(s): Nuclear Energy—Research

Oil and Gas Industry Initiatives
http://www.ftc.gov/ftc/oilgas/
Sponsor(s): Federal Trade Commission (FTC)
Description: As stated on the site, "this website describes the FTC's oversight of the petroleum industry, with special sections on our activities related to merger enforcement, anticompetitive nonmerger activity, and gasoline price data." The site provides FTC reports on gasoline pricing and mergers in the petroleum industry.
Subject(s): Antitrust Law; Petroleum

U.S. Petroleum Reserves
http://www.fe.doe.gov/programs/reserves/
Sponsor(s): Energy Department—Fossil Energy Office
Description: This Web site provides profiles of the Strategic Petroleum Reserve and the much smaller Northeast Home Heating Oil Reserve and Naval Petroleum and Oil Shale Reserves. For the Strategic Petroleum Reserve, the site has data on current inventory, general location of the secure storage sites, information on expanding the reserve, and information about when and why crude oil has been released from the reserve.
Subject(s): Petroleum
Publication(s): *Strategic Petroleum Reserve Annual Report*, E 1.84

UTILITIES

Rural Utilities Service (RUS)
http://www.rurdev.usda.gov/Utilities_LP.html
Sponsor(s): Agriculture Department (USDA)—Rural Utilities Service (RUS)
Description: RUS supports the expansion and maintenance of electric, telecommunications, water, and waste disposal utilities in rural areas. Information about the RUS Web site is divided into sections covering the Electric Program, the Water and Environmental Program, and the Telecommunications Program. Each major section includes program information and contacts.
Subject(s): Distance Learning—Grants; Rural Development; Rural Utilities; Telemedicine—Grants; Water Treatment

SEPA: Southeastern Power Administration
http://www.sepa.doe.gov/
Sponsor(s): Energy Department—Southeastern Power Administration
Description: SEPA is responsible for marketing the electric power and energy generated at reservoirs operated by the U.S. Army Corps of Engineers in Georgia, Florida, Alabama, Mississippi, southern Illinois, Virgin-

ia, Tennessee, Kentucky, North Carolina, and South Carolina. Its Web site includes rate schedules, a system map, and information about how hydroelectricity works.

Subject(s): Hydroelectric Power

SmartGrid.gov

http://www.smartgrid.gov/

Sponsor(s): Federal Smart Grid Task Force

Description: A smart grid is an advanced version of the electrical grid network of technologies that delivers electricity from power plants to consumers in their homes and offices. SmartGrid.gov explains the technology basics. It describes government-funded projects for research, investment, and workforce training. The Web site also has a wealth of background information on the topic, as well as Recovery Act Smart Grid programs.

Subject(s): Electricity

Southwestern Power Administration

http://www.swpa.gov/

Sponsor(s): Energy Department—Southwestern Power Administration

Description: The Southwestern Power Administration is responsible for marketing the hydroelectric power produced at 24 U.S. Army Corps of Engineers multipurpose dams. Its Web site has information about how the Southwestern Power Administration operates and its rate schedules, estimated power generation, and acquisitions information.

Subject(s): Hydroelectric Power

Tennessee Valley Authority (TVA)

http://www.tva.gov/

Sponsor(s): Tennessee Valley Authority (TVA)

Description: TVA is a federal corporation and public power company. It operates fossil fuel and nuclear power plants and manages a system of dams. The Energy section of the site describes TVA's power sources, transmission system, and right-of-way lands. The Environment section includes environmental reviews of TVA projects under the National Environmental Policy Act (NEPA). The site also covers river management and TVA's recreational lakes. For information on TVA's role in encouraging economic development, the site links to http://www.tvaed.com/.

Subject(s): Electricity; Utilities (Energy)

Western Area Power Administration (WAPA)

http://www.wapa.gov/

Sponsor(s): Energy Department—Western Area Power Administration (WAPA)

Description: WAPA markets and delivers hydroelectric power in the central and western United States. The Power Marketing and Transmission sections provide detailed background information. The About section has financial data and annual reports. The Energy Services section is designed for customers. The Web site also has information on WAPA's Electric Power Training Center, which is open to public enrollment. Other sections offer news, acquisitions information, Federal Register notices, and links to Web pages for each WAPA region.

Subject(s): Hydroelectric Power; West (United States)
Publication(s): *Energy Services Bulletin*

TEN

Engineering and Technology

Engineering and technology Web sites from the federal government cover a broad range of applications and goals, such as aerospace research and development, computer security, telecommunications regulations, technical assistance for manufacturers, industrial standards, and technology transfer and commercialization. Sponsors of these Web sites include the military, the Energy Department, and the National Institute of Standards and Technology (NIST). Researchers may also want to check the Science chapter of the book, particularly the Scientific and Technical Information section and the Space section, for additional sites of interest.

Subsections in this chapter are Communications, Engineering, and Technology.

COMMUNICATIONS

FCC Enforcement Bureau
http://www.fcc.gov/eb/
Sponsor(s): Federal Communications Commission (FCC)—Enforcement Bureau
Description: The FCC's regulatory enforcement arm implements rules regarding consumer protection, local competition enforcement, and public safety/homeland security. In the What We Do section, the bureau explains its work on consumer telephone issues, local telephone competition enforcement, indecent or obscene broadcasts, wireless 911 violations, communications equipment marketing violations, and other areas. The bureau's Web site has instructions on filing complaints about amateur radio interference, indecent broadcasts, and other topics. The site also has current news and documents.
Subject(s): Broadcasting—Laws; Telecommunications—Laws

FCC International Bureau
http://www.fcc.gov/ib/
Sponsor(s): Federal Communications Commission (FCC)—International Bureau
Description: The International Bureau administers the FCC's international telecommunications policies and obligations. Its Web site includes information about bureau contacts and current FCC actions. The Applications section includes Earth Station Licensing information, fee filing guides, and a link to file pleadings. The Industry Information section contains news related to the World Trade Organization Basic Telecommunications Agreement and the annual circuit status reports for U.S. facilities-based international common carriers. The Resources section provides a long list of reference information, including foreign ownership guidelines, international agreements, rules for foreign carriers, and Significant Satellite Rulemakings.
Subject(s): Telecommunications—International
Publication(s): *Foreign Ownership Guidelines for FCC Common Carrier and Aeronautical Radio Licenses*

FCC Media Bureau
http://www.fcc.gov/mb/
Sponsor(s): Federal Communications Commission (FCC)—Media Bureau
Description: The FCC Media Bureau manages policy and licensing programs relating to electronic media, including cable television, broadcast television, and radio. This Web site carries news on regulatory, licensing, and merger developments. The Official Documents section includes documents from the Media Bureau and from its recent predecessors, the Mass Media Bureau and the Cable Services Bureau. The site also provides quarterly tallies of broadcast stations, information on political programming rules, and a "Significantly Viewed" list of television stations. Media Bureau databases include CDBS (licensing information for radio and RV broadcast stations) and COALS (Cable Operations and Licensing System).
Subject(s): Broadcasting—Regulations

FCC Office of Engineering and Technology (OET)
http://www.fcc.gov/oet/
Sponsor(s): Federal Communications Commission (FCC)—Office of Engineering and Technology
Description: OET is concerned with the policies and regulations for frequency allocation, spectrum usage, advanced communications technologies, and other matters related to communications engineering. Major sections of its Web site focus on information about radio frequency

safety, radio spectrum allocation, and the authorization of equipment using the radio frequency spectrum. The OET Docket Information page provides access to FCC orders, notices, and press releases. It also links to mapping resources, technical documents, and a database of equipment authorizations.

Subject(s): Communications Technology—Regulations

FCC Public Safety and Homeland Security Bureau

http://www.fcc.gov/pshs/

Sponsor(s): Federal Communications Commission (FCC)—Public Safety and Homeland Security Bureau

Description: The FCC Public Safety and Homeland Security Bureau was established in 2006 to coordinate FCC activities related to public safety, homeland security, national security, emergency management and preparedness, and disaster management. The Web site covers topics such as the public safety communications spectrum, emergency communications planning, 911 call centers, and related advisory groups and safety groups. The site also has an online clearinghouse of public safety communications information.

Subject(s): Communications—Policy; Disaster Preparedness; Homeland Security

FCC Tribal Initiatives

http://www.fcc.gov/indians/

Sponsor: Federal Communications Commission (FCC)

Description: This site describes FCC programs to overcome the lack of telecommunications availability and use on tribal lands. The site includes the FCC "Statement of Policy on Establishing a Government-to-Government Relationship with Indian Tribes." It also covers specific issues such as tower and antenna siting, tribal lands bidding credits for telecommunications services, and financial assistance.

Subject(s): Telecommunications—Policy; American Indians

FCC Wireless Telecommunications Bureau

http://wireless.fcc.gov/

Sponsor(s): Federal Communications Commission (FCC)—Wireless Telecommunications Bureau

Description: The Wireless Telecommunications Bureau handles FCC domestic wireless telecommunications programs and policies for cellular, paging, maritime mobile, and other wireless communications services. Its Web site includes statements, public notices, and other documents. Other sections within the site include Auctions, Licensing, Towers and Antennas, and Wireless Services. The Wireless Services section links to FCC information for over 30 services, including amateur radio, Wireless Communications Service (WCS), and Broadband Radio Service (BRS).

Subject(s): Wireless Communications—Regulations

FCC's Parents' Place

http://www.fcc.gov/parents/

Sponsor(s): Federal Communications Commission (FCC)

Description: The FCC created this Web site to help parents understand and monitor their children's use of communications technology, including cell phones, television, and the Internet. The site includes sections on children's television programming, parental controls, online safety, blocking objectionable content on mobile devices, and more.

Subject(s): Communications Technology

Federal Communications Commission (FCC)

http://www.fcc.gov/

Sponsor: Federal Communications Commission (FCC)

Description: The FCC regulates interstate and international communications by radio, television, wire, satellite, and cable. The FCC Web site provides centralized access to information about the commission and its work, along with biographies of its commissioners and links to the FCC bureaus, offices, and advisory committees. The home page also features current FCC news and a link to the Web version of the *Federal Communications Commission Daily Digest*, which is also available via e-mail delivery. The Daily Digest is a synopsis of commission orders, news releases, speeches, public notices, and all other FCC documents released each business day, with links to the full-text versions of each document. Issues are archived and kept online from June 1994 onward. The FCC offers a variety of finding aids for its Web site and documents collections.

Subject(s): Telecommunications—Regulations

Publication(s): *FCC Forms*, CC 1.55/2

Federal Communications Commission Daily Digest, CC 1.56

Statistics of Communications Common Carriers, CC 1.35

Telephone Directory, FCC, CC 1.53

Institute for Telecommunication Sciences (ITS)

http://www.its.bldrdoc.gov/

Sponsor(s): Commerce Department—National Telecommunications and Information Administration (NTIA)

Description: ITS is the research and engineering branch of the National Telecommunications and Information Administration (NTIA). The Web site's Programs section links to information on such projects as the Audio Quality Research, Video Quality Research, Wireless Networks, and Radio Frequency Interference Monitoring System projects. It also links to information about technology transfer and ITS cooperative research and development agreements (CRADAs). The Publications section offers access to a variety of NTIA reports.

Subject(s): Communications Technology—Research
Publication(s): *ITS Technical Progress Report*, C 60.14

National Broadband Plan

http://www.broadband.gov/
Sponsor: Federal Communications Commission (FCC)
Description: In the context of the Internet, the word "broadband" in the most general sense refers to a network with transmission speeds and capacity better than today's average. The FCC's National Broadband Plan, the centerpiece of this Web site, proposes strategies for stimulating private sector competition to expand capacity and coverage of the nation's networks. The report was mandated by Congress in 2010. The FCC used a number of strategies, such as workshops, to gather input from across the United States.

The Broadband.gov Web site is also available in Spanish. The Executive Summary is available in Spanish, Chinese (Simplified), Thai, Vietnamese, Korean, Tagalog, and Samoan.

Subject(s): Internet—Policy

National Telecommunications and Information Administration (NTIA)

http://www.ntia.doc.gov/
Sponsor(s): Commerce Department—National Telecommunications and Information Administration (NTIA)
Description: NTIA, an Executive Branch agency within the Department of Commerce, is principally responsible for domestic and international telecommunications and information policy issues. The NTIA Web site has information about the administration, its publications, and its press releases. Much of the information on the site is found on the pages for NTIA's component offices, such as the page for Spectrum Management. The Grants section, under Topics, includes information on the Public Telecommunications Facilities Program (PTFP), Public Safety Interoperable Communications (PSIC), and other grant programs. The NTIA Web site also links to extensive information about the Broadband Technology Opportunities Program grants funded through the Recovery Act of 2009.

Subject(s): Internet—Policy; Telecommunications—Policy

Publication(s): *Manual of Regulations & Procedures for Federal Radio Frequency Management (Redbook)*, C 60.8:R 11/

United States Frequency Allocations: The Radio Spectrum (Wall Chart), C 60.16:R 11

Reboot.FCC.gov
http://reboot.fcc.gov/
Sponsor: Federal Communications Commission (FCC)
Description: The FCC launched Reboot.FCC.gov to discuss improvements for the commission and its Web site and to spotlight initiatives and reforms. The Initiatives section of the site introduces new FCC Web content. The Reform section discusses improvements in FCC systems, data, and external communications.
Subject(s): Communications Technology—Regulations

USDA Telecommunications Program
http://www.usda.gov/rus/telecom/
Sponsor(s): Agriculture Department (USDA)—Rural Development
Description: The Rural Development Telecommunications Program assists with financing for rural America's telecommunications infrastructure. The program provides loans and grants in the areas including broadband connectivity, distance learning, and telemedicine. Program materials on the Web site include grant and loan applications and a list of materials acceptable for use on the telecommunications systems of borrowers.
Subject(s): Telecommunications

ENGINEERING

Chemical Propulsion Information Analysis Center
http://www.cpia.jhu.edu/
Sponsor(s): Defense Department—Chemical Propulsion Information Analysis Center (CPIAC)
Description: This Department of Defense Information Analysis Center is a clearinghouse for information on chemical, electrical, and nuclear propulsion for missile, rocket, and space and gun propulsion systems. In the Products section, the Web site includes the CPIAC *Bulletin* and listings of other CPIAC publications and databases. Database access is granted only to those that meet the eligibility requirements listed on the site. For the general public, the site offers propulsion news items from non-restricted sources.
Subject(s): Information Analysis Centers; Propulsion Technology; Rockets
Publication(s): *Bulletin*

Coastal and Hydraulics Laboratory (CHL)
http://chl.erdc.usace.army.mil/
Sponsor(s): Army—Army Corps of Engineers

Description: The U.S. Army Corps of Engineers Coastal and Hydraulics Laboratory (CHL) conducts research and development in civil engineering related to shorelines, coastal structures, water flow, and waterways navigation. The CHL Web site provides information on its research programs, data and software publications research and development applications, research facilities, and organizational structure. CHL capabilities are organized by area of expertise, such as dredging, estuaries, flood control, and coastal structures.

Subject(s): Civil Engineering—Research; Waterways—Research

Publication(s): *Coastal and Hydraulics Engineering Technical Notes*

Construction Engineering Research Laboratory (CERL)

http://www.erdc.usace.army.mil/Locations/
ConstructionEngineeringResearchLaboratory.aspx

Alternate URL(s)

http://www.cecer.army.mil/

Sponsor(s): Army—Army Corps of Engineers—Engineer Research and Development Center (ERDC)

Description: CERL conducts research in civil engineering and environmental quality to support sustainable military installations for the army. The Web site has information about CERL, its leadership, and its facilities and products.

Subject(s): Civil Engineering—Research

Engineer Research and Development Center (ERDC)

http://www.erdc.usace.army.mil/

Sponsor(s): Army—Army Corps of Engineers—Engineer Research and Development Center (ERDC)

Description: ERDC specializes in engineering and environmental sciences in support of the military and for domestic projects. ERDC and its laboratories are concerned with the engineering and science aspects of coastal environments and hydraulics, flood control and storm damage reduction, cold regions, construction, engineering geology, environmental cleanup and restoration, information technology, geospatial systems, and military support. The Web site links to each of the ERDC laboratory Web sites.

Subject(s): Civil Engineering; Defense Research

Engineering at LLNL

http://www-eng.llnl.gov/

Sponsor(s): Energy Department—Lawrence Livermore National Laboratory (LLNL)

Description: The Engineering at LLNL Web site highlights the engineering projects underway at the Lawrence Livermore National Laboratory. Designed for potential clients and the general public, the site covers such LLNL specialties as biotechnology, materials engineering, and precision engineering,

Subject(s): Engineering Research; National Laboratories

Hollings Manufacturing Extension Partnership (MEP)

http://www.nist.gov/mep/

Sponsor(s): Commerce Department—Technology Administration (TA)—National Institute of Standards and Technology (NIST)

Description: The Hollings Manufacturing Extension Partnership (MEP), named for Sen. Ernest Frederick "Fritz" Hollings, is a network of extension centers and experts who offer technical and business assistance to smaller manufacturers. Its Web site describes the program and offers a directory of participating extension centers.

Subject(s): Manufacturing

Manufacturing Engineering Laboratory (MEL)

http://www.nist.gov/el/

Sponsor(s): Commerce Department—Technology Administration (TA)—National Institute of Standards and Technology (NIST)

Description: MEL focuses on measurements and standards issues in parts manufacturing. The laboratory's divisions are Materials and Structural Systems, Energy and Environment, Fire Research, Intelligent Systems, and Systems Integration, with the offices of Applied Economics, National Earthquake Hazards Reduction Program (NEHRP), National Windstorm Impact Reduction Program, and Smart Grid. Each division provides information on the technology in its realm. The Web site also provides information by topics, such as disaster resilience, robotics and automation, and supply chain integration. The Products and Services section of the site has information on software products and guest researcher opportunities.

Subject(s): Manufacturing Technology

Manufacturing Technology Program (ManTech)

https://www.dodmantech.com/

Sponsor: Defense Department

Description: ManTech focuses on improved processes in the production of weapons systems. The site describes program activities in such areas as metals, composites, and electronics research. The site also includes information on the program's funding, relevant legislation, business opportunities, and achievements.

Subject(s): Manufacturing Technology

Publication(s): *Defense News*

Manufacturing & Technology News

National Institute of Standards and Technology (NIST)

http://www.nist.gov/

Sponsor(s): Commerce Department—Technology Administration (TA)— National Institute of Standards and Technology (NIST)

Description: NIST, an agency within the Department of Commerce, seeks to promote economic growth by working with industry to develop and apply technology, measurements, and standards. One of their major projects is to develop standards to enable the nation's move to a "smart grid," a modernized electric power infrastructure; the work is discussed at http://www.nist.gov/smartgrid/. The NIST Web site provides information from the agency's ten specialized laboratories, including Building and Fire Research, Electronics and Telecommunications, and Information Technology. The site also organizes NIST's work by general topic, such as bioscience and health, energy, quality, and transportation.

The site also accesses the NIST online databases and NIST publications.

Subject(s): Research and Development; Research Laboratories; Standards and Specifications

Publication(s): *Checking the Net Contents of Packaged Goods (Handbook 133)*, C 13.11:133/4

Directory of NVLAP Accredited Laboratories, C 13.58/7

Federal Information Processing Standards Publications (FIPS Pubs) Index, C 13.52:58/INDEX

Journal of Research of the National Institute of Standards and Technology, C 13.22

NIST Special Publications (800 Series), C 13.10:800

NIST Tech Beat, C 13.46/3

Specifications, Tolerances, and Other Technical Requirements for Weighing and Measuring Devices (Handbook 44), C 13.11/2

SRM (Standard Reference Materials), C 13.48/4-3

Uniform Laws and Regulations in the Areas of Legal Metrology and Engine Fuel Quality (Handbook 130), C 13.11:130/

Standards.gov

http://standards.gov/

Sponsor(s): Commerce Department—Technology Administration (TA)— National Institute of Standards and Technology (NIST)

Description: Standards.gov provides background information on standards (including a legal definition of "standards" for the purposes of the Web site) and assistance in locating information about the use of standards in government. The site focuses on federal agency use of standards for regulatory and procurement purposes. The Federal Agency Info section links to agency Web sites about standards, the Interagency

Committee on Standards Policy (ICSP), and federal standards-related laws, policies, and guidance.

Subject(s): Standards and Specifications

U.S. Army Corps of Engineers Cold Regions Research and Engineering Laboratory (CRREL)

http://www.erdc.usace.army.mil/Locations/
ColdRegionsResearchandEngineeringLaboratory.aspx

Sponsor(s): Army—Army Corps of Engineers—Engineer Research and Development Center (ERDC)

Description: CRREL conducts scientific and engineering research on cold temperature environments. The Facilities and Products section of the site links to information resources such as the Ice Jam Clearinghouse and the Cold Regions Bibliography. Information on academic and business opportunities with CRREL is also provided.

Subject(s): Engineering Research; Research Laboratories

U.S. Army Corps of Engineers Headquarters (USACE)

http://www.usace.army.mil/

Sponsor(s): Army—Army Corps of Engineers

Description: The U.S. Army Corps of Engineers (USACE) provides engineering services for military construction and civil works projects in areas such as flood control and waterway navigation and emergency response. The Library section includes links to the USACE libraries, publication listings, and maps information. The Media section links to news releases, fact sheets, and videos and images. The Web site also has information on USACE locations and business opportunities, and a blog by the Commanding General of USACE.

The Army Corps of Engineers has an extensive network of Web sites. To discover the full range of content available, use the organizational and geographic district links in the About Us section.

Subject(s): Civil Engineering; Waterways

Publication(s): *Engineer Circulars*
Engineer Manuals
Engineer Regulations

TECHNOLOGY

Biometrics Consortium (Biometrics.org)

http://www.biometrics.org/

Sponsor(s): Commerce Department—National Institute of Standards and Technology (NIST) National Security Agency (NSA)

Description: The Biometrics Consortium, according to the Web site, "exists to faciiltate scientific and technical (S&T) interchanges between the U. S. federal government and outside entities on biometric and other identity technologies in support of Defense, Homeland Security, Identity Management, Border Crossing, and Electronic Commerce." The consortium organizes an annual conference in the fall. Its Web site includes sections for information about government activity and standards activity, as well as other biometrics resources and an introduction to biometrics. Biometric.org is the sister site of Biometrics.gov, which is described in a separate entry.

Subject(s): Biometrics — Research

Biometrics Resource Center Website

http://www.itl.nist.gov/div893/biometrics/

Sponsor(s): Commerce Department — National Institute of Standards and Technology (NIST)

Description: NIST is part of the government's Biometric Consortium. This Web describes the biometrics research activities of NIST's Information Technology Laboratory and offers links to Biometric Consortium conference information and to related government Web sites.

Subject(s): Biometrics — Research

Biometrics.gov

http://biometrics.gov/

Sponsor(s): White House — National Science and Technology Council (NSTC)

Description: Biometrics.gov serves as the federal government's central Web site for information on biometric technologies and federal biometrics activities. The site includes an extensive introduction to biometrics and publications, presentations from the NSTC's Subcommittee on Biometrics, Presidential Directives that have a direct or indirect biometric component, and inventory of relevant federal programs.

Subject(s): Biometrics

Publication(s): *NSTC Policy for Enabling the Development, Adoption, and Use of Biometric Standards*

Registry of USG Recommended Biometric Standards

Digital Preservation

http://www.digitalpreservation.gov/

Sponsor: Library of Congress

Description: Digital Preservation is the Web site for the National Digital Information Infrastructure and Preservation Program (NDIIPP), a collaborative effort led by the Library of Congress to develop a national strategy to collect, preserve, and make available digital content. The Web site has information on NDIIP's over 300 partner institutions and their digital preservation initiatives. The Web site features access to many of the tools and services created by project partners, as well as reports, video presentations, and podcasts. The site also has a section on personal archiving for individuals who would like to preserve their own digital creations.

Subject(s): Archives; Digital Libraries; Information Technology

Digital TV Transition
http://www.dtv.gov/
Sponsor: Federal Communications Commission (FCC)
Description: This special FCC Web site was created to educate consumers about the 2009 switch from analog format to digital by full-power television broadcast stations. The site now has basic consumer information on digital television. It is also available in Spanish.

Subject(s): Television

Energy Science and Technology Software Center (ESTSC)
http://www.osti.gov/estsc/
Sponsor(s): Energy Department—Scientific and Technical Information Office
Description: ESTSC licenses and distributes federally funded scientific and technical software developed by the national laboratories, Department of Energy contractors, and other developers. This Web site serves as the central catalog and order site. The software available is highly technical and specialized, with titles such as "Unsaturated Groundwater and Heat Transport Model" and "Simulation Program for Non-isothermal Multiphase Reactive Geochemical Transport."

Subject(s): Software; Technology Transfer

Energy Sciences Network (ESnet)
http://www.es.net/
Sponsor(s): Energy Department—Lawrence Berkeley National Laboratory (LBL)
Description: ESnet is a high-speed network, funded by the Department of Energy (DOE), that provides network and collaboration services in support of the agency's research missions. ESnet is used by researchers at national laboratories, universities, and other institutions and provides direct connections to all major DOE sites with high performance speeds. Major sections of the Web site include Network R&D (Research and Development) and News & Publications.

Information Technology Laboratory (ITL)
http://www.itl.nist.gov/
Sponsor(s): Commerce Department—Technology Administration (TA)—National Institute of Standards and Technology (NIST)
Description: This NIST laboratory develops the tests and test methods used by researchers and scientists to measure, compare, and improve

information technology systems. Detailed information is available on its Web site, organized by research area: advanced network technologies, computer security, information access, applied and computational mathematics, software and systems, and statistical engineering. The site also has information on the laboratory's role as an ANSI standards developer.

Subject(s): Information Technology—Research
Publication(s): *Engineering Statistics e-Handbook*
ITL Bulletin, C 13.76

Information Technology Portal

http://www.nist.gov/information-technology-portal.cfm
Sponsor(s): Commerce Department—National Institute of Standards and Technology (NIST)
Description: The NIST Information Technology Portal links to NIST research, news, and publications on a broad range of technologies. Topics covered by the portal include biometrics, computer forensics, computer security, conformance testing, and cybersecurity.
Subject(s): Information Technology

Nanotechnology at NIH

http://www.nih.gov/science/nanotechnology/
Sponsor: National Institutes of Health (NIH)
Description: This site provides basic information about nanotechnology and about the nanotechnology research and resources at NIH.
Subject(s): Nanotechnology—Research

NASA Advanced Supercomputing Division (NAS)

http://www.nas.nasa.gov/
Sponsor(s): National Aeronautics and Space Administration (NASA)—Ames Research Center (ARC)—Advanced Supercomputing Division (NAS)
Description: NAS provides research, development, and delivery of high-end computing services and technologies to facilitate NASA mission success. The Web site describes projects running on the NASA supercomputers and provides—under the Publications heading—links to NAS technical reports.
Subject(s): High Performance Computing

NASA Independent Verification and Validation Facility (IV&V)

http://www.ivv.nasa.gov/
Sponsor: National Aeronautics and Space Administration (NASA)
Description: The IV&V Facility was established in 1993 to ensure the safety and reliability of the agency's mission-critical software and systems. The Web site has information about this process in the IV&V Services section. Other sections provide information about the facility's mis-

sion and organization, research, education programs, and annual workshop.

Subject(s): Software

NASA Innovative Partnerships Office

http://www.nasa.gov/offices/oct/partnership/index.html

Sponsor: National Aeronautics and Space Administration (NASA)

Description: NASA's Innovative Partnerships Office administers programs to advance the commercialization and transfer of NASA technology. The Web site provides information on partnership programs and development, how to partner with NASA, and intellectual property management. Information on technology transfer and innovation is also listed.

Subject(s): Space Technology; Technology Transfer

Publication(s): *Spinoff*, NAS 1.1/4

Technology Innovation magazine, NAS 1.95

NASA Technology Transfer Program

http://technology.nasa.gov/

Sponsor: National Aeronautics and Space Administration (NASA)

Description: NASA TechFinder highlights the NASA technologies that have commercial potential. A Success Stories section describes NASA spinoffs into the commercial sector.

Subject(s): Space Technology; Technology Transfer

National Coordination Office for Information Technology Research and Development

http://www.nitrd.gov/

Sponsor: National Coordination Office for Information Technology Research and Development (NITRD)

Description: The National Coordination Office (NCO) for Information Technology Research and Development supports planning, budget, and assessment activities for the federal information technology R&D program. The Web site has information from both the NCO and the Networking and Information Technology Research and Development (NITRD) Program it supports. The organizations work to promote U.S. deployment of advanced information technologies. The site has information on the work of each of its interagency groups, including Cyber Security and Information Assurance, High End Computing, and Large Scale Networking. The site also has the annual *Supplement to the President's Budget*, which coordinates the information technology R&D plans of multiple agencies.

Subject(s): Information Technology—Research

Publication(s): *Harnessing the Power of Digital Data for Science and Society*
Supplement to the President's Budget (Blue Book)

National Energy Research Scientific Computing Center (NERSC)

http://www.nersc.gov/
Sponsor(s): Energy Department—Lawrence Berkeley National Laboratory (LBL)
Description: NERSC provides high-performance computing services to scientists supported by the Department of Energy Office of Science. Its Web site provides information on NERSC computing resources, research projects, and publications. Although the computing resources of NERSC are limited to authorized scientists, the center's technical reports and presentations on the Web site may be of interest to other scientists.

Although the computing resources of NERSC are limited to authorized scientists, the NERSC site provides some information for non-affiliated users interested in computational sciences and high-performance computing.
Subject(s): High Performance Computing; Scientific Research

National Geological and Geophysical Data Preservation Program (NGGDP)

http://datapreservation.usgs.gov/
Sponsor(s): Interior Department—U.S. Geological Survey (USGS)
Description: NGGDP was established to set up an archive of geography-related data, maps, well logs, and other information; to create a national catalog of this data; and to assist state geological surveys with their data. The Web site outlines the work being led by NGGDP in these areas.
Subject(s): Data Storage; Geology

National Nanotechnology Initiative (NNI)

http://www.nano.gov/
Sponsor(s): White House—National Science and Technology Council (NSTC)
Description: NNI is a multi-agency effort to coordinate federal research and development in nanoscale science, engineering, and technology. The NNI Web site includes information on available funding opportunities for nanotechnology R&D, the areas of research focus for NNI, current research news, and information about nanotechnology safety issues. The site also describes educational outreach programs for various educational levels.
Subject(s): Nanotechnology—Research
Publication(s): *NNI Supplement to the President's 2013 Budget*

National Vulnerability Database (NVD)

http://nvd.nist.gov/

Sponsor(s): Homeland Security Department—National Cyber Security Division; Commerce Department—Technology Administration (TA)—National Institute of Standards and Technology (NIST)

Description: NVD provides current information about threats to computer security. NVD includes databases of security checklists, security related software flaws, misconfigurations, product names, and impact metrics. The Web site also has a statistics generation engine to graph and chart vulnerability characteristics.

Subject(s): Computer Security

NIST Computer Security Resource Clearinghouse (CSRC)

http://csrc.ncsl.nist.gov/

Sponsor(s): Commerce Department—Technology Administration (TA)—National Institute of Standards and Technology (NIST)

Description: CSRC is designed to collect and disseminate computer security information and resources to help users, systems administrators, managers, and security professionals better protect their data and comply with the Federal Information Systems Management Act (FISMA). Most of the information on the site can be found in the Projects/Research sections: Cryptographic Technology, Education Outreach, FISMA & Other Initiatives, Identity Management & Access Control, Security Automation & Vulnerability Management, Systems & Emerging Technologies, and Validation Programs & Advanced Testing. Publications on the CSRC site include Federal Information Processing Standards (FIPS) information. The Drivers section covers the legal and regulatory framework governing federal information security practices.

Subject(s): Computer Security
Publication(s): *FIPS Publications*, C 13.52

Section 508

http://www.section508.gov/

Sponsor: General Services Administration (GSA)

Description: Section 508 of the Rehabilitation Act requires federal agencies to make their electronic and information technology accessible to people with disabilities. This GSA-sponsored Web site provides the guidance and explanations of Section 508 requirements to help both agencies and vendors comply with the law.

Subject(s): World Wide Web—Laws

Technology Innovation Program (TIP)

http://www.nist.gov/tip/

Sponsor(s): Commerce Department—National Institute of Standards and Technology (NIST)

Description: TIP supports high-risk, high-reward research in areas determined to be of critical national need. The Web site has information on the current competition for TIP funding and on past funded projects.

Subject(s): Research and Development—Grants

Usability.gov

http://usability.gov/

Sponsor(s): National Institutes of Health (NIH)—National Cancer Institute (NCI)

Description: This information, sponsored by NCI, is distilled into the online guidebook available on this Web site along with other usability resources.

This site is an excellent resource for people learning about or working in the field of Web site design.

Subject(s): World Wide Web

Publication(s): *Research-Based Web Design and Usability Guidelines*, HE 1.2

US-CERT

http://www.us-cert.gov/

Sponsor(s): Homeland Security Department— National Cyber Security Division

Description: US-CERT (United States Computer Emergency Readiness Team) is a partnership between the Department of Homeland Security and the public and private sectors that was established to protect the nation's Internet infrastructure. The site offers several security alert services deliverable by e-mail or RSS feed and excellent security publications for the average user.

Subject(s): Computer Security

ELEVEN

Environment and Nature

The Environmental Protection Agency, the Department of the Interior, and the Commerce Department's National Oceanic and Atmospheric Administration sponsors public Web sites with data, science, policy, and educational information related to the environment. Sites from these and other agencies are included in this section. Outdoor recreation information can be found in the Culture and Recreation chapter. Atmospheric sciences sites are in the Science and Space chapter.

Subsections in this chapter are Environmental Law, Environmental Policy, Environmental Protection, Environmental Science, Geography, Natural Resources, Pollutants and Waste, and Weather.

ENVIRONMENTAL LAW

Enforcement and Compliance History Online (ECHO)
  http://echo.epa.gov/
  Sponsor(s): Environmental Protection Agency (EPA)
  Description: ECHO is an EPA information system that provides violation and enforcement information on approximately 800,000 facilities under key environmental statutes. From the home page, users can search by ZIP code or address to find regulated facilities and display their inspection and enforcement history. The More Search Options button enables additional search criteria, including facility name, EPA region, county, and state. Searches can be filtered by a number of characteristics, such as whether the facility has had violations, is on Indian land, is near the U.S.-Mexico border, or has a certain percentage of minority population within a three-mile radius. Specific types of data, such as compliance on hazardous waste or compliance with water rules, can also be searched

separately. Facilities identified in search results can be located on Google maps.

EPA provides detailed document and guides to the data, and the data fields on tables link to helpful descriptions.

Subject(s): Environmental Law

Environmental Appeals Board

http://www.epa.gov/eab/

Sponsor(s): Environmental Protection Agency (EPA)

Description: The Environmental Appeals Board handles administrative appeals under all of the major environmental statutes administered by the EPA. The Web site carries published decisions and lists of decisions reviewed by the federal courts or pending federal court review. It includes guidance documents and *A Citizens' Guide to EPA's Environmental Appeals Board*.

Subject(s): Environmental Law

Publication(s): *A Citizens' Guide to EPA's Environmental Appeals Board Environmental Appeals Board Practice Manual*, EP 1.8

EPA Laws, Regulations, Guidance & Dockets

http://www.epa.gov/lawsregs/

Sponsor(s): Environmental Protection Agency (EPA)

Description: This EPA page links to information on environmental regulations organized by environmental topic and business sector. The page also links to significant regulatory guidance documents and to the major federal laws and executive orders that EPA administers. Background information includes sections on how EPA writes regulations, how to comment on proposed regulations, and how EPA enforces environmental laws.

Subject(s): Environmental Protection—Regulations

National Environmental Policy Act (NEPA)

http://www.nepa.gov/

Alternate URL(s)

http://ceq.hss.doe.gov/

Sponsor(s): White House—Council on Environmental Quality (CEQ)

Description: This site provides news and information from the Council on Environmental Quality (CEQ) related to implementation of NEPA. The site has statutes, regulations, executive orders, and regulatory guidance concerning NEPA. The Legal Corner section has NEPA-related case law and litigation statistics. The site also provides NEPA reports and publications, including *The Citizen's Guide to the National Environmental Policy Act*.

Subject(s): Environmental Impact Statements; Environmental Law

Publication(s): *The Citizen's Guide to the National Environmental Policy Act*

National Environmental Policy Act (NEPA)

http://nepa.energy.gov/

Sponsor(s): Environmental Protection Agency (EPA)

Description: This Web site summarizes DOE's activities related to NEPA. Documents available on the site include relevant Records of Decision, Notices of Intent, and NEPA Annual Planning Summaries. The site also provides environmental impact statement schedules, a public meeting calendar, information for NEPA contractors, and the *Lessons Learned* quarterly report. The site also covers NEPA compliance guidance. A notice on the site regarding secure documents advises: "Categorical exclusions are categories of actions that DOE has determined, by regulation, do not individually or cumulatively have a significant effect on the human environment and for which, therefore, neither an environmental assessment nor an environmental impact statement normally is required." These restricted-access documents can be requested in hard copy format.

Subject(s): Environmental Law

Regulatory Development and Retrospective Review Tracker (Reg DaRRT)

http://yosemite.epa.gov/opei/RuleGate.nsf/

Sponsor(s): Environmental Protection Agency (EPA)

Description: This Web site includes rules that have not yet been proposed, those that are open for public comment, those for which EPA is working on a final rule, and those that have been recently finalized. Researchers can find rules with an advanced search, or sort them by topic, rulemaking phase, or effect. Under Get Alerts, the site provides over a dozen RSS newsfeeds, including for new rules added to the Gateway, newly opened comment periods, and notice of the final rule.

Subject(s): Environmental Law

ENVIRONMENTAL POLICY

American Indian Tribal Portal

http://www.epa.gov/tribalportal/

Sponsor(s): Environmental Protection Agency (EPA)

Description: This Web site serves as a central access point for EPA information specifically relevant to tribal governments. The site links to EPA Indian policies, EPA tribal programs, and agency tribal contacts. It also links to general information on environmental grants, laws, and regulations.

Subject(s): American Indians

Bureau of Oceans and International Environmental and Scientific Affairs (OES)

http://www.state.gov/e/oes/

Sponsor(s): State Department

Description: OES coordinates U.S. foreign policy related to science, the environment, and the world's oceans. The Web site presents remarks, reports, and press releases related to topics such as climate change, biodefense, science and technology cooperation, sustainable development, fisheries, polar affairs, and water issues. The site also links to Web pages for the State Department's regional environmental hubs located in selected U.S. embassies around the world. Links to the bureau's Facebook, Twitter, and Flickr pages are prominently displayed on the home page.

   Subject(s): Oceans—Policy; Science and Technology Policy—International; Environmental Policy—International

Bureau of Safety and Environmental Enforcement (BSEE)

http://bsee.gov/

Sponsor(s): Interior Department

Description: As of October 2011, the former Bureau of Ocean Energy Management, Regulation and Enforcement (BOEMRE) was reorganized and replaced with the Bureau of Ocean Energy Management (BOEM) and the Bureau of Safety and Environmental Enforcement (BSEE).

   According to the Web site, "BSEE works to promote safety, protect the environment, and conserve resources offshore through vigorous regulatory oversight and enforcement." The Inspections & Enforcement section includes information about programs and civil penalties and appeals. The Technology & Research section has links to information about the National Offshore Training Center and OHMSETT—The National Oil Spill Response and Renewable Energy Test Facility. Procurement business opportunities can be found in the About BSEE section.

   Subject(s): Safety; Environmental Policy

Council on Environmental Quality (CEQ)

http://www.whitehouse.gov/ceq/

Alternate URL(s)

http://www.whitehouse.gov/administration/eop/ceq/

Sponsor(s): White House—Council on Environmental Quality (CEQ)

Description: CEQ coordinates federal environmental efforts and oversees federal agency implementation of the environmental impact assessment process. The CEQ Web site has been expanded under the new administration. It includes press releases, a FOIA page, and information on CEQ initiatives such as Gulf Coast Ecosystem Restoration, America's Great Outdoors, and the Climate Change Adaptation Task Force. The

Initiatives section also includes information on the administration's update of Principles and Guidelines for Water and Land Related Resources Implementation Studies.

Subject(s): Environmental Protection—Policy; National Environmental Policy Act

Defense Environmental Network and Information Exchange (DENIX)

http://www.denix.osd.mil/

Sponsor(s): Defense Department—Office of the Under Secretary of Defense (Installations and Environment)

Description: DENIX is a centralized resource for environment, safety, and occupational health policy and guidance information for the entire Department of Defense. Topical sections on the Web site, under Programs, Performance, and Conferences & Training. The site also provides information on international agreements and on policies from the armed services.

Some sections of the Web site may be available only to authorized users.

Subject(s): Defense Administration; Environmental Protection—Policy; Historic Preservation

EPA National Center for Environmental Economics (NCEE)

http://yosemite.epa.gov/ee/epa/eed.nsf/pages/homepage

Sponsor(s): Environmental Protection Agency (EPA)—National Center for Environmental Economics

Description: NCEE conducts economic research and analysis related to environmental issues, such as economic incentives for protecting the environment and the benefits and costs of environmental policies and regulations. The site has information on NCEE's reports and working papers, seminars and workshops, grants and funding, and an extensive catalog of Web sites concerning environmental economics.

Subject(s): Economics; Environmental Protection—Policy

It's Our Environment

http://blog.epa.gov/blog/

Sponsor(s): Environmental Protection Agency (EPA)

Description: The official blog of the EPA is written by a variety of EPA employees. Topics range from consumer issues, such as asthma or recycling, to the scientific, such as radiation monitoring, and also cover policy and environmental education issues. Comments in accordance with their posted comment policy are encouraged and an RSS subscription feed is available.

Subject(s): Environmental Policy; Blogs

Morris K. Udall and Stewart L. Udall Foundation

http://www.udall.gov/

Sponsor(s): Morris K. Udall Foundation

Description: The Morris K. Udall and Stewart L. Udall Foundation is an Executive Branch agency created by Congress to honor Congressman Morris Udall's service in the House of Representatives. The foundation provides for internships, scholarships, and fellowships, most with a focus on public service, the environment, and Native Americans. The foundation also runs the U.S. Institute for Environmental Conflict Resolution. The Web site includes information on these and other Udall Foundation programs.

Subject(s): Environmental Education; American Indians; Scholarships

Office of Cooperative Environmental Management

http://www.epa.gov/ocem/

Sponsor(s): Environmental Protection Agency (EPA)

Description: EPA's Office of Cooperative Environmental Management coordinates the work of the numerous federal advisory committees concerned with environmental issues. The Web site provides information and documents from each of the committees.

Subject(s): Environmental Policy

Office of Natural Resources Revenue (ONRR)

http://www.onrr.gov/

Sponsor(s): Interior Department—Bureau of Ocean Energy Management, Regulation, and Enforcement (BOEMRE)

Description: During the reorganization and renaming of the Minerals Management Service in 2010, ONRR took over the responsibilities of Minerals Revenue Management (MRM) program. As stated on the Web site, the office "is a trustee of royalty assets from Indian trust properties and is an advocate for the interests of Indian mineral owners. In conjunction with the Bureau of Indian Affairs, ONRR provides revenue management services for mineral leases on American Indian lands. Money collected is returned – 100 percent – to respective Indian tribes and individual Indian mineral owners through the Office of Trust Funds Management."

Subject(s): Natural Resources Management

Office of the Federal Environmental Executive (OFEE)

http://www.ofee.gov/

Sponsor(s): White House—Office of the Federal Environmental Executive (OFEE)

Description: OFEE promotes environmental practices, such as recycling and procurement of recycled products, in the federal government.

This site has news and information about the office. Many OFEE documents are located at a second site, http://fedcenter.gov.

Subject(s): Recycling

Tribal Energy and Environmental Information Clearinghouse (TEEIC)

http://teeic.anl.gov/

Sponsor(s): Energy Department—Argonne National Laboratory (ANL)—Interior Department

Description: TEEIC provides information about the environmental effects of energy development on tribal lands. One section of the site offers impact, mitigation, regulatory, and case study information by type of energy, such as coal or wind. A second section focuses on guidance for conducting project-specific impact assessments and monitoring. The third section covers federal laws, regulations, and Executive Orders that may apply to energy development activities on tribal lands.

Subject(s): American Indians

ENVIRONMENTAL PROTECTION

America's National Wildlife Refuge System

http://www.fws.gov/refuges/

Sponsor(s): Interior Department—Fish and Wildlife Service (FWS)

Description: This Fish and Wildlife Service Web site has online visitor information for each of the National Wildlife Refuges. The site also provides information on the National Wildlife Refuge System, lands and planning, wildlife and habitat management, budget information, and relevant federal regulations.

Subject(s): Conservation (Natural Resources); Wildlife

Publication(s): *Refuge Update*, I 49.44/6

Coastal Program

http://www.fws.gov/coastal/

Sponsor(s): Interior Department—Fish and Wildlife Service (FWS)

Description: The Coastal Program works to conserve fish and wildlife and their habitats in the bays, estuaries, and watersheds around the U.S. coastline. The Web site has information about program activities, including the National Coastal Wetlands Conservation Grants.

Subject(s): Coastal Ecology

Coastal Management Office

http://www.csc.noaa.gov/

Sponsor(s): Commerce Department—National Oceanic and Atmospheric Administration (NOAA)—Office for Coastal Management

Description: As stated on the Web site, "NOAA's Office of Ocean and Coastal Resource Management and the Coastal Services Center joined forces to become the new Office for Coastal Management." The office helps state and local coastal resource management programs by providing them with data, tools, training, and technical assistance. The Web site has information broken down by region, including Northeast & Mid-Atlantic, Great Lakes, West Coast, and Pacific Islands. Its programs include the National Estuarine Research Reserves, Digital Coast, Coral Reef Conservation, and Coastal Zone Management.

Subject(s): Coastal Ecology; Remote Sensing

Division of Bird Habitat Conservation
http://birdhabitat.fws.gov

Sponsor(s): Interior Department—Fish and Wildlife Service (FWS)

Description: This Fish and Wildlife Service division supports bird habitat conservation partnerships through the North American Wetlands Conservation Act grants program and other programs. The site has sections on the North American Waterfowl Management Plan, the U.S. Shorebird Conservation Plan, and other bird conservation plans.

Subject(s): Birds; Conservation (Natural Resources)—Grants

Earth Day
http://www.epa.gov/earthday/

Alternate URL(s)

http://www.earthday.gov/

Sponsor(s): Environmental Protection Agency (EPA)

Description: This site is a portal for government information on Earth Day, celebrated every April 22nd. The site has information on Earth Day activities, environmental practices, and links to environmental volunteer opportunities. It features a number of links to EPA lesson plans.

Subject(s): Environmental Education

Environmental Protection Agency (EPA)
http://www.epa.gov/

Sponsor(s): Environmental Protection Agency (EPA)

Description: The central EPA Web site provides information resources on science and policy related to the environment, environment-related health issues, climate, ecosystems, pollution, hazardous substances, water quality, and more. The major sections of the site are: Learn the Issues, Science & Technology, Laws & Regulations, and About EPA. Click on the A-Z Index link in the upper right corner of the home page to use the helpful index and other finding aids, such as quick links to the most popular topics, links to EPA's regional Web sites, and a list of EPA databases and software.

The home page features EPA news and the site's blog, Greenversations. The Science & Technology section organizes EPA research areas by topic. The Laws & Regulations section has environmental laws and regulations, information on how to comment on regulations, and regulatory guidance and enforcement information.

As with other Cabinet-level agencies, EPA provides a Recovery Act section and an Open Government section its site. The EPA Web site has Spanish, Chinese, Vietnamese, and Korean versions. It also has a mobile version for smartphone access at http://m.epa.gov/

Subject(s): Environmental Protection

Publication(s): *EPA National Catalog of Publications*, EP 1.21
Inventory of U.S. Greenhouse Gas Emissions and Sinks, EP 1.115
National Biennial RCRA Hazardous Waste Report, EP 1.104/3
National Water Quality Inventory Report to Congress, EP 2.17/2
The Benefits and Costs of the Clean Air Act, EP 4.31
Toxic Chemical Release Inventory Reporting Form R Instructions, EP 5.22/3
Toxic Release Inventory, EP 5.22/2
Tribal Air, EP 4.67

Estuary Education

http://estuaries.noaa.gov/

Sponsor(s): Commerce Department—National Oceanic and Atmospheric Administration (NOAA)

Description: This educational Web site explains the environmental importance of estuaries. It includes a section for students and provides curriculum guides for teachers.

Subject(s): Coastal Ecology; Environmental Education

Estuary Restoration Act & NOAA

http://era.noaa.gov/

Sponsor(s): Commerce Department—National Oceanic and Atmospheric Administration (NOAA)

Description: NOAA is one of five federal agencies serving on an interagency council charged with implementing the Estuary Restoration Act (ERA). This site provides information on project funding and the Estuary Habitat Restoration Strategy. It also has information on the law and on the Estuary Habitat Restoration Council.

Subject(s): Wetlands

Marine Protected Areas of the United States

http://oceanservice.noaa.gov/ecosystems/mpa/

Sponsor(s): Commerce Department—National Oceanic and Atmospheric Administration (NOAA)

Description: This site provides a classification system for the various types of marine protected areas (MPAs), including their conservation focus and levels of environmental protection. The Multimedia section includes photos, infographics, and podcasts. The site also has organizational information on the National MPA Center and the Advisory Committee.

The MPA Web site provides multiple approaches to rich content on science, policy, regulation, enforcement, and many other topics related to MPAs.

Subject(s): Coastal Ecology; Marine Life

Migratory Bird Conservation Commission

http://www.fws.gov/refuges/realty/mbcc.html

Sponsor(s): Migratory Bird Conservation Commission

Description: The Migratory Bird Conservation Commission considers any recommendations by the Secretary of the Interior for the purchase or rental of land for the Fish and Wildlife Service. It also considers the establishment of any new waterfowl refuges. The Web site has information on the commission, its members, its annual report, the Migratory Bird Conservation Fund, and related topics.

Subject(s): Birds; Conservation (Natural Resources)

National Estuaries Restoration Inventory (NERI)

https://neri.noaa.gov/

Sponsor(s): Commerce Department—National Oceanic and Atmospheric Administration (NOAA)

Description: NERI collects information on estuary habitat restoration projects across the country. Projects can be searched by location, restoration technique, and other factors.

Subject(s): Coastal Ecology

National Estuarine Research Reserve System

http://nerrs.noaa.gov/

Sponsor(s): Commerce Department—National Oceanic and Atmospheric Administration (NOAA)—National Ocean Service

Description: Areas in the National Estuarine Research Reserve System are protected for long-term research, water-quality monitoring, education, and coastal zone management. The Web site has profiles of the designated areas and the programs offered under the Reserve System. Featured education programs include the National Estuarine Research Reserve System's Graduate Research Fellowships and the Coastal Training Program.

Subject(s): Environmental Education; Environmental Protection; Rivers and Streams

National Marine Sanctuaries

http://sanctuaries.noaa.gov/

Sponsor(s): Commerce Department—National Oceanic and Atmospheric Administration (NOAA)—National Weather Service

Description: The National Marine Sanctuary System provides resource protection, coordinates scientific research on the sanctuaries, and facilitates multiple uses of the national marine sanctuaries. Its colorful Web site includes sections on marine expeditions, maritime heritage, visiting sanctuaries, and volunteer opportunities. The Management and Resource Protection section has relevant regulations, permit information, and an ocean etiquette guide. The Science section includes Condition Reports for each sanctuary, updated every five years, and the Conservation Series of published articles. The multimedia *Encyclopedia of the Sanctuaries* and sanctuary maps are in the Multimedia section.

Subject(s): Marine Sanctuaries

Publication(s): *Conservation Series*, C 55.443
National Marine Sanctuaries State of the Sanctuary Report

National Wild and Scenic Rivers System

http://www.rivers.gov/

Sponsor(s): Interior Department—National Park Service (NPS)

Description: The Wild and Scenic Rivers Act (Public Law 90-542) is intended to protect selected rivers, keeping them free-flowing and preserving the general character of a river. This site describes the Scenic Rivers program and lists protected rivers. A kids' page is linked at the top of the home page.

Subject(s): Rivers and Streams

Natural Resources Conservation Service (NRCS)

http://www.nrcs.usda.gov/

Sponsor(s): Agriculture Department (USDA)—Natural Resources Conservation Service (NRCS)

Description: NRCS provides expertise in conserving soil, water, and other natural resources. The site's Topics section points to information on such topics as air, soils, water, and energy. It includes Field Office Technical Guides (FOTGs) with soil and conservation profiles. The Programs section has an inventory of financial assistance programs for conservation of wetlands, farm and ranch lands, grasslands, and other purposes. It also provides information on program funding and allocations by state. The Newsroom section includes state program news and photos. A smaller version of the site is available in Spanish.

Subject(s): Conservation (Natural Resources); Environmental Protection

Publication(s): *NRCS This Week*

Ocean Service Office of Restoration and Response (OR&R)

http://response.restoration.noaa.gov/

Sponsor(s): Commerce Department—National Oceanic and Atmospheric Administration (NOAA)—National Ocean Service

Description: OR&R provides scientific support for oil and chemical spill response and damage assessments in coastal waters. Their Web site has information for emergency responders, research institutions, the general public, and students and teachers. It links to closely related Web sites, such as its Damage Assessment, Remediation, and Restoration Program (DARRP) and the NOAA Restoration Center site. The OR&R Web site also links to its own portal, IncidentNews, which has news, photos, and other information about selected oil spills where OR&R provided support. IncidentNews contains information on thousands of historical incidents spanning 30 years.

Subject(s): Oceans; Oil Spills

Office of Protected Resources

http://www.nmfs.noaa.gov/pr/

Sponsor(s): Commerce Department—National Oceanic and Atmospheric Administration (NOAA)—National Marine Fisheries

Description: The NOAA Fisheries Office of Protected Resources coordinates the protection, conservation, and restoration of marine mammals, endangered species, their habitats, and marine-protected areas. This Web site provides legal and regulatory information on the Marine Mammals Protection Act (MMPA) and the Endangered Species Act (ESA), and a listing of threatened and endangered species. The site also has program descriptions, permit information, and a section for educators and students.

Subject(s): Endangered Species; Marine Life; Marine Mammals

U.S.-Mexico Border 2020

http://www.epa.gov/usmexicoborder/

Sponsor(s): Environmental Protection Agency (EPA)

Description: U.S.-Mexico Environmental Program (Border 2020) is a U.S.-Mexico binational program focusing on cleaning the air, providing safe drinking water, reducing the risk of exposure to hazardous waste, and ensuring emergency preparedness along the U.S.-Mexico border. The Web site has information on regional and border-wide working groups and on measuring conditions. The site is also available in Spanish, Chinese, Vietnamese, and Korean.

Subject(s): Environmental Protection; Mexico

United States Coral Reef Task Force

http://www.coralreef.gov/

Sponsor(s): Interior Department; Commerce Department—National Oceanic and Atmospheric Administration (NOAA)

Description: The Coral Reef Task Force, established by executive order, is an interagency task force co-chaired by the Interior Department and NOAA. This site has information about the responsibilities of the task force, its meetings, documents, working groups, and available grants.

Subject(s): Coral Reefs

ENVIRONMENTAL SCIENCE

Air Resources Laboratory (ARL)

http://www.arl.noaa.gov/

Sponsor(s): Commerce Department—National Oceanic and Atmospheric Administration (NOAA)—Office of Oceanic and Atmospheric Research

Description: The Air Resources Laboratory (ARL) focuses on air quality and climate research. The site describes current research, work of the ARL divisions, and climate and meteorological data.

This site will be primarily of interest to atmospheric scientists for the data and information on atmospheric and air quality modeling.

Subject(s): Air Quality—Research; Atmospheric Sciences

Atlantic Oceanographic and Meteorological Laboratory (AOML)

http://www.aoml.noaa.gov/

Sponsor(s): Commerce Department—National Oceanic and Atmospheric Administration (NOAA)—Office of Oceanic and Atmospheric Research

Description: AOML conducts research in oceanography, tropical meteorology, atmospheric and oceanic chemistry, and acoustics. The site provides online access to the lab's data sets. The Publications section provides a searchable catalog of AOML-authored publications dating back to 1985.

Subject(s): Hurricanes—Research; Meteorology—Research; Oceanography—Research

Bureau of Ocean Energy Management (BOEM)

http://www.boem.gov/

Sponsor(s): Interior Department

Description: As of October 2011, the former Bureau of Ocean Energy Management, Regulation and Enforcement (BOEMRE) was reorganized and replaced with the Bureau of Ocean Energy Management (BOEM) and the Bureau of Safety and Environmental Enforcement (BSEE).

BOEM's mission is to explore and develop offshore resources. Key responsibilities include the assessment duties of the Five Year Outer Continental Shelf (OCS) Oil and Natural Gas Leasing Program, offshore renewable energy programs, environmental stewardship, and sand and gravel negotiated agreements. The Newsroom section links to fact sheets, congressional testimony, press releases, and speeches.

Subject(s): Energy—Regulations; Natural Gas; Natural Resources Management; Oceans

Climate Change

http://epa.gov/climatechange/

Sponsor(s): Environmental Protection Agency (EPA)

Description: The EPA Climate Change Web site provides a non-technical overview of global climate change, its causes and effects, and associated policy issues. Major sections of the site include Learn the Issues, Science & Technology, Laws & Regulations, and About EPA. The site also offers a glossary of climate change terms.

Subject(s): Climatology; Climate Change

Coastal and Marine Geology Program

http://marine.usgs.gov/

Sponsor(s): Interior Department—U.S. Geological Survey (USGS)

Description: The Coastal and Marine Geology Program promotes understanding of marine and coastal geologic systems, addressing issues relating to environmental quality, public safety, and natural resources. The online newsletter *Sound Waves* has much of the current program information available at the site. Much of the rest of the content is organized as a database, allowing researchers to specify their topic or region of interest. The database includes research projects, educational material, photographs, movies, maps, publications, and data set. Topics include beaches, sediments, erosion, mapping, remote sensing, minerals, and oil and gas. The site also links to field centers in California, Florida, and Massachusetts.

Subject(s): Coastal Ecology; Geology

Publication(s): *Sound Waves*, I 19.171

Strategic Science for Coral Ecosystems 2007–2011

CSCOR: Center for Sponsored Coastal Ocean Research

http://www.cop.noaa.gov/

Sponsor(s): Commerce Department—National Oceanic and Atmospheric Administration (NOAA)

Description: NOAA's Center for Sponsored Coastal Ocean Research (CSCOR) manages a competitive research program to support understanding of complex coastal systems. CSCOR research focuses on the causes of ecosystem change: climate change, extreme natural events, pollution, invasive species, and land and resources use. The Web site includes grants information and a database of sponsored research summaries. The Publications section includes fact sheets and the Decision Analysis Series.

Subject(s): Coastal Ecology—Grants

Publication(s): *NOAA Coastal Ocean Program, Decisions Analysis Series,* C 55.49/3

Earth Observatory

http://earthobservatory.nasa.gov/

Sponsor(s): National Aeronautics and Space Administration (NASA)—Goddard Space Flight Center (GSFC)

Description: The Earth Observatory Web site is a NASA outreach effort to provide satellite imagery and scientific information about Earth to the public. The site is appropriate for the high school through undergraduate science levels, or for any non-specialist interested in the topic. The Earth Observatory provides NASA images and data mapped onto global image maps. (Check the image use policy link at the bottom of the page for information about copying images from the site.) The Web site also has feature articles and news, with a focus on the global climate and environmental changes.

Subject(s): Environmental Education; Remote Sensing

Global Change Master Directory

http://gcmd.gsfc.nasa.gov/

Sponsor(s): National Aeronautics and Space Administration (NASA)

Description: NASA's Global Change Master Directory (GCMD) is a catalog of Earth science data sets and services pertaining to global change research. The GCMD database has over 34,000 descriptions of earth science data sets and services. An interface for browsing the dataset descriptions organizes them by topics such as agriculture, atmosphere, biosphere, climate indicators, oceans, and Sun.

This well-constructed directory can assist researchers in finding data sets and serve as a model for similar Web projects.

Subject(s): Climate Research; Data Products

Global Change Research Program

http://www.globalchange.gov/

Sponsor(s): White House

Description: The United States Global Change Research Program coordinates federal research on changes in the global environment and their implications for society. Multiple federal agencies participate in the program, which is run by a steering committee and overseen by the Executive Office of the President. The Web site describes the two research priorities, national climate assessment and human health. The site links to news from the program, from international organizations, and to climate change coverage by news media around the world. The site also has an image gallery and materials for educators.

Subject(s): Climate Change

National Centers for Environmental Prediction (NCEP)

http://www.ncep.noaa.gov/

Sponsor(s): Commerce Department—National Oceanic and Atmospheric Administration (NOAA)

Description: This site links to the Web sites for the component NCEP centers: the Aviation Weather Center, the Climate Prediction Center, the Environmental Modeling Center, the Ocean Prediction Center, the Space Weather Prediction Center, the Storm Prediction Center, the National Hurricane Center, and NCEP Central Operations. Each of these publishes images, data, and information related to its specialty.

Most maps and data presented at the Prediction Center sites may be beyond the scope of anyone who is not a professional meteorologist, but some of the sites—such as the Storm Prediction Center—carry information that will be of interest to a broader audience.

Subject(s): Meteorology; Weather Forecasts

National Environmental Satellite, Data, and Information Service (NESDIS)

http://www.nesdis.noaa.gov/

Sponsor(s): Commerce Department—National Oceanic and Atmospheric Administration (NOAA)—National Environmental Satellite, Data, and Information Service (NESDIS)

Description: NESDIS manages environmental satellites, disseminates the data they collect, and conducts related research. The About NESDIS, Satellites, Data Centers, and Resources sections of the NESDIS Web site have information on satellite operations and development.

Subject(s): Environmental Science; Satellites

National Ocean Service (NOS)

http://www.nos.noaa.gov/

Sponsor(s): Commerce Department—National Oceanic and Atmospheric Administration (NOAA)—National Ocean Service

Description: NOS is the primary civil agency within the federal government responsible for the health and safety of the nation's coastal and oceanic environment. Topics include coral reef conservation, oil and chemical spills, coastal monitoring and observations, national estuarine research reserves, global positioning, and tides and currents. The Education section offers lesson plans and online tutorials on corals, tides and water levels, and related topics. The NOS Web site also links to the Web sites for other NOS offices and programs, such as the International Program Office and the Office of Coast Survey.

Subject(s): Oceanography

National Oceanic and Atmospheric Administration (NOAA)

http://www.noaa.gov/

Sponsor(s): Commerce Department—National Oceanic and Atmospheric Administration (NOAA)

Description: With information on issues such as climate, fisheries, and the ocean, the NOAA Web site is a major resource for the environmental sciences. Beyond providing current news and agency information, this central NOAA site best serves as a finding tool for the substantive content on the sites of NOAA's component divisions and offices. Subject access is provided by links to Weather, Oceans, Climate, Coasts, Fisheries, Charting, Research, and Satellites. The NOAA in Your State section has a map of NOAA activities relevant to each U.S. state.

Subject(s): Atmospheric Sciences; Environmental Science; Oceanography

National Oceanographic Data Center

http://www.nodc.noaa.gov/

Sponsor(s): Commerce Department—National Oceanic and Atmospheric Administration (NOAA)—National Environmental Satellite, Data, and Information Service (NESDIS)

Description: The National Oceanographic Data Center provides public access to global oceanographic and coastal data, products, and information. Click on "Access Data" on the home page to reach the Archived Data, CD-ROMs, Publications, and Online Store sections. Available data sets cover ocean currents, plankton, salinity, sea level, and more. The site features the popular "Coastal Water Temperature Guide," which reports near real-time temperature the U.S. coastal regions and makes them available as RSS feeds or viewable on maps.

Subject(s): Oceanography

National Water and Climate Center

http://www.wcc.nrcs.usda.gov/

Sponsor(s): Agriculture Department (USDA)—Natural Resources Conservation Service (NRCS)

Description: The NRCS National Water and Climate Center provides water and climate information and technology to support natural resource conservation. The center's Web site supplies detailed water supply forecasts, snow data, and climate reports at the regional and local levels.

Subject(s): Climate Research; Water Supply

National Wetlands Inventory Center (NWIC)
  http://www.fws.gov/wetlands/
  Sponsor(s): Interior Department—Fish and Wildlife Service (FWS)
  Description: NWIC studies and reports on the nation's wetlands and deepwater habitats. NWIC's Web site focuses on wetlands mapping standards, mapping tools, and geospatial wetlands digital data. The Web site features a Wetlands Mapper, under Wetlands Data, to support the integration of digital map data with other information. The Status and Trends section of the site includes NWIC national, state, and regional reports on the status of wetlands.
  Subject(s): Wetlands
  Publication(s): *Status and Trends of Wetlands in the Conterminous United States*, I 49.2

NOAA Commissioned Officer Corps
  http://www.noaacorps.noaa.gov/
  Sponsor(s): Commerce Department—National Oceanic and Atmospheric Administration (NOAA)
  Description: Members of the NOAA Corps are part of the United States uniformed services and may serve in the armed forces during times of war. Their usual occupations include operating NOAA ships, flying aircraft, managing research projects, conducting diving operations, and serving in staff positions. They are professionals in such fields as oceanography, meteorology, and fisheries science. This Web site provides information on the NOAA Corps organization and operations along with recruiting information.
  Subject(s): Environmental Science

NOAA Earth System Research Laboratory (ESRL)
  http://www.esrl.noaa.gov/
  Sponsor(s): Commerce Department—National Oceanic and Atmospheric Administration (NOAA)
  Description: NOAA's Earth System Research Laboratory (ESRL) was formed in 2005 through the consolidation of six NOAA research organizations. "ESRL researchers monitor the atmosphere, study the physical and chemical processes that comprise the Earth system, and integrate those findings into environmental information products." (from the Web site) The site provides access to data sets and describes ESRL research at its labs, observatories, and field programs. A link beneath the site search box leads to a catalog of ESRL peer-reviewed publications.
  Subject(s): Climate Research; Meteorology—Research

NOAA Research
  http://www.research.noaa.gov/

Sponsor(s): Commerce Department—National Oceanic and Atmospheric Administration (NOAA)

Description: This site links to extensive information on NOAA research activities. NOAA Research includes internal research laboratories, programs for undersea research and ocean exploration, a grants program through the Climate Program Office, and external research at Sea Grant universities and programs.

Subject(s): Environmental Science—Research

NOAA's National Centers for Coastal Ocean Science (NCCOS)

http://coastalscience.noaa.gov/

Sponsor(s): Commerce Department—National Oceanic and Atmospheric Administration (NOAA)—National Centers for Coastal Ocean Science

Description: NCCOS conducts and supports research, monitoring, assessment, and technical assistance for managing coastal ecosystems. The Web site links to information from each of these centers. The site presents the centers' research, publications, and data. Research described on the site covers such topic as coral reefs, estuaries, pollution, and invasive species. Grants and funding information is provided in the Funding section.

Subject(s): Coastal Ecology; Oceans—Research

NSCEP/NEPIS—Publications Gateway

http://www.epa.gov/ncepihom/

Sponsor(s): Environmental Protection Agency (EPA)

Description: This site provides indexed access to free online and print publications from EPA. It is a combination of what were previously two separate Web sites, National Service Center for Environmental Publications (NSCEP)—for print publications—and National Environmental Publications Internet Site (NEPIS)—for digitized publications. The database can be searched and browsed.

Subject(s): Environmental Protection; Publications Catalogs

Pacific Marine Environmental Laboratory (PMEL)

http://www.pmel.noaa.gov/

Sponsor(s): Commerce Department—National Oceanic and Atmospheric Administration (NOAA)—Office of Oceanic and Atmospheric Research

Description: PMEL carries out interdisciplinary scientific investigations in oceanography and atmospheric sciences. The site has sections for Research, Publications, Data, Theme Pages, and Infrastructure. Theme pages explore such topics as the North Pacific Ocean, the Arctic, and ocean seismicity. Featured topics include tsunamis, acoustics, and engineering. The Publications page offers a search of PMEL publications by year, author, title, citation, abstract, division, and media type.

Subject(s): Atmospheric Sciences—Research; Oceanography—Research

Physical Oceanography Distributed Active Archive Center

http://podaac.jpl.nasa.gov

Sponsor(s): National Aeronautics and Space Administration (NASA)—Jet Propulsion Laboratory (JPL)

Description: The Physical Oceanography Distributed Active Archive Center is a component of the NASA Earth Observing System Data Information System (EOSDIS). The center is responsible for archiving and distributing satellite data relevant to the physical state of the ocean. The site has a data catalog and specialized data tools.

While most of the data is for the use of scientists, the site also has links to educational Web sites and products.

Subject(s): Oceanography

Smithsonian Tropical Research Institute

http://www.stri.org/

Sponsor(s): Smithsonian Institution

Description: The Smithsonian Tropical Research Institute is based in Panama. In addition to its own scientific staff, the institute hosts visiting scholars and students conducting research on the ecology and behavior of tropical plants and animals, and on man's impact in the tropics. The Web site has information on the institute's research, facilities, academic programs, and opportunities for visiting scientists. The institute's research data is available in the Bioinformatics section.

Subject(s): Environmental Science—Research

Upper Midwest Environmental Sciences Center (UMESC)

http://www.umesc.usgs.gov/

Sponsor(s): Interior Department—U.S. Geological Survey (USGS)

Description: UMESC is a river-related inventory, monitoring, research, spatial analysis, and information-sharing program. One of its main program areas is the Long-Term Resource Monitoring Program (LTRMP) of the Upper Mississippi River System and adjoining geographic areas. The Maps, Tools, and Databases section includes a variety of environmental datasets, photographs, and maps for the Mississippi River. The Science Programs section is organized into sections for aquatic sciences, river inventory and monitoring, invasive species, and terrestrial sciences. The Outreach and Education section has a variety of educational material on the Mississippi River.

This site provides access to a substantial amount of information for researchers on fish and wildlife, vegetation, invertebrates, water quality, water levels, sediments, contaminants, and nutrients, as well as access to aerial and satellite photography, software, scientific publications, and geographic information systems maps, quadrangles, and figures.

Subject(s): Rivers and Streams—Research

GEOGRAPHY

EarthExplorer

http://earthexplorer.usgs.gov

Sponsor(s): Interior Department

Description: EarthExplorer is a system for finding and ordering satellite images, cartographic products, and high resolution scanned images from photographs through USGS. EarthExplorer provides cross inventory search capabilities and secured e-commerce support for product orders. Users may log in as guests or as registered users; registration is required to order and download data.

EROS Data Center

http://eros.usgs.gov/

Sponsor(s): Interior Department

Description: The Earth Resources Observation and Science (EROS) Center is a data management, systems development, and research center for the USGS Geography Discipline. The Web site provides consolidated access to aerial photography, satellite, imagery, digital maps, land use data, and specialized data tools. The Science section provides research information related to climate change, landscape dynamics, hazards and disasters, and international activities. The site also links to extensive information and data from remote sensing programs.

Subject(s): Maps and Mapping; Remote sensing

Federal Geographic Data Committee (FGDC)

http://www.fgdc.gov/

Sponsor(s): Federal Geographic Data Committee (FGDC)

Description: The Federal Geographic Data Committee is "an interagency committee that promotes the coordinated development, use, sharing, and dissemination of geospatial data on a national basis." (from the Web site) The FGDC coordinates the National Spatial Data Infrastructure (NSDI), which encompasses policies, standards, and procedures for organizations to cooperatively produce and share geospatial data. Web site sections include Metadata, Standards, Policy & Planning, Training, and Grants. The Standards section covers FGDC standards projects, processes, and publications.

Subject(s): Geography

Geographic Names Information System

http://geonames.usgs.gov/domestic/

Sponsor(s): Interior Department—U.S. Geological Survey (USGS)

Description: The GNIS database has federally recognized names of physical and cultural geographic features in the United States and its territories. Geographic features are defined broadly and include populated places, as well as airports, cemeteries, mines, lakes, rivers, streams, schools, beaches, and parks. For each feature, GNIS provides the official name, geographic coordinates, state and county, and feature type. GNIS assigns each geographic feature a unique Feature ID "as the only standard Federal key for accessing, integrating, or reconciling feature data from multiple data sets." (from the Web site) Compressed files of the data can be downloaded from the site. The site also has an online form for proposing geographic name changes or new names.

Subject(s): Geography; Reference

GEONet Names Server

http://geonames.nga.mil/gns/html/

Sponsor(s): Defense Department—National Geospatial-Intelligence Agency (NGA)

Description: The GNS database is the official repository of foreign place names and undersea feature names, such as the Great Barrier Reef, approved by the U.S. Board on Geographic Names. (A notice on the site states, "The names, variants, and associated data may not reflect the views of the United States Government on the sovereignty over geographic features.") GEONet covers place names for all areas of the world except the United States and Antarctica, which are maintained by the United States Geological Survey Geographic Names Information System (http://geonames.usgs.gov/).

Subject(s): Geography; Reference

GeoPlatform.gov

http://www.geoplatform.gov/

Sponsor(s): Federal Geographic Data Committee (FGDC)

Description: GeoPlatform.gov is part of an interagency initiative to provide a open platform for geographic data, software, services, and applications. It is intended to provide dynamic mapping capabilities to governments at all levels and to the general public. GeoPlatform.gov was initially launched to provide mapping services related to the April 2010 BP oil spill.

Subject(s): Maps and Mapping; Oil Spills

National Geodetic Survey (NGS)

http://www.ngs.noaa.gov/

Sponsor(s): Commerce Department—National Oceanic and Atmospheric Administration (NOAA)—National Ocean Service

Description: NGS develops and maintains the National Spatial Reference System (NSRS), a national coordinate system that defines latitude, longitude, height, scale, gravity, and orientation throughout the United States, including how these values change with time. The Web site describes NGS services and programs, such as the Continuously Operating Reference Station (CORS) network and the Height Modernization Program.

Subject(s): Geodesy; Maps and Mapping

National Geospatial Programs Office (NGPO)

http://www.usgs.gov/ngpo/

Sponsor(s): Interior Department—U.S. Geological Survey (USGS)

Description: NGPO, established in 2004, is responsible for all USGS-led geospatial programs, such as The National Map and the Center of Excellence for Geospatial Information Science (CEGIS). NGPO works to promote a National Spatial Data Infrastructure for consistent means to share geographic data between parties. The Web site has news and program information.

Subject(s): Maps and Mapping

Publication(s): *The National Map*

National Map

http://nationalmap.gov/

Sponsor(s): Interior Department—U.S. Geological Survey (USGS)

Description: "The *National Map* is a collaborative effort among the USGS and other Federal, State, and local partners to improve and deliver topographic information for the Nation. It has many uses ranging from recreation to scientific analysis to emergency response. The *National Map* is easily accessible for display on the Web, as products and services, and as downloadable data. The geographic information available from the *National Map* includes orthoimagery (aerial photographs), elevation, geographic names, hydrography, boundaries, transportation, structures, and land cover." (from the Web site) The *National Map* Web site includes a viewer for the data. The Products and Services section has information on current and planned future maps, images, and mapping services.

Subject(s): Maps and Mapping

Publication(s): *Research Agenda for Geographic Information Science at the United States Geological Survey*

Office of Coast Survey

http://www.nauticalcharts.noaa.gov/

Sponsor(s): Commerce Department—National Oceanic and Atmospheric Administration (NOAA)—National Ocean Service

Description: The Coast Survey is the official U.S. chart-making agency. It manages nautical chart data collections and information programs. The NOAA charts can be viewed at the site or ordered online. The Nautical Charts & Pubs section also links to explanatory information, historical maps and charts, and major data portals such as nowCOAST and Tides and Currents; GIS products are listed in a separate section. The site also covers development of new charting technologies, current hydrography projects, and data on submerged wrecks.

Subject(s): Maps and Mapping; Oceans—Research

NATURAL RESOURCES

Alaska Science Center

http://alaska.usgs.gov/

Sponsor(s): Interior Department—U.S. Geological Survey (USGS)

Description: The USGS Alaska Science Center conducts monitoring, research, and assessments of natural resources issues and natural hazards in Alaska and the region. Under Science, the site links to relevant information in the areas of biology, geography, geology, and water, among other features. The Products section has a publications catalog and a link to the Alaska Geospatial Data Clearinghouse.

Subject(s): Wildlife—Research; Alaska—Research

America's Great Outdoors

http://americasgreatoutdoors.gov/

Sponsor(s): White House

Description: According to the Web site, AGO was launched by President Obama in order that "conservation solutions should rise from the American people – that the protection of our natural heritage is a nonpartisan objective shared by all Americans." Under Reports, the site links to fact sheets on subjects including private lands, public lands, and historic preservation, as well as to the full *America's Great Outdoors Report*. Comments are allowed on certain features of the site.

Subject(s): Conservation (Natural Resources)

Publication(s): *The America's Great Outdoors Report*

Animal Welfare

http://www.aphis.usda.gov/animal_welfare/

Sponsor(s): Agriculture Department (USDA)—Animal and Plant Health Inspection Service (APHIS)

Description: This APHIS Web site is concerned with the latest news about the Animal Welfare Act, Horse Protection Act, and related issues. The site includes publications, animal research facility reports, regulations, and forms.

Subject(s): Animals—Regulations

Animal Welfare Information Center (AWIC)

http://www.nal.usda.gov/awic/

Sponsor(s): Agriculture Department (USDA)—National Agricultural Library (NAL)

Description: AWIC compiles links to information about the welfare of farm, lab, circus, and zoo animals, as well as companion animals (pets) to assist with regulatory compliance. The site has information on laws, policies, and guidelines, and links to related databases and Web sites. Linked resources come from both government and non-government sources. AWIC also maintains RSS feeds for news about animal welfare.

Subject(s): Animals

BLM National Wild Horse and Burro Program

http://www.blm.gov/wo/st/en/prog/whbprogram.html

Sponsor(s): Interior Department—Bureau of Land Management (BLM)

Description: The Bureau of Land Management manages wild horses and burros on public lands. The Web site outlines myths and facts about the program, program statistics, and current plans for funding and managing the program. The site includes information from the Wild Horse and Burro Advisory Board and about wild horse and burro adoption. The site also links to information on state-level wild horse and burro programs.

Subject(s): Wild Horses

Bureau of Land Management (BLM)

http://www.blm.gov/

Sponsor(s): Interior Department—Bureau of Land Management (BLM)

Description: BLM administers U.S. public lands, which are primarily in the Western states. The site's What We Do section links to BLM activities in the areas of energy, fire, grazing, and land use planning. The What We Do programs list also includes information on abandoned mine lands, cultural and paleontological resources, General Land Office records, law enforcement, the National Landscape Conservation System (NLCS), rights-of-way, and more. The Information Center section includes news, laws, regulations, policies, and publications. BLM's annual

Public Land Statistics report online provides statistics on federal lands, their commercial uses, recreational uses, conservation, and related topics. The Information Center's Online Services subsection has information on researching BLM records and on doing business with BLM or public lands. The site's home page features a clickable U.S. map as the interface to public lands information for states or regions.

Subject(s): Public Lands
Publication(s): *Public Land Statistics*, I 53.1/2

Bureau of Reclamation

http://www.usbr.gov/

Sponsor(s): Interior Department—Bureau of Reclamation (USBR)

Description: The subtitle of this Web site is "Managing Water in the West." The Bureau of Reclamation manages dams and reservoirs in the western states and produces hydroelectric power. The Web site's Projects and Facilities Database includes information about reclamation power plants, projects, and major reclamation dams. The Programs and Activities section of the site serves as an index to many other reclamation activities, including desalination, cultural resources management, hydroelectric research, and materials engineering and research. The Water Operations section links to the Web sites for BLM regional offices representing the Great Plains, Lower Colorado, Upper Colorado, Mid-Pacific, and Pacific Northwest. Each regional site has information on its dams, reservoirs, projects, news, and publications.

Subject(s): Hydroelectric Power; Water Supply

Department of the Interior (DOI)

http://www.doi.gov/

Sponsor(s): Interior Department

Description: The Interior Web site serves primarily as a portal to the sites for the department's many component agencies, such as the Bureau of Indian Affairs, the National Park Service, the U.S. Fish and Wildlife Service, and the U.S. Geological Survey. The main page features news and RSS feeds from Interior and its component agencies. Like other major departments and agencies, the Interior has a section for Recovery Act information and for Open Government Initiative information on its Web site.

The site is well organized and its multiple access points to various DOI resources make it easy to use.

Subject(s): Natural Resources; Public Lands
Publication(s): *People, Land & Water*, I 1.116

Endangered Species

http://www.fws.gov/endangered/

Sponsor(s): Interior Department—Fish and Wildlife Service (FWS)

Description: This Fish and Wildlife Service site provides a broad collection of news and information on endangered species and the Endangered Species Act (ESA). The Endangered Species lists for animals and plants, as well as proposals for changes to the list, can be found in the Species section of the site. The Species section also has a map for finding endangered species by state and information on critical habitats. The site also provides extensive information in the For Landowners section. The Laws & Policies and Library sections have *Federal Register* notices and documents related to the Endangered Species Act. The Web site also has information on grants and a section for kids.

Subject(s): Endangered Species; Native Plants

Publication(s): *Endangered Species Bulletin*, I 49.77

Recovery Plans, I 49.2

Fish and Wildlife Service (FWS)

http://www.fws.gov/

Sponsor(s): Interior Department—Fish and Wildlife Service (FWS)

Description: FWS aims to conserve, protect, and enhance fish, wildlife, plants, and their habitats. The Web site features current news on its varied programs, such as endangered species, the Federal Duck Stamp Program, and the National Wildlife Refuge System. Quick links lead to information on FWS coastal programs, environmental contaminants, fisheries and habitat conservation, grants, hunting, law enforcement, Native American issues, permits, policy and directives, wetlands, and more.

Subject(s): Birds; Conservation (Natural Resources)—Laws; Fisheries; Natural Resources Management; Wildlife

Publication(s): *Digest of Federal Resource Laws of Interest to the U.S. Fish and Wildlife Service*, I 49.2

Eddies: Reflections on Fisheries Conservation, I 49.118

Fish and Wildlife News, I 49.88

National Survey of Fishing, Hunting, and Wildlife-Associated Recreation, I 49.98

Fort Collins Science Center Online

http://www.fort.usgs.gov/

Sponsor(s): Interior Department—U.S. Geological Survey (USGS)

Description: Scientists at this USGS biological science center study the ecosystems of the mountain, desert, and semi-arid western United States in support of land managers and natural resource decision makers. Programs described on the Web site include Invasive Species Science, Ecosystem Dynamics, Information Science, Trust Species and Habitat, and Policy Analysis and Science Assistance. The Products section has publications, software, and data.

Subject(s): Environmental Science—Policy; Wildlife—Research; West (United States)

National Interagency Fire Center (NIFC)
http://www.nifc.gov/
Sponsor(s): Agriculture Department (USDA)—Forest Service (USFS)
Interior Department
Description: NIFC in Idaho is the national support center for wildland firefighting. In addition to the Forest Service and relevant Interior Department agencies, Fire Center participants include the National Park Service, U.S. Fire Administration, and the nongovernmental National Association of State Foresters (NASF), in addition to other agencies. The Web site features current wildland fire news, wildland fire statistics, policies, and prevention and education information. It also links to wildland fire training programs.
Subject(s): Firefighting; Forest Fires

National Wetlands Research Center
http://www.nwrc.usgs.gov/
Sponsor(s): Interior Department—U.S. Geological Survey (USGS)
Description: Located in Lafayette, LA, the National Wetlands Research Center has expertise in plant, wetland, and animal ecology, as well as remote sensing, geographic information systems, information technologies, and water quality analysis. The site provides a directory of experts on such topics as coastal marsh dieback and coastal prairie management and restoration. It also links to data, maps, publications, and topical sections, such as one on Louisiana land change.
Subject(s): Wetlands

National Wildlife Health Center (NWHC)
http://www.nwhc.usgs.gov/
Sponsor(s): Interior Department—U.S. Geological Survey (USGS)
Description: NWHC provides information, technical assistance, and research on national and international wildlife health issues. The Web site's home page features links to information on current issues, such as avian influenza and chronic wasting disease. The Disease Information section discusses major wildlife health concerns, with links to reports and Web resources for each. NWHC publications online include fact sheets, quarterly wildlife mortality reports, and wildlife health bulletins.
Subject(s): Wildlife—Research
Publication(s): *Field Manual of Wildlife Diseases*, I 19.210
Quarterly Wildlife Mortality Report, I 19.213/2

NOAA's Coral Reef Information System (CoRIS)

http://coris.noaa.gov/

Sponsor(s): Commerce Department—National Oceanic and Atmospheric Administration (NOAA)—National Ocean Service

Description: This portal to NOAA coral reef information and data products has a variety of data sets, reference resources, and information on coral reef biology and environmental threats. A Professional Exchanges section offers access to NOAA's Coral Health and Monitoring Program (CHAMP) electronic discussion list. The Data & Publications section has a searchable catalog of coral ecosystem data sets and NOAA papers and reports along with links to other coral reef Web sites. The site also has information about coral reef biology, diseases and hazards, and a glossary of coral reef terminology.

Subject(s): Coral Reefs

Publication(s): *The State of Coral Reef Ecosystems of the United States and Pacific Freely Associated States,* C 55.13/2

Northern Prairie Wildlife Research Center

http://www.npwrc.usgs.gov/

Sponsor(s): Interior Department—U.S. Geological Survey (USGS)

Description: Part of the USGS Biological Research Division, staff at the Northern Prairie Wildlife Research Center study the species and ecosystems of the Great Plains region. In the Biological Resources section of this site, resources are organized by geography, type (e.g., checklists, identification tools, distribution maps), and taxon (e.g., waterfowl, mammals, and fish).

Subject(s): Conservation (Natural Resources)—Research; Wildlife—Research; Butterflies

NPS: Explore Nature

http://www.nature.nps.gov/

Sponsor(s): Interior Department—National Park Service (NPS)

Description: This National Park Service site links to information on natural resource conservation and science activities in the parks. Extensive environment and science coverage is provided in sections on air resources, biological resources, geologic resources, natural sounds and night skies, water resources, and more. Special features include the Climate Change Response Program, the National Natural Landmarks Program, coral reefs in National Parks, and the National Park Service Planning, Environment, and Public Comment (PEPC) site. The Web site also links to nature-focused sites hosted by individual parks.

Subject(s): Conservation (Natural Resources); Parks and Reserves

Publication(s): *Natural Resource Year in Review,* I 29.1/4
Park Science, I 29.3/4-2

NWISWeb Water Data for the Nation

http://waterdata.usgs.gov/nwis/

Sponsor(s): Interior Department—U.S. Geological Survey (USGS)

Description: NWISWeb has current and historic data on the quantity, quality, distribution, and movement of surface and underground waters in the United States. Use the drop-down menu to view information for a particular state or territory.

Subject(s): Water Supply

Office of Surface Mining (OSM)

http://www.osmre.gov/

Sponsor(s): Interior Department—Surface Mining Office

Description: OSM has the responsibility of reclaiming abandoned mines and protecting the environment and people during coal mining and reclamation. Major sections link to legal, regulatory, and science and technology information related to the missions of regulating coal mines; reclaiming abandoned mine lands; and applying sound science. The Resources section includes directives, grants, forms, FAQs, and other documents. The How Do I? section provides links for reporting an emergency, finding a regulator, and other OSM-related tasks.

Subject(s): Coal; Mining Reclamation

Office of Water, EPA

http://www.epa.gov/OW/

Sponsor(s): Environmental Protection Agency (EPA)—Water Office

Description: As the primary EPA agency overseeing regulatory issues relating to clean water, the Office of Water's Web site features a variety of resources related to drinking water, water pollution, watersheds, and wastewater management. Major sections—listed toward the bottom of the home page—are Drinking Water & Ground Water, Wastewater Management, and Wetlands, Oceans, & Watersheds. The site also includes sections for Laws & Regulations, Grants & Funding, Resources & Performance, Science & Technology, and Education & Training.

Subject(s): Drinking Water; Water Pollution

Patuxent Wildlife Research Center (PWRC)

http://www.pwrc.usgs.gov/

Sponsor(s): Interior Department—U.S. Geological Survey (USGS)

Description: PWRC, located in Maryland, is one of 17 research centers of the U.S. Geological Survey. The center focuses on coastal and wetlands ecology and on migratory birds and waterfowl. The center operates national wildlife inventory and monitoring programs and is responsible for the North American Bird Banding Program. The Web site addresses these topics and includes sections on research and education and a photo gallery of birds, animals, and habitats.

This site will be useful for anyone getting involved with an inventory and monitoring program as well as for those interested in some of the species for which monitoring programs are available.

Subject(s): Birds; Wildlife

Water Resources of the United States

http://water.usgs.gov/

Sponsor(s): Interior Department—U.S. Geological Survey (USGS)

Description: As one of the major subject-oriented USGS Web sites, Water Resources of the United States covers USGS materials related to water use, surface water, ground water, and water quality. It links to the Web sites for USGS water resources programs. The primary divisions of this site include Data, Publications, Maps/GIS, Software, Multimedia, Education, and Programs. Information is organized by locale in the site's Water Science by State feature.

Subject(s): Water

POLLUTANTS AND WASTE

AirCompare

http://www.epa.gov/aircompare/

Sponsor(s): Environmental Protection Agency (EPA)

Description: AirCompare enables U.S. county and state comparisons of air quality. It also provides air quality information for groups such as asthma sufferers and for the general population. Information is not available from all counties. An interagency group provides the data.

Subject(s): Air Quality

Chemical Safety and Hazard Investigation Board (CSB)

http://www.csb.gov/

Sponsor(s): Chemical Safety And Hazard Investigation Board

Description: CSB is an independent, scientific investigatory board that works to determine the causes of chemical accidents. CSB also investigates chemical hazards. The CSB Web site features current news and reports of current investigations, available via RSS. It also has reports of completed investigations and recommendations.

Subject(s): Chemical Industry; Industrial Accidents

Publication(s): *Investigations and News*, Y 3.C 42/2:16

Department of Energy Hanford Site

http://www.hanford.gov/

Sponsor(s): Energy Department—River Protection Office

Description: Hanford, formerly a plutonium production complex, is now one of the world's largest environmental cleanup projects. The project is being managed by the DOE as it explores ways of handling Hanford's tank waste retrieval, treatment, and disposal, as well as restoring the Columbia River Corridor where the plant is located. The Web site includes the plant history, resources for reporters, a list of contractors, a calendar of public meetings, and official documents.

Subject(s): Environmental Cleanup; Nuclear Waste

DOE Environmental Management
http://www.em.doe.gov/
Sponsor(s): Energy Department
Description: The Energy Department's Office of Environmental Management manages the cleanup of radioactive, chemical, and other hazardous waste left after years of nuclear weapons production. The Web site lists current projects and links to completed projects.

Subject(s): Environmental Cleanup; Nuclear Waste

Envirofacts Data Warehouse
http://www.epa.gov/enviro/
Sponsor(s): Environmental Protection Agency (EPA)
Description: Envirofacts provides a central location for access to major environmental databases from the EPA. Databases include Toxics Release Inventory (TRI), Safe Drinking Water Information System, Permit Compliance System, Brownfields Management System, Compensation and Liability Information System (CERCLIS), and many others. Researchers can choose individual databases or search multiple databases at once. Searches are also organized by general topic, such as land, air, or water.

Subject(s): Pollutants; Databases

EPA Air and Radiation
http://www.epa.gov/oar/
Sponsor(s): Environmental Protection Agency (EPA)—Air and Radiation Office
Description: The Office of Air and Radiation's Web site includes links to project and programs in the fields of fuel economy, Clean School Bus USA, the SmartWay Transport Partnership, the National Clean Diesel Campaign, and other issues. News releases and standards also are linked, and the Clean Air Act and the Atomic Energy Act are referenced.

Federal Remediation Technologies Roundtable (FRTR)
http://www.frtr.gov/
Sponsor(s): Federal Remediation Technologies Roundtable
Description: FRTR is an interagency working group supporting collaboration among the federal agencies involved in hazardous waste site remediation. The Web site features a section on Remediation Optimization and a variety of tools, information, and case studies to help with

selecting the best technology for remediation tasks. FRTR meeting information and publications are also online.

Subject(s): Environmental Cleanup

Publication(s)s: *Abstracts of Remediation Case Studies*, EP 1.2:AB 8

Green Vehicle Guide

http://www.epa.gov/greenvehicles/

Sponsor(s): Environmental Protection Agency (EPA)—Air and Radiation Office

Description: This online guide rates the environmental performance of recent car models. Consumers can look up the score for a specific model and make of automobile or browse by type of vehicle, such as pickup or minivan. The best environmental performers earn the EPA SmartWay designation. The site includes explanations of the rankings and information on auto emissions.

Subject(s): Motor Vehicles

Hazardous Information Programs

http://www.aviation.dla.mil/UserWeb/aviationengineering/HazInfo/

Sponsor(s): Defense Department—Defense Logistics Agency (DLA)

Description: The Hazardous Information Programs provide guidance to Defense Department personnel on safely handling and transporting hazardous materials. The Hazardous Technical Information Service (HTIS) on the site serves the defense community, but its HTIS Bulletin, news items, and Web links are available to the public. The Hazardous Materials Information Resource System (HMIRS), the central repository for information on hazardous materials used by the Defense Department, is described on the site but can only be accessed by authorized personnel.

Subject(s): Hazardous Waste

Publication(s): *HTIS (Hazardous Technical Information Services) Bulletin*, D 7.2/3

Storage and Handling of Hazardous Materials, D 7.6/4

Hazardous Waste Clean-Up Information (CLU-IN)

http://clu-in.org/

Sponsor(s): Environmental Protection Agency (EPA)

Description: The CLU-IN Web site provides information about innovative treatment technologies to the hazardous waste remediation community. The site has databases on Remediation and Characterization and Monitoring, as well as technology descriptions and selection tools in these areas. Users with a professional interest in environmental technology can subscribe to e-mail delivery of several newsletters including *Technology News and Trends* or receive an RSS feed of CLU-IN news. Major sections of the site include Contaminants, Issues (e.g., brownfields, mining sites), Strategies & Initiatives, Vendors & Developers, and Training & Events (including online seminars).

Subject(s): Environmental Cleanup
Publication(s): *Technology News and Trends*, EP 1.10/3

Office of Chemical Safety and Pollution Prevention, EPA (OCSPP)

http://www.epa.gov/opptsmnt/

Sponsor(s): Environmental Protection Agency (EPA)—Prevention, Pesticides and Toxic Substances Office

Description: OCSPP is involved in protecting public health and the environment from potential risk from toxic chemicals. The office promotes pollution prevention and the public's right to know about chemical risks and evaluates pesticides and chemicals to safeguard children and other vulnerable members of the population, as well as threatened species and ecosystems. The office implements the Federal Insecticide, Fungicide, and Rodenticide Act (FIFRA), the Federal Food, Drug and Cosmetic Act (FFDCA), the Toxic Substances Control Act (TSCA), and the Pollution Prevention Act.

Subject(s): Pesticides; Toxic Substances

Office of Pollution Prevention and Toxics, EPA (OPPT)

http://www.epa.gov/opptintr/

Sponsor(s): Environmental Protection Agency (EPA)—Prevention, Pesticides, and Toxic Substances Office

Description: OPPT has primary responsibility for administering the Toxic Substances Control Act and the Pollution Prevention Act. The site links to information on OPPT's work in assessment of new chemicals in the marketplace, regulation of High Production Volume (HPV) chemicals, and many other areas.

Subject(s): Toxic Substances

Office of Solid Waste and Emergency Response, EPA (OSWER)

http://www.epa.gov/swerrims/

Sponsor(s): Environmental Protection Agency (EPA)—Solid Waste and Emergency Response Office

Description: OSWER provides policy, guidance, and direction for the EPA solid waste and emergency response programs. The site covers such topics as Superfund and federal facility cleanups, brownfields, landfills, underground storage tanks, safe waste management, grants and funding, and environmental emergencies.

Subject(s): Environmental Cleanup; Hazardous Waste
Publication(s): *Tribal Solid Waste Journal*, EP 1.17:530-N/

RadTown USA

http://www.epa.gov/radtown/

Sponsor(s): Environmental Protection Agency (EPA)

Description: RadTown USA provides educational information about radiation. It uses an interactive graphic of a town to show everyday sources of radiation. Sections of Radtown discuss personal exposure, use of radioactive materials, radiation-treated materials, radioactive waste, natural radiation, and security applications of radiation.

Subject(s): Radiation

RestoretheGulf.gov

http://www.restorethegulf.gov/

Sponsor(s): Homeland Security Department—Coast Guard

Description: RestoretheGulf.gov is the official federal portal for the information on the Deepwater BP oil spill response and recovery. The information is provided by multiple agencies, including the U.S. Coast Guard. The site has current news, health and safety, and assistance information.

Savannah River Site (SRS)

http://www.srs.gov/

Alternate URL(s)

http://www.srs.gov/general/srs-home.html

Sponsor(s): Energy Department

Description: A former production site for weapons-grade nuclear materials, SRS is now focused on management of the nuclear stockpile and nuclear materials and on related environmental issues. The Web site's Programs section describes each program at SRS and provides related documents. The Documents & Publications section includes a library of environmental reports about SRS.

Subject(s): Nuclear Weapons

Publication(s): *Savannah River Site Environmental Report*, E 1.2:SA 9/3/

Superfund Program

http://www.epa.gov/superfund/

Sponsor(s): Environmental Protection Agency (EPA)—Solid Waste and Emergency Response Office

Description: This EPA portal for the Superfund environmental cleanup program covers information about the program, the individual Superfund sites, law and policy documents, liability and enforcement, community involvement, training, regional contacts, databases, and the cleanup process. It also links to a clickable map (under Superfund Sites Where You Live). The Web site has a version available in Spanish.

Subject(s): Environmental Cleanup

Publication(s): *National Priorities List (Superfund)*, EP 1.107/3
Records of Decision (Superfund)

Tox Town

http://toxtown.nlm.nih.gov/
Sponsor(s): National Institutes of Health (NIH)—National Library of Medicine (NLM)
Description: Tox Town is an educational site about toxic chemicals, designed for a general audience. The site uses a graphical pathway image to serve as an interface to toxicity information from such agencies as the National Institutes of Health and the Environmental Protection Agency. It has modules for a city, town, farm, shipping port, and the U.S.-Mexico border. Modified versions of the content are provided in Spanish and in a text-only version. Tox Town also has teaching resources and an alphabetical index of information on the site.
Subject(s): Toxic Substances

ToxFAQs™: Toxic Substances Portal

http://www.atsdr.cdc.gov/toxfaqs/index.asp
Sponsor(s): Health and Human Services Department—Toxic Substances and Disease Registry Agency
Description: ToxFAQs™ offers fact sheets on hazardous substances and the effects of exposure on human health. The information is excerpted from the ATSDR Toxicological Profiles and Public Health Statements. Much of the core material at the ToxFAQs™ site is also available in Spanish.
Subject(s): Hazardous Waste; Toxic Substances

TribalAIR

http://www.epa.gov/oar/tribal/
Sponsor(s): Environmental Protection Agency (EPA)—Air and Radiation Office
Description: This site from the EPA's Office of Air and Radiation provides information about air quality programs in Indian Country. It includes regional contacts, training schedules, regulations, and success stories from tribal environmental professionals in the Tribe to Tribe section. The *Tribal Air Newsletter* is also available in full text.

EPA also maintains a Web site for its American Indian Tribal Portal at http://www.epa.gov/tribalportal/.
Subject(s): Air Quality; American Indians
Publication(s): *Tribal Air Newsletter*, EP 4.67

TTNWeb Technology Transfer Network

http://www.epa.gov/ttn/

Sponsor(s): Environmental Protection Agency (EPA)—Air and Radiation Office

Description: TTNWeb provides centralized access to the technical information available on the Web from the EPA's Office of Air Quality Planning and Standards. The linked Web sites concern air pollution science, technology, regulation, measurement, and prevention. Sites include Emissions Test Methods and Information, National Ambient Air Quality Standards, and Inventories and Emission Factors.

Subject(s): Air Quality; Technology Transfer

WEATHER

AIRNow

http://airnow.gov/

Sponsor(s): Environmental Protection Agency (EPA)

Description: AIRNow offers daily Air Quality Index (AQI) forecasts and real-time AQI conditions for over 300 cities across the United States. AIRNow is an interagency Web site sponsored by the Environmental Protection Agency (EPA), the National Oceanic and Atmospheric Administration (NOAA), the National Aeronautics and Space Administration (NASA), the National Association of Clean Air Agencies, and the National Park Service (NPS), along with Canada and U.S. partner agencies in tribal, state, and local governments. Detailed local observations and forecasts on the site come from the partner agencies. The EnviroFlash feature provides e-mail or pager notification of current air quality conditions in many cities and towns in the United States.

AQI data can be downloaded from AIRNow in Keyhole Markup Language (KML) format, allowing the data to be used in 3D viewers such as Google Earth. Some content is available in Spanish.

Subject(s): Air Quality

Aviation Weather Center (AWC)

http://aviationweather.gov/

Sponsor(s): Commerce Department—National Oceanic and Atmospheric Administration (NOAA)—National Weather Service

Description: The Aviation Weather Center has forecasts, advisories, and observations for pilots. Observations include *Pilot Reports (PIREPs)*, *Meteorological Aviation Reports (METARs)*, and radar and satellite imagery. An Aviation Links section includes other aviation weather sites and Volcanic Ash Advisory Centers.

Subject(s): Aviation; Weather Forecasts

Climate Analysis Branch (CAB)

http://www.esrl.noaa.gov/psd/psd1/

Sponsor(s): Commerce Department—National Oceanic and Atmospheric Administration (NOAA)

Description: CAB, within NOAA's Earth System Research Laboratory, researches the causes of observed climate variations. CAB researches topics such as El Nino/La Nina and U.S. precipitation anomalies. Their Web site provides climate and weather data and interactive tools to chart or map the data.

Subject(s): Climate Research; El Nino

Climate Prediction Center

http://www.cpc.ncep.noaa.gov/

Sponsor(s): Commerce Department—National Oceanic and Atmospheric Administration (NOAA)—National Weather Service

Description: The Climate Prediction Center maintains a continuous watch on climate fluctuations and attempts to diagnose and predict them. This Web site provides climatological information, with highlights on long-term temperature and climate outlooks, U.S. Hazards Assessment, and U.S. Drought Assessment. The Outreach section has the center's publications, educational materials, and a climate glossary.

Subject(s): Climatology; El Nino; Weather Forecasts

Publication(s): *Climate Diagnostics Bulletin (monthly)*, C 55.194

Proceedings of the Climate Diagnostics and Prediction Workshop, C 55.2:C 61/3/

Global Systems Division

http://www.esrl.noaa.gov/gsd/

Sponsor(s): Commerce Department—National Oceanic and Atmospheric Administration (NOAA)

Description: Global Systems Division conducts research to develop global environmental information and forecast technology products. After development, technologies are transferred to National Weather Service, other government agencies, the commercial and general aviation communities, and others. The Web site describes the Global Systems Division's projects and products.

Subject(s): Meteorology—Research; Technology Transfer

Heat Island Effect

http://www.epa.gov/heatislands/

Sponsor(s): Environmental Protection Agency (EPA)

Description: The term "heat island" describes the phenomenon of urban and suburban temperatures that are two to ten degrees Fahrenheit hotter than nearby rural areas. This Web site provides information on the effect, research results, and energy use and health impacts. It also features a section on ameliorative measures, such as installing green roofing and planting trees.

Subject(s): Climate Research

National Climatic Data Center (NCDC)

http://www.ncdc.noaa.gov/

Alternate URL(s)

http://www.ncdc.noaa.gov/oa/ncdc.html

Sponsor(s): Commerce Department—National Oceanic and Atmospheric Administration (NOAA)—National Environmental Satellite, Data, and Information Service (NESDIS)

Description: As the world's largest active archive of weather data, NCDC produces numerous climate publications and data sets and makes a wide variety of information available on this site. Users may search for weather station data for a particular location or use a clickable map interface

NCDC presents various different catalogs and subsets of its products via links or online purchase. Some of the online data and publications require a paid subscription, with exemptions for education, military, and government use.

NCDC provides an enormous amount of information and data. The Web site manages to make it accessible by offering multiple well-designed approaches to the content.

Subject(s): Climatology; Data Products; Weather

Publication(s): *Climatological Data (various states)*, C 55.214/51

Hourly Precipitation Data: Various States and Countries, C 55.216/45

Local Climatological Data: Various States , C 55.286/6-54

Monthly Climatic Data for the World, C 55.211

Monthly State, Regional, and National Cooling Degree Days, Weighted by Population, C 55.287/60-3

Monthly State, Regional, and National Heating Degree Days, Weighted by Population, C 55.287/60-2

Storm Data (monthly), C 55.212

National Data Buoy Center (NDBC)

http://seaboard.ndbc.noaa.gov/

Sponsor(s): Commerce Department—National Oceanic and Atmospheric Administration (NOAA)—National Weather Service

Description: The National Data Buoy Center site provides buoy-measured environmental data and an overview of the NDBC. Current (Real-Time) Meteorological and Oceanographic Data are available for locations along the coasts of North America, Hawaii, the Caribbean, Brazil, Chile, France, Great Britain, and the Western Pacific. Historical data are also available, grouped by station ID. Other sections of the site include Station Status and Observations, and information on the Dial-a-Buoy program that provides station information over the telephone. The site also provides RSS feeds of observation data and a page designed specifically for mobile phone access.

Subject(s): Oceans; Weather Forecasts

National Hurricane Center—Tropical Prediction Center

http://www.nhc.noaa.gov/

Sponsor(s): Commerce Department—National Oceanic and Atmospheric Administration (NOAA)—National Weather Service

Description: The Tropical Prediction Center Web site features data, graphs, and other information on tropical cyclones and hurricanes. The site offers advisories that can be delivered via e-mail, RSS feed, or to mobile devices. Menu items on the home page include Marine Forecasts, Cyclone Forecasts, and Outreach & Education. This site covers conditions in the Atlantic and Eastern Pacific regions, and the latest forecasts are featured prominently, as are the site's Facebook and Twitter pages. It also links to tropical cyclone centers worldwide.

This is the key government Web site to consult during hurricane season.

Subject(s): Hurricanes

National Severe Storms Laboratory (NSSL)

http://www.nssl.noaa.gov/

Sponsor(s): Commerce Department—National Oceanic and Atmospheric Administration (NOAA)—Office of Oceanic and Atmospheric Research

Description: The NSSL site describes research and development work concerning forecasting, radar, and warnings. The Research Tools has a topical list of NSSL fields. The site also has an Education section with a "Severe Weather 101" primer and other content for children.

Subject(s): Tornadoes; Weather—Research
Publication(s): *NSSL Briefings*

National Weather Service (NWS)

http://www.weather.gov/

Sponsor(s): Commerce Department—National Oceanic and Atmospheric Administration (NOAA)—National Weather Service

Description: The National Weather Service (NWS) collects weather data and provides forecasts for the United States and surrounding waters. The NWS home page features a color-coded map of current weather warnings and advisories in the United States. A city/state name search box gives quick access to local short-and long-term weather forecasts, current conditions, and radar and satellite images. The Forecast section links to the forecasts available on NOAA Web sites, including hurricanes, fire, marine, aviation, and river flows. The Weather Safety section takes a similar approach, linking to NOAA Weather Radio and to safety information related to storms, heat, lightning, hurricanes, tornadoes, rip currents, and floods. Publications designed for the general public are available online in HTML and PDF formats. Some forecast information is available in Spanish.

The Organization section, under About, has links to the Web sites for the many NWS regional offices and centers, each of which provides a wealth of local U.S. data.

While the NWS data repository is vast, this Web site makes the most popular data easily accessible.

Subject(s): Meteorology; Weather Forecasts

National Weather Service Marine Forecasts

http://www.nws.noaa.gov/om/marine/home.htm

Sponsor(s): Commerce Department—National Oceanic and Atmospheric Administration (NOAA)—National Weather Service

Description: This gateway site links to marine weather forecast information. Shortcuts are provided to marine forecasts in text or graphic formats. Preparedness information on such topics as rip currents and thunderstorms is also provided.

Subject(s): Maritime Transportation; Weather Forecasts

Publication(s): *Mariner's Weather Log Magazine*, C 55.135

NOAA Tides and Currents

http://tidesandcurrents.noaa.gov/

Sponsor(s): Commerce Department—National Oceanic and Atmospheric Administration (NOAA)—National Ocean Service

Description: Tides and Currents is the Web site for the Center for Oceanographic Products and Services (CO-OPS). The center collects, analyzes, and distributes historical and real-time observations and predictions of water levels, coastal currents, and other meteorological and oceanographic data. The Web site features a zoomable data retrieval map and station list for finding all CO-OPS information by locale. CO-OPS programs include the Physical Oceanographic Real-Time System (PORTS) that integrates observed and predicted data for mariners. CO-OPS also manages the National Current Observation Program (NCOP). Tide data and predictions are available on the site. The Education section includes lesson plans about tides.

Subject(s): Oceanography

NOAA Weather Radio (NWR)

http://www.nws.noaa.gov/nwr/

Sponsor(s): Commerce Department—National Oceanic and Atmospheric Administration (NOAA)—National Weather Service

Description: NOAA Weather Radio (NWR) is a nationwide network of radio stations broadcasting continuous weather information that can be picked up by special radio receivers. This site has station listings, coverage maps, and consumer information on radio receivers. Other sections explain NWR's role as an "all hazards" radio network—broadcasting non-weather emergency information when requested by state or local state officials. The site is also available in Spanish.

Subjects: Disasters and Emergencies; Weather

NOAAWatch

http://www.noaawatch.gov/

Sponsor(s): Commerce Department—National Oceanic and Atmospheric Administration (NOAA)

Description: NOAAWatch, subtitled "NOAA's All Hazard Monitor," features current national weather news, charts, and imagery, and links to weather forecasts and warnings. Specific sections cover air quality, droughts, earthquakes, excessive heat, fire weather, flooding, hurricanes/ tropical weather, oil and chemical spills, tsunamis, volcanoes, and more.

Subjects: Weather forecasts

Storm Prediction Center (SPC)

http://www.spc.noaa.gov/

Sponsor(s): Commerce Department—National Oceanic and Atmospheric Administration (NOAA)—National Weather Service

Description: Storm Prediction Center provides forecasts for severe thunderstorms and tornadoes over the contiguous United States. The SPC also monitors heavy rain, heavy snow, and fire weather events across the United States. Their Web site reports on and maps current storm, tornado, fire, and convective watches. The Outreach section features extensive information about tornadoes and derechos. The Organization section on the top menu bar links to regional centers with more detailed local information. SPC also provides RSS feeds for tornado and severe thunderstorm watches, fire weather outlooks, and other topics.

Subject(s): Tornadoes; Weather Forecasts

Tsunami

http://www.tsunami.noaa.gov/

Sponsor(s): Commerce Department—National Oceanic and Atmospheric Administration (NOAA)

Description: The NOAA Tsunami Web site is largely concerned with the agency's responsibility for the nation's Tsunami Warning System. The site provides detailed background information about how tsunamis occur and about NOAA's role in forecasting tsunamis. It includes sections on current tsunami observations and data, tsunami preparedness and response, and public education. The Web site also has photos and animations of tsunamis.

Subject(s): Oceans

TWELVE

Government and Politics

This chapter covers some of the federal government's most familiar roles, such as tax collector, mail carrier, employer, purchaser, and provider of emergency relief.

Subsections in this chapter are Democracy, Government Administration, Government Business, Government Employees, Government Finance, Government Services, Intergovernmental Relations, and Public Policy.

DEMOCRACY

Campaign Finance Reports and Data
http://www.fec.gov/disclosure.shtml
Sponsor(s): Federal Election Commission (FEC)
Description: The FEC's campaign finance retrieval system includes financial data for candidates, campaign committees, and political action committees (PACs). Data can be viewed online or downloaded. Images of the actual campaign finance disclosure filings are also online. The site provides data on "electioneering communications," a category of political broadcast advertisements that became regulated under the Bipartisan Campaign Reform Act (BCRA) of 2002 (Public Law 107-155, also known as McCain-Feingold). The FEC has a Disclosure Data Blog on the site to report on content updates.

While the FEC site is easy to use, researchers may also want to try the nongovernment Open Secrets Web site at http://www.opensecrets.org. Open Secrets downloads FEC data and adds value, with an emphasis on current data and newsworthy reports.
Subject(s): Campaign Funds; Elections

Civics and Citizenship Toolkit

http://www.uscis.gov/citizenship/organizations/civics-and-citizenship-toolkit

Sponsor(s): Homeland Security Department—Citizenship and Immigration Service (USCIS)

Description: The Civics and Citizenship Toolkit publication is the product of a project to assist U.S. immigrants and is overseen by USCIS. The kit is distributed through public libraries, which can request a single, free copy using the Web site.

Subject(s): Citizenship; Civics Education

Core Documents of U.S. Democracy

http://www.fdsys.gov/

Alternate URL(s)

http://www.gpo.gov/libraries/core_docs.htm

Sponsor(s): Government Printing Office (GPO)

Description: With input from government documents librarians, GPO has developed a selective list of important current and historical government publications to feature as having "free, permanent, public access" on the GPO Access Web site. Although GPO aims to provide the same access to many other documents, these have been selected as being essential to an informed democratic process. The selection includes the Constitution of the United States of America, the Bill of Rights, the Declaration of Independence, Supreme Court decisions, congressional bills and the Congressional Record, the United States Code, the Budget of the United States Government, the Federal Register, and the Code of Federal Regulations. GPO began offering these documents on its new FDsys.gov system in late 2010; they are currently on the GPO Access Web site as well.

Subject(s): Government Publications

Democratic National Committee

http://www.democrats.org/

Sponsor(s): Democratic National Committee (DNC)

Description: The national Democratic Party Web site features news on politics and policy, a blog, Twitter feeds, and a directory of local party organizations throughout the United States. Interactive features focus on online voter registration, fundraising, volunteering, and interning. The site also has a version available in Spanish.

Subject(s): Political Parties

Election Assistance Commission (EAC)

http://www.eac.gov/

Sponsor(s): United States Election Assistance Commission

Description: The EAC was established by the Help America Vote Act of 2002 (HAVA) to provide guidance and funding to improve the administration of federal elections. Its Web site features information about HAVA and the competitive grant programs authorized by HAVA to improve the administration of elections. The Payments and Grants section has updates to the state HAVA plans originally filed in 2004. The EAC site also has information on the testing and certification of voting systems, resources for elections officials, the National Mail Voter Registration Form, and helpful information for voters. Information is available in Spanish, Vietnamese, and other languages.

Subject(s): Elections—Regulations

Electioneering Communications Database

http://gullfoss2.fcc.gov/ecd/

Sponsor(s): Federal Communications Commission (FCC)—Media Bureau

Description: This Web site is intended to help political campaigns comply with a provision of the Federal Election Campaign Act of 1971, which requires candidates who spend more than $10,000 on an "electioneering communication" during any calendar year to file a statement with the Federal Election Commission. The database helps users determine if their broadcasts qualify as an electioneering communications.

Subject(s): Elections—Regulations

Electoral College

http://www.archives.gov/federal-register/electoral-college/

Sponsor(s): National Archives and Records Administration (NARA)—Electoral College

Description: The National Archives oversees the Electoral College and provides this Web site to inform the public about how its works. The site features statistics and summaries of the votes in the Electoral College for every presidential election since the election of George Washington. Other features include the Make a Prediction tool and Frequently Asked Questions. Users can also view the states' certificates for their electors and for the electors' votes.

Subject(s): Electoral College

Federal Election Commission (FEC)

http://www.fec.gov/

Sponsor(s): Federal Election Commission (FEC)

Description: FEC is an independent regulatory agency whose mission is to disclose campaign finance information, enforce provisions of the law such as the limits and prohibitions on contributions, and oversee the public funding of presidential elections. The Campaign Finance Disclosure Portal section of the site provides finance data for candidates, campaign committees, and political action committees. The Enforcement Matters section has audit reports and a database of documents related to completed enforcement cases. The Law, Regulations and Procedures section has FEC advisory opinions, information on FEC litigation, and information on major campaign laws. Other sections include Meetings and Hearings and Help with Reporting and Compliance. A section called Quick Answers discusses frequently asked-about issues that typically come from candidates, state party committees, researchers, and the general public.

Subject(s): Campaign Funds—Laws; Voting—Statistics

Publication(s): *Campaign Guide for Congressional Candidates and Committees*, Y 3.EL 2/3

Campaign Guide for Corporations and Labor Organizations, Y 3.El 2/3

Campaign Guide for Nonconnected Committees , Y 3.EL 2/3

Campaign Guide for Political Party Committees , Y 3.El 2/3

Record Newsletter, Y 3.EL 2/3

Selected Court Case Abstracts, Y 3.EL 2/3

The FEC and the Federal Campaign Finance Law, Y 3.EL 2/3

Federal Voting Assistance Program (FVAP)

http://www.fvap.gov/

Sponsor(s): Defense Department—Federal Voting Assistance Program (FVAP)

Description: FVAP provides U.S. citizens worldwide with a broad range of nonpartisan information and assistance to facilitate their participation in the voting process, regardless of where they work or live. Located within the Department of Defense, FVAP is responsible for serving military personnel, their families, and other U.S. citizens residing outside the United States. The main page of the site is designed for U.S. voters who are overseas, but the site also has sections for local elections officials and voting assistance officers. The site includes instructions for civilian and military voters and supplies an online version of the federal postcard application for voter registration and absentee ballots.

Subject(s): Voting

Improving U.S. Voting Systems

http://vote.nist.gov/

Sponsor(s): Commerce Department—Technology Administration (TA)—National Institute of Standards and Technology (NIST)

Description: NIST was charged with advising the Election Assistance Commission on the development of technical guidelines for voting systems. This Web site provides news, background, and research reports related to the development of the technical guidelines.

Subject(s): Voting

Republican National Committee

http://www.gop.com/

Sponsor(s): Republican National Committee (RNC)

Description: The RNC Web site has sections on how to become active in supporting the party, how to register to vote online, and how to make contributions online. The site also has a directory of the Republican Party's state offices, blogs, and issue statements.

Subject(s): Political Parties

Tax Information for Political Organizations

http://www.irs.gov/Charities-&-Non-Profits/Political-Organizations

Sponsor(s): Treasury Department—Internal Revenue Service (IRS)

Description: This IRS Web page focuses on reporting and disclosure requirements for political parties, campaign committees, and political action committees, which fall under section 527 of the Internal Revenue Code.

Subject(s): Campaign Funds

GOVERNMENT ADMINISTRATION

Administrative Conference of the United States

http://www.acus.gov/

Sponsor(s): Administrative Conference of the United States (ACUS)

Description: Established in 1968, the Administrative Conference was not funded by Congress between 1995 and 2010. Currently, ACUS develops recommendations to improve the fairness and effectiveness of rulemaking and other activities of federal agencies. The Web site provides information on the agency's activities and organization.

Subject(s): Regulatory Policy

Chief Information Officers (CIO) Council

http://www.cio.gov/

Sponsor(s): Chief Information Officers Council

Description: The CIO Council is the principal interagency forum focused on federal agency management of information technology. The site provides information on council membership, meetings, and projects. It links to blogs written by members of different federal agencies.

Subject(s): Information Technology

Federal Executive Boards (FEBs)

http://www.feb.gov/

Sponsor(s): Office of Personnel Management (OPM)

Description: FEBs coordinate many of the activities carried out by federal agency regional offices, which are located outside the national capital area. Based in 28 cities and regions and with a large federal presence, FEBs operate under the direction of OPM and are concerned with coordination in such areas as management strategies, personnel programs, and community relations. This Web site provides background information about the boards and links to each of the local FEB Web sites.

Subject(s): Government Administration

General Services Administration (GSA)

http://www.gsa.gov/

Sponsor(s): General Services Administration (GSA)

Description: GSA procures and manages federal office space, vehicles, technology, and supplies. The agency also sells off surplus government property. GSA's activities are described in this Web site's Buildings & Real Estate and Products & Services sections under What GSA Offers. In the same section, the Policy & Regulations content covers GSA's role in setting rules for management of federal acquisitions, real property, travel, and more. The Doing Business with GSA section provides details on opportunities for selling services and supplies to the federal government. While GSA mostly works with federal agencies or government contractors, the site includes a section for citizens and consumers, including information on consumer issues and government surplus property sales. Other popularly requested information includes federal per diem rates, the Federal Acquisition Regulations, forms, and procurement information for vendors.

Because GSA is involved in a wide range of activities, first-time users may wish to browse the site map to become familiar with the variety of information available on the site.

Subject(s): Government Administration; Government Procurement; Public Buildings

Publication(s): *Federal Acquisition Regulation*, GS 1.6/10

Federal Fleet Report, GS 2.18

Federal Supply Schedule (by Group), GS 2.7/4

Federal Travel Regulation, GS 1.6/8-2

Forms (GSA), GS 1.13

Index of Federal Specifications, Standards and Commercial Item Descriptions, GS 2.8/2

Worldwide Geographic Location Codes, GS 1.34

IDManagement.gov

http://www.idmanagement.gov/

Sponsor(s): General Services Administration (GSA)

Description: IDManagement.gov provides news and background information on the security technology and procedures the federal government is applying to its operations. The Web site features sections on the Homeland Security Presidential Directive 12 (HSPD-12) Policy for a

Common Identification Standard for Federal Employees and Contractors, Federal Public Key Infrastructure (FPKI), and other solutions.

Subject(s): Computer Security; Homeland Security

IGnet—Federal Inspectors General

http://www.ignet.gov/

Sponsor(s): Office of Government Ethics (OGE)

Description: IGnet is a gateway site that serves the federal inspectors general (IG) community, whose members are the offices of the inspectors general that conduct audits, investigations, and inspections. The site includes a directory of agency inspector generals, links to their Web sites, and information about the role of the IGs.

IGnet provides a broad range of materials for both IG employees and for whistleblowers interested in contacting one of the IG offices.

Subject(s): Inspectors General

Publication(s): *The Journal of Public Inquiry*, PREX 2.36/3

Office of Government Ethics (OGE)

http://www.usoge.gov/

Sponsor(s): Office of Government Ethics (OGE)

Description: OGE coordinates activities in the Executive Branch related to the prevention of conflicts of interest on the part of government employees and the resolution of conflicts of interest that do occur. The site features information for the general public, for international interests, and for the media. The Financial Disclosure section has subsections for public and confidential disclosure. The Laws & Regulations section provides the complete text of applicable executive orders, Federal Register issuances, employee standards of conduct, and statutes and regulations related to the Executive Branch ethics program.

The OGE site also has substantial information about agency model practices, easily accessible by clicking on the Site Index link.

Subject(s): Ethics in Government; Government Employees—Regulations

Publication(s): *Compilation of Federal Ethics Laws*, Y 4.G 74/9

Standards of Ethical Conduct for Employees of the Executive Branch, Y 3.ET 3

Office of Governmentwide Policy (OGP)

http://www.gsa.gov/ogp/

Sponsor(s): General Services Administration (GSA)—Office of Governmentwide Policy (OGP)

Description: OGP was created to consolidate all of GSA's governmentwide policy-making activities within one central office. These activities include acquisitions, government travel, and internal management systems. The site links to OGP's component offices, such as the Office of

Acquisition Policy, the Office of Executive Councils, and the Office of Travel, Transportation, and Asset Management.

Subject(s): Government Administration—Policy; Government Procurement—Policy

Office of Management and Budget (OMB)

http://www.whitehouse.gov/omb/

Sponsor(s): Office of Management and Budget (OMB)

Description: OMB assists the president in overseeing the preparation of the federal budget and supervises budget administration in executive branch agencies. In addition, OMB oversees the administration's procurement, financial management, information, and regulatory policies. OMB's Web site covers each of these areas of responsibility.

Primary sections of the site include The Budget, Management, Regulation & Information Policy, Legislative Information, and OMBlog. The site includes *OMB Circulars*, the *OMB Bulletin*, OMB memoranda, and privacy guidance for executive agencies. Documents under The Budget section include budget supplementals and amendments. The Regulation & Information Policy section includes information about federal statistical programs and standards, regulatory policy, information policy, and e-government.

OMB news releases, circulars, and Statements of Administration Policy are available as RSS feeds.

In addition to the collection of federal budget documents, this site is useful for the availability of the *OMB Circulars*, such as *OMB Circular A-130*, which establishes administration policy for the management of federal information resources, and *OMB Circular A-76*, which concerns federal policy for the competition of commercial activities. OMB's *Statements of Administration Policy*, found in the Legislative Information section, will be helpful to those tracking bills in which the administration has a strong interest.

Subject(s): Budget of the U.S. Government; Government Administration

Publication(s): *Budget of the Unites States Government*, PREX 2.8/8

Mid-Session Review of the . . . Budget, PREX 2.31

OMB Bulletin, PREX 2.3

OMB Circulars, PREX 2.4

Statements of Administration Policy on Non-Appropriations and Appropriations Bills, PREX 2.2

The Statistical Program of the United States Government, PREX 2.10/3

OMB Blog

http://www.whitehouse.gov/omb/blog/

Sponsor(s): Office of Management and Budget (OMB)

Description: The OMB Blog is written by the office's staffers. The blog discusses government budget policy, regulatory policy, and other topics within OMB's purview. It is not open for comments. Entries can be shared via e-mail and Twitter. An RSS subscription service is available.

Subject(s): Budget of the U.S. Government—Policy; Blogs

Performance.gov
> http://www.performance.gov/
> **Sponsor(s):** White House
> **Description:** Performance.gov tracks the performance of federal agencies in regard to contract spending, proper and improper payments, real estate streamlining and downsizing, technological productivity, and personnel performance. The site includes information about the areas of focus, links to participating agencies, a frequently asked questions section, and a link to provide feedback.
> **Subject(s):** Performance Evaluation

Treasury Inspector General for Tax Administration (TIGTA)
> http://www.treasury.gov/tigta/
> **Sponsor(s):** Treasury Department—Treasury Inspector General for Tax Administration (TIGTA)
> **Description:** TIGTA provides independent oversight of Internal Revenue Service (IRS) activities, serving in effect as an inspector general for the IRS. The TIGTA Web site explains the office's role and posts copies of its audit reports and congressional testimony. The site also has information about the TIGTA hotline and an online form for reporting any knowledge of IRS waste, fraud, or abuse.
> **Subject(s):** Inspectors General; Taxation
> **Publication(s):** *Semiannual Report to Congress (TIGTA)*, T 1.1/6

United States Government Manual
> http://www.fdsys.gov/
> **Alternate URL(s)**
> http://www.gpo.gov/fdsys/browse/collection.action?collectionCode=GOVMAN
> **Sponsor(s):** National Archives and Records Administration (NARA)
> **Description:** The official, annual *United States Government Manual* is a descriptive directory of the executive, legislative, and judicial agencies of the federal government. It also includes information on quasi-official agencies; international organizations; and boards, commissions, and committees. The manual is available on the Government Printing Office FDsys online service for 1995-1996 to the present. Content is available in text and PDF versions, but only the PDF version contains the agency organization charts and other graphics. The manual can be directly accessed at the alternate URL listed above.

The strength of the *United States Government Manual* lies in the descriptions of the agencies, how they were established, what they do, and the nature of their primary divisions, as well as in the publication's helpful appendixes. As with the print edition, users of the online version of this reference classic will want to check more frequently updated sources—such as agency Web sites—for current personnel and organizational information.

Subject(s): Federal Government; Directories
Publication(s): *United States Government Manual*, AE 2.108/2

GOVERNMENT BUSINESS

AbilityOne
http://www.abilityone.gov/
Sponsor(s): Committee for Purchase From People Who Are Blind or Severely Disabled
Description: Through federal procurement policies, the AbilityOne program (formerly known as Javits-Wagner-O'Day or JWOD) generates jobs and training opportunities for people who are blind or have other severe disabilities. AbilityOne is administered by the Committee for Purchase From People Who Are Blind or Severely Disabled, an independent federal agency. Its Web site includes information about the committee, relevant laws and notices, a procurement list, program contacts, and information about how to participate.
Subject(s): Disabilities; Government Procurement—Policy

Acquisition Central
http://www.acquisition.gov/
Sponsor(s): General Services Administration (GSA)
Description: The Acquisition Central Web site is a central collection point for news, reference, and regulatory information needed by individuals and organizations involved in government contracting and procurement. It links to the Federal Acquisition Regulations (FAR) and to Web sites relevant to contractor performance evaluations, bid protests, individual agency procurement, and professional development for government contracting personnel.
Subject(s): Government Procurement; Military Procurement
Publication(s): *Federal Acquisition Regulation*, GS 1.6/10

Acquisition One Source
http://www.secnav.navy.mil/rda/OneSource/Pages/default.aspx
Sponsor(s): Navy
Description: Acquisition One Source provides authoritative acquisitions policy, regulations, and other information of interest to the Navy

acquisitions and procurement community. Information is grouped under subjects such as Bridge Contract Policy, Business Opportunities, and Strategic Sourcing.

Subject(s): Military Procurement

Civilian Board of Contract Appeals (CBCA)

http://www.cbca.gsa.gov/

Sponsor(s): General Services Administration (GSA)—Civilian Board of Contract Appeals (CBCA)

Description: The CBCA hears and decides contract disputes between government contractors and executive agencies for all agencies except the Department of Defense, Army, Navy, Air Force, National Aeronautics and Space Administration (NASA), United States Postal Service, Postal Rate Commission, and Tennessee Valley Authority. The Web site has copies of the board's decisions and rules of procedure. It also carries decisions from the boards it superseded.

Subjects(s): Government Contracts

Commission on Wartime Contracting

http://www.wartimecontracting.gov

Alternate URL(s)

http://cybercemetery.unt.edu/archive/cwc/20110929213815/

http://www.wartimecontracting.gov/

Sponsor(s): Congress—Commission on Wartime Contracting in Iraq and Afghanistan

The Commission on Wartime Contracting in Iraq and Afghanistan, established by Congress, issued an interim report in 2009 and its final report in 2011. "The Commission is required to study, assess and make recommendations concerning wartime contracting for the reconstruction, logistical support, and the performance of security functions in Iraq and Afghanistan. The Commission's major objectives include a thorough assessment of the systemic problems identified with interagency wartime contracting, the identification of instances of waste, fraud and abuse, and ensuring accountability for those responsible." (from the Web site) The Web site has commission briefings, hearings, special reports, and a meetings schedule.

This Web site was archived in December 2011. It is hosted by the University of North Texas on behalf of the National Archives and Records Administration.

Subject(s): Military Procurement

Publication(s): *At What Risk? Correcting Over-Reliance on Contractors in Contingency Operations*

Defense Logistics Agency Disposition Services

http://www.dispositionservices.dla.mil/

Sponsor(s): Defense Department—Defense Reutilization and Marketing Service (DRMS)

Description: Due to the launch of the We Are DLA initiative in 2010, the Defense Logistics Agency Disposition Services Web site was established. With headquarters in Michigan, the Disposition Services division is involved with the disposal of excess property from military services, selling DoD surplus property, and maintaining environmental conscientiousness. Sections include information on such topics as turn-in documentation; property searches for military, state, federal, and special programs; and property for sale to the public.

Subject(s): Surplus Government Property

DLA Land and Maritime

http://www.dscc.dla.mil/

Sponsor(s): Defense Department—Defense Logistics Agency (DLA)

Description: DLA Land and Maritime, a Department of Defense procurement and supply center, offers information about military procurement and about buying from and selling to the center. The site links to the DLA-EBS Internet Bid Board System (DIBBS) and to the DoD EMALL (Electronic Mall) system.

Subject(s): Military Procurement

eSRS: Electronic Subcontracting Reporting System

http://www.esrs.gov/

Sponsor(s): General Services Administration (GSA)

Description: The Federal Funding Accountability and Transparency Act of 2006, Public Law 109-282, requires subcontract award data as part of the USAspending.gov database. (USAspending.gov is described in a separate entry.) The Electronic Subcontracting Reporting System, or eSRS, collects this data from federal government contractors.

Subject(s): Government Contracts

FedBizOpps

http://www.fedbizopps.gov/

Alternate URL(s)

http://www.fbo.gov/

Sponsor(s): General Services Administration (GSA)

Description: FedBizOpps is the central clearinghouse for information about federal government procurement notices in excess of $25,000. Vendors seeking government business opportunities on FedBizOpps can search the full-text versions of notices and limit searches by agency, set-aside code, date range, and other criteria. The site provides subscribers with free e-mail notification of procurement announcements. Online videos demonstrate how to use FedBizOpps.

Subject(s): Government Contracts; Government Procurement

Federal Acquisition Jumpstation

http://prod.nais.nasa.gov/pub/fedproc/home.html

Sponsor(s): National Aeronautics and Space Administration (NASA)

Description: The Federal Acquisition Jumpstation provides a simple list of links to federal agency Web pages concerned with procurement, contracts, and grants.

Subject(s): Government Procurement

Federal Acquisition Regulation (FAR)

http://www.acquisition.gov/far/

Sponsor(s): General Services Administration (GSA)

Description: This version of FAR provides access to HTML, zipped HTML, and PDF versions of the regulations. It includes PDF files of Federal Acquisition Circulars in both their looseleaf and Federal Register printing formats. There are also special sections for proposed rules and for Small Entity Compliance Guidelines. Users can subscribe to the Acquisition News e-mail service to receive news of circulars, proposed rules, public meetings, and other information about FAR-related issues.

Subject(s): Government Procurement—Regulations

Publication(s): *Federal Acquisition Regulation*, GS 1.6/10

Federal Acquisition Service (FAS)

http://www.gsa.gov/fas

Sponsor(s): General Services Administration (GSA)

Description: FAS was formed in late 2006 by combining the Federal Technology Service with the Federal Supply Service. FAS offers procurement services for federal government agencies. Its Web site has information about the organization and links to its component offices.

Subject(s): Government Procurement

Federal Laboratory Consortium for Technology Transfer

http://www.federallabs.org/

Sponsor(s): Federal Laboratory Consortium (FLC)

Description: The Federal Laboratory Consortium for Technology Transfer helps to move the federal laboratories' research and development into the U.S. private sector. On the Web site, the FLC's tool for locating technology allows users to request technical assistance and be partnered with the appropriate laboratory. The site also has a searchable directory of FLC laboratories, as well as a link to the FLC Facebook page.

Subject(s): Technology Transfer

Federal Procurement Data System — Next Generation
https://www.fpds.gov/fpdsng_cms/index.php/en/
Sponsor(s): General Services Administration (GSA)
Description: The Federal Procurement Data System — Next Generation (FPDS-NG) is the central repository of statistical information about
federal executive branch contracting. It contains detailed information
about contract awards over $3,000. Free registration is required to search
the data, which is also available free of charge. Selected reports and "top
requests" (such as Recovery Act contracts) are available from the main
page without signing in.
    FPDS-NG, launched with fiscal year 2004 data, was designed to meet
the need for faster reporting of contract actions. Since then, the federal
government has launched the USAspending.gov Web site for both
contracts and assistance (grants and loans) reporting. The USAspend-
ing.gov contract information is based on FPDS-NG data.
    Subject(s): Government Contracts

GovSales.gov
http://www.govsales.gov/
Sponsor(s): General Services Administration (GSA)
Description: The tagline for GovSales.gov is "The Official Site to Find
U.S. Government Property." The site has separate sections for each type
of goods, including real estate, computers, and industrial. See the FAQs
section on the top menu bar for important information about registering
and bidding.
    Subject(s): Government Auctions; Surplus Government Property

GSA Advantage!
https://www.gsaadvantage.gov/
Sponsor(s): General Services Administration (GSA)
Description: This GSA Web site, for use by federal government agencies only, is an online shopping and supply site. Authorized users can use
government credit cards to purchase products from the Federal Supply
Service. Non-registered users can browse the products catalog.
    Subject(s): Government Procurement

iEdison
http://www.iedison.gov/
Sponsor(s): National Institutes of Health (NIH)
Description: Government grantees and contractors are required to
report any government-funded inventions to the federal agency that
made the award. Interagency Edison, or iEdison, is an online system
designed to streamline the administrative tasks involved in complying
with this requirement. It can be used to report to a number of agencies,

including the Department of Energy and the National Institutes of Health.

Subject(s): Intellectual Property

NASA Acquisition Internet Service

http://prod.nais.nasa.gov/

Sponsor(s): National Aeronautics and Space Administration (NASA)

Description: The NASA Acquisition Internet Service Web site provides a central online point of contact for businesses interested in NASA acquisitions and procurement opportunities. The site includes the annual NASA acquisition forecasts and the NASA Procurement Data View (NPDV) system. The site also offers an e-mail alert system for news about NASA opportunities.

Subject(s): Government Procurement

SBIR and STTR Awards

http://www.sbir.gov/past-awards

Sponsor(s): Small Business Administration (SBA)

Description: The Small Business Innovation Research and Small Business Technology Transfer programs are competitive funding programs that encourage innovative research and development in small businesses and nonprofit research institutions. They are offered by agencies with large research and development budgets and are coordinated by SBA. This section of the SBIR/STTR site provides graphical demographic breakdowns of past award winners.

Subject(s): Small Business—Grants

Small and Disadvantaged Business Utilization (OSDBU)

http://www.dm.usda.gov/smallbus/

Sponsor(s): Agriculture Department (USDA)—Small and Disadvantaged Business Utilization Office (OSDBU)

Description: The mission of OSDBU is to assist small businesses with the Department of Agriculture's contracting process. Its Web site includes a directory of subcontracting opportunities, the USDA Forecast of Business Opportunities, and small business community events.

Subject(s): Government Procurement; Small Business

Publication(s): *USDA Forecast of Business Opportunities*

SUB-Net

http://web.sba.gov/subnet/

Sponsor(s): Small Business Administration (SBA)

Description: This Web site was designed primarily as a place for businesses to post solicitations and notices. Prime contractors can use SUB-Net to post subcontracting opportunities. These may or may not be reserved for small business and they may include either solicitations or other notices, such as notices of sources sought for teaming partners and subcontractors on future contracts. Small businesses can use this site to identify opportunities in their areas of expertise. Major sections of the Web site are Search, Post, and Help.

Subject(s): Government Contracts

System for Award Management (SAM)

http://www.ccr.gov/

Sponsor(s): Defense Department; General Services Administration (GSA)

Description: The SAM Web site is a single point of access and registration for vendors who want to do business with the federal government. The site includes a section for user guides and helpful hints and space for news and announcements.

Subject(s): Defense Contracting; Government Procurement

UNICOR—Federal Prison Industries, Inc.

http://www.unicor.gov/

Sponsor(s): Federal Prison Industries, Inc.

Description: The UNICOR Web site allows the federal government and contractors to buy goods and services from Federal Prison Industries (FPI), Inc., whose primary mission is the productive employment of inmates. The site has an online product catalog with browsing and ordering capabilities. It also provides substantial background information on the Inmate Training Programs.

Subject(s): Government Procurement; Prisoners

USA.gov Government Sales and Auctions

http://www.usa.gov/shopping/shopping.shtml

Sponsor(s): General Services Administration (GSA)

Description: The USA.gov Web site section that deals with government sales and auctions describes it purpose as one that allows users to "buy new, seized, and surplus merchandise and real estate from the government." This portal to other government Internet resources is divided into the following sections: Federal Government Surplus and Seized Property Sales; State and Local Surplus Property Sales; Government Stores - Souvenirs, Books, and Gifts; and Sales, by Federal Agency, which serves as an index to the sales-related pages on agency Web sites.

Subject(s): Government Auctions; Surplus Government Property

USDA Procurement

http://www.dm.usda.gov/procurement/

Sponsor(s): Agriculture Department (USDA)

Description: This procurement site from the Department of Agriculture's Departmental Management provides guidance on the department's highly decentralized procurement activities. The site provides news, updates, the Acquisition Toolkit, information on policy and regulations, and links to related USDA information.

Subject(s): Government Procurement

GOVERNMENT EMPLOYEES

Federal Labor Relations Authority (FLRA)

http://www.flra.gov/

Sponsor(s): Federal Labor Relations Authority (FLRA)

Description: FLRA is an independent agency responsible for administering the labor-management relations program for federal employees. Its Web site includes information about filing a case with FLRA and the types of cases it handles. It also carries the decisions made by FLRA and the statutes and regulations under which it does its work.

Subject(s): Government Employees; Labor-Management Relations

Publication(s): *Decisions of the Federal Labor Relations Authority*, Y 3.F 31/21-3:10-4/

Federal Retirement Thrift Investment Board (FRTIB)

http://www.frtib.gov/

Sponsor(s): Federal Retirement Thrift Investment Board

Description: The Federal Retirement Thrift Investment Board administers the Thrift Savings Plan (TSP) for federal employees. Its Web site includes a Reading Room with the board's annual TSP audit report and other frequently requested documents. The site also links to TSP contact information and publications.

Subject(s): Government Employees

FedScope

http://www.fedscope.opm.gov/

Sponsor(s): Office of Personnel Management (OPM)

Description: FedScope is a central access point for data about the federal government's civilian workforce. Its Web site provides flexible retrieval of aggregate statistics extracted from OPM's Central Personnel Data File on topics including length of service, gender and age, pay grades, work schedules, and employment location. The Employment Statistics link on the top menu leads to electronic publications compiling historical trends and data. Data products are typically available in PDF and spreadsheet formats.

It may be particularly helpful for users to review the About Our Data and Data Source/Definitions sections before using the FedScope data in analyses.

Subject(s): Government Employees—Statistics
Publication(s): *Employment and Trends*, PM 1.15

FedsHireVets.gov

http://fedshirevets.gov/
Sponsor(s): Office of Personnel Management (OPM)
Description: FedsHireVets.gov is part of the Veterans Employment Initiative, established by executive order in 2009. The Web site is intended to be a central source for federal employment information for veterans, transitioning service members and their families, and federal hiring managers. The site has a section for individuals looking for a job and for agency human resources personnel looking to hire. It also has a directory of Veteran Employment Program Offices.
Subject(s): Veterans

Merit Systems Protection Board (MSPB)

http://www.mspb.gov/
Sponsor(s): Merit Systems Protection Board (MSPB)
Description: MSPB serves as guardian of the federal government's merit-based system of employment, primarily by hearing and deciding appeals from federal employees concerning removals and other major personnel actions. The board also hears and decides other types of civil service cases, reviews significant actions and regulations of the Office of Personnel Management, and conducts studies of the merit systems. Its Web site includes additional descriptive information about the board, along with links to decisions, studies, and information on how to file an appeal.
Subject(s): Government Employees; Labor-Management Relations
Publication(s): *Decisions of U.S. Merit Systems Protection Board*, MS 1.10

National Personnel Records Center (NPRC)

http://www.archives.gov/st-louis/
Alternate URL(s)
http://www.archives.gov/veterans/military-service-records/
Sponsor(s): National Archives and Records Administration (NARA)
Description: NPRC in St. Louis is a central repository for federal civil service and military personnel records. Its Web site describes the collections and how to request information. The records themselves are not available online. A special site, eVetRecs, allows veterans and the next of kin of deceased veterans to request records online. The eVetRecs site is available at the alternate URL listed above.
Subject(s): Government Employees; Veterans

Office of Compliance

http://www.compliance.gov/

Sponsor(s): Office of Compliance

Description: The Office of Compliance is an independent agency that was established by the Congressional Accountability Act of 1995 to protect the safety, health, and workplace rights of covered employees in the legislative branch. Its Web site includes information about employee rights, the directives of the board of directors, regulations, and procedural rules.

Subject(s): Labor Law; Legislative Branch—Regulations

Office of Personnel Management (OPM)

http://www.opm.gov/

Sponsor(s): Office of Personnel Management (OPM)

Description: As the federal government personnel office, OPM is a primary source for information about working for the federal government. OPM displays the current operating status of the federal government (for example, for holidays) and features sections for federal job seekers, federal employees, retirees, and human resources practitioners. The OPM Web site's home page links directly to the most requested pages, including the USAJOBS employment Web site, the Feds Hire Vets site, forms, wages and salaries, and information on retirement benefits. Links to reports to the president and to Congress, to Inspector General reports, and to the OPM Publications database can be found under News. Use the site's helpful subject index to find additional information.

Subject(s): Government Employees; Personnel Management

Publication(s): *CSRS and FERS Handbook for Personnel and Payroll*, PM 1.14/3-3

Demographic Profile of the Federal Workforce, PM 1.10/2-3

Employment and Trends as of . . . (bimonthly), PM 1.15

Federal Equal Opportunity Recruitment Program, Report to Congress, PM 1.42

Guide to Personnel Data Standards, PM 1.14/3

Guide to Processing Personnel Actions, PM 1.14/3-4

Position Classification Standards, PM 1.30

Salary Tables, Executive Branch of the Government, PM 1.9

Presidential Management Fellows Program

http://www.pmf.gov/

Sponsor(s): Office of Personnel Management (OPM)

Description: The Presidential Management Fellows Program is designed to recruit for public service a variety of outstanding citizens interested in the leadership and management of public policies and programs. This site provides information on the program and how to apply.

Subject(s): Government Employees

Salaries and Wages

http://www.opm.gov/policy-data-oversight/pay-leave/salaries-wages/#url=2015

Sponsor(s): Office of Personnel Management (OPM)

Description: This official OPM Web site for government-wide pay programs for federal employees has information about the General Schedule (GS), Law Enforcement Pay Schedules, and the Memorandum on Executive Order for 2015 Pay Schedules. It provides a variety of resources. Most of the schedules are presented in PDF format. The following schedules are available: General Schedule and Locality Pay Tables, Law Enforcement Officer (LEO) General Schedule Locality Pay Tables, Executive & Senior Level Employee Pay Tables, and Special Rate Tables.

Subject(s): Government Employees; Pay and Benefits

Telework.gov

http://www.telework.gov/

Sponsor(s): Office of Personnel Management (OPM)

Description: Telework.gov provides guidance, policies, procedures, and studies related to telecommuting for federal government employees.

Subject(s): Government Employees—Policy

Publication(s): *Status of Telework in the Federal Government*

Thrift Savings Plan (TSP)

http://www.tsp.gov/

Sponsor(s): Federal Retirement Thrift Investment Board

Description: TSP is a retirement savings plan for federal civilian employees and for uniformed services members. This site offers basic information about the service, participation, and retirement planning.

Subject(s): Government Employees

U.S. Office of Special Counsel (OSC)

http://www.osc.gov/

Sponsor(s): Office of Special Counsel (OSC)

Description: OSC is an independent federal investigative and prosecutorial agency that is responsible for protecting federal employees and applicants from prohibited personnel practices, especially reprisal for whistleblowing. The agency is also concerned with adherence to the Hatch Act, which restricts political activity by federal government employees. Major sections of its Web site explain prohibited personnel practices, whistleblower procedures and protections, and Hatch Act rules. The site also covers the Uniformed Services Employment and Reemployment Rights Act (USERRA), which prohibits discrimination against persons because of their service in the Armed Forces Reserve, the National Guard, or other uniformed services. The site provides summaries of a variety of successful Special Counsel cases. The Resources section includes OSC publications and the Public Filing documents associated with recently closed whistleblower cases.

Subject(s): Government Employees—Laws; Hatch Act

Publication(s): *Annual Reports to Congress from the U.S. Office of Special Counsel*, MS 2.1

GOVERNMENT FINANCE

Budget of the United States Government

http://www.whitehouse.gov/omb/budget/

Alternate URL(s)

http://www.fdsys.gov/

Sponsor(s): Office of Management and Budget (OMB)

Description: OMB provides the full-text version of the current U.S. budget, supporting documents, and additional information online. Most of the files are available in PDF format, with some tables available in spreadsheet format. The Government Printing Office's FDsys.gov Web service has copies of the budget online for the past several years; it can be accessed at the alternate URL above. The FDsys system provides the extra functionality of a word search across the U.S. budgets.

Subject(s): Budget of the U.S. Government; Government Finance

Publication(s): *Analytical Perspectives*, PREX 2.8/5

Budget of the United States Government, PREX 2.8

Budget of the United States Government, Appendix, PREX 2.8

Economic Report of the President, Pr 42.9

Historical Tables, Budget of the United States Government, PREX 2.8/8

Mid-Session Review of The Budget, PREX 2.31

Bureau of the Fiscal Service

http://www.fiscal.treasury.gov/

Sponsor(s): Treasury Department

Description: The Bureau of the Fiscal Service was established in October 2012 through the merging of the Treasury's Bureau of the Public Debt and the Financial Management Service. The Bureau of the Fiscal Service operates the government's collections and deposit systems; uses the sale of Treasury bonds, notes, and bills to borrow the money needed to operate the government; provides access to TreasuryDirect (described in a separate entry), where Treasury securities can be purchased online; and offers administrative, reporting, and other finance-related managerial services. The site provides information about the bureau's reports, publications, and programs.

Department of the Treasury
http://www.treasury.gov/
Sponsor(s): Treasury Department
Description: The Treasury Department's Web site provides current news and links to the issues handled by the department. The "Treasury For . . ." section links to information for the general public, business, financial institutions, and government. The Initiatives section provides information about such topics as Wall Street reform and housing finance reform. Data and charts can be found under Resource Center. The Treasury Notes blog can be found under Connect With Us and on the right-hand site of the home page, while a link to Treasury auctions can be found on the home page.
Subject(s): Government Finance

Federal Accounting Standards Advisory Board (FASAB)
http://www.fasab.gov/
Sponsor(s): Federal Accounting Standards Advisory Board (FASAB)
Description: FASAB is a federal advisory committee responsible for establishing generally accepted accounting principles for federal entities. FASAB publishes the *FASAB Handbook of Federal Accounting Standards and Other Pronouncements, as Amended*, interpretations, and technical bulletins. Along with background information, its Web site has a newsletter that reports board meeting highlights.
Subject(s): Accounting
Publication(s): *Statements of Federal Financial Concepts and Standards, Pronouncements as Amended*

Federal Financing Bank (FFB)
http://www.ustreas.gov/ffb/
Sponsor(s): Treasury Department—Federal Financing Bank
Description: FFB is a government corporation that works under the general supervision of the secretary of the Treasury. FFB coordinates federal and federally assisted borrowing from the public with the overall financial and economic goals of the government. Its Web site includes information about FFB's operations, press releases, and financial statements.
Subject(s): Government Finance

Follow the Money: GAO's Oversight of the Recovery Act
http://www.gao.gov/recovery/
Sponsor(s): Government Accountability Office (GAO)

Description: As they are required by the Recovery Act, the GAO reports on aspects of management and spending under the act. The site provides GAO's reviews of how Recovery Act funds are being spent in a sample of states and whether they are achieving the act's goals.

Subject(s): Government Finance

Internal Revenue Service (IRS)

http://www.irs.gov/

Sponsor(s): Treasury Department—Internal Revenue Service (IRS)

Description: The intended audience for the official Web site of the IRS is the average U.S. taxpayer. Special sections also lead to information for businesses, charities and nonprofits, government entities, tax professionals, and users concerned with retirement plans and tax-exempt bonds. A Spanish-language version of the site is available. The section for individuals includes instructions, forms and publications, and resources for electronic filing through the IRS e-file program. The site's News & Events section links to media contacts, IRS guidance, news, and information about tax scams.

The IRS site, one of the most heavily used federal Web sites, is well organized and provides multiple points of access to major sections and resources. The site map can help users find specific information.

Subject(s): Income Tax; Tax Forms; Taxation

Publication(s): *Armed Forces' Tax Guide*, T 22.44/2:3/

Federal Employment Tax Forms, T 22.44/2

Federal Tax Forms, T 22.51

Internal Revenue Bulletin, T 22.23

Internal Revenue Manual, T 22.2/15-3

Statistics of Income Bulletin, T 22.35/4:

Taxpayer Information Publications, T 22.44/2

Your Rights as a Taxpayer, T 22.44/2:1/

Tax Statistics

http://www.irs.gov/uac/Tax-Stats-2

Sponsor(s): Treasury Department—Internal Revenue Service (IRS)

Description: The Tax Statistics Web page serves as a central access point for a variety of statistics about IRS operations aggregated from filings with the IRS. Major sections include Business Tax, Charitable, Compliance, Individual Tax, and (Statistics) by Form. A special Tax Stats Topics section includes statistics on estate and gift tax returns and research on taxpayer compliance.

Subject(s): Taxation—Statistics

Publication(s): *IRS Annual Data Book*, T 22.1

Taxpayer Advocate Service

http://www.irs.gov/Advocate

Sponsor(s): Treasury Department—Internal Revenue Service (IRS)

Description: The Taxpayer Advocate Service was created to ensure that taxpayer complaints not resolved through the normal channels could be resolved fairly and efficiently, and to recommend system changes based on the experiences that occur while reviewing these complaints. This Web site provides information about the service and how to use it. The site also has the taxpayer advocate's annual report to Congress, which details the most frequent taxpayer complaints and makes recommendations for improvement.

Subject(s): Income Tax

Publication(s): *National Taxpayer Advocate's Objectives Report to Congress*

National Taxpayer Advocate's Annual Report to Congress

TreasuryDirect

http://www.treasurydirect.gov/

Sponsor(s): Treasury Department—Bureau of the Public Debt

Description: TreasuryDirect has three separate sections: Individuals, Financial Institutions (institutional investors), and Government. The section for individuals allows customers to set up an account with the Department of the Treasury; purchase Treasury bills, bonds, and notes; participate in Treasury security auctions; convert paper savings bonds to electronic; and otherwise manage their accounts.

The section for institutional investing focuses on Treasury auctions, but also provides access to online account services and relevant information. The Government section describes programs specifically for government entities, such as the Federal Investments Program and the State and Local Government Series (SLGS) securities program.

Subject(s): Treasury Bills; Treasury Bonds; Treasury Notes

U.S. Chief Financial Officers Council (CFOC)

https://cfo.gov/

Sponsor(s): U.S. Chief Financial Officers Council

Description: Members of the CFOC are the chief financial officers of the largest federal agencies and senior officials of the Office of Management and Budget and the Department of the Treasury. The CFOC Web site includes a membership list, council charter, news, documents, and meetings information. The Resources section links to the annual financial reports of the Cabinet departments and major agencies.

Subject(s): Government Finance

GOVERNMENT INFORMATION

CENDI
http://cendi.dtic.mil/
Sponsor(s): CENDI
Description: CENDI is a working group of federal scientific and technical information (STI) managers. (It is named for the initial four entities that formed the group: the Department of Commerce, the Department of Energy, NASA, and the Defense Information Managers Group.) This Web site has CENDI publications, materials from CENDI workshops, and information from CENDI working groups. Topics covered include digital libraries, copyright, technology assessments, and current federal STI projects.

Despite CENDI's specialized mission and membership, the content available on this site may also be useful to digital library managers outside the realms of federal and scientific/technical information.

Subject(s): Digital Libraries; Government Information

Data.gov
http://data.gov/
Sponsor(s): Chief Information Officers Council
Description: Launched in May 2009, Data.gov is a portal to more than 132,000 free federal government data sets. The site also links to Web tools for data extraction, for porting data and information to Web sites through a widget, and for other data tasks. The Data section provides browsing capability for items from a number of sources.

Federal Digital System (FDsys)
http://www.fdsys.gov/
Sponsor(s): Government Printing Office (GPO)
Description: The Federal Digital System, or FDsys.gov, provides online access to federal documents and information produced by the Government Printing Office. FDsys was launched in early 2009 as a replacement for the GPO Access Web site, and all content was transferred by the end of 2011.

As the official source for electronic formats of core U.S. government documents, FDsys.gov is an essential resource.

Subject(s): Congressional Documents; Government Publications; Presidential Documents

Government Printing Office (GPO)
http://www.gpo.gov/
Sponsor(s): Government Printing Office (GPO)
Description: As stated on its Web site, GPO is "the Federal Government's official, digital, secure resource for producing, procuring, catalog-

ing, indexing, authenticating, disseminating, and preserving the official information products of the U.S. Government." The site has information about GPO, its print and electronic information services for agencies, its network of federal depository library partners, new government publications, and contract opportunities for printing. It also links to the online Catalog of U.S. *Government Publications,* online bookstore, and GPO's Ben's Guide to U.S. Government for Kids.

GPO has migrated content from its original online database system, GPO Access, to the Federal Digital System (FDsys) at http://fdsys.gpo.gov/. The GPO.gov site links directly to FDsys.

Subject(s): Government Publications

Information Security Oversight Office (ISOO)

http://www.archives.gov/isoo/

Sponsor(s): National Archives and Records Administration (NARA)

Description: ISOO is responsible for policy and operations related to classifying, declassifying, and safeguarding national security information. ISOO's annual report compiles statistics on agency classification and declassification activities. Its Web site describes the scope of the office's authority and responsibilities and provides relevant policy documents, ISOO notices, and security forms. ISOO activities described on the site include the Interagency Security Classification Appeals Panel (ISCAP), the National Industrial Security Program (NISP), and the Controlled Unclassified Information (CUI) Office.

Subject(s): Information Policy; National Security—Regulations

Publication(s): *ISOO (Information Security Oversight Office) Annual Reports,* AE 1.101/3

National Archives and Records Administration (NARA)

http://www.archives.gov/

Sponsor(s): National Archives and Records Administration (NARA)

Description: NARA oversees the archival records of the executive, congressional, and judicial branches of the federal government. Its Web site describes these holdings and provides online access to selected digital collections. The Research Our Records section of the site offers an introduction to the archives' contents and explains how to search for materials. The Web version of the *Guide to Federal Records in the National Archives of the United States* allows users to search the guide or enter a record group number directly. The site also has information for genealogists and in this section provides tips on researching census records, military records, immigration records (ship passenger lists), naturalization records, and land records. The site's alphabetical subject index provides quick links to specific collections. Links at the bottom of the home page lead to the information the site provides in Spanish, as well as relevant social media pages.

NARA's Web site explains the agency's varied responsibilities and includes equally varied content. For example, NARA houses the Office of the Federal Register, which is responsible for publishing public laws and the Federal Register, and also for coordinating the Electoral College. NARA's Information Security Oversight Office works with security classification policies for government and industry. NARA also oversees the Presidential Libraries. Aside from the Presidential Libraries, NARA has locations across the country; the site links to NARA Research Centers, regional archives, and affiliated archives located outside of Washington, D.C., in the Research Our Records section.

For archivists, the Records Managers section offers news and information pertaining to federal records management policy; a separate section covers document preservation. For educators and students, the site provides lesson plans, an introductory research activity, and more. The Architect of the United States maintains a news blog, which links to other NARA blogs, at http://blogs.archives.gov/aotus/.

This site is unusual in the scope of materials available. While very little actual archival material is online, NARA has put selected high-interest items on the site.

Subject(s): Archives

Publication(s): *Citing Records in the National Archives of the United States*, AE 1.113:17/

Guide to Federal Records in the National Archives of the United States, AE 1.108:G 94/

NARA Bulletins, AE 1.103

National Archives, Calendar of Events, AE 1.129

Prologue, GS 4.23

Quarterly Compilation of Periodical Literature Reflecting the Use of Records in the National Archives, AE 1.128

National Declassification Center (NDC)

http://www.archives.gov/declassification/

Sponsor(s): National Archives and Records Administration (NARA)

Description: NDC, part of the National Archives, works to improve the declassification process and to implement standard declassification training for records determined to have permanent historical value. The Web site includes key policy documents, information on declassification, and the center's bi-annual status report.

Subject(s): Declassified Documents

Publication(s): *Bi-annual Report on Operations of the National Declassification Center*

National Technical Information Service (NTIS)

http://www.ntis.gov/

Alternate URL(s)

http://www.ntis.gov/search/

Sponsor(s): Commerce Department—Technology Administration (TA)—National Technical Information Service (NTIS)

Description: NTIS is one of the major government publishing agencies and features hundreds of thousands of publications related to scientific, technical, engineering, and business information that have been produced by or for the U.S. government. However, since NTIS is run on a cost recovery basis, many of its services require payment.

NTIS provides a search engine to find items in its large collection of reports for sale. Direct access to the search engine is at the alternate URL listed above.

Subject(s): Government Publications; Scientific and Technical Information; Publication Catalogs

Office of Information and Privacy (OIP)

http://www.usdoj.gov/oip/oip.html

Sponsor(s): Justice Department

Description: OIP manages the Department of Justice's responsibilities related to the Freedom of Information Act (FOIA) and the Privacy Act. These responsibilities include coordinating and implementing policy development and government-wide compliance for FOIA, compliance by the Justice Department for the Privacy Act, and the decisions on all appeals from denials of access to information under those acts by any component of the Justice Department. Its Web site includes online access to reference documents, including the *DOJ Annual FOIA Report*.

Subject(s): Freedom of Information Act

Publication(s): *DOJ Annual FOIA Report*, J 1.1/11

FOIA Post, J 1.58/1

Justice Department Guide to the Freedom of Information Act, J 1.8/2

Office of Information and Regulatory Affairs (OIRA)

http://www.whitehouse.gov/omb/inforeg/

Sponsor(s): Office of Management and Budget (OMB)

Description: In addition to its important responsibilities in the area of regulatory policy, OIRA is concerned with government information collection and management. The site also has a section that provides federal government statistical programs and standards, including the schedule of release dates for principal federal economic indicators. The Information Policy section of the OIRA Web site covers information policy documents, federal Web site standards guidance, privacy guidance, the Government Paperwork Elimination Act, and the Freedom of Information Reform Act.

OIRA reviews draft federal regulations from federal agencies and articulates the administration's regulatory policy. Documents related to these activities can be found in the Regulatory Matters section of the OIRA site.

Subject(s): Government Information—Policy; Regulatory Policy

Office of the Federal Register

http://www.ofr.gov/

Sponsor(s): National Archives and Records Administration (NARA)—Federal Register Office

Description: The Office of the Federal Register prepares the official texts for federal regulatory materials, federal laws, presidential documents, and the U.S. Government Manual. The Web site serves as a portal linking to the government Web sites hosting the online version of these documents. The Public Inspection Desk section of the site provides access to the documents (notices, regulations, and other items) that will appear in the next day's Federal Register and selected documents scheduled for later issues.

The office has several other roles in addition to its responsibilities as an official legal information service. It administers and maintains the Web site for the Electoral College. It also compiles Privacy Act Issuances, through which federal agencies disclose any information system containing personally identifiable information and explain how individuals can access records about themselves. These issuances are available on the office's site.

Subject(s): Laws; Privacy—Regulations

Publication(s): *Compilation, Privacy Act Issuances,* AE 2.106/4-2

Public Interest Declassification Board (PIDB)

http://www.archives.gov/declassification/pidb/

Sponsor(s): National Archives and Records Administration (NARA)

Description: PIDB advises the president and Executive Branch officials on issues related to the review and declassification of national security documents to serve the public interest and contribute to an accurate archival record. Its Web site includes the board's enabling legislation, meeting minutes, and recommendations.

Subject(s): Government Information—Policy; National Security

U.S. Government Bookstore

http://bookstore.gpo.gov/

Sponsor(s): Government Printing Office (GPO)

Description: GPO's sales catalog can be searched by keyword or browsed by topic on this Web site. Documents can be ordered online. The site also features a list of government best sellers.

Subject(s): Government Publications; Publication Catalogs

Publication(s): *Sales Product Catalog,* GP 3.22/7

United States Government Blog

http://blog.usa.gov/

Sponsor(s): General Services Administration (GSA)—Citizen Services and Communications Office

Description: This blog highlights useful government information and services for Americans' everyday lives. Typical topics include history, nutrition, financial matters, and tracking current events. Bloggers are employees of the General Services Administration (GSA). Comments are allowed, and entries can be Tweeted or liked on Facebook.

Subject(s): Government Services; Blogs

XML.Gov

http://xml.fido.gov/

Sponsor(s): Chief Information Officers Council

Description: This Web site is maintained by a federal government staff group in order to facilitate implementation of XML technology in government information systems. (XML is a standard for structured documents and data on the Internet.) In addition to information about government activities and events in this area, the site also has sections related to XML standards, guidelines, and tutorials.

Subject(s): World Wide Web

GOVERNMENT SERVICES

Citizens' Stamp Advisory Committee (CSAC)

http://about.usps.com/who-we-are/leadership/stamp-advisory-committee.htm

Sponsor(s): Postal Service (USPS)

Description: CSAC is the mechanism by which subjects are selected to be featured on U.S. postage stamps. CSAC receives recommendations, evaluates them, and makes recommendations to the postmaster general. This U.S. Postal Service Web site has information about CSAC, a list of current committee members, and the formal criteria for stamp subject selection.

Subject(s): Postage Stamps

Federal Emergency Management Agency (FEMA)

http://www.fema.gov/

Sponsor(s): Homeland Security Department—Federal Emergency Management Agency (FEMA)

Description: The FEMA Web site features news and victim assistance information for any current disasters in the United States. The site also provides information about how to prepare for emergencies ranging from floods to terrorist threats, how to apply for disaster assistance, and how to keep safe and recover after a disaster. Audience-specific sections provide information and resources for businesses, emergency personnel, homeowners, livestock owners, volunteers, kids, and others. The About FEMA section has a leadership directory. Information about grants can be found in the Topics & Audience section. The site map is an alphabetical index providing quick access to resources, including FEMA programs such as the National Fire Academy, the National Fire Incident Reporting System, the National Flood Insurance Program, and urban search-and-rescue programs. The FEMA Web site is also available in Spanish, Vietnamese, and other languages and has a mobile version.

Subject(s): Disaster Assistance

Publication(s): *Are You Ready? A Guide to Citizen Preparedness*, FEM 1.8/3:34/

FEMA News Releases, FEM 1.28

Flood Insurance Manual, FEM 1.8

National Flood Insurance Program Community Status Book, FEM 1.210

FirstGov for Seniors

http://www.seniors.gov/

Sponsor(s): Social Security Administration (SSA)

Description: The mission of FirstGov for Seniors is to provide one comprehensive Web site where seniors can go to find health and security information and services. The site is arranged by topic, such as Consumer Protection, Health, Retirement, and Money and Taxes. Each topic has links to relevant Web sites.

Subject(s): Senior Citizens

FloodSmart.gov

http://www.floodsmart.gov/

Alternate URL(s)

http://www.fema.gov/business/nfip/

Sponsor(s): Homeland Security Department—Federal Emergency Management Agency (FEMA)

Description: FloodSmart.gov has consumer information on flood risk, preparing for flooding, and flood insurance. The Web site is sponsored by the National Flood Insurance Program (NFIP). The main NFIP Web page is located at the alternate URL above.

Subject(s): Flood Insurance

GovLoans.gov

http://govloans.gov/

Sponsor(s): Labor Department

Description: GovLoans.gov is a central location for information about federal loan programs. Major sections cover topics such as agriculture, business, disaster relief, education, housing, and veterans' loans. The site is a cooperative effort between the Departments of Agriculture, Commerce, Education, Housing and Urban Development, and Veterans Affairs, as well as the Small Business Administration. It is hosted by the Department of Labor's GovBenefits.gov Web site. GovLoans.gov is also available in Spanish.

Subject(s): Government Loans

LEP.gov

http://www.lep.gov/

Sponsor(s): Federal Interagency Working Group on Limited English Proficiency

Description: The LEP.gov Web site was created by the Federal Interagency Working Group on Limited English Proficiency. The site offers information and guidance for language access to federal and federally assisted programs, with three major target audiences: federal agencies, recipients of federal funds, and community organizations. The site provides policy guidance, directories of translator and interpreter organizations, demographic data, and program news. Information in other languages, including Spanish, is available on the site.

Subject(s): Civil Rights—Regulations; Language Groups

Postal Regulatory Commission (PRC)

http://www.prc.gov/

Sponsor(s): Postal Regulatory Commission (PRC)

Description: PRC is an independent regulatory agency that reviews Postal Service requests for changes in postal rates. The Reference and Reports/Data sections hav statistical reports made by the Postal Service to PRC on topics such as personnel, payroll, and productivity.

Subject(s): Postal Service—Regulations

United States Postal Service (USPS)

http://www.usps.com/

Sponsor(s): Postal Service (USPS)

Description: The USPS Web site provides information, such as a directory of post offices, and online services for the general public and businesses. Online services include stamp sales, a postage rate calculator, and package tracking. The site's Forms and Publications section, which is accessed through a link at the bottom of the page, has over 100 U.S. postal forms in PDF format.

USPS videos and press releases are available in the About USPS Home section. This section includes the annual report as well.

Subject(s): Postal Service

Publication(s): *Comprehensive Statement on Postal Operations*, P 1.2:P 84/

Domestic Mail Manual, P 1.12/11

International Mail Manual, P 1.10/5
Postal Bulletin, P 1.3

INTERGOVERNMENTAL RELATIONS

Advisory Commission on Intergovernmental Relations (ACIR)
http://www.library.unt.edu/gpo/acir/acir.htm
Sponsor(s): Advisory Commission on Intergovernmental Relations (ACIR) University of North Texas Libraries
Description: ACIR was established by Congress in 1959 to study the relationships between local, state, and federal government. The commission was closed in 1996. The University of North Texas Libraries maintains this Web site to provide permanent public access to the electronic publications that were available on the ACIR Web site. It includes editions of Significant Features of Fiscal Federalism, a reference tool for data on state and federal revenues and expenditures and federal spending in the states. All serial publication volumes from 1976 through 1994 are available online, with other documents from the 1960s to the 1990s available as well.

The ACIR materials are accessible thanks to a partnership between the University of North Texas Libraries and the U.S. Government Printing Office to provide permanent public access to the electronic Web sites and publications of defunct U.S. government agencies and commissions.
Subject(s): Intergovernmental Relations
Publication(s): *Intergovernmental Perspective,* Y 3.AD 9/8:11/
Significant Features of Fiscal Federalism, Y 3.AD 9/8:18/

Code Talk
http://www.hud.gov/offices/pih/ih/codetalk/
Sponsor(s): Housing and Urban Development (HUD)—Office of Native American Programs (ONAP)
Description: Code Talk is an interagency Web site that was established to deliver electronic information from government agencies and other organizations to Native American communities. The name is based on the Native American Code Talkers, who were heroes of the two World Wars. The site is hosted on the Department of Housing and Urban Development (HUD) Web site and includes detailed information about American Indian housing programs and federal program news.
Subject(s): American Indians
Publication(s): *National Directory of the Tribally Designated Housing Entities and Tribes*

Federal, State, and Local Governments (Census)
http://www.census.gov/govs/

Sponsor(s): Commerce Department—Economics and Statistics Administration (ESA)—Census Bureau

Description: This Web site brings together information from Census Bureau programs that cover local, state, and federal governments and their finances. Featured data sources include the *Census of Governments* and *State Government Tax Collections Survey*. The site has survey forms, publications, summary reports, and press releases. Statistics are available under topical headings such as Government Employment and Payroll, Government Finance Statistics, Tax Statistics, and Federal Spending. There are options to view national or individual state data, and reports can be downloaded in spreadsheet format or as a flat ASCII file.

Subject(s): Government Employees—Statistics; Government Finance—Statistics; State Government—Statistics

Publication(s): *Census of Governments*, GP 3.22/2
Government Finance and Employment Classification Manual
Public Elementary-Secondary Education Finances, C 3.191/2-10

Indian Affairs
http://www.indianaffairs.gov/

Sponsor(s): Interior Department—Bureau of Indian Affairs (BIA)

Description: The Indian Affairs Web site provides information from the Bureau of Indian Affairs (BIA) and the Bureau of Indian Education (BIE). BIA manages land held in trust by the United States for American Indian tribes and Alaska Natives. BIE provides education services to American Indian students. The Web site describes BIA structure and mission, services, and current BIA tribal consultations. The What We Do section of the site organizes BIA activities by topic, such as economic development, education, gaming, and justice services. The site's Document Library includes the *Tribal Leaders Directory*, the *Guide to Tracing Your American Indian Ancestry*, and the *FR Notice - Indian Entities Recognized and Eligible to Receive Services From the US BIA*.

Subject(s): American Indians

Publication(s): *FR Notice - Indian Entities Recognized and Eligible to Receive Services From the US BIA*
Guide to Tracing Your American Indian Ancestry

Office of the Special Trustee for American Indians (OST)
http://www.doi.gov/ost/index.cfm

Sponsor(s): Interior Department—Office of the Special Trustee for American Indians (OST)

Description: OST was created by law in 1994 to improve the accountability and management of Indian funds held in trust by the federal government. The Web site provides current news, information for Indian

Trust beneficiaries, and Trust documents. It has a special section on the Cobell v. Salazar legal settlement concerned with trust fund mismanagement.

Subject(s): American Indians

Office of Tribal Justice (OTJ)
http://www.usdoj.gov/otj/
Sponsor(s): Justice Department—Tribal Justice Office
Description: The Office of Tribal Justice (OTJ) was established in 1995 with the purpose of increasing the responsiveness of the Department of Justice to the concerns of the American Indian Nations, individual Indians, and others interested in Indian affairs. The Web site's About the Office section has the Department of Justice Sovereignty Policy and related policy documents. The site's Selected Resources section links to information from the Justice Department and other federal agencies on American Indian law enforcement, corrections, courts, and other issues.

Subject(s): American Indians

Tax Information for Indian Tribal Governments
http://www.irs.gov/Government-Entities/Indian-Tribal-Governments
Sponsor(s): Treasury Department—Internal Revenue Service (IRS)
Description: This Web site is designed for use by tribes and is maintained by the IRS Indian Tribal Governments office. The site addresses topics such as employment taxes, casino issues, and fraud and abusive schemes. The site also includes news and compliance guidance.

Subject(s): American Indians

PUBLIC POLICY

John C. Stennis Center for Public Service
http://www.stennis.gov/
Sponsor(s): Stennis Center for Public Service
Description: The John C. Stennis Center for Public Service was created by Congress in 1988 to promote public service in the United States at all levels of government. The center is governed by a board of trustees appointed by the Democratic and Republican leaders in the U.S. Senate and House of Representatives. The Web site has information about the center's programs and its namesake. Programs described include the Civil Military Leadership Program, the Emerging Congressional Staff Leaders Program, the Stennis Fellows Program, and the Stennis Student Congress.

Subject(s): Fellowships; Civics Education

Woodrow Wilson International Center for Scholars

http://www.wilsoncenter.org/

Sponsor(s): Woodrow Wilson International Center for Scholars

Description: The Wilson Center supports scholarship linked to public policy. The center offers fellowships and special opportunities for research and writing with a focus on history, political science, and international relations. As a public/private partnership, the center receives roughly one-third of its operating funds from federal appropriations. The Web site has information about current Wilson Center projects and publications, and audio files of its weekly radio program, "Dialogue." The site also carries essays and other items from the center's journal, *The Wilson Quarterly*. In the About section, the site offers information on applying for a fellowship or internship with the center.

Subject(s): Fellowships; Public Policy—Research; Social Science Research

Publication(s): *The Wilson Quarterly*

THIRTEEN

Health and Safety

Government health sciences Web sites serve everyone from research scientists to clinicians and the general public. Health science professionals have used government Web sites to expand a tradition of disseminating research information. Government information on the Web has also been a boon to the average citizen seeking authoritative medical information written in layman's terms. This chapter includes the full range, as well as information on nutrition, safety, and health care finance.

Subsections in this chapter are Conditions and Treatment, Health Care Finance, Health Occupations, Health Policy and Promotion, Health Research, Medical Information, Medicine and Medical Devices, Nutrition, and Safety.

CONDITIONS AND TREATMENT

AIDS.gov

http://www.aids.gov/

Sponsor(s): Health and Human Services Department

Description: AIDS.gov is a portal to government HIV/AIDS information and resources. The site links to information on a wide range of resources on federal programs and policies, such as the Presidential Advisory Council on HIV/AIDS (PACHA), research, grants, and international issues. AIDS.gov also has an extensive HIV/AIDS Basics section discussing prevention and treatment. Some resources are available in Spanish.

AIDS.gov makes extensive use of social media in its How to Use New Media section, providing a blog, podcasts, Twitter feed, Facebook page, and other outlets for AIDS information. The blog is described in a separate entry.

331

AIDS.gov Blog

http://blog.aids.gov/

Sponsor(s): Health and Human Services Department

Description: The AIDS.gov blog is intended to assist individuals, organizations, and government officers concerned with public health promotion and particularly with AIDS awareness. Comments are allowed, and articles can be shared via Twitter, Facebook, and Google+.

Subject(s): AIDS

AIDSinfo

http://aidsinfo.nih.gov/

Sponsor(s): Health and Human Services Department

Description: AIDSinfo is a user-friendly Web site with well-designed sections on drugs, clinical trials, related health topics, and guidelines for prevention and treatment. The HIV/AIDS Health Topics section is a portal to information from government and a variety of other sources on all of these aspects of AIDS treatment. The Mobile Resources & Tools section provides a live chat feature and a place to order publications. Some publications are available in Spanish.

Subject(s): AIDS

Alzheimer's Disease Education and Referral (ADEAR) Center

http://www.nia.nih.gov/alzheimers

Sponsor(s): National Institutes of Health (NIH)—National Institute on Aging (NIA)

Description: The ADEAR Center is operated as a service of the National Institute on Aging. It is an information clearinghouse for health professionals, people with Alzheimer's disease, their families, and the general public. The Web site provides information on the disease and news of current research and clinical trials, with links to Alzheimer's research centers. The site also offers an e-mail service for news updates.

Subject(s): Alzheimer's Disease

Publication(s): *Alzheimer's Disease Progress Report, HE 20.3869 Alzheimer's Disease: Unraveling the Mystery*

Autism Information

http://www.hhs.gov/autism/

Sponsor(s): Health and Human Services Department

Description: The Autism Information page provides general information on autism spectrum disorders (ASDs) and links to more specific information on federal Web sites. The site covers topics such as signs and symptoms, screening and diagnosis, treatment options, causes and risk factors, and research and clinical trials. The page also links to publications from the Interagency Autism Coordinating Committee (IACC) at http://www.iacc.hhs.gov/.

Subject(s): Diseases and Conditions

Cancer Control PLANET
http://cancercontrolplanet.cancer.gov/
Sponsor(s): Health and Human Services Department
Description: Cancer Control PLANET is designed specifically for professional cancer control planners, program staff, and researchers. Its Web site is a portal to information needed in developing cancer control programs; it links primarily to information compiled by the federal government. The site is sponsored by the American Cancer Society and by Department of Health and Human Services agencies, including the National Cancer Institute and the Centers for Disease Control and Prevention.
Subject(s): Cancer; Public Health

Cancer Information Service (CIS)
http://www.cancer.gov/aboutnci/cis
Sponsor(s): National Institutes of Health (NIH)—National Cancer Institute (NCI)
Description: CIS is a free, public service set up to answer individual questions about cancer. The LiveHelp link provides an instant messaging service. In addition to providing information about CIS, the site links to cancer news, resources, and publications. CIS also operates a toll free number, 1-800-4-CANCER.
Subject(s): Cancer

CDC Cancer Prevention and Control
http://www.cdc.gov/cancer/dcpc/about/
Alternate URL(s)
http://www.cdc.gov/cancer/
Sponsor(s): Health and Human Services Department—Centers for Disease Control and Prevention (CDC)—Cancer Prevention and Control Division
Description: The CDC Cancer Prevention and Control Web site provides state and national statistics, fact sheets, program information, and publications related to cancer. The Prevention section has information about screening tests and risk reduction, while the Cancer Survivorship section has information for caregivers and survivors. The site also has a Spanish-language version available.
The alternate URL brings users to a page of information about gynecological cancers and the CDC's work regarding their prevention and treatment.
Subject(s): Cancer—Statistics
Publication(s): *United States Cancer Statistics*, HE 20.7045

CDC National Prevention Information Network (NPIN)
http://www.cdcnpin.org/

Sponsor(s): Health and Human Services Department—Centers for Disease Control and Prevention (CDC)—National Center for HIV/AIDS, Viral Hepatitis, STD, and TB Prevention (NCHHSTP)

Description: NPIN focuses on control and prevention of HIV/AIDS, viral hepatitis, sexually transmitted diseases (STDs), and tuberculosis (TB). NPIN has databases of relevant organizations, conferences, and private and government funding opportunities for community-based and HIV/AIDS, STD, and TB service organizations. The site offers RSS feeds for daily news, conference announcements, and funding opportunity announcements and a display of its Twitter, Facebook, LinkedIn, Google+, and Pinterest pages on the home page.

Subject(s): AIDS; HIV Infections; Sexually Transmitted Diseases; Tuberculosis

Publication(s): *CDC HIV/STD/TB Prevention News Update*, HE 20.7318

Centers for Disease Control and Prevention (CDC)
http://www.cdc.gov/

Sponsor(s): Health and Human Services Department—Centers for Disease Control and Prevention (CDC)

Description: The CDC is concerned with public health, disease prevention and control, environmental health, and health promotion and education. Its main Web site has information about the agency with links to all of CDC's component centers, institutes, and offices. The site features current public health topics of interest. The Diseases & Conditions section is a gateway to extensive CDC information under categories such as ADHD, cancer, and diabetes. The Data and Statistics section brings together news and links for CDC's many statistical compilation, including pediatric growth charts. The Publications section includes the *Morbidity and Mortality Weekly Report* and the journals *Emerging Infectious Diseases* and *Preventing Chronic Disease*. The CDC Web site has a Spanish-language version.

CDC offers a version of its site for mobile Internet devices, as well as several apps, a news feed, Facebook and Twitter links, and numerous RSS feeds.

This main CDC page serves as a starting point for finding extensive information on various diseases, disease statistics, and disease prevention. The site offers an A to Z index, search engine, dynamic links to the most-visited pages, and entry point by audience type such as individuals, researchers, and businesses. The information is well organized and the pages are easy to navigate.

Subject(s): Diseases and Conditions; Epidemiology; Public Health

Publication(s): *Advance Data from the Vital and Health Statistics*, HE 20.6209/3

Emerging Infectious Diseases, HE 20.7817
Fact Sheets (NCHSTP-HIV/AIDS Prevention Division), HE 20.7320/3
Health Information for International Travelers, HE 20.7315
MMWR Recommendation and Reports, HE 20.7009/2-2
Morbidity and Mortality Weekly Report, HE 20.7009
National Vital Statistics Report (monthly), HE 20.6217
Preventing Chronic Disease, HE 20.7620
Summary of Sanitation Inspection of International Cruise Ships, HE 20.7511

Diabetes Public Health Resource

http://www.cdc.gov/diabetes/

Sponsor(s): Health and Human Services Department—Centers for Disease Control and Prevention (CDC)—National Center for Chronic Disease Prevention and Health Promotion (NCCDPHP)

Description: This site communicates practical information on diabetes prevention and control. It includes a diabetes fact sheet, frequently asked questions, diabetes statistics, and information on state-based diabetes prevention and control programs. The Newsroom section has CDC statements, press releases, and congressional testimony related to diabetes. The site also has a Spanish-language version available.

Subject(s): Diabetes

Eldercare Locator

http://www.eldercare.gov

Sponsor(s): Health and Human Services Department—Administration on Aging (AoA)

Description: According to the Web site, "The Eldercare Locator . . . is a nationwide service that connects older Americans and their caregivers with information on senior services." The site provides searches by topic or ZIP code, and in the Resources section, information about such topics as long-term care planning and benefits for older adults, caregivers, and professionals. Fact sheets and news are also available in this section, and links to relevant social media pages are also provided.

Subject(s): Senior Citizens

Flu.gov

http://www.flu.gov/

Sponsor(s): Health and Human Services Department

Description: Flu.gov is the main government interagency Web site, hosted by the Department of Health and Human Services, for the public to learn about influenza vaccination, prevention, and treatment. It has information for special populations, such as seniors. During flu season, the site has a national directory of flu shot providers. Flu.gov also provides planning and communications guides for schools, businesses, local governments, and others.

Subject(s): Diseases and Conditions; Public Health

GulfLINK

http://www.gulflink.osd.mil/

Sponsor(s): Defense Department—Office of the Special Assistant for Gulf War Illnesses

Description: GulfLINK has news and information on illnesses reported by veterans of the Persian Gulf War of 1991. The Library section of the site includes case narratives, *Environmental Exposure Reports*, and RAND research reports. The site also has information on services for veterans, medical evaluation programs, and a summary of medical issues relating to symptoms among Gulf War veterans.

Subject(s): Gulf War Disease

HIV/AIDS Surveillance Reports

http://www.cdc.gov/hiv/library/reports/surveillance/

Sponsor(s): Health and Human Services Department—Centers for Disease Control and Prevention (CDC)—National Center for HIV/AIDS, Viral Hepatitis, STD, and TB Prevention (NCHHSTP)

Description: These annual reports contain detailed statistics on the incidence of HIV and AIDS in the United States, including data by state, metropolitan statistical area, mode of exposure to HIV, sex, race/ethnicity, age group, vital status, and case definition category.

Subject(s): AIDS—Statistics; HIV Infections—Statistics

Publication(s): *HIV/AIDS Surveillance Report*, HE 20.7320

Influenza (Flu)

http://www.cdc.gov/flu/

Sponsor(s): Health and Human Services Department—Centers for Disease Control and Prevention (CDC)

Description: Seasonal flu is the single topic of this Web site. It provides information on the flu vaccine, antiviral drugs, and flu symptoms and treatment in general. The Web site has sections for health care professionals, parents, business, people at high risk, and other special groups. A link to CDC Flu's Twitter feed is also provided. The CDC Web site is available in a Spanish-language version.

Subject(s): Diseases and Conditions

National Center for HIV/AIDS, Viral Hepatitis, STD, and TB Prevention (NCHHSTP)

http://www.cdc.gov/nchhstp/

Sponsor(s): Health and Human Services Department—Centers for Disease Control and Prevention (CDC)—National Center for HIV/AIDS, Viral Hepatitis, STD, and TB Prevention (NCHHSTP)

Description: The NCHHSTP Web site features current disease research news and data, with information for researchers, patients, public health professionals, and the public. The site provides extensive background information on specific Sexually Transmitted Diseases (STDs), HIV/AIDS, Viral Hepatitis, and Tuberculosis (TB). The State Health Profiles section of the site has statistics and program information about HIV/AIDS, Viral Hepatitis, STDs, and TB for all 50 states and the District of Columbia. The site also has information on global HIV/AIDS.

Subject(s): AIDS; HIV Infections; Sexually Transmitted Diseases
Publication(s): *HIV/AIDS Surveillance Report*, HE 20.7320
Reported Tuberculosis in the United States, HE 20.7310
Sexually Transmitted Disease Surveillance, HE 20.7309/2
TB Notes, HE 20.7310/2

National Center for PTSD

http://www.ptsd.va.gov/
Sponsor(s): Veterans Affairs Department (VA)

Description: The VA's National Center for Post-Traumatic Stress Disorder (PTSD) provides this Web site as an educational resource concerning PTSD and other consequences of traumatic stress. The primary audiences are veterans and their families, researchers, and mental health care providers. The Web site offers information on assessment, treatment, and VA services. In addition to combat stress, reactions to trauma caused by natural disasters, abuse, and other factors are discussed. The site offers free online access to PILOTS, a database indexing the literature on PTSD and other mental health consequences of exposure to traumatic events.

Subject(s): Mental Health; Veterans
Publication(s): *PTSD Research Quarterly*, VA 1.94

National Diabetes Education Program (NDEP)

http://www.ndep.nih.gov/
Sponsor(s): National Institutes of Health (NIH)

Description: NDEP is a partnership of NIH, the Centers for Disease Control and Prevention (CDC), and over 200 public and private organizations to promote awareness of diabetes prevention and control. The site has a wealth of background information on diagnosis, prevention, and treatment. It includes resources for health, education, and business professionals. Publications can be ordered online for free in English, Spanish, and more than 15 other languages.

Subject(s): Diabetes

National Heart, Lung, and Blood Institute (NHLBI)

http://www.nhlbi.nih.gov/

Sponsor(s): National Institutes of Health (NIH)—National Heart, Lung, and Blood Institute (NHLBI)

Description: NHLBI organizes resources into sections for the public and for health professionals. The section for the public links to fact sheets and publications on heart and vascular diseases, lung diseases, and blood diseases. The site also links to educational material on high blood cholesterol, high blood pressure, overweight and obesity, and heart attack warning signs. Sections for professionals cover information including clinical practice guidelines, scientific reports, and continuing education. The site also carries announcements of technology transfer opportunities and clinical trials.

Subject(s): Heart Disease—Research

Publication(s): *Morbidity and Mortality: Chart Book on Cardiovascular, Lung, and Blood Diseases,* HE 20.3226

National HIV and STD Testing Resources

http://www.hivtest.org/

Sponsor(s): Health and Human Services Department—Centers for Disease Control and Prevention (CDC)

Description: The site features a nationwide database of testing locations for detecting HIV and other sexually transmitted diseases, along with information about the tests. It provides information in both English and Spanish.

Subject(s): HIV Infections

National Kidney Disease Education Program (NKDEP)

http://www.nkdep.nih.gov/

Sponsor(s): National Institutes of Health (NIH)—National Institute of Diabetes and Digestive and Kidney Disease (NIDDK)

Description: The NKDEP site has sections for patients and the public, health professionals, and laboratory professionals. Each section provides detailed information on different aspects of kidney disease diagnosis and care. The site also has a Spanish-language version.

Subject(s): Kidney Disease

NIH Senior Health

http://nihseniorhealth.gov/

Sponsor(s): National Institutes of Health (NIH)—National Institute on Aging (NIA)

Description: The NIH Senior Health Web site is a joint project of the National Institute on Aging and the National Library of Medicine to produce Web content for seniors that is designed in an age-appropriate style. The site uses large print and breaks content into short segments. Topics include Arthritis, Exercise, Osteoporosis, Taking Medicines, and more. Some sections include short video clips with the option of reading the video transcript.

Subject(s): Alzheimer's Disease; Senior Citizens

Office of Cancer Survivorship
http://dccps.nci.nih.gov/ocs/
Alternate URL(s)
http://cancercontrol.cancer.gov/ocs/
Sponsor(s): National Institutes of Health (NIH)—National Cancer Institute (NCI)
Description: This Web site is designed for researchers, health professionals, advocates, and cancer survivors and their families. Topics include cancer survivorship research, possible late effects of treatment, and clinical practice follow-up guidelines. The site provides reports, fact sheets, information on research funding, news, and conference information.
Subject(s): Cancer

Office of Rare Diseases (ORDR)
http://rarediseases.info.nih.gov/
Sponsor(s): National Institutes of Health (NIH)—Office of Rare Diseases
Description: The Office of Rare Diseases is concerned with research on rare, or orphan, diseases, defined as diseases or conditions affecting fewer than 200,000 persons in the United States. The Web site provides resources on research, clinical trials, conferences, patient support groups, and relevant genetics information for rare diseases. Information is also available in Spanish.
Subject(s): Diseases and Conditions—Research

Organ Donation
http://www.organdonor.gov/
Sponsor(s): Health and Human Services Department—Health Resources and Services Administration (HRSA)
Description: This Department of Health and Human Services Web site provides general information on the process of organ and tissue donation and information on how to sign up. It features a downloadable donor card and brochure. The site also covers transplantation basics and how to avoid the risk of needing a transplant. The sections entitled Materials & Resources and Legislation have information on research grants, the National Organ Transplant Act, and organ transplant policy.
Subject(s): Medical Information

President's Malaria Initiative (PMI)
http://www.fightingmalaria.gov/
Sponsor(s): Agency for International Development (USAID)
Description: PMI is an interagency effort to fund malaria treatment and prevention in 15 African counties. It is led by USAID and includes the Department of Health and Human Services, the Department of State, the White House, and other agencies. Its Web site includes program information and statistics, profiles of malaria conditions in the target countries, and information on topics such as mosquito nets and anti-malarial drugs.
Subject(s): Malaria

SAMHSA: Substance Abuse and Mental Health Service Administration Publication Ordering
http://ncadi.samhsa.gov/
Sponsor(s): Health and Human Services Department—Substance Abuse and Mental Health Services Administration (SAMHSA)
Description: The Web site for the SAMHSA National Clearinghouse provides a wealth of information resources on mental health, substance abuse, prevention, and treatment. Publications can be located by selecting the intended audience, drug name, treatment, or location. Some publications are available in Spanish.
Subject(s): Substance Abuse
Publication(s): *Substance Abuse Treatment Advisory*, HE 20.429/5
Substance Abuse Treatment Facility Locator, HE 20.410/3
Tips for Teens about . . . , HE 20.8002:T 49/

HEALTH CARE FINANCE

Centers for Medicare and Medicaid Services (CMS)
http://www.cms.gov/
Sponsor(s): Health and Human Services Department—Centers for Medicare and Medicaid Services
Description: CMS runs the Medicare program and oversees the federal portions of Medicaid and the Children's Health Insurance Program (CHIP). The CMS Web site has information on the programs it administers, which also include portions of the Health Insurance Portability and Accountability Act. The Regulations and Guidance section includes CMS program manuals, rulings, transmittals, regulatory updates, and extensive background on major laws. The extensive and varied information in the Research, Statistics, Data and Systems section includes Medicare enrollment tables, Medicare Current Beneficiary Survey, national health expenditure data, program data sets, and the new Medicare & Medicaid Research Review journal. The site also provides administrative informa-

tion by provider type, such as hospice or home health agency. The site's FAQs section has a searchable database of answers to common questions.

Much of the information on the CMS site is relevant to health care providers and program administrators. For consumer information on Medicare, see Medicare.gov at http://www.medicare.gov. For consumer information on SCHIP, see Insure Kids Now at http://www.insurekidsnow.gov. For information on the new health care reform law, see http://www.healthcare.gov/. Each of these sites is listed elsewhere in this book.

Subject(s): Health Care Finance; Medicaid; Medicare
Publication(s): *Active Projects Report*, HE 22.16/2
CMS Online Manual System, HE 22.8/23
CMS Rulings, HE 22.38
Data Compendium, HE 22.511
Medicare & Medicaid Research Review
Skilled Nursing Facility Manual, HE 22.8/3

Children's Health Insurance Program (CHIP)

http://www.cms.gov/home/chip.asp
Sponsor(s): Health and Human Services Department—Centers for Medicare and Medicaid Services
Description: The Children's Health Insurance Program (CHIP) is jointly financed by the federal and state governments and is administered by the states. This Web site has information on the Children's Health Insurance Program Reauthorization Act (CHIPRA) of 2009, CHIP dental coverage, and national CHIP policy.

This site is intended for program administrators. Consumer information on the program is available from the federal Web site Insure Kids Now at http://www.insurekidsnow.gov.

Subject(s): Health Insurance; Child Health and Safety

Health Care—Veterans Health Administration

http://www1.va.gov/health/
Sponsor(s): Veterans Affairs Department (VA)—Veterans Health Administration (VHA)
Description: The VHA Web site is part of the larger Veterans Administration site. It provides consumer-oriented information and services, with sections on applying for care, refilling a prescription, finding a VA health facility, a crisis prevention hotline for veterans, and more. In the A-Z index, the site links to VHA information on specific topics, such as dental care, prescriptions, prosthetics and sensory aids, health promotion, and VA medical research.

Subject(s): Veterans
Publication(s): *VA Research Currents*, VA 1.107

HealthCare.gov

http://www.healthcare.gov/

Sponsor(s): Health and Human Services Department

Description: HealthCare.gov is designed to help consumers navigate the health insurance market and learn about the Patient Protection and Affordable Care Act (Public Law 111-148). The site also has information on the new law tailored to families with children, individuals, people with disabilities, young adults, and seniors. A section called Find Insurance Options Now links to specific health insurance plans based on your home state and demographic information, such as age range, employment or self-employment status, and presence of children. The site also covers preventative care and links to online tools to compare the quality of hospitals, nursing homes, and dialysis facilities.

Subject(s): Health Insurance

Insure Kids Now

http://www.insurekidsnow.gov/

Sponsor(s): Health and Human Services Department—Health Resources and Services Administration (HRSA)

Description: This site links to information on children's health insurance programs in each state and offers answers to a variety of questions about insurance for children. Sections include Medicaid and CHIP Basics, Learn About Programs in Your State, and Questions & Answers. A Spanish-language version of the site is available.

Subject(s): Health Insurance; Child Health and Safety

Medicare Payment Advisory Commission (MedPAC)

http://www.medpac.gov/

Sponsor(s): Congress—Medicare Payment Advisory Commission (MedPAC)

Description: MedPAC is a nonpartisan congressional advisory body charged with providing policy advice and technical assistance for Medicare payment policies. Major sections of the Web site are About MedPAC, Public Meetings, Documents, and Research Areas. The home page includes a clickable calendar with upcoming events.

Subject(s): Medicare—Policy

Publication(s): *Data Book: Healthcare Spending and the Medicare Program*, Y 3.M 46/3

Report to Congress: Aligning Incentives in Medicare, Y 3.M 46/3

Medicare.gov

http://www.medicare.gov/

Sponsor(s): Health and Human Services Department—Centers for Medicare and Medicaid Services

Description: This official Medicare site for consumers features Medicare pamphlets and publications, news, and basic explanations of various aspects of Medicare. Sections cover information about Medicare enrollment, plan choices, the prescription drug plan, long-term care, preventive services, billing, and appeals. Under Forms, Help & Resources, the site offers Web tools to help consumers find, compare, or evaluate services, such as doctors, nursing homes, Medigap policies, home health care, prescription drug plans, and dialysis facilities. The site features the annual consumer guide *Medicare and You*.

Medicare.gov has a Spanish-language version, a large-text version, and a printable version. The site also links to an access screen for My-Medicare.Gov, a personal Medicare beneficiary portal.

Subject(s): Medicare; Nursing Homes
Publication(s): *Guide to Choosing a Nursing Home*, HE 22.8:N 93/
Medicare and You, HE 22.8/16
Medicare Hospice Benefits, HE 22.21/5

TRICARE, Military Health System

http://www.tricare.mil/
Sponsor(s): Defense Department—TRICARE Management Activity
Description: TRICARE is the health care benefit for the military. This Web site provides information and documents for TRICARE beneficiaries and providers, including a directory of providers. TRICARE beneficiaries can also log into the TRICARE Online service to conduct transactions such as scheduling appointments.
Subject(s): Health Insurance; Military Medicine

HEALTH OCCUPATIONS

Bureau of Health Professions

http://bhpr.hrsa.gov/
Sponsor(s): Health and Human Services Department—Health Resources and Services Administration—Health Professions Bureau
Description: The mission of the Bureau of Health Professions is to ensure that health care professionals deliver quality services to all geographic areas and to all segments of society. Topics covered on the site include grants, scholarships/loans, the National Center for Health Workforce Analysis, and designated Health Professional Shortage Areas. The Health Workforce Analysis topic features data on the U.S. population of physicians, nurses, and other health workers.
Subjects: Health Occupations—Grants; Medical Schools—Grants

Medical Reserve Corps (MRC)

http://www.medicalreservecorps.gov/

Sponsor(s): Health and Human Services Department—Public Health and Science Office—Surgeon General; USA Freedom Corps

Description: MRC consists of local units of volunteer medical and public health professionals organized to assist their communities during emergencies and to promote public health. The MRC Web site has information on volunteering, a directory of MRC units, program news, information on joining or forming a unit, and guidance for existing units. The MRC's program office is headquartered in the Office of the U.S. Surgeon General.

Subject(s): Disaster Preparedness; Public Health

National Health Service Corps (NHSC)

http://nhsc.hrsa.gov/

Sponsor(s): Health and Human Services Department—Health Resources and Services Administration (HRSA)—Health Professions Bureau

Description: NHSC recruits primary care clinicians for medically underserved areas. It offers financial assistance to medical students who will practice in underserved areas, as well as work experiences and residencies. The site has online applications and information about NHSC programs.

Subject(s): Health Care

National Practitioner Data Bank

http://www.npdb-hipdb.hrsa.gov/

Sponsor(s): Health and Human Services Department—Health Resources and Services Administration (HRSA)—Health Professions Bureau

Description: The full title of this Web site is "National Practitioner Data Bank—Healthcare Integrity and Protection" (NPDB—HIPDB). NPDB compiles records of malpractice and other adverse reports filed against physicians, dentists, and other health care practitioners. HIPDB compiles reports of fraud and abuse in health insurance and health care delivery. Neither database is fully available to the general public. A modified version of the data bank file, containing selected information and no identification data, may be downloaded from the site. Under Resources, the site links to annual reports, the publicly accessible file, and summary statistics from NPDB and HIPDB.

Subject(s): Health Care—Regulations; Health Occupations—Regulations

Publication(s): *National Practitioner Data Bank Guidebook*, HE 20.9308: D 26/

Uniformed Services University of the Health Sciences (USUHS)

http://www.usuhs.mil/

Sponsor(s): Defense Department—Uniformed Services University of the Health Sciences (USUHS)

Description: According to the Web site, USUHS's mission "is to train, educate and prepare uniformed services health professionals, officers, and leaders to directly support the Military Health System, the National Security and National Defense Strategies of the United States, and the readiness of our Armed Forces." This Web site provides basic information about the university, its School of Medicine, Graduate School of Nursing, and university research.

Subject(s): Medical Schools; Military Medicine

HEALTH POLICY AND PROMOTION

Administration on Aging (AoA)

http://www.aoa.gov/

Sponsor(s): Health and Human Services Department—Administration on Aging (AoA)

Description: The AoA Web site features resources for the elderly, their families, and professionals who work with the elderly. The main page presents sections for aging statistics, AoA programs, and grant opportunities. The online Eldercare Locator is a nationwide directory assistance service designed to help older persons and caregivers locate local support services. Covered topics include benefits, long-term care, Medicare, and information resources. The Newsroom has social media features, information for the press, and other services related to the aging. The Web site also offers statistics on the aging population.

Subject(s): Senior Citizens

American Indian Health

http://americanindianhealth.nlm.nih.gov/

Sponsor(s): National Institutes of Health (NIH)—National Library of Medicine (NLM)

Description: The mission of this NLM-sponsored site is "to bring together health and medical resources pertinent to the American Indian population including policies, consumer health information, and research." The site links to Web resources from the federal government, academia, and health profession organizations. Information covered includes health care access, traditional healing, environmental health, and research. A Health Topics section points to similar specialized resources.

Subject(s): Health Promotion; American Indians

Asian American Health

http://asianamericanhealth.nlm.nih.gov/

Sponsor(s): National Institutes of Health (NIH)—National Library of Medicine (NLM)

Description: This is a portal to health information on the Internet for the diverse Asian-American population. Major sections cover common diseases and conditions, complementary and alternative medicine, and behavioral and mental health issues. The site provides numerous health pamphlets in Asian languages. Links are also organized by population, such as Chinese and Filipino.

Subject(s): Asian Americans

Bioethics Resources on the Web

http://bioethics.od.nih.gov/

Sponsor(s): National Institutes of Health (NIH)

Description: This NIH site links to Web sites, documents, regulations, news, conferences, and other information about bioethics issues. Many of the resources are from NIH itself, but sources also include other federal agencies and organizations. The topics covered include human subject research, privacy, conflicts of interest, and genetic testing.

Subject(s): Bioethics

Bioethics.gov

http://bioethics.gov/

Sponsor(s): Health and Human Services Department; White House

Description: The Presidential Commission for the Study of Bioethical Issues was created by executive order in November 2009 and continued to hold meetings through 2012. The Web site has news and transcripts from the commission's hearings. The commission's report was released on March 19, 2013. It contains recommendations on pediatric medical countermeasure research.

Subject(s): Bioethics—Policy

Center for Global Health

http://www.cdc.gov/globalhealth/

Sponsor(s): Health and Human Services Department—Centers for Disease Control and Prevention (CDC)

Description: The Center for Global Health focuses on collaborating with other nations and international organizations to promote healthy lifestyles and to prevent high rates of disease, disability, and death in the global health arena. The Web site spotlights efforts focusing on global AIDS, malaria, influenza, polio, and global disease detection. The site describes numerous other initiatives in such areas as environmental health, migration and quarantine, and foodborne infections. The site also has information on International Health Regulations, global training opportunities, and global health funding.

Subject(s): Health Care—International

Children's Health Protection

http://yosemite.epa.gov/ochp/ochpweb.nsf/

Sponsor(s): Environmental Protection Agency (EPA)—Children's Health Protection Office

Description: Children face special and increased risks from exposure to environmental pollutants. This Web site explains the risks and how to minimize them. A section called What You Can Do to Protect Children from Environmental Risks is available in English, Spanish, Vietnamese, Korean, and Chinese. The site also offers publications, regulatory information, data, and other extensive coverage of the topic.

Subject(s): Child Health and Safety; Environmental Health

Publication(s): *America's Children and the Environment*, EP 1.2

Chronic Disease Prevention

http://www.cdc.gov/chronicdisease/

Sponsor(s): Health and Human Services Department—Centers for Disease Control and Prevention (CDC)—National Center for Chronic Disease Prevention and Health Promotion (NCCDPHP)

Description: NCCDPHP works to reduce the incidence of such chronic diseases as diabetes, cancer, and heart disease. Chronic disease programs also address topics such as arthritis, tobacco use, nutrition and physical activity, and teen pregnancy. The agency's Web site describes its various programs, grants, research, and public health surveillance. The site has summary facts and graphs derived from its surveillance programs for behavioral risk factors, youth risk behavior, cancer registries, and pregnancy risks. State profiles include statistical profiles.

Subject(s): Health Promotion; Preventive Health Care

Publication(s): *Preventing Chronic Disease*, HE 20.7620

Community Health Status Indicators (CHSI)

http://www.cdc.gov/CommunityHealth/

Sponsor(s): Health and Human Services Department

Description: The CHS Web site presents over 3,000 county health status profiles representing each county in the United States excluding territories. Users can also make customized brochures with the county's health indicators and download the data for their own projects. CHSI is a project of the Health and Human Services Department and several nonprofit health associations.

Subject(s): Health Statistics

Consumer Health Information

http://www.fda.gov/ForConsumers/default.htm

Sponsor(s): Health and Human Services Department—Food and Drug Administration (FDA)

Description: The FDA compiles a wide variety of consumer health information on this Web site. The site has consumer news, recalls, and product alerts, with an RSS news feed and e-mail service for updates. The news covers drugs, medical devices, cosmetics, food, and other products under FDA regulation. The site also has a section providing fraud alerts and guidance. The Consumer Information by Audiences section has tips for patients, women, health educators, and others. Some online publications are available in both English and Spanish.

Subject(s): Consumer Information

Health Resources and Services Administration (HRSA)

http://www.hrsa.gov/

Sponsor(s): Health and Human Services Department—Health Resources and Services Administration (HRSA)

Description: HRSA works to expand health care access for the uninsured, underserved, and special needs populations. HRSA concerns include health care for uninsured people, people living with HIV/AIDS, maternal health, rural health, organ transplants and donations, and emergency preparedness. The site includes information on current and past grants and an online grant application process. Under the Data & Statistics heading, data about Shortage Areas, the Organ Transplantation Program, and the National Health Service Corps is available.

Two important pages are linked from the top banner. The Questions link leads to a knowledge base of frequently asked questions. The A-Z Index is a useful tool for navigating the site.

The HRSA Web site provides extensive information on the many programs they operate, providing information for administrators and users of health care, researchers, and policy makers.

Subject(s): Public Health

Health.gov

http://www.health.gov/

Sponsor(s): Health and Human Services Department—Public Health and Science Office—Disease Prevention and Health Promotion Office

Description: This health gateway site consists of links to federal health initiatives information, government health agency sites, and other government-produced information. Site content is also available in Spanish.

Subject(s): Health and Safety

Healthy People 2020

http://www.healthypeople.gov/

Sponsor(s): Health and Human Services Department

Description: This site has information on the Healthy People 2020 national health promotion initiative. A major part of the effort is to establish metrics for measuring progress in the population's health. The Topics & Objectives section breaks down the program's goals by health topic.

Subject(s): Health and Safety—Statistics; Health Promotion

Publication(s): *Healthy People 2020 Consortium Toolkit*, HE 20.2

Healthy Youth

http://www.cdc.gov/healthyyouth/

Sponsor(s): Health and Human Services Department—Centers for Disease Control and Prevention (CDC)—National Center for Chronic Disease Prevention and Health Promotion (NCCDPHP)

Description: This site deals with both school practices to promote student health and health issues relevant to adolescents. It provides school health education resources, school health policies, statistics, and an evaluation and planning tool called School Health Index. Specific health topics include asthma, obesity, injury and violence, and sexual risk behaviors.

Subject(s): Adolescents; Health Promotion; School Safety

HRSA Primary Health Care

http://www.bphc.hrsa.gov/

Sponsor(s): Health and Human Services Department—Health Resources and Services Administration (HRSA)—Primary Health Care Bureau

Description: The site describes the Health Center Program, which is designed to provide primary health care services to medically underserved communities and vulnerable populations. The site has a directory of health care centers, information on how public and private nonprofit health care organizations may apply to receive funding under the program, and related policy and administrative information. The site's Uniform Data System has statistics on program operation, including information on health care for the homeless, migrants, and public housing residents.

Subject(s): Hospitals and Clinics—Grants

HRSA Telehealth

http://www.hrsa.gov/telehealth/

Sponsor(s): Health and Human Services Department—Health Resources and Services Administration (HRSA)

Description: This site describes telehealth as "the use of electronic information and telecommunications technologies to support long-distance clinical health care, patient and professional health-related education, public health and health administration." The site features tele-health-related publications and grants information.

Subject(s): Telemedicine

Indian Health Service (IHS)

http://www.ihs.gov/
Alternate URL(s)
http://info.ihs.gov/
Sponsor(s): Health and Human Services Department—Indian Health Services (IHS)
Description: IHS is the primary federal agency responsible for providing health care services to American Indians and Alaska Natives. Major sections of the IHS Web site include About IHS, Locations, For Patients, For Providers, Community Health, Career Opportunities, and Newsroom. The About IHS section includes legal and policy information, publications, and organizational overviews. The Web site includes a search engine, frequently asked questions, and an A-Z index.

The alternate URL above links directly to IHS Fact Sheets, a user-friendly site with basic information on topics such as behavioral health, diabetes, Indian health disparities, and IHS budget planning with tribes.

Subject(s): Health Care; American Indians
Publication(s): *Indian Health Manual*
The IHS Primary Care Provider, HE 20.320

Interagency Autism Coordinating Committee (IACC)

http://iacc.hhs.gov/
Sponsor(s): Health and Human Services Department
Description: IACC, a federal advisory committee, coordinates all aspects of the Department of Health and Human Services's involvement with autism spectrum disorders (ASDs). IACC meetings, which are open to the public, are summarized on the Meetings & Events page. The site also includes sections on the various IACC subcommittees, as well as reports and meetings from non-IACC sources.

Subject(s): Mental Health

Let's Move!

http://www.letsmove.gov/
Sponsor(s): White House—First Lady's Office
Description: Let's Move, an initiative of First Lady Michelle Obama, is a public health promotion campaign aimed at kids. The Web site has practical information on exercising and eating right. It also has guides to action for parents, schools, kids, and other audiences. The site has a

blog and links to social media pages, and the About Let's Move section has news releases, photos, and videos.

Subject(s): Physical Fitness

National Committee on Vital and Health Statistics (NCVHS)

http://www.ncvhs.hhs.gov/

Sponsor(s): Health and Human Services Department—National Committee on Vital and Health Statistics

Description: NCVHS is concerned with the quality of the health data and statistics that inform national health policy, including issues of privacy and confidentiality. Reports, recommendations, and meeting recordings from the full committee and its working groups are available on the Web site.

Subject(s): Medical Information—Policy

NIDA for Teens: The Science Behind Drug Abuse

http://teens.drugabuse.gov/

Sponsor(s): National Institutes of Health (NIH)—National Institute on Drug Abuse (NIDA)

Description: NIDA for Teens is designed to provide adolescents ages 11 through 15 (as well as their parents and teachers) with science-based facts about how drugs affect the brain and body. The site includes fact sheets on specific drugs and classes of drugs, teens' questions, informative blog postings, and interactive online activities.

Subject(s): Adolescents; Drug Abuse

Publication(s): *Mind over Matter: The Brain's Response to . . .* , HE 20.3958

Office of Lead Hazard Control and Healthy Homes (OLHCHH)

http://portal.hud.gov/hudportal/HUD?src=/program_offices/healthy_homes

Sponsor(s): Department of Housing and Urban Development

Description: OLHCHH provides funding to state and local government entities in order to eradicate the threat of lead poisoning in homes. The site has links to associated programs and grants, information about such topics as lead and radon, and direct links to popular related posts.

Subject(s): Lead Poisoning

Office of National AIDS Policy (ONAP)

http://www.whitehouse.gov/administration/eop/onap

Sponsor(s): White House

Description: The Web site for the White House Office of National AIDS Policy maintains a blog reporting policy and program developments and provides information on the National HIV/AIDS Strategy.

Subject(s): AIDS—Policy

Office of Population Affairs (OPA)

http://www.hhs.gov/opa/

Sponsor(s): Health and Human Services Department—Public Health and Science Office—Population Affairs Office

Description: OPA operates programs concerned with reproductive health, family planning, and adolescent pregnancy. Its Web site offers sections on health topics, such as contraception, and on OPA activities, such as grant programs and funding. The Legislation Mandates section, under Title X Family Planning, has the full text of the statutes and regulations under which OPA operates.

Subject(s): Family Planning, Reproductive Health

Office of Rural Health Policy (ORHP)

http://ruralhealth.hrsa.gov/

Sponsor(s): Health and Human Services Department—Health Resources and Services Administration (HRSA)

Description: This Web site for ORHP provides information on the federal government grants, policy, and research focused on improving health conditions in rural America. It also reports on the Border Health Initiative. For further information, the site links to rural health publications and related Web sites.

Subject(s): Rural Health—Policy

Office of the Assistant Secretary for Planning and Evaluation (ASPE)

http://aspe.hhs.gov/

Sponsor(s): Health and Human Services Department

Description: ASPE advises the secretary of HHS on policy development, strategic planning, policy research, and economic analyses. The main portion of the home page is set up to perform literature searches on 40 topics of concern to ASPE, such as child welfare, disability, insurance, and substance abuse. The In the Spotlight section covers topics such as Affordable Care Act research and poverty and income statistics. A section called Most Popular links to the HHS Poverty Guidelines.

Subject(s): Health Care—Policy; Social Services—Policy

Office of the Surgeon General

http://www.surgeongeneral.gov/

Sponsor(s): Health and Human Services Department—Public Health and Science Office—Surgeon General

Description: The Surgeon General's Web site has current and historical information on the office, including portraits and biographies of all previous surgeons general. It contains speeches made by the surgeon general, testimony before Congress, and general information on public health priorities such as preventing childhood obesity. The site has the full texts of reports issued by the surgeon general.

The Initiatives section provides information about the office's tobacco, prevention, breastfeeding support, and family health history reports.

Subject(s): Public Health—Policy

Publication(s): *Bone Health and Osteoporosis: A Report of the Surgeon General*, HE 20.2

Mental Health: Culture, Race, and Ethnicity, A Supplement to Mental Health: A Report of the Surgeon General, HE 20.402

Oral Health in America: A Report of the Surgeon General, HE 20.3402

Preventing Tobacco Use Among Youth and Young Adults

Public Health Reports, HE 20.30

Reducing Tobacco Use: A Report of the Surgeon General, HE 20.7602

Surgeon General's Call to Action to Prevent and Decrease Overweight and Obesity, HE 20.2

Surgeon General's Call to Action to Prevent Suicide, HE 20.2

Surgeon General's Call to Action to Promote Sexual Health and Responsible Sexual Behavior, HE 1.2

The Health Consequences of Involuntary Exposure to Tobacco Smoke: A Report of the Surgeon General, HE 20.7002

The Health Consequences of Smoking: A Report of the Surgeon General, HE 20.7002

Women and Smoking: A Report of the Surgeon General, HE 20.7615

Youth Violence: A Report of the Surgeon General, HE 20.2

Office of the U.S. Global AIDS Coordinator

http://www.state.gov/s/gac/

Sponsor(s): State Department—Office of the U.S. Global AIDS Coordinator

Description: As stated on the Web site, "The U. S. Global AIDS Coordinator's mission is to lead implementation of the U.S. President's Emergency Plan for AIDS Relief (PEPFAR)." The site provides basic information on the office. For more information on the plan, see http://www.pepfar.gov/.

Subject(s): AIDS—International

Publication(s): *The President's Emergency Plan for AIDS Relief*, S 1.2

President's Council on Bioethics

http://www.bioethics.gov/

Sponsor(s): President's Council on Bioethics

Description: Established in 2001, the council is charged with advising the president on bioethical issues that may emerge as a consequence of advances in biomedical science and technology. The Web site includes a council meeting schedule, meeting agendas, and news. The site also has the reports from previous bioethics commissions.

Subject(s): Bioethics—Policy; Presidential Advisors

President's Council on Physical Fitness, Sports & Nutrition
http://www.fitness.gov/

Sponsor(s): President's Council on Physical Fitness and Sports

Description: Established by executive order in 1956, the President's Council on Physical Fitness and Sports promotes physical fitness and sports participation for Americans of all ages. In June 2010, the name of the council was updated to the President's Council on Physical Fitness, Sports & Nutrition. The Web site has information on the history, mission, and membership of the council under the About PCFSN section. The Resource Center section includes the quarterly PCFSN Research Digests, a summary of the latest scientific information on issues relating to physical activity.

Subject(s): Physical Fitness; Sports

Publication(s): *PCFSN Research Digests*

President's Emergency Plan for AIDS Relief
http://www.pepfar.gov/

Sponsor(s): White House

Description: PEPFAR involves strategic funding to combat HIV/AIDS in over 120 countries. The Web site includes information on participating countries, implementing agencies, policy guidance, reports to Congress, and PEPFAR reports. Links to PEPFAR social media pages are also provided.

Subject(s): AIDS—International; Foreign Assistance; HIV Infections—International

President's New Freedom Commission on Mental Health
http://govinfo.library.unt.edu/mentalhealthcommission/

Sponsor(s): White House—President's New Freedom Commission on Mental Health

Description: The President's New Freedom Commission on Mental Health was charged with studying the U.S. mental health service delivery system and advising the president on methods to improve it. The Commission presented its final report in July 2003. The commission's Web site has been archived at the address above thanks to a partnership between the University of North Texas Libraries and the U.S. Government Printing Office.

Subject(s): Mental Health—Policy

Publication(s): *Achieving the Promise: Transforming Mental Health Care in America*, PR 43.8

Reports of the Surgeon General

http://profiles.nlm.nih.gov/NN/

Sponsor(s): National Institutes of Health (NIH)—National Library of Medicine (NLM)

Description: This site carries the full texts of all official surgeon general reports, beginning with 1964's *Smoking and Health: A Report of the Surgeon General*, the first report given. The National Library of Medicine has digitized these along with conference proceedings, pamphlets, photographs, and brochures from the Office of the Surgeon General. A search engine provides full text or fielded search options. Historical information on the office and on U.S. public health supplements the reports.

Subject(s): Public Health—Policy

Smokefree.gov

http://www.smokefree.gov/

Sponsor(s): National Institutes of Health (NIH)—National Cancer Institute (NCI)

Description: NCI maintains this Web site to help smokers quit and to disseminate free anti-smoking materials. Under Talk to an Expert, the site lists toll-free numbers and instant messaging services available for information and advice on quitting.

Subject(s): Smoking

Specialized Information Services (SIS) Division

http://www.sis.nlm.nih.gov/

Sponsor(s): National Institutes of Health (NIH)—National Library of Medicine (NLM)

Description: The SIS Division is responsible for information resources and services in toxicology, environmental health and toxicology, chemistry, HIV/AIDS, and topics in regard to special population groups. Its Web site features information products in each of these areas. The Web site also includes information from the SIS Outreach and Special Populations Branch, which focuses on improving access to quality health information in special populations.

Subject(s): Health Promotion; Environmental Health

State Cancer Legislative Database Program (SCLD)

http://www.scld-nci.net/

Sponsor(s): National Institutes of Health (NIH)—National Cancer Institute (NCI)

Description: NCI monitors cancer-related state legislation and maintains the State Cancer Legislative Database of cancer-related bills and resolutions enacted or adopted in the United States at the state level. The site also provides fact sheets, newsletters, and presentations on the topic.

Subject(s): Cancer—Legislation

Publication(s): *SCLD (State Cancer Legislative Database) Update*, HE 20.3182/9-2

SCLD Fact Sheets, HE 20.3182/9-3

Substance Abuse and Mental Health Services Administration (SAMHSA)

http://www.samhsa.gov/

Sponsor(s): Health and Human Services Department—Substance Abuse and Mental Health Services Administration (SAMHSA)

Description: SAMHSA administers grants, programs, training, and public education campaigns to assist those working to combat substance abuse and mental illness. The Web site's Topics section organizes SAMHSA program information into subject areas, such as co-occurring disorders, health reform, suicide prevention, the SAMHSA Syringe Exchange Program, and the National Children's Mental Health Awareness Day. The site also links to treatment center directories. The Data section offers reports and data from the National Survey on Drug Use & Health (NSDUH) and the Drug Abuse Warning Network (DAWN), and other sources. SAMHSA has RSS feeds for announcements of new publications, and awareness campaigns. The site is also available in Spanish.

Subject(s): Mental Health; Substance Abuse

Publication(s): *Drug Abuse Warning Network (DAWN)*, HE 20.416/3

National Household Survey on Drug Abuse, HE 20.417/5

Youth Tobacco Prevention

http://www.cdc.gov/tobacco/youth/

Sponsor(s): Health and Human Services Department—Centers for Disease Control and Prevention (CDC)—National Center for Chronic Disease Prevention and Health Promotion (NCCDPHP)

Description: This CDC site links to an extensive list of resources about young people and smoking. Resources include research reports, content especially for children, and materials (such as videos and program guides) for adults responsible for organizing anti-smoking campaigns for children.

Subject(s): Smoking; Tobacco; Kids' Pages

HEALTH RESEARCH

Agency for Healthcare Research and Quality (AHRQ)

http://www.ahrq.gov/

Sponsor(s): Health and Human Services Department—Healthcare Research and Quality Agency

Description: AHRQ supports research to improve the quality of health care, reduce its cost, and broaden access to essential services. Its

Web site features a wide range of resources in sections including Health Care Information, For Patients & Consumers, Research Tools & Data, and Funding & Grants. Some consumer publications are available in Spanish.

Subject(s): Health Policy

Publication(s): *AHRQ Publications Catalog,* HE 20.6509/3

MEPS (Medical Expenditure Panel Survey) Highlights, HE 20.6517/6

MEPS (Medical Expenditure Panel Survey) Research Findings, HE 20.6517/9

Arctic Health

http://arctichealth.org/

Sponsor(s): National Institutes of Health (NIH)—National Library of Medicine (NLM)

Description: NLM's Arctic Health Web site is a central point for information on Arctic health and environment. The site has research and publications databases and covers such topics as diseases, traditional medicine, climate change, and telemedicine. Arctic Health, which defines the Arctic as encompassing all or portions of Alaska, Canada, Greenland/Denmark/Faroe Islands, Iceland, Norway, Sweden, Finland, and Russia, is built on the premise that the populations of these countries are subject to a unique set of health and environmental challenges. Along with NLM, the site is co-sponsored by University of Alaska Anchorage's Health Sciences Information Service.

Subject(s): Arctic Regions

Armed Forces Medical Examiner System (AFMES)

http://www.afmes.mil/

Sponsor(s): Defense Department

Description: In accordance with the Base Realignment, AFMES has taken over forensic toxicology case submissions for the Armed Forces Institute of Pathology, which was disestablished in September 2011. AFMES's mission is to provide full services in the areas of forensic pathology, forensic toxicology, DNA technology and identification, and mortality surveillance for the Department of Defense. Forms are available for requesting autopsy reports and DNA analysis.

Subject(s): Forensics; Toxicology (Medicine)

Cancer.gov Clinical Trials

http://www.cancer.gov/clinicaltrials

Sponsor(s): National Institutes of Health (NIH)—National Cancer Institute (NCI)

Description: This NCI site provides information on cancer-related clinical trials. A database of trials can be searched by type of cancer, type of trial, and location of trial. The site also has educational materials about clinical trials and information from recent clinical trials.

Subject(s): Cancer; Clinical Trials

Center for Information Technology (CIT)

http://cit.nih.gov/

Sponsor(s): National Institutes of Health (NIH)

Description: According to the Web site, "In 1998 the Center for Information Technology (CIT) was formed, combining the functions of the DCRT, the Office of Information Resources Management (OIRM), and the Telecommunications Branch." Major sections of the Web site for CIT, which is part of NIH, include CIT Service Catalog, Information Security, Support, Science, IT Policies, and About CIT. The Science Catalog includes a list of tools and resources and computational SIGs. The About CIT section includes sections with information for collaborators and partners, job seekers, scientists, staff, "techies," vendors, and visitors.

Subject(s): Information Technology

Center for Scientific Review (CSR)

http://public.csr.nih.gov/Pages/default.aspx

Sponsor(s): National Institutes of Health (NIH)

Description: CSR is NIH's gateway for grant applications and review. Proposals are examined for their merit from a scientific standpoint. News and reports can be found in the About CSR section. Other major sections include Applicant Resources, Reviewer Resources, NIH Program Resources, Study Sections, Rosters and Meetings, and Employment.

Subject(s): Grants; Health Research

ClinicalTrials.gov

http://clinicaltrials.gov/

Sponsor(s): National Institutes of Health (NIH)—National Library of Medicine (NLM)

Description: NLM has developed this site to provide patients, family members, and the public with current information about clinical research studies sponsored privately and by the federal government. ClinicalTrials.gov currently contains over 188,000 trials with locations in over 189 countries. Users may search the database by disease or condition, location of the trial, study type, and other criteria.

Subject(s): Clinical Trials—International

Environmental Health Perspectives: EHP Online

http://www.ehponline.org/

Sponsor(s): National Institutes of Health (NIH)—National Institute of Environmental Health Sciences (NIEHS)

Description: The EHP Online site provides free access to the NIEHS peer-reviewed journal Environmental Health Perspectives and its Chinese-language edition. Issues of the journal are online from 1972 to the present. EHP offers updates via RSS news feeds and e-mail alerts. Podcasts are also available. Paid subscriptions are required for the print version of the journal.

Subject(s): Environmental Health

Publication(s): *Environmental Health Perspectives*, HE 20.3559/2

Epidemic Intelligence Service (EIS)

http://www.cdc.gov/eis/

Sponsor(s): Health and Human Services Department—Centers for Disease Control and Prevention (CDC)

Description: EIS is a surveillance and response unit for all types of epidemics in the United States and throughout the world. EIS employs physicians and other health specialists seeking a postgraduate program of service and on-the-job training in the practice of epidemiology. The site includes information about EIS's work and program eligibility.

Subject(s): Epidemiology; Public Health—Research

Fogarty International Center (FIC)

http://www.fic.nih.gov/

Sponsor(s): National Institutes of Health (NIH)—John E. Fogarty International Center (FIC)

Description: FIC promotes international cooperation and advanced study in the biomedical sciences. It fosters research partnerships between American scientists and their foreign counterparts through research and training grants, fellowships, exchange awards, and international agreements. The Web site provides information on these activities and on FIC programs. The site also lists available grant opportunities.

Subject(s): Biological Medicine—Grants; Medical Research—International

Publication(s): *Global Health Matters*, HE 20.3718

HMO Cancer Research Network

http://crn.cancer.gov/

Sponsor(s): National Institutes of Health (NIH)—National Cancer Institute (NCI)

Description: The HMO Cancer Research Network is a consortium funded by NCI to conduct research on cancer prevention, early detection, treatment, long-term care, and surveillance. The Web site identifies the participating health plans and research centers and describes the nature of the research. Research areas include prevention and screening, epidemiology of prognosis and outcomes, health care quality and cost, and communications and dissemination.

Subject(s): Cancer—Research

National Cancer Institute (NCI)
http://www.cancer.gov/
Sponsor(s): National Institutes of Health (NIH)—National Cancer Institute (NCI)
Description: The NCI Web site provides information on over 100 types of cancer. It has a cancer drug dictionary. The site also includes sections on research programs, research funding, clinical trials information, statistics, news, and free informational booklets to download. Some information is available in Spanish. The About NCI section has links to NCI's main divisions, to its advisory boards, and to information on legislation and funding related to cancer research. The Cancer Statistics section has information on the public-use Surveillance, Epidemiology, and End Results (SEER) data program, described elsewhere in this chapter. State cancer profiles, maps and graphs of cancer data, and Web-based interfaces to querying cancer data are also provided.

NCI's Web site is easy to navigate and is an important starting point for many cancer information needs.

Subject(s): Cancer
Publication(s): *Cancer | Changing the Conversation: The Nation's Investment in Cancer Research - 2012*, HE 20.3190
Cancer Mortality Maps, HE 20.3152:M 84/4
Cancer Progress Report, HE 20.3172/3
DCEG (Division of Cancer Epidemiology and Genetics) Linkage, HE 20.3196
NCI Annual Fact Book, HE 20.3174
NCI Cancer Bulletin, HE 20.3153/4
Report of the President's Cancer Panel, HE 20.3168/5

National Center for Advancing Translational Sciences (NCATS)
http://www.ncats.nih.gov/
Sponsor(s): National Institutes of Health (NIH)
Description: According to the Web site, "The mission of the National Center for Advancing Translational Sciences (NCATS) at the National Institutes of Health (NIH) is to catalyze the generation of innovative methods and technologies that will enhance the development, testing and implementation of diagnostics and therapeutics across a wide range of human diseases and conditions." NCATS has three major program areas: Clinical and Translational Science, Rare Disease Research and Therapeutics, and Re-engineering Translational Sciences. Major sections

include Research (with a program index), Funding & Notices, News & Events, and Policy Issues.

Subject(s): Health Research

National Center for Complementary and Alternative Medicine (NCCAM)

http://nccam.nih.gov/

Sponsor(s): National Institutes of Health (NIH)—National Center for Complementary and Alternative Medicine

Description: NCCAM is concerned with health care practices that are outside the realm of conventional medicine as practiced in the United States. Its Web site describes research grant opportunities and priorities and the clinical trials it conducts. The Health Info section addresses popular topics, such as acupuncture and homeopathy. It also has information for the consumer on choosing alternative medicines or treatments. Some consumer information is available in Spanish.

Subject(s): Alternative Medicine

Publication(s): *NCCAM Clinical Digest*

National Center for Toxicological Research (NCTR)

http://www.fda.gov/nctr/

Sponsor(s): Health and Human Services Department—Food and Drug Administration (FDA)—National Center for Toxicological Research (NCTR)

Description: NCTR conducts peer-reviewed scientific research in support and anticipation of the FDA's regulatory needs. Initiatives include programs in food safety, bioinformatics, biostatistics, computational toxicology, and nanotechnology. NCTR research divisions include biochemical toxicology, microbiology, neurotoxicology, personalized nutrition and medicine, and veterinary services.

Subject(s): Biotechnology—Research; Toxicology (Medicine)—Research

Publication(s): *Regulatory Research Perspectives*, HE 20.4051

National Center on Minority Health and Health Disparities (NCMHD)

http://ncmhd.nih.gov/

Sponsor(s): National Institutes of Health (NIH)—National Center on Minority Health and Health Disparities

Description: NCMHD supports programs involving basic and clinical research, training, and the dissemination of health information to reduce disparities in health for minority population groups. This site has information about the office, its programs, and news.

Subject(s): Medical Research—Policy; Minority Groups

National Council on Disability (NCD)

http://www.ncd.gov/

Sponsor(s): National Council on Disability

Description: NCD is an independent agency that works with Congress and the Executive Branch on disability-related policy. The NCD Policy Areas section, under About Us, details the wide variety of issues on which the agency works. Educational sources can be found in the Resources section.

Subject(s): Disability

National Eye Institute (NEI)

http://www.nei.nih.gov/

Sponsor(s): National Institutes of Health (NIH)—National Eye Institute (NEI)

Description: NEI supports research to prevent and treat eye diseases and other vision disorders. The Health Information section includes fact sheets and guides written at the consumer level. These cover glaucoma, macular degeneration, diabetic eye disease, eye anatomy, and other topics. Many of the guides are also available in Spanish. The site also has information on research funding and on the public awareness campaigns supported by NEI.

Subject(s): Vision Disorders—Research

National Institute of Allergy and Infectious Diseases (NIAID)

http://www.niaid.nih.gov/

Sponsor(s): National Institutes of Health (NIH)—National Institute of Allergy and Infectious Diseases (NIAID)

Description: NIAID supports and conducts basic research in immunology, microbiology, and infectious disease. On its Web site, users can explore research on AIDS, allergic diseases, asthma, biodefense, E. coli, hepatitis, influenza, malaria, tuberculosis, and more. Agency information on this site includes research grant announcements and NIAID laboratory profiles. On the research side, the site describes each research activity and related clinical trials, news, and resources. The Web site has a detailed A-Z index for its health and research topics.

Subject(s): AIDS—Research; Allergies—Research; Diseases and Conditions—Research; Medical Research—Grants

National Institute of Arthritis and Musculoskeletal and Skin Diseases (NIAMS)

http://www.niams.nih.gov/

Sponsor(s): National Institutes of Health (NIH)—National Institute of Arthritis and Musculoskeletal and Skin Diseases (NIAMS)

Description: The NIAMS Web site provides health information, information about basic research, clinical and epidemiologic research, research databases, and grant opportunities in the fields of rheumatology, orthopedics, dermatology, metabolic bone diseases, heritable disorders of bone and cartilage, inherited and inflammatory muscle diseases, and sports medicine. The Health Information section includes pamphlets on such conditions as acne, arthritis, back pain, fibromyalgia, gout, knee problems, lupus, osteoporosis, vitiligo, and sports injuries. The site also has a Spanish-language version available, as well as information in Chinese.

Subject(s): Arthritis—Research; Diseases and Conditions—Research; Medical Research—Grants

National Institute of Biomedical Imaging and Bioengineering (NIBIB)

http://www.nibib.nih.gov/

Sponsor(s): National Institutes of Health (NIH)—National Institute of Biomedical Imaging and Bioengineering (NIBIB)

Description: NIBIB supports research to develop innovative technologies that improve health care. The Web site includes information on funding opportunities, training, and job vacancies. It also has a directory of NIBIB Biomedical Technology Resource Centers throughout the United States. A version of the site is also available in Spanish.

Subject(s): Biotechnology; Medical Computing

National Institute of Child Health and Human Development (NICHD)

http://www.nichd.nih.gov/

Sponsor(s): National Institutes of Health (NIH)—National Institute of Child Health and Human Development (NICHD)

Description: NICHD's full name is the Eunice Kennedy Shriver National Institute of Child Health and Human Development. It conducts research, clinical trials, and epidemiological studies related to the health of the human growth, development, and reproductive processes. The Web site has information about NICHD, its divisions, grants and contracts, intramural research, and fellowships. The News & Health section has information on numerous child health and human development topics.

Subject(s): Reproductive Health—Research; Child Health and Safety—Research

National Institute of Dental and Craniofacial Research (NIDCR)

http://www.nidcr.nih.gov/

Sponsor(s): National Institutes of Health (NIH)—National Institute of Dental and Craniofacial Research (NIDCR)

Description: The NIDCR Web site offers a substantial collection of documents and information on dental research. Major sections include Oral Health, Clinical Trials, Research, Grants & Funding, and Careers & Training. Under Research, the Tools for Researchers subsection links to specialized databases and research centers related to microbiology and immunology and to craniofacial development. The Oral Health section links to publications and resources on topics such as fluoride, smokeless tobacco, temporomandibular joint and muscle disorders, and oral complications of systemic diseases. The site also has sections for finding low-cost dental care, oral health statistics, and material in Spanish.

Subject(s): Dental Health—Research

National Institute of Diabetes and Digestive and Kidney Disease (NIDDK)

http://www.niddk.nih.gov/

Sponsor(s): National Institutes of Health (NIH)—National Institute of Diabetes and Digestive and Kidney Disease (NIDDK)

Description: The NIDDK Web site features information on disorders studied by the agency, including diabetes, digestive diseases, endocrine diseases, hematologic diseases, kidney diseases, nutrition and obesity, and urologic diseases. Sections include Health Education, Research & Funding for Scientists, and News. Spanish-language pamphlets are also available.

Subject(s): Diabetes—Research; Medical Research—Grants; Kidney Disease—Research

Publication(s): *Kidney Disease Research Updates*, HE 20.3324/2-2
NIDDK Information Clearinghouses Publications Catalog, HE 20.3316
Prevent Diabetes Problems, HE 20.3326

National Institute of Environmental Health Sciences (NIEHS)

http://www.niehs.nih.gov/

Sponsor(s): National Institutes of Health (NIH)—National Institute of Environmental Health Sciences (NIEHS)

Description: NIEHS, an institute for research on environment-related diseases, links to a wide variety of information for health researchers, the general public, and teachers. The site identifies diseases and conditions, such as asthma and lung disease, that may be strongly related to environmental exposures. It also describes NIEHS scientific and clinical research, research grants, and research databases. For teachers and students, the site has a Science Education section under Health & Education.

Subject(s): Toxicology (Medicine)—Research; Environmental Health—Research

Publication(s): *Environmental Factor Newsletter*

National Institute of Mental Health (NIMH)

http://www.nimh.nih.gov/

Sponsor(s): National Institutes of Health (NIH)—National Institute of Mental Health (NIMH)

Description: NIMH conducts and funds research on mental and behavioral disorders, and works to educate the public on mental health topics. The site has information on NIMH grants and on its intramural research. The Health Topics section links to specific areas of NIMH research, such as autism spectrum disorder, eating disorders, and schizophrenia. For the public, the NIMH site also has information on medications, coping with traumatic events, getting help, and suicide prevention. For researchers, the site provides information on grants and research contracts. Some information is available in Spanish.

Subject(s): Brain—Research; Mental Health—Research

National Institute of Neurological Disorders and Stroke (NINDS)

http://www.ninds.nih.gov/

Sponsor(s): National Institutes of Health (NIH)—National Institute of Neurological Disorders and Stroke (NINDS)

Description: NINDS supports biomedical research on disorders of the brain and nervous system. For researchers, the site has information on research funding, research plans, and the text of workshop and conference proceedings. The Disorders A-Z section of the site is an extensive guide to numerous neurological disorders, such as Alzheimer's disease, autism, epilepsy, multiple sclerosis, Parkinson's disease, and stroke. The site also has a Spanish-language version.

National Institute of Nursing Research

http://www.ninr.nih.gov/

Sponsor(s): National Institutes of Health (NIH)— National Institute of Nursing Research (NINR)

Description: The NINR site features information on the broad range of nursing research. The site includes sections for About NINR, News & Information, Research & Funding, and Training. News & Information has NINR-supported investigator publications and summaries of NINR-supported research, as well as articles and podcasts. The Research & Funding section has grant information, information on NINR supported projects, and information about NINR intramural and extramural research. The Training section is designed for training researchers.

Subject(s): Nursing—Research

National Institute on Aging (NIA)

http://www.nia.nih.gov/

Sponsor(s): National Institutes of Health (NIH)—National Institute on Aging (NIA)

Description: NIA provides leadership in aging research (including Alzheimer's disease research), training, health information dissemination, and other programs related to aging. The site has information on research funding opportunities and research training support. The Research and Funding section offers further details on NIA research areas and funding opportunities. The Health and Aging Section has publications and a directory of related organizations. Under About NIA, the site also has information on the National Advisory Council on Aging, which reviews applications for funding and training and makes recommendations to NIA regarding research plans. Some information is available in Spanish.

Subject(s): Medical Research—Grants; Senior Citizens

National Institute on Alcohol Abuse and Alcoholism (NIAAA)

http://www.niaaa.nih.gov/

Sponsor(s): National Institutes of Health (NIH)—National Institute on Alcohol Abuse and Alcoholism (NIAAA)

Description: NIAAA conducts and supports research and education to reduce alcohol-related problems in the population. The NIAAA site features the sections About NIAAA, Publications & Multimedia, Research, Alcohol & Your Health, News & Events, and Grant Funding. Publications include the full text of the bulletin Alcohol Alert, along with pamphlets and research monographs.

Subject(s): Alcohol Abuse

Publication(s): *Alcohol Alert*, HE 20.8322

Alcohol Research, HE 20.8309

NIAAA Spectrum Webzine

National Institute on Deafness and Other Communication Disorders (NIDCD)

http://www.nidcd.nih.gov/

Sponsor(s): National Institutes of Health (NIH)—National Institute on Deafness and Other Communication Disorders (NIDCD)

Description: NIDCD conducts and supports research about the normal and disordered processes of hearing, balance, smell, taste, voice, speech, and language. The Web site has information on the institute and its research grants programs. The section on NIDCD research describes its work in such areas as the biophysics and mechanics of sensory cells and gene structure and function. The Health Info section has resources for the general public on topics such as ear infections, hearing aids, balance disorders, dysphagia, and stuttering. Some resources in this section are available in Spanish.

Subject(s): Hearing Disorders—Research

Publication(s): *Directory of Organizations, National Institute on Deafness*, HE 20.3660/2

National Institute on Disability and Rehabilitation Research (NIDRR)

http://www.ed.gov/about/offices/list/osers/nidrr/index.html

Sponsor(s): Education Department—Special Education and Rehabilitative Services Office—National Institute on Disability and Rehabilitation Research (NIDRR)

Description: NIDRR sponsors disability research and works with other federal agencies that conduct disability research through the Interagency Committee on Disability Research (ICDR). The Publications, Products, Research and Statistics section of the site provides links to publications and databases, including the Traumatic Brain Injury Database and the Spinal Cord Injury Database. The Programs and Projects section lists projects currently funded by NIDRR.

Subject(s): Disabilities—Research

Publication(s): *Program Directory, National Institute on Disability and Rehabilitation Research*, ED 1.215

National Institute on Drug Abuse (NIDA)

http://www.drugabuse.gov/

Sponsor(s): National Institutes of Health (NIH)—National Institute on Drug Abuse (NIDA)

Description: NIDA supports research and education to reduce drug abuse and addiction. The Drugs of Abuse section on the NIDA Web site provides fact sheets, statistics, and information on drug testing and treatment research. The site has a section for researchers with information on grants, funding, ongoing research, and clinical trials, as well as sections for medical and health professionals, parents and teachers, and students and young adults. It also provides extensive information in Spanish.

The NIDA Web site is easy to use and a recommended first stop for non-technical information on the science of drug abuse and addiction.

Subject(s): Drug Abuse

Publication(s): *Addiction Science & Clinical Practice*, HE 20.3972:
NIDA Notes, HE 20.3967
NIDA Research Report Series, HE 20.3965/2

National Institutes of Health (NIH)

http://www.nih.gov/

Sponsor(s): National Institutes of Health (NIH)

Description: The NIH Web site is a key starting point for finding government-related health sciences information. Sections include Health Information, Grants & Funding, News & Events, Research & Training, Institutes at NIH, and About NIH. The About NIH section covers its mission, organization, leadership, staff, and budget. The Institutes at NIH section links to the many component NIH organizations. The Health Information section has resources for the general public on health topics, clinical studies, and drug information, with links to health databases and health hotlines.

The Grants & Funding section features NIH funding opportunities and application kits, grants policy, and award data. New funding announcements can be viewed online or sent automatically via e-mail or RSS feed. The Research & Training section covers NIH intramural research news, postdoctoral and clinical training opportunities, and laboratory research resources. The News & Events section has news, social media links, and podcasts. The site also has a Spanish-language version.

The NIH is a significant health sciences and medical research institution. This central NIH site contains excellent information about the NIH and its component organizations. More importantly, the site links to an important body of NIH resources in the health sciences for the general public, health science researchers, and health science professionals. Many of the NIH component Web sites are listed in this publication.

Subject(s): Diseases and Conditions—Research; Medical Research—Grants

Publication(s): *NIH Almanac*, HE 20.3016
NIH Guide for Grants and Contracts, HE 20.3008/2
NIH News in Health, HE 20.3038/2
NIH Record, HE 20.3007/3
NIH Telephone and Service Directory, HE 20.3037

National Institutes of Health Public Access

http://publicaccess.nih.gov

Sponsor(s): National Institutes of Health (NIH)

Description: Peer-reviewed journal manuscripts based on NIH-funded research are required to be submitted to the NIH PubMed Central online repository. This site provides an explanation of the policy and instructions for compliance.

Subject(s): Publishing—Policy; Health Research—Policy

National Toxicology Program (NTP)

http://ntp.niehs.nih.gov/

Sponsor(s): National Institutes of Health (NIH)—National Institute of Environmental Health Sciences (NIEHS)

Description: NTP is an interagency program conducting toxicity/carcinogenicity studies on agents suspected of posing hazards to human health. Hundreds of chemical studies are on file, and much of this information is available on the NTP Web site.

This site contains a significant amount of toxicological data for researchers and those interested in the scientific basis for the regulation of toxic chemicals.

Subject(s): Toxicology (Medicine)—Research

Publication(s): *Report on Carcinogens*, HE 20.3562

NCI-Frederick (National Cancer Institute at Frederick)

http://ncifrederick.cancer.gov/

Sponsor(s): National Institutes of Health (NIH)—National Cancer Institute (NCI)

Description: NCI-Frederick is one of the main NCI cancer research centers. It focuses on direct research to help identify the causes of cancer, AIDS, and related diseases. Under the Science heading, the NCI-Frederick Web site links to its laboratories, branches, programs, and investigators. The site also has information on its support services, training, and a visitor's guide.

Subject(s): Cancer—Research

NIH Center for Scientific Review

http://www.csr.nih.gov/

Sponsor(s): National Institutes of Health (NIH)

Description: The Center for Scientific Review receives all grant applications sent to NIH and organizes the peer review groups for a majority of the research grants. The Web site has a section with resources for grant applicants and a section for those serving in peer review study sections.

Subject(s): Grants Management; Health Research—Grants
Publication(s): *Peer Review Notes*, HE 20.3045

NIH Clinical Center

http://www.cc.nih.gov/

Sponsor(s): National Institutes of Health (NIH)

Description: The NIH Clinical Center is a specialized research hospital at the National Institutes of Health. It is involved in a variety of clinical studies, and the Web site features a section about participating in these. For researchers and physicians, the site has information about research opportunities, information for referring physicians, summary information on research activities, and other resources.

Subject(s): Clinical Medicine

NIH Common Fund

http://nihroadmap.nih.gov

Sponsor(s): National Institutes of Health (NIH)

Description: The NIH Common Fund is an effort by NIH to identify and pursue areas that the agency must address as a whole, rather than leaving them to be addressed by the individual institutes within NIH. Sample Common Fund Programs include clinical research training, nanomedicine, and structural biology. The Web site provides background on the target areas and has information on funding opportunities, workshops, and news within the targeted research areas.

Subject(s): Health Research—Policy

NIH Office of the Director

http://www.nih.gov/icd/od/

Sponsor(s): National Institutes of Health (NIH)

Description: The director of NIH oversees the director's office and 27 institutes and centers. The Office of the Director web site has information about the director, communications, policy, research, administration, and funding. The site also links to pages for the Office of Federal Advisory Committee Policy (OFACP), with a separate link for NIH-only access.

Subject(s): Health Policy

Office of Animal Care and Use

http://oacu.od.nih.gov/

Sponsor(s): National Institutes of Health (NIH)

Description: This office provides oversight of animal care and use at NIH. The site is designed as an informational resource for NIH scientists and others at NIH involved in biomedical research. It includes information on NIH policy, guidelines, regulations, and standards, as well as information on health and safety issues.

Subject(s): Animals; Biological Medicine—Research

Office of Behavioral and Social Sciences Research (OBSSR)

http://obssr.od.nih.gov/

Sponsor(s): National Institutes of Health (NIH)—Office of Behavioral and Social Sciences Research

Description: OBSSR promotes research into how behavioral and social factors, such as family environment or cognitive issues, influence health. The Web site explains this field of research and lists opportunities for education and funding in the field.

Subject(s): Mental Health—Research; Social Science Research

Office of Disease Prevention (ODP)

https://prevention.nih.gov/

Sponsor(s): National Institutes of Health (NIH)

Description: ODP coordinates preventive medical research across NIH centers and with agencies and organizations outside NIH. The Web site has information about prevention research at NIH.

Subject(s): Preventive Health Care—Research

Profiles in Science

http://profiles.nlm.nih.gov/

Sponsor(s): National Institutes of Health (NIH)—National Library of Medicine (NLM)

Description: NLM's Profiles in Science Web site presents information on 20th-century leaders in biomedical research and public health. For each profiled person, the site includes biographical information and a collection of digitized materials, such as manuscripts, journal articles, photographs, and video clips.

Subject(s): Biographies; Health Research—History

Research Portfolio Online Reporting Tool (RePORT)

http://report.nih.gov/

Sponsor(s): National Institutes of Health (NIH)

Description: RePORT provides reports and data on the research activities of NIH. The site has a searchable database of NIH reports and most frequently requested statistical reports, such as average research grant size. The site's Categorical Spending section reports total spending by topic, such as heart disease or genetics. The centerpiece of the Web site is RePORTER, which enables detailed searching of a repository of NIH-funded research projects and provides access to publications and patents resulting from NIH funding.

Subject(s): Health Research

Publication(s): *NIH Data Book*

Stem Cell Information

http://stemcells.nih.gov/

Sponsor(s): National Institutes of Health (NIH)

Description: This NIH site includes information on research, federal policy, and frequently asked questions about stem cell research. The Research Topics section provides an overview of research at NIH and non-NIH institutions. The Info Center section offers substantial background information on stem cells and stem cell research, including a glossary and links to external Web sites that cover ethical issues of stem cell research. Another section covers related federal policy, statements, and legislation.

Subject(s): Biology—Research

MEDICAL INFORMATION

CDC Wonder on the Web

http://wonder.cdc.gov/

Sponsor(s): Health and Human Services Department—Centers for Disease Control and Prevention (CDC)

Description: CDC Wonder on the Web provides a single point of access to a variety of CDC reports, guidelines, and numeric public health data. The numeric databases can provide the numbers and rates for many diseases and health occurrences, including sexually transmitted diseases, cancer cases, and types of mortality and births in the United States. A list of topics covered on CDC Wonder is available by major area (such as communicable diseases) and in an alphabetical list.

Subject(s): Public Health—Statistics

Evaluating Internet Health Information
   http://www.nlm.nih.gov/medlineplus/webeval/
   Sponsor(s): National Institutes of Health (NIH)—National Library of Medicine (NLM)
   Description: This site provides a tutorial on evaluating the health information that can be found on the Web. The tutorial can be viewed online or downloaded for use without an Internet connection.
   Subject(s): Internet

healthfinder®
   http://www.healthfinder.gov/
   Sponsor(s): Health and Human Services Department
   Description: The healthfinder® Web site is designed to assist consumers in finding government health information on the Internet. It links to selected publications, databases, Web sites, support and self-help groups, and government health agencies. The site has consumer health news available by e-mail or as an RSS newsfeed, in English and Spanish. A version of the site is also available in Spanish.
   This site is an excellent starting point for finding health information and information about health services at the consumer's level, rather than the more technical information available elsewhere for medical practitioners and researchers.
   Subject(s): Health Care; Medical Information; Finding Aids

HealthIT.gov
   http://www.healthit.gov/
   Sponsor(s): Health and Human Services Department
   Description: This umbrella site provides information on the efforts of federal and state government and private partnerships to implement electronic management of medical information. The site is a joint effort between the Office of the National Coordinator for Health Information Technology (ONC) and the Agency for Health Research and Quality (AHRQ); more agencies may also join. The site also states that it "makes it possible for health care providers to better manage patient care through secure use and sharing of health information." Major topics include health IT funding opportunities, programs, federal advisory committees, and regulatory guidance. It also has a blog called Health IT Buzz.
   Subject(s): Medical Records

Lister Hill National Center for Biomedical Communications
   http://lhncbc.nlm.nih.gov/
   Sponsor(s): National Institutes of Health (NIH)—National Library of Medicine (NLM)

Description: Lister Hill specializes in health care communication, computing, and information sciences. The Web site features their work in biomedical informatics, multimedia visualization, knowledge and language processing, and other areas. The site carries related journal articles and technical publications.

Subject(s): Information Technology—Research; Medical Computing—Research

MedlinePlus

http://medlineplus.gov/

Alternate URL(s)

http://m.medlineplus.gov/

Sponsor(s): National Institutes of Health (NIH)—National Library of Medicine (NLM)

Description: MedlinePlus, the main NLM consumer health information Web site, presents information on hundreds of diseases and conditions, along with a guide to medications and supplements. The core of the site is the Health Topics section, a portal to a wide range of health issues. For each medical condition, MedlinePlus provides basic information and any other resources that may be useful to the public, such as surgery videos or interactive tutorials. For those who wish to go directly to the videos, there is a Videos & Cool Tools section. The site also has a dictionary search (medical terms), directories (doctors, dentists, and hospitals), and health news. MedlinePlus also features RSS feeds and links to its Twitter feed. The alternate URL above is for the mobile smart phone version of MedlinePlus.

MEDLINEplus is an outstanding resource for current, non-technical information on diseases, health conditions, medication, health supplements, and other medical topics. The site's design and content are both exemplary.

Subject(s): Medical Information; Pharmaceuticals; Databases

Publication(s): *MEDLINEplus*, HE 20.3629

NIH MedlinePlus Magazine, HE 20.3629/2

NIH MedlinePlus Salud Magazine

Morbidity and Mortality Weekly Report (MMWR)

http://www.cdc.gov/mmwr/

Sponsor(s): Health and Human Services Department—Centers for Disease Control and Prevention (CDC)

Description: The *Morbidity and Mortality Weekly Report (MMWR)*, along with its associated reports, is a standard and authoritative resource for detailed health statistics. The online version presents the full text of each issue of the *MMWR* from February 1982 (volume 31, issue 5) onward, with one issue from 1981 available. Individual components and issues of the MMWR series, such as the Summary of Notifiable Diseases, can be browsed in the MMWR Publications section. The weekly publication is also available as an RSS feed. Podcasts are also offered on the site.

The CDC has done a commendable job of converting this essential publication to an online format and organizing the Web site so that it is relatively easy to find current articles and back issues.

Subject(s): Diseases and Conditions—Statistics; Vital Statistics

Publication(s): *MMWR CDC Surveillance Summaries*, HE 20.7009/2
MMWR Recommendation and Reports, HE 20.7009/2-2
Morbidity and Mortality Weekly Report, HE 20.7009

National Center for Health Statistics (NCHS)

http://www.cdc.gov/nchs/

Sponsor(s): Health and Human Services Department—Centers for Disease Control and Prevention (CDC)—National Center for Health Statistics (NCHS)

Description: NCHS is the lead agency for U.S. health statistics. Major sections of the site cover NCHS surveys and data collection, Publications derived from the data, and downloadable data sets and data analysis tools. Major surveys conducted by NCHS include the *National Health Care Survey (NHCS)* and *National Health and Nutrition Examination Survey (NHANES)*. NCHS also maintains the National Vital Statistics System (NVSS).

NCHS Web site menus provide a layered access to data and reports—from raw data to prepared fact sheets. The home page makes it easy to find the most frequently used information.

Subject(s): Health and Safety—Statistics; Health Care—Statistics; Vital Statistics

Publication(s): *Health, United States*, HE 20.7042/6
International Classification of Diseases, HE 22.41/2
Life Tables, HE 20.6215
National Hospital Discharge Survey, HE 20.6209/7
National Vital Statistics Report, HE 20.6217
Vital and Health Statistics, HE 20.6209
Where to Write for Vital Records, HE 20.6210/2

National Health Information Center (NHIC)

http://www.health.gov/nhic/

Sponsor(s): Health and Human Services Department—Public Health and Science Office—Disease Prevention and Health Promotion Office

Description: NHIC, a health information referral service, produces this Web site featuring health information for health professionals and consumers. The Health Information Resource Database includes about 1,600 organizations and government offices that provide health information upon request. The Publications area has information on the annual National Health Observances and a list of toll-free numbers for health information. NHIC also supports the healthfinder® Web site; health care consumers will want to check that site for additional information.

Subject(s): Health Promotion

Publication(s): *Federal Health Information Centers and Clearinghouses*, HE 20.34/2:IN 3/2/

National Health Observances, HE 20.2:H 34/

National Rehabilitation Information Center (NARIC)

http://www.naric.com/

Sponsor(s): Education Department—Special Education and Rehabilitative Services Office—National Institute on Disability and Rehabilitation Research (NIDRR)

Description: Funded by NIDRR, NARIC collects and disseminates the results of federally funded research projects in the area of disability and rehabilitation. The site tailors this information for three audiences: the general public, researchers, and NIDRR grantees. The information for researchers includes REHABDATA, an extensive database of literature abstracts covering physical, mental, and psychiatric disabilities; independent living; vocational rehabilitation; special education; assistive technology; and other issues related to people with disabilities. REHABDATA also has the full text access of original research documents that are the direct result of government-funded research.

Subject(s): Disabilities—Research

Publication(s): *NIDRR Program Directory*, ED 1.215

NLM Gateway

http://gateway.nlm.nih.gov/

Sponsor(s): Lister Hill National Center for Biomedical Communications (LHNCBC); National Institutes of Health (NIH)—National Library of Medicine (NLM)

Description: The NLM Gateway has been mostly transitioned out to a pilot program from the Lister Hill National Center for Biomedical Communications, focusing on the Meeting Abstracts and Health Services Research Projects in Progress (HSRProj) databases. The About link on the page lists the databases formerly contained in the Gateway and the URLs at which they can be accessed.

Subject(s): Medical Information; Databases

PubMed

http://www.ncbi.nlm.nih.gov/PubMed/

Sponsor(s): National Institutes of Health (NIH)—National Library of Medicine (NLM)

Description: PubMed is part of the Entrez Retrieval System operated by NLM's National Center for Biotechnology Information (NCBI). It searches more than 24 million citations to biomedical literature. The citations are from MEDLINE and additional life science sources. PubMed also includes links to sites providing full-text articles and other related resources. Other PubMed services include the MeSH (Medical Subject Heading Browser) Database, Citation Matcher (single and batch), Clinical Queries (for physicians), and LinkOut, which links to a wide variety of relevant web-accessible online resources. A mobile version of PubMed is also available.

PubMed is a central resource for searching life sciences literature.

Subject(s): Medical Information; Medline

PubMed Central (PMC)

http://www.pubmedcentral.nih.gov/

Sponsor(s): National Institutes of Health (NIH)—National Library of Medicine (NLM)

Description: PMC is a free digital archive of biomedical and life sciences journal literature. Participating journals deposit their content with PMC, but copyright is retained by the journal or authors (as appropriate). An RSS feed provides news on new journals added to PMC.

Subject(s): Biological Medicine—Research; Life Sciences—Research

Surveillance, Epidemiology, and End Results (SEER) Program

http://seer.cancer.gov/

Sponsor(s): National Institutes of Health (NIH)—National Cancer Institute (NCI)

Description: The SEER program collects and publishes cancer incidence and survival data from a number of population-based cancer registries. Its data and publications are available on this Web site. The Cancer Statistics section provides an introduction to cancer statistics and access to simplified quick reference tools, such as Fast Stats and State Cancer Profiles. The Datasets & Software section links to the SEER data, statistical software resources, and supporting materials.

Subject(s): Cancer—Statistics

Publication(s): *SEER Cancer Statistics Review*, HE 20.3186

United States Cancer Statistics, HE 20.7045:

TOXNET

http://toxnet.nlm.nih.gov/

Sponsor(s): National Institutes of Health (NIH)—National Cancer Institute (NCI)

Description: TOXNET is a group of databases on toxicology, hazardous chemicals, and related areas. The site allows users to search the databases separately or together. Hosted databases include the Hazardous Substances Data Bank (HSDB), Chemical Carcinogenesis Research Information Service (CCRIS), International Toxicity Estimates for Risk (ITER), and the Developmental and Reproductive Toxicology Database (DART).

The site also links to TOXMAP, an NLM service that maps the Environmental Protection Agency's (EPA) Toxics Release Inventory (TRI) data.

Subject(s): Chemical Information; Toxic Substances

United States Renal Data System (USRDS)

http://www.usrds.org/

Sponsor(s): Health and Human Services Department—Centers for Medicare and Medicaid Services; National Institutes of Health (NIH)—National Institute of Diabetes and Digestive and Kidney Disease (NIDDK)

Description: USRDS is a national data system that collects, analyzes, and distributes information about end-stage renal disease (ESRD) in the United States. The organization's work is funded by Department of Health and Human Services agencies—the National Institute of Diabetes and Digestive and Kidney Diseases and the Centers for Medicare and Medicaid Services. The site includes an annual data report on end-stage renal disease in the United States and the Renal Data Extraction and Referencing (RenDER) System database.

Subject(s): Kidney Disease—Statistics

Publication(s): *United States Renal Data System, Annual Data Report,* HE 20.3325

Visible Human Project®

http://www.nlm.nih.gov/research/visible/

Sponsor(s): National Institutes of Health (NIH)—National Library of Medicine (NLM)

Description: NLM's Visible Human Project® has created digital image datasets of the normal male and female human body. The site includes detailed information on the project and on other projects based on the visible human data set. It provides information on how to obtain the data, including the license agreement. Translations are available in Finnish, German, Russian, and Belorussian.

Subject(s): Human Anatomy and Physiology; Medical Computing

VitalStats

http://www.cdc.gov/nchs/VitalStats.htm

Sponsor(s): Health and Human Services Department—Centers for Disease Control and Prevention (CDC)—National Center for Health Statistics (NCHS)

Description: VitalStats is a central location for data on births and perinatal mortality.

Subject(s): Health Care—Statistics; Vital Statistics

Who Cares: Sources of Information About Health Care Products and Services
http://www.ftc.gov/whocares
Sponsor(s): Federal Trade Commission (FTC)
Description: The Who Cares Web site provides consumer information on medicine and medical services, and information on how to file a consumer complaint. A section on fraud and scams discusses medical ID theft, Medicare fraud, miracle cures, and other topics. The site is also available in Spanish.
Subject(s): Consumer Information

MEDICINE AND MEDICAL DEVICES

DailyMed
http://dailymed.nlm.nih.gov/
Sponsor(s): National Institutes of Health (NIH)—National Library of Medicine (NLM)
Description: DailyMed provides FDA-approved labels (package insert information) for more than 48,000 marketed drugs. Label information can be e-mailed from the site or all drug labels can be downloaded at once. DailyMed also has an RSS feed for notification of updates to the database.
Subject(s): Pharmaceuticals

Drug Information Portal
http://druginfo.nlm.nih.gov/
Sponsor(s): National Institutes of Health (NIH)—National Library of Medicine (NLM)
Description: The Drug Information Portal serves as a starting point for finding information about prescription and over-the-counter drugs. It includes drugs from the time they are entered into clinical trials through their entry in the U.S. market place. The site links to Web sites and databases for drug information from such government agencies as the National Institutes of Health and the Food and Drug Administration. The resources can also be searched by name or by category, such as antibiotics.
Subject(s): Pharmaceuticals

Drugs
http://www.fda.gov/Drugs/default.htm
Sponsor(s): Health and Human Services Department—Food and Drug Administration (FDA)—Center for Drug Evaluation and Research (CDER)

Description: This Web site provides information for consumers, medical professionals, and the pharmaceutical industry. It features a number of databases, including the "Orange Book" of approved drugs, the National Drug Code Directory, and the Adverse Event Reporting Program. The wealth of information on the site is organized into several major sections: Drug Approvals and Databases; Drug Safety and Availability; Development and Approval Process (Drugs); Guidance, Compliance & Regulatory Information; News & Events; and Science and Research (Drugs).

Subject(s): Pharmaceuticals

Publication(s): *Electronic Orange Book: Approved Drug Products with Therapeutic Equivalence Evaluations*, HE 20.4715

National Drug Code Directory, HE 20.4012

Drugs@FDA

http://www.accessdata.fda.gov/scripts/cder/drugsatfda/

Sponsor(s): Health and Human Services Department—Food and Drug Administration (FDA)—Center for Drug Evaluation and Research (CDER)

Description: Drugs@FDA has information on U.S. approved and tentatively approved prescription and over-the-counter drugs intended for human use. It also has information on drugs removed from the U.S. market for reasons besides safety or effectiveness. (The Web site's FAQ provides a more complete list of drug types that are included and excluded.) Drugs@FDA can be used to find labels for approved drugs, generic drug products for a brand name drug, therapeutically equivalent drug products for a brand name or generic drug product, consumer information for drugs approved, drugs with a specific active ingredient, and the approval history of a drug. The Web site also offers a downloadable file of the Drugs@FDA database.

Subject(s): Over-The-Counter Drugs; Pharmaceuticals

Electronic Orange Book

http://www.accessdata.fda.gov/scripts/cder/ob/

Sponsor(s): Health and Human Services Department—Food and Drug Administration (FDA)—Center for Drug Evaluation and Research (CDER)

Description: This online version of *Approved Drug Products with Therapeutic Equivalence Evaluations*, known as the *FDA Orange Book*, includes information on prescription drugs, over-the-counter drugs, and discontinued drugs. Users can search by the following categories: Active Ingredient, Applicant Holder, Proprietary Name, Patent Number, or Application Number. The result categories include Active Ingredient, Dosage Form and Route, Applicant Holder, Proprietary Name, Strength, Application Number, and Reference Listed Drug. The Patent Search page can also display recently added patents and patent delistings.

This is a useful database for verifying FDA approval of a drug and for determining the length of time for which it has been approved. Read the Frequently Asked Questions section for important information about how often the database is updated.

Subject(s): Pharmaceuticals

Publication(s): *Approved Drug Product with Therapeutic Equivalence Evaluations (Orange Book)*, HE 20.4715

FDA Notices of Judgment Collection

http://archive.nlm.nih.gov/fdanj/

Sponsor(s): National Institutes of Health (NIH)—National Library of Medicine (NLM)

Description: As described on the site, "The FDA Notices of Judgment Collection is a digital archive of the published notices judgment for products seized under authority of the 1906 Pure Food and Drug Act." The collection spans 1908 to 1964 and covers the legal document related to food, drugs, medical devices, and cosmetics.

Subject(s): Health Products—Laws; Medicine and Medical Devices—Regulations

Food and Drug Administration (FDA)

http://www.fda.gov/

Sponsor(s): Health and Human Services Department—Food and Drug Administration (FDA)

Description: The FDA regulates the quality and safety of food, drugs, cosmetics, medical devices, biologics (such as vaccines), animal feed, veterinary drugs, radiation-emitting products (such as tanning lamps), and tobacco products. The FDA Web site features news, recalls and safety alerts, statutes and regulations, and a variety of paths to information on its regulated product areas. Press releases, recall notices, and alerts are available as RSS feeds. The site links to the specialized offices that make up the FDA, the FDA field offices, and the FDA advisory committees. Specific sections of the Web site are tailored to consumers, industry, health professionals, and state and local officials. Some consumer health publications are available in Spanish.

The FDA site is well designed, with multiple paths to find all of the information the agency provides on the Web. Use the A to Z subject index to find specific information quickly.

Subject(s): Food—Regulations; Pharmaceuticals—Regulations

Publication(s): *FDA Compliance Program Guidance Manual*, HE 20.4008
FDA Enforcement Reports, HE 20.4039

Medical Devices

http://www.fda.gov/MedicalDevices/

Sponsor(s): Health and Human Services Department—Food and Drug Administration (FDA)—Center for Devices and Radiological Health (CDRH)

Description: CDRH is concerned with the safety and regulation of medical devices and electronic products that produce radiation. Web site sections include Products and Medical Procedures, Medical Device Safety, Device Advice: Comprehensive Regulatory Assistance, Science and Research (Medical Devices), News and Events (Medical Devices), and Resources for You (Medical Devices). The products profiled include LASIK eye surgery, surgical staplers, hearing aids, infusion pumps, home healthcare products, tanning devices, and medical devices for children.

Subject(s): Medical Devices—Regulations; Radiation—Regulations

MedWatch: FDA Safety Information and Adverse Event Reporting Program

http://www.fda.gov/medwatch/

Sponsor(s): Health and Human Services Department—Food and Drug Administration (FDA)

Description: MedWatch provides information and alerts about the safety of medical products to both health care professionals and the public. MedWatch also allows both of these groups to report problems related to medical products to the FDA. Users can subscribe to receive MedWatch alerts by e-mail or RSS feed.

Subject(s): Medicine and Medical Devices—Regulations

Vaccines and Immunizations

http://www.cdc.gov/vaccines/

Sponsor(s): Health and Human Services Department—Centers for Disease Control and Prevention (CDC)—National Center for Immunization and Respiratory Diseases (NCIRD)

Description: This CDC Web site provides information on immunization and vaccine safety for the general public, parents, travelers, health care professionals, local governments, immunization program managers, and others. It includes immunization schedules and information on vaccine safety and vaccination records. The site also has information on requirements and laws, and recommendations from the Advisory Committee on Immunization Practices. The Vaccination Coverage and Surveillance section has data from the National Immunization Survey and other sources. Publications include *Vaccine Information Statements* and the *Epidemiology and Prevention of Vaccine-Preventable Diseases*, known as the *Pink Book*.

This CDC site provides organized access to a tremendous amount of information on vaccines and immunizations. It should be a first stop for general research in this area.

Subject(s): Immunization

Publication(s): *Epidemiology and Prevention of Vaccine-Preventable Diseases (Pink Book)*, HE 20.7970

Vaccine Information Statements, HE 20.7962

NUTRITION

Center for Food Safety and Applied Nutrition (CFSAN)

http://www.fda.gov/Food/

Sponsor(s): Health and Human Services Department—Food and Drug Administration (FDA)—Center for Food Safety and Applied Nutrition (CFSAN)

Description: CFSAN is responsible for the safety and proper labeling of food and cosmetics. The site has information on national food safety programs, food facility registration, consumer advice, information for industry, and updates on food and cosmetics laws and regulations. Information on the site covers such topics as biotechnology, cosmetics, dietary supplements, food labeling and nutrition, foodborne illness, import and exports, pesticides and chemical contaminants, and seafood (including the *Regulatory Fish Encyclopedia*). The site links to information on inspections, compliance, enforcements, and recalls.

The CFAN site provides relevant and practical content for consumers, industry, health professionals, legal experts, and others.

Subject(s): Food Safety; Cosmetics—Regulations

Publication(s): *Food Code*, HE 20.4002

Interstate Certified Shellfish Shippers List, HE 20.4014

Regulatory Fish Encyclopedia, HE 20.4002

The Bad Bug Book: Foodborne Pathogenic Microorganisms and Natural Toxins Handbook, HE 20.4508

Center for Nutrition Policy and Promotion (CNPP)

http://www.usda.gov/cnpp/

Sponsor(s): Agriculture Department (USDA)—Center for Nutrition Policy and Promotion (CNPP)

Description: CNPP is the focal point within USDA for scientific research linked with the nutritional needs of the public. Project links include Dietary Guidelines for Americans, the Healthy Eating Index, and Nutrient Content of the U.S. Food Supply.

Subject(s): Dietary Guidelines; Nutrition

Publication(s): *Cost of Food at Home Estimated for Food Plans at Four Cost Levels*, A 98.19/2

Dietary Guidelines for Americans, A 1.77:232/
Expenditures on Children by Families: Annual Report, A 1.38
Nutrient Content of the U.S. Food Supply, A 1.87:55

ChooseMyPlate.gov

http://www.choosemyplate.gov/

Sponsor(s): Agriculture Department (USDA)

Description: ChooseMyPlate.gov is a federal initiative to provide the general public with nutritional guidance. The site provides an image of a plate and the proportions of fruits, vegetables, grains, and proteins that should be added to it. Other reference sources discuss such topics as weight management and physical activity. The SuperTracker tool allows users to plan and analyze their diet and activity choices.

Subject(s): Nutrition

Dietary Supplements Labels Database

http://www.dsld.nlm.nih.gov/dsld/

Sponsor(s): National Institutes of Health (NIH)—National Library of Medicine (NLM)

Description: This database provides ingredient and health claim information from the product labels of over 7,000 selected brands of dietary supplements. The information can be searched or browsed by brand name, active ingredient, and manufacturer. The database also links to ingredient fact sheets (when available). The site links to warnings and recalls from the Food and Drug Administration (FDA) and provides helpful background information on dietary supplements.

Subject(s): Dietary Supplements

Food and Nutrition Information Center (FNIC)

http://www.nal.usda.gov/fnic/

Sponsor(s): Agriculture Department (USDA)—National Agricultural Library (NAL)

Description: The FNIC Web site says that the center "provides credible, accurate, and practical resources for nutrition and health professionals, educators, government personnel, and consumers." Topics include food safety, food labeling, dietary guidance, weight and obesity, and food composition. The site provides numerous resources and databases to further nutrition education. The site also has an RSS feed combining food and nutrition news from USDA and other federal government sources.

Subject(s): Nutrition

Fruits and Vegetables

http://www.fruitsandveggiesmatter.gov/

Sponsor(s): National Institutes of Health (NIH)—National Cancer Institute (NCI)

Description: This health promotion Web site touts the benefits of eating fruits and vegetables. It includes nutrient information and tips for using fruits and vegetables to maximize weight management.

Subject(s): Fruit; Nutrition; Vegetables

Healthy Meals Resource System

https://healthymeals.nal.usda.gov/

Sponsor(s): Agriculture Department (USDA)

Description: This site has a wealth of resources on child nutrition and food safety. Materials discuss nutrition education, menu planning, HealthierUS School Challenge resources, and professional and career resources.

While the site is designed for day care providers who participate in the USDA's Child and Adult Care Food Program, parents and others will also find the recipes and educational activity ideas useful.

Subject(s): Child Care; Nutrition; Recipes

Nutrition.gov

http://www.nutrition.gov/

Sponsor(s): Agriculture Department (USDA)

Description: Nutrition.gov is a portal Web site for government information on nutrition. It organizes links to nutrition information from many federal agencies into sections such as Smart Nutrition 101, Weight Management, Dietary Supplements, and Food Assistance Programs. The site serves consumers, nutrition educators, health providers, and researchers.

Subject(s): Nutrition

Office of Dietary Supplements (ODS)

http://ods.od.nih.gov/

Sponsor(s): National Institutes of Health (NIH)—Office of Dietary Supplements

Description: ODS promotes scientific research in the area of dietary supplements. The Web site describes ODS programs, research, and funding. ODS does not have granting authority but co-sponsors research with other institutes. In the Research & Funding section, the ODS Web site provides resources such as the Computer Access to Research on Dietary Supplements (CARDS) Database and the Dietary Supplement Ingredient Database (DSID). The Health Information section has information for the consumer, including information on health claims and labeling. The site also offers a newsletter and more than 60 fact sheets on specific dietary supplements, including botanical supplements, vitamins, and minerals.

This site provides extensive information for health professionals and consumers. The ODS booklet "How To Evaluate Health Information on the Internet: Questions and Answers" should be of assistance to many consumers—even beyond those with an interest in dietary supplements.

Subject(s): Dietary Supplements; Nutrition—Research
Publication(s): *Dietary Supplements Fact Sheets*
The Scoop: A Newsletter for Consumers

SNAP-Ed Connection

http://snap.nal.usda.gov/

Sponsor(s): Agriculture Department (USDA)—National Agricultural Library (NAL)

Description: The SNAP-Ed Connection Web site is designed for Supplemental Nutrition Assistance Program (SNAP) nutrition education providers, but it includes excellent resources for users looking for nutrition information. The Resource Library section has Resource Finder database of educational and training materials on topics such as dietary guidelines, meal planning, food purchasing, and weight control. The site also has a recipe database of recipes submitted by nutrition and health professionals. Other materials on the site, such as state program links and professional development materials, will primarily be of interest to the site's intended audience of nutrition educators.

Subject(s): Nutrition; Recipes

WIC Works Resource System

http://wicworks.nal.usda.gov/

Sponsor(s): Agriculture Department (USDA)

Description: This site offers resources for state-based professionals facilitating the USDA's Special Supplemental Nutrition Program for Women, Infants, and Children (known as WIC). WIC Works is a clearinghouse for educational and promotional materials about nutrition for WIC program clients.

Subject(s): Nutrition

SAFETY

Air Force Rescue Coordination Center (AFRCC)

http://www.1af.acc.af.mil/units/afrcc/

Sponsor(s): Air Force—Air Combat Command (ACC)

Description: AFRCC is the single federal agency responsible for coordinating search and rescue (SAR) activities in the continental United States. AFRCC also coordinates search and rescue agreements, plans, and policy. This Web site describes their structure and operations. The AFRCC SAR Links section includes Web links to other federal and private search and rescue organizations. AFRCC annual reports provide detailed reporting and statistics on the previous year's missions.

Subject(s): Search and Rescue

CDC Emergency Preparedness and Response

http://www.bt.cdc.gov/

Sponsor(s): Health and Human Services Department—Centers for Disease Control and Prevention (CDC)

Description: This CDC portal site links to a broad range of practical information about health and safety emergencies. Major categories are Bioterrorism, Chemical Emergencies, Radiation Emergencies, Natural Disasters, Caring for Children, and Recent Incidents.

Subject(s): Disaster Preparedness

Disaster Information Management Research Center

http://sis.nlm.nih.gov/dimrc.html

Sponsor(s): National Institutes of Health (NIH)—National Library of Medicine (NLM)

Description: Disaster Information Management Research Center provides disaster health information resources and research to assist public health officials, healthcare providers, special populations, and the public. The site links to information from NLM and other Web sites about such topics as bioterrorism, earthquakes, and public health preparations for mass gatherings.

Subject(s): Disaster Assistance; Public Health

DisasterAssistance.gov

http://www.disasterassistance.gov/

Sponsor(s): Federal Emergency Management Agency (FEMA)

Description: DisasterAssistance.gov is the federal government's portal to information about disaster assistance and services from state and federal government and from nongovernment sources. The site also has advice and referrals for Americans affected by disaster when in a foreign country.

Subject(s): Disaster Assistance

Food Safety

http://www.fns.usda.gov/fns/food_safety.htm

Sponsor(s): Agriculture Department (USDA)—Food and Nutrition Service (FNS)

Description: This site compiles information on food safety and security related to the assistance programs administered by FNS. Resources include guidance for food service in schools and the latest food product recall information. The federal government also maintains a multi-agency food safety portal for consumers at http://foodsafety.gov.

Subject(s): Food Safety

Food Safety and Inspection Service (FSIS)

http://www.fsis.usda.gov/

Sponsor(s): Agriculture Department (USDA)—Food Safety and Inspection Service (FSIS)

Description: FSIS is the public health regulatory agency in the USDA responsible for ensuring that meat, poultry, and egg products are safe, wholesome, and accurately labeled. Major topics covered by the FSIS Web site include food safety education, food safety science, regulations and policies, FSIS recalls, and food defense and emergency response. The site has information on federal and state inspection programs, compliance assistance, news on food safety issues in the United States. Background on the Codex Alimentarius Commission (the international mechanism for guarding safety in food trade) is provided on the site. The FSIS Recalls section lists current food recalls, which are voluntary actions by a manufacturer or distributor. It also has information on how to report a food problem. The site has numerous fact sheets covering such topics as safe food handling, food labeling, and meat, poultry, and egg preparation. Other publications can be found in the FOIA Electronic Reading Room section, which is linked from the bottom of the page. The site is also available in Spanish.

For users concerned with food safety issues, this site offers easy access to relevant information.

Subject(s): Food Safety

FoodSafety.gov

http://www.foodsafety.gov/

Sponsor(s): Health and Human Services Department—Food and Drug Administration (FDA)—Center for Food Safety and Applied Nutrition (CFSAN)

Description: FoodSafety.gov is a gateway to selected food safety-related information on government Web sites. The site provides practical guidance on keeping food safe, seasonal food handling advice, types of food poisoning, and where to report a problem. The site also has information on inspections and compliance guidance for the food industry. The News & Features section includes product recall alerts and food safety news from multiple federal agencies concerned with different aspects of food safety.

Subject(s): Food Safety

Healthy Homes and Lead Hazard Control
http://www.hud.gov/offices/lead/
Sponsor(s): Housing and Urban Development (HUD)—Office of Healthy Homes and Lead Hazard Control
Description: This HUD office works to eliminate lead-based paint hazards in privately owned and low-income housing. The site focuses on regulations, enforcement, grants information, technical training, and technical studies and guidelines. It also includes information on mold and moisture.
Subject(s): Home Maintenance; Lead Poisoning

Household Products Database
http://householdproducts.nlm.nih.gov/
Sponsor(s): National Institutes of Health (NIH)—National Library of Medicine (NLM)
Description: This database of over 14,000 consumer brands provides information on the chemicals the products contain, any ill effects those chemicals may cause, and what first aid steps should be taken if necessary. It also provides the manufacturer's toll free number, the products' health and flammability ratings, and tips for handling and disposal. The database can be searched by product or ingredient. Product sections include Auto Products, Pesticides, Landscape/Yard, Pet Care, and more.
Subject(s): Chemical Information; Product Safety
Publication(s): *Material Safety Data Sheets*, D 5.302

Lead in Paint, Dust, and Soil
http://www.epa.gov/lead/
Sponsor(s): Environmental Protection Agency (EPA)—Prevention, Pesticides and Toxic Substances Office
Description: This EPA Web site provides information on lead poisoning and where lead is likely to be a hazard. The site also has relevant regulations, guidelines for professionals who deal with lead-based paint, information on the National Lead Information Center hotline, and links to other EPA resources on lead hazards.
Subject(s): Lead Poisoning

National Center for Injury Prevention and Control (NCIPC)
http://www.cdc.gov/injury/
Sponsor(s): Health and Human Services Department—Centers for Disease Control and Prevention (CDC)—National Center for Injury Prevention and Control (NCIPC)
Description: NCIPC seeks to reduce morbidity, disability, mortality, and costs associated with injuries outside the workplace. Its Web site features data and statistics, fact sheets, research and funding information, and publications. Topical categories include Violence Prevention, Trau-

matic Brain Injury, Motor Vehicle Safety, Prescription Drug Overdose, and Home & Recreational Safety. The site's WISQARS™ (Web-based Injury Statistics Query and Reporting System) database provides customized reports of injury-related data. The Data and Statistics section also links to a national inventory of injury data systems.

Subject(s): Injuries; Safety

U.S. Fire Administration (USFA)

http://www.usfa.dhs.gov/

Sponsor(s): Homeland Security Department—Federal Emergency Management Agency (FEMA)—U.S. Fire Administration

Description: As part of FEMA, USFA works to reduce life and economic losses due to fire, arson, and related emergencies. The Web site has current fire news and information on firefighter fatalities, fire statistics, and the National Fire Department Census Database. It also features a searchable database of hotels and motels that meet fire and life federal safety requirements. Major sections include Grants & Funding, Data Publications & Library, Operations Management & Safety, Fire Prevention & Public Education, and Training & Professional Development. A version of the site is available in Spanish.

Subject(s): Fire Prevention; Firefighting—Grants

Publication(s): *Fire in the United States*, FEM 1.117

Firefighter Fatalities, FEM 1.116

FOURTEEN

International Relations

This chapter includes a number of Web sites from the State Department and other agencies whose work involves international assistance, immigration control, diplomacy, or other topics related to the U.S. role in the world. The field of international relations often intersects with those of defense and commerce. Researchers may want to check the Defense and Intelligence chapter and the International Trade section of the Business and Economics chapter for additional Web sites of interest. Also, the Education chapter has a section on International Education.

Subsections in this chapter are Arms Control, Country Information, Diplomacy, Foreign Policy, International Migration and Travel, and International Relations.

ARMS CONTROL

Bureau of Verification, Compliance, and Implementation (VCI)
http://www.state.gov/t/vci/
Sponsor(s): State Department—Verification, Compliance, and Implementation Bureau
Description: VCI works to ensure compliance with international arms control, nonproliferation, and disarmament agreements and commitments. VCI reports to Congress on other nations' compliance. The bureau also reports in the Federal Register, noting any sanctions against countries providing controlled technology to Iran, North Korea, or Syria. The Web site has information on the New Strategic Arms Reduction Treaty (New START) and copies of other treaties and agreements concerned with nonproliferation and disarmament.
Subject(s): Arms Control; Nonproliferation

Publication(s): *Adherence to and Compliance with Arms Control, Nonproliferation, and Disarmament Agreements and Commitments*
World Military Expenditures and Arms Transfers, S 22.116

Chemical Weapons Convention Web Site
http://www.cwc.gov/
Sponsor(s): Commerce Department—Bureau of Industry and Security (BIS)
Description: This Web site brings together background information, regulations, documents, and reports related to U.S. compliance with the Chemical Weapons Convention. The treaty affects U.S. private industries that produce, process, consume, import, or export dual-use chemicals that could be used to produce chemical weapons. The Declarations section of the site includes handbooks and forms to assist companies with compliance. More publications are available in the Outreach section.
Subject(s): Chemical Warfare

Nonproliferation and Disarmament Fund (NDF)
http://www.state.gov/t/isn/ndf/
Sponsor(s): State Department—Nonproliferation Bureau
Description: NDF was established to enable quick responses to stop the proliferation of nuclear, biological, and chemical weapons; weapons of mass destruction; and advanced conventional weapons. The NDF Web site provides basic information on the fund, its legal authority, and projects.
Subject(s): Arms Control; Nonproliferation
Publication(s): *NDF Annual Report*

COUNTRY INFORMATION

Bilateral Relations Fact Sheets
http://www.state.gov/r/pa/ei/bgn/
Sponsor(s): State Department
This popular series of brief country profiles comes from the Department of State. Each country's edition is consistently formatted and contains facts and narrative on aspects of the geography.

This series is useful for bringing together basic historical, political, social, and economic information for each country, and the online version's HTML format makes it easy to link to referenced resources. However, be sure to check the date of the latest revision for each country; there may have been significant changes in a country since the last update.
Subject(s): Foreign Countries; History
Publication(s): *Background Notes (various countries)*; S 1.123

Country Studies: Area Handbook Series

http://lcweb2.loc.gov/frd/cs/cshome.html

Sponsor(s): Library of Congress

Description: These books, alternatively known as *Country Studies* or Army *Area Handbooks*, are excellent sources for detailed—if dated—information on other countries. Each publication in the series covers a particular foreign country, describing and analyzing its political, economic, social, and national security systems and institutions and examining the interrelationships of those systems and the ways they are shaped by cultural factors. Each study was written by a multidisciplinary team of social scientists. Intended as background material for the U.S. Army, the series includes such countries as North Korea and Kazakhstan but does not cover Canada, France, or the United Kingdom. This site offers full-text search capabilities across all or any combination of the available books. Country Studies has not been updated since 1998 because the Army discontinued funding for the project. The Web site's FAQ section discusses the funding situation.

Although these books have not been updated to reflect current events, they remain valuable reference tools for the cultural and historical information they provide. Each study also includes a selective bibliography for further research. Due to the unique publication history of the *Country Studies*, the FAQ section should be consulted as a reference.

Subject(s): Foreign Countries; History

Publication(s): *Country Studies Series*

World Factbook

https://www.cia.gov/library/publications/the-world-factbook/

Sponsor(s): Central Intelligence Agency (CIA)

Description: The CIA's *World Factbook* is a standard reference for country information. Information and data on the site is updated throughout the year. For each country, the *World Factbook* provides a map, a color image of the national flag, and a profile that includes reference information about the country's geography, population, government, economy, communications, transportation, military, and transnational issues. The *World Factbook* has prepared tables ranking the countries on certain numerical data, such as total population. Appendices include an extensive list of international organizations and acronyms and a conversion table for weights and measures.

Given its authority and frequent updates, the *World Factbook* Web site is a recommended online reference tool.

Subject(s): Foreign Countries

Publication(s): *World Factbook*, PREX 3.15

DIPLOMACY

Broadcasting Board of Governors
http://www.bbg.gov/
Sponsor(s): International Broadcasting Bureau
Description: The Broadcasting Board of Governors is an independent federal agency responsible for all non-military, international broadcasting by the U.S. government. The board's Web site describes each of the international broadcasting services in operation: the Voice of America (VOA), Alhurra, Radio Sawa, Radio Free Europe/Radio Liberty (RFE/RL), the Middle East Broadcasting Networks (MBN), Radio Free Asia (RFA), and Radio and TV Marti. Each is assisted by the International Broadcasting Bureau (IBB). The Web site also has press releases and board meeting reports.
Subject(s): Broadcasting—International

Bureau of Diplomatic Security (DS)
http://www.state.gov/m/ds/
Sponsor(s): State Department—Diplomatic Security Bureau
Description: The Bureau of Diplomatic Security (DS) is the security and law enforcement arm of the Department of State. DS manages the security programs that protect U.S. personnel working in U.S. diplomatic missions around the world. DS also assists foreign embassies and consulates in the United States with security and manages immunity issues for foreign diplomats in the United States. They investigate passport and visa fraud and manage the Department of State's personnel security clearance program. The Web site describes each aspect of the DS mission in detail and provides current information about its activities. The News and Information section includes fact sheets and press releases.
Subject(s): Terrorism
Publication(s): *Antiterrorism Assistance Program: Report to Congress for Fiscal Year . . . ,* S 1.138/3
Political Violence Against Americans, S 1.138/2

Department of State
http://www.state.gov/
Sponsor(s): State Department
Description: The home page of the Department of State Web site features current news, latest Tweets, and videos of recent department events. Toward the bottom of the page, there is a link to a subject index of the content on the site. The Web site has direct links to popular sections: Media Center, Travel, Careers, Business, Youth and Education, and About State. The Media section links to the *Daily Press Briefings*, videos, and press releases. The Travel section covers passports, visas, and international travel warnings. The Business section covers trade issues and

State support for businesses. The Youth and Education section includes information on educational and cultural exchange programs, State Department and U.S. diplomatic history, and intercountry adoption. The About State section includes biographies of State Department officials, organizational information, department publications, and directories such as Key Officers at Foreign Service Posts and U.S. Embassies and Consulates. Other major sections of the site address the policy roles of the State Department in arms control, economics, democracy abroad, foreign aid, and additional issues.

This site provides a wealth of information about international issues.

Subject(s): Diplomacy; Foreign Policy

Publication(s): *Annual Report on International Religious Freedom*, S 1.151
Background Notes, S 1.123
Battling International Bribery, S 1.2:B 31/
Country Commercial Guides, S 1.40/7
Country Reports on Economic Policy and Trade Practices, Y 4.IN 8/16:C 83/
Country Reports on Human Rights Practices, Y 4.IN 8/16-15
Country Reports on Terrorism, S 1.138
Department of State Standardized Regulations (DSSR), S 1.76/3
Diplomatic List, S 1.8
Foreign Affairs Manual & Foreign Affairs Handbooks, S 1.40/2
Foreign Consular Offices in the United States, S 1.69/2
Foreign Relations of the United States, S 1.1
International Narcotics Control Strategy Report, S 1.146
Key Officers of Foreign Service Posts, S 1.40/5
Patterns of Global Terrorism, S 1.138
Semiannual Report to Congress, Office of Inspector General, S 1.1/6
State Magazine, S 1.118
Telephone Directory, S 1.21
Treaties in Force, S 9.14
Treaty Actions, S 9.14/2
United States Participation in the United Nations, S 1.70/8
Victims of Trafficking and Violence Protection Act: Trafficking in Persons Report, S 1.152

DipNote

http://blogs.state.gov/
Sponsor(s): State Department
Description: DipNote is the State Department's official blog. The term "DipNote" refers to a diplomatic note, a form for communication between national governments. Blog entries are regularly written by employees in many different sections of State, including foreign service offers posted abroad, ambassadors, and headquarters staff. Comments are permitted.
Subject(s): Diplomacy; Blogs

Frontline Diplomacy: Foreign Affairs Oral History Collection

http://memory.loc.gov/ammem/collections/diplomacy/

Sponsor(s): Library of Congress

Description: Part of the Library of Congress American Memory on-line collection, this set of interview transcripts is entitled "Frontline Diplomacy: The Foreign Affairs Oral History Collection of the Association for Diplomatic Studies and Training." The interviews with State Department Foreign Service officers and other officials are mostly from the 1940s to the 1990s. The collection can be searched by word or browsed by topic or author.

Subject(s): Diplomacy—History

Japan-United States Friendship Commission (JUSFC)

http://www.jusfc.gov/

Sponsor(s): Japan-United States Friendship Commission

Description: JUSFC administers a trust fund for promoting scholarly, cultural, and public affair activities between the United States and Japan. Its Web site has information on JUSFC grants, fellowships, and the Creative Artists Program.

Subject(s): Culture—Grants; International Education—Grants; Japan

Office of the Chief of Protocol

http://www.state.gov/s/cpr/

Sponsor(s): State Department

Description: This Web site details the varied responsibilities of the Department of State's chief of protocol and features information about major diplomatic events both in the United States and abroad. Reference material on the site includes the Diplomatic List, accredited diplomatic officers of foreign embassies within the United States and a directory of foreign consular offices in the United States.

Subject(s): Diplomacy

Publication(s): *Diplomatic List*, S 1.8

Foreign Consular Offices in the United States, S 1.69/2

Open World Leadership Center

http://www.openworld.gov/

Sponsor(s): Open World Leadership Center

Description: The Open World Leadership Center, an independent entity in the legislative branch, enables emerging political and civic leaders from Russia and other former Soviet Union countries to work with their U.S. counterparts. Open World also sponsors a cultural program. This Web site provides information about program activities, grants for hosting organizations, countries authorized to participate, and program donors.

Subject(s): Cultural Exchanges; Russia

U.S. Agency for International Development (USAID)

http://www.usaid.gov/

Sponsor(s): Agency for International Development (USAID)

Description: USAID is an independent agency that provides economic development and humanitarian assistance around the world. The USAID Web site has information about the agency, its work and locations, policy documents, press releases, contracting and acquisition opportunities, and agency employment. Its many program areas include HIV/AIDS treatment and prevention, democracy and governance training, Food for Peace, American Schools and Hospitals Abroad, literacy, microenterprise development, Women in Development, and the Denton Program for transporting humanitarian donations on U.S. military cargo planes. Information about these and other programs is provided in the Our Work section.

The site links to statistical sources such as *U.S. Overseas Loans and Grants* (also known as *The Greenbook*) and the U.S. Official Development Assistance Database. About USAID also links to the Development Experience Clearinghouse.

Subject(s): Foreign Assistance

Publication(s): *U.S. Official Development Assistance Database*
U.S. Overseas Loans & Grants Online (Greenbook)
USAID FrontLines, S 18.63

U.S. Diplomacy Center (USDC)

http://diplomacy.state.gov/

Sponsor(s): State Department—Public Affairs Bureau

Description: USDC organizes exhibits, educational programs, and events to demonstrate the role of the State Department and both current and historic U.S. diplomacy. USDC draws from its collection of over 6,000 artifacts to create exhibits at its own facilities and at other U.S. and international sites; a selection can be viewed on the Web site. The Education Programs section includes classroom materials and content designed to inform students about the State Department and diplomatic careers.

Subject(s): Diplomacy—History; Museums

USEmbassy.Gov

http://usembassy.gov/

Sponsor(s): State Department

Description: This Web site provides information about U.S. embassies, consulates, and diplomatic missions abroad. The site is broken down by region for easy reference. Information about citizen services, visas, and travel warnings can also be accessed from this starting point.

Subject(s): Diplomacy; Embassies

United States Institute of Peace (USIP)
http://www.usip.org/
Sponsor(s): United States Institute of Peace (USIP)
Description: USIP is an independent, nonpartisan federal institution created and funded by Congress to strengthen the nation's capacity to promote the peaceful resolution of international conflict. The Web site describes USIP programs such as the Center for Conflict Analysis and Prevention and the Center for Mediation and Conflict Resolution. The Issue Areas section of the site organizes USIP information by topic, such as economics and conflict education, post-conflict and peacekeeping activities, religion and peacemaking, and rule of law. The site also has information on USIP subject specialists, grants and fellowships, and education and training programs. The Publications and Tools section of the site encompasses the USIP Library, publications catalog, reports, and online bookstore.
Subject(s): International Relations—Research; Peace
Publication(s): *Peace Watch*, Y 3.P 31:15-2/
Peaceworks, Y 3.P 31
Special Reports, Y 3.P 31:20/

United States Mission to International Organizations in Vienna (UNVIE)
http://vienna.usmission.gov/
Sponsor(s): State Department
Description: UNVIE works with the cluster of UN and UN-related agencies headquartered in Vienna. These include the International Atomic Energy Agency (IAEA), the Preparatory Commission for the Comprehensive Test Ban Treaty Organization, and the Wassenaar Arrangement. The UNVIE Web site provides news and fact sheets, links to relevant documents, and UNVIE statements.
Subject(s): International Organizations

United States Mission to the OECD
http://usoecd.usmission.gov/
Sponsor(s): State Department
Description: The Organisation for Economic Co-operation and Development (OECD) in Paris works to foster cooperation among advanced market-based democracies. Along with information about the current ambassador to the OECD, this Web site summarizes U.S. goals and work in current issue areas. Current issues include energy, governance, and combating corruption.
Subject(s): International Economic Relations; International Organizations

United States Mission to the OSCE

http://osce.usmission.gov/

Sponsor(s): State Department

Description: The Organization for Security and Co-operation in Europe (OSCE) is a regional security organization with 57 participating nations from Europe, Central Asia, and North America and 11 additional partner countries. The Web site for the U.S. Mission to the OSCE in Vienna explains the work, history, and goals of the OSCE and the U.S. objectives in the organization. It includes U.S. statements to the OSCE Permanent Council.

Subject(s): International Relations; Europe—Policy; International Organizations

United States Mission to the United Nations (USUN)

http://usun.state.gov/

Sponsor(s): State Department

Description: The U.S. Representative to the United Nations, along with several deputies who serve with ambassador rank, represents the United States in meetings with the United Nations. This Web site provides information about the work of the ambassadors and staff in the U.S. mission to the United Nations, which uses the acronym USUN. The site provides official statements, press releases, blog entries, and background information on a wide range of foreign policy issues.

Subject(s): Diplomacy; International Organizations

Vietnam Education Foundation (VEF)

http://home.vef.gov/

Sponsor(s): Vietnam Education Foundation

Description: VEF provides opportunities for Vietnamese nationals to pursue graduate and postgraduate studies in science and technology in the United States and for American citizens to teach in the same fields of study in Vietnam. Its Web site provides news and information about the program.

Subject(s): International Education; Vietnam

Voice of America (VOA)

http://www.voanews.com/

Sponsor(s): International Broadcasting Bureau

Description: VOA is an international broadcasting service funded by the U.S. government. VOA programs, which cover U.S. news, information, and culture, are produced and broadcasted in English and nearly 50 other languages via radio, satellite, and the Internet. The VOA Web site highlights daily VOA newswire stories and broadcasts, and provides news in RSS feeds and webcasts. The Programs section lists the VOA's radio and TV offerings, and the site offers a pronunciation guide for international names and places in the news. VOA also offers VOA Mobile, an all-text version of top stories for use on Web-enabled handheld devices. Links to VOA's social media feeds are included on the home page.

Subject(s): Broadcasting—International; News Services
Publication(s): *VOA Program Guide*, B 2.10

FOREIGN POLICY

Bureau of African Affairs
http://www.state.gov/p/af/
Sponsor(s): State Department—African Affairs Bureau
Description: The Bureau of African Affairs is concerned with sub-Saharan Africa policy. In the Regional Topics section, the bureau's Web site has press releases and documents on such issues as the African Growth and Opportunity Act and AIDS relief. The site also has biographies of chiefs of mission and other senior State Department principals in Africa.
Subject(s): Africa—Policy

Bureau of Economic, Energy, and Business Affairs
http://www.state.gov/e/eeb/
Sponsor(s): State Department—Economic and Business Affairs Bureau
Description: The Department of State's Bureau of Economic, Energy, and Business Affairs is responsible for coordinating U.S. foreign economic policy. The bureau's Web site describes its work in supporting U.S. business in foreign markets, negotiating at economic summits and with international organizations, combating bribery in international commerce, coordinating economic sanctions policy, and making recommendations for national energy security. Material from the bureau and its component offices covers such specific topics as Internet freedom, conflict diamonds, Open Skies Agreements, and Free Trade Agreements.
Subject(s): International Economic Relations—Policy

Bureau of Near Eastern Affairs
http://www.state.gov/p/nea/
Sponsor(s): State Department—Near Eastern Affairs Bureau
Description: The Bureau of Near Eastern Affairs is concerned with policy toward Algeria, Bahrain, Egypt, Iran, Iraq, Israel, Jordan, Kuwait, Lebanon, Libya, Morocco, Oman, Palestinian Territories, Qatar, Saudi Arabia, Syria, Tunisia, United Arab Emirates, and Yemen. The Regional Topics section of its Web site includes information on Iraq, Middle East

peace, and the Middle East Partnership Initiative (MEPI). The subsection on Middle East peace includes key remarks, briefings, and press releases.

Subject(s): Middle East—Policy

Bureau of South and Central Asian Affairs

http://www.state.gov/p/sca/

Sponsor(s): State Department—South and Central Asian Affairs Bureau

Description: The Bureau of South and Central Asian Affairs is concerned with policy toward the countries of Afghanistan, Bangladesh, Bhutan, India, Kazakhstan, Kyrgyzstan, Maldives, Nepal, Pakistan, Sri Lanka, Tajikistan, Turkmenistan, and Uzbekistan. The site provides news releases and biographies of the U.S. ambassadors in the region, along with links to the bureau's social media pages.

Subject(s): Asia—Policy

Bureau of Western Hemisphere Affairs

http://www.state.gov/p/wha/

Sponsor(s): State Department—Western Hemisphere Affairs Bureau

Description: The Bureau of Western Hemisphere Affairs is concerned with policy toward the region including Canada, Mexico, Central and South America, and the Caribbean island nations. The Web site features sections on Hemispheric Security and the U.S. Mission to the Organization of American States. The Regional Topics section links to information on free trade agreements, the Caribbean Basin Security Initiative, the Summit of the Americas, and other initiatives.

Subject(s): North America—Policy; South America—Policy; Caribbean—Policy

Foreign Relations of the United States

http://history.state.gov/historicaldocuments

Alternate URL(s)

http://digicoll.library.wisc.edu/FRUS/

Sponsor(s): State Department

Description: The *Foreign Relations of the United States (FRUS)* series, published by the Department of State's Office of the Historian, is a compilation of U.S. foreign policy documents beginning with the Lincoln administration in 1861. Documents selected for inclusion come from the State Department and other sources, including the intelligence agencies and private papers. Under the Historical Documents heading, the State Department Web site provides a description of the series, a list of all of its volumes, information about print volumes sold by the Government Printing Office, and the status of their work on the series. The State Department also provides the full texts of volumes starting with the Truman administration; these are available in HTML format. Online volumes can be searched by keyword.

The alternate URL listed above links to a FRUS digitization project at the University of Wisconsin–Madison Libraries. This site has scanned copies of the FRUS for 1861 through 1960 (with some gaps). The set can be browsed by volume or searched by keyword.

Subject(s): Foreign Policy — History
Publication(s): *Foreign Relations of the United States*, S 1.1

Office of the Historian (State Department)

http://history.state.gov/

Sponsor(s): State Department

Description: "The Office of the Historian is responsible, under law, for the preparation and publication of the official documentary history of U.S. foreign policy in the Foreign Relations of the United States series." (from the Web site) The Web site provides the Foreign Relations of the United States series online along with a wealth of other historical resources. Content includes biographies and records of official travel for all former Secretaries of State, U.S. visits by foreign heads of state from 1874 onward, foreign travels by former U.S. presidents, the status of U.S. diplomatic relations with each country of the world, and a guide to the diplomatic archives of other countries.

Subject(s): Foreign Policy — History
Publication(s): *Foreign Relations of the United States*

INTERNATIONAL MIGRATION AND TRAVEL

Bureau of Population, Refugees, and Migration (PRM)

http://www.state.gov/g/prm/

Sponsor(s): State Department — Population, Refugees, and Migration Bureau

Description: PRM has primary responsibility for formulating policies on population, refugees, and migration, and for administering U.S. refugee assistance and admissions programs. The Web site includes background information and news releases. It also has funding information for nongovernmental organizations that carry out relief services overseas.

Subject(s): Refugees — Policy

CDC Travel Information

http://www.cdc.gov/travel/

Sponsor(s): Health and Human Services Department — Centers for Disease Control and Prevention (CDC)

Description: This Web site provides health risk information by travel destination. It contains information about diseases and disease outbreaks, including avian influenza; vaccine recommendations; insect protection; special needs travelers; and cruise ship and air travel. The site also links to CDC's *Yellow Book* (*Health Information for International Travel*). The site has travel notices for specific countries on its home page.

Subject(s): Diseases and Conditions—International; Tourism

Publication(s): *Health Information for International Travel (Yellow Book)*, HE 20.7818

Executive Office for Immigration Review (EOIR)

http://www.justice.gov/eoir/

Sponsor(s): Justice Department—Executive Office for Immigration Review

Description: EOIR conducts immigration court proceedings, appellate reviews, and administrative hearings in individual cases. This Web site contains information about the EOIR and its organization and activities. The site includes a national directory of immigration courts.

Subject(s): Immigration Law

Publication(s): *Immigration Judge Benchbook*
Statistical Year Book, Executive Office for Immigration Review

Immigration Statistics

http://www.dhs.gov/immigration-statistics

Sponsor(s): Homeland Security Department—Citizenship and Immigration Service (USCIS)

Description: This site compiles links to publications, data tables, and other sources of statistics related to migration to the United States. Statistics cover immigration, naturalization, refugees, asylum seekers, the illegal immigrant population, applications for immigration benefits, and related topics. The main page of the site features new releases.

Subject(s): International Migration—Statistics

Publication(s): *Estimates of the Unauthorized Immigrant Population Residing in the United States*
Immigration Enforcement Actions
Yearbook of Immigration Statistics, HS 8.15

Office of Refugee Resettlement (ORR)

http://www.acf.hhs.gov/programs/orr/

Sponsor(s): Health and Human Services Department—Administration for Children and Families (ACF)

Description: ORR provides assistance to people fleeing persecution in their homelands. Its Web site describes the programs, policy, grants, and funding of ORR and explains the legal definition of refugee status and who is eligible for benefits. It covers special programs such as those for unaccompanied refugee minors and has a directory of state-level refugee coordinators. A Refugee Arrival Data subsection reports on refugee arrivals by country of origin and by U.S. state.

Subject(s): Refugees

Travel.State.Gov

http://travel.state.gov/

Sponsor(s): State Department—Consular Affairs Bureau

Description: The Bureau of Consular Affairs, which maintains this Web site, is concerned with the safety of U.S. citizens in foreign countries. The bureau issues passports for U.S. citizens traveling abroad and visas for foreign citizens traveling to the United States. Travel.State.Gov has practical news, advice, and fact sheets about travel safety, applying for a passport, and U.S. visa programs. The site supplies consular information sheets for each country, which summarize entry requirements, local health and safety information, customs regulations, and registering with the local U.S. embassy or consulate. It also contains official Travel Warnings and Public Announcements for specific countries or regions. The Legal Considerations section has clear explanations of legal issues related to Americans abroad (such as those pertaining to judicial assistance), citizenship and nationality, and law enforcement. The Web site also has a section on addressing international parental child abduction cases.

The Bureau of Consular Affairs site provides simple, straightforward access to essential travel information. The passport and visa information is particularly thorough and includes links to the necessary forms.

Subject(s): Passports; Visas

U.S. Citizenship and Immigration Services (USCIS)

http://www.uscis.gov/

Sponsor(s): Homeland Security Department—Citizenship and Immigration Service (USCIS)

Description: The responsibilities of USCIS include asylum and refugee processing, naturalization, special immigration status programs, and issuance of immigration documents. The Web site provides easy access to guidance, forms, legal information, online services, and current news. It links to the E-Verify system for employers who need to check the immigration status of job applicants. Major sections on the home page address the green card (permanent residency), citizenship, immigrant family issues, working in the U.S., refugees and asylum, international adoption, and citizenship for members of the U.S. military. The site's Laws section has the text of relevant laws, regulations, administrative decisions, and policy memoranda. It also links to sources for free legal services. The USCIS site is available in Spanish.

Subject(s): Citizenship; Immigration Law

Publication(s): *A Guide to Naturalization*, HS 8.8

Learn About the United States: Quick Civics Lessons, HS 8.2

USCIS Civics Flash Cards, HS 8.2
Welcome to the United States: A Guide for New Immigrants, HS 1.8

INTERNATIONAL RELATIONS

Commission on Security and Cooperation in Europe (CSCE)
http://www.csce.gov/

Sponsor(s): Commission on Security and Cooperation in Europe (CSCE)

Description: CSCE, better known as the U.S. Helsinki Commission, is an independent government agency created by Congress. It monitors and encourages compliance with the Helsinki Accords/Final Act and other commitments of the countries participating in the Organisation for Security and Co-operation in Europe (OSCE). The commission's Web site includes information about the CSCE and OSCE and the full texts of the commission's press releases, hearings, briefings, and statements.

Subject(s): Human Rights

Congressional-Executive Commission on China (CECC)
http://www.cecc.gov/

Sponsor(s): Congressional-Executive Commission on China (CECC)

Description: CECC was established to monitor the human rights situation and development of the rule of law in China. Its Web site has information about the commission and records of their hearings and roundtables. It includes information on Chinese law, a directory of Chinese legal provisions, and a database of prisoners of conscience in China.

Subject(s): Human Rights; China—Policy

Publication(s): *China Human Rights and Rule of Law Update*, Y 4.C 44

Defense Security Cooperation Agency (DSCA)
http://www.dsca.mil/

Sponsor(s): Defense Department—Defense Security Cooperation Agency (DSCA)

Description: DSCA assists U.S. allies through foreign military sales, training, and technical and humanitarian assistance. The DSCA Web site provides background information on the agency and its organizational components and features announcements of major foreign military arms sales. The Publications section (under Resources) provides links to the key policy and legal documents on foreign military assistance.

While much of the DSCA Web site is technical in nature and written for a very specific audience, researchers will find this to be a valuable source for U.S. security assistance and arms transfer policy and regulatory information.

Subject(s): International Relations; National Defense—Policy

Publication(s): *DSCA Facts Book: Foreign Military Sales, Foreign Military Construction Sales and Military Assistance Facts,* D 1.66

Department of Justice Activities in Iraq
http://www.justice.gov/archive/iraq/index.html
Sponsor(s): Justice Department
Description: Justice Department employees serve throughout the Republic of Iraq on projects to facilitate the rule of law. This Web site provides information on the projects and working groups, including the Rule of Law Counselor, the Major Crimes Task Force (MCTF), and the International Criminal Investigative Training Assistance Program (ICITAP). The site also lists job openings with the Iraq offices.
Subject(s): Iraq

Famine Early Warning Systems Network (FEWS NET)
http://www.fews.net/
Sponsor(s): Agency for International Development (USAID)
Description: FEWS NET provides information and analysis on food security conditions in African nations, Central America, Haiti, Yemen, and other counties. FEWS NET is funded by USAID and implemented through a partnership with other federal and international organizations. Its Web site highlights food emergency announcements and warnings, drought and flood hazard assessments, market conditions, and remote-sensing imagery of rainfall and vegetation on the African continent. The site has versions in French, Spanish, and Portuguese.
Subject(s): Famine; Africa; Middle East; Central America; Caribbean
Publication(s): *FEWS Special Report,* S 18.68/2
Food Security Updates, ID 1.20

Foreign Agents Registration Act (FARA)
http://www.fara.gov/
Alternate URL(s)
http://www.fara.gov/quick-search.html
Sponsor(s): Justice Department—National Security Division (NSD)
Description: FARA requires that individuals and organizations lobbying on behalf of foreign business or foreign government interests register with the Department of Justice. The Foreign Agents Registration Unit, within Justice's National Security Division, has responsibility for administering the act. This Web site has information for those who need to register as well as for those interested in researching FARA registrations.

In 2007, Justice made FARA registrations available in an online, searchable database; the quick search is available at the alternate URL listed above. Searchers should read the document search help and understand the FARA statute to use the database most productively.
Subject(s): Lobbyists—Regulations

Publication(s): *Report of the Attorney General to the Congress of the United States on the Administration of the Foreign Agents Registration Act . . . (semiannual)*, J 1.30

House Democracy Partnership
http://hdac.house.gov/
Sponsor(s): Congress—House of Representatives
Description: As stated on the Web site, the mission of the House Democracy Assistance Commission is "to support the development of effective, independent, and responsive legislative institutions." The site includes the commission's news and a list of "partner legislatures" participating in the program.
Subject(s): Democracy—International; Foreign Assistance

Inter-American Foundation (IAF)
http://www.iaf.gov/
Sponsor(s): Inter-American Foundation (IAF)
Description: IAF is an independent agency that provides assistance to Latin America and the Caribbean by awarding grants directly to local organizations throughout the region. Its Web site features sections entitled About the IAF, Our Work, Apply for Grants, Resources, and Partners. The site is available in Spanish, Portuguese, and Creole.
Subject(s): Foreign Assistance; South America
Publication(s): *Inter-American Foundation Annual Report*, Y 3.IN 8/25

Middle East Partnership Initiative (MEPI)
http://www.mepi.state.gov/
Sponsor(s): State Department
Description: MEPI supports reform in the areas of politics, economics, education, and women's issues in the Middle East. Its Web site provides background information and details about its organization and structure. The site also links to the Web sites for the Abu Dhabi and Tunis regional offices, as well as grant application information.
Subject(s): Foreign Assistance; Middle East

Millennium Challenge Corporation (MCC)
http://www.mcc.gov/
Sponsor(s): Millennium Challenge Corporation
Description: MCC, a government corporation, works with countries to promote sustainable economic growth and reduce poverty through investments in areas such as agriculture, education, and private sector development. Countries are selected to receive aid based on their performance in governing justly, investing in their citizens, and encouraging economic freedom. The Web site provides information on MCC, its lead-

ership, selection criteria, country activities, and business and procurement.

Subject(s): International Economic Development

Office of Global Criminal Justice (GCJ)

http://www.state.gov/j/gcj/

Sponsor(s): State Department—War Crimes Issues Office

Description: As described on the Web site, GCJ, formerly the Office of War Crimes "advises the Secretary of State and other elements of the United States government on the prevention of, and response to, atrocity crimes. The Office provides advice and expertise on transitional justice, including ways to ensure justice and accountability for genocide, crimes against humanity, and war crimes, as well as other grave human rights violations." The site provides information on recent war crimes tribunals, such as the International Criminal Tribunal for Rwanda.

Subject(s): War Crimes

Office of the Coordinator for Counterterrorism

http://www.state.gov/s/ct/

Sponsor(s): State Department—Counterterrorism Office

Description: The Department of State's Office of the Coordinator for Counterterrorism develops U.S. counterterrorism policy and coordinates U.S. efforts to improve counterterrorism cooperation with foreign governments. Its Web site includes statements on U.S. policy and describes the office's programs. The site also provides the annual publication Country Reports on Terrorism, the list of State Sponsors of Terrorism, and explanations of the terrorist designation lists.

Subject(s): Terrorism—Policy

Publication(s): *Country Reports on Terrorism*, S 1.138

Overseas Security Advisory Council (OSAC)

http://www.osac.gov/

Sponsor(s): Overseas Security Advisory Council

Description: OSAC was established to promote security cooperation and communication between the U.S. government and U.S. private sector companies and organizations that operate abroad. OSAC services are for registered constituent organizations and some Web site content is available only to registered constituents. The OSAC Web site provides unclassified information, such as daily news of foreign events and reports on topics such as crime and security trends in foreign countries. The Country Councils section of the site provides links to the Web pages for each of the over 50 regional OSAC councils.

Subject(s): Terrorism; Crime Prevention—International

U.S.-China Economic and Security Review Commission (USCC)

http://www.uscc.gov/

Sponsor(s): United States-China Security Review Commission

Description: USCC was created to review the national security implications of trade and economic ties between the United States and the People's Republic of China. Its Web site has hearings schedules, congressional testimony, and annual reports. The site also has directories of the commissioners and staff and copies of research papers and trade data and analyses.

Subject(s): International Economic Relations; China—Policy

United States Commission on International Religious Freedom

http://www.uscirf.gov/

Sponsor(s): United States Commission on International Religious Freedom

Description: The Commission on International Religious Freedom is a federal government commission established to monitor the status of religious freedom in other nations and make policy recommendations to the president, secretary of state, and Congress. The commission issues an annual report on religious persecution around the world; current and past reports are available on their Web site. The commission maintains lists of Countries of Particular Concern and a country Watch List, available on this site. The site also has additional information about the commission and its hearings, press releases, congressional testimony, and relevant legislation.

Subject(s): Human Rights

Publication(s): *Annual Report of the United States Commission on International Religious Freedom*, Y 3.R 27:1/

United States Mission to NATO

http://nato.usmission.gov/

Sponsor(s): Defense Department—State Department

Description: The Department of State and Department of Defense have a combined United States Mission to the North Atlantic Treaty Organization (NATO). This Web site has current speeches and statements from the U.S. ambassador to NATO and current news from the U.S. government on security issues.

Subject(s): International Agreements

FIFTEEN

Law and Law Enforcement

Web sites concerning law and law enforcement are primarily sponsored by the Justice Department and the federal courts. The Justice Department in particular has a very broad role in legal matters, covering topics from legal practices to community policing to homeland security. This chapter has a similarly broad scope. However, some subject-specific Web sites, such as sites about environmental law, can be found in the relevant subject chapters in this book.

Subsections in this chapter are Areas of Law, Courts and the Judicial System, Crime and Enforcement, and Laws and Legal Information.

AREAS OF LAW

ADA Home Page—Information and Technical Assistance on the Americans with Disabilities Act
http://www.ada.gov/
Sponsor(s): Justice Department—Civil Rights Division
Description: The Department of Justice's central Web site for the Americans with Disabilities Act (ADA) compiles a wide range of information for audiences such as the general public, businesses, and state and local governments. The site provides a catalog of publications about ADA regulations, technical assistance, information about ADA enforcement actions, information for state and local governments, and links to other federal agency Web sites with disability information. Some publications are available in Spanish. The Contact Us section lists the Justice Department's toll-free ADA hotlines, 800-514-0301 (voice) and 800-514-0383 (TDD).

New features on the site, found under the New on ADA.gov section, include recent settlement agreements, complaints, and consent degrees.

This site's broad scope will make it of interest to anyone concerned with ADA compliance and information.

Subject(s): Americans with Disabilities Act (ADA)

Publication(s): *Enforcing the ADA, A Status Report from the Department of Justice*, J 1.106

Administrative Decisions and Other Actions

http://www2.lib.virginia.edu/govtinfo/fed_decisions_agency.html

Sponsor(s): University of Virginia Library

Description: This university Web site is a finding aid for administrative actions that fall outside the usual scope of the Code of Federal Regulations and the Federal Register. Its lengthy list includes links to items such as the advisory opinions from the Consumer Product Safety Commission, Department of Energy directives, Federal Labor Relations Authority decisions, Food and Drug Administration enforcement reports, and Postal Service administrative decisions.

Maintained at the University of Virginia Library's Government Information Resources site, this page fills an important niche for finding legal information on the Web.

Subject(s): Administrative Law; Finding Aids

Alcohol Policy Information System (APIS)

http://alcoholpolicy.niaaa.nih.gov/

Sponsor(s): National Institutes of Health (NIH)—National Institute on Alcohol Abuse and Alcoholism (NIAAA)

Description: APIS compiles detailed information on state and federal law and policy on alcohol topics. Issues covered include underage drinking, retail sales, alcoholic beverage control, taxation, and transportation laws. The site also tracks changes in laws and policies and provides a national summary of state laws and regulations related to underage drinking and access to alcohol. The Maps and Charts section displays statistical and 50-state data on topics such as taxation, transportation, and blood alcohol concentration limits.

Subject(s): Alcohol—Laws

Antitrust Division

http://www.usdoj.gov/atr/

Sponsor(s): Justice Department—Antitrust Division

Description: The Antitrust Division promotes competition through enforcement of the antitrust laws. The division's Web site provides full-text antitrust cases and information about the division and its activities. The Public Documents section links to selected appellate briefs (back to 1993), international information, Economic Analysis Group Papers, policy statements and guidelines, and other publications. The Antitrust Case Filings page includes cases from December 1994 onward, which are arranged alphabetically. The site has a Report Violations section and a home page link to reporting possible antitrust violations.

Subject(s): Antitrust Law

Civil Rights Division

http://www.usdoj.gov/crt/

Sponsor(s): Justice Department—Civil Rights Division

Description: The Civil Rights Division of the Justice Department enforces federal statutes prohibiting discrimination. Pages for each of the division's organizational sections hold most of the content at the site. The organizational sections—under the About the Division heading—are Appellate, Criminal, Disability Rights, Education, Employment, Federal Coordination and Compliance, Housing and Civil Enforcement, Office of Special Counsel for Immigration-Related Unfair Employment Practices, Policy and Strategy, Special Litigation, and Voting. Each section typically includes background material on the relevant area of practice, statutes enforced, and cases or briefs. The Publications section has material on a wide range of topics not covered elsewhere on the site, such as the pamphlet "Federal Protections Against National Origin Discrimination," which is available in 16 languages.

Subject(s): Civil Rights—Laws

Comptroller General Decisions and Opinions

http://www.gao.gov/legal/index.html

Sponsor(s): Government Accountability Office (GAO)—Comptroller General

Description: The GAO comptroller general issues decisions regarding use of federal appropriations, government contract bid protests, and major federal regulations. This site provides access to summaries and full texts of recent decisions in HTML and PDF formats.

Subject(s): Government Contracts—Regulations

Publication(s): *Decisions of the Comptroller General*, GA 1.5/A-2

Copyright Office

http://www.copyright.gov/

Sponsor(s): Library of Congress—Copyright Office

Description: The U.S. Copyright Office Web site includes information on copyright law, searching existing copyright records, and registering a work for copyright protection. The site also highlights hot topics and provides an RSS feed of copyright news. The Publications section of the site has copies of the office's circulars, brochures, and forms. One-page fact sheets cover specific topics such as fair use, international copyright, and how to register specific types of works, such as books, music, and photographs. The site also has information on licensing, preregistration, and recording documents about a copyright with the Copyright Office.

The About section includes basic information and an organizational chart.

Subject(s): Copyright Law; Intellectual Property

Publication(s): *Annual Report of the Register of Copyrights*, LC 3.1
Catalog of Copyright Entries, LC 3.6/6
Copyright Basics, LC 3.4/2
Copyright Information Circulars, LC 3.4/2
Copyright Law of the United States, LC 3.4/2
Forms, Copyright Office, LC 3.14
NewsNet, LC 3.4/3

Copyright Royalty Board (CRB)

http://www.loc.gov/crb/

Sponsor(s): Library of Congress

Description: The Copyright Royalty Board (CRB) was created by the Copyright Royalty and Distribution Reform Act of 2004 (Public Law 108-419). The CRB consists of three permanent copyright royalty judges. The Web site has information on rate and distribution proceedings, CRB notices in the Federal Register, and forms for filing royalty fee claims for cable, satellite, and digital audio recording devices and media.

Subject(s): Copyright Law

Department of Justice

http://www.justice.gov/

Sponsor(s): Justice Department

Description: The central Web site for the Department of Justice links to the department's 50-plus component divisions and programs. Under Resources, the site brings together the department's publications, forms, and information on notable cases, such as *United States v. Bernard L. Madoff*. The News section includes videos and the department's blog. This central Justice Web site also has information on the department's grants, business opportunities, and careers.

The home page of the site features an Action Center with links such as Report a Crime; Locate a Prison, Inmate, or Sex Offender; Find Sales of Seized Property; and Report and Identify Missing Persons. As a Cabinet department, Justice also maintains information on its Recovery Act Programs and Open Government Plan.

This well-organized site is easy to navigate.

Subject(s): Law and Law Enforcement

Publication(s): *Office of Inspector General Semiannual Report to Congress*, J 1.1/9
United States Attorneys' Bulletin, J 31.12
United States Attorneys' Manual, J 1.8:AT

Department of Labor Office of Administrative Law Judges (OALJ)

http://www.oalj.dol.gov/

Sponsor(s): Labor Department—Office of Administrative Law Judges (OALJ)

Description: The Labor Department's administrative law judges preside over cases related to many of the department's programs, such as black lung benefits and longshore workers' compensation. The office also includes the Board of Contract Appeals (BCA). Decisions and other online documents are organized in the Library Collections section by program area, with subheadings including Davis-Bacon Act and Service Contract Act, Longshore, Black Lung, Whistleblower, and Immigration. They can also be searched by complainant or employer name, date, and OALJ case number.

Subject(s): Labor Law

Publication(s): *Judges' Benchbook of the Black Lung Benefits Act*, L 1.2

Disability Rights Section

http://www.justice.gov/crt/about/drs/

Sponsor(s): Justice Department—Civil Rights Division

Description: The Disability Rights Section is concerned with enforcement of the Americans with Disabilities Act (ADA) and related federal law. The Web sites covers enforcement issues, compliance assistance, certification of building codes, and other regulatory topics.

Subject(s): Disabilities—Laws

Publication(s): *Disability Rights Online News*
Enforcing the ADA: A Status Report, J 1.106:
Guide to Disability Rights Laws, J 1.109/2

Federal Mine Safety and Health Review Commission (FMSHRC)

http://www.fmshrc.gov/

Sponsor(s): Federal Mine Safety and Health Review Commission (FMSHRC)

Description: FMSHRC is an independent adjudicative agency that provides administrative trial and appellate review of legal disputes arising under the Federal Mine Safety and Health Amendments Act of 1977. Sections featured at the site include About FMSHRC, Decisions, Review Commission Arguments & Meetings, the Mine Act & Procedural Rules, Reports & Budget Submissions, Cases on Review, and FOIA. The site also has information and cases related to the Mine Improvement and New Emergency Response Act of 2006 (Public Law 109-236, known as the MINER Act).

Subject(s): Mining—Laws

Publication(s): *Decisions, Federal Mine Safety and Health Review Commission*, Y 3.M 66:9/

First Freedom Project

http://www.firstfreedom.gov/

Sponsor(s): Justice Department—Civil Rights Division

Description: This Justice Department site provides information on the laws protecting religious liberty in such areas as education, employment, and housing. It also provides fact sheets and brochures for distribution.

Subject(s): Civil Rights; Religion—Laws

Publication(s): *Religious Freedom in Focus Newsletter*

Report on Enforcement of Laws Protecting Religious Freedom: Fiscal Years 2001–2006, J 1.2

Foreign Claims Settlement Commission

http://www.usdoj.gov/fcsc/

Sponsor(s): Justice Department—Foreign Claims Settlement Commission

Description: The Foreign Claims Settlement Commission is a quasi-judicial independent agency within the Department of Justice. The commission rules on claims of U.S. nationals against foreign governments. The Web site has information on the commission, special claims programs, and copies of the annual report.

Subject(s): International Law

Publication(s): *Annual Report to Congress, Foreign Claims Settlement Commission,* J 1.1/6

Historical Publication(s) of the United States Commission on Civil Rights

http://www.law.umaryland.edu/marshall/usccr/index.asp

Sponsor(s): University of Maryland. Thurgood Marshall Law Library

Description: This site provides access to PDF copies of Civil Rights Commission documents that are in the collection of the University of Maryland Thurgood Marshall Law Library. It includes a selection of documents dating back to the Civil Rights Act of 1957, which created the original Civil Rights Commission.

Subject(s): Civil Rights

Military Commissions

http://www.defenselink.mil/news/commissions.html

Sponsor(s): Defense Department

Description: This site provides material related to operating military commissions, also called military tribunals, and the Military Commissions Act. As stated in the law, the Military Commissions Act "establishes procedures governing the use of military commissions." The Web site includes the *Manual for Military Commissions* and related press materials.

Subject(s): Military Justice
Publication(s): *Manual for Military Commissions*

Military Legal Resources
http://www.loc.gov/rr/frd/Military_Law/
Sponsor(s): Library of Congress—Federal Research Division (FRD)
Description: This Library of Congress site provides access to a growing collection of historic, digitized military legal resources, including: the Military Law Review, 1958 to 2012; Geneva Conventions materials; *Manuals for Courts-Martial*; and *The Army Lawyer*, from 1971 to 2012. Historical military legal documents are also grouped under headings for the Indian Wars Era, the Civil War Era, the World War II Era, the Korean War Era, and the Vietnam War Era. They are selected from the collection of the U.S. Army Judge Advocate General's Legal Center and School Library in Charlottesville, VA.
Subject(s): Military History; Military Justice
Publication(s): *Manual for Courts-Martial, United States*, D 1.15:
Military Law Review, D 101.22
The Army Lawyer, D 101.22/32

National Indian Gaming Commission (NIGC)
http://www.nigc.gov/
Sponsor(s): National Indian Gaming Commission
Description: NIGC is an independent federal regulatory agency established by the Indian Gaming Regulatory Act of 1988 (Public Law 100-497). The Web site includes an overview of the commission and the laws and regulations with which it is concerned. The Reading Room section includes National Indian Gaming Commission decisions, enforcement actions, approved gaming ordinances, a list of tribal gaming locations, and more.
Subject(s): Gambling—Regulations; American Indians

Occupational Safety and Health Review Commission (OSHRC)
http://www.oshrc.gov/
Sponsor(s): Occupational Safety and Health Review Commission (OSHRC)
Description: OSHRC is an independent federal agency created to decide contests of citations or penalties resulting from OSHA inspections. The commission functions as an administrative court, with established procedures for conducting hearings, receiving evidence, and rendering decisions by its administrative law judges. Its Web site has recent decisions by the commission and administrative law judges. Other sections include Rules, Publications, and Budget.
Subject(s): Labor Law; Workplace Safety—Laws
Publication(s): *Guide to Review Commission Procedures*, Y 3.OC 1:8 P

OSHRC Decisions. ALJ Decisions., Y 3.OC 1:10-5/

Office of Legal Counsel

http://www.justice.gov/olc/

Sponsor(s): Justice Department—Office of Legal Counsel

Description: The Office of Legal Counsel drafts legal opinions of the attorney general and provides legal advice for the White House and Executive Branch agencies. The office also reviews draft executive orders and proclamations for legality. The Web site has the text of selected opinions and memoranda from the office from 1992 onward.

Subject(s): Legal Issues

Publication(s): *Opinions of the Office of Legal Counsel,* J 1.5/4

Privacy and Civil Liberties Office

http://www.usdoj.gov/pclo/

Sponsor(s): Justice Department—Deputy Attorney General

Description: The mission of the Privacy and Civil Liberties Office is to ensure that the Justice Department is compliant with laws and policies regarding personal privacy and the protection of individual civil liberties. The Web site has information on the Privacy Act of 1974, including an updated guide. The Resources section of the site has the text of laws and Office of Management and Budget policies regarding privacy. The site also has completed DOJ Privacy Impact Assessments, conducted when an agency makes new plans to use information technology to collect or share content that may include personally identifiable information.

Subject(s): Privacy

Publication(s): *Overview of the Privacy Act of 1974,* J 1.2:P 93/16

U.S. Commission on Civil Rights (USCCR)

http://www.usccr.gov/

Sponsor(s): Civil Rights Commission

Description: USCCR investigates and reports on discrimination because of race, color, religion, sex, age, disability, or national origin. The USCCR Web site includes commission news, meeting transcripts, State Advisory Committee terms, congressional testimony, and information on filing a complaint. Topics covered on the site include voting rights, educational opportunities, ending campus anti-Semitism, and access to health care.

Subject(s): Civil Rights

United States Access Board

http://www.access-board.gov/

Sponsor(s): Access Board

Description: The United States Access Board is an independent federal agency whose mission is to promote accessibility for people with disabilities. Its Web site has information on accessibility guidelines, standards, and enforcement of the Architectural Barriers Act (ABA). The Guidelines and Standards section includes information on relevant laws and policies.

Subject(s): Americans with Disabilities Act (ADA)

Publication(s): *Access Currents Newsletter*, Y 3.B 27:16/

ADA Accessibility Guidelines for Buildings and Facilities (ADAAG), Y 3.B 27:8 AM

USDA Office of the Assistant Secretary for Civil Rights

http://www.ascr.usda.gov/

Sponsor(s): Agriculture Department (USDA)—Civil Rights Office

Description: The USDA Office of the Assistant Secretary for Civil Rights handles complaints regarding employment discrimination for USDA staff and program discrimination for those served by USDA programs. The Web site has information on how to file a complaint and has the full text of directives and regulations. The site is also available in Spanish.

Subject(s): Civil Rights; Employment Discrimination

COURTS AND THE JUDICIAL SYSTEM

Civil Division

http://www.justice.gov/civil/

Sponsor(s): Justice Department—Civil Division

Description: The Civil Division represents the United States, its departments and agencies, members of Congress, Cabinet officers, and other federal employees in litigation. The Web site includes sections for each of the division's branches under the About the Division heading, including Appellate, Commercial Litigation, Consumer Protection Branch, Federal Programs, Immigration Litigation, and Torts. The Torts Branch section includes the Aviation and Admiralty Section; the Environmental Tort Litigation Section; the Federal Tort Claims Act Litigation Section; and the Constitutional and Specialized Torts Litigation Section.

Subject(s): Litigation

Court of Appeals. (01) First Circuit

http://www.ca1.uscourts.gov/

Sponsor(s): Court of Appeals. (01) First Circuit

Description: The First Circuit covers Maine, Massachusetts, New Hampshire, Puerto Rico, and Rhode Island. The court's official site has a database of its opinions and dockets. The site also features the court calendar, rules and procedures, forms and notices, and links to the Web sites of other courts in the First Circuit.

Subject(s): Federal Appellate Courts

Court of Appeals. (02) Second Circuit

http://www.ca2.uscourts.gov/

Sponsor(s): Court of Appeals. (02) Second Circuit

Description: The Second Circuit covers Connecticut, Vermont, and New York. The court's official site has opinions issued within the past 30 days. Opinions can be browsed by date range or searched by case name or docket number. The official site also offers a court directory, forms, and the Federal Rules of Appellate Procedure and Local Rules of the Second Circuit.

Subject(s): Federal Appellate Courts

Court of Appeals. (03) Third Circuit

http://www.ca3.uscourts.gov/

Alternate URL(s)

http://vls.law.vill.edu/Locator/3/

Sponsor(s): Court of Appeals. (03) Third Circuit

Description: The Third Circuit covers Delaware, New Jersey, Pennsylvania, and the Virgin Islands. At its official site, the court has its most current opinions, searchable by keyword. A much more comprehensive source is available at the Villanova University School of Law site (listed here as the alternate URL). Villanova has the full texts of the decisions from the Third Circuit from May 1994 to the present.

The court's site also has a Death Penalty Information section, listing the appeals status and history for individuals given a death sentence in courts within the Third Circuit.

Subject(s): Federal Appellate Courts

Court of Appeals. (04) Fourth Circuit

http://www.ca4.uscourts.gov/

Sponsor(s): Court of Appeals. (04) Fourth Circuit

Description: The Fourth Circuit covers Maryland, North Carolina, South Carolina, Virginia, and West Virginia. The Court of Appeals site has its opinions online going back to 1996; it also offers an e-mail alert service for new opinions.

Subject(s): Federal Appellate Courts

Court of Appeals. (05) Fifth Circuit

http://www.ca5.uscourts.gov/

Sponsor(s): Court of Appeals. (05) Fifth Circuit

Description: The Fifth Circuit covers Louisiana, Mississippi, and Texas. The official Fifth Circuit Court of Appeals Web site includes published and unpublished opinions released from 1992 to the present. The cases can be searched by date, docket number, and keyword. Researchers can sign up for an RSS feed or download opinions from recent years. The site also includes dockets, calendars, and a practitioner's guide.

Subject(s): Federal Appellate Courts

Court of Appeals. (06) Sixth Circuit

http://www.ca6.uscourts.gov/

Sponsor(s): Court of Appeals. (06) Sixth Circuit

Description: The Sixth Circuit covers Kentucky, Michigan, Ohio, and Tennessee. The Web site has a database of published opinions issued since July 1999 and unpublished opinions issued since October 2004. The site also has dockets, forms, fee information, and links to the Sixth Circuit district courts.

Subject(s): Federal Appellate Courts

Court of Appeals. (07) Seventh Circuit

http://www.ca7.uscourts.gov/

Sponsor(s): Court of Appeals. (07) Seventh Circuit

Description: The Seventh Circuit covers Illinois, Indiana, and Wisconsin. This site has searchable access to its opinions and oral arguments; searching is by case number or date. The Seventh Circuit provides an RSS feed for all new opinions or for opinions by a judge.

Subject(s): Federal Appellate Courts

Court of Appeals. (08) Eighth Circuit

http://www.ca8.uscourts.gov/

Sponsor(s): Court of Appeals. (08) Eighth Circuit

Description: The Eighth Circuit covers Arkansas, Iowa, Minnesota, Missouri, Nebraska, North Dakota, and South Dakota. Online documents include opinions and oral arguments. The site also has the court calendar, rules, and publications. The Circuit Library section provides news and links to the Eighth Circuit courts.

Subject(s): Federal Appellate Courts

Court of Appeals. (09) Ninth Circuit

http://www.ca9.uscourts.gov/

Sponsor(s): Court of Appeals. (09) Ninth Circuit

Description: The Ninth Circuit covers Alaska, Arizona, California, Hawaii, Idaho, Montana, Nevada, Oregon, Washington, Guam, and the Northern Mariana Islands. Opinions can be browsed by date or case number. The site has added audio files of oral arguments before the Ninth Circuit; they are available online the day after the oral argument is made. The Ninth Circuit offers RSS feeds for its opinions, memoranda, cases of interest, and announcements. Other sections of the site include the court calendar, rules, and status of pending cases.

Subject(s): Federal Appellate Courts

Court of Appeals. (10) Tenth Circuit
http://www.ca10.uscourts.gov/
Alternate URL(s)
http://ca10.washburnlaw.edu/
Sponsor(s): Court of Appeals. (10) Tenth Circuit
Description: The Tenth Circuit covers Colorado, Kansas, New Mexico, Oklahoma, Utah, and Wyoming. This official site features information on the circuit, links to current opinions, and a link to the Bankruptcy Appellate Panel (BAP) of the Tenth Circuit. Opinions can be browsed back to 1995. Enhanced access to opinions is available at the alternate URL provided above.
Subject(s): Federal Appellate Courts

Court of Appeals. (11) Eleventh Circuit
http://www.ca11.uscourts.gov/
Sponsor(s): Court of Appeals. (11) Eleventh Circuit
Description: The Eleventh Circuit covers Alabama, Florida, and Georgia. On the Web site, published opinions are available from 1995 to the present. The site has an RSS news feed that announces new published opinions. Unpublished opinions are online from April 2005 to present. The site also includes a fee schedule, court rules, and links to district and bankruptcy court sites within the Eleventh District.
Subject(s): Federal Appellate Courts

Court of Appeals. District of Columbia Circuit
http://www.cadc.uscourts.gov/
Alternate URL(s)
http://www.ll.georgetown.edu/federal/judicial/cadc.cfm
Sponsor(s): Court of Appeals. (00) District of Columbia Circuit
Description: The D.C. Circuit Court of Appeals hears appeals from the U.S. District Court for the District of Columbia and also for many federal administrative agencies. The court's Web site carries its opinions going back to 1997. Georgetown University's Law Library site, the alternate URL provided here, carries the opinions going back to April 1995.

Due to the jurisdiction of the court, researchers will find this site useful for documents in high-profile cases involving the federal government.
Subject(s): Federal Appellate Courts

Court of Appeals. Federal Circuit
http://www.cafc.uscourts.gov/
Alternate URL(s)
http://www.ll.georgetown.edu/federal/judicial/cafed.cfm
Sponsor(s): Court of Appeals. (00) Federal Circuit

Description: The U.S. Court of Appeals for the Federal Circuit has nationwide jurisdiction to hear appeals in specialized claims cases, including patent cases. The Web site has background information on the court and its workload statistics. The court's site carries its opinions from 2004 to the present and posts recordings of its oral arguments. The Georgetown University's Law Library Web site, which can be found at the alternate URL above, has opinions available back to July 1995.

Subject(s): Federal Appellate Courts

Federal Judicial Center (FJC)

http://www.fjc.gov/

Sponsor(s): Federal Judicial Center (FJC)

Description: FJC conducts research on federal court operations and history, and it manages training programs for federal judges and court employees. FJC publishes research, analysis, and training products on such topics as alternative dispute resolution, court management, federal judges, and probation and pretrial services. Many of these publications are available online. Educational materials online include an orientation site called "Inside the Federal Courts." The Federal Judicial History section includes biographies of federal judges since 1789 and a history of landmark legislation affecting the courts.

Subject(s): Federal Courts

Publication(s): *Benchbook for U.S. District Court Judges*, JU 13.2
Catalog of Publications, Federal Judicial Center, JU 13.11/2
Federal Courts and What They Do, JU 13.2
Federal Securities Law, JU 13.2
Primer on the Jurisdiction of the U.S. Court of Appeals, Ju 13.9
Reference Manual on Scientific Evidence, JU 13.8

FindLaw: Cases and Codes: U.S. Circuit Courts

http://www.findlaw.com/casecode/courts/

Sponsor(s): Findlaw, Inc.

Description: FindLaw—a free, nongovernment Web site—offers this section with cases from all the circuit courts. Most are searchable by docket number, party name, or words in the text. The cases can also be browsed by date. FindLaw also provides a court directory for each circuit and a link to recent related blog posts.

Like their Supreme Court database, FindLaw's Circuit Court site is an easy-to-use tool for searching for recent opinions. In addition, the site links to other Web sites that provide judicial opinions online.

Subject(s): Federal Courts; Finding Aids

FindLaw: Supreme Court Opinions

http://www.findlaw.com/casecode/supreme.html

Sponsor(s): Findlaw, Inc.

Description: FindLaw, a nongovernment finding aid for Internet law sources, features Supreme Court opinions in HTML format back to 1893, volume 150 of the U.S. Reports. The opinions have hypertext links from references to other cases available through FindLaw.

This is an excellent, free source for Supreme Court opinions on the Web.

Subject(s): Supreme Court

History of the Federal Judiciary

http://www.fjc.gov/history/home.nsf

Sponsor(s): Federal Judicial Center (FJC)

Description: The History of the Federal Judiciary Web site presents basic reference information about the history of the federal courts and the judges who have served on the federal courts since 1789. Major sections on this site include Judges of the United States Courts, to search for judges by name or browse by alphabetical listing, and Courts, Caseloads, and Jurisdictions, which contains information on historical court caseloads.

Legal Services Corporation (LSC)

http://www.lsc.gov/

Sponsor(s): Legal Services Corporation (LSC)

Description: LSC is a private, nonprofit corporation established by Congress to provide civil legal assistance to low-income people. The Congress section has information about funding, hearings, and votes. State information can be found in the Local Programs Section.

Subject(s): Legal Assistances

Publication(s): *Annual Report*

Office of Legal Policy

http://www.justice.gov/olp/

Sponsor(s): Justice Department—Office of Legal Policy

Description: The Office of Legal Policy develops and promotes the legal policy initiatives of the president and the Justice Department and reviews Justice Department regulations. The office also assists with filling certain judicial vacancies. The site includes current information and statistics on judicial vacancies and the nominations made to fill them.

Subject(s): Judges; Laws—Policy

PACER Service Center

http://www.pacer.uscourts.gov/

Sponsor(s): Administrative Office of the U.S. Courts

Description: "Public Access to Court Electronic Records (PACER) is an electronic public access service that allows users to obtain case and docket information online from federal appellate, district, and bankruptcy courts, and the PACER Case Locator. PACER is provided by the Federal Judiciary in keeping with its commitment to providing public access to court information via a centralized service." (from the Web site) The service is fee based and is financed through the collection of these user fees. Registration is required. The type of information available through case dockets on PACER includes listing of all parties and participants in the case, a chronology of case events, appellate court opinions, and judgments or case status. The main sections include Register, Find a Case, E-File, and Quick Links.

The Administrative Office of the United States Courts halted a 2008 pilot project to provide free access to PACER in selected federal government depository libraries. The fees charged by PACER are a topic of current debate.

Subject(s): Federal Courts; Databases

State Justice Institute (SJI)

http://www.sji.gov/

Sponsor(s): State Justice Institute

Description: SJI is a federally funded organization established by Congress to award grants to improve the state court system. The Web site has information on available grants and news releases.

Subject(s): Court Administration—Grants

Publication(s): *E-SJI News*

U.S. Court of Appeals for the Armed Forces

http://www.armfor.uscourts.gov/

Sponsor(s): Court of Appeals for the Armed Forces

Description: The United States Court of Appeals for the Armed Forces has appellate jurisdiction over members of the armed forces on active duty and others subject to the Uniform Code of Military Justice. This site provides information about the court and access to online opinions. Opinions are available back to October 1996; access is by date. The site also has information on court history, jurisdiction, judges, rules, and scheduled hearings.

Subject(s): Military Justice

U.S. Court of Appeals for Veterans Claims

http://www.uscourts.cavc.gov/

Sponsor(s): Court of Appeals for Veterans Claims

Description: The court reviews final decisions of the Board of Veterans' Appeals, which largely consist of cases concerning entitlement to benefits. The court's Web site has information on how to appeal, court rules, forms, and fees. Orders and opinions are online from 2000 to present, with archives for previous years. Audio files for oral arguments are online beginning with 2005.

Subject(s): Veterans

U.S. Courts: The Federal Judiciary

http://www.uscourts.gov/

Sponsor(s): Administrative Office of the U.S. Courts

Description: The Administrative Office of the U.S. Courts maintains this site about the U.S. federal court system, including the U.S. Supreme Court, courts of appeals, district courts, and bankruptcy courts. A Court Locator is featured on the home page. The Federal Courts section offers an excellent overview and information on topics such as bankruptcy law, appointment of legal counsel, probation, and the jury service. The site also has information on federal judgeships, judicial vacancies, and judicial appointments, and statistics on court operations, bankruptcy proceedings, and wiretap approvals. Other sections cover court rules, forms, fees, and a selection of educational resources for teachers and students.

The site includes press releases, the publication *Journalist's Guide* and the newsletter "The Third Branch."

Subject(s): Court Administration

Publication(s): *Federal Court Management Statistics*, JU 10.14

Federal Probation Journal, JU 10.8

Journalist's Guide

The Federal Court System in the U.S., JU 10.2

The Third Branch, Bulletin of the Federal Courts, JU 10.3/2

Understanding the Federal Courts, JU 10.2

Wiretap Report, JU 10.19

United States Attorneys Office

http://www.usdoj.gov/usao/

Sponsor(s): Justice Department—United States Attorneys

Description: The United States attorneys, working under the attorney general, conduct most of the trial work in which the United States is a party. The Web site has a directory of the 93 United States Attorneys stationed throughout the United States, Puerto Rico, the Virgin Islands, and Guam. The site describes the Executive Office for United States Attorneys, which serves as a liaison between the Department of Justice and the attorneys. The Executive Office for United States Attorneys includes the Crime Victims' Rights Ombudsman, with information on the Crime Victims' Rights Act and procedures for complaints under the Act. The Web site is also available in Spanish.

Subject(s): Litigation

United States Bankruptcy Courts

http://www.uscourts.gov/bankruptcycourts.html

Sponsor(s): Administrative Office of the U.S. Courts

Description: Federal courts have exclusive jurisdiction over bankruptcy cases. This Web site has information on federal bankruptcy courts and copies of official bankruptcy forms. The Bankruptcy Resources section includes information on credit counseling, filing fees, fee waivers, and filing for bankruptcy without an attorney.

Subject(s): Bankruptcy Court

Publication(s): *Bankruptcy Basics*, JU 10.2:B 22/3/

United States Court of Federal Claims

http://www.uscfc.uscourts.gov/

Sponsor(s): Court of Federal Claims

Description: The Court of Federal Claims is authorized to primarily hear money claims founded upon the Constitution, federal statutes, executive regulations, or contracts, with the United States. As described on the site, many of the cases before the court concern complex tax refund disputes, government contracts, natural resource issues, civilian and military pay, and Indian tribe and Nation claims. Published and unpublished decisions are available on the Web site. The site also has information on rules, forms, fees, and the court's Office of Special Masters, which handles claims under the National Vaccine Injury Compensation Program.

Subject(s): Federal Courts

United States Court of International Trade

http://www.cit.uscourts.gov/

Sponsor(s): Court of International Trade

Description: The United States Court of International Trade handles litigation rising out of international trade disputes and within their jurisdiction of the United States. The court's Web site has sections for the weekly court calendar, court staff directory, rules and forms, and biographies of the judges. Slip opinions are online for 1999 forward.

Subject(s): Federal Courts; International Trade—Laws

United States Court Resources

http://www.washlaw.edu/uslaw/judicial.html

Sponsor(s): Washburn University. School of Law

Description: United States Court Resources is a section of the Web site WashLaw: Legal Research on the Web. It links to the free sources of federal case law on the Internet and complementary information on the federal judiciary.

Subject(s): Federal Courts

United States Sentencing Commission (USSC)

http://www.ussc.gov/

Sponsor(s): Sentencing Commission

Description: USSC was created by the Sentencing Reform Act of 1984 to reduce disparities in federal sentences. The commission is an independent agency in the judicial branch. In the Publications section, the commission's Web site has the *Federal Sentencing Guidelines Manual* and its amendments, and provides federal sentencing statistics by state, district, and circuit. The commission also has information on its training materials for teaching sentencing guidelines applications to judges, attorneys, and others.

Subject(s): Sentencing

Publication(s): *Federal Sentencing Guidelines Manual*, Y 3.SE 5:8 G 94/ *Sourcebook of Federal Sentencing Statistics*, Y 3.SE 5:1/

United States Tax Court

http://www.ustaxcourt.gov/

Sponsor(s): Tax Court

Description: The United States Tax Court, a federal court established by Congress under Article I of the Constitution, provides a judicial forum for affected persons to dispute "tax deficiencies" as determined by the Commissioner of Internal Revenue, prior to payment of the disputed amounts. The site has sections for Today's Opinions, Opinions Search, Forms, Rules, Fees/Charges, and general information about contacts and frequently asked questions. The Opinions Search section offers a search of past opinions by release date, petitioner's name, judge, and opinion type, and sorted by case name or release date. The Taxpayer Information section is a guide to the process for those who represent themselves before the court.

Subject(s): Federal Courts; Taxation—Laws

United States Trustee Program

http://www.justice.gov/ust/

Sponsor(s): Justice Department

Description: The United States Trustee Program oversees the bankruptcy process to ensure legal and procedural compliance. The Trustee Web site provides basic information for individuals, including a bankruptcy information sheet translated into over 17 languages besides English and a directory of Trustee Program offices nationwide. The site has information on the Bankruptcy Abuse Prevention and Consumer Protection Act of 2005 (Public Law 109-8), notice of any proposed regulations, and additional resources for practitioners. The Press & Public Affairs section includes bankruptcy fact sheets and bankruptcy statistics.

Subject(s): Bankruptcy

Publication(s): *United States Trustee Manual*

CRIME AND ENFORCEMENT

AMBER Alert

http://www.amberalert.gov/

Sponsor(s): Justice Department—Justice Programs Office

Description: AMBER Alerts are local systems for alerting the public when a child has been abducted. This site includes program information, statistics, and answers to frequently asked questions. It also provides State AMBER Alert contacts and information on the wireless AMBER Alert service.

Subject(s): Kidnapping

Publication(s): *Amber Advocate*, J 32.28

America's Most Wanted Criminals

http://www.usa.gov/Citizen/Topics/MostWanted.shtml

Sponsor(s): General Services Administration (GSA)

Description: USA.gov presents this compilation of links to most-wanted lists from nine U.S. and international sources. It also provides links to state and national sex offender search registries and information about missing children.

Subject(s): Criminals

ATF Online - Bureau of Alcohol, Tobacco, Firearms, and Explosives

http://www.atf.gov/

Sponsor(s): Justice Department—Bureau of Alcohol, Tobacco, Firearms, and Explosives

Description: As part of the Homeland Security Act of 2002, the Bureau of Alcohol, Tobacco, Firearms, and Explosives (ATF) was transferred from the Treasury Department to the Justice Department in early 2003. Certain functions of the ATF remain with Treasury in the Alcohol and Tobacco Tax and Trade Bureau, or TTB. See the separate entry for the TTB Web site for more information.

ATF is a law enforcement organization charged with enforcing federal laws and regulations relating to alcohol and tobacco, firearms, explosives, and arson. Each topic has a section discussing enforcement, regulations, and other information. The Publications section includes ATF circulars, bulletins, delegation orders, and fact sheets.

Subject(s): Law Enforcement; Wanted People

Publication(s): *ATF Industry Circulars*, T 70.10

Federal Explosives Licensee (FEL) Newsletter

Federal Firearms Licensee (FFL) Newsletter, T 70.18

Firearms Publications, T 70.14

Attorney General

http://www.usdoj.gov/ag/

Sponsor(s): Justice Department—Attorney General

Description: The attorney general is the head of the Justice Department and the chief law enforcement officer of the federal government. This site describes the office and has some biographical information on the current attorney general. It also provides links to speeches, testimony, annual reports, and the office's FOIA section.

Subject(s): Law Enforcement

Publication(s): *Assessment of U.S. Government Activities to Combat Trafficking in Persons*, J 1.2

Report and Recommendations of the Presidential Task Force on Controlled Unclassified Information

Bureau of Justice Assistance (BJA)

http://www.ojp.usdoj.gov/BJA/

Sponsor(s): Justice Department—Justice Programs Office

Description: BJA supports local criminal justice agencies throughout the United States, offering grants, training, and technical assistance. The site offers information on funding and training opportunities. Program information is available in the Topics section under topical headings such as Adjudication, Corrections, Crime Prevention, and Justice Information Sharing.

Subject(s): Law Enforcement—Grants

Bureau of Justice Statistics (BJS)

http://www.ojp.usdoj.gov/bjs/

Sponsor(s): Justice Department—Bureau of Justice Statistics (BJS)

Description: BJS collects and reports data on law enforcement, crime, and corrections at the federal, state, and local levels. The Web site provides the data in multiple formats, such as prepared reports and statistical tables, spreadsheets, and data sets to download. Data products and publications are organized under topics including corrections, courts and sentencing, crime type, justice employment and expenditure, law enforcement, and victims.

BJS also supports grants programs for state, local, and tribal governments to assist with criminal justice statistics programs at those levels.

Subject(s): Criminal Justice—Statistics; Prisons—Statistics

Publication(s): *Background Checks for Firearm Transfers*, J 29.11:F

Bureau of Justice Statistics Publications Catalog, J 29.14/2

Capital Punishment, J 29.11/3

Census of State and Federal Corrections Facilities, J 29.16

Compendium of Federal Justice Statistics, J 29.20

Criminal Victimization (A National Crime Victimization Survey Report), J 29.11/10

Federal Justice Statistics, J 29.11/18:

Federal Law Enforcement Officers, J 29.11:L

Felony Defendants in Large Urban Counties, J 29.2:F
Felony Sentences in State Courts, J 29.11/11
Felony Sentences in the United States, J 29.11/11-2
HIV in Prisons and Jails, J 29.11:P 93/
Indicators of School Crime and Safety, ED 1.347
Jails in Indian Country, J 29.11/5-3:
Local Police Departments, J 29.2:P 75/
Prisoners, J 29.11/7
Prosecutors in State Courts, J 29.11/15
Sourcebook of Criminal Justice Statistics, J 29.9/6
State Court Sentencing of Convicted Felons, J 29.11/11-3
Survey of State Criminal History Information Systems, J 29.9/8:H 62/

Community Relations Service (CRS)
http://www.usdoj.gov/crs/
Sponsor(s): Justice Department—Community Relations Service
Description: CRS was established by the Civil Rights Act of 1964 to help communities resolve serious racial or ethnic conflicts. Major sections of the Web site include Frequently Asked Questions (under Resources). The About CRS section has a list of CRS regional and field offices. CRS is involved with such topics as hate crimes and police use of force.
Subject(s): Dispute Resolution; Mediation

Computer Crime & Intellectual Property Section (CCIPS)
http://www.cybercrime.gov/
Sponsor(s): Justice Department—Criminal Division
Description: This Web site for the Justice Department's CCIPS reports on relevant policy developments, cases, guidance, laws, and documents in the areas of computer crime, intellectual property protection, and electronic evidence.
Subject(s): Computer Security; Intellectual Property

Coordinating Council on Juvenile Justice and Delinquency Prevention
http://www.juvenilecouncil.gov/
Sponsor(s): Coordinating Council on Juvenile Justice and Delinquency Prevention
Description: The Coordinating Council on Juvenile Justice and Delinquency Prevention is an independent body within the Executive Branch. It coordinates federal programs concerning juvenile delinquency prevention, programs and activities that detain or care for unaccompanied juveniles, and programs relating to missing and exploited children. Its Web site has information on the council, its members, its meetings, and links to relevant grant programs.
Subject(s): Child Welfare; Juvenile Delinquency; Juvenile Justice

COPS Office: Grants and Resources for Community Policing

http://www.cops.usdoj.gov/

Sponsor(s): Justice Department—Community Oriented Policing Services

Description: The COPS Office makes grants to state and local law enforcement agencies to advance community policing. The Web site has information on the grants and training available. It also covers community policing topics such as gangs and school safety.

Subject(s): Police-Community Relations—Grants

Publication(s): *Community Policing Dispatch*, J 1.107

Criminal Division

http://www.usdoj.gov/criminal/

Sponsor(s): Justice Department—Criminal Division

Description: The Department of Justice's Criminal Division enforces and prosecutes federal criminal law. Most of the information on the Web site can be reached through the Organizations link under About the Division. The organization chart links to information on the Narcotic and Dangerous Drug Section, the Fraud Section, the Capital Case Unit, the Organized Crime and Gang Section, and other sections. The Task Forces subsection also links to information on special task forces, such as the Hurricane Katrina Fraud Task Force and the Organized Crime Drug Enforcement Task Forces. The Public Services subsection has information on topics such as the Child Exploitation and Obscenity Section and the Human Rights and Special Prosecutions Section.

Subject(s): Crime; Law Enforcement

Cyber Crime

http://www.fbi.gov/cyberinvest/cyberhome.htm

Sponsor(s): Justice Department—Federal Bureau of Investigation (FBI)

Description: The FBI is concerned with stopping computer network intrusions, online sexual predators, online operations that target U.S. intellectual property, and organized criminal enterprises engaging in Internet fraud. The Cyber Crime Web site has FBI news and initiatives in these areas. It also carries advice to the public about protection from computer crime.

Subject(s): Computer Security

Dru Sjodin National Sex Offender Public Registry

http://www.nsopw.gov/

Sponsor(s): Justice Department

Description: The National Sex Offender Public Registry is a cooperative effort between the state agencies hosting public sexual offender registries and the federal government. It can be searched by name, county, city/town, and ZIP code. The site provides background information that should be consulted before using the database. It covers what may legally constitute a sex offense and warns about the differences in registries from state to state. The site also has a lengthy "conditions of use" statement under the Search section that includes individual state, territory, and tribal conditions of use for the information.

The Web site was renamed the Dru Sjodin National Sex Offender Public Registry in October 2006 in memory of Dru Sjodin, a college student who was murdered in North Dakota by a convicted sex offender.

Subject(s): Criminals

Drug Enforcement Administration (DEA)

http://www.justice.gov/dea/

Sponsor(s): Justice Department—Drug Enforcement Administration (DEA)

Description: The DEA Web site focuses on information about current illegal drug threats and recent DEA enforcement actions. Topical sections include Prevention, Drug Info (including fact sheets), and Topics of Interest. The Operations section links to information about diversion control, training, and programs. The Press Room section includes links to speeches, testimony, and a multimedia resource library.

Subject(s): Drug Control; Law Enforcement

Publication(s): *Drugs of Abuse,* J 24.2

Guidelines for the Cleanup of Clandestine Drug Laboratories, J 24.8

Microgram Bulletin, J 24.31

Microgram Journal, J 24.31/2

Speaking Out Against Drug Legalization, J 24.2

Federal Bureau of Investigation (FBI)

http://www.fbi.gov/

Sponsor(s): Justice Department—Federal Bureau of Investigation (FBI)

Description: For an overview of the FBI's work, see this site's What We Investigate header, which is in the About Us section. It links to substantial information on FBI programs in counterterrorism, counterintelligence, public corruption, civil rights, organized crime, white collar crime, art theft, and other areas. Other sections of the Web site cover crime prevention tips, the FBI's Most Wanted, laboratory services, information technology initiatives, agency history, and directories of FBI field and overseas offices. The site also has an online form for submitting tips about suspected criminal activity.

The Freedom of Information Act section, linked from the bottom of each page, can be accessed directly at http://foia.fbi.gov. It has an index to the popularly requested FOIA documents in its Washington FOIA reading room, with links to those documents that have been digitized and put online. An Electronic Reading Room section, the Vault, has online documents organized alphabetically and by topic.

Because information is spread throughout the many sections of this site, first-time users may want to consult the site map.

Subject(s): Crime Detection; Law Enforcement; Wanted People
Publication(s): *Crime in the United States*, J 1.14/7-8
FBI Laboratory Annual Report, J 1.14/27
FBI Law Enforcement Bulletin, J 1.14/8
Forensic Science Communications, J 1.14/18-2
Handbook of Forensic Services, J 1.14/18-3
Hate Crime Statistics, J 1.14/7-9
Law Enforcement Officers Killed and Assaulted, J 1.14/7-6

Federal Bureau of Prisons (BOP)

http://www.bop.gov/
Sponsor(s): Justice Department—Federal Bureau of Prisons
Description: BOP is responsible for the federal prison system and federal inmates. The BOP Web site has the Inmate Locator database of federal inmates incarcerated from 1982 to present. It also has a Facility Locator and links to Web pages for each of the facilities operated by the Bureau of Prisons. The Inmate Matters section covers topics such as medical care, substance abuse treatment, preparation for release, and the Victim/Witness Notification Program. The site also has information on employment and acquisition opportunities.

Subject(s): Prisons
Publication(s): *Legal Resource Guide to the Federal Bureau of Prisons*
State of the Bureau, J 16.1
Weekly Population Report, J 16.32

Federal Law Enforcement Training Center (FLETC)

http://www.fletc.gov/
Sponsor(s): Homeland Security Department—Federal Law Enforcement Training Center (FLETC)
Description: FLETC is the federal government's centralized law enforcement training organization. Its Web site includes a list of locations and FLETC news. The FLETC site will be of interest primarily to those considering FLETC training.

Subject(s): Homeland Security; Law Enforcement
Publication(s): *Federal Law Enforcement Informer*, HS 1.17

Financial Crimes Enforcement Network (FinCEN)

http://www.fincen.gov/
Sponsor(s): Treasury Department
Description: FinCEN supports law enforcement investigations into domestic and international financial crimes and money laundering. The

agency works with the law enforcement (local, national, and international), financial, and regulatory communities on information sharing in the network. The site has regulatory guidance on the Bank Secrecy Act (BSA) and the USA PATRIOT Act. FinCEN's *SAR Activity Review* of statistical data from the Suspicious Activity Report forms filed by various financial institutions is available, along with reports on suspected mortgage fraud. The FinCEN Advisory Publications, which often focus on financial transactions with specific countries, are also on the site.

The Web site has specific guidance sections for depository institutions, casinos, Money Services Businesses (MSBs), the insurance industry, securities and futures, and the precious metals/jewelry industry.

Subject(s): Financial Crimes; Money Laundering

Publication(s): *FinCEN Advisory*, T 22.3/4

SAR Activity Review, T 1.67/3

SAR Activity Review by the Numbers, T 1.67/4

Identity Theft

http://www.ftc.gov/idtheft/

Sponsor(s): Federal Trade Commission (FTC)

Description: This site serves as a central point for government information on identity theft, which occurs when someone appropriates personal information without that person's knowledge to commit fraud or other crimes. The FTC provides detailed information for consumers, businesses, law enforcement, the media, and members of the military. Consumer information is available in Spanish.

Subject(s): Identity Theft

Immigration and Customs Enforcement (ICE)

http://www.ice.gov/

Sponsor(s): Homeland Security Department—Immigration and Customs Enforcement (ICE)

Description: ICE has investigation and law enforcement responsibilities within the Department of Homeland Security. ICE is concerned with such issues as illegal shipments, drug trafficking, and immigrant smuggling. Most information about the agency's operations is in the Investigations section. Topics include the detention and removal of illegal aliens, intelligence analysis, intellectual property rights, and combating human smuggling, trafficking in persons, and clandestine terrorist travel. The Newsroom section of the site includes links to fact sheets on ICE programs, federal regulation notices, the *Cornerstone Reports* series, and the latest IPR (Intellectual Property Rights) Center Report. Basic information about ICE is available in Spanish.

Subject(s): Customs (Trade); Homeland Security; Immigration Law

Publication(s): *Cornerstone Reports*

Internet Crime Complaint Center
http://www.ic3.gov/

Sponsor(s): Justice Department—Federal Bureau of Investigation (FBI)

Description: The Internet Crime Complaint Center is a partnership between the FBI, the Bureau of Justice Assistance, and the National White Collar Crime Center. The Web site describes current Internet crime schemes and has a form for filing a complaint online. In the Press Room section, the center's annual report provides statistics on complaints by state.

Subject(s): Fraud; Internet

Justice Information Sharing
http://it.ojp.gov/

Sponsor(s): Justice Department—Justice Programs Office

Description: This Justice Department site provides a central location for news, documents, funding information, data and technology standards, and policy related to sharing information and intelligence among law enforcement, public safety, and private sector officials at all levels. The National Initiatives section covers Fusion Centers and the National Information Exchange model. The site also has information on privacy and civil liberties as related to justice information sharing.

Subject(s): Government Information; Law Enforcement Policy

JUSTNET—Justice Technology Information Network
http://www.justnet.org/

Sponsor(s): Justice Department—National Institute of Justice (NIJ)—National Law Enforcement and Corrections Technology Center (NLECTC)

Description: JUSTNET is the home page for the National Law Enforcement and Corrections Technology Center (NLECTC), which assists state and local law enforcement and corrections personnel with technology, equipment, and information systems. The Web site describes NLECTC programs in technology assistance, equipment testing and evaluation, and training assistance. Resources such as journal articles, government Web sites, and grants programs are organized by technology, including communications, crime mapping, explosives, forensics, and personal protective equipment.

Subject(s): Law Enforcement—Grants

Publication(s): *TechBeat*, J 28.37

National Center on Elder Abuse (NCEA)
http://www.ncea.aoa.gov/

Sponsor(s): Health and Human Services Department—Administration on Aging (AoA)

Description: NCEA serves as a national resource center on the prevention of elder mistreatment. The Web site provides federal, state, and community outreach information resources for families, caregivers, and communities. The site has a directory of elder abuse hotlines and adult protective services (APS) and information on state APS laws. The site also features a calendar with conferences, events, and training.

Subject(s): Senior Citizens

National Criminal Justice Reference Service (NCJRS)

https://www.ncjrs.gov/index.html

Sponsor(s): Justice Department—National Criminal Justice Reference Service (NCJRS)

Description: NCJRS compiles resource information from federal agencies involved in law enforcement research and policy. It responds to queries from law enforcement and corrections officials, lawmakers, judges and court personnel, and researchers. The NCJRS Web site houses numerous publications on a wide range of criminal justice and law enforcement topics. It also provides access to the NCJRS Abstracts Database with summaries of more than 220,000 justice and substance abuse publications.

Other topical links on the main page include Corrections, Courts, Crime, Crime Prevention, Drugs, Justice System, Juvenile Justice, Law Enforcement, and Victims. These topic sections include links to publications, Department of Justice seminars, and related resources. The NCJRS site also includes a list of federal grants relating to criminal justice.

The vast number of publications available from the NCJRS site makes it a leading source for criminal justice statistics and reports. Many of the publications are available directly from the individual agencies. NCJRS provides centralized access.

Subject(s): Criminal Justice

Publication(s): *NCJRS Abstracts Database,* J 28.31/2-2

National Institute of Corrections (NIC)

http://nicic.gov/

Sponsor(s): Justice Department—Federal Bureau of Prisons

Description: NIC provides training, technical assistance, information services, and program development assistance to federal, state, and local corrections agencies. Publications announcements are in the About Us section. The Library section provides access to many of NIC's digital resources and a directory of other corrections Web sites, as well as e-mail and RSS subscription options.

Subject(s): Criminal Justice; Prisons

National Institute of Justice (NIJ)

http://www.ojp.usdoj.gov/nij/

Sponsor(s): Justice Department—National Institute of Justice (NIJ)

Description: NIJ supports research, evaluation, and demonstration programs, development of technology, and national and international information dissemination in the area of criminal justice. Program topics include biometrics, forensic DNA, communications technologies, body armor, and crime mapping. The Web site has information on the institute, its programs, funding opportunities, and publications.

Subject(s): Criminal Justice—Research

Publication(s): *Geography and Public Safety Bulletin*, J 28.3/5
National Institute of Justice Annual Report to Congress, J 28.1
National Institute of Justice Journal, J 28.14/2-2

National Missing and Unidentified Persons System (NamUs)

http://www.namus.gov/

Sponsor(s): Justice Department—Justice Programs Office

Description: NamUs is a national repository for the names of missing persons and the records of people who have died but not been identified. A database for unclaimed persons lists decedents whose names are known but whose next of kin has not been identified. The database is made available to the general public and law enforcement to help solve cases. Registration is not required to search the database, but registered users can take advantage of advanced features. The site explains the issues of missing persons and unidentified decedents in an online video and in the About NamUs section.

Subject(s): Crime Detection; Missing Children

Office for Victims of Crime (OVC)

http://www.ojp.usdoj.gov/ovc/

Sponsor(s): Justice Department—Justice Programs Office

Description: OVC was established by the 1984 Victims of Crime Act to oversee grants, training, and other programs that benefit victims of crime. Major sections include Grants & Funding, Help for Crime Victims, Library & Multimedia, News & Features, Help for Providers, Public Awareness, and Crime Victims' Rights. The Help for Crime Victims section directs users to resources, particularly nongovernment organizations and their Web sites, that can assist with such areas as child abuse, elder abuse, sexual abuse, white collar crime, and stalking. It also features an online directory of crime victim services.

Much of the funding and technical assistance information on the OVC Web site is for professionals and organizations that manage victim assistance programs. The Help for Victims section can be of direct interest to individuals.

Subject(s): Victims of Crime

Publication(s): *Directory of International Crime Victim Compensation Programs*, J 34.10

OVC Fact Sheets, J 34.4

OVC National Directory of Victim Assistance Funding Opportunities, J 34.10/2

OVC's Legal Series Bulletins, J 34.3/3

Office of Child Support Enforcement (OCSE)

http://www.acf.hhs.gov/programs/cse/

Sponsor(s): Health and Human Services Department—Administration for Children and Families (ACF)—Child Support Enforcement Office

Description: Child support enforcement is conducted primarily at the state level. OCSE supports state and local efforts to locate participants in child support cases, collect child support payments, and enforce child support orders. The Web site has information on available grants, state child support Web sites, and services for finding participants in child support cases. Some materials, such as a handbook for the party seeking child support, are available in Spanish as well as English.

Subject(s): Child Support

Publication(s): *Child Support Enforcement Handbook,* T 22.44/2

Child Support Report, HE 24.9

Office of Justice Programs (OJP)

http://www.ojp.usdoj.gov/

Sponsor(s): Justice Department—Justice Programs Office

Description: OJP provides federal assistance to the nation's justice system. OJP and its program bureaus are responsible for collecting statistical data and conducting analyses, identifying emerging criminal justice issues, providing technical assistance and training, evaluating program results, and disseminating information to state and local governments. The Web site has sections on funding resources and on technical and training assistance. The OJP Topics section has detailed information on resources in specific areas such as juvenile justice and corrections.

Subject(s): Criminal Justice—Research; Law Enforcement—Grants

Publication(s): *Office of Justice Programs Resource Guide,* J 1.8/2

Office of Juvenile Justice and Delinquency Prevention (OJJDP)

http://www.ojjdp.gov/

Sponsor(s): Justice Department—Justice Programs Office

Description: OJDPP supports states and communities in their work to prevent and control juvenile crime. Featured sections of the site include Topics, Funding, Programs, Publications, State Contacts, and Statistics. The Topics section organizes OJJDP publications, programs, funding opportunities, and events by subject. Topics include child protection, corrections/detention, delinquency prevention, schools, and offenses/offender. The publications catalog links to full-text publications on the NCJRS site.

Subject(s): Juvenile Delinquency; Juvenile Justice
Publication(s): *OJJDP Bulletin*, J 32.21/2-2
OJJDP Fact Sheets, J 32.21
OJJDP News @ a Glance, J 32.25

Office of Terrorism and Financial Intelligence (TFI)

http://www.treasury.gov/about/organizational-structure/offices/
Pages/Office-of-Terrorism-and-Financial-Intelligence.aspx
Sponsor(s): Treasury Department
Description: TFI develops policies, regulations, and strategies to guard financial systems against illegal use and to target the use of financial systems by terrorists. Topics covered by the Web site include freezing terrorist assets and protecting charities from misuse by terrorist organizations.
Subject(s): Financial Crimes; Terrorism

Office of the Deputy Attorney General

http://www.justice.gov/dag/
Sponsor(s): Justice Department—Deputy Attorney General
Description: This page features the deputy attorney general's speeches, congressional testimony, and publications.
Subject(s): Law Enforcement Policy
Publication(s): *Health Care Fraud and Abuse Control Program Annual Report* J 1.1/13

Office on Violence Against Women

http://www.ovw.usdoj.gov/
Sponsor(s): Justice Department
Description: The Office on Violence Against Women was established as a source for assistance to female victims of violence. The Web site links to resources and publications on help for victims (including hotline numbers), domestic violence, sexual assault, and stalking. The site also has information on grant programs, federal laws, and the National Advisory Committee on Violence Against Women.
Subject(s): Domestic Violence; Victims of Crime

Office to Monitor and Combat Trafficking in Persons

http://www.state.gov/g/tip/
Sponsor(s): State Department
Description: The Office to Monitor and Combat Trafficking in Persons is concerned with preventing abusive smuggling of men, women, and children across international borders. The Web site provides background information on the issue, U.S. laws on trafficking in persons, and government-funded anti-trafficking programs.
Subject(s): International Crimes

Publication(s): *Trafficking in Persons Report,* S 1.152

Project Safe Childhood
http://www.projectsafechildhood.gov/
Sponsor(s): Justice Department
Description: Project Safe Childhood is designed to strengthen the investigation and prosecution of sexual exploitation crimes committed against children. The Web site provides detailed information on the program and news and reports related to the victimization of youth.
Subject(s): Children

Project Safe Neighborhoods
http://www.psn.gov/
Sponsor(s): Justice Department
Description: Project Safe Neighborhoods is a national, state, and local effort to reduce gun and gang violence. Federal support comes in the form of funding, grants, law enforcement training, and technology. This Web site provides background information on the project and links to related publications and topics.
Subject(s): Guns; Crime Prevention

Sourcebook of Criminal Justice Statistics
http://www.albany.edu/sourcebook/
Sponsor(s): Justice Department—Bureau of Justice Statistics (BJS); University of Albany
Description: The *Sourcebook of Criminal Justice Statistics* is a key Justice Department reference publications that presents over 600 tables of data from over 100 sources. This university site has made the *Sourcebook* available online and the data is continuously updated. Data tables are in PDF and spreadsheet formats. The Sourcebook is no longer issued in print; the site has an archive of past *Sourcebook* editions going back to 1994.
Subject(s): Criminal Justice—Statistics
Publication(s): *Sourcebook of Criminal Justice Statistics,* J 29.9/6

STRYVE - Striving to Reduce Youth Violence Everywhere
http://vetoviolence.cdc.gov/apps/stryve/
Sponsor(s): Health and Human Services Department—Centers for Disease Control and Prevention (CDC)
Description: STRYVE is a "national initiative, led by the Centers for Disease Control and Prevention (CDC), which takes a public health approach to preventing youth violence before it starts." (from the Web site) The Web site's Resources section features news, definitions, and other resources on the topic. The site also links to online training and a training calendar.
Subject(s): Juvenile Delinquency

U.S. Customs and Border Protection

http://www.cbp.gov/xp/cgov/border_security/border_patrol/

Sponsor(s): Homeland Security Department—Customs and Border Protection Bureau

Description: The U.S. Border Patrol Web presence is part of a larger section on border security on the Department of Homeland Security Web site. The overall mission of the Border Patrol is to detect and prevent the illegal entry of aliens into the United States. The site also has a section on Border Patrol history.

Subject(s): Homeland Security—International Borders

Publication(s): *2012–2016 Border Patrol Strategic Plan*

U.S. Border Patrol Weekly Blotter

U.S. Marshals Service

http://www.justice.gov/marshals/

Sponsor(s): Justice Department—Marshals Service

Description: The U.S. Marshals Service, in existence since 1789, today has a range of duties including court security, fugitive investigations, and the sale of properties seized and forfeited by federal law enforcement agencies. The Web site emphasizes news of current fugitives and recent captures. Other sections of the site cover the U.S. Marshals duties, the long and eventful history of the service, the Asset Forfeiture Program (including current asset sales), prisoner transportation and custody issues, court and witness security, and service of process. The site also has career information, a detailed directory of the local district offices, and an RSS feed for news releases.

Subject(s): Law Enforcement; Wanted People

U.S. National Central Bureau of Interpol

http://www.justice.gov/usncb/

Sponsor(s): Justice Department

Description: The U.S. National Central Bureau of Interpol acts as the U.S. representative to the International Criminal Police Organization (INTERPOL) on behalf of the U.S. attorney general. Among its responsibilities, the bureau distributes INTERPOL notices on fugitives, lost persons, stolen art and cultural objects, organized crime groups, and other matters. The Web site has information on the bureau's mission, organization, and programs.

Subject(s): International Crimes; Wanted People

U.S. Postal Inspection Service

https://postalinspectors.uspis.gov/

Sponsor(s): Postal Service (USPS)—Postal Inspection Service

Description: The U.S. Postal Inspection Service is a federal law enforcement agency with the security and enforcement responsibilities for the U.S. mail and U.S. Postal Service workers. Major sections of the Web site concern mail fraud, identity theft, mail theft, child exploitation, and dangerous mail (for example, hazardous substances). The site also has a list of the U.S. Postal Inspection Service's most wanted criminals with links to their wanted posters.

Subject(s): Postal Service; Wanted People

United States Park Police

http://www.nps.gov/uspp/

Sponsor(s): Interior Department—National Park Service (NPS)

Description: This site describes the history, role, and activities of the United States Park Police, law enforcement officers with jurisdiction in National Park Service areas and certain government properties. The site describes the field operations (including horse mounted police), icon protection branch (protecting Golden Gate Bridge and other American cultural icons), and the investigative branch. The site also features the Park Police Most Wanted List and phone numbers for their offices.

Subject(s): National Parks and Reserves; Police

United States Parole Commission

http://www.usdoj.gov/uspc/

Sponsor(s): Justice Department—Parole Commission

Description: The United States Parole Commission makes parole determinations in certain federal offender cases, District of Columbia Code violation cases, Uniform Code of Military Justice offender cases, and for certain state probationers and parolees who have been placed in the federal witness protection program. The site describes the commission and its specific jurisdiction. Sections include Victim/Witness Program, USPC FOIA, News, and Resources. Questions such as "How does the Commission determine if someone is eligible for parole?" and "What happens at a parole hearing?" are addressed in the Frequently Asked Questions section.

Subject(s): Prisoners

LAWS AND LEGAL INFORMATION

Code of Federal Regulations (CFR)

http://www.fdsys.gov/

Alternate URL(s)

http://www.ecfr.gov

Sponsor(s): National Archives and Records Administration (NARA)—Federal Register Office—Government Printing Office (GPO)

Description: As described by the Government Printing Office (GPO), The Code of Federal Regulations (CFR) "is the codification of the general and permanent rules published in the Federal Register by the departments and agencies of the Federal Government. It is divided into 50 titles that represent broad areas subject to Federal regulation." The CFR on GPO's FDsys.gov online system is a digital version of the printed edition. Content is updated annually when the print volumes are updated. Past editions, going back to 1996, are kept online.

GPO has also developed a complementary online version, called e-CFR. The e-CFR is available at the alternate URL listed above. The e-CFR text is continually updated with new federal regulations.

Researchers using either version of the CFR should read the online background information to learn how the regulations are updated.

Subject(s): Legal Information—Regulations
Publication(s): *Code of Federal Regulations*, AE 2.106/3

Federal Register

http://www.gpo.gov/fdsys/browse/collection.action?collectionCode= FR

Sponsor(s): National Archives and Records Administration (NARA)—Federal Register Office—Government Printing Office (GPO)

Description: The Federal Register is the official daily publication for rules, proposed rules, and notices of Federal agencies and organizations, as well as executive orders, presidential proclamations, and other presidential documents. Federal Register issues are available on the Government Printing Office FDsys online system for 1994 to the present. The issues are compiled by the National Archives and put online by the Government Printing Office.

The newer Federal Register Web site, Federal Register 2.0, which provides users with a more interactive interface, is listed in a separate entry.

Subject(s): Legal Information—Regulations
Publication(s): *Federal Register*, AE 2.106

Federal Register 2.0

http://www.federalregister.gov/

Sponsor(s): National Archives and Records Administration (NARA)—Federal Register Office—Government Printing Office (GPO)

Description: The new Federal Register 2.0 Web site is intended to make it easier to find and comment on federal regulations. Researchers can do a word search or browse regulations by the issuing agency's name. Researchers can also browse by topic and set up an RSS news feed of new items in that topic area.

The online version through the GPO is on the FDsys.gov Web site and is described in a separate entry.

Subject(s): Laws—Regulations

Global Legal Monitor (GLM)

http://www.loc.gov/lawweb/servlet/lloc_news?home

Sponsor(s): Library of Congress—Law Library of Congress

Description: GLM features international legal news by topic and by country. The Law Library of Congress introduced GLM, an online publication, in 2006. News updates are available as an RSS feed, and all news can be search by topic, country, and date.

Subject(s): Legal Information—International

Office of the Law Revision Counsel

http://uscode.house.gov/

Sponsor(s): Congress—House of Representatives—Office of the Law Revision Counsel

Description: "The United States Code is a consolidation and codification by subject matter of the general and permanent laws of the United States. It is prepared by the Office of the Law Revision Counsel of the United States House of Representatives." (from the Web site) The Law Revision Counsel makes the U.S. Code available online for searching, browsing, or downloading. The site also features the office's classification tables, which show where recently enacted laws will appear in the U.S. Code and which sections of the code have been amended by those laws.

See also the separate entry for the U.S. Code Web site, which is sponsored by the Legal Information Institute.

Subject(s): Laws

Public and Private Laws

http://www.fdsys.gov/

Alternate URL(s)

http://www.gpo.gov/fdsys/browse/collection.action?collectionCode=PLAW

Sponsor(s): Government Printing Office (GPO)

Description: The GPO's FDsys Web site has a database of public and private laws enacted from 1995 to the present. Laws are available in both text and PDF formats. Most laws are Public Laws. Private laws are enacted to assist citizens that have been injured by government programs or who are appealing an executive agency ruling such as deportation.

Select "Public and Private Laws" from the FDsys menu or access it directly from the alternate URL listed above.

Subject(s): Laws

Public Laws

http://www.archives.gov/federal-register/laws/

Sponsor(s): National Archives and Records Administration (NARA)—Federal Register Office

Description: Public laws are published by the National Archive's Office of the Federal Register. This Web page explains how laws are numbered and printed. Users can view a list of laws from the current session of Congress or sign up to receive automatic e-mail announcements of new public law numbers.

Subject(s): Laws

RegInfo.gov

http://reginfo.gov/

Sponsor(s): General Services Administration (GSA)—Office of Management and Budget (OMB)

Description: RegInfo.gov is a finding aid for federal regulatory information and learning how to track regulations throughout the process. The site features the Regulatory Review Dashboard, an interactive graph for finding regulations currently under review. The site links to key online resources for regulatory information such as the Federal Register and the Code of Federal Regulations, Small Business Administration Regulatory Alerts, and the Unified Agenda of Federal Regulatory and Deregulatory Actions.

RegInfo.gov is a useful portal site for official regulatory documents and information on the federal regulatory process.

Subject(s): Regulatory Policy; Finding Aids

Publication(s): *Unified Agenda of Federal Regulatory and Deregulatory Actions*, GS 1.6/11-2

Regulations.gov

http://www.regulations.gov/

Sponsor(s): Environmental Protection Agency (EPA)

Description: Regulations.gov is intended to make it easier for the general public to participate in the federal regulations review process. The site is an interagency effort led by the EPA. Users can search by word, agency, and other facets to find proposed and final regulations currently open for comment. Search results include a docket ID, Federal Register citation and date for when the regulation was first published, and final date for comments. The results also have links to view the Federal Register announcement in text or PDF formats and a link to a Web form for submitting comments. The full docket of materials includes the text of public comments in accordance with the policies of the individual agencies. Prepared searches to make it easy to find newly issued regulatory proposals and regulations with a comment period that is ending soon.

Subject(s): Regulatory Policy

U.S. Code

http://www.law.cornell.edu/uscode/

Alternate URL(s)

http://www.gpo.gov/fdsys/browse/collectionUScode.action?collectionCode=USCODE

Sponsor(s): Legal Information Institute (LII)

Description: Cornell University's Legal Information Institute (LII) offers this popular and free interface for searching the U.S. Code. The code can be searched by word, by title and section number, or browsed. The site also features a table of popular names of laws, such as Voting Rights Act and Railroad Retirement Act. Where these laws can easily be linked to one part of the code, LII does so.

The U.S. Code can also be accessed and browsed on GPO's FDsys system at the alternate URL listed above.

Subject(s): Laws

Publication(s): *United States Code*

SIXTEEN

Legislative Branch

The United States Congress is comprised of two chambers, 535 Member offices, over forty committees, various legislative and operational offices, and several major congressional support agencies. Most of these entities have their own Web site. In addition, many private and educational sites help to spread and interpret congressional information. This chapter describes major legislative branch Web sites and other useful finding aids for legislative information. The Web sites for individual Members of Congress and congressional committees are listed in appendixes A and B at the end of this book.

Subsections in this chapter are Congress, Congressional Support Agencies, and Legislative Information.

CONGRESS

Biographical Directory of the United States Congress
http://bioguide.congress.gov/
Sponsor(s): Congress
Description: For over a century, the *Biographical Directory of the United States Congress* has provided valuable information about the more than 13,000 individuals who have served in the national legislature, including members of the Continental Congress, the Senate, and the House of Representatives from 1774 to the present. Congress offers an online version of this historical resource that goes beyond the scope of the printed *Biographical Directory* by including images and extended information about research collections relating to each member. The online version is also continuously updated. The biographies may be searched by name, position (e.g., senator or Speaker of the House), party, and state.
Subject(s): Members of Congress; Biographies

Publication(s): *Biographical Directory of the United States Congress*

Black Americans in Congress

http://history.house.gov/Exhibitions-and-Publications/BAIC/Black-Americans-in-Congress/

Sponsor(s): Congress—House of Representatives—Office of the Clerk

Description: As described on the site, Black Americans in Congress features "biographical profiles of former African-American Members of Congress, links to information about current black Members, essays on institutional and national events that shaped successive generations of African Americans in Congress, and images of each individual Member, supplemented by other historical photos." The Educational Resources section of the site includes lesson plans and fact sheets on African American congressional "firsts." It is based on the publication *Black Americans in Congress, 1870–2007.*

Subject(s): African Americans—History; Lesson Plans

Committee on House Administration

http://cha.house.gov/

Sponsor(s): Congress—House of Representatives

Description: Although other congressional committees do not receive a separate entry in this section, the Committee on House Administration is featured here because of several reference resources available on the site. It provides a directory of Congressional Member Organizations, such as the Congressional Arts Caucus, the Law Enforcement Caucus, and the Military Veterans Caucus. The site also has information from the Commission on Congressional Mailing Standards, known as the Franking Commission, which regulates issues related to outgoing congressional mail.

Subject(s): House of Representatives

Congressional Directory

http://www.gpo.gov/fdsys/browse/collection.action?collectionCode=CDIR

Alternate URL(s)

http://www.gpo.gov/help/sample_searches_and_urls_for_congressional_directory.htm

Sponsor(s): Congress—Joint Committee on Printing

Description: The *Congressional Directory*, the official directory of Congress, has been published since 1888. The Government Printing Office has made it available online on their FDsys Web site for the 105th Congress (1997–1998) to the 113th Congress (2013–2014). Each edition of the *Congressional Directory* can be searched by keyword or browsed by section. The online edition is typically updated once before the next edition appears in print.

The alternate URL listed above provides tips from the GPO about searching for entries in the *Congressional Directory*.

The publishing schedule of the *Congressional Directory* makes it less valuable as a source of current contact information than as a source of historical reference. Useful lists in the Statistical Information section of each edition include: joint sessions of Congress for 1789 to present; House impeachments of judges, presidents, and members of Congress; and political divisions in the House and Senate from 1855 onward.

Subject(s): Congressional Information

Publication(s): *Congressional Directory*, GP 3.22/2:228/

Guide to House and Senate Members

http://www.memberguide.gpoaccess.gov/

Alternate URL(s)

http://www.gpo.gov/fdsys/

Sponsor(s): Government Printing Office (GPO) Congress—House of Representatives—Congress—Senate

Description: The House of Representatives and the Senate each feature directory pages of members and committees on their Web sites. Among the various free congressional directories online, these naturally tend to be the most current and authoritative. In addition to the official listings and links to members' Web sites, the House directories page includes information on current vacancies and member addresses formatted as downloadable mailing labels. The Senate features a list that can be sorted by name, state, or party. The Senate listing includes e-mail addresses. The House offers a Write Your Representative feature for finding and e-mailing your House member.

The data come from the *Pictorial Directory* and the *Congressional Directory*. These publications are available at the alternate URL listed above.

Subject(s): Members of Congress; Directories

History of the United States Capitol

http://www.access.gpo.gov/congress/senate/capitol/

Sponsor(s): Congress—Architect of the Capitol

Description: The full-text version of the *History of the United States Capitol: A Chronicle of Design, Construction, and Politics*, a 2002 book by architectural historian William C. Allen, is available in PDF format on this GPO Access Web site. The book, which was sponsored by Congress and printed as a Senate document, includes numerous illustrations and photographs, as well as a bibliography.

Subject(s): Capitol Building—History

Publications: *History of the United States Capitol: A Chronicle of Design, Construction, and Politics*, Y 1.1/2:SERIAL 14620

House Democratic Leader
http://www.democraticleader.gov/
Sponsor(s): Congress—House of Representatives
Description: The Web site for House Democratic Leader Nancy Pelosi includes an Issues section, which is broken down into such topics as energy independence, health care, and education. The site also includes a calendar (under Resources), a biography of Pelosi, and a Newsroom section with press releases, speeches, and reports.
Subject(s): House of Representatives

House of Representatives—Committee Offices
http://www.house.gov/committees/
Sponsor(s): Congress—House of Representatives
Description: This Web page provides links to all of the House committee Web sites. The content of these sites can vary tremendously from one committee to the next. Most include a list of committee members and information on the committee's jurisdiction and schedule. Most provide live webcasts of hearings, but not all provide archives of past hearings. The sites, managed by the committee's majority party, typically link to a Web site for the committee's minority party members.

The House committee Web sites can be useful sources for current legislative information and of information about the programs within their jurisdiction. Many of the sites, however, could be improved with more timely provisions of hearings transcripts or availability of archived hearing webcasts.
Subject(s): Congressional Committees

House Statement of Disbursements
http://disbursements.house.gov/
Sponsor(s): Congress—House of Representatives
Description: According to the Web site, "The Statement of Disbursements (SOD) is a quarterly public report of all receipts and expenditures for U.S. House of Representatives Members, Committees, Leadership, Officers, and Offices." It is published by the Chief Administrative Officer of the House. It has been published in print since 1964 and is recently available online in PDF format. The Web site has the SOD for July 2009 forward.

This document is fairly technical and specific to House disbursements. Be sure to review the supporting documentation for help in reading the statements.
Subject(s): House of Representatives

Lobbying Disclosure—House

http://lobbyingdisclosure.house.gov/

Sponsor(s): Congress—House of Representatives—Office of the Clerk

Description: The House provides this Web site for those who must by law register with the House Clerk's Office and file regular reports on their lobbying activities.

Prior to 2008, the House did not make copies of the disclosure reports available online. Changes in the reporting system were brought about in compliance with the Honest Leadership and Open Government Act of 2007, described on this site. An alternative for lobbying data is the nonprofit OpenSecrets.org Lobby database at http://www.opensecrets.org/lobby/.

Subject(s): Lobbyists

Lobbying Disclosure—Senate

http://www.senate.gov/pagelayout/legislative/g_three_sections_with_teasers/lobbyingdisc.htm

Alternate URL(s)

http://www.senate.gov/legislative/Public_Disclosure/LDA_reports.htm

Sponsor(s): Congress—Senate—Secretary of the Senate

Description: For those who wish to lobby the Senate, this Web page provides access to filing forms and information about compliance with lobbying disclosure law. It also links to databases of lobbyists' disclosure filings. One database is for the standard (LD-1/LD-2) quarterly report; the other is for a relatively new semiannual report (LD-203) of payments for honorary contributions, event hosting costs, and other contributions. The alternate URL above is a direct link to the disclosure filings search page.

An alternative for lobbying data is the nonprofit OpenSecrets.org Lobby database at http://www.opensecrets.org/lobby/.

Subject(s): Lobbyists

Majority Whip

http://www.majoritywhip.house.gov/

Sponsor(s): Congress—House of Representatives—Office of the House Majority Whip

Description: The Majority Whip is responsible for marshaling the votes of members of the majority party in the House. The whip's Web site is used to keep members informed about upcoming legislation and floor votes; researchers can also use it for this purpose. The site also links to a blog, recent video, and a Twitter feed. A new mobile app, WhipCast, provides current congressional updates.

Subject(s): Legislation

Office of the Clerk

http://clerk.house.gov/

Sponsor(s): Congress—House of Representatives—Office of the Clerk

Description: The Clerk of the House is charged with a variety of procedural and administrative duties. The clerk's Web site includes information about the office itself, along with a wealth of congressional information associated with the clerk's duties. The site includes directories of members of Congress, leadership offices, committees, and subcommittees; House legislative activity schedules; legislative procedure information; roll call vote results; congressional history; congressional election statistics; and public disclosure information, such as members' financial disclosure reports and official foreign travel and expenditures reports. It also carries the official list of congressional office vacancies and current tallies of party alignment in the House and Senate.

Subject(s): Congressional Information; Legislative Procedure

Senate Majority Leader

http://www.reid.senate.gov/

Sponsor(s): Congress—Senate

Description: Senator Mitch McConnell (R-Ky.) is the current majority leader of the Senate. This site includes a Leadership section with links to the pages of other Senate members who hold leadership roles.

Subject(s): Senate

Senate Minority Leader

http://www.reid.senate.gov/

Sponsor(s): Congress—Senate

Description: The site for the Senate's minority leader, Senator Harry Reid (D-Utah), includes information about the senator and his bills and actions in the Senate.

Subject(s): Senate

Speaker's Blog

http://www.speaker.gov/blog

Sponsor(s): Congress—House of Representatives

Description: The blog for the Speaker of the House links to analysis of congressional and presidential initiatives. Comments are permitted.

Speaker.gov

http://www.speaker.gov/

Sponsor(s): Congress—House of Representatives

Description: The Web site for the Speaker of the House, Rep. John Boehner (R-Ohio), includes photos and video, a biography of Boehner, and information about legislative initiatives. Links to social media pages and a blog (described in a separate entry) are also available.

Subject(s): House of Representatives

United States House of Representatives

http://www.house.gov/

Sponsor(s): Congress—House of Representatives

Description: The House of Representatives Web site includes a wealth of current legislative and policy information. The site provides quick links to House member Web sites, which typically have information about their House district and representational services for constituents of the district. The House site also links to individual House committee Web sites, which report on legislation within their jurisdiction. Links for finding and writing to local representatives are provided in the upper right-hand corner of the home page.

Other sections of the site link to House schedule information, sources for legislative and legal research, House members' voting information, information for kids and students, visitor information, and the Web sites for legislative branch agencies.

Subject(s): House of Representatives

United States Senate

http://www.senate.gov/

Sponsor(s): Congress—Senate

Description: The United States Senate Web site is a source for both current legislative news and historical Senate information. The major sections of the site are Senators, Committees, Legislation & Records, Art & History, Visitors, and Reference. As with the House site, the content of individual member and committee sites varies, and the committee sites typically carry hearings schedules and some form of testimony.

The Legislation and Records section links to Senate votes, schedules, lobbying disclosure reports, and guides to the legislative process. The Active Legislation subsection identifies currently active bills and labels them by topic. The Nominations section performs a similar role and includes lists of nominations by status, nominations withdrawn, and nominations failed or returned.

In the Reference section, the Senate Library offers a Virtual Reference Desk (VRD) with information about topics including filibustering, Senate traditions, congressional medals and honors, the Senate Page program, and women and minorities in the Senate. This section also has reference statistics and lists (including a list of the longest-serving senators), bibliographies, research guides, and a glossary. The Art & History section is particularly rich with historical information and images.

Subject(s): Senate

United States Senate: Committees Home
http://www.senate.gov/pagelayout/committees/d_three_sections_with_teasers/committees_home.htm
   Sponsor(s): Congress—Senate
   Description: The Senate's home page for its committees features direct links to the committees' Web sites, committee membership lists, and a schedule of upcoming committee hearings and meetings. It also provides background information about the committee system and offers links to related Web sites. To avoid entering the long URL above, go to the Senate.gov home page and click on "Committees."
   Subject(s): Congressional Committees

Women in Congress
http://womenincongress.house.gov/
   Sponsor(s): Congress—House of Representatives—Office of the Clerk
   Description: The Women in Congress site features historical and current information about female members of the House and Senate. It includes biographical profiles, historical essays, and historical data such as a list of women who have been elected to party leadership positions. The Education section features lesson plans.
   Subject(s): Lesson Plans; Women—History

CONGRESSIONAL SUPPORT AGENCIES

Architect of the Capitol (AOC)
http://www.aoc.gov/
   Sponsor(s): Congress—Architect of the Capitol
   Description: The Architect of the Capitol (AOC) is responsible for the maintenance, operation, development, and preservation of the United States Capitol Complex, which includes the Capitol and its grounds, the congressional office buildings, the Library of Congress buildings, the Supreme Court building, the Capitol Power Plant, and other facilities. Major sections of this Web site include Explore Capitol Hill, Plan Your Visit, and About AOC.

   The Explore Capitol Hill section provides extensive information about the history, art, and architecture of the Capitol Building, supplemented by historic and contemporary photographs and illustrations. The new Capitol Visitor Center has a small Web site of its own, http://www.visitthecapitol.gov/, with maps and information on booking a tour.

   The detailed current and historical information on this site makes it a useful resource for reference or research. It will be of interest to tourists as well as students of history, government, art, architecture, and historical preservation.
   Subject(s): Capitol Building

Congressional Budget Office (CBO)

http://www.cbo.gov/

Sponsor(s): Congressional Budget Office (CBO)

Description: CBO provides Congress with the analyses needed for economic and budget decisions and with the information and estimates required for the congressional budget process. The CBO Web site has the full-text versions of its many publications, including economic forecasts, budget projections, analysis of the president's budget, CBO testimony before Congress, and cost estimates for bills reported by congressional committees. The Topics sections has drop-down menus that allow users to browse publications by topic, congressional session, budget function, and publication type. The CBO Web site offers RSS feeds and the option to create a customized My CBO page.

CBO publications provide a wealth of information on the federal budget and on tax and spending proposals. Outside of its regular budget report series, CBO publishes special reports on policy and program topics such as funding for homeland security and the outlook for Social Security.

Subject(s): Budget of the U.S. Government; Congressional Support Agencies

Publication(s): *An Analysis of the President's Budgetary Proposals for Fiscal Year . . .* , Y 10.19

Budget Options, Y 10.2

Historical Effective Federal Tax Rates, Y 10.2:H 62

Monthly Budget Review, Y 10.21/2

The Budget and Economic Outlook: An Update, Y 10.17:

The Budget and Economic Outlook: Fiscal Years . . . , Y 10.13

Unauthorized Appropriations and Expiring Authorizations, Y 10.22

Congressional Oversight Panel

http://cybercemetery.unt.edu/archive/cop/20110401223205/http:/www.cop.senate.gov/

Sponsor(s): Congress—Congressional Oversight Panel

Description: The Congressional Oversight Panel, which ceased operation in early 2011, was established in 2008 by the Emergency Economic Stabilization Act (Public Law 110-343). The panel's Web site, now archived in the University of North Texas's CyberCemetery, provided news, reports, and testimony related to congressional oversight of actions taken by the Treasury Department and financial institutions and their effect on the economy. The Web site also has biographies of the panel members, who were appointed by House and Senate minority and majority leadership.

Subject(s): Banking Regulation; Finance—Regulations

Congressional Research Service Employment Opportunities
http://www.loc.gov/crsinfo/
Sponsor(s): Library of Congress—Congressional Research Service (CRS)
Description: The Congressional Research Service is a legislative support agency located within the Library of Congress. Its mission is to provide nonpartisan analysis and research services to Congress. The purpose of its Web site is to provide information about job openings, internships, and other employment options. Basic background and research information about CRS is also provided. Because CRS works exclusively for Congress, this employment page is its only official public site.
Subject(s): Congressional Support Agencies

CRS Reports—UNT Libraries
http://digital.library.unt.edu/explore/collections/CRSR/
Sponsor(s): University of North Texas Libraries
Description: The goal of the CRS Reports project at the University of North Texas Libraries is to provide permanent public access to CRS Reports that have been available at a variety of different Web sites since 1990. The reports can be searched or browsed by topic. Subject indexing of the reports uses the CRS Legislative Indexing Vocabulary, supplemented with Library of Congress Subject Headings.

This University of North Texas (UNT) Web site was launched at about the same time as the Open CRS Network Web site, which is also described in this publication. The Open CRS Network site is focused on expanding the number of CRS Reports in the public domain and lobbying for better public access to these reports. This UNT Libraries Web site brings greater historical coverage, search capabilities, subject indexing, and the goal of permanent public access to past CRS Reports.
Subject(s): Legislative Information

Government Accountability Office (GAO)
http://www.gao.gov/
Sponsor(s): Government Accountability Office (GAO)
Description: GAO is the investigative arm of Congress. It examines the use of public funds and evaluates federal programs and activities to help the Congress in oversight, policy, and funding decisions. Its Web site features the full-text versions of GAO Reports and Testimony and recent comptroller general decisions and opinions. E-mail alert lists and RSS news feeds are offered to notify subscribers when new reports or decisions are published. GAO's FraudNET service allows the public to report allegations of waste, fraud, abuse, or mismanagement of federal funds; the site provides an online form for reporting such allegations. The GAO Web site also features information from their biennial report to Congress on federal programs at high risk for waste, fraud, and abuse. In

addition, GAO has a section explaining their role in Recovery Act oversight and to provide related reports. GAO also offers a mobile app for the Android operating system.

Subject(s): Congressional Support Agencies; Government Administration

Publication(s): *Abstracts of Reports and Testimony*, GA 1.16/3-3
Decisions of the Comptroller General, GA 1.5/A-2
Financial Report of the United States Government, T 63.113/3
GAO Reports, GA 1.13
Government Auditing Standards (Yellow Book), GA 1.2
High-Risk Series: An Update, GA 1.13
Month in Review, GA 1.16/3
Principles of Federal Appropriations Law (Red Book), GA 1.14
Today's Reports, GA 1.16/7

Office of Congressional Ethics (OCE)

http://oce.house.gov/
Sponsor(s): Congress—House of Representatives
Description: As stated on the Web site, OCE is "an independent, nonpartisan entity charged with reviewing allegations of misconduct against Members, officers, and staff of the United States House of Representatives and, when appropriate, referring matters to the House Committee on Ethics." OCE was established by House resolution in 2008. The Web site lists the board of directors members and provides copies of ethics rules documents, board meeting minutes, and reports. It also connects to OCE blog postings.
Subject(s): Ethics in Government

Office of Technology Assessment: The OTA Legacy

http://www.princeton.edu/~ota/
Sponsor(s): Office of Technology Assessment (OTA)
Description: After Congress terminated its Office of Technology Assessment (OTA) at the end of 1995, the official OTA Web site ceased. This Princeton University site makes archived OTA information available to the public. It provides the full text of OTA publications arranged by title, year, and topic, as they were on the official OTA site. The Technology Assessment and the Work of Congress section describes the history and operations of OTA, including speeches and news reports about its role.
Subject(s): Science and Technology Policy
Publications: *OTA Reports*, Y 3.T 22/2

U.S. Capitol Visitor Center

http://www.visitthecapitol.gov/
Sponsor(s): Congress—Architect of the Capitol

Description: The new U.S. Capitol Visitor Center, on the east side of the Capitol Building, hosts tours and exhibits. The Web site has information on planning a visit to the Capitol, with a special section for schools and teachers planning field trips. Information about Congress is also provided.

Subject(s): Capitol Building

LEGISLATIVE INFORMATION

A Century of Lawmaking for a New Nation: U.S. Congressional Documents and Debates, 1774–1875

http://memory.loc.gov/ammem/amlaw/lawhome.html

Sponsor(s): Library of Congress

Description: Congressional documents from the Continental Congress through 1875 are available to search, browse, and display on this Web site, courtesy of the Library of Congress and its Law Library. The digitized collection includes the *Journals of the Continental Congress* (1774–1789); the *Letters of Delegates to Congress* (1774–1789); the *Records of the Federal Convention of 1787*, or Farrand's Records; and the Debates in the Several State Conventions on the Adoption of the Federal Constitution (1787–1788), or Elliot's Debates; the journals of the House of Representatives (1789–1875) and the Senate (1789–1875), including the *Senate Executive Journal* (1789–1875); the *Journal of William Maclay* (1789–1791); the debates of Congress as published in the *Annals of Congress* (1789–1824), the *Register of Debates* (1824–1837), the *Congressional Globe* (1833–1873), and the Congressional Record (1873–1875); the *Statutes at Large* (1789–1875); the *American State Papers* (1789–1838); and congressional bills and resolutions for selected sessions beginning with the 6th Congress (1799) in the House of Representatives and the 16th Congress (1819) in the Senate. It also includes selected documents from the *U.S. Serial Set* from 1833 through 1916.

The site provides tips on using, searching, and viewing the collection. A search button for "All Titles" leads to a search page with many options, including searching one specific title or a combination of several titles. Browse options are also presented on the search page. The title page for each document includes links to a citation guide and basic historical background on the document.

This collection provides substantial public access to the documentary history of American democracy.

Subject(s): Congress — History; Congressional Documents

Center for Legislative Archives

http://www.archives.gov/records_of_congress/

Sponsor(s): National Archives and Records Administration (NARA)

Description: The Center for Legislative Archives is the repository for historically valuable congressional records at the National Archives and Records Administration. The center, located in Washington, D.C., holds more than 170,000 cubic feet of records, dating from the first Congress to modern Congresses. The official records from the committees of the House of Representatives and the Senate—the standing, select, special, and joint committees, which Congress uses to accomplish the majority of its work—represent the core holdings of the center. It also holds some collections from legislative support agencies, such as federal government publications from the Government Printing Office. The site provides various online finding guides, which can be searched by keyword.

Most of the holdings are not available online. A few have been digitized and are available in the Featured Document subsection (under the Resources section). The Other Congressional Collections subsection, also under Resources, links to a directory of congressional members' personal papers collections, most of which are held at archival institutions other than NARA. The Web site also links to information from the Advisory Committee on the Records of Congress.

Subject(s): Congressional Documents

C-SPAN.org

http://www.c-span.org/

Sponsor(s): C-SPAN

Description: The cable television industry created C-SPAN (Cable-Satellite Public Affairs Network) in 1979 to provide live, gavel-to-gavel coverage of the House of Representatives. Senate coverage started in 1986, when the Senate began televising its proceedings. C-SPAN currently offers audio and video of floor proceedings and some hearings over the Internet. Online users can browse the schedules for C-SPAN's cable and radio stations and receive public affairs and congressional programming online.

C-SPAN has grown to include more educational and video material. The C-SPAN Web site includes the C-SPAN Classroom, the C-SPAN Video Library archives, and the First Ladies section. The Resources section includes links to numerous public affairs Web sites.

Subject(s): Congressional Information; Legislative Procedure

How Our Laws Are Made

http://thomas.loc.gov/home/lawsmade.toc.html

Sponsor(s): Congress—House of Representatives; Library of Congress

Description: This classic guide provides a readable and non-technical outline of the numerous steps in the federal lawmaking process. It is available online as a single PDF file or as a chapter-divided HTML file.

The HTML version of this classic is organized to make it relatively easy for users to read the entire work or browse relevant sections.

Subject(s): Legislative Procedure
Publication(s): *How Our Laws are Made*, Y 1.1/7

Legislative Resources on FDsys

http://www.fdsys.gov/
Sponsor(s): Government Printing Office (GPO)
Description: FDsys.gov is GPO's online system. FDsys provides access to many congressional documents, including House and Senate bills, congressional committee reports, the *Congressional Record*, the *Congressional Directory*, and the *Congressional Pictorial Directory*.
    Subject(s): Congressional Documents; Databases
    Publication(s): *Calendar of United States House of Representatives and History of Legislation*, Y 1.2/2
    Cannon's Precedents of the House of Representatives
    Congressional Directory, Y 4.P 93/1:1
    Congressional Pictorial Directory, Y 4.P 93/1:1 P/
    Congressional Record, X 1.1/A
    Constitution of the United States of America: Analysis and Interpretation, Y 1.1/3
    Constitution, Jefferson's Manual, and Rules of the House of Representatives, Y 1.1/7
    Deschler's Precedents of the United States House of Representatives, Y 1.1/2
    Hinds' Precedents of the House of Representatives
    House Practice: A Guide to the Rules, Precedents, and Procedures of the House (Brown), Y 1.2
    Riddick's Senate Procedure, Y 1.1/3
    Senate Calendar of Business (daily), Y 1.3/3
    Senate Manual, Y 1.1/3

LLSDC's Legislative Source Book

http://www.llsdc.org/sourcebook/
Sponsor(s): Law Librarians' Society of Washington, DC, Inc.
Description: The Legislative Interest Section of the Law Librarians' Society of Washington, DC, has compiled a variety of useful legislative research tools developed by its members. Many are unique to this Web site. They include a guide to researching federal legislative histories, an overview of the *Congressional Record* and its predecessor publications, and instructions for finding and establishing direct links to documents online at THOMAS and GPO FDsys. It is a reverse chronological correlation of congressional session numbers.
    This site will be of interest to government documents librarians and serious legislative researchers.
    Subject(s): Congressional Documents; Legislation—Research

THOMAS: Legislative Information on the Internet
http://thomas.loc.gov/
Alternate URL(s)
http://www.thomas.gov/
Sponsor(s): Library of Congress
Description: THOMAS, a service of the Library of Congress that acts under the direction of the Congress, makes U.S. legislative information freely available on the Internet. The Bill Summary and Status database is the core THOMAS database; it is available for the 93rd Congress (1973) to the present. It tracks the action on each bill in Congress, provides links to the full-text version of the bill and related debate in the Congressional Record, and identifies congressional sponsor or co-sponsor, amendments to the bill, and any related bills. The Congressional Record database on THOMAS includes the full-text versions of the Record (from 1989 onward) and its index (from 1995 onward). The Committee Reports database has reports from 1995 onward. THOMAS also has databases of Presidential Nominations (from 1987 to the present) and Treaties (largely from 1975 to the present), both of which are handled by the Senate.

In addition to its core databases, THOMAS links to a variety of legislative research tools and educational information about the legislative process.

This is one of the most widely used Internet sources for legislative information. While it does not yet deliver all the information that some users might desire, it does make a significant body of legislative documentation easily available to the public.
Subject(s): Legislation; Databases
Publication(s): Congressional Record, X 1.1/A
House Bills, Y 1.4/6
House Concurrent Resolutions, Y 1.4/9
House Joint Resolutions, Y 1.4/8
House Resolutions, Y 1.4/7
How Our Laws are Made, Y 1.1/7
Senate Bills, Y 1.4/1
Senate Concurrent Resolutions, Y 1.4/4
Senate Joint Resolutions, Y 1.4/3
Senate Printed Amendments, Y 1.4/5
Senate Resolutions, Y 1.4/2

SEVENTEEN

Presidency

The Obama Administration is the third presidential administration to maintain a White House Web site. It is the first to have a blog and to use the site to link to an official White House presence on such third-party social media sites as Facebook and Flickr. This chapter includes Web sites sponsored by the current presidential administration as well as finding aids for presidential documents from this and other administrations.

Subsections in this chapter are Current Administration and Presidential Information.

CURRENT ADMINISTRATION

Council of Economic Advisers (CEA)
http://whitehouse.gov/cea/
Alternate URL(s)
http://www.whitehouse.gov/administration/eop/cea/
Sponsor(s): Council of Economic Advisers (CEA)
Description: CEA, which consists of one chairman and two members, advises the president of the United States on domestic and international economic policy and assists in the preparation of the *Economic Report of the President*. The CEA Web site describes the mission and operations of the council and links to current CEA publications and the text of the chairman's speeches. The Fact Sheets & Reports section includes the quarterly report on the Economic Impact of the American Recovery and Reinvestment Act of 2009. CEA publications include the monthly *Economic Indicators*, and the CEA Web site links to this document.

Subject(s): Economic Statistics; Economic Policy; Presidential Advisors

Publication(s): *Economic Indicators*, Y 4.EC 7:EC 7/

Economic Report of the President, Pr 42.9

Domestic Policy Council
http://www.whitehouse.gov/administration/eop/dpc/
Sponsor(s): White House—Domestic Policy Council
Description: The Domestic Policy Council manages the president's domestic policy agenda. Its Web site provides a brief description of the council's history and work and has a leadership biography.
Subject(s): Presidential Advisors; Public Policy

First Lady Michelle Obama
http://www.whitehouse.gov/firstlady/
Alternate URL(s)
http://www.whitehouse.gov/administration/michelle_obama/
Sponsor(s): White House—First Lady's Office
Description: The First Lady's Web site provides a biography, photographic portrait, related videos, and news releases.
Subject(s): First Lady

Middle Class Task Force
http://www.AStrongMiddleClass.gov
Alternate URL(s)
http://www.whitehouse.gov/strongmiddleclass/
Sponsor(s): White House—Vice President's Office
Description: The White House Web site describes the White House Task Force on the Middle Class as a "major initiative targeted at raising the living standards of middle-class, working families in America." The Web site has task force reports and a task force blog.
Subject(s): Social Welfare; Vice President
Publication(s): *Middle Class Task Force Annual Report*

National Security Council (NSC)
http://www.whitehouse.gov/administration/eop/nsc/
Alternate URL(s)
http://www.whitehouse.gov/nsc/
Sponsor(s): National Security Council (NSC)
Description: NSC is the president's forum for considering national security and foreign policy matters with his senior national security advisers and cabinet officials. The NSC Web site describes the NSC's role and history. It also provides information on cybersecurity and the new Cybersecurity Coordinator office.
Subject(s): National Security—Policy; Presidential Advisors

Office of Administration
http://www.whitehouse.gov/administration/eop/oa/

Alternate URL(s)

http://www.whitehouse.gov/oa/

Sponsor(s): White House—White House Office of Administration

Description: The Office of Administration provides administrative support services to all units within the Executive Office of the President (EOP). These services include financial management and information technology support, human resources management, library and research assistance, facilities management, and procurement. Its Web site features information about the component offices within the EOP, the history of the office, and the White House Preservation Office.

Subject(s): White House (Mansion)

Vice President Joe Biden

http://www.whitehouse.gov/vicepresident/

Alternate URL(s)

http://www.whitehouse.gov/administration/vice_president_biden/

Sponsor(s): White House—Vice President's Office

Description: Vice President Joe Biden's Web site includes his biography. The vice president is authorized to nominate individuals to the United States Military, Naval, and Air Force Academies; the Web site links to information and an application form.

Subject(s): Vice President

White House

http://www.whitehouse.gov/

Sponsor(s): White House

Description: The White House Web site combines current news and policy statements from the administration with historical information relating to both the building and the Executive Office of the Presidency. In addition to a White House blog, current content is provided in sections called Briefing Room, Issues, and The Administration. The Briefing Room provides news releases and the text of press briefings; the president's weekly address; presidential executive orders, memoranda, and proclamations; presidential speeches and statements; press briefings; the president's and vice president's daily schedules; legislation before the president; visitor access records; and a listing of the status of many of the presidential nominations and appointments. The Issues section summarizes the Obama Administration's policies on major topics, such as defense and health care. The Administration section has biographies of Cabinet members and leading White House staff.

The White House section provides historical information about the mansion and other buildings, biographies of past presidents and first ladies, information on White House tours and events, and more. The Our Government section provides an overview of the structure of American federal, state, and local government. The White House Web site includes a search engine and links to relevant social media pages.

The White House Web site should be the first stop online for users seeking current presidential news, statements, and documents; biographies of elected and appointed White House officials; and historical information about the White House and its occupants.

Subject(s): First Lady; Presidency; White House (Mansion)

White House Blog

http://www.whitehouse.gov/blog/

Sponsor(s): White House

Description: The Obama Administration is the first presidential administration to use the blog format on the White House Web site. The blog reports on presidential initiatives, presidential speeches, White House events, and the work of the Cabinet secretaries. Posts are written by members of the White House staff and by members of the President's Cabinet. The blog is not open for comments.

Subject(s): President; Blogs

White House Fellows Program

http://www.whitehouse.gov/about/fellows/

Sponsor(s): White House

Description: The nonpartisan White House Fellows Program was established by President Lyndon B. Johnson in 1964 to provide early-career professionals with firsthand experience in governing the nation. Each fellow works full time for one year as a special assistant to a cabinet member or senior presidential adviser. This Web site provides information about the program, selection criteria, the application process, and the current class of fellows.

Subject(s): Fellowships; Public Policy

White House Military Office

http://www.whitehouse.gov/administration/eop/whmo/

Sponsor(s): White House

Description: The White House Military Office units include the White House Communications Agency, Presidential Airlift Group, White House Medical Unit, Camp David, Marine Helicopter Squadron One, Presidential Food Service, and the White House Transportation Agency. The Web site explains the role and responsibilities of the White House Military Office, with a section about its history.

Subject(s): President

PRESIDENTIAL INFORMATION

American Presidency Project

http://www.presidency.ucsb.edu/

Sponsor(s): University of California, Santa Barbara

Description: Although it is an unofficial Web site, the American Presidency Project Web site provides a more complete collection of certain key presidential documents than can be found elsewhere on the publicly accessible Web. The site contains the following: Public Papers of the Presidents, (1929–1933, 1945–2007, and 2009); State of the Union addresses, (1790–present); inaugural addresses (1789–present); transcripts from presidential candidate debates (1960–present); and other related documents. The site also has presidential elections results from 1789–present, numerous presidential statistics (number of vetoes, job approval ratings, and more), and audio and video of presidents' speeches.

Subject(s): Presidential Documents

Codification of Presidential Proclamations and Executive Orders

http://www.archives.gov/federal-register/codification/

Sponsor(s): National Archives and Records Administration (NARA)—Federal Register Office

Description: The Office of the Federal Register presents this online version of the Codification of Presidential Proclamations and Executive Orders, which covers proclamations and executive orders issued by presidents from April 13, 1945, through January 20, 1989. Documents that had no legal effect on January 20, 1989, are excluded. The Disposition Tables Numeric Index section lists all the documents back to 1945, noting whether the documents have been revoked or superseded, or have become otherwise obsolete. Earlier proclamations and executive orders are included if they were amended or otherwise affected by documents issued during the 1945–1989 period.

Subject(s): Executive Orders; Presidential Documents

Publication(s): *Codification of Presidential Proclamations and Executive Orders*, AE 2.113:

Compilation of Presidential Documents

http://www.presidentialdocuments.gov/

Alternate URL(s)

http://www.fdsys.gov/

Sponsor(s): National Archives and Records Administration (NARA)—Federal Register Office—Government Printing Office (GPO)

Description: The Compilation of Presidential Documents provides access to the text of the presidents' speeches, bill signing statements, executive orders, proclamations, communications to Congress, and other presidential materials released by the White House Press Secretary. It includes both the Daily Compilation of Presidential Documents and its predecessor, the Weekly Compilation of Presidential Documents. The Daily Compilation began on January 29, 2009. Copies of the Weekly Compilation are online from 1993 to January 20, 2009. The content is published by the National Archives and made available through the Government Printing Office's FDsys system.

Subject(s): Presidential Documents
Publication(s): *Daily Compilation of Presidential Documents,* AE 2.109
Weekly Compilation of Presidential Documents, AE 2.109

Executive Orders Disposition Tables

http://www.archives.gov/federal-register/executive-orders/disposition.html
Sponsor(s): National Archives and Records Administration (NARA)—Federal Register Office
Description: This Web site provides online citations and status information for executive orders issued by presidents from 1937 through the present. The Disposition Tables include the executive order number, signing date, Federal Register citation, title, amendments (if any), and current status (where applicable).
Subject(s): Executive Orders; Presidential Documents

First Ladies

http://www.whitehouse.gov/about/first_ladies/
Sponsor(s): White House
Description: This page presents brief biographies of all first ladies from Dolley Madison to Michelle Obama.
Subject(s): First Lady; Biographies

Office of the Pardon Attorney

http://www.justice.gov/pardon/
Sponsor(s): Justice Department—Office of the Pardon Attorney
Description: The Office of the Pardon Attorney reviews requests for presidential pardons for federal criminal offenses. Its Web site includes application forms, regulations, and background information relating to clemency petitions. The site also provides clemency statistics from 1900 onward and lists of clemency recipients from 1989 onward.
Subject(s): Pardons

Presidential Directives and Executive Orders

http://www.fas.org/irp/offdocs/direct.htm
Sponsor(s): Federation of American Scientists (FAS)
Description: This Web site, maintained by a nonprofit research organization, focuses on intelligence-related presidential directives and executive orders from the Truman administration to the present. Copies of

documents that are not still classified are available on this site. The site also links to helpful background information on presidential directives.

Subject(s): Intelligence; Presidential Documents

Public Papers of the Presidents of the United States

http://www.fdsys.gov/

Alternate URL(s)

http://www.gpo.gov/fdsys/browse/collection.action?collectionCode= PPP

Sponsor(s): National Archives and Records Administration (NARA)—Federal Register Office—Government Printing Office (GPO)

Description: *Public Papers of the Presidents of the United States*, a printed volume series that compiles the messages and papers of the presidents, beginning with the Hoover administration. GPO has put the series online beginning with the 1991 volume in the George H. W. Bush administration. Each volume in the series contains the papers and speeches of the president of the United States that were issued by the Office of the Press Secretary during the specified time period.

Select "Browse Collections" under the right-hand menu, and then select "Public Papers of the Presidents of the United States" for access. The collection can also be accessed at the alternate URL listed above.

Subject(s): Presidential Documents

Publication(s): *Public Papers of the President*, AE 2.114

EIGHTEEN

Science and Space

The federal government is involved in basic and applied science, in helping to disseminate scientific information, and in encouraging scientific research in academia and other research centers. Many Web sites in this chapter present highly specialized and technical information.

Subsections in this chapter include Life Sciences, National Laboratories, Physical Sciences, Science Agencies and Policy, Scientific and Technical Information, and Space.

LIFE SCIENCES

Biological Resources Division at USGS
http://biology.usgs.gov/

Sponsor(s): Interior Department—U.S. Geological Survey (USGS)

Description: This site links to the Web sites for each major USGS biology program and to the Web sites for regional USGS Science Centers. Program topics covered in depth include biological informatics, ecosystems, fisheries, invasive species, wildlife, and the status and trends of biological resources. Featured links lead to information about climate and land use change, core science systems, ecosystems, energy and minerals and environmental health, natural hazards, science quality and integrity, and water.

Given the broad scope of USGS programs, this site offers one of the best government starting points for general biological and ecosystem information.

Subject(s): Natural Resources—Research

Computational Bioscience and Engineering Laboratory (CBEL)
http://dcb.cit.nih.gov/cbel/
Sponsor(s): National Institutes of Health (NIH)
Description: CBEL's work addresses areas requiring high-performance parallel computing, with projects in areas such as biomedical imaging, human genetic linkage analysis, and computationally intensive statistical applications. Its Web site features links to the lab's divisions, job opportunities, and research studies.
Subject(s): Medical Computing—Research

DOE Joint Genome Institute (JGI)
http://jgi.doe.gov/
Sponsor(s): Energy Department—Joint Genome Institute (JGI)
Description: JGI is a cooperative effort involving the Department of Energy's Lawrence Berkeley, Lawrence Livermore, Los Alamos, Oak Ridge, and Pacific Northwest National Laboratories, along with the Hudson Alpha Institute for Biotechnology. Operated by the University of California, the institute works on genetic sequencing research to further the Energy Department's missions related to clean energy generation and environmental characterization and cleanup. The Web site highlights current projects and links to specialized research sections on topics such as fungal genomics and plant genomics. The Education section describes higher education opportunities sponsored by JGI.
Subject(s): Energy—Research; Genomics—Research

Genomics.energy.gov
http://genomics.energy.gov/
Sponsor(s): Energy Department—Science Office
Description: Genomics.energy.gov consolidates information on the genome programs of the Department of Energy's Office of Science. It features links to the Web sites on Human Genome Project Information (project completed in 2003) and the Microbial Genome Program Archive. The image gallery provides free images.
Subject(s): Genomics—Research

Integrated Taxonomic Information System (ITIS)
http://www.itis.gov/
Sponsor(s): Agriculture Department (USDA)
Description: ITIS is an excellent tool for looking up the taxonomic names and common names of the biota of North America. (Biota refers to all the plant and animal life in an area.) ITIS is a partnership of U.S., Canadian, and Mexican agencies, organizations, and taxonomic specialists that cooperate on the development of a scientifically credible list of biological names. The ITIS database can be searched by scientific name, common name, or taxonomic serial number (TSN). The records in the

database include scientific name, common name, synonym, taxonomic serial number, author, and credibility rating. The full database, or custom reports from it, can be downloaded.

Subject(s): Biological Names

Laboratory of Neurosciences

http://www.grc.nia.nih.gov/branches/lns/

Sponsor(s): National Institutes of Health (NIH)—National Institute on Aging (NIA)

Description: The goal of basic research at the Laboratory of Neurosciences is to establish methods for preventing and treating age-related neurological disorders, such as Alzheimer's disease and Parkinson's disease. Links to information from each of the lab's research programs are at the bottom of the page, as are links to staff publications.

Subject(s): Neurology—Research

Laboratory of Structural Biology

http://www.niehs.nih.gov/research/atniehs/labs/lsb/

Sponsor(s): National Institutes of Health (NIH)—National Institute of Environmental Health Sciences (NIEHS)

Description: The lab's mission is to provide insights into the biological processes that impact human environmental health. The site has information on the lab's facilities, scientists, and research groups. The research groups specialize in such areas as macromolecular structure and mass spectrometry.

Subject(s): Molecular Biology—Research

NASA Astrobiology

http://astrobiology.nasa.gov/

Sponsor(s): National Aeronautics and Space Administration (NASA)—Ames Research Center (ARC)

Description: Astrobiology is the study of the origin, evolution, distribution, and destiny of life in the universe. It uses multiple scientific disciplines and space technologies. The Web site's About Astrobiology section links to information on the four elements of the program: the NASA Astrobiology Institute, Exobiology and Evolutionary Biology, Astrobiology Science and Technology for Exploring Planets, and Astrobiology Science and Technology Instrument Development. The site also links to publications and education programs. The Web site also profiles astrobiology projects on space exploration missions.

Subject(s): Astrobiology

Publication(s): *Astrobiology Journal*

NASA Life Sciences Data Archive

http://lsda.jsc.nasa.gov/

Sponsor(s): National Aeronautics and Space Administration (NASA)—Johnson Space Center (JSC)

Description: The Life Sciences Data Archive is a searchable collection of information and data sets from space flight experiments funded by NASA. The growing archive includes documentation from experiments flown since 1961 that include human, animal, or plant studies. The archive can be searched by mission, experiment, research area, and other parameters. The Web site also describes current and historical research. Online books in the reading room include Biomedical Results of Apollo.

Subject(s): Astrobiology—Research; Human Space Exploration—Research

Publication(s): *Biomedical Results of Apollo*, NAS 1.21
Life into Space: Space Life Sciences Experiments, NAS 1.21

National Center for Biotechnology Information (NCBI)

http://www.ncbi.nlm.nih.gov/

Sponsor(s): National Institutes of Health (NIH)—National Library of Medicine (NLM)

Description: NCBI conducts basic and applied research in computational molecular biology and maintains a variety of databases related to their work. This site describes and links to numerous NCBI databases and software tools. Literature databases include PubMed, PubMed Central, and Online Mendelian Inheritance in Man (OMIM). Molecular and genome databases include GenBank, Nucleotide, and BLAST. The site has an alphabetical index of all the linked databases and information resources. At the top of the page, researchers can use the search box to search one or all of the NCBI-provided databases.

This is an important site for genome and genetic sequence researchers. The site provides access to multiple databases with detailed help files to assist with database searches. NCBI gives multiple means of accessing the data.

Subject(s): Genomics—Research; Molecular Biology—Research; Databases

Publication(s): *NCBI News*, HE 20.3624/2

National Human Genome Research Institute (NHGRI)

http://www.genome.gov/

Sponsor(s): National Institutes of Health (NIH)—National Human Genome Research Institute (NHGRI)

Description: NHGRI led the now-completed Human Genome Project, and currently focuses its genomic research on human health and disease issues. This site brings together news, research reports, and educational resources related to the institute's work. In addition to profiles of each research branch, the Research at NHGRI section has information about NHGRI clinical trials, online databases developed at the institute, and publications by NHGRI researchers. The Research Funding section links to information on current opportunities. The Health section has information on genetic and rare diseases, and educational information for health professionals. The Issues in Genetics section covers such topics as privacy, ethics, genetic discrimination, and policy issues.

Subject(s): Genomics—Research

National Institute of General Medical Sciences (NIGMS)

http://www.nigms.nih.gov/

Sponsor(s): National Institutes of Health (NIH)—National Institute of General Medical Sciences (NIGMS)

Description: NIGMS supports basic biomedical research that is not targeted at specific diseases, but instead lays the foundation for advances in disease diagnosis, treatment, and prevention. The Web site spotlights findings from NIGMS-funded research. Major sections of the site are Research Funding, Research Training, News & Meetings, Science Education, and About NIGMS. The Publications section, within the News section, offers a number of science education booklets aimed at the general public.

Subject(s): Biological Medicine—Research

Publication(s): *Findings, NIGMS*, HE 20.3470

PubChem

http://pubchem.ncbi.nlm.nih.gov/

Sponsor(s): National Institutes of Health (NIH)—National Library of Medicine (NLM)

Description: PubChem contains the chemical structures of small organic molecules and information on their biological activities. The PubChem system consists of several information tools: PubChem Substance, PubChem Compound, PubChem BioAssay, and a chemical structure similarity search tool.

Subject(s): Molecular Biology

NATIONAL LABORATORIES

Argonne National Laboratory

http://www.anl.gov/index.html

Sponsor(s): Energy Department—Argonne National Laboratory (ANL)

Description: The Energy Department's Argonne National Laboratory, located just outside of Chicago, maintains a Web site with a mix of information on research, technology transfer, and career opportunities. Major sections include Energy, Environment, Security, User Facilities, Science, and Commercialization. Research at Argonne concerns basic science, energy resources, environmental management, and national security. The site provides links to Argonne's social media pages and YouTube channel.

Subject(s): Nuclear Energy—Research; Research Laboratories; Scientific Research

Publication(s): *Argonne Now*

Brookhaven National Laboratory (BNL)

http://www.bnl.gov/world/

Sponsor(s): Energy Department—Brookhaven National Laboratory (BNL)

Description: BNL carries out and supports research in a multitude of scientific disciplines, including high energy physics, materials science, environmental sciences, and nonproliferation. Its Web site serves as a gateway to information on its many research projects, facilities (including the Relativistic Heavy Ion Collider), and divisional sites.

Because the BNL site includes so much information on so many projects and fields of science, the A to Z site index may be a helpful tool for discovering information on the site.

Subject(s): Particle Accelerators; Research Laboratories

Publication(s): *Brookhaven Bulletin*, E 1.12/2-3

Fermi National Accelerator Laboratory (Fermilab)

http://www.fnal.gov/

Sponsor(s): Energy Department—Fermi National Accelerator Laboratory

Description: Fermilab is a research lab with a focus on high-energy physics and the fundamental nature of matter and energy. It is known for its particle accelerator, the Tevatron. The Science section summarizes the lab's accomplishments and major research areas, such as particle physics, neutrino physics, and the dark matter of the cosmos. The site also has information on the many educational programs offered at each level of learning.

Subject(s): Particle Accelerators; Physics—Research; Research Laboratories

Publication(s): *Fermilab Today*
Symmetry, E 1.92/3

Lawrence Berkeley National Laboratory

http://www.lbl.gov/

Sponsor(s): Energy Department—Lawrence Berkeley National Laboratory (LBL)

Description: The Berkeley Lab conducts basic research in a wide range of fields. Current areas of interest highlighted on the lab's Web site include energy efficiency, climate change, computational science, and energy bioscience. The site has profiles for each research division and for the national user research facilities. The site also has information on educational opportunities and technology transfer, and a creative video glossary featuring lab scientists explaining scientific terminology, such as "galactic emissions" and "cellular senescence." The Web site has an extensive A-Z index for its content.

Subject(s): Physics—Research; Research Laboratories

Lawrence Livermore National Laboratory (LLNL)

http://www.llnl.gov/

Sponsor(s): Energy Department—Lawrence Livermore National Laboratory (LLNL)

Description: LLNL research areas include nuclear sciences, defense technology, energy, computation, and materials sciences. The Web site links to research information under the categories Defense, Energy, Intelligence, and Nonproliferation. Other sections cover Weapons, Bio-Security, and Counterterrorism. The site's Publications section (under News) includes the lab's published research papers, reports, and periodicals, with issues of *Science and Technology Review* as far back as 1994 (when it appeared under its previous title, *Energy and Technology Review*).

The LLNL site provides a substantial amount of online full-text documents of interest to researchers. The site should be the starting point for anyone seeking more information about the lab's programs or its areas of expertise.

Subject(s): Nuclear Weapons—Research; Research Laboratories

Publication(s): *Science and Technology Review: Lawrence Livermore Laboratory*, E 1.53

Los Alamos National Laboratory (LANL)

http://www.lanl.gov/

Sponsor(s): Energy Department—Los Alamos National Laboratory (LANL)

Description: Created to help in the development of nuclear weapons, the central mission of the Los Alamos National Laboratory is national security. It has stewardship of the nation's nuclear stockpile and conducts research related to this role. The lab Web site describes it work in sections on such areas as global security, environmental sciences, and strategic science. Publications on the site *include 1663: Los Alamos Science and Technology Magazine*. Other sections on the site cover procurement, technology transfer, and educational opportunities.

Subject(s): Nuclear Weapons; Physics—Research; Research Laboratories

Publication(s): *1663: Los Alamos Science and Technology Magazine,* E 1.96
Actinide Research Quarterly, E 1.96/4
Nuclear Weapons Journal

Oak Ridge National Laboratory (ORNL)
http://www.ornl.gov/
Sponsor(s): Energy Department—Oak Ridge National Laboratory (ORNL)
Description: Oak Ridge National Laboratory is a multiprogram science and technology laboratory. ORNL research focuses on neutron science, energy, high-performance computing, biological systems, and national security. The About ORNL section has information on organizational structure, leadership, procurement, and ORNL history since its founding in World War II.
Subject(s): Research Laboratories; Scientific Research
Publication(s): *Oak Ridge National Laboratory Review,* E 1.28/17

Pacific Northwest National Laboratory (PNNL)
http://www.pnl.gov/
Sponsor(s): Energy Department—Pacific Northwest National Laboratory (PNNL)
Description: PNNL conducts research in chemical and molecular sciences, biological systems sciences, climate change science, applied materials science and engineering, applied nuclear science and technology, and other areas. Work at the lab is described in the Research section of its Web site. Other sections describe the lab's facilities, educational opportunities, staffing, business resources, and technology licensing program. The Publications section includes archived material from the lab's former magazine, *Breakthroughs,* and a database of materials published since 1998 by PNNL staff or by external researchers using PNNL facilities.
Subject(s): Research Laboratories
Publication(s): *Breakthroughs,* E 1.53/5

Sandia National Laboratories
http://www.sandia.gov/
Sponsor(s): Energy Department—Sandia National Laboratories
Description: Sandia focuses on research and development related to national security goals. Sections of the Sandia site discusses activities in areas such as nuclear weapons, energy, defense systems, and homeland security. The News section has links to news releases, corporate information, and Sandia publications.
Subject(s): Research Laboratories; Weapons Research
Publication(s): *Sandia Technology Magazine,* E 1.20/5

Savannah River National Laboratory (SRNL)

http://srnl.doe.gov/

Sponsor(s): Energy Department—Savannah River National Laboratory

Description: SRNL is the applied research and development laboratory at the Energy Department's Savannah River Site. The Web site describes the major areas of the lab's research focus: environmental stewardship, clean energy, and national security. Research capabilities in related technologies, such as hydrogen storage and radioactive chemical processing, are also described.

Subject(s): Energy—Research; Research Laboratories

PHYSICAL SCIENCES

Alaska Volcano Observatory (AVO)

http://www.avo.alaska.edu/

Sponsor(s): Interior Department—U.S. Geological Survey (USGS)

Description: AVO is a federal, state, and university partnership to monitor Alaska's volcanoes. The Web site describes the monitoring, hazard assessments, and volcano research conducted by AVO. The Volcano Information section features an interactive map of Alaskan volcanoes and a database of eruption events. The Current Volcanic Activity section includes webcams and volcano activity notifications.

This well-designed site has content for those with general interest in volcanoes and for those in the scientific and Alaskan regional communities.

Subject(s): Volcanoes

Publication(s): *Catalog of the Historically Active Volcanoes of Alaska,* I 19.76

Summary of Events and Response of the Alaska Volcano Observatory, I 19.76

Cascades Volcano Observatory (CVO)

http://vulcan.wr.usgs.gov/

Sponsor(s): Interior Department—U.S. Geological Survey (USGS)

Description: CVO watches volcanoes and other natural hazards, including earthquakes, landslides, and debris flows in the western United States. The CVO Web site has current status reports and other reports on volcanoes in the Cascade Range, including Mount Rainier and Mount St. Helens. The site features maps, photos, hazard assessment reports, and information on living with volcanoes and visiting volcanoes. The Education section includes materials that will be of interest to students, teachers, and the general public, including seminar announcements.

Subject(s): Volcanoes

Chemoinformatics Tools and Services
  http://cactus.nci.nih.gov/
  Sponsor(s): National Institutes of Health (NIH)
  Description: This collaborative Web site includes chemical information databases, software tools, and links to other chemistry-related databases. It features a Chemical Structure Lookup Service (CSLS) for discovering whether a structure occurs in any of the public and commercial
databases the service has checked. The National Cancer Institute's Com-
puter-Aided Drug Design (CADD) Group hosts the site.
  The site is open to the general public; however, the About section of
the Web site states, "The information is not geared toward the general
public, and will probably be most useful for researchers working with, or
interested in, chemical information."
  Subject(s): Chemical Information

Earth Observing System (EOS) (NASA)
  http://eospso.gsfc.nasa.gov/
  Sponsor(s): National Aeronautics and Space Administration
(NASA)—Goddard Space Flight Center (GSFC)—Earth Observing System (EOS) Project Science Office
  Description: EOS consists of a science component and a data system
supporting a coordinated series satellites for global observations of the
land surface, biosphere, solid earth, atmosphere, and oceans. The main
categories of this Web site are Missions, Data, Communications, People,
and *The Earth Observer* newsletter. The site also links to sources for images of the Earth from space.
  Subject(s): Planetary Science
  Publication(s): *The Earth Observer*

Earth Observing System (NOAA)
  http://www.noaa.gov/eos.html
  Sponsor(s): Commerce Department—National Oceanic and Atmos-
pheric Administration (NOAA)
  Description: This NOAA site provides information about the emerg-
ing Global Earth Observation System of Systems (GEOSS). It links to
related Web sites, such as the U.S. Group on Earth Observations (US-
GEO) site and the Intergovernmental Group on Earth Observations
(GEO) site.
  NASA also provides a Web page on Earth observing systems, and this
is described in a separate entry.
  Subject(s): Planetary Science

Earthquake Hazards Program

http://earthquake.usgs.gov/

Sponsor(s): Interior Department—U.S. Geological Survey (USGS)

Description: The mission of the Earthquake Hazards Program is to understand the characteristics and effects of earthquakes and to apply this knowledge to reduce deaths, injuries, and property damage from earthquakes. The Web site features reports and maps of current earthquakes, past earthquakes, and significant earthquakes in history. The site also has information on U.S. and global seismic networks for monitoring and recording quakes. The Research section of the site includes scientific data and software and reports of ongoing research projects. A sections of interest to the general public is Learn, for children and teachers. The site also links to regional information from program sites in the Pacific Northwest, Northern California, Southern California, the Intermountain West, and the Central and Eastern U.S.

With everything from earthquake shakemaps and photos to research data to science fair project ideas, this USGS site is a good place to start an earthquake information search.

Subject(s): Earthquakes

Environmental Molecular Sciences Laboratory

http://www.emsl.pnl.gov/

Sponsor(s): Energy Department—Environmental Molecular Sciences Laboratory (EMSL)

Description: The EMSL national research laboratory conducts fundamental research in molecular and computational sciences, particularly in relation to energy technologies. The Science section of the Web site describes lab research in the areas of biological interactions and dynamics, geochemistry/biogeochemistry, and the science of interfacial phenomena. The Web site also describes the lab's capabilities and cites science journal articles in which all or part of the research was carried out using EMSL resources.

Subject(s): Research Laboratories; Scientific Research

Geology Research and Information

http://geology.usgs.gov/

Sponsor(s): Interior Department—U.S. Geological Survey (USGS)

Description: U.S. Geological Survey Geology Discipline covers natural hazards, Earth resources, and geologic processes. The site provides a central point for geology-related publications and for links to all related USGS programs. The programs are grouped into four categories: Natural Resources, which include Energy and Minerals programs; Hazards, which include Earthquakes, Landslides, Geomagnetism, the Global Seismic Network, and Volcanoes; and Landscape and Coasts, which has Geologic Mapping and Coastal Marine Geology. A fourth category, Other, has Astrogeology and Data Preservation information. Each section leads to detailed information about the program and the science involved. The site also has geologic databases, software, and standards information.

Subject(s): Geology

Geophysical Fluid Dynamics Laboratory (GFDL)

http://www.gfdl.noaa.gov/

Sponsor(s): Commerce Department—National Oceanic and Atmospheric Administration (NOAA)—Office of Oceanic and Atmospheric Research

Description: GFDL is a research laboratory focusing on the physical processes influencing the behavior of the atmosphere and the oceans as complex fluid systems. The Research section of the site includes resources from project groups for Atmospheric Physics, Chemistry, and Climate; Climate and Ecosystems; Climate Diagnostics; Climate Change, Variability, and Predictions; Oceans and Climate; and Weather and Atmospheric Dynamics. The site also provides bibliographies of GFDL published articles and presentations.

Subject(s): Atmospheric Sciences—Research; Climatology—Research

Goddard Earth Sciences (GES) Data and Information Services Center

http://daac.gsfc.nasa.gov/

Sponsor(s): National Aeronautics and Space Administration (NASA)—Goddard Space Flight Center (GSFC)

Description: The NASA Goddard Earth Sciences (GES) Data and Information Services Center (DISC) provides Earth science data, information, and services to scientists and students. Goddard's archive includes data on precipitation and hydrology and on atmospheric composition and dynamics. The Web site provides access to the data and related tools and describes recent Earth observations.

Subject(s): Atmospheric Sciences—Research; Data Products

Harvard-Smithsonian Center for Astrophysics

http://cfa-www.harvard.edu/

Sponsor(s): Harvard-Smithsonian Center for Astrophysics

Description: The Harvard-Smithsonian Center for Astrophysics is a collaboration between the Smithsonian Astrophysical Observatory and the Harvard College Observatory to study the basic physical processes that determine the nature and evolution of the universe. The Web site has information about the center, its research, and its facilities.

Subject(s): Astrophysics—Research

Hawaiian Volcano Observatory (HVO)

http://hvo.wr.usgs.gov/

Sponsor(s): Interior Department—U.S. Geological Survey (USGS)

Description: HVO conducts research on the volcanoes of Hawaii and works with emergency-response officials to protect people and property from earthquakes and volcano-related hazards. The site has information on current activity, history, and hazards for Mauna Loa and Kilauea volcanoes. Other sections cover earthquakes, other volcanoes, and volcanic hazards. The site also features *Volcano Watch*, a weekly newsletter for the general public that is written by scientists at the HVO.

This site will be of great interest to anyone living on or visiting the Big Island of Hawaii, and it provides educational information for anyone else interested in volcanoes and volcanology.

Subject(s): Volcanoes
Publication(s): *Volcano Watch*, I 19.170

High Energy Astrophysics Science Archive Research Center (HEASARC)

http://heasarc.gsfc.nasa.gov/

Sponsor(s): National Aeronautics and Space Administration (NASA)—Goddard Space Flight Center (GSFC)

Description: The purpose of HEASARC is to support a multimission archive facility in high energy astrophysics for scientists all over the world. HEASARC has data from multiple observatories covering 30 years of X-ray and gamma-ray astronomy. The data from space-borne instruments are provided along with tools to analyze multiple datasets. The HEASARC Web site also has astronomy information for the public, students, and teachers.

Primarily intended for professional astronomers and astrophysicists, the HEASARC Web site does offer some content for the general public and the educational community.

Subject(s): Astrophysics—Research

Jefferson Lab

http://www.jlab.org/

Sponsor(s): Energy Department—Thomas Jefferson National Accelerator Facility

Description: The Thomas Jefferson National Accelerator Facility (Jefferson Lab) is a nuclear physics research laboratory built to probe the nucleus of the atom to learn more about the quark structure of matter. The lab is funded by the Energy Department's Office of Science, the City of Newport News, and the Commonwealth of Virginia. The Jefferson Lab's Web site features information about its scientific program as well as resources for K–12 education.

Subject(s): Nuclear Physics—Research; Particle Accelerators; Research Laboratories

NASA Astrophysics Data System (ADS)
http://adswww.harvard.edu/
Sponsor(s): Harvard-Smithsonian Center for Astrophysics; National Aeronautics and Space Administration (NASA)
Description: ADS is a NASA-funded project maintaining three sets of bibliographic databases: Astronomy and Astrophysics, Physics, and preprints in Astronomy (ArXiv e-prints). All are available to search or browse at this site. The site also has a current awareness e-mail service called myADS.
Subject(s): Astrophysics

NASA Goddard Institute for Space Studies (GISS)
http://www.giss.nasa.gov/
Sponsor(s): National Aeronautics and Space Administration (NASA)—Goddard Space Flight Center (GSFC)—Goddard Institute for Space Studies (GISS)
Description: GISS is a NASA research institute that emphasizes a broad, interdisciplinary study of global environmental change. A key objective of its research is the prediction of atmospheric and climate changes in the 21st century. Research themes described on the Web site include global climate modeling, planetary atmospheres, and atmospheric chemistry. The site also includes sections on Datasets & Images, Publications, Software, Education, and About GISS.
Subject(s): Climate Change—Research

National Earthquake Information Center (NEIC)
http://neic.usgs.gov/
Alternate URL(s)
http://earthquake.usgs.gov/regional/neic/
Sponsor(s): Interior Department—U.S. Geological Survey (USGS)
Description: NEIC identifies its mission as "to provide and apply relevant earthquake science information and knowledge for reducing deaths, injuries, and property damage from earthquakes through understanding of their characteristics and effects and by providing the information and knowledge needed to mitigate these losses." (from the Web site) The site includes earthquake catalogs and bulletins, and the *International Registry of Seismograph Stations*.
Subject(s): Earthquakes
Publication(s): *International Registry of Seismograph Stations*
Routine Mining Seismicity in the United States

National Geophysical Data Center (NGDC)
http://www.ngdc.noaa.gov/

Sponsor(s): Commerce Department—National Oceanic and Atmospheric Administration (NOAA)—National Environmental Satellite, Data, and Information Service (NESDIS)

Description: The mission of NGDC is to prepare and provide geophysical data sets that are in the public domain. Data groups include bathymetry and topography, marine geology and geophysics, natural hazards, geomagnetic data and models, Earth observations from space, and space weather and solar events. Much of the data is available online; some data sets can be purchased on DVD-ROM. Other sections of the Web site include Education and News.

The site contains numerous data products of use to research professionals in the relevant disciplines; it also contains a selection of educational products for the general public.

Subject(s): Data Products; Environmental Science

National Radio Astronomy Observatory (NRAO)

http://www.nrao.edu/

Sponsor(s): National Science Foundation (NSF)—National Radio Astronomy Observatory (NRAO)

Description: The NRAO designs, builds, and operates state-of-the-art radio telescope facilities for use by the scientific community. The NRAO Web site has extensive information about each of its sites in Virginia, West Virginia, Arizona, Chile, and New Mexico. The Image Gallery section includes galaxies, stars, comets, black holes, telescopes, and historical photographs of telescopes and astronomers.

Subject(s): Astronomy; Observatories

Naval Oceanography Portal

http://www.usno.navy.mil/

Sponsor(s): Navy

Description: This portal Web site links to sites available from the component commands of the United States Naval Meteorology and Oceanography Command. Linked sites include the U.S. Naval Observatory, the Joint Typhoon Warning Center, the Naval Oceanography Operations Command, the Fleet Numerical Meteorology and Oceanography Center, and the Naval Oceanographic Office. Topical sections of the site include time, Earth orientation, astronomy, meteorology, oceanography, and ice.

Subject(s): Oceanography

New Brunswick Laboratory

http://science.energy.gov/nbl/

Sponsor(s): Energy Department—Security Office

Description: The New Brunswick Laboratory is a federal lab specializing in the science of measuring nuclear materials. This site describes the mission and programs of the lab. Programs include Nuclear Safeguards and Nonproliferation Support, Measurement Development, Measurement Evaluation, Measurement Services, and Certified Reference Materials.

Subject(s): Chemistry Research; Standards and Specifications

NIST Physics Laboratory

http://physics.nist.gov/

Sponsor(s): Commerce Department—Technology Administration (TA)—National Institute of Standards and Technology (NIST)

Description: The Physics Laboratory supports industry by providing measurement services and research for electronic, optical, and radiation technologies. The site links to detailed information from each of the research divisions: Electromagnetics, Quantum Electronics and Photonics, Quantum Measurement, Quantum Physics, Radiation Physics, Semiconductor and Dimensional Metrology, Sensor Science, Time and Frequency, and the Office of Weights and Measures. The Product/Services section of the site features the following subsections: Measurements and Calibrations, General Interest, Special Publications and Tutorials, the Official U.S. Time, and Physical Reference Data.

Subject(s): Physics—Research; Standards and Specifications

Ocean Surface Topography from Space

http://topex-www.jpl.nasa.gov/

Sponsor(s): National Aeronautics and Space Administration (NASA)—Jet Propulsion Laboratory (JPL)

Description: This site describes NASA research and missions related to ocean topography. It has information on the TOPEX/Poseidon Mission, a partnership between the United States and France to monitor global ocean topography, discover the links between the oceans and atmosphere, and improve global climate predictions. The follow-on missions, called Jason-1 and Jason-2, are also described in detail.

The Web site is a rich source of educational information on the effects of oceans on our climate, weather events such as El Nino/La Nina, and the satellite missions and data. The site's Sea Level Viewer presents images of the Earth during events such as the Indian Ocean tsunami in 2004 and Hurricane Katrina in 2005.

Subject(s): Climate Research; Oceans—Research

Princeton Plasma Physics Laboratory (PPPL)

http://www.pppl.gov/

Sponsor(s): Energy Department—Princeton Plasma Physics Laboratory (PPPL)

Description: PPPL is concerned with fusion energy and plasma physics research. PPPL is managed by Princeton University for the Energy

Department. The site features information about the lab, its research, and its equipment. The Fusion Basics section (under About) provides extensive information for the interested public. The Research section describes current projects.

Subject(s): Plasma Physics—Research
Publication(s): *PPPL News*, E 1.103/2

SOHO: The Solar and Heliospheric Observatory

http://soho.nascom.nasa.gov/
Sponsor(s): National Aeronautics and Space Administration (NASA)
Description: SOHO is a cooperative project of NASA and the European Space Agency to study the sun and solar wind. Major sections of the SOHO Web site are the data and archive and a solar image gallery. The About section discusses the mission history. The site's Publications page includes a SOHO bibliography and publications database, SOHO documentation, and links to privately published online journals that cover solar physics research.

Subject(s): Solar-Terrestrial Physics; Sun

Stanford Linear Accelerator Center (SLAC)

http://www.slac.stanford.edu/
Sponsor(s): Energy Department—Stanford Linear Accelerator Center (SLAC)
Description: SLAC, operated by Stanford University for the Energy Department, conducts high-energy physics research. This site provides an introduction to SLAC and its programs. The Research section provides detail on the center's research in accelerator physics, astrophysics and cosmology, materials and nanoscience, and other areas.

Subject(s): Particle Accelerators; Physics—Research; Research Laboratories

T-2 Nuclear Information Service

http://t2.lanl.gov/
Sponsor(s): Energy Department—Los Alamos National Laboratory (LANL)
Description: Run by the Nuclear Physics Group of the Theoretical Division of Los Alamos National Lab, this site covers nuclear modeling, nuclear data, cross sections, nuclear masses, nuclear astrophysics, radioactivity, radiation shielding, data for medical radiotherapy, data for high-energy accelerator applications, and data and codes for fission and fusion systems. Available categories include Library, Seminars, and topic-area sections, such as Cosmology and Astrophysics.

The very technical nature of this data means that the site will primarily be of interest to nuclear physicists.

Subject(s): Nuclear Physics

United States Naval Observatory (USNO)

http://www.usno.navy.mil/USNO

Sponsor(s): Navy—Naval Observatory (USNO)

Description: USNO is responsible for measuring the positions and motions of Earth, the sun, the moon, planets, stars, and other celestial objects; providing astronomical data; determining precise time; measuring the Earth's rotation; and maintaining the Master Clock for the United States. The Astronomical Applications section of the Web site includes popular reference information, such as daily sun and moon rise and set times for locations worldwide, a map of world time zones, solar and lunar eclipse information, and an online astronomical almanac. Other sections of the site provide USNO information in the areas of astrometry, Earth orientation, and precise time. The site also links to the James M. Gilliss Library and to tour information.

Subject(s): Astronomy; Observatories

Volcano Hazards Program

http://volcanoes.usgs.gov/

Sponsor(s): Interior Department—U.S. Geological Survey (USGS)

Description: This central site for the USGS Volcano Hazards Program includes information on the status of volcanic activity in the United States, including a volcanic status map and a list of current alerts. The Hazards section of the site discusses aspects of volcanic eruptions, including volcanic gases and volcanic ash. The Observatories section links to extensive information from the regional observatories in Washington State/Oregon, Hawaii, Alaska, and the Mariana Islands. It also links to information on the Volcano Disaster Assistance Program (VDAP). The Web site also has a Learn section with information for teachers and students.

For checking either current activity or historical eruptions, this is a great starting point for finding information on volcanoes.

Subject(s): Volcanoes

SCIENCE AGENCIES AND POLICY

National Aeronautics and Space Administration (NASA)

http://www.nasa.gov/

Sponsor(s): National Aeronautics and Space Administration (NASA)

Description: The central NASA Web site provides information about the agency and links to the numerous other Web sites and resources

NASA maintains. Major sections of the site include News (news releases, budget, and reports), Missions (current, past, and future), Multimedia (images, videos, and NASA TV), About NASA (locations, organizations, and research opportunities), and Connect (links to NASA's presence on such sites as Flickr and YouTube). The NASA home page highlights current news, Twitter updates, and popular features. Audience-specific views of the NASA Web content are available for the general public (the default), educators, students, and the media. The News heading links to the major sections about shuttle and station, solar system, universe, aeronautics, Earth, technology, and NASA history and people.

Subject(s): Space
Publication(s): *NASA Strategic Plan*, NAS 1.15

National Science Advisory Board for Biosecurity (NSABB)

http://osp.od.nih.gov/office-biotechnology-activities/biosecurity/nsabb

Alternate URL(s)

http://www.biosecurityboard.gov/

Sponsor(s): National Science Advisory Board for Biosecurity (NSABB)
Description: The NSABB is an interagency board chartered with minimizing the risk of misuse of life sciences research technologies, particularly as a threat to public health and national security. The Web site has NSABB news, members, and meeting schedules and webcasts.

Subject(s): Scientific Research—Policy; Life Sciences—Policy

National Science and Technology Council (NSTC)

http://www.whitehouse.gov/administration/eop/ostp/nstc

Sponsor(s): White House—National Science and Technology Council (NSTC)
Description: NSTC was formed in 1993 to coordinate science and technology policy across multiple White House and executive branch departments. The Web site has information on council members, meetings, and reports.

Subject(s): Science and Technology Policy

National Science Board (NSB)

http://www.nsf.gov/nsb/

Sponsor(s): National Science Foundation (NSF)—National Science Board (NSB)
Description: NSB is the governing board for the NSF and serves as national science policy adviser to the president and Congress. The Web site has information on NSB membership, meetings, and the honorary science awards it bestows.

Subject(s): Science—Policy

National Science Foundation (NSF)

http://www.nsf.gov/

Sponsor(s): National Science Foundation (NSF)

Description: As one of the government's major scientific agencies, NSF promotes science and engineering research and education. NSF, an independent federal agency, supports scientists, engineers, and educators directly through their own home institutions (typically universities and colleges). The site's main sections provide information about funding opportunities and awards. The site also includes a wealth of publications and data from NSF, particularly on science and engineering education, funding, and the workforce. A Discoveries section profiles discoveries and innovations that began with NSF support.

Subject(s): Science Education; Scientific Research—Grants

Publication(s): *Graduate Students and Postdoctorates in Science and Engineering*, NS 1.22/11

National Patterns of R&D Resources, NS 1.22/2

NSF Current Newsletter

Science and Engineering Indicators, NS 1.28/2

Science and Engineering State Profiles, NS 1.22/12

Women, Minorities, and Persons with Disabilities in Science and Engineering, NS 1.49

Office of Science

http://science.energy.gov/

Sponsor(s): Energy Department

Description: The Department of Energy's Office of Science is the gateway to the agency's scientifically focused research, analysis, and information. Its six core programs include Advanced Scientific Computing Research, Basic Energy Sciences, Biological and Environmental Research, Fusion Energy Sciences, High Energy Physics, and Nuclear Physics. An interactive grants map can be found under the Universities heading, and a list of related facilities is located in the Laboratories section.

Subject(s): Science

Office of Science and Technology Policy (OSTP)

http://www.ostp.gov/

Sponsor(s): White House—Office of Science and Technology Policy (OSTP)

Description: Established in 1976, OSTP serves as a source of scientific and technological analysis and judgment for the president with respect to major policies, plans, and programs of the federal government. The Web site offers general information on the organization and activities of OSTP. Along with current news and the OSTP Blog, the site has information on the administration policy on science and technology issues and on the federal research and development budget.

Subject(s): Science and Technology Policy

OSTP Blog

http://blog.ostp.gov/

Sponsor(s): White House—Office of Science and Technology Policy (OSTP)

Description: The OSTP blog discusses policy making from a science and technology perspective. An RSS subscription feed is available.

Subject(s): Science and Technology Policy; Blogs

President's National Medal of Science

http://www.nsf.gov/nsb/awards/nms/medal.htm

Sponsor(s): National Science Foundation (NSF)

Description: The National Medal of Science was established by Congress in 1959 as a Presidential Award to be given to individuals "deserving of special recognition by reason of their outstanding contributions to knowledge in the physical, biological, mathematical, or engineering sciences." (from the Web site) In 1980, Congress expanded this recognition to include the social and behavioral sciences. This site features information on nomination procedures, new award announcements, former medalists, and members of the President's Committee. The site also links to information on the National Medal of Technology and Innovation, administered by the Patent and Trademark Office.

Subject(s): Science—Awards and Honors

Research.gov

http://www.research.gov/

Sponsor(s): National Science Foundation (NSF)

Description: Research.gov has information for and about researchers working under a federal grant. The Research.gov program is led by the National Science Foundation; NSF partners include NASA and Defense Department research agencies. The site's Research Spending and Results database has information on research awards active in fiscal year 2007 and beyond with total obligations of $25,000 or more. The site also provides online tools specifically for federal research grant recipients.

Subject(s): Scientific Research—Grants

Science of Science Policy

http://www.scienceofsciencepolicy.net/

Sponsor(s): White House—Office of Science and Technology Policy (OSTP)

Description: The Science of Science Policy Web site is designed to develop and promote a scientifically rigorous and quantitative basis for science policy. The Web site provides a forum for government officials, academics, and other science researchers to learn about and share information on using scientific methods to evaluate science policy. Under SCISP Program, award descriptions are available.

Subject(s): Scientific Research—Policy

Publication(s): *Science of Science Policy: A Federal Research Roadmap,* PREX 23.14

U.S. Arctic Research Commission

http://www.arctic.gov/

Sponsor(s): United States Arctic Research Commission

Description: The Arctic Research Commission was established to set the national goals and priorities for the federal basic and applied scientific research plan for the Arctic. This Web site has information on current commission news, meetings, and publications. Publications include research goals reports and Arctic boundary maps.

Subject(s): Scientific Research—Policy

Publication(s): *USARC Report on Goals and Objectives for Arctic Research* , NS 1.2

U.S. Geological Survey (USGS)

http://www.usgs.gov/

Sponsor(s): Interior Department—U.S. Geological Survey (USGS)

Description: As one of the government's primary scientific agencies, the USGS offers a broad range of scientific material on its Web site. USGS provides scientific and safety information about such natural hazards as landslides, earthquakes, and volcanoes. USGS also studies natural resources, such as minerals. Science in Your Backyard links to USGS information—such as flood or drought watches—for each state, the District of Columbia, Puerto Rico, and the U.S. Virgin Islands. The Social Media section includes a consolidated list of USGS podcasts and RSS newsfeeds on topics such as earthquake news, volcano watches, and satellite imagery updates. The Maps, Imagery, and Publications section centralizes access to the many USGS Web pages that provide catalogs or collections of USGS information products. The Web site also has a substantial science-related Education section.

The USGS home page provides multiple access points to its rich collection of scientific resources and publications.

Subject(s): Geography; Geology; Natural Resources; Scientific Research

Publication(s): *Geographic Names Information System,* I 19.16/2
National Hydrography Dataset, I 19.127
National Landcover Data Set, I 19.168
USGS Circulars, I 19.4/2

SCIENTIFIC AND TECHNICAL INFORMATION

DOE Patents Database

http://www.osti.gov/doepatents/

Sponsor(s): Energy Department—Scientific and Technical Information Office

Description: The DOE Patents database provides information on patents resulting from research and development funded by the Department of Energy. When possible, the database records provide the full text of the patent from DOE or link to the information at the United States Patent and Trademark Office. The site is intended to demonstrate the Energy Department's contributions to the sciences.

Subject(s): Inventions; Research and Development

NASA Scientific and Technical Information (STI)

http://www.sti.nasa.gov/

Sponsor(s): National Aeronautics and Space Administration (NASA)

Description: NASA defines STI as basic and applied research results from the work of scientists, engineers, and others. The NASA Scientific and Technical Information Program disseminates STI from NASA research and other sources to the public. This site offers databases, documents, and new reports announcements. The major asset on the site is the NASA Technical Reports Server (NTRS), which covers NASA materials such as reports, journal articles, conference and meeting papers, and technical videos. NTRS also includes records from the National Advisory Committee for Aeronautics (NACA) database; NACA, NASA's predecessor, was operational from 1917 to 1958. In addition, NTRS includes the NASA Image eXchange (NIX) collection and material from outside organizations, such as the European Space Agency (ESA).

Other free STI resources on the site include NASA's *Spinoff* magazine and a database of abstracts for every successfully commercialized NASA technology published in *Spinoff*. The site also offers two current awareness services announcing newly released and newly acquired STI: the Selected Current Aerospace Notices (SCAN) service and Scientific and Technical Aerospace Reports (STAR). An RSS feed is available for tracking new STI from NASA and for the STI blog.

The NTRS is a major bibliographic database of broad interest to the engineering and scientific communities. NTRS and the other services offered by NASA's STI program make this site a key resource for scientific and technical literature.

Subject(s): Scientific and Technical Information; Databases

Publication(s): *NASA Technical Reports Server (NTRS)*, NAS 1.12/2-2

Scientific and Technical Aerospace Reports (STAR), NAS 1.9/4

Spinoff, NAS 1.1/4

National Science Digital Library (NSDL)
  http://nsdl.org/
  Sponsor(s): National Science Foundation (NSF)
  Description: NSDL is a National Science Foundation program. The NSDL goal is to provide "high quality online educational resources for teaching and learning, with current emphasis on the sciences, technology, engineering, and mathematics (STEM) disciplines—both formal and informal, institutional and individual, in local, state, national, and international educational settings." (from the Web site) NSDL collections focus on science portal sites that provide material for educators or students. In addition to the NSDL contents, the site provides a wealth of related resources for teachers.
  Subject(s): Science Education

National Technical Reports Library (NTRL)
  http://www.ntis.gov/products/ntrl.aspx
  Sponsor(s): Commerce Department—National Technical Information Service (NTIS)
  Description: Most Web sites described in this book can be used free of charge. The National Technical Reports Library (NTRL), however, requires a paid subscription because the responsible agency, NTIS, operates on a cost-recovery basis. NTRL has over 3 million citations to government-funded technical reports. Most of the collection dates from the 1970s onward.
  Some Federal Depository Libraries provide public access to NTRL; to find the nearest depository library, see http://catalog.gpo.gov/fdlpdir/FDLPdir.jsp.
  Subject(s): Scientific and Technical Information

NIST Data Gateway
  http://srdata.nist.gov/gateway/
  Sponsor(s): Commerce Department—Technology Administration (TA)—National Institute of Standards and Technology (NIST)
  Description: The NIST Data Gateway links to over 80 databases from the National Institute of Standards and Technology. As stated on the site, "these data cover a broad range of substances and properties from many different scientific disciplines." Specific resources include the Atomic Spectra Database (ASD), *Engineering Statistics Handbook*, CODATA Fundamental Physical Constants, and the *NIST Chemistry WebBook*. The site also lists NIST databases that are available for purchase or subscription.
  Subject(s): Engineering Research; Scientific and Technical Information; Databases

Public Technical Reports

http://www.dtic.mil/dtic/search/tr/

Sponsor(s): Defense Department—Defense Technical Information Center (DTIC)

Description: The scope of the Public Technical Reports database includes defense research topics, the basic sciences, and specific documents such as conference papers and patent applications. It provides access to citations to unclassified unlimited documents entered into DTIC's Technical Reports Collection since 1960 and to online copies of many documents published after 1990.

Subject(s): Scientific and Technical Information; Databases

Science Inventory

http://cfpub.epa.gov/si/

Sponsor(s): Environmental Protection Agency (EPA)

Description: The EPA's Science Inventory site is a database of EPA scientific and technical projects and scientific activities. Database entries include project descriptions, products produced, types of peer review, links to related work, and contacts for additional information. The database can be searched by word. Researchers can subscribe to an RSS feed of all new entries or set up a customized RSS feed based on a word search or topic.

Subject(s): Research and Development

Science Tracer Bullets Online

http://www.loc.gov/rr/scitech/tbs.html

Alternate URL(s)

http://www.loc.gov/rr/scitech/

Sponsor(s): Library of Congress

Description: The Library of Congress Science Tracer Bullets are research guides for finding books, journal articles, Internet resources, and other literature on specific science and technology topics. The guides cover such topics as careers in science, earthquakes and earthquake engineering, introductory physics, global warming and climate change, and science fair projects.

The tracer bullets range from one year to over ten years old. Only the newest bullets include Internet resources. While much of the research guidance is still worthwhile, researchers should remember that more current resources are probably available. Consult the home page of Science Reference Services for additional science research guides at the alternate URL.

Subject(s): Science—Research

Publication(s): *LC Science Tracer Bullet Series*, LC 33.10

Science.gov

http://www.science.gov/

Sponsor(s): Energy Department—Scientific and Technical Information Office

Description: Science.gov represents a collaborative effort by a group of government agencies to select and share the best of their online science information. Science.gov accesses over 60 databases and more than 2,200 science Web sites. The Energy Department's Office of Scientific and Technical Information (OSTI), listed here as the search capabilities sponsor, hosts the site. The science resources can be browsed by topic or searched by word. The search feature allows users to select a combination of government science Web sites and databases to search. Users can also set up e-mail alerts based on search topics. Indexed resources in science.gov include the Energy Citations Database, NASA Technical Reports Server, PubMed, and National Science Foundation publications. Science.gov also has science news and special collections of links on topics such as science conferences and internships and fellowships.

Science.gov allows for easy discovery of science and technical information that is distributed through government Web sites.

Subject(s): Scientific and Technical Information; Databases

SPACE

Aeronautics Research Mission Directorate (ARMD)

http://www.aeronautics.nasa.gov/

Sponsor(s): National Aeronautics and Space Administration (NASA)—Aeronautics Research Mission Directorate

Description: ARMD is concerned with cutting-edge aeronautics research. The Programs section of the ARMD Web sites describes work in the following areas: Fundamental Aeronautics Program, Airspace Systems Program, Aviation Safety Program, Aeronautics Test Program, and Integrated Systems Research Program. The Reference Materials section has ARMD publications and related NASA publications. The Education section has resources on aeronautics for all levels of students.

Subject(s): Aerospace Engineering—Research

Ames Research Center

http://www.nasa.gov/centers/ames/

Sponsor(s): National Aeronautics and Space Administration (NASA)—Ames Research Center (ARC)

Description: NASA's Ames Research Center in California specializes in researching and developing new technologies in such fields as supercomputing, nanotechnology, fundamental space biology, biotechnology, and human factors research. The Research section of the site provides information on current projects. The Research section also links to information on collaborative efforts such as NASA Research Park and the NASA Astrobiology Institute.

Subject(s): Space Sciences—Research; Space Technology—Research

Astronomy Resources at STScI

http://www.stsci.edu/resources/

Sponsor(s): Space Telescope Science Institute

Description: The Space Telescope Science Institute (STScI) is one of the astronomy centers operated by the Association of Universities for Research in Astronomy, Inc., (AURA) for NASA. It is responsible for the scientific operation of the Hubble Space Telescope and will also be supporting the James Webb Space Telescope (JWST) for NASA; each one is described in detail at this site. Other main categories at this Web site include News and Education, Data Archives, News and Outreach, Events, and Future Missions and Initiatives Support.

Subject(s): Astronomy; Telescopes

Cassini-Huygens Mission

http://saturn.jpl.nasa.gov/index.cfm

Sponsor(s): National Aeronautics and Space Administration (NASA)—Jet Propulsion Laboratory (JPL)

Description: The Cassini spacecraft orbiting Saturn has completed both its initial mission and first extended mission to explore the Saturn System. Its second extended mission, called the Solstice Mission, has a projected end date of 2017. The Web site has mission news, Saturn images, and information about Cassini. It also has educational materials and a link to the mission's Twitter feed.

Subject(s): Spacecraft; Saturn

Chandra X-Ray Observatory

http://chandra.harvard.edu/

Sponsor(s): National Aeronautics and Space Administration (NASA)—Marshall Space Flight Center (MSFC)

Description: Chandra X-Ray Observatory is an orbiting space telescope launched in 1999. Chandra captures X-ray images from high-energy regions of the universe, such as the remnants of exploded stars. This Web site, operated for NASA by the Harvard-Smithsonian Center for Astrophysics, serves as a center for information on Chandra's status and discoveries.

Subject(s): Astrophysics; Telescopes

Columbia Accident Investigation Board (CAIB)

http://govinfo.library.unt.edu/caib/

Alternate URL(s)
http://caib.nasa.gov/
Sponsor(s): Columbia Accident Investigation Board
Description: The Columbia Accident Investigation Board (CAIB) was established to determine actual or probable causes of the failure of NASA's Columbia space shuttle on February 1, 2003. The Web site includes the final report, information on board members, the board charter, press releases, transcripts of press briefings, and minutes of any public meetings. It is archived at the University of North Texas Libraries' Cyber-Cemetery.
Subject(s): Space Shuttle
Publication(s): *Columbia Accident Investigation Board Final Report*, NAS 1.2:C 72/V.1-6

Compton Gamma Ray Observatory Science Support Center (CGRO)
http://cossc.gsfc.nasa.gov/docs/cgro/
Sponsor(s): National Aeronautics and Space Administration (NASA)—Goddard Space Flight Center (GSFC)
Description: CGRO, in service from 1991 to 2000, was the second of NASA's four Great Observatories. The Web site has sections for the CGRO data archive, data analysis, and the CGRO instruments. It also has an Education & Public Info section that details CGRO discoveries.
Subject(s): Astronomy; Telescopes

Crustal Dynamics Data Information System (CDDIS)
http://cddis.gsfc.nasa.gov/
Sponsor(s): National Aeronautics and Space Administration (NASA)—Goddard Space Flight Center (GSFC)
Description: According to the Web site, CDDIS "continues to support the space geodesy and geodynamics community through NASA's Space Geodesy Project as well as NASA's Earth Science Enterprise." This site offers access to CDDIS data sets, programs, and reports.
This site will primarily be of interest to researchers in this field.
Subject(s): Geodesy

Eclipse Home Page
http://eclipse.gsfc.nasa.gov/eclipse.html
Sponsor(s): National Aeronautics and Space Administration (NASA)—Goddard Space Flight Center (GSFC)
Description: This site provides details on total and partial solar and lunar eclipses around the world. It includes eclipse maps, listings, path coordinates, explanations, and predication information. The site also has information on lunar eclipses and planetary transits across the sun.

The clear organization of this site makes it an excellent reference source on the topic.

Subject(s): Eclipses; Sun

Galileo Legacy Site

http://solarsystem.nasa.gov/galileo/

Sponsor(s): National Aeronautics and Space Administration (NASA)—Jet Propulsion Laboratory (JPL)

Description: NASA's Galileo mission ended when the spacecraft impacted Jupiter on September 2003 as planned. The Galileo site provides an extensive collection of information on the Galileo spacecraft and the planet Jupiter. The site also includes images, mission details, and educational resources.

Subject(s): Jupiter; Spacecraft

Glenn Research Center

http://www.nasa.gov/centers/glenn/

Sponsor(s): National Aeronautics and Space Administration (NASA)—Glenn Research Center

Description: Formerly known as the Lewis Research Center, the Glenn Research Center was renamed after John H. Glenn, former astronaut and U.S. senator. Spaceflight systems, aeronautics, and aeropropulsion technologies are the center's focus. The Web site describes the center's work related to the space station and shuttle, moon and Mars missions, technology, and aeronautics. The site also has sections on education and on doing business with the center.

Subject(s): Aerospace Engineering—Research; Space Technology—Research

Publication(s): *AeroSpace Frontiers*

Goddard Space Flight Center (GSFC)

http://www.nasa.gov/centers/goddard/

Sponsor(s): National Aeronautics and Space Administration (NASA)—Goddard Space Flight Center (GSFC)

Description: GSFC specializes in developing and operating unmanned scientific spacecraft conducting research on the Earth, sun, and universe. The Web site describes past, present, and future missions supported by Goddard. It includes feature stories and videos highlighting Earth and space observations. Other sections of the site cover Goddard's educational programs and business opportunities.

Subject(s): Space Sciences; Space Technology

Publication(s): *Goddard View*, NAS 1.104

GRIN—Great Images in NASA

http://grin.hq.nasa.gov/

Sponsor(s): National Aeronautics and Space Administration (NASA)—History Office

Description: GRIN is a collection of over a thousand photographs of significant historical interest from both NASA and its predecessor, the National Advisory Committee for Aeronautics (NACA). The images, all in JPEG format, can be searched by a variety of factors, such as keyword, date range, and GRIN number. While most of the images are not protected by copyright, the Copyright Information section (under How to Use GRIN) should be reviewed for information on usage restrictions.

The emphasis of this selective collection is on NASA history. Researchers looking for a broader collection of images may also wish to check the NASA Image eXchange (NIX) and NASA Multimedia Gallery Web sites. Both are linked from the GRIN home page.

Subject(s): Aerospace Engineering—History; Photography; Space—History

International Space Station (ISS)

http://www.nasa.gov/mission_pages/station/main/

Sponsor(s): National Aeronautics and Space Administration (NASA)

Description: This central Web site for ISS has news, mission and crew profiles, images, interactive features, and science information. The News & Media Resources section includes press kits, briefing materials, and documents related to the station. Interactive features on the site include an animated reference guide. Links to ISS's social media pages are also provided.

Subject(s): Space Stations

James Webb Space Telescope (JWST)

http://www.jwst.nasa.gov/

Sponsor(s): National Aeronautics and Space Administration (NASA)—Goddard Space Flight Center (GSFC)

Description: JWST is the planned successor to the Hubble Space Telescope. This Web site gives an overview of the project, news, science goals, and mission hardware. The section specifically for scientists includes the *Webb Update* newsletter and has information for astronomers who would like to learn more about using JWST for their research programs. The Web site also has images, videos, animations, and educational games about the telescope.

Subject(s): Astronomy; Telescopes—Research

Publication(s): *Webb Update*

Jet Propulsion Laboratory (JPL)

http://www.jpl.nasa.gov/

Sponsor(s): National Aeronautics and Space Administration (NASA)—Jet Propulsion Laboratory (JPL)

Description: JPL is the lead U.S. center for robotic exploration of the solar system. Major subject links on the JPL Web site include News, Missions, Images, Galleries, Public Events, Follow JPL, and About. The Missions page profiles specific robotic spacecraft, such as Voyager and the Mars Global Surveyor, and the accomplishments of their missions. It includes current, past, present, and proposed missions with JPL involvement. The News section provides press releases, mission fact sheets, and a JPL blog. The site has a well-stocked Education section, with information for teachers and students.

Subject(s): Planets; Space technology

Johnson Space Center (JSC)

http://www.nasa.gov/centers/johnson/home/

Alternate URL(s)

http://www.jsc.nasa.gov/

Sponsor(s): National Aeronautics and Space Administration (NASA)—Johnson Space Center (JSC)

Description: Programs at the JSC in Texas focus on human spaceflight, the International Space Station (ISS), the Mission Control Center, and astronaut training. The About Johnson section links to information on each of these topics, including the NASA Astronaut Corps. The Johnson News section includes status reports for the ISS. The Education section provides news and information about JSC education programs and about internships at JSC.

Most of the material on this site is geared toward the public, the press, and business users. It is also an excellent site for students and teachers to find material for education related to humans in space, manned space flights, and basic astronomy.

Subject(s): Astronauts; Human Space Exploration; Spacecraft

Kennedy Space Center (KSC)

http://www.nasa.gov/centers/kennedy/home/

Alternate URL(s)

http://www.ksc.nasa.gov/

Sponsor(s): National Aeronautics and Space Administration (NASA)—Kennedy Space Center (KSC)

Description: NASA's KSC in Florida has primary responsibility for ground turnaround, support, and launch of the space shuttle and its payloads, including elements for the International Space Station (ISS).

The Web site has information on shuttle and KSC history. Other rockets also launch from KSC, and the site provides status reports.

Subject(s): Space Shuttle; Space Stations; Rockets

Lunar and Planetary Sciences at the NSSDC

http://nssdc.gsfc.nasa.gov/planetary/

Sponsor(s): National Aeronautics and Space Administration (NASA)—Goddard Space Flight Center (GSFC)

Description: The National Space Science Data Center (NSSDC) is responsible for the collection, storage, and distribution of lunar and planetary images and other data to scientists, educators, and the general public. The site offers a separate page for each planet and for the moon, asteroids, and comets. Each of these separate pages features fact sheets, images, a Frequently Asked Questions file, other resources, and information on spacecraft missions to that specific astral body.

This site offers a substantial body of textual and pictorial information for all the planets in our solar system. Information is available at many levels and for many audiences, from children to research scientists. It is worth a visit from anyone in search of basic information or images of the planets, the moon, asteroids, or comets.

Subject(s): Planetary Science; Planets

Marshall Space Flight Center (MSFC)

http://www.nasa.gov/centers/marshall/

Sponsor(s): National Aeronautics and Space Administration (NASA)—Marshall Space Flight Center (MSFC)

Description: The Marshall Space Flight Center in Alabama develops space transportation and propulsion systems and oversees science and hardware development for the International Space Station. Its Web site provides a broad range of technical and background information on the many projects, scientific disciplines, and specific space flight missions with which the center is involved. Major sections of the Web site include Beyond Earth, Learning About Marshall, Expanding the Science Frontier, and Capabilities. The site also has a history of the center.

Subject(s): Microgravity; Propulsion Technology; Space Technology

NASA Armstrong Flight Research Center (DFRC)

http://www.nasa.gov/centers/armstrong/home/index.html

Sponsor(s): National Aeronautics and Space Administration (NASA)—Dryden Flight Research Center (DFRC)

Description: Armstrong Flight Research Center, located on Edwards Air Force Base in California, is responsible for flight research and flight testing. Web site sections include About Us, Capabilities and Facilities, Aircraft Operations Facility, Education, Multimedia, History, and Doing Business with Us. The Multimedia section has an archive of digitized photos, movies, and drawings of many of the unique research aircraft flown at the facility from the 1940s to the present.

Subject(s): Aerospace Engineering—Research; Aircraft—Research

NASA Exploration Systems Mission Directorate (ESMD)

http://exploration.nasa.gov/

Sponsor(s): National Aeronautics and Space Administration (NASA)—Exploration Systems Mission Directorate

Description: ESMD leads the agency's human and robotic exploration programs. The site has information about human health and safety on long space missions and research about the best methods for safe human space travel. The site links to several social media pages.

Subject(s): Human Space Exploration; Space Technology

NASA Headquarters

http://www.nasa.gov/centers/hq/home/

Sponsor(s): National Aeronautics and Space Administration (NASA)

Description: NASA Headquarters in Washington, D.C., manages the space flight centers, research centers, and other NASA installations. Under the heading Organization, the site links to headquarters leaders and NASA mission directorates, the NASA budget and reports, and business and research opportunities.

Subject(s): Space

NASA History Division

http://history.nasa.gov/

Sponsor(s): National Aeronautics and Space Administration (NASA)—History Office

Description: The NASA History Program, dating back to 1958, documents and preserves the agency's history. The site includes a brief history of NASA—including that of its predecessor, NACA—and an extensive topical index to historical information distributed on the many NASA Web sites. The Publications section lists print publications about NASA history, many of which are also available online, and links to NASA's own electronic publications about the agency history.

Subject(s): Spacecraft—History

Publication(s): *Apollo by the Numbers: A Statistical Review*, NAS 1.21
The Problem of Space Travel: The Rocket Motor, NAS 1.21

NASA Image eXchange (NIX)

http://data.nasa.gov/nasa-image-exchange/

Sponsor(s): National Aeronautics and Space Administration (NASA)

Description: NIX is a central search engine for many of the agency's distributed online multimedia collections. The collections can be searched by word. Images can also be browsed with a hierarchical menu of topics.

Subject(s): Photography; Space

NASA Langley Research Center (LaRC)

http://www.nasa.gov/centers/langley/

Sponsor(s): National Aeronautics and Space Administration (NASA)—Langley Research Center (LaRC)

Description: NASA's Langley Research Center, located in Virginia, has long been a major center for aeronautics research. The Web site provides news, images, and information related to this research and also highlights Langley contributions to space exploration and science. The Work with Langley section has information on procurement and technology transfer.

Subject(s): Aerospace Engineering—Research

NASA Lunar Science Institute (NLSI)

http://lunarscience.arc.nasa.gov/

Sponsor(s): National Aeronautics and Space Administration (NASA)—Ames Research Center (ARC)

Description: NLSI is managed by the NASA Ames Research Center but has dispersed teams across the nation working on research activities related to NASA's lunar exploration goals. The Web site provides information on the research teams and lunar science. It also has a section for the Lunar Science Forum.

Subject(s): Moon—Research

NASA Multimedia

http://www.nasa.gov/multimedia/

Sponsor(s): National Aeronautics and Space Administration (NASA)

Description: NASA Multimedia presents a selection of NASA images, 3D images, videos, podcasts, and interactive presentations. In the Images section, check the image usage guidelines before using material from this site; the guidelines cover images, audio, video, and other formats.

This NASA site makes it easy to find images and video recordings tied to recent NASA news. For a more extensive collection, see the NASA Image eXchange (NIX) site, which is described elsewhere in this section.

Subject(s): Space

NASA Science

http://science.hq.nasa.gov/

Sponsor(s): National Aeronautics and Space Administration (NASA)—Space Science Mission Directorate

Description: NASA's Science Mission Directorate offers this Web site with detailed information on the agency's science strategy and science missions. The Web site describes each science mission and organizes science topics in sections for Earth, Heliophysics, Planets, and Astrophysics. The site has audience-specific sections for researchers, educators, kids, teens, and "citizen scientists." The Web site also has science news.

Subject(s): Space Sciences

NASA Shuttle

http://www.nasa.gov/mission_pages/shuttle/main/index.html

Sponsor(s): National Aeronautics and Space Administration (NASA)—Spaceflight Office

Description: The final Space Shuttle mission took place in July 2011, and the Space Shuttle Discovery was turned over to the Smithsonian in April 2012. The Web site has information on the final flights and on past missions. Under several Missions subheadings, the Shuttle Archives section documents the crew, payloads, and timeline for previous missions back to 1981. Other subsections include Behind the Scenes, Launch & Landing, and Vehicle Structure.

Subject(s): Space Shuttle

NASA Tech Briefs

http://www.techbriefs.com/tech-briefs

Sponsor(s): Tech Briefs Media Group

Description: *NASA Tech Briefs* publishes information on commercially significant technologies developed in the course of NASA research and development. The publication is a joint publishing venture of NASA and Tech Briefs Media Group, which runs this Web site. The site also offers free downloadable Technical Support Packages (TSPs) with further information on the innovations described in the *NASA Tech Briefs*.

Subject(s): Space Technology; Technology Transfer

Publication(s): *NASA Tech Briefs*, NAS 1.29/3-2

NASA White Sands Test Facility (WSTF)

http://www.nasa.gov/centers/wstf/

Sponsor(s): National Aeronautics and Space Administration (NASA)—Johnson Space Center (JSC)

Description: NASA's White Sands Test Facility (WSTF) in New Mexico is operationally part of the NASA Johnson Space Center. The facility tests rocket propulsion systems, propellants and hazardous fluids, and materials and components used in spaceflight. It also serves as the primary training area for space shuttle pilots practicing landings. The Web site describes WSTF capabilities in each of these areas.

Subject(s): Aerospace Engineering; Propulsion Technology

National Space Science Data Center (NSSDC)

http://nssdc.gsfc.nasa.gov/

Sponsor(s): National Aeronautics and Space Administration (NASA)—Goddard Space Flight Center (GSFC)

Description: National Space Science Data Center serves as the permanent archive for space science data from NASA spaceflight missions. The data are related to the fields of astronomy and astrophysics, solar and space plasma physics, and planetary and lunar science. The site has an online Master Catalog of available data and resources. Some resources are available online; others must be ordered. The data are intended for use by the professional scientific community.

Subject(s): Space Sciences

Publication(s): *SPACEWARN Bulletin*, NAS 1.37/3

NSPIRES—NASA Research Opportunities

http://nspires.nasaprs.com/external/

Sponsor(s): National Aeronautics and Space Administration (NASA)

Description: NSPIRES stands for NASA Solicitation and Proposal Integrated Review and Evaluation System. The Web site is an online service center for each stage in the NASA research solicitation and award process. Users can search for open, closed, past, and future NASA research announcements and view the list of proposals selected to conduct NASA research, including the principal investigator, institution, and proposal title. Extensive guidance is provided in the NSPIRES Help section.

Subject(s): Scientific Research—Grants; Space—Research

Office of Space Commercialization

http://www.space.commerce.gov/

Sponsor(s): Commerce Department—National Oceanic and Atmospheric Administration (NOAA)

Description: "The Office of Space Commercialization is the principal unit for space commerce policy activities within the Department of Commerce. Its mission is to foster the conditions for the economic growth and technological advancement of the U.S. commercial space industry." (from the Web site) The Web site outlines space commercialization policy, particularly in the areas of remote sensing and space transportation. Topical sections bring together information on various specializations, such as satellite navigation and new entrepreneurial initiatives.

Subject(s): Space Technology

Planetary Data System (PDS)

http://pds.jpl.nasa.gov/

Sponsor(s): National Aeronautics and Space Administration (NASA)—Space Science Mission Directorate

Description: PDS is an archive of peer-reviewed data products from NASA planetary missions, astronomical observations, and laboratory measurements. The site includes sections for data services information, tools to manage the downloaded data, and documentation and manuals. PDS is managed by a system of nodes—NASA offices and university consortia—with specialties in the planetary disciplines. Links to each node's specialized Web site are in the left column of the PDS home page. While most of the content is for scientists, the site also has a section with resources for students and educators.

Subject(s): Planetary Science—Research

Solar System Exploration

http://sse.jpl.nasa.gov/

Sponsor(s): National Aeronautics and Space Administration (NASA)—Jet Propulsion Laboratory (JPL)

Description: The Jet Propulsion Lab's Solar System Exploration Web site is a public outreach effort with a wealth of information on the Earth's solar system and on planetary science. It profiles current and past planetary missions and includes a multimedia section with images. Most of the site is written for the general public of high school or adult age, but it also provides sections for kids and for educators.

This is a colorful and well-designed site with fresh content for space enthusiasts and amateur astronomers.

Subject(s): Planetary Science

Space Calendar

http://www2.jpl.nasa.gov/calendar/

Sponsor(s): National Aeronautics and Space Administration (NASA)—Jet Propulsion Laboratory (JPL)

Description: JPL's Space Calendar covers space-related activities and historical anniversaries for the coming year, with more than 5,200 links to related Web pages. The calendar includes launch dates, conferences, and celestial events such as eclipses. The site also offers calendar archives for the past several years.

This is an excellent resource for amateur astronomers and those interested in the history of space exploration.

Subject(s): Space—History

Space Operations

http://www.nasa.gov/directorates/somd/

Sponsor(s): National Aeronautics and Space Administration (NASA)—Space Operations Mission Directorate

Description: The NASA Space Operations Mission Directorate directs space flight operations, space launches and space communications, and other systems in operation. Major sections of the site include Education and Outreach, Shuttle Retirement, and Space Flight Awareness. Each operation is covered in detail. The site also links to the NASA SkyWatch application for determining when to view the space station from selected cities around the world.

Subject(s): Human Space Exploration; Space Shuttle; Space Stations

Space Weather Prediction Center

http://www.swpc.noaa.gov/

Sponsor(s): Commerce Department—National Oceanic and Atmospheric Administration (NOAA)—Office of Oceanic and Atmospheric Research

Description: As stated on the Web site, "Space Weather impacts numerous facets of everyday life, from where airplanes can safely fly, to how accurately a farmer plows his field. In addition, there are a large variety of phenomena that are driven by the variability of the sun over periods ranging from hours to years. SWPC provides information for novices and experts alike about the impacts and phenomena of Space Weather." The Web site's About Space Weather section reports on geomagnetic storms, solar radiation storms, radio blackouts, and the latest alerts and advisories. The Education/Outreach (under Media and Resources) section has classroom materials, brief papers on topics such as the ionosphere and radio wave propagation, and general information on space weather, including a Web page in Spanish.

Subject(s): Space Environment; Sun

Spitzer Space Telescope

http://www.spitzer.caltech.edu/spitzer/

Sponsor(s): National Aeronautics and Space Administration (NASA)—Jet Propulsion Laboratory (JPL)

Description: The Spitzer Space Telescope is a cryogenically-cooled infrared observatory. It is the final element of what are called NASA's four "Great Observatories," the others being the Hubble Space Telescope, Compton Gamma-Ray Observatory, and Chandra X-Ray Observatory. The Mission section of the site provides detailed information on the project's history, mission, science, and technology. The site also has project news and a large image gallery.

Subject(s): Astronomy; Telescopes

Stennis Space Center (SSC)

http://www.nasa.gov/centers/stennis/

Alternate URL(s)

http://www.ssc.nasa.gov/

Sponsor(s): National Aeronautics and Space Administration (NASA)—Stennis Space Center (SSC)

Description: SSC is NASA's primary center for testing large rocket propulsion systems and for developing remote sensing technology. These programs are detailed in the Missions section of the Web site. Under Multimedia, the site has a retrieval system for images related to work at SSC. The site also has information about Stennis education and business opportunities.

Subject(s): Propulsion Technology; Remote Sensing; Rockets

Voyager

http://voyager.jpl.nasa.gov/

Sponsor(s): National Aeronautics and Space Administration (NASA)—Jet Propulsion Laboratory (JPL)

Description: This site covers the missions of the Voyager-1 and Voyager-2 spacecraft, both launched in 1977 and now heading out of the solar system. The site has information on the science, spacecraft, and images of the Voyager missions.

Subject(s): Spacecraft

Wallops Flight Facility

http://www.nasa.gov/centers/wallops/home/index.html

Sponsor(s): National Aeronautics and Space Administration (NASA)—Wallops Flight Facility

Description: Wallops Flight Facility is responsible for the launch and operation of suborbital and small orbital payloads that support space-based research focused on Earth. It supports NASA's Sounding Rocket and Scientific Balloon Programs. The Web site describes the Wallops programs, facilities, business opportunities, education outreach, and history.

Subject(s): Rockets

NINETEEN

Social Welfare

The federal government develops programs and policies and administers grants in areas such as housing, community development, volunteer services, and welfare. This chapter includes agency Web sites that either serve the customers of such programs, or compile information on such programs.

Subsections in this chapter are Child Welfare, Economic Development, Housing, Social Services, and Volunteerism and Charities.

CHILD WELFARE

Administration for Children and Families (ACF)

http://www.acf.hhs.gov/

Sponsor(s): Health and Human Services Department—Administration for Children and Families (ACF)

Description: ACF is a federal agency that funds state, local, and tribal organizations that provide family assistance (welfare), child support, childcare, Head Start, child welfare, and other services related to children and families. Its Web site presents program and agency information under sections including About, Find Help, Programs, Grants & Funding, and Data & Research. Program information and resources organized under the Programs heading include information about children and youths, families, and emergency response and recovery.

The ACF Web site is a well organized and informative resource for child and family welfare federal programs. The program's research, data, and statistics information should be of interest to social service researchers.

Subject(s): Child Welfare; Early Childhood Education; Families; Welfare

Adoption.State.Gov

http://adoption.state.gov/

Sponsor(s): State Department—Children's Issues Office

Description: This site provides information on the international adoption process for Americans wishing to adopt a child from another country. It has sections on the Hague Convention on Intercountry Adoption, visas, country information, and the adoption process.

Subject(s): Adoption—International

Child Welfare Information Gateway

http://www.childwelfare.gov/

Sponsor(s): Health and Human Services Department—Administration for Children and Families (ACF)—Children's Bureau

Description: The Child Welfare Information Gateway is a Web portal to information on such topics as child abuse and neglect, out-of-home care, and adoption. Resources include the National Foster Care & Adoption Directory, statistics on child neglect issues, summaries of state laws, and links to relevant national organizations. Core information and some publications are available in Spanish.

Subject(s): Child Welfare

ChildCare.gov

http://childcare.gov/

Sponsor(s): Health and Human Services Department—Administration for Children and Families (ACF)—Child Care Bureau

Description: ChildCare.gov links to information about child care and early learning from federal government and government-sponsored sources. The site is designed for the general public, with special sections for parents, child care providers, researchers, and policy makers. It includes information on finding, choosing, and paying for child care; running a child care business; and topics such as the Head Start program and childproofing. Information is available in Spanish.

Subject(s): Child Care; Early Childhood Education

Family and Youth Services Bureau (FYSB)

http://www.acf.hhs.gov/programs/fysb/

Sponsor(s): Health and Human Services Department—Administration for Children and Families (ACF)—Family and Youth Services Bureau (FYSB)

Description: FYSB provides runaway and homeless youth service grants to local communities. It also funds research and demonstration projects. The FYSB divisions described on the Web site include Family Violence Prevention and Services, Special Projects for Runaway and

Homeless Youth, and Adolescent Pregnancy Prevention. Links to resources and funding opportunities are also provided.

Subject(s): Adolescents; Social Services—Grants

Publication(s): *Report to Congress on the Youth Programs of the Family and Youth Services Bureau*

National Clearinghouse on Families and Youth (NCFY)

http://www.ncfy.com/

Sponsor(s): Health and Human Services Department—Administration for Children and Families (ACF)—Family and Youth Services Bureau (FYSB)

Description: NCFY provides information on youth development, family violence prevention, abstinence education, and mentoring children of prisoners. The site is intended to support Family and Youth Service Bureau grantees and organizations interested in youth programming and policy. NCBY links to its own publications and an online database of summaries of publications from other sources. The site also has an online newsletter, *Youth Initiatives Update*.

Subject(s): Adolescents; Families

Publication(s): *Youth Initiatives Update*

National Responsible Fatherhood Clearinghouse (NFRC)

http://www.fatherhood.gov/

Sponsor(s): Health and Human Services Department—Administration for Children and Families (ACF)

Description: NRFC collects, organizes, and provides access to research, policies, best practices, and other information to support ACF-funded grantees in the Promoting Responsible Fatherhood program. Some information is available in Spanish, including information on the President's Fatherhood and Mentoring Initiative. The site also links to the DadTalk blog.

Subject(s): Families

Office of Child Care

http://www.acf.hhs.gov/programs/ccb/

Sponsor(s): Health and Human Services Department—Administration for Children and Families (ACF)—Child Care Bureau

Description: The Office of Child Care administers federal funds to states, territories, and tribes to help low-income families obtain quality child care. The site has policy and regulatory guidance documents and technical assistance information for the local governments administering the funds. It links to resources for childcare providers and for parents seeking quality child care. The site provides statistics on the Child Care and Development Fund.

Subject(s): Child Care

Women, Infants, and Children (WIC)
  http://www.fns.usda.gov/wic/
  Sponsor(s): Agriculture Department (USDA)—Food and Nutrition Service (FNS)
  Description: "WIC provides Federal grants to States for supplemental foods, health care referrals, and nutrition education for low-income pregnant, breastfeeding, and non-breastfeeding postpartum women, and to infants and children who are found to be at nutritional risk." (from the Web site) The Web site serves multiple audiences, including WIC applicants, state program administrators, and food manufacturers wishing to participate in the program.
  Subject(s): Nutrition—Grants; Pregnancy

ECONOMIC DEVELOPMENT

Administration for Native Americans (ANA)
  http://www.acf.hhs.gov/programs/ana/
  Sponsor(s): Health and Human Services Department—Administration for Children and Families (ACF)
  Description: As stated on the Web site, the Administration for Native Americans (ANA) has a mission to promote "self-sufficiency for Native Americans by providing discretionary grant funding for community based projects, and training and technical assistance to eligible tribes and native organizations." The site has information on grant programs and awards, emergency preparedness, and funding opportunities. Special initiatives include the Social and Economic Development Strategies (SEDS) and Native American language preservation and maintenance projects.
  Subject(s): Indigenous Peoples; Social Welfare; American Indians

Appalachian Regional Commission (ARC)
  http://www.arc.gov/
  Sponsor(s): Appalachian Regional Commission (ARC)
  Description: ARC supports economic and social development in the Appalachian region, which spans the spine of the Appalachian Mountains from southern New York to northern Mississippi. It includes all of West Virginia and parts of 12 other states: Alabama, Georgia, Kentucky, Maryland, Mississippi, New York, North Carolina, Ohio, Pennsylvania, South Carolina, Tennessee, and Virginia. The ARC Web site lists the individual counties that make up Appalachia. The site also features news about ARC and the Appalachian region and ARC's *Appalachia Magazine*.
  Subject(s): Rural Development
  Publication(s): *Appalachia Magazine*, Y 3.AP 4/2:9-2; County Economic Status and *Distressed Areas in Appalachia*, Y 3.AP 4/2:17

Consumer Financial Protection Bureau (CFPB)

http://www.consumerfinance.gov/

Sponsor(s): Federal Reserve

Description: CFPB is an independent Federal Reserve agency. According to its Web site, its mission is "to make markets for consumer financial products and services work for Americans—whether they are applying for a mortgage, choosing among credit cards, or using any number of other consumer financial products," through the application of education, enforcement, and research. The Get Assistance section informs consumers about protecting against credit discrimination, getting mortgage help, and other procedures. The home page provides links to the bureau's Facebook page and Twitter feed.

Subject(s): Consumer Information; Finance

Economic Development Administration (EDA)

http://www.eda.gov/

Sponsor(s): Commerce Department—Economic Development Administration (EDA)

Description: EDA gives grants to local communities for infrastructure and business development. Its Web site provides a full list of EDA contacts and links to the administration's social media pages. The Newsroom section lists press releases in reverse chronological order.

Subject(s): Economic Development—Grants

National Rural Development Partnership (NRDP)

http://www.rurdev.usda.gov/CEDP-NRDP.html

Sponsor(s): Agriculture Department (USDA)—Rural Business-Cooperative Service (RBS)

Description: NRDP promotes rural development through partnerships with local, state, tribal, and federal governments, as well as for-profit and nonprofit organizations. This site features information about NRDP, its accomplishments, and congressional updates. It also links to state and national partners and other rural development sites.

Subject(s): Rural Development

Office of Economic Adjustment (OEA)

http://www.oea.gov/

Sponsor(s): Defense Department—Office of Economic Adjustment (OEA)

Description: OEA provides adjustment assistance to communities affected by a military base closure, base expansion, or contract and program cancellations. The Web site has assistance information and resources related to planning for local development authorities, for growth management organizations, and for supporting compatible uses. The

About Us section includes news, project highlights, and information on the Economic Adjustment Committee, an interagency group that helps to coordinate federal intergovernmental assistance to local communities.

Subject(s): Economic Development

Recovery.gov

http://www.recovery.gov/

Sponsor(s): White House—Recovery Accountability and Transparency Board

Description: Recovery.gov is the central federal government Web site reporting on spending under the American Recovery and Reinvestment Act (Public Law 111-5), or Stimulus Bill. It tracks the disposition of funds and provides information on the geographic impact of the stimulus. The main section of the site, entitled "What Is Recovery.gov?," provides links to the programs it oversees.

Subject(s): Economic Policy

Rural Information Center (RIC)

http://ric.nal.usda.gov/

Sponsor(s): Agriculture Department (USDA)—National Agricultural Library (NAL)

Description: RIC is a specialized information and referral service within the National Agricultural Library. In the About RIC section, the RIC site links to information on rural resources and funding sources and RIC's own database, Federal Funding Sources for Rural Areas Database. The RIC Web site also provides a documented definition of "rural" for major federal programs.

The RIC Web site is an excellent starting point for those researching rural development topics for grant-writing or other purposes. It can be of assistance to rural governments, grant-seekers, small farms, and nonprofit organizations.

Subject(s): Rural Development—Research

Publication(s): *Rural Information Center Publication Series,* A 17.29

USDA Rural Development

http://www.rurdev.usda.gov/

Sponsor: Agriculture Department (USDA)

Description: The Rural Development Web site links to information on its major program areas: businesses, cooperatives, community development, energy, utilities, and housing. It includes current notices of funding availability and program news. The site also carries regulations, forms, and publications. Some publications are available in Spanish, and a version of the site is also available in Spanish.

Subject(s): Rural Development

HOUSING

Department of Housing and Urban Development (HUD)

http://www.hud.gov/

Sponsor(s): Housing and Urban Development (HUD)

Description: HUD's Web site describes the agency's programs in housing and community development. Under the heading State Info, the site has information for residents of each of the 50 states, the District of Columbia, Puerto Rico, and the Virgin Islands. Another main section of the site, Topic Areas, provides information on numerous topics, including avoiding foreclosure, buying a home, fair lending practices, homes for sale, housing discrimination, housing research and data sets, rental assistance, and veterans information. Under Resources, the site has an extensive online library of information and tools including a Loan Estimator Calculator, a Lender Locator, and a database of HUD-approved appraisers. The site also has an A to Z index and is available in Spanish.

As with other Cabinet agencies, HUD has Recovery Act and Open Government sections on its Web site.

This site provides valuable resources on housing to the general public.

Subject(s): Community Development; Housing

Publication(s): *Labor Relations Letters*, HH 1.117

Legal Opinions of the Office of General Counsel (annual), HH 1.86

Federal Housing Administration (FHA)

http://portal.hud.gov/

Sponsor(s): Housing and Urban Development (HUD)—Office of Housing

Description: FHA provides mortgage insurance on single-family, multifamily, manufactured homes, and hospital loans made by FHA-approved lenders. Under Resources, the Web site has sections for consumers, lenders, real estate professionals, appraisers, builders, inspectors, and counseling services. The site also include information on the FHA National Servicing Center, which helps homeowners by working with lenders to find solutions to avoid foreclosure. The FHA Web site provides detailed information on its programs, products, services, and rule. It also links to state Web sites.

Subject(s): Home Mortgages

Federal Housing Finance Agency (FHFA)

http://www.fhfa.gov/

Sponsor: Federal Housing Finance Agency (FHFA)

Description: Created in 2008, FHFA oversees Fannie Mae, Freddie Mac, and the Federal Home Loan Banks. It replaces Office of Federal Housing Enterprise Oversight (OFHEO), the Federal Housing Finance Board (FHFB), and the government-sponsored enterprise team (GSE) mission office at the Department of Housing and Urban Development (HUD). The Web site includes FHFA regulations and agency guidance. The House Price Index (HPI) section of the site includes current HPI data reports, downloadable data in text and spreadsheet formats, and historical reports.

Subject(s): Housing Finance

Foreclosure Resource Center

http://www.stlouisfed.org/foreclosure/

Sponsor(s): Federal Reserve—Federal Reserve Bank of St. Louis

Description: The Federal Reserve provides a *Foreclosure Survival Guide* for consumers and a Mitigation Toolkit for communities. The site provides additional links to home foreclosure information for consumers, communities, and financial institutions.

Subject(s): Home Mortgages

Ginnie Mae

http://www.ginniemae.gov/

Sponsor(s): Housing and Urban Development (HUD)—Government National Mortgage Association (Ginnie Mae)

Description: Ginnie Mae, a wholly owned government corporation within HUD, aims to help provide affordable, government-insured mortgages to American families. Its Web site includes information for investors, homeowners, and mortgage-backed securities issuers, as well as information about Ginnie Mae. The site also has information on the history of Ginnie Mae and on the relevant statutes and regulations.

Subject(s): Housing Finance

HUD User

http://www.huduser.org/

Sponsor(s): Housing and Urban Development (HUD)—Policy Development and Research Office

Description: HUD User is the primary source for federal government reports and information about housing policy and programs, building technology, economic development, urban planning, and other housing-related topics. Web site sections include About PD&R, Research & Publications, Data Sets, Initiatives, and Quick Links. The Bibliographic Database links to information on thousands of reports, articles, case studies, and other research literature related to housing and community development. The Data Sets section includes the original electronic data sets from the American Housing Survey and other housing research initiatives. The About PD&R section features the current research and initiatives of the Office of Policy Development and Research.

Subject(s): Community Development—Research; Housing—Research; Databases

Publication(s): *Cityscape*, HH 1.75/2
ResearchWorks, HH 1.75/4
U.S. Housing Market Conditions (quarterly), HH 1.120/2

HUDCLIPS
http://www.hud.gov/hudclips/
Alternate URL(s)
http://www.hud.gov/offices/adm/hudclips/
Sponsor(s): Housing and Urban Development (HUD)
Description: HUDCLIPS (HUD's Client Information and Policy System) is a password-accessible, searchable online database that contains the entire inventory of official HUD policies, procedures, announcements, forms, and other materials. The site provides HUD forms in PDF format; some of these forms are also available in Spanish. Other documents on HUDCLIPS include HUD handbooks, letters, guidebooks, notices, bulletins, housing policy documents, and legal opinions.
Subject(s): Housing; Publication Catalogs

Making Home Affordable
http://makinghomeaffordable.gov/
Alternate URL(s)
http://makinghomeaffordable.gov/spanish/
Description: MakingHomeAffordable.gov is the central Web site for information on government programs to help homeowners afford their mortgages to promote financial stability. Major sections of the site cover eligibility, finding a HUD-approved housing counselor, and applying for the applying for the Home Affordable Modification Program. The Learning Center section provides practical information for borrowers, including information about avoiding scams. The site is available in Spanish at the alternate URL listed above.

United States Interagency Council on Homelessness
http://usich.gov/
Alternate URL(s)
http://makinghomeaffordable.gov/spanish/
Sponsor(s): Interagency Council on Homelessness
Description: Nineteen federal departments and agencies are members of the Interagency Council on Homelessness. The council coordinates federal policy and programs on homelessness and employs regional coordinators to work with state and local governments. The Web site provides information on the council's activities, programs to reduce homelessness, state and local initiatives, and news about funding and technical assistance. The council's fact sheets are in the Resources section.
Subject(s): Homelessness

Publication(s): *Opening Doors: Federal Strategic Plan to Prevent and End Homelessness* PR 44.8:D 72

VA Loan Guaranty Home Loan Program
http://www.benefits.va.gov/homeloans/
Alternate URL(s)
http://www.homeloans.va.gov/
Sponsor(s): Veterans Affairs Department (VA)
Description: The VA Loan Guaranty Service is the organization within the Veterans Benefits Administration charged with the responsibility of administering the home loan program. The VA home loan program helps veterans finance the purchase of homes through favorable loan terms and competitive interest rates. The Web site provides information for home buyers, lenders, loan servicers, and real estate professionals. It has online videos, pamphlets, and disaster advice for VA borrowers. The site also has information on grants for specially adapted housing.
Subject(s): Housing Finance; Veterans

SOCIAL SERVICES

Administration on Developmental Disabilities (AIDD)
http://www.acf.hhs.gov/programs/add/
Sponsor(s): Health and Human Services Department—Administration for Children and Families (ACF)
Description: ADD coordinates service programs for those with developmental disabilities (defined as physical or mental impairments that begin before age 22 and restrict a person's ability to perform basic tasks for self-sufficiency). The site provides AIDD publications and program guidance and describes AIDD's major programs and program outcomes. The AIDD Programs section of the site links to institutional resources such as state councils on developmental disabilities and state protection and advocacy systems.
Subject(s): Disabilities

Benefits.gov
http://www.benefits.gov/
Alternate URL(s)
http://www.govbenefits.gov/
Sponsor(s): Labor Department
Description: Benefits.gov is a multi-agency effort to provide a single Web site for users with questions about government benefits. The site can help users find benefits information without having to know which agency to contact. One of its major features is a benefit finder; the user answers a series of questions to determine eligibility for specific govern-

ment benefits. (The site does not ask for identifying information, such as name or Social Security number.) A Spanish-language version is available.

Although the site is managed by a multi-agency partnership, the Department of Labor takes the "managing partner" role.

Subject(s): Social Welfare

Campaign to Rescue and Restore Victims of Human Trafficking

http://www.acf.hhs.gov/trafficking/

Sponsor(s): Health and Human Services Department—Administration for Children and Families (ACF)

Description: The Health and Human Services Department is responsible for helping victims of human trafficking become eligible to receive benefits and services. This Web site provides information on the department's campaign to locate human trafficking victims. It provides campaign toolkits for social service organizations, health care providers, and law enforcement officers. The site also links to other agency program Web sites concerned with human trafficking.

Subject(s): International Crimes

Catalog of Federal Domestic Assistance (CFDA)

http://www.cfda.gov/

Sponsor(s): General Services Administration (GSA)—Office of Governmentwide Policy (OGP)

Description: This online version of the classic print document, Catalog of Federal Domestic Assistance (CFDA), is a searchable version of the catalog. CFDA describes a broad range of federal assistance programs, including formula-based grants, guaranteed loans, insurance, counseling, training, information services, and donation of goods. The site has a separate database to highlight Recovery Act programs. Most of the programs are not for direct assistance to individuals, but rather for state and local governments, Indian tribal governments, or other organizations that administer the distribution of aid. Catalog entries include a program identifier number, description, eligibility requirements, program contact information, and details on the application and awards process.

With the advanced search feature, users of the catalog can search programs by keyword, type of assistance, type of entity eligible for the assistance, descriptive subject area or function, deadline for application, and more. Programs can be listed by agency or easily retrieved by CFDA program number. The General Info section of the site includes important resources such as a guide to writing grant proposals, explanations of the types of assistance in the CFDA, and a link for those who want to store and use the CFDA data at their own site.

Subject(s): Government Loans; Grants

Publication(s): *Catalog of Federal Domestic Assistance*, PREX 2.20

Center for Faith-Based and Neighborhood Partnerships (Education)
http://www.ed.gov/about/inits/list/fbci/
Sponsor(s): Education Department
Description: This is one of the Centers for Faith-Based and Neighborhood Partnerships, which work with 13 federal agencies; these centers were created to encourage new participation in federal grant programs. The Web site includes information on program goals, news, and partnership funding.
Subject(s): Education Funding; Grants

Center for Faith-Based and Neighborhood Partnerships (HHS)
http://www.hhs.gov/fbci/
Sponsor(s): Health and Human Services Department
Description: The HHS Center for Faith-Based and Neighborhood Partnerships works to encourage the participation of religious and neighborhood organizations in the department's many service programs for those in need. The site has information on the partnership center and opportunities for faith-based and community organizations.
Subject(s): Grants; Social Services

Center for Faith-Based and Neighborhood Partnerships (HUD)
http://www.hud.gov/offices/fbci/
Sponsor(s): Housing and Urban Development (HUD)
Description: The HUD Center for Faith-Based and Community Initiatives Web site has information on grants and technical assistance for nonprofits, as well as other housing-related resources.
Subject(s): Grants; Social Services

Center for Faith-Based and Neighborhood Partnerships (Labor)
http://www.dol.gov/cfbnp/
Sponsor(s): Labor Department
Description: This Web site carries news on worker issues, the Labor Department's grants, and recent grant awards. Information is available in Spanish, Chinese, and Vietnamese.
Subject(s): Employment—Policy; Grants

Department of Health and Human Services (HHS)
http://www.hhs.gov/
Sponsor(s): Health and Human Services Department
Description: The HHS Web site is a gateway to information on all of the health and social services programs overseen by the department. Major sections of the site cover federal grants and funding, services for families, disease prevention, disease information, and public health emergency preparedness. The site also links to regulations, policies, and guide-

lines relevant to HHS. The About HHS section links to HHS regional offices, and the HHS Secretary section links to speeches and testimony. The site's home page features links to the Web sites for major initiatives, such as HealthCare.gov and FoodSafety.gov. For navigating the abundance of information at HHS.gov, the site has a search engine, frequently asked questions section, and an A-Z index. Like other Cabinet agencies, HHS has Open Government and Recovery Act information on its site.

This site is a good starting point for HHS programs and initiatives.

Subject(s): Public Health; Social Services

Disability.gov

https://www.disability.gov/

Sponsor(s): White House

Description: Disability.gov is a portal to federal Web sites and programs of concern to persons with disabilities. The site is divided into topical sections, including Benefits, Community Life, Civil Rights, Emergency Preparedness, Employment, Education, Health, Housing, Transportation, and Technology.

Subject(s): Disabilities

FindYouthInfo.gov

http://www.findyouthinfo.gov/

Sponsor(s): Interagency Working Group on Youth Programs

Description: FindYouthInfo.gov is designed to help community organizations in their efforts to support youth. It provides tools to find existing federal and local resources and to develop local programs and partnerships. The site is sponsored by a working group of 12 federal agencies, including the White House Office of Drug Control Policy, the Corporation for National and Community Service, the Department of Justice, and the Department of Housing and Urban Development.

Subject(s): Adolescents

Food and Nutrition Service (FNS)

http://www.fns.usda.gov/fns/

Sponsor(s): Agriculture Department (USDA)—Food and Nutrition Service (FNS)

Description: FNS manages programs including School Meals; the Women, Infants, and Children (WIC) Program; the Supplemental Nutrition Assistance Program (SNAP, formerly the Food Stamp Program); Food Assistance for Disaster Relief; and Food Distribution (including emergency food assistance). The Web site provides information on the regulations, statistics, and forms related to the programs. A Nutrition Education section, under Research, highlights federal programs and resources in this area. The Newsroom section includes links to each program's publications. Other sections cover Forms, Programs, and Data. The site also has a Spanish-language version.

Subject(s): Food Stamps; Nutrition; School Meal Programs

Publication(s): *Disaster Manual,* A 98.8

WIC Program and Participants Characteristics, A 98.17

Food Distribution Programs

http://www.fns.usda.gov/fdd/

Sponsor(s): Agriculture Department (USDA)—Food and Nutrition Service (FNS)

Description: The Food Distribution programs provide commodity distribution and other nutrition assistance to low-income families, emergency feeding programs, Indian Reservations, and the elderly. The Web site offers information primarily for food commodity providers. The Help section includes a site map and A to Z index for the site. The site is also available in Spanish.

Subject(s): Food Aid

HIV/AIDS Programs

http://hab.hrsa.gov/

Sponsor(s): Health and Human Services Department—Health Resources and Services Administration (HRSA)

Description: This site focuses on the federal programs funded under the Ryan White Comprehensive AIDS Resources Emergency (CARE) Act. CARE Act programs are designed to help individuals with HIV who lack the health insurance and financial resources necessary for their care. The programs include health care and support, grants, training, and technical assistance. This site provides detailed information on the CARE Act and on applying for and managing the program grants. It also provides program data, including state profiles.

Subject(s): AIDS; HIV Infections

Publication(s): *HRSA Care Action,* HE 20.9516

House Ways and Means Committee Prints

http://www.gpoaccess.gov/wmprints/index.html

Sponsor(s): Government Printing Office (GPO); Congress—House Committee on Ways and Means

Description: The House Committee on Ways and Means has jurisdiction over most programs authorized by the Social Security Act, and its special publications can be useful sources of information on entitlement and benefits programs. Of particular use for reference and research is the committee print *Background Material and Data on Programs Within the Jurisdiction of the Committee on Ways and Means,* popularly known as the *Green Book,* now hosted on the GPO's FDsys Web site. This document is a unique collection of program descriptions and historical data on a wide variety of social and economic topics, including Social Security, employment, earnings, welfare, child support, health insurance, the elderly, families with children, poverty, and taxation. The Ways and Means Committee also produces the *Compilation of the Social Security Laws, Including the Social Security Act, as Amended, and Related Enactments.*

While the *Green Book* and other prints are often updated, they are not issued every year or even every session of Congress.

Subject(s): Social Security—Statistics; Welfare—Statistics
Publication(s): *Compilation of the Social Security Laws . . .* , Y 4.W 36
Green Book, Y 4.W 36

Low Income Home Energy Assistance Program (LIHEAP)

http://www.acf.hhs.gov/programs/liheap/
Alternate URL(s)
http://liheap.ncat.org/
Sponsor(s): Health and Human Services Department—Administration for Children and Families (ACF)
Description: LIHEAP is a federally funded program that helps low-income households with their home energy bills for heating or cooling. Its Web site provides information for consumers who may be eligible for LIHEAP, as well as for professionals who coordinate LIHEAP programs in states, tribal areas, and localities. The site has information on funding and on applying for assistance. Instructions on applying are available in Spanish and English. The Web site also has regulatory guidance, policy information, and program statistics.

The alternate URL above links to the LIHEAP Clearinghouse, a network for parties interested in low-income energy issues and a repository for information on the topic.

Subject(s): Energy Prices and Costs

Migrant and Seasonal Farm Workers

http://www.doleta.gov/Farmworker/
Sponsor(s): Labor Department—Employment and Training Administration (ETA)
Description: The Department of Labor maintains this Web site for their National Farmworker Jobs Program (NFJP). The program provides funding to community-based organizations and public agencies that assist migrant and seasonal farmworkers with job skills training, housing, and health care. The Web site has information on the program, grant

awards, and state allocations, as well as information on the National Monitor Advocate System.

Subject(s): Farms and Farming; Job Training—Grants

Office of Faith-Based and Neighborhood Partnerships

http://www.whitehouse.gov/administration/eop/ofbnp

Sponsor(s): White House

Description: This White House office coordinates the work of the Federal Centers for Faith-Based and Community Initiatives. The centers help community organizations find and apply for federal grants and implement grant awards to serve their communities. The site outlines the offices' policy goals and features a Partnership Blog.

Subject(s): Grants; Social Services

Office of Family Assistance (OFA)

http://www.acf.hhs.gov/programs/ofa/

Sponsor(s): Health and Human Services Department—Administration for Children and Families (ACF)

Description: OFA administers the Temporary Assistance for Needy Families (TANF) welfare program. Along with non-technical overviews of how TANF works, the site provides legislative, regulatory, and technical documents related to the program. The TANF Program section links to data on TANF finances, demographics of recipients, and work participation rates of recipients.

OFA also administers the Healthy Marriage program. The Web site provides information for funding information and research.

Subject(s): Welfare

Publication(s): *Annual Report to Congress/Temporary Assistance to Needy Families*, HE 25.11

Office of University Partnerships (OUP)

http://www.oup.org/

Sponsor(s): Housing and Urban Development (HUD)

Description: OUP functions as a national clearinghouse for disseminating information about HUD's Community Outreach Partnership Centers Program. HUD established OUP in 1994 to encourage university-community partnerships. The Web site's grantee database lists current and past grant recipients by state. The Research & Publications section includes more information on research and links to related Web sites. Other sections cover data, initiatives, and events.

Subject(s): Community Development—Grants

Publication(s): *Diversity Works*
Research in Focus

Poverty Guidelines, Research, and Measurement

http://aspe.hhs.gov/poverty/

Sponsor(s): Health and Human Services Department

Description: This site provides the text of the current HHS poverty guidelines, as published annually in the Federal Register. A table lists the actual dollar figures going back to 1982 and links to the guidelines going back to 1996. The site explains the difference between the "poverty threshold" issued by the Census Bureau and the "poverty guidelines" issued by HHS. The site includes papers and articles about how poverty can be measured and how it has been measured over time. It also links to academic research centers studying poverty.

This is an essential site for checking the current poverty guidelines, particularly since it includes additional explanatory information and context.

Subject(s): Poverty

Social Security Administration (SSA)

http://www.socialsecurity.gov/

Sponsor(s): Social Security Administration (SSA)

Description: The SSA's central Web site leads to a wealth of information and online services from the agency. Major programs involve such subjects as retirement, survivors, disability, SSI, and Medicare. Other sections on the home page link to SSA's online services, tools for calculating benefits, a directory of local Social Security Offices, forms and publications, and program news. The home page also features a menu to select answers to common questions and information tailored to specific groups (such as attorneys, press, and wounded warriors).

Other Languages, located on the top menu of the home page, links to the SSA Multilanguage Gateway. Consumer information is available there in 17 languages, including Spanish, Arabic, Chinese, French, Portuguese, Farsi, Korean, and Russian. Each section also has information on interpreter services. A Spanish-language version of the site is available directly on the home page.

The design of the SSA's main Web page makes it easy to find information on popular topics. The site also has a search engine. For specific topics, one of the most helpful tools may be the FAQs menu on the home page. The FAQs section can also be accessed directly at http://ssa-custhelp.ssa.gov/.

Subject(s): Social Security

Publication(s): *Actuarial Notes*, SSA 1.25

Actuarial Studies, SSA 1.25/2

Annual Report of the Board of Trustees of the OASDI Trust Funds, SSA 1.1/4

Annual Statistical Supplement to the Social Security Bulletin, SSA 1.22/2

Compilation of Social Security Laws . . ., Y 4.W 36:10-3/

Congressional Statistics, SSA 1.1/9
Fast Facts and Figures About Social Security, SSA 1.26
Income of the Population 55 or Older, SSA 1.30
Program Operations Manual System (POMS), SSA 1.8/2
Seguro Social, hechos sobre cupones de alimentos, SSA 1.2:F 73/2/
Seguro Social, Seguridad de Ingreso Suplementario Para Extranjeros, SSA 1.2:N 73/
Social Security Bulletin, SSA 1.22
Social Security Handbook, SSA 1.8/3
Social Security Programs Throughout the World , SSA 1.24
Social Security Rulings, HE 3.44/2
What You Need to Know When You Get Retirement or Survivors Benefits . . . , SSA 1.20

Social Security Advisory Board
http://www.ssab.gov/
Sponsor(s): Social Security Advisory Board
Description: The Social Security Advisory Board is an independent, bipartisan board whose purpose is to advise the president, Congress, and the commissioner of Social Security on the Social Security and Supplemental Security Income programs. Its Web site has information on the board's authority and operations and has brief biographies of its members. The board's reports are online in full text back to 1997.
Subject(s): Social Security
Publication(s): *Social Security Advisory Board Annual Report, 2013*
Unsustainable Cost of Health Care, Y 3.2

Social Security Online — For Women
http://www.ssa.gov/women/
Sponsor(s): Social Security Administration (SSA)
Description: This site provides SSA program information on retirement, survivors, disability, and Supplemental Security Income benefits relevant to women. Information is organized into categories that correspond to the various life stages of women: Working Women, Women Who Receive Social Security Benefits, Brides, New Mothers, Wives, Divorced Women, Caregivers, and Widows.
Subject(s): Social Security; Women

Supplemental Nutrition Assistance Program (SNAP)
http://www.fns.usda.gov/snap/
Sponsor(s): Agriculture Department (USDA)—Food and Nutrition Service (FNS)
Description: SNAP, formerly known as the Food Stamp Program, helps low-income people and families buy food. The Web site has program application forms and information for recipients and for retail

stores. The site also has nutrition education materials, regulations and policy information, and data such as state-level participation. The site is also available in Spanish.

Subject(s): Food Stamps

The Work Site

http://www.ssa.gov/work/

Sponsor(s): Social Security Administration (SSA)

Description: This site describes the voluntary Ticket to Work program and other programs useful to persons with disabilities who want to try to work. The site has information and documents for both beneficiaries and service providers.

Subject(s): Disabilities; Employment

Title V Information System (TVIS)

https://mchdata.hrsa.gov/tvisreports/

Sponsor(s): Health and Human Services Department—Health Resources and Services Administration (HRSA)—Maternal and Child Health Bureau

Description: TVIS electronically captures data from annual Title V Block Grant applications and reports. Title V of the Social Security Act covers a major federal block grant program funding health promotion efforts for mothers, infants, and children. Reports available on the site include *Financial Data for the Most Recent Year*, *Program Data for the Most Recent Year*, and *Measurement and Indicator Data*.

Subject(s): Reproductive Health—Statistics; Child Health and Safety—Statistics

Publication(s): *Title V: A Snapshot of Maternal and Child Health*, HE 20.9202

Unemployment Insurance

http://workforcesecurity.doleta.gov/unemploy/

Sponsor(s): Labor Department—Employment and Training Administration (ETA)

Description: Each state administers a separate unemployment insurance (UI) program within guidelines established by federal law. This Department of Labor Web site provides a centralized location for information on the federal-state program. The site provides extensive information on available programs, laws and regulations, statistics, budget, and reemployment services. The site also links to each state office responsible for administering unemployment insurance.

Subject(s): Unemployment Insurance

United We Ride

http://www.unitedweride.gov/

Sponsor(s): Federal Interagency Coordinating Council on Access and Mobility (CCAM)

Description: The federal United We Ride initiative coordinates grants to states to improve transportation options for groups such as the elderly, low-income individuals, or disabled persons. The site provides program policy and funding information, a section on assessment and planning, and strategies for improving citizens' mobility. Publications are in the Resources section of the site.

Subject(s): Transportation Funding

USAID: Faith-Based and Community Initiatives

http://www.usaid.gov/who-we-are/organization/independent-offices/office-faith-based-and-community-initiatives

Sponsor(s): Agency for International Development (USAID)

Description: The Office of Faith-Based and Community Initiatives at USAID uses this page to highlight relevant information and to provide resources for interested organizations. USAID works in such areas as global health, disaster response, and food aid.

Subject(s): Foreign Assistance; Grants

USDA Faith-Based and Neighborhood Partnerships

http://www.usda.gov/wps/portal/usda/usdahome?navid=FBCI

Alternate URL(s)

http://www.usda.gov/fbci/

Sponsor(s): Agriculture Department (USDA)

Description: This USDA site highlights opportunities for faith-based and community organizations in USDA grant programs. The site highlights opportunities in the areas of reducing hunger, revitalizing rural communities, and helping to conserve natural resources.

Subject(s): Grants; Social Services

VOLUNTEERISM AND CHARITIES

AmeriCorps

http://www.americorps.gov/

Sponsor(s): Corporation for National and Community Service—Americorps

Description: AmeriCorps is a program of the Corporation for National and Community Service. AmeriCorps volunteers serve on education, public safety, health, and environmental assistance projects and are eligible for an education-related stipend. The Web site has news and information for potential volunteers and for organizations seeking AmeriCorps assistance. Major sections of the site describe AmeriCorps VISTA

(Volunteers in Service to America), AmeriCorps NCCC (National Civilian Community Corps), and Americorps State and National.

Subject(s): Volunteerism

Citizen Corps

http://www.citizencorps.gov/

Sponsor: USA Freedom Corps

Description: Citizen Corps, part of USA Freedom Corps, was created to help coordinate volunteer activities that work to prepare communities to respond to emergency situations. Under Our Partners (which can be found under the Citizen Corps tab on the home page), the Web site describes the major programs that Citizen Corps supports: CERT (Community Emergency Response Teams), VIPs (Volunteers in Police Service), USAonWatch, the Fire Corps, the Corporation for National and Community Service (CNCS), and the Medical Reserve Corps (MRC). The site also links to emergency preparedness guidance.

Subject(s): Volunteerism

Corporation for National and Community Service (CNCS)

http://www.nationalservice.gov/

Sponsor(s): Corporation for National and Community Service

Description: CNCS is a federal corporation governed by a board of directors. CNCS programs include AmeriCorps, Learn and Serve America, Senior Corps, and a number of special initiatives. The Web site has prominent links to the Web sites for its programs and information about how to volunteer. The About Us section has information on staff and organizational structure, fact sheets, relevant laws and regulations, and the annual report to Congress. Other sections are directed to organizations needing assistance and individuals seeking to volunteer. The site also covers developments such as Recovery Act funding and the Edward M. Kennedy Serve America Act.

Subject(s): Volunteerism

Search for Charities

http://www.irs.gov/Charities-&-Non-Profits/Exempt-Organizations-Select-Check

Sponsor(s): Treasury Department—Internal Revenue Service (IRS)

Description: This site began an online version of IRS Publication 78 Cumulative List of Organizations, which is no longer published in print by the IRS. It can be searched to see if a particular organization is exempt from federal taxation and if contributions to them are tax deductible. It can be searched by name, city, or state. On the search page, be sure to check for links to helpful background before conducting a search.

To reach this resource without typing in the URL listed above, go to the IRS home page and click on the Charities tab and then the Search for Charities link.

Subject(s): Charities

Senior Corps

http://www.seniorcorps.gov/

Sponsor(s): Corporation for National and Community Service—Senior Corps

Description: Senior Corps is a program of the Corporation for National and Community Service involving volunteers ages 55 and older. The Web site describes its major programs, such as Senior Companions and the Retired and Senior Volunteer Program (RSVP). The site has information for potential volunteers and for organizations seeking assistance from Senior Corps.

Subject(s): Senior Citizens; Volunteerism

United We Serve

http://serve.gov/

Sponsor(s): Corporation for National and Community Service

Description: Serve.gov was launched in April 2009 in coordination with the signing of the Edward M. Kennedy Serve America Act (Public Law 111-13). The Web site provides a clearinghouse of volunteer opportunities available to Americans in the United States and worldwide. Organizations may also post their volunteer needs on the site.

Subject(s): Volunteerism

Volunteer.Gov/Gov

http://www.volunteer.gov/gov/

Sponsor: Interior Department

Description: The goal of Volunteer.Gov/Gov is to connect people with public service volunteer opportunities. Users can view descriptions of volunteer opportunities by type, city, and state and apply for positions online. Volunteer.Gov/Gov is an interagency effort. The Department of the Interior manages the Web site.

Subject(s): Volunteerism

TWENTY

Transportation

Although some aspects of transportation are handled at the state and local levels, the federal government still plays a major role in transportation funding, policy, regulation, and research. This chapter covers many modes of transportation and includes Web sites that are intended for consumers as well as sites for transportation operators and makers of transportation policy. Web sites concerning transportation security are listed in the Homeland Security section of the Defense and Intelligence chapter.

Subsections in this chapter are Aviation, Maritime Transportation, Mass Transit, Surface Transportation, Transportation Policy and Research, and Transportation Safety.

AVIATION

Federal Aviation Administration (FAA)

http://www.faa.gov/

Sponsor(s): Transportation Department—Federal Aviation Administration (FAA)

Description: FAA is responsible for the safety of civil aviation. Its Web site includes the following sections: Aircraft, Airports, Air Traffic (with airport status and airline on-time statistics), Data & Research (aviation and commercial space statistics, research funding), Licenses & Certificates, Regulations & Policies, and Training & Testing (aviation schools). The About FAA section links to field and regional offices and information on current FAA initiatives. The site has audience-specific sections for airline pilots, pilots, mechanics, and others, and an A-Z index for locating specific information on the site.

Subject(s): Aviation—Regulations; Aviation Safety—Regulations

Publication(s): *Administrator's Fact Book*, TD 4.20/2
Advisory Circular Checklist, TD 4.8/5
Air Traffic Publications Library, TD 4.78
Airplane Flying Handbook, TD 4.8/2
Airworthiness Directives, TD 4.10/6:
FAA Safety Briefing, TD 4.9
Federal Aviation Regulations, TD 4.6
National Plan Integrated Airport Systems, TD 4.33/3

Flight Delay Information

http://www.fly.faa.gov/

Sponsor(s): Transportation Department—Federal Aviation Administration (FAA)

Description: The Air Traffic Control System Command Center provides this interactive U.S. map for information on flight delays. As stated on the Web site, "the status information provided on this site indicates general airport conditions; it is not flight-specific."

Flight Standards Service

http://www.faa.gov/about/office_org/headquarters_offices/avs/offices/afs/

Sponsor(s): Transportation Department—Federal Aviation Administration (FAA)

Description: The FAA's Flight Standards Service maintains this Web site to provide FAA safety-related information for pilots and others regarding flying, airlines, and aircraft. The site has information on its safety programs and the Civil Aviation Registry, which is responsible for the registration of United States civil aircraft and certification of airmen.

William J. Hughes Technical Center

http://www.faa.gov/about/office_org/headquarters_offices/ang/offices/tc/

Sponsor(s): Transportation Department—Federal Aviation Administration (FAA)

Description: The William J. Hughes Technical Center is an aviation research, development, engineering, testing, and evaluation facility located in New Jersey. Center activities involve testing and evaluation in air traffic control, communications, navigation, airports, and aircraft safety and security, as well as long-range R&D projects. This Web site includes an overview of the center's work and facility.

Subject(s): Aviation Safety—Research

MARITIME TRANSPORTATION

Federal Maritime Commission (FMC)

http://www.fmc.gov/

Sponsor(s): Federal Maritime Commission (FMC)

Description: The FMC is responsible for the regulation of shipping in the foreign trades of the United States. Its Web site is designed for providers and consumers of international shipping services. The Agreement Notices & Library section, under Databases & Services, allows for browsing Agreement Notices by carrier, country, type of agreement, and more. The Web site also links to SERVCON, the commission's electronic filing system.

Subject(s): Shipping—Regulations

Publication(s): *Commonly Used Commission Forms (Federal Maritime Commission)*, FMC 1.13

Formal Docket Decisions, FMC 1.10/2

Maritime Administration (MARAD)

http://marad.dot.gov/

Sponsor(s): Transportation Department—Maritime Administration (MARAD)

Description: The Department of Transportation's MARAD promotes the U.S. Merchant Marine for waterborne commerce and as a naval and military auxiliary in time of war or national emergency. The Ports section of the site covers port security, infrastructure, conveyance, and licensing. The Education section features maritime career information, the Adopt a Ship program, and a page for kids. Statistics provided in the Resources section of the site cover the cruise industry, waterborne foreign trade, flags of registry, and vessel calls at U.S. port by vessel type. This section also has publications, including forms, policy papers, and a *Glossary of Shipping Terms* and Maritime Laws.

Subject(s): Merchant Marine; Shipping—Statistics

Publication(s): *Glossary of Shipping Terms*, TD 11.2

Maritime Laws, TD 11.6

National Maritime Center

http://www.uscg.mil/nmc/

Sponsor(s): Homeland Security Department—Coast Guard

Description: This Web site serves as a central location for information on merchant marine licenses, certificates of registry, and merchant mariner documents (issued to unlicensed personnel who support the operation of a vessel). It includes background information and checklists, applications and forms, and a user fee schedule.

Subject(s): Merchant Marine—Regulations

Saint Lawrence Seaway Development Corporation (SLSDC)

http://www.seaway.dot.gov/
Alternate URL(s)
http://www.greatlakes-seaway.com/
Sponsor(s): Transportation Department—Saint Lawrence Seaway Development Corporation (SLSDC)
Description: SLSDC works to ensure the safe transit of vessels through the two U.S. locks and navigation channels of the Saint Lawrence Seaway System. SLSDC works cooperatively with the Canadian Saint Lawrence Seaway Management Corporation, and many of the links on this site lead to a binational Web site run by both corporations (see the alternate URL listed above). The site includes press releases, Seaway Notices, and the toll schedule. Annual reports from 1997 onward are available under a separate heading.
Subject(s): Shipping
Publication(s): *Seaway Handbook*
SLSDC Newsletter

USCG Navigation Center

http://www.navcen.uscg.gov/
Sponsor(s): Homeland Security Department—Coast Guard
Description: The U.S. Coast Guard Navigation Center provides navigation services that promote safe transportation and support the commerce of the United States. The site features information on navigation rules, maritime telecommunications, global positioning systems (GPS), differential global positioning systems (DGPS), Local Notices to Mariners (LMNs), and the LORAN C service. The site also provides the *Light List*, a list of U.S. lights, sound signals, buoys, day beacons, and other aids to navigation.
Subject(s): Maritime Transportation
Publication(s): *Light List*, TD 5.9
Local Notice to Mariners, HS 7.19/6

MASS TRANSIT

Federal Transit Administration (FTA)

http://www.fta.dot.gov/
Sponsor(s): Transportation Department—Federal Transit Administration (FTA)
Description: FTA assists in the planning, development, and financing of public transportation. Its Web site provides information on transit planning, safety, and security programs. The site also has major sections on FTA grant programs, including Recovery Act information, and on research and technical assistance. The About FTA section has agency

budget and contracting information. The News section provides press releases, procurement news, congressional testimony, and administrator's policy letters. The site also provides transit laws and regulations, as well as regulatory guidance. The Publications section includes FTA reports to Congress, other publications, and a transit glossary.

Subject(s): Mass Transit; Transportation—Grants

Publication(s): *Annual Report on New Starts: Proposed Allocations of Funds for FY ...*, TD 7.1/2

Statistical Summaries: FTA Grant Assistance Programs, TD 7.2:G 76/2/

Status of the Nation's Highways, Bridges, and Transit, TD 2.30/5

National Transit Database

http://www.ntdprogram.gov/

Sponsor(s): Transportation Department—Federal Transit Administration (FTA)

Description: The National Transit Database is the Federal Transit Administration's primary national database for statistics on the transit industry. Information is available in spreadsheet and PDF formats and includes financial data, ridership counts, and safety reports. The data is intended for transit planning purposes and is also used in the formula allocations of federal transit funds.

Subject(s): Mass Transit—Statistics

Publication(s): *National Transit Database*, TD 7.11/2-2

SURFACE TRANSPORTATION

Amtrak

http://www.amtrak.com/

Sponsor(s): Amtrak (National Railroad Passenger Corporation)

Description: Passengers can use the Amtrak Web site to plan rail excursions, book trips, and check on train schedules. Main sections and tabs include Tickets, Timetables, Stations, and Routes. Amtrak, officially named the National Passenger Railroad Corporation, is a federally chartered for-profit public corporation. For information about its operations and finances, see the About Amtrak (with the employee newsletter *Amtrak Ink*) and News and Media sections, linked at the bottom of each page. The site is also available in Spanish, French, and German.

Subject(s): Amtrak; Railroads

Publication(s): *Amtrak Ink*

Central Federal Lands Highway Division

http://www.cflhd.gov/

Sponsor(s): Transportation Department—Federal Highway Administration (FHWA)

Description: The Federal Lands Highway Program administers highway programs in cooperation with other federal agencies and provides transportation engineering services for highways and bridges that are on (or provide access to) federally owned lands. The Central Federal Lands Highway Division has responsibility for most states west of the Mississippi River, excepting those in the far northwestern United States. Its jurisdiction also includes Hawaii and American Samoa. This site contains related information in its Projects, Programs, Contracting, Resources, and Employment sections. The Projects section lists projects by state and provides links to construction documents.

Subject(s): Highways and Roads; West (United States)

Eastern Federal Lands Highway Division (EFLHD)

http://www.efl.fhwa.dot.gov/

Sponsor(s): Transportation Department—Federal Highway Administration (FHWA)

Description: The Federal Lands Highway Program provides transportation engineering services for highways and bridges that are on (or provide access to) federally owned lands and administers highway programs in cooperation with other federal agencies. The Eastern Division serves 31 states east and immediately west of the Mississippi River, Puerto Rico, the District of Columbia, and the Virgin Islands. The site provides detailed information on current projects and public notices, planning, road design and technology, and contracts.

Subject(s): Highways and Roads

Federal Highway Administration (FHWA)

http://www.fhwa.dot.gov/

Sponsor(s): Transportation Department—Federal Highway Administration (FHWA)

Description: The FHWA Web site offers a wide range of information related to the nation's highways and roads. The home page highlights Recovery Act information, monthly traffic volume trends, and the Fast Lane blog from the secretary of transportation. Also highlighted are FHWA's Facebook page and YouTube channel. The site links to information about roads and bridges, highway funding, environment, road operations and congestion, road users (bicyclists, motorcycles), safety, international issues, and federal and Indian lands. Other major sections of the site cover legislation, regulations and regulatory guidance, statistics, publications, business opportunities, and news. The Briefing Room section displays press releases, speeches, and testimony.

Subject(s): Highways and Roads

Publication(s): *Highway Statistics* , TD 2.23

Status of the Nation's Highways, Bridges, and Transit, TD 2.30/5

Federal Railroad Administration (FRA)

http://www.fra.dot.gov/

Sponsor(s): Transportation Department—Federal Railroad Administration (FRA)

Description: FRA consolidates government support of railroad activities and provides regulation and research for improved railroad safety. The site includes sections for Railroad Safety, Rail Network Development, Research & Development, and Grants & Loans.

Subject(s): Railroad Safety; Railroads—Regulations

Highways for LIFE

http://www.fhwa.dot.gov/hfl/

Sponsor(s): Transportation Department—Federal Highway Administration (FHWA)

Description: Highways for LIFE is a Federal Highway Administration grant program for states to build "longer-lasting highway infrastructure using innovations to accomplish the fast construction of efficient and safe highways and bridges." (from the Web site) This site describes the program, projects, technology transfer, and funding opportunities.

Subject(s): Highways and Roads

Publication(s): *Innovator Newsletter*, TD 2.89

National Traffic and Road Closure Information

http://www.fhwa.dot.gov/trafficinfo/

Sponsor(s): Transportation Department—Federal Highway Administration (FHWA)

Description: This FHWA site centralizes access to government and commercial road condition and traffic information Web sites nationwide. It also links to each state's 511 travel conditions Web site and to sites reporting on weather and conditions.

Subject(s): Highways and Roads

Surface Transportation Board (STB)

http://www.stb.dot.gov/

Sponsor(s): Transportation Department—Surface Transportation Board (STB)

Description: STB is an independent adjudicatory body within the Department of Transportation. The board is responsible for the economic regulation of interstate surface transportation, primarily railroads. Its Web site features sections including Rail Consumers (shippers, receivers, rail car owners, and rail car manufacturers), Industry Data (economic and merger data), and Environmental Matters (regulations, cases, and correspondence). The site also has STB decisions and notices, transcripts and statements from STB hearings, and relevant correspondence.

Subject(s): Railroads

Publication(s): *Surface Transportation Board Reports: Decisions of the Surface Transportation Board*, TD 13.6/2

Vehicle Technologies Office
http://www.eere.energy.gov/vehiclesandfuels/
Sponsor(s): Energy Department—Energy Efficiency and Renewable Energy Office
Description: The Vehicle Technologies Office focuses on technologies for cleaner and more fuel-efficient cars and other road vehicles. The site describes technology developments related to hybrid vehicles, energy storage, power electronics, advanced combustion engines, fuels and lubricants, and materials technologies. The About the Vehicles Technology Office section provides organizational contacts and links to the national laboratories working on vehicle technologies. Grants are described in the Financial Opportunities section, and publications are listed in the News section.
Subject(s): Motor Vehicles—Research

Western Federal Lands Highway Division
http://www.wfl.fhwa.dot.gov/
Sponsor(s): Transportation Department—Federal Highway Administration (FHWA)
Description: The Federal Lands Highway Program administers highway programs in cooperation with other federal agencies and provides transportation engineering services for the highways and bridges that are on, or provide access to, federally owned lands. The Western Federal Lands Highway Division serves Oregon, Washington, Idaho, Montana, Alaska, and the Yellowstone and Grand Teton National Parks in Wyoming. This site has information on programs, projects, and contracting opportunities in the region.
Subject(s): Highways and Roads; West (United States)

TRANSPORTATION POLICY AND RESEARCH

Bureau of Transportation Statistics (BTS)
http://www.bts.gov/
Sponsor(s): Transportation Department—Research and Innovative Technology Administration (RITA)
Description: The BTS Web site is a central source for U.S. transportation data collected by BTS and other agencies. The home page features current news and data releases. The Data and Statistics section covers numerous areas, including airlines, border crossings, freight data, household commuting and travel, and bridge data. The BTS Publications section (under Library) links to many free, online statistical reports. The

External Links section (under Library) links to other government and private sources of statistics. Under Subject Areas, the site provides background information and reports on key areas such as congestion, connectivity, and safety.

A major portal to transportation statistics, TranStats, is in the Data and Statistics section of the BTS Web site. TranStats is described in a separate entry in this chapter.

Subject(s): Transportation—Statistics
Publication(s): *Air Carrier Traffic Statistics*, TD 12.15/5
Pocket Guide to Transportation, TD 12.8/2
Transportation Statistics Annual Report, TD 12.1
TranStats, TD 12.19

Center for Transportation Analysis

http://cta.ornl.gov/cta/

Sponsor(s): Energy Department—Oak Ridge National Laboratory (ORNL)

Description: CTA conducts research and development for many aspects of transportation. The Research Areas section on the CTA Web site includes subsections on Aviation Safety and Air Traffic Management Analysis, Defense Transportation, Energy and Environmental Policy Analysis, Intelligent Transportation Systems, and many other topics. The site also has a publications directory and an extensive list of links to related Web sites.

Subject(s): Energy Consumption—Research; Transportation—Research

Department of Transportation (DOT)

http://www.dot.gov/

Sponsor(s): Transportation Department

Description: DOT is concerned with the safety and efficiency of the nation's transportation systems. The DOT Web site home page links to its component agencies, including the Federal Aviation Administration, the Federal Transit Administration, Federal Railroad Administration, the Maritime Administration, and others. The home page highlights popular search topics, such as DOT numbers for motor carriers, airline complaints, trucking company complaints, and car safety information. As with other departments, DOT provides an online section with Recovery Act information.

The home page of the DOT site provides quick access to major issues and to its component agencies.

Subject(s): Transportation

Intelligent Transportation Systems (ITS)

http://www.its.dot.gov

Sponsor(s): Transportation Department—Research and Innovative Technology Administration (RITA)

Description: According to the Web site, "The U.S. Department of Transportation's (U.S. DOT) Intelligent Transportation Systems (ITS) Program aims to bring connectivity to transportation through the application of advanced wireless technologies—powerful technologies that enable transformative change." The ITS Web site also discusses the specific role of its Joint Program Office, which coordinates ITS initiative with other Transportation Department offices, such as the Federal Highway Administration and the Federal Transit Administration. The ITS Web site provides information about the office's research and projects. The Press Room section contains news and information about public meetings and events.

Subject(s): Transportation Policy and Research

John A. Volpe National Transportation Center

http://www.volpe.dot.gov/

Sponsor(s): Transportation Department

Description: The John A. Volpe National Transportation Systems Center conducts research and development, engineering, and analysis on transportation and logistics topics. The center's expertise includes environmental issues, safety engineering, noise and vibration, and Global Positioning Systems (GPS). The Information Resources section includes reports, technical papers, and articles published by Volpe Center staff. The Volpe Center receives no federal appropriations and works on a fee-for-service basis. Its site also has information about doing business with the center for clients and for vendors.

Subject(s): Engineering Research; Transportation—Research

Publication(s): *Volpe Highlights*, TD 10.15/2

Office of Research, Development & Technology (RDT)

http://www.rita.dot.gov/rdt/

Sponsor(s): Transportation Department—Research and Innovative Technology Administration (RITA)

Description: RDT is responsible for hosting and moderating the collaboration between the Transportation Department's research clusters, awarding and overseeing grant administration, and coordinating the department's research, development activities, and investments. The site provides links to current research topics and maps of research facilities, including those involved in alternative fuel, hydrogen, remote sensing, and cold region rural transportation research. The University Transportation Centers section links to lists of national and regional centers and related news and publications.

Subject(s): Transportation Policy and Research

Research and Innovative Technology Administration (RITA)

http://www.rita.dot.gov/

Sponsor(s): Transportation Department—Research and Innovative Technology Administration (RITA)

Description: RITA is charged with coordinating Department of Transportation research programs and advancing the use of innovative transportation technologies. Its Web site includes links to RITA's component offices, such as the Bureau of Transportation Statistics, the Transportation Safety Institute, and Intelligent Transportation Systems.

Subject(s): Transportation—Research

Transportation and Climate Change Clearinghouse

http://climate.dot.gov/

Sponsor(s): Transportation Department—Center for Climate Change and Environmental Forecasting

Description: This clearinghouse Web site provides access to reports and information on the relationship between transportation practices—particularly greenhouse gas emissions—and climate change. Reports are from state and federal government, international organizations, and the private sector.

Subject(s): Greenhouse Gases; Transportation—Research; Climate Change

TranStats

http://www.transtats.bts.gov/

Sponsor(s): Transportation Department—Bureau of Transportation Statistics (BTS)

Description: TranStats offers organized access to over 100 transportation-related databases, as well as the social and demographic data sets commonly used in transportation analysis. The data comes from federal agencies and several transportation-related organizations. The data sets are packaged with basic documentation. The TranStats Web site offers downloading in comma-separated file format and provides some interactive mapping applications. Transportation modes covered by the data sets include aviation, highway, mass transit, rail, bike/pedestrian, pipeline, and others. The site also has a schedule of upcoming data releases.

Subject(s): Transportation—Statistics; Databases

Publication(s): *Directory of Transportation Data Sources*, TD 1.9/4:

TRANSPORTATION SAFETY

ATVSafety.gov

http://www.atvsafety.gov/

Sponsor(s): Consumer Product Safety Commission (CPSC)

Description: This site provides safety tips for using all-terrain vehicles (ATVs). It has national and state injury statistics and information on state laws regarding ATVs.

Subject(s): Vehicle Safety

Distracted Driving

http://www.distraction.gov/

Sponsor(s): Transportation Department—National Highway Traffic Safety Administration (NHTSA)

Description: This site is part of a safety campaign warning against visual, manual, and cognitive distractions for drivers, particularly the use of handheld electronic devices while driving. The site provides information on relevant state laws, research, and Department of Transportation initiatives.

Subject(s): Traffic Safety

FARS Encyclopedia

http://www-fars.nhtsa.dot.gov/

Sponsor(s): Transportation Department—National Highway Traffic Safety Administration (NHTSA)

Description: The FARS Encyclopedia presents data from the Fatality Analysis Reporting System (FARS). FARS collects data on all vehicle crashes in the United States that occur on a public roadway and involve a fatality. The Web site provides statistics from 1994 to the most current year available, including state-by-state statistics and maps.

Subject(s): Accidents (Motor Vehicles)—Statistics

Federal Motor Carrier Safety Administration (FMCSA)

http://www.fmcsa.dot.gov/

Sponsor(s): Transportation Department—Federal Motor Carrier Safety Administration

Description: FMCSA's mission is to "educe crashes, injuries and fatalities involving large trucks and buses." (from the Web site) For regulated carriers, the site has online registration for USDOT Numbers, Operating Authority, and Registration Requirements. The Safety section has company safety records and information on cargo securement and hazardous material security. The Data and Statistics subsection has a variety of motor carrier safety statistics, including a table relating the costs of accidents, and a schedule of free webinars.

Subject(s): Trucking; Transportation Safety

FHWA Safety Program

http://safety.fhwa.dot.gov/

Sponsor(s): Transportation Department—Federal Highway Administration (FHWA)

Description: FHWA's Office of Safety focuses on highway engineering to promote road safety. The Web site covers road design research and other topics, such as public education, accident statistics, laws and guidelines, and safety technologies. Special sections discuss the safety of pedestrians, bicyclists, older drivers, intersections, and routes to school. The site also links to resources for states and localities.

Subject(s): Accidents (Motor Vehicles); Highways and Roads; Safety

Publication(s): *Pedestrian Forum Newsletter*, TD 2.2:P 34/

National Highway Traffic Safety Administration (NHTSA)

http://www.nhtsa.dot.gov/

Sponsor(s): Transportation Department—National Highway Traffic Safety Administration (NHTSA)

Description: NHTSA sets and enforces safety performance standards for motor vehicles and assists state and local governments with grants for local highway safety programs. The NHTSA Web site has information about product recalls, crash test results, consumer complaints, technical service bulletins, and defects investigations for cars, child seats, tires, and auto equipment. There are car and tire safety tips, as well as regulatory information on such topics as fuel economy, child seats, safety standards, and air bags. The Driving Safety section covers topics such as distracted driving, driver education, impaired driving, child passengers, school buses, and pedestrian and bicycle safety. The NHTSA site also includes extensive data related to traffic safety.

This site offers a substantial collection of information about the government's testing of vehicles and its auto safety ratings and makes it accessible for consumers. The site also brings together grants, regulatory, and state and national legislative information concerning motor vehicle standards and traffic safety.

Subject(s): Motor Vehicles—Regulations; Traffic Safety; Vehicle Safety

Publication(s): *Traffic Techs*, TD 8.63

National Transportation Safety Board (NTSB)

http://www.ntsb.gov/

Sponsor(s): National Transportation Safety Board (NTSB)

Description: The NTSB Web site features information about its programs and the primary areas of safety in which the NTSB works. These programs include aviation, highway, marine, railroad, pipeline, and hazardous materials. The News & Events section includes documents from recent major investigations and information about board meetings and public hearings. The Safety Advocacy section provides the most wanted list, safety alerts, safety recommendations, and safety studies. The Disaster Assistance section explains the role of NTSB in coordinating responses from federal, state, and local governments and the airlines to meet the needs of disaster victims and their families.

Subject(s): Accidents (Motor Vehicles)—Statistics; Safety; Transportation

Publication(s): *Aviation Accident Reports,* TD 1.112
Hazardous Materials Accident Briefs, TD 1.128/2
Hazardous Materials Accident Reports, TD 1.129
Highway Accident Briefs, NTSB-HAB (series), TD 1.117/2
Highway Accident Reports, TD 1.117
Marine Accident Reports, TD 1.116
Pipeline Accident Briefs, NTSB-PAB (series), TD 1.118/3
Pipeline Accident Reports, TD 1.118
Railroad Accident Briefs, NTSB-RAB (series), TD 1.112/5
Railroad Accident Reports, TD 1.112/3

NHTSA Child Passenger Safety (CPS)

http://www.nhtsa.gov/Safety/CPS

Sponsor(s): Transportation Department—National Highway Traffic Safety Administration (NHTSA)

Description: This Web site promotes public awareness of the value of using proper car safety seats for children. The site provides a guide to help choose the right seat for the child's size and information about reporting a child seat or vehicle defect.

Subject(s): Child Health and Safety

Pipeline and Hazardous Materials Safety Administration (PHMSA)

http://www.phmsa.dot.gov/

Sponsor(s): Transportation Department—Pipeline and Hazardous Materials Safety Administration (PHMSA)

Description: PHMSA is responsible for the safe and secure movement of hazardous materials shipments by all modes of transportation, including through pipeline infrastructure. The Pipeline Safety section includes information on compliance and enforcement, safety training, data and statistics, and more.

Subject(s): Toxic Substances; Transportation Safety

SaferCar.gov

http://www.safercar.gov/

Sponsor(s): Transportation Department—National Highway Traffic Safety Administration (NHTSA)

Description: SaferCar.gov provides information about vehicle safety for drivers and car shoppers. Topics covered include tires, air bags, and rollover prevention. Also listed is information about the government's "5-star safety ratings." It also has information about reported defects and recalls and a child seat safety inspection locator, searchable by state and ZIP code.

Subject(s): Motor Vehicles

Transportation Safety Institute

http://www.tsi.dot.gov/

Sponsor(s): Transportation Department—Research and Innovative Technology Administration (RITA)

Description: The Transportation Safety Institute is a self-funding federal agency that provides safety and security training to both the public and private sectors. The institute provides training related to mass transit, aviation, multi-modal safety, and traffic safety. Its Web site provides a course catalog and detailed information about each of its program areas.

Subject(s): Transportation Security; Transportation Safety

TSA Blog

http://blog.tsa.gov/

Sponsor(s): Homeland Security Department—Transportation Security Administration (TSA)

Description: The TSA uses its blog "to communicate with the public about all things TSA related." (from the Web site) Bloggers are TSA employees. Comments are encouraged.

Subject(s): Homeland Security; Blogs

USCG Boating Safety Resource Center

http://www.uscgboating.org/

Sponsor(s): Homeland Security Department—Coast Guard

Description: This Web site, provided by the Coast Guard, is a resource for boaters and those who keep the waterways safe. Links are provided for reporting boating accidents and for navigation rules. The Recalls and Safety Defects section links to tools for reporting defects in boating products and notices of recalls. Boating laws can be found under the Regulations section. The NBSAC section provides information about joining the National Boating Safety Advisory Council, as well as a link to the Homeport Web site. The Statistics section presents information on such topics as accident rates and the prevalence of life jackets and their use.

Subject(s): Boating Safety

TWENTY-ONE

Beyond the Federal Web—Nongovernmental Web Sites

While the preceding chapters have provided information about government Internet sites, this final chapter takes a look at related, but no less valuable, sources that come from non-federal sources. These resources cover a wide range of topics—in fact, their scope mirrors that of all of the preceding chapters—and come from a multitude of different types of organizations. The common thread between these sites is their relevance to the subjects published by the federal agencies.

Sources for the Web sites include nongovernmental organizations, advocacy organizations and "think tanks," social welfare and justice organizations, multinational and binational initiatives, science and technology cooperatives, and international organizations.

Africa Fighting Malaria
http://www.fightingmalaria.org/#
Sponsor(s): Africa Fighting Malaria
Description: ALM, founded in 2000, works to increase the efficiency and effectiveness of malaria treatment. The What We Do section contains editorials, papers, and testimony, while the Initiatives section has information about malarial countries and donor programs.
Subject(s): Malaria

American Aging Association
http://www.americanagingassociation.org/
Sponsor(s): American Aging Association
Description: According to the Web site, "The American Aging Association is a group of experts dedicated to understanding the basic mechanisms of aging and the development of interventions in age-related dis-

ease to increase healthy lifespan for all." This site has information about the association's history and initiatives. It also provides access to the association's journal, *AGE: Journal of the American Aging Association*.

Subject(s): Senior citizens

Publication(s): *AGE: Journal of the American Aging Association*

American Association of Retired People (AARP)

http://www.aarp.org/

Sponsor(s): American Association of Retired People (AARP)

Description: AARP was established to help older Americans (age 50 and above) improve their quality of life. The home page features a long list of links with information about such subjects as caregiving, job hunting, Social Security and Medicare, and AARP discounts. News, videos, and opinion pieces are also accessible from the home page. Sections toward the top of the page break down the subjects even further, with links for Health, Work & Retirement, Money, Home & Family, Entertainment, Food, Travel, Politics, and Games. Links at the top of the page lead to *AARP The Magazine* and the *AARP Bulletin*.

Subject(s): Senior citizens

Publication(s): *AARP The Magazine*

AARP Bulletin

American Bar Association

http://www.americanbar.org/aba.html

Sponsor(s): American Bar Association

Description: The ABA has nearly 400,000 members nationwide. Its Web site includes information about the association, information about membership, and other resources for lawyers. The Advocacy section has information about ABA's policy initiatives and its governmental and legislative work. Amicus curiae briefs are also available in this section.

Subject(s): Law and legal information

American Civil Liberties Union (ACLU)

http://www.aclu.org/

Sponsor(s): American Civil Liberties Union (ACLU)

Description: Much of the ACLU Web site's information can be found right on its home page. Recent news stories and blog postings are highlighted, while toward the bottom of the page, topic sections for issues such as capital punishment, free speech, human rights, HIV/AIDS, racial justice, and religion and belief each provide multiple links to related content. A drop-down menu is available to help users find issues of interest.

Subject(s): Civil rights

American Heart Association

http://www.heart.org/HEARTORG/

Sponsor(s): American Heart Association

Description: The home page of the American Heart Association's Web site provides insight into its initiatives and programs, with a tabbed menu for new topics, most searched topics, and most popular topics. Also included are an online "Heart and Stroke Encyclopedia" reference tool, as well as a section for the warning signs of these diseases. Sections for educators and caregivers can be found toward the top of the page. The Healthcare/Research section has membership information and documents for health care professionals.

Subject(s): Health promotion; Heart disease

American Lung Association

http://www.lung.org/

Sponsor(s): American Lung Association

Description: This Web site, subtitled "Fighting for Air," contains informative sections about lungs and lung disease. Under Your Lungs, users can find anatomical information and warning signs of lung disease. The section also discusses lung issues in the context of the Affordable Care Act. The Healthy Air section discusses the subject in the contexts of schools, homes, workplaces, and the outdoors.

Subject(s): Air Quality; Diseases and Conditions

American Medical Association

http://www.ama-assn.org/ama

Sponsor(s): American Medical Association

Description: According to the Web site, AMA's mission is "to promote the art and science of medicine and the betterment of public health." The Resources section provides links to information about such topics as continuing medical education, medical ethics, the Physician Consortium for Performance Improvement, legal issues, and health information technology. In this section, resources are also organized for audiences, including patients, physicians, residents, and medical students. Newsletters and events can be found in the Advocacy section. A link to the JAMA Network, which is described in a separate entry, can be found in the Publications section.

The Education section contains a multitude of information for students on such topics as careers in health care, becoming a physician, and finding a position.

Subject(s): Health and Safety; Health Care; Public Health

American Psychiatric Association

http://www.psych.org/

Sponsor(s): American Psychiatric Association

Description: The American Psychiatric Association, comprising more than 33,000 psychiatrists worldwide, is the largest organization of its kind in the world. The Web site has sections for Physicians, Residents, Medical Students, Public, and Researchers. The Mental Health section has a drop-down menu for finding further information on psychiatric topics and people in psychiatry. The Advocacy & Newsroom section has links to news, videos, and position statements.

Subject(s): Psychiatry

American Red Cross

http://www.redcross.org/

Sponsor(s): American Red Cross

Description: The American Red Cross's Web site contains extensive information about its initiatives and activities. Under What We Do, the site links to sections for disaster relief, supporting military families, health and safety training and education, and the lifesaving benefits of blood. The News & Events section has a calendar of events, local and national Twitter feeds, Facebook postings, and recent press releases. The home page has direct links for donating blood, obtaining assistance, and volunteering.

Subject(s): Disaster Assistance; Health and Safety

Amnesty International

http://www.amnestyusa.org/

Sponsor(s): Amnesty International

Description: Amnesty International is an organization that works to assert human rights throughout the global community. The Our Work section has information about the organization's issues and campaigns, countries in which it works, and cases and victories. Under About Us, two initiatives are featured: advocacy for the Arms Trade Treaty and its analysis of the human rights situation in Aleppo, Syria. The home page includes links to Amnesty International's Facebook and Twitter pages, as well as its blog. The site is available in Spanish.

Subject(s): Human Rights

Anti-Defamation League

http://www.adl.org/

Sponsor(s): Anti-Defamation League

Description: As stated on the Web site, "fights anti-Semitism and all forms of bigotry, defends democratic ideals and protects civil rights for all." The home page provides links to the league's social media pages.

The Combating Hate section offers the "Responding to Hate: A Toolkit for Action." The league's centennial occurred in 2013.

Subject(s): Civil Rights; Anti-defamation

Asia-Pacific Economic Cooperation

http://www.apec.org/

Sponsor(s): Asia-Pacific Economic Cooperation

Description: APEC is an international forum promoting open trade and economic cooperation. Established in 1989 in response to the growing interdependence among Asia-Pacific economies, its members are located in the Pacific Rim and include the United States. The Web site provides links to relevant topics and publications. Its Topics section links to APEC's work in specific fields, such as agriculture, health, and trade facilitation.

Subject(s): Military Training and Education; Asia—Policy; Defense Research

Association of Southeast Asian Nations (ASEAN)

http://www.asean.org/

Description: Association of Southeast Asian Nations (ASEAN)

ASEAN was established in 1967, and its member states currently include Brunei, Cambodia, Indonesia, Laos, Malaysia, Myanmar (Burma), The Philippines, Singapore, Thailand, and Vietnam. Under ASEAN Member States, the Web site provides country information and links to each one's relevant international ministry or office. The Resources section provides users with access to relevant ASEAN and ASEAN-related statistics, publications, and speeches. The Calendar section lists public holidays and official meetings.

Subject(s): International Economic Relations

Publication(s): *ASEAN Human Rights Declaration—AHRD*

Association of Universities for Research in Astronomy, Inc.

http://www.aura-astronomy.org/

Sponsor(s): Association of Universities for Research in Astronomy, Inc.

Description: AURA is comprised of 40 national institutions and four international entities. The organization's mission, according to the Web site, is " to establish, nurture, and promote public observatories and facilities that advance innovative astronomical research." Its home page features links to major initiatives, such as the James Webb Space Telescope, as well as community projects, such as the NSF Science Folio Review. AURA's facilities include the Gemini Observatory, the Large Synoptic Survey Telescope (LSST), the National Optical Astronomical Observatory

(NOAO), the National Solar Observatory (NSO), and the Space Telescope Science Institute (STScI), which are all also described in this publication.
Subject(s): Astronomy; Space

CARE International
http://www.care-international.org/
Sponsor(s): CARE International
Description: CARE's member countries have helped the organization work to fight poverty in 90 countries around the world. In addition to participating in relief during emergencies such as conflict or natural disasters, CARE works on the following issues: agriculture and natural resources, climate change, education, health, HIV/AIDS, nutrition, economic development, and water, sanitation, and environmental health. More information about the topics can be found in the CARE's Work section. Media releases and featured articles can be found in the News section. The United States' country-specific CARE Web site can be accessed at http://www.care.org/.
Subject(s): Poverty

Center for International Trade & Security
http://cits.uga.edu/
Sponsor(s): University of Georgia
Description: This University of Georgia facility's mission is to research issues related to trade technologies and security. Its home page links to a list of current issues of interest and news, with a featured article on the Arms Trade Treaty, which was signed by the United Nations General Assembly in April 2013. A Student Opportunities section links to application materials for the center's programs.
Subject(s): Security

Center for Restorative Justice and Peacemaking
http://www.cehd.umn.edu/ssw/rjp/
Sponsor(s): University of Minnesota
Description: The Center for Restorative Justice & Peacemaking's mission, according to the Web site, is "to provide supports and resources to program leaders, practitioners, and workshop participants so they can maintain and strengthen restorative dialogue on all levels. To do this in a comprehensive way, our center does a variety of activities and services." The center's Community Peacemaking Project combats hate crimes and political intolerance, and it has also partnered on similar issues with Northern Ireland's Seeds of Hope organization. The Web site contains information about the center's initiatives and training programs.
Subject(s): Peace; Crime Prevention

Commission on Security and Cooperation in Europe (CSCE)

http://www.csce.gov/

Description: Commission on Security and Cooperation in Europe (CSCE)

CSCE, better known as the U.S. Helsinki Commission, is an independent government agency created by Congress. It monitors and encourages compliance with the Helsinki Accords/Final Act and other commitments of the countries participating in the Organisation for Security and Co-operation in Europe (OSCE). The commission's Web site includes information about the CSCE and OSCE and the full texts of the commission's press releases, hearings, briefings, and statements.

Subject(s): Human rights

Congressional Quarterly Roll Call

http://corporate.cqrollcall.com/

Sponsor(s): Economist Group

Description: CQ Roll Call is a subscription-based service that provides users with legislation and policy tracking. Major sections include News, Analysis & Schedules; Legislation; and Advocacy & Engagement Solutions. Related products, including *CQ Weekly* and subscriptions to the congressionally oriented *Roll Call* newspaper, which is described in a separate entry, are available for purchase.

Subject(s): News Services
Publication(s): *CQ Weekly*

Corporation for Public Broadcasting (CPB)

http://www.cpb.org/

Sponsor(s): Corporation for Public Broadcasting (CPB)

Description: CPB is a private, nonprofit corporation that was created by Congress in 1967. It receives partial funding through annual congressional appropriations and, in turn, funds public television and radio programming. The About CPB section of this Web site includes leadership profiles, CPB's annual reports, and financial information. The Programs & Projects section has a directory of CPB-funded programs for television, radio, and the Web.

Subject(s): Broadcasting

Democratic Congressional Campaign Committee (DCCC)

http://dccc.org/

Sponsor(s): Democratic Congressional Campaign Committee (DCCC)

Description: The DCCC Web site's home page features links to the committee's blog, video clips, and related news. Information about

registering to vote can be found under the Action Center link. The home page provides links to the DCCC's social media pages and mobile site.
Subject(s): Political Parties

Democratic Senatorial Campaign Committee (DSCC)
http://www.dscc.org/
Sponsor(s): Democratic Senatorial Campaign Committee (DSCC)
Description: The DSCC Web site features news, recent Tweets, and a race tracker (for election season). A map on the home page provides information on campaigns for the 2016 elections. Job and internship information can be found in the About section. The site also links to the DSCC's social media pages.
Subject(s): Political Parties

Doctors Without Borders/Médecins Sans Frontières
http://www.doctorswithoutborders.org/
Sponsor(s): Doctors Without Borders/Médecins Sans Frontières
Description: Doctors Without Borders/Médecins Sans Frontières has a presence in more than 60 countries, where they provide medical relief to regions facing issues such as epidemics, armed conflicts, malnutrition, natural disasters, and lack of access to health care. Stories from the field and aid worker blogs can be found in the Our Work section. Another section discusses working with the organization. The News & Stories section contains research articles, opinions, and reports.
Subject(s): Medicine; Physicians

Export-Import Bank of the United States
http://www.exim.gov/
Sponsor(s): Export-Import Bank of the United States
Description: The Export-Import Bank offers export financing for U.S. businesses. The Products section of its Web site provides information about the bank's working capital financing, export credit insurance, loan guarantees, and direct loans. Application forms and instructions on applying are included with the information. The site also features sections for specific audiences, including small businesses.
Subject(s): Finance; International Trade

Federation of American Scientists (FAS)
https://www.fas.org/
Sponsor(s): Federation of American Scientists (FAS)
Description: FAS is a private, nonprofit group concerned with public policy. While this Web site is not an official government source of information, the collection is valuable for the ease of access it provides to these documents. Featured issue areas include biosecurity, Earth systems, government secrecy, and nuclear information. The Policy Action section

provides links to FAS's social media pages, video clips, and an e-mail signup for news releases.

FAS sponsors a Presidential Directives and Executive Orders page that is described elsewhere in this publication. This page, which can be found at http://www.fas.org/irp/offdocs/direct.htm, contains related documents from the Truman administration through the Obama administration.

Subject(s): Presidential Documents; Security

G8 Information Centre
  http://www.g8.utoronto.ca/
  Sponsor(s): University of Toronto
  Description: This site organizes and provides access to materials and sites related to the G8, its summits, and other meetings. The G8 refers to a group of eight major market-oriented democracies. The site's home page features recent news and social media posts (from sites such as Twitter), as well as links to frequently asked questions, such as "What is the G8?" Links to its sponsoring institutions and to publications can be found toward the bottom of the home page. Publications offered include governance working papers and the Ashgate Series. The home page also offers resources for teaching.
  Subject(s): International Economic Relations
  Publication(s): *Ashgate Series*

Gemini Observatory
  http://gemini.edu/
  Sponsor(s): Association of Universities for Research in Astronomy, Inc.
  Description: The Gemini Observatory consists of twin telescopes located in Hawaii and Chile. The observatory is the creation of a six-country partnership, including the United States, Canada, Chile, Australia, Brazil, and Argentina. A Science section provides more information about Gemini's technology, science, operation, and data. Under Public/Images, access is provided to podcasts, education and outreach materials, and an image gallery.
  Subject(s): Astronomy; Telescopes
  Publication(s): *Gemini Focus*

Habitat for Humanity® International
  http://www.habitat.org/
  Sponsor(s): Habitat for Humanity® International
  Description: Habitat for Humanity is dedicated to providing low-income families worldwide with safe and affordable housing by either building or renovating dwellings. Habitat trains volunteers and the prospective homeowner families to assist in the building and renovation

tasks. Under Where We Build, Web site users can find a map and directory of Habitat sites by region. The Stories & Multimedia section links to the organization's blog and to Habitat World magazine.

Subject(s): Housing; Housing Subsidies
Publication(s): *Habitat World*

Hague Conference on Private International Law (HCCH)

http://www.hcch.net/index_en.php
Sponsor(s): Hague Conference on Private International Law (HCCH)
Description: HCCH, which consists of 78 members (77 countries and the European Union), works to develop means of unifying countries in the context of private international law. One of its major functions is to have its Conventions ratified and enacted. HCCH adopted 38 Conventions between 1951 and 2008. The United States ratified the Hague Convention on Intercountry Adoptions in 2007. The Web site's FAQ section presents a wealth of introductory information on topics ranging from "What is a Special Commission of the Hague Conference?" to "How does a State become a Member of the Hague Conference?" The site is available in 24 languages, including French, Spanish, Polish, and Dutch.

Subject(s): International Law

Homeland Security Studies & Analysis Institute

http://www.homelandsecurity.org/
Sponsor(s): Analytic Services, Inc.
Description: The Homeland Security Studies & Analysis Institute, a FFDRC (federally funded research and development center) operated on behalf of the Department of Defense, is concerned with the following areas: Counterterrorism, Borders, and Immigration; Resilience and Emergency Preparedness/Response; and Departmental Integration/Unification. The News & Resources section has publications, news articles, and a spotlight for current projects. The home pages includes an events schedule, a call for paper submissions, and the organization's most recent tweets.

Subject(s): Homeland Security

Humane Society of the United States

http://www.humanesociety.org/
Sponsor(s): Humane Society of the United States
Description: Animal welfare is the focus of the Humane Society, and this site has a plethora of information about its activities. The home page includes top news stories and feeds from the Humane Society's Facebook and Twitter pages. A drop-down menu on the home page allows users to learn facts about specific animals and adoption. The Animals section includes information about pets and wild animals, as well as information

about animal care. The Magazines section includes links to publications including *All Animals* and *Animal Sheltering*.

Subject(s): Animals
Publication(s): *All Animals*

Inter-American Development Bank

http://www.iadb.org/

Sponsor(s): Inter-American Development Bank (IDB)

Description: The Inter-American Development Bank was established to help accelerate economic and social development in Latin America and the Caribbean. Its Web site features categories including Doing Business, Accountability, Our Organization, and Resources. Under Data, the site offers searchable statistics and indicators for Latin American and Caribbean countries. The Publications section includes technical notes, working papers, and policy briefs. The site has a Spanish-language version.

Subject(s): International Economic Development; South America; Caribbean

International Bureau of Education (IBE)

http://www.ibe.unesco.org/

Sponsor(s): United Nations—United Nations Educational, Scientific, and Cultural Organization (UNESCO)

Description: IBE is a UNESCO center for information and research in the field of education, focusing currently on the management of curricula change for the 21st century. This Web site features sections including Themes, Areas of Action, and Services. The site is available in Spanish, French, and other languages.

Subject(s): Education Research—International

International Criminal Court (ICC)

http://www.icc-cpi.int/EN_Menus/icc/Pages/default.aspx

Sponsor(s): International Criminal Court (ICC)

Description: According to the Web site, ICC is "the first permanent, treaty based, international criminal court established to help end impunity for the perpetrators of the most serious crimes of concern to the international community." Its seat is at The Hague in The Netherlands. The Situations and Cases section breaks down the court's cases by country.

Subject(s): International Crimes; International Law

International Governmental Organizations

http://www.library.northwestern.edu/govpub/resource/internat/igo.html

Sponsor(s): Northwestern University

Description: According to the Web site, "This unit has been a federal depository library for more than a century and features such materials as Congressional reports and hearing transcripts, census information, statistics and studies generated by federal agencies, and presidential papers." Items in the collection include publications and documents from the European Union, international organizations such as IMF, and maps from such agencies as NOAA and USGS. Not all materials are available in the online catalog.

Subject(s): Finding Aids; International Organizations

International Monetary Fund (IMF)

http://www.imf.org/

Sponsor(s): International Monetary Fund (IMF)

Description: IMF is an international organization established to promote international monetary cooperation, exchange stability, and economic growth. Its Web site features sections such as About the IMF, News, Data, Publications, Research, and Countries. The Publications page provides search and browse access to IMF print and online publications. A fair number of publications are accessible online. The Research tab links users to a variety of indicators and reports. Available material includes the World Economic Outlook (WEO) Reports, Global Financial Stability Reports (GFSR), and WEO Databases. The Country Info section arranges publications and reports by country. Also in this section, the IMF Data Mapper ® comprises a clickable, interactive map that displays the findings of IMF Datasets.

Subject(s): International Economic Relations; Monetary Policy—International

Publication(s): *World Economic Outlook (WEO) Reports*
Global Financial Stability Reports (GFSR)

JAMA Network

http://jamanetwork.com/public/about.aspx

Sponsor(s): American Medical Association

Description: The JAMA (Journal of the American Medical Association) Network, a subscription-based service, provides search tools for finding videos, articles, and other journal products. A mobile version is available.

Subject(s): Health and Safety; News Services

James Martin Center for Nonproliferation Studies (CNS)

http://cns.miis.edu/index.htm

Sponsor(s): Middlebury College

Description: CNS's research focuses on weapons of mass destruction (WPD) and the training of individuals to prevent their dissemination. The Publications section includes the center's *Nonproliferation Review* and

WMD Junction products. The Students section provides information about obtaining a master's degree and about internships, while the Programs section has links to such components as the Chemical and Biological Weapons Nonproliferation Program (CBWNP) and the East Asia Nonproliferation Program (EANP).

Subject(s): Arms Control; Nonproliferation; Trade Laws and Regulations; Weapons of Mass Destruction

Publication(s): *Nonproliferation Review*

WMD Junction

Large Synoptic Survey Telescope (LSST)

http://www.lsst.org/lsst/

Sponsor(s): LSST Corporation

Description: The LSST, subtitled on the Web site as "the widest, fastest, deepest eye of the new digital age," uses a three-billion pixel digital camera to study objects such as near-Earth asteroids. Information sections on the site include areas for the public and for scientists. A Gallery section provides both photos and videos, and an FAQ section answers questions about the technology for the public. This section also has a link to a scientist FAQ.

Subject(s): Astronomy; Telescopes

League of Conservation Voters (LCV)

http://www.lcv.org/

Sponsor(s): League of Conservation Voters (LCV)

Description: According to the Web site, "LCV works to turn environmental values into national, state and local priorities. LCV, in collaboration with [its] state LCV partners, advocates for sound environmental laws and policies, holds elected officials accountable for their votes and actions, and elects pro-environment candidates who will champion our priority issues." Information about its initiatives is broken down by topic in the Issues section, with sections ranging from hardrock mining to toxic chemicals. A States section has local contact information.

Subject(s): Conservation (Natural Resources); Environmental Protection

Millennium Challenge Corporation (MCC)

http://www.mcc.gov/

Sponsor(s): Millennium Challenge Corporation

Description: MCC, a government corporation, works with countries to promote sustainable economic growth and reduce poverty through investments in areas such as agriculture, education, and private sector development. Countries are selected to receive aid based on their performance in governing justly, investing in their citizens, and encouraging economic freedom. The Web site provides information on MCC, its leadership, selection criteria, country activities, and business and procurement.

Subject(s): International Economic Development

Mothers Against Drunk Driving

http://www.madd.org/

Sponsor(s): Mothers Against Drunk Driving

Description: MADD, formed to combat drunk driving and underage drinking, provides a wealth of information on its site. The home page links to its social media profiles and provides information about its initiatives, such as Walk Like MADD and the Victim/Survivor Tributes. Under Victim Services, users can find information about victims' compensation and funding, links to other victims, and *MADDvocate Magazine*. The Get Involved section describes how users can donate, volunteer, and find a local chapter of MADD.

Subject(s): Alcohol Abuse

Publication(s): *MADDvocate Magazine*

National American Indian Court Judges Association (NAICJA)

http://www.naicja.org/

Sponsor(s): National American Indian Court Judges Association (NAICJA)

Description: NAICJA, founded in 1969, was established to help strengthen the tribal justice system. The organization's focus includes education about tribal justice, national advocacy, providing networking and membership opportunities, and improving cooperation between the state, federal, and tribal judicial systems. The Web site has information about membership, training, and events, as well as links to NAICJA's Facebook and YouTube accounts.

Subject(s): Judicial System; Tribal Governments

National Association for the Advancement of Colored People (NAACP)

http://www.naacp.org/

Sponsor(s): National Association for the Advancement of Colored People (NAACP)

Description: NAACP, which celebrated its centennial in 2009, was founded in order to fight racial discrimination. Its Web site has a plethora of information about its causes and programs. Under Advocacy & Issues, users can find information on topics such as civic engagement, climate justice, and media diversity. A richly detailed History section provides users with background on the association. Publications, financial reports, legal dockets, and amicus briefs can be found under Resources. A menu on the right-hand side of the home page allows users to look up their local NAACP chapters. The menu below links to NAACP's social media pages.

Subject(s): Civil Rights

National Center for Missing and Exploited Children (NCMEC)

http://www.missingkids.com

Sponsor(s): National Center for Missing and Exploited Children (NCMEC)

Description: Founded in 1984, NCMEC serves as a clearinghouse of information on missing children and child exploitation. The top of the home page has a link to active AMBER Alerts (described in a separate entry). Under How You Can Help, information about a 24-hour hotline is provided for users to report a missing child or a case of possible child exploitation. RSS feeds and an eNews signup can be found in the Stay Informed section.

Subject(s): Child Abuse; Children

National Center for Victims of Crime (NCVC)

http://www.victimsofcrime.org/

Sponsor(s): National Center for Victims of Crime

Description: NCVC works to advocate for the rights and protections of crime victims and to supply them with information, services, and advocacy. Its mission also encompasses related education and training. The NCVC Web site provides information on the center's programs and initiatives. Under Help for Crime Victims, national hotlines, information on coping with trauma and grief, and a local assistance directory are provided. The Library section contains publications and relevant statistics.

Subject(s): Victims of Crime

National Indian Justice Center (NIJC)

http://www.nijc.org/

Sponsor(s): National Indian Justice Center (NIJC)

Description: NJIC was established "in order to establish an independent national resource for Native communities and tribal government." (from the Web site) The Projects/Surveys section provides links to current initiatives, such as Communities Empowering Native Youth and the Tribal Traffic Safety Justice Liaison Project. Training manuals and videos are available in the Publications section, and the Resources section links to outside organizations that might be of interest to users, including the California Indian Museum and the Native American Bar Association.

Subject(s): Judicial System; Tribal Governments

National Journal

http://www.nationaljournal.com/

Sponsor(s): National Journal Group, Inc.

Description: The *National Journal* is a publication focused on politics and policy. Its Web site offers sections for the topics of which the publication offers the most coverage: White House, Politics, Congress, Health Care, Energy, Defense, and Tech.

Subject(s): News Services
Publication(s): *National Journal*

National Optical Astronomical Observatory (NOAO)

http://www.noao.edu/

Sponsor(s): Association of Universities for Research in Astronomy, Inc.

Description: As stated on the Web site, "NOAO is the US national research & development center for ground-based night-time astronomy. [Its] mission is to provide public access to qualified professional researchers to forefront scientific capabilities on telescopes operated by NOAO as well as other optical and infrared telescopes. Today, these telescopes range in aperture size from 2-m to 10-m." Its observatories are located in Chile and Arizona, and it is involved with the Gemini telescopes, which are described elsewhere in this publication. It has a special section for astronomers, an image gallery, and an education- and outreach-oriented section with information for such audiences as middle school teachers, undergraduates, and citizens.

Subject(s): Astronomy; Telescopes

National Organization for Women (NOW)

http://www.now.org/

Sponsor(s): National Organization for Women (NOW)

Description: NOW, which has half a million contributing members and 550 chapters nationwide, was founded in 1966 to advocate for issues pertaining to women's rights. A history of the organization and a section of frequently asked questions can be found by accessing the About the Foundation link. An issues box on the left-hand side of the home page links to major initiatives, such as ending gender discrimination and promoting diversity/ending racism. The site has links to blog posts and a tool for finding one's local chapter.

Subject(s): Women

National Republican Congressional Committee (NRCC)

http://www.nrcc.org/

Sponsor(s): National Republican Congressional Committee

Description: The NRCC Web site features news and opinions relevant to the committee's mission and focus. Links for blog entries and videos can be found in the upper right-hand part of the home page.

Subject(s): Political Parties

National Republican Senatorial Committee (NRSC)

http://www.nrsc.org/

Sponsor(s): National Republican Senatorial Committee: NRSC

Description: The NRSC Web site features current news stories and links to the NRSC's social media pages.

Subject(s): Political Parties

National Security Archive

http://www.gwu.edu/~nsarchiv/

Sponsor(s): National Security Archive

Description: The National Security Archive is a private, independent research institute and library located at George Washington University in Washington, D.C. Despite the official-sounding name, it is not a government agency. The archive collects and publishes declassified documents acquired through the Freedom of Information Act (FOIA). Only a fraction of the archive's holdings are online; nevertheless, the online offerings are significant. The documents section of the site includes "electronic briefing books," collections of scanned declassified documents along with National Security Archive analysis. The collections are grouped by topic, such as nuclear history. These online briefing books are free; other formal collections and analysis are available for purchase. The FOIA (Freedom of Information) section of the site includes the downloadable guide "Effective FOIA Requesting for Everyone" and information on document classification. The National Security Archive provides a valuable research service offline, with its archive of declassified U.S. documents obtained through FOIA and its own print and microform publications. The online collections meet some popular information needs and present documents with contextual commentary identifying the people and events related to the documents.

Subject(s): Declassified Documents; Foreign Policy—Research; Freedom of Information Act

Publication(s): *Effective FOIA Requesting for Everyone*

National Solar Observatory (NSO)

http://www.nso.edu/

Sponsor(s): Association of Universities for Research in Astronomy, Inc.

Description: The prime objective of the NSO is to study the sun, with facilities located in Arizona and New Mexico. A Current Images section provides views of the sun, as well as relevant NSO data. Data sets are provided in the Digital Library section. The data, according to the Web site, consist of "the Kitt Peak Vacuum telescope magnetograms and spectroheliograms; the Fourier Transform Spectrometer transformed spectra, the Sacramento Peak Evans Facility spectroheliograms and coronal scans, and solar activity indices."

Subject(s): Space; Sun

North Atlantic Treaty Organization (NATO)

http://www.nato.int/cps/en/natolive/index.htm

Sponsor(s): North Atlantic Treaty Organization (NATO)

Description: NATO is an alliance of independent nations committed to each other's defense. The NATO Web site features news, speeches, and videos on current NATO activities. The Organization section features information on the structure of NATO and links to the national information servers of member countries. The NATO A-Z index contains a thematic index that links to information about such topics as human trafficking, NATO in Afghanistan, and NATO and the fight against terrorism.

While only a small subset of their printed publications is available, the Web site provides a significant collection of documents from and about NATO. It is an excellent source of information on the organization.

Subject(s): Military Forces—International

Publication(s): *NATO Handbook; NATO Review*

Nuclear Threat Initiative (NTI)

http://www.nti.org/

Sponsor(s): Nuclear Threat Initiative (NTI)

Description: According to the Web site, "The Nuclear Threat Initiative (NTI) is a nonprofit, nonpartisan organization with a mission to strengthen global security by reducing the risk of use and preventing the spread of nuclear, biological, and chemical weapons and to work to build the trust, transparency, and security that are preconditions to the ultimate fulfillment of the Non-Proliferation Treaty's goals and ambitions." In this capacity, NTI has created the now-independent World Institute for Nuclear Security (WINS) and the Middle East Consortium on Infectious Disease Surveillance. The institute also provides support to Kazakhstan for the securing and dispersal of its uranium stores. The Threats sections of the Web site breaks down issues topically, with sections for nuclear, biological, chemical, and radiological threats.

Subject(s): Nonproliferation; Nuclear Weapons

Open Secrets

http://www.opensecrets.org/

Sponsor(s): Center for Responsive Politics

Description: According to the Web site, Open Secrets, which was launched after the 1996 elections, "is the nation's premier research group tracking money in U.S. politics and its effect on elections and public policy." Frequently cited by Washington, D.C., and national media outlets, the Web site serves as a clearinghouse of information regarding many of the different roles that money plays in politics. The site also provides access to the Open Secrets Blog, which is described in a separate entry. Issue profiles can be found in the News & Analysis section, while information about PACs and lobbying can be found in the Influence & Lobbying section. The Take Action section provides users with a list of issues on which the Center for Responsive Politics is currently working. The Community link under Resources provides access to the organization's social media pages.

Open Secrets Blog

http://www.opensecrets.org/news/

Sponsor(s): Center for Responsive Politics

Description: This blog, subtitled "Investigating Money in Politics," examines both politicians and organizations under the scope of its mission. Comments are allowed.

Subject(s): Money; Politics; Blogs

Organisation for Economic Co-operation and Development (OECD) Online

http://www.oecd.org/

Sponsor(s): Organisation for Economic Co-operation and Development (OECD)

Description: OECD Online contains descriptive information about the OECD, its activities, and its member countries. Major categories include About OECD, Countries, Topics, Data, and Publications. Key topics available on the home page include restoring public finance, boosting jobs and skills, restoring public trust, and new sources of growth. There is free access to many online documents including the OECD Observer and OECD Outlooks. The site contains useful descriptive information about the OECD and a useful collection of free online publications and statistics.

Subject(s): International Economic Development

Publication(s): *OECD Outlooks*

Organisation for Security and Co-operation in Europe (OSCE)

http://www.osce.org/

Sponsor(s): Organisation for Security and Co-operation in Europe (OSCE)

Description: OSCE is a regional security organization that consists of 57 European, North American, and Central Asian member states. Its security issues portfolio includes such topics as arms control, border management, combating human trafficking, counterterrorism, conflict resolution, education, good governance, and environmental activities. OSCE news can be found in the Newsroom section.

Subject(s): International Organizations; Security

Organization of American States
http://www.oas.org/

Sponsor(s): Organization of American States (OAS)

Description: The OAS Web site features information on the organization and its involvements. Major sections include About the OAS, Topics, Strategic Partners, Member States, Media Center, Documents, and Calendar. The Strategic Partners section links to information about the Trust for the Americas, Consortium of Universities, Pan American Development Foundation (PADF), Joint Summit Working Group, and YABT. The site is available in English, Spanish, French and Portuguese.

Subject(s): South America; Caribbean

Publication(s): *Américas*

Organization of the Petroleum Exporting Countries (OPEC)
http://www.opec.org/

Sponsor(s): Organization of the Petroleum Exporting Countries (OPEC)

Description: OPEC is an organization of oil-exporting nations dedicated to the stability and prosperity of the petroleum market. The OPEC Web site features sections such as About Us, Press Room, Data/Graphs, Publications, 50th Anniversary, and Multimedia. The Publications section highlights major reports and bulletins.

Subject(s): Petroleum—International

Publication(s): *OPEC Annual Report*

Pantex Plant
http://www.pantex.com/Pages/default.aspx

Sponsor(s): Consolidated Nuclear Security, LLC

Description: As stated on the Web site, "Pantex Plant's key role is to ensure the safety, security and reliability of the nation's nuclear stockpile . . . excess weapons are dismantled, surveillance is conducted on the stockpile and aging weapons are maintained through the Life Extension Programs." Community involvement and emergency preparation information is available under the About Pantex heading. The site also has procurement information, as well as a section for employment.

Subject(s): Nuclear Weapons

Partners in Health
http://www.pih.org/

Sponsor(s): Partners in Health

Description: Partners in Health, which was created to provide health care to people living in poverty worldwide, features resources and tools for health care professionals. The Our Work section has links to the organization's priority health programs: Cancer & Chronic Diseases, Child Health, Cholera, Ebola, Community Health Workers, HIV/AIDS, Mental Health, Nursing, Surgery, Tuberculosis, and Women's Health. The News section features recent articles. Links to the organization's social media pages are also provided on the site.

Subject(s): Health Care; Poverty

Partnership for the National Trails System

http://www.pnts.org/

Sponsor(s): Partnership for the National Trails System

Description: PNTS is a collective of nonprofit trail organizations and federal agencies working together in order to preserve, complete, protect, and oversee 30 National Scenic and Historic Trails contained within the National Trails System. Its Web site includes news and a quarterly publication about recent relevant events. A Youth Gateway section has a blog for young adults and related job postings.

Subject(s): National Parks and Reserves

Publication(s): *Pathways*

Politico

http://www.politico.com/

Sponsor(s): Politico LLC

Description: *Politico*'s focus is on Washington-based news, particularly Congress, public policy, and the White House. The publication was founded in 2007. Its Web site links to current news articles, blog posts, and Politico Pro, a subscription-based service that offers enhanced access to coverage.

Subject(s): News Services

Publication(s): *Politico*

Presidential Directives and Executive Orders

http://www.fas.org/irp/offdocs/direct.htm

Sponsor(s): Federation of American Scientists (FAS)

Description: This Web site, maintained by a nonprofit research organization, focuses on intelligence-related presidential directives and executive orders from the Truman administration to the present. Copies of documents that are not still classified are available on this site. The site also links to helpful background information on presidential directives.

Subject(s): Intelligence; Presidential Documents

RAND Corporation
http://www.rand.org/
Sponsor(s): RAND Corporation
Description: Founded more than 60 years ago, RAND's mission is to improve policymaking and decision making through research and analysis. The Research section denotes topics with which the corporation works, including public safety, health and health care, and terrorism and homeland security. News releases, announcements, a calendar, and the blog can be found in the Newsroom section.
Subject(s): Education; Health and Safety; Homeland Security

Roll Call
http://www.rollcall.com/
Sponsor(s): Economist Group
Description: Roll Call is a newspaper dedicated to coverage of the workings of Capitol Hill. Its home page links to news, opinions, and blogs. The newspaper also publishes its annual *"Roll Call* Fabulous 50," a list of what it dubs "Capitol Hill's leading staffers."
Subject(s): News services
Publication(s): *Roll Call*

Sierra Club
http://www.sierraclub.org/
Sponsor(s): Sierra Club
Description: The motto of the Sierra Club is "explore, enjoy and protect the planet." Users can find information about some of the organization's issues, including protection of America's waters and facilitating resilient habitats. The news section links to the Sierra Club's blogs, e-mail newsletters, and other publications. The Local Chapters & Events section has state-by-state chapter information.

Southern Poverty Law Center (SPLC)
http://www.splcenter.org/
Sponsor(s): Southern Poverty Law Center (SPLC)
Description: Founded in 1971, SPLC's mission is to eradicate hate crimes and bigotry-motivated violence. Its Web site provides information about the center's history and its target issues (at-risk children, hate and extremism, immigrant justice, and LGBT rights). The Teaching Tolerance section describes this program, an anti-prejudice education-oriented program that takes place in school classrooms. A link to *Teaching Tolerance* magazine is also provided.
Publication(s): *Teaching Tolerance*

Stimson Center

http://www.stimson.org/

Sponsor(s): Stimson Center

Description: The Stimson Center's research and outreach work toward the goals of establishing international peace and security, building stability throughout the regions of the world, and reducing the presence of weapons of mass destruction. In its Programs section, topical initiatives are grouped into three categories: Transnational Threats, Regional Security, and Effective Institutions. The Topics section provides further information about its research and analysis in such areas as border security, biological and chemical weapons, energy, and humanitarian issues.

Subject(s): Nonproliferation; Peace

Stockholm International Peace Research Institute (SIPRI)

http://www.sipri.org/

Sponsor(s): Stockholm International Peace Research Institute (SIPRI)

Description: SIPRI, established in 1996, "is an independent international institute dedicated to research into conflict, armaments, arms control and disarmament." Issues are organized topically on the home page, with sections for Regional and Global Security, Armed Conflict and Conflict Management, and Military Spending and Armaments. Available databases include the SIPRI Multilateral Peace Operations Database and the SIPRI Arms Transfers Database.

Subject(s): Nonproliferation; Arms Control; Security

The Hill

http://thehill.com/

Sponsor(s): News Communications, Inc.

Description: *The Hill* is a media source for information, news, and opinions about Capitol Hill and Congress. Subscription services are available. The home page also links to related blogs.

Subject(s): News services

U.S-Mexico Border 2020

http://www.epa.gov/usmexicoborder/

Sponsor(s): Environmental Protection Agency (EPA)

Description: U.S.-Mexico Environmental Program (Border 2020) is a U.S-Mexico binational program focusing on cleaning the air, providing safe drinking water, reducing the risk of exposure to hazardous waste, and ensuring emergency preparedness along the U.S-Mexico border. The Web site has information on regional and border-wide working groups and on measuring conditions and progress in the board region. The site is also available in Spanish, Chinese, Vietnamese, and Korean.

Subject(s): Environmental Protection; Mexico

UN Refugee Agency (UNHCR)

http://www.unhcr.org/cgi-bin/texis/vtx/home

Sponsor(s): UN Refugee Agency (UNHCR)

Description: Established in 1950, UNHCR is charged with protecting refugees and resolving refugee situations. The Who We Help section provides clarity on the groups of refugees assisted, and information about refugees is broken down into topical demographic groups, such as stateless people and internally displaced people. A photo gallery can be found in the News & Views section, and research, statistics, and publications are available in the Resources section. The site is available in Arabic, Chinese, Spanish, French, and Russian.

Subject(s): Refugees

UNESCO World Heritage Centre

http://whc.unesco.org/en/list

Sponsor(s): United Nations—United Nations Educational, Scientific, and Cultural Organization (UNESCO)

Description: The UNESCO World Heritage Centre is committed to the preservation of places of significant natural and/or cultural importance. This Web site provides information about the initiative, a list of UNESCO World Heritage sites (complete with map), a list of sites potentially in danger of damage or eradication, and information about its activities and volunteer organizations.

Subject(s): Cultural Artifacts; Culture

UNICOR—Federal Prison Industries, Inc.

http://www.unicor.gov/

Sponsor(s): Federal Prison Industries, Inc.

Description: The UNICOR Web site allows the federal government and contractors to buy goods and services from Federal Prison Industries (FPI), Inc., whose primary mission is the productive employment of inmates. The site has an online product catalog with browsing and ordering capabilities. It also provides substantial background information on the Inmate Training Programs.

Subject(s): Government Procurement; Prisoners

Union of Concerned Scientists (UCS)

http://www.ucsusa.org/

Sponsor(s): Union of Concerned Scientists (UCS)

Description: UCS's mission, according to the Web site, is to "develop and implement innovative, practical solutions to some of our planet's most pressing problems—from combating global warming and developing sustainable ways to feed, power, and transport ourselves, to fighting misinformation and reducing the threat of nuclear war." The Take Action section of the site provides science-related "Action Alerts" and tips and tools for activists seeking to connect with policy makers and media outlets. The top of the page offers a link to UCS's blog, and the Publications section includes documents on a variety of topics, such as *Catalyst* magazine and the *Earthwise* newsletter.

Subject(s): Government Procurement; Prisoners
Publication(s): *Catalyst*
Earthwise

United Nations (UN)
http://www.un.org/
Sponsor(s): United Nations
Description: This main United Nations site features information and documents about the UN. Aside from organization and program information, the site includes an extensive news center, UN Webcast section, and the educational section. Other sections link to the main bodies of the UN, such as the General Assembly, Security Council, and Economic and Social Council. A section called Global Issues organizes UN resources by topic, such as AIDS, Climate Change, Disarmament, Human Rights, Peace and Security, Refugees, and Terrorism. The Member States section includes a list with date of admission to the UN, as well as links to Permanent Missions and to non-member states maintaining Permanent Observer Missions at UN Headquarters. The Publications section of the site includes sales publications and online versions of popular UN publications. The Documents section has meeting records, Security Council resolutions, *Journal of the United Nations*, press releases, and other documents.

Subject(s): International Relations
Publication(s): *African Renewal*
Journal of the United Nations
UN Chronicle

United Nations Children's Fund Works for Children Worldwide (UNICEF)
http://www.unicef.org/
Sponsor(s): United Nations — United Nations Children's Fund (UNICEF)
Description: UNICEF presents a site filled with information on international children's rights, the health and well-being of children, the abuse of children, and other material related to children. The site features the following main categories: What We Do, Who We Are, Focus Areas, Where We Work, and Press Centre. Links to UNICEF's Facebook, Twitter, and YouTube pages are provided. Focus areas include such topics as child survival and development, basic education and gender equality, children and HIV/AIDS, and child protection. The UNICEF sites are a

treasure trove of information about children and UNICEF's activities on behalf of children.

Subject(s): Child Welfare; International
Publication(s): *The Progress of Nations*
The State of the World's Children
UNICEF Annual Report

United Nations Climate Change Portal

http://www.un.org/climatechange/

Sponsor(s): United Nations—World Meteorological Organization (WMO)

Description: This page discusses the UN's actions regarding climate change. The UN Climate Voices section features interviews with UN officials involved with climate change initiatives, and the Publications section links to related UN-issued reports.

Subject(s): Climate Change

United Nations Educational, Scientific and Cultural Organization (UNESCO)

http://www.unesco.org/

Sponsor(s): United Nations—United Nations Educational, Scientific, and Cultural Organization (UNESCO)

Description: UNESCO, founded in 1945, has 195 members and 8 associate members, with more than 50 field offices around the world. UNESCO's slate of topics is diverse, with major programs including natural sciences, education, social and human sciences, and communications and information. Each topical section links to news, events, and other related materials. The Media subsection includes press releases, advisories, and multimedia content, such as photos and videos. The site is available in Spanish, French, Russian, Chinese, Arabic, and Portuguese. One of UNESCO's major initiatives is its World Heritage Centre program, which is described in a separate entry.

Subject(s): Culture; Education; Science

Wisconsin Project on Nuclear Arms Control

http://www.wisconsinproject.org/

Sponsor(s): Wisconsin Project on Nuclear Arms Control

Description: The aim of the Wisconsin Project on Nuclear Arms Control is to control and prevent the spread of long-rage missiles and weapons of mass destruction. Its products include the Risk Report database, which compiles information on companies around the world suspected of contributing to the creation and building of weapons of mass destruction; the Iran Watch, which tracks that country's weapons capabilities; and the Iraq Watch, which focuses on disarmament.

Subject(s): Arms Control; Nuclear Weapons; Weapons of Mass Destruction

Woodrow Wilson International Center for Scholars

http://www.wilsoncenter.org/

Sponsor(s): Woodrow Wilson International Center for Scholars

Description: The Wilson Center supports scholarship linked to public policy. The center offers fellowships and special opportunities for research and writing with a focus on history, political science, and international relations. As a public/private partnership, the center receives roughly one-third of its operating funds from federal appropriations. The Web site has information about current Wilson Center projects and publications, and audio files of its weekly radio program, "Dialogue." The site also carries essays and other items from the center's journal, *The Wilson Quarterly*. In the About section, the site offers information on applying for a fellowship or internship with the center.

Subject(s): Fellowships; Public Policy—Research; Social Science Research

Publication(s): *The Wilson Quarterly*

World Bank

http://www.worldbank.org/

Sponsor(s): World Bank

Description: This site concentrates on information about the World Bank, its programs, and constituent organizations. Sections include Data, Research, Learning, News, Projects & Operations, and Publications. A Countries section provides detailed data on countries of the world. The Projects & Operations section allows users to browse topics and issues by country/area, sector, and theme.

Subject(s): International Economic Development

World Health Organization (WHO)

http://www.who.int/en/

Sponsor(s): United Nations—World Health Organization (WHO)

Description: WHO is a UN agency focusing on global health issues. The WHO site features the major categories: Health Topics, Data, Media Centre, Publications, Countries, Programmes, Governance, and About WHO. The Countries section gives a health profile of member nations. The Media Centre section links to fact sheets on global health topics such as African trypanosomiasis (sleeping sickness), Chagas disease, dengue, malaria, and tobacco use.

Subject(s): Health and Safety—International

Publication: *WHO Weekly Epidemiological Record*

World Intellectual Property Organization (WIPO)

http://www.wipo.int/portal/index.html.en

Sponsor(s): United Nations—World Intellectual Property Organization (WIPO)

Description: The site, subtitled "Encouraging Creativity and Innovation," includes sections such as About IP, Inside WIPO, IP Services, Policy, Cooperation, and Reference. The IP Services section has information on such topics as developing laws and standards, copyright issues, and the economics of IP, or intellectual property. Case studies, country profiles, databases, documents, and publications can be found in the Reference section. The site is available in Spanish, French, Russian, Arabic, and Chinese.

Subject(s): Intellectual Property—International

World Meteorological Organization (WMO)

http://www.wmo.int/pages/index_en.html

Sponsor(s): United Nations—World Meteorological Organization (WMO)

Description: The World Meteorological Organization is a United Nations agency that promotes the effective use worldwide of meteorological and hydrological information, notably in weather and water resource prediction and in climatology. The home page features current news, weather forecasts and warnings, recent and upcoming events, and a link to the MyWorld Weather App for iPhone and Android. The site's Media Centre section has news, press releases, and podcasts. The site is available in Arabic, Chinese, French, Russian, and Spanish.

Subject(s): Meteorology—International

World Trade Organization (WTO)

http://www.wto.org/

Sponsor(s): World Trade Organization (WTO)

Description: The WTO Web site feature Trade Topics; About WTO; Documents, Data, and Resources; and News and Events. Under Trade Topics, the page organizes information under the headings Goods, Services, Intellectual Property, Building Trade Capacity, Doha Development Agenda, Trade Monitoring, and Dispute Settlement. The Documents and Resources section links to an online bookstore and key WTO publications.

Subject(s): International Trade

Publication(s): *International Trade Statistics*

World Wildlife Fund (WWF)
http://worldwildlife.org/
Sponsor(s): World Wildlife Fund (WWF)
Description: With a presence in over 100 countries, the WWF strives to support conservation and natural protection issues. Under About Us, the News & Press section includes news articles, press releases, and contact information for the media. The Places section breaks down WWF initiatives by region/area. Information about partnerships and projects can be found in Our Work.
Subject(s): Animals; Conservation (Natural Resources)

Appendix A

List of Members of the 114th Congress

Alabama

Sen. Jeff Session (R)
http://sessions.senate.gov/

Sen. Richard C. Shelby (R)
http://shelby.senate.gov/

Rep. Bradley Byrne (R-01)
http://byrne.house.gov/

Rep. Martha Roby (R-02)
http://roby.house.gov/

Rep. Mike Rogers (R-03)
http://mikerogers.house.gov/

Rep. Robert Aderholt (R-04)
http://aderholt.house.gov/

Rep. Mo Brooks (R-05)
http://brooks.house.gov/

Rep. Gary Palmer (R-06)
http://palmer.house.gov/

Rep Terri A. Sewell (D-07)
http://sewell.house.gov/

Alaska

Sen. Daniel Sullivan (R)
http://sullivan.senate.gov/

Sen. Lisa Murkowski (R)

http://murkowski.senate.gov/

Rep. Don Young (R-At Large)
http://donyoung.house.gov/

American Samoa

Rep. Amata Radewagen (R-At Large)
http://radewagen.house.gov/

Arizona

Sen. Jeff Flake (R)
http://www.flake.senate.gov/

Sen. John McCain (R)
http://mccain.senate.gov/

Rep. Ann Kirkpatrick (D-01)
http://kirkpatrick.house.gov/

Rep. Martha McSally (R-02)
http://mcsally.house.gov/

Rep. Raúl Grijalva (D-03)
http://quayle.house.gov/

Rep. Paul Gosar (R-04)
http://gosar.house.gov/

Rep. Matt Salmon (R-05)
http://salmon.house.gov/

Rep. David Schweikert (R-06)

http://schweikert.house.gov/

Rep. Ruben Gallego (D-07)
http://www.rubengallego.house.
gov/

Rep. Trent Franks (R-08)
http://franks.house.gov/

Rep. Kyrsten Sinema (D-09)
http://sinema.house.gov/

Arkansas

Sen. John Boozman (R)
http://boozman.senate.gov/

Sen. Tom Cotton (R)
http://cotton.senate.gov/

Rep. Rick Crawford (R-01)
http://crawford.house.gov/

Rep. French Hill (R-02)
http://hill.house.gov/

Rep. Steve Womack (R-03)
http://womack.house.gov/

Rep. Bruce Westerman (R-04)
http://westerman.house.gov/

California

Sen. Barbara Boxer (D)
http://www.boxer.senate.gov/

Sen. Dianne Feinstein (D)
http://www.feinstein.senate.gov/

Rep. Doug LaMalfa (R-01)
http://lamalfa.house.gov/

Rep. Jared Huffman (D-02)
http://huffman.house.gov/

Rep. John Garamendi (D-03)
http://garamendi.house.gov/

Rep. Tom McClintock (R-04)
http://mcclintock.house.gov/

Rep. Mike Thompson (D-05)
http://mikethompson.house.gov/

Rep. Doris O. Matsui (D-06)
http://matsui.house.gov/

Rep. Ami Bera (D-07)
http://bera.house.gov/

Rep. Paul Cook (R-08)
http://cook.house.gov/

Rep. Jerry McNerney (D-09)
http://mcnerney.house.gov/

Rep. Jeff Denham (R-10)
http://denham.house.gov/

Rep. Mark DeSaulnier (D-11)
http://desaulnier.house.gov/

Rep. Nancy Pelosi (D-12)
http://pelosi.house.gov/

Rep. Barbara Lee (D-13)
http://lee.house.gov/

Rep. Jackie Speier (D-14)
http://speier.house.gov/

Rep. Eric Swalwell (D-15)
http://swalwell.house.gov/

Rep. Jim Costa (D-16)
http://costa.house.gov/

Rep. Mike Honda (D-17)
http://honda.house.gov/

Rep. Anna G. Eshoo (D-18)
http://eshoo.house.gov/

Rep. Zoe Lofgren (D-19)
http://lofgren.house.gov/

Rep. Sam Farr (D-20)
http://www.farr.house.gov/

Rep. David Valadao (R-21)
http://valadao.house.gov/

Rep. Devin Nunes (R-22)
http://nunes.house.gov/

Rep. Kevin McCarthy (R-23)
http://kevinmccarthy.house.gov/

Rep. Lois Capps (D-24)
http://capps.house.gov/

Rep. Steve Knight (R-25)
http://knight.house.gov/

Rep. Julia Brownley (D-26)
http://juliabrownley.house.gov/

Rep. Judy Chu (D-27)
http://chu.house.gov/

Rep. Adam Schiff (D-28)
http://schiff.house.gov/

Rep. Tony Cárdenas (D-29)
http://cardenas.house.gov/

Rep. Brad Sherman (D-30)
http://bradsherman.house.gov/

Rep. Pete Aguilar (D-31)
http://aguilar.house.gov/

Rep. Grace Napolitano (D-32)
http://napolitano.house.gov/

Rep. Ted Lieu (D-33)
http://lieu.house.gov/

Rep. Xavier Becerra (D-34)
http://becerra.house.gov/

Rep. Norma Torres (D-35)
http://torres.house.gov/

Rep. Raul Ruiz (D-36)
http://ruiz.house.gov/

Rep. Karen Bass (D-37)
http://bass.house.gov/

Rep. Linda Sanchez (D-38)
http://lindasanchez.house.gov/

Rep. Ed Royce (R-39)
http://royce.house.gov/

Rep. Lucille Roybal-Allard (D-40)
http://roybal-allard.house.gov/

Rep. Mark Takano (D-41)
http://takano.house.gov/

Rep. Ken Calvert (R-42)
http://calvert.house.gov/

Rep. Maxine Waters (D-43)
http://waters.house.gov/

Rep. Janice Hahn (D-44)
http://hahn.house.gov/

Rep. Mimi Walters (R-45)
http://walters.house.gov/

Rep. Loretta Sanchez (D-46)
http://lorettasanchez.house.gov/

Rep. Alan Lowenthal (D-47)
http://lowenthal.house.gov/

Rep. Dana Rohrabacher (R-48)
http://rohrabacher.house.gov/

Rep. Darrell Issa (R-49)
http://issa.house.gov/

Rep. Duncan D. Hunter (R-50)
http://hunter.house.gov/

Rep. Juan Vargas (D-51)
http://vargas.house.gov/

Rep. Scott Peters (D-52)
http://scottpeters.house.gov/

Rep. Susan Davis (D-53)
http://susandavis.house.gov/

Colorado

Sen. Michael F. Bennet (D)
http://www.bennet.senate.gov/

Sen. Cory Gardner (R)
http://gardner.senate.gov/

Rep. Diana DeGette (D-01)
http://degette.house.gov/

Rep. Jared Polis (D-02)
http://polis.house.gov/

Rep. Scott Tipton (R-03)
http://tipton.house.gov/

Rep. Ken Buck (R-04)
http://buck.house.gov/

Rep. Doug Lamborn (R-05)
http://lamborn.house.gov/

Rep. Mike Coffman (R-06)
http://coffman.house.gov/

Rep. Ed Perlmutter (D-07)
http://perlmutter.house.gov/

Connecticut

Sen. Richard Blumenthal (D)
http://www.blumenthal.senate.gov/

Sen. Christopher Murphy (D)
http://www.murphy.senate.gov/

Rep. John B. Larson (D-01)
http://www.larson.house.gov/

Rep. Joe Courtney (D-02)
http://courtney.house.gov/

Rep. Rosa DeLauro (D-03)
http://delauro.house.gov/

Rep. Jim Himes (D-04)
http://himes.house.gov/

Rep. Elizabeth Esty (D-05)
http://esty.house.gov/

Delaware

Sen. Thomas R. Carper (D)
http://carper.senate.gov/

Sen. Christopher A. Coons (D)
http://coons.senate.gov/

Rep. John Carney (D-At Large)
http://johncarney.house.gov/

District of Columbia

Del. Eleanor Holmes Norton (D-At Large)
http://norton.house.gov/

Florida

Sen. Bill Nelson (D)
http://www.billnelson.senate.gov/

Sen. Marco Rubio (R)
http://www.rubio.senate.gov/

Rep. Jeff Miller (R-01)
http://jeffmiller.house.gov/

Rep. Gwen Graham (D-02)
http://graham.house.gov/

Rep. Ted Yoho (R-03)
http://yoho.house.gov/

Rep. Ander Crenshaw (R-04)
http://crenshaw.house.gov/

Rep. Corinne Brown (D-05)
http://corrinebrown.house.gov/

Rep. Ron DeSantis (R-06)
http://desantis.house.gov/

Rep. John Mica (R-07)
http://mica.house.gov/

Rep. Bill Posey (R-08)
http://posey.house.gov/

Rep. Alan Grayson (D-09)
http://grayson.house.gov/

Rep. Daniel Webster (R-10)
http://webster.house.gov/

Rep. Richard Nugent (R-11)
http://nugent.house.gov/

Rep. Gus M. Bilirakis (R-12)
http://bilirakis.house.gov/

Rep. David Jolly (R-13)
http://jolly.house.gov/

Rep. Kathy Castor (D-14)
http://castor.house.gov/

Rep. Dennis Ross (R-15)
http://dennisross.house.gov/

Rep. Vern Buchanan (R-16)
http://buchanan.house.gov/

Rep. Tom Rooney (R-17)
http://rooney.house.gov/

Rep. Patrick Murphy (D-18)
http://patrickmurphy.house.gov/

Rep. Curt Clawson (R-19)
http://clawson.house.gov/clerk.
house.gov/

Rep. Alcee L. Hastings (D-20)
http://alceehastings.house.gov/

Rep. Ted Deutch (D-21)
http://teddeutch.house.gov/

Rep. Lois Frankel (D-22)
http://frankel.house.gov/

Rep. Debbie Wasserman Schultz
(D-23)
http://wassermanschultz.house.
gov/

Rep. Frederica Wilson (D-24)
http://wilson.house.gov/

Rep. Mario Diaz-Balart (R-25)
http://mariodiazbalart.house.gov/

Rep. Carlos Curbelo (R-26)
http://curbelo.house.gov/

Rep. Ileana Ros-Lehtinen (R-27)
http://ros-lehtinen.house.gov/

Georgia

Sen. David Perdue (R)
http://perdue.senate.gov/index.cfm

Sen. Johnny Isakson (R)
http://www.isakson.senate.gov/

Rep. Buddy Carter (R-01)
http://buddycarter.house.gov/

Rep. Sanford D. Bishop, Jr. (D-02)
http://bishop.house.gov/

Rep. Lynn A. Westmoreland (R-03)
http://westmoreland.house.gov/

Rep. Henry C. "Hank" Johnson (D-04)
http://hankjohnson.house.gov/

Rep. John Lewis (D-05)
http://johnlewis.house.gov/

Rep. Tom Price (R-06)
http://tomprice.house.gov/

Rep. Robert Woodall (R-07)
http://woodall.house.gov/

Rep. Austin Scott (R-08)
http://austinscott.house.gov/

Rep. Doug Collins (R-09)
http://dougcollins.house.gov/

Rep. Jody Hice (R-10)
http://hice.house.gov/

Rep. Barry Loudermilk (R-11)
http://loudermilk.house.gov/

Rep. Rick Allen (R-12)
http://allen.house.gov/

Rep. David Scott (D-13)
http://davidscott.house.gov/

Rep. Tom Graves (R-14)
http://tomgraves.house.gov/

Guam

Del. Madeleine Bordallo (D-At Large)
http://bordallo.house.gov/

Hawaii

Sen. Mazie K. Hirono (D)
http://www.hirono.senate.gov/

Sen. Brian Schatz (D)
http://www.schatz.senate.gov/

Rep. Mark Takai (D-01)
http://takai.house.gov/

Rep. Tulsi Gabbard (D-02)
http://gabbard.house.gov/

Idaho

Sen. Mike Crapo (R)
http://crapo.senate.gov/

Sen. James E. Risch (R)
http://risch.senate.gov/

Rep. Raul R. Labrador (R-01)
http://labrador.house.gov/

Rep. Mike Simpson (R-02)
http://simpson.house.gov/

Illinois

Sen. Richard J. Durbin (D)
http://www.durbin.senate.gov/

Sen. Mark Kirk (R)
http://www.kirk.senate.gov/

Rep. Bobby L. Rush (D-01)
http://rush.house.gov/

Rep. Robin Kelly (D-02)
http://robinkelly.house.gov/

Rep. Daniel Lipinski (D-03)
http://www.lipinski.house.gov/

Rep. Luis Gutierrez (D-04)
http://gutierrez.house.gov/

Rep. Mike Quigley (D-05)
http://quigley.house.gov/

Rep. Peter J. Roksam (R-06)
http://roskam.house.gov/

Rep. Danny K. Davis (D-07)
http://www.davis.house.gov/

Rep. Tammy Duckworth (D-08)
http://duckworth.house.gov/

Rep. Jan Schakowsky (D-09)
http://schakowsky.house.gov/

Rep. Bob Dold (R-10)
http://dold.house.gov/

Rep. Bill Foster (D-11)
http://foster.house.gov/

Rep. Mike Bost (R-12)
http://bost.house.gov/

Rep. Rodney Davis (R-13)
http://rodneydavis.house.gov/

Rep. Randy Hultgren (R-14)
http://hultgren.house.gov/

Rep. John Shimkus (R-15)
http://shimkus.house.gov/

Rep. Adam Kinzinger (R-16)
http://kinzinger.house.gov/

Rep. Cheri Bustos (D-17)
http://bustos.house.gov/

Vacant, District 18

Indiana

Sen. Daniel Coats (R)
http://coats.senate.gov/

Sen. Joe Donnelly (D)
http://www.donnelly.senate.gov/

Rep. Peter Visclosky (D-01)
http://visclosky.house.gov/

Rep. Jackie Walorski (R-02)
http://walorski.house.gov/

Rep. Marlin Stutzman (R-03)
http://stutzman.house.gov/

Rep. Todd Rokita (R-04)
http://rokita.house.gov/

Rep. Susan W. Brooks (R-05)
http://susanwbrooks.house.gov/

Rep. Luke Messer (R-06)
http://messer.house.gov/

Rep. André Carson (D-07)
http://carson.house.gov/

Rep. Larry Bucshon (R-08)
http://bucshon.house.gov/

Rep. Todd Young (R-09)
http://toddyoung.house.gov/

Iowa

Sen. Chuck Grassley (R)
http://grassley.senate.gov/

Sen. Joni Ernst (R)
http://www.ernst.senate.gov/

Rep. Rod Blum (R-01)
http://blum.house.gov/

Rep. David Loebsack (D-02)
http://loebsack.house.gov/

Rep. David Young (R-03)
http://davidyoung.house.gov

Rep. Steve King (R-04)
http://steveking.house.gov/

Kansas

Sen. Jerry Moran (R)
http://www.moran.senate.gov/

Sen. Pat Roberts (R)
http://www.roberts.senate.gov/

Rep. Tim Huelskamp (R-01)
http://huelskamp.house.gov/

Rep. Lynn Jenkins (R-02)
http://lynnjenkins.house.gov/

Rep. Kevin Yoder (R-03)
http://yoder.house.gov/

Rep. Mike Pompeo (R-04)
http://pompeo.house.gov/

Kentucky

Sen. Mitch McConnell (R)
http://www.mcconnell.senate.gov/

Sen. Rand Paul (R)
http://www.paul.senate.gov/

Rep. Ed Whitfield (R-01)
http://whitfield.house.gov/

Rep. S. Brett Guthrie (R-02)
http://guthrie.house.gov/

Rep. John A. Yarmuth (D-03)
http://yarmuth.house.gov/

Rep. Thomas Massie (R-04)
http://massie.house.gov/

Rep. Harold Rogers (R-05)
http://halrogers.house.gov/

Rep. Andy Barr (R-06)
http://barr.house.gov/

Louisiana

Sen. Bill Cassidy (R)
http://www.cassidy.senate.gov/

Sen. David Vitter (R)
http://www.vitter.senate.gov/

Rep. Steve Scalise (R-01)
http://scalise.house.gov/

Rep. Cedric Richmond (D-02)
http://richmond.house.gov/

Rep. Charles W. Boustany, Jr. (R-03)
http://boustany.house.gov/

Rep. John Fleming (R-04)
http://fleming.house.gov/

Rep. Ralph Abraham (R-05)
http://abraham.house.gov/

Rep. Garret Graves (R-06)
http://garretgraves.house.gov/

Maine

Sen. Susan M. Collins (R)
http://collins.house.gov/

Sen. Angus S. King, Jr. (I)
http://www.king.senate.gov/

Rep. Chellie Pingree (D-01)
http://pingree.house.gov/

Rep. Bruce Poliquin (D-02)
http://poliquin.house.gov/

Maryland

Sen. Benjamin L. Cardin (D)
http://www.cardin.senate.gov/

Sen. Barbara A. Mikulski (D)
http://www.mikulski.senate.gov/

Rep. Andy Harris (R-01)
http://harris.house.gov/

Rep. C. A. Dutch Ruppersberger (D-02)
http://ruppersberger.house.gov/

Rep. John P. Sarbanes (D-03)
http://sarbanes.house.gov/

Rep. Donna F. Edwards (D-04)
http://donnaedwards.house.gov/

Rep. Steny H. Hoyer (D-05)
http://hoyer.house.gov/

Rep. John Delaney (D-06)
http://delaney.house.gov/

Rep. Elijah Cummings (D-07)
http://cummings.house.gov/

Rep. Chris Van Hollen (D-08)
http://vanhollen.house.gov/

Massachusetts

Sen. Edward J. Markey (D)
http://www.markey.senate.gov/

Sen. Elizabeth Warren (D)
http://www.warren.senate.gov/

Rep. Richard E. Neal (D-01)
http://neal.house.gov/

Rep. James McGovern (D-02)
http://mcgovern.house.gov/

Rep. Niki Tsongas (D-03)
http://tsongas.house.gov/

Rep. Joseph P. Kennedy III (D-04)
http://kennedy.house.gov/

Rep. Katherine Clark (D-05)
http://katherineclark.house.gov/

Rep. Seth Moulton (D-06)
http://moulton.house.gov/

Rep. Michael E. Capuano (D-07)
http://capuano.house.gov/

Rep. Stephen F. Lynch (D-08)
http://lynch.house.gov/

Rep. William Keating (D-09)
http://keating.house.gov/

Michigan

Sen. Gary Peters (D)
http://www.peters.senate.gov/

Sen. Debbie Stabenow (D)
http://www.stabenow.senate.gov/

Rep. Dan Benishek (R-01)
http://benishek.house.gov/

Rep. Bill Huizenga (R-02)
http://huizenga.house.gov/

Rep. Justin Amash (R-03)
http://amash.house.gov/

Rep. John Moolenaar (R-04)
http://moolenaar.house.gov/

Rep. Daniel Kildee (D-05)
http://dankildee.house.gov/

Rep. Fred Upton (R-06)
http://upton.house.gov/

Rep. Tim Walberg (R-07)
http://walberg.house.gov/

Rep. Mike Bishop (R-08)
http://mikebishop.house.gov/

Rep. Sander Levin (D-09)

http://levin.house.gov/

Rep. Candice Miller (R-10)
http://candicemiller.house.gov/

Rep. Dave Trott (R-11)
http://trott.house.gov/

Rep. Debbie Dingell (D-12)
http://debbiedingell.house.gov/

Rep. John Conyers, Jr. (D-13)
http://conyers.house.gov/

Rep. Brenda Lawrence (D-14)
http://lawrence.house.gov/

Minnesota

Sen. Al Franken (D)
http://www.franken.senate.gov/

Sen. Amy Klobuchar (D)
http://www.klobuchar.senate.gov/

Rep. Timothy J. Walz (D-01)
http://walz.house.gov/

Rep. John Kline (R-02)
http://kline.house.gov/

Rep. Erik Paulsen (R-03)
http://paulsen.house.gov/

Rep. Betty McCollum (D-04)
http://mccollum.house.gov/

Rep. Keith Ellison (D-05)
http://ellison.house.gov/

Rep. Tom Emmer (R-06)
http://emmer.house.gov/

Rep. Collin C. Peterson (D-07)
http://collinpeterson.house.gov/

Rep. Rick Nolan (D-08)
http://nolan.house.gov/

Mississippi

Sen. Thad Cochran (R)
http://www.cochran.senate.gov/

Sen. Roger F. Wicker (R)
http://www.wicker.senate.gov/

Vacant, District 1

Rep. Bennie G. Thompson (D-02)
http://benniethompson.house.gov/

Rep. Gregg Harper (R-03)
http://harper.house.gov/

Rep. Steven Palazzo (R-04)
http://palazzo.house.gov/

Missouri

Sen. Roy Blunt (R)
http://www.blunt.senate.gov/

Sen. Claire McCaskill (D)
http://www.mccaskill.senate.gov/

Rep. William "Lacy" Clay, Jr. (D-01)
http://lacyclay.house.gov/

Rep. Ann Wagner (R-02)
http://wagner.house.gov/

Rep. Blaine Luetkemeyer (R-03)
http://luetkemeyer.house.gov/

Rep. Vicky Hartzler (R-04)
http://hartzler.house.gov/

Rep. Emanuel Cleaver (D-05)
http://cleaver.house.gov/

Rep. Sam Graves (R-06)
http://graves.house.gov/

Rep. Billy Long (R-07)
http://long.house.gov/

Rep. Jason Smith (R-08)
http://jasonsmith.house.gov/

Montana

Sen. Jon Tester (D)
http://www.tester.senate.gov/

Sen. Steve Daines (R)
http://www.daines.senate.gov/

Rep. Ryan Zinke (R-At Large)
http://zinke.house.gov/

Nebraska

Sen. Deb Fischer (R)
http://www.fischer.senate.gov/

Sen. Ben Sasse (R)
http://www.sasse.senate.gov/

Rep. Jeff Fortenberry (R-01)
http://fortenberry.house.gov/

Rep. Brad Ashford (D-02)
http://ashford.house.gov/

Rep. Adrian Smith (R-03)
http://www.adriansmith.house.gov/

Nevada

Sen. Dean Heller (R)
http://www.heller.senate.gov/

Sen. Harry Reid (D)
http://www.reid.senate.gov/

Rep. Dina Titus (D-01)
http://titus.house.gov/

Rep. Mark Amodei (R-02)
http://amodei.house.gov/

Rep. Joe Heck (R-03)
http://heck.house.gov/

Rep. Cresent Hardy (R-04)
http://hardy.house.gov/

New Hampshire

Sen. Kelly Ayotte (R)
http://www.ayotte.senate.gov/

Sen. Jeanne Shaheen (D)
http://www.shaheen.senate.gov/

Rep. Frank Guinta (R-01)
http://guinta.house.gov/

Rep. Ann Kuster (D-02)
http://kuster.house.gov/

New Jersey

Sen. Cory A. Booker (D)
http://www.booker.senate.gov/

Sen. Robert Menendez (D)
http://www.menendez.senate.gov/

Donald Norcross (D-01)
http://norcross.house.gov

Rep. Frank LoBiondo (R-02)
http://lobiondo.house.gov/

Rep. Tom MacArthur (R-03)

http://macarthur.house.gov/

Rep. Chris Smith (R-04)
http://chrissmith.house.gov/

Rep. Scott Garrett (R-05)
http://garrett.house.gov/

Rep. Frank Pallone, Jr. (D-06)
http://pallone.house.gov/

Rep. Leonard Lance (R-07)
http://lance.house.gov/

Rep. Albio Sires (D-08)
http://sires.house.gov/

Rep. Bill Pascrell, Jr. (D-09)
http://pascrell.house.gov/

Rep. Donald Payne, Jr. (D-10)
http://payne.house.gov/

Rep. Rodney Frelinghuysen (R-11)
http://frelinghuysen.house.gov/

Rep. Bonnie Watson Coleman
(D-12)
http://watsoncoleman.house.gov/

New Mexico

Sen. Martin Heinrich (D)
http://www.heinrich.senate.gov/

Sen. Tom Udall (D)
http://www.tomudall.senate.gov/

Rep. Michelle Lujan Grisham
(D-01)
http://lujangrisham.house.gov/

Rep. Steve Pearce (R-02)
http://pearce.house.gov/

Rep. Ben R. Lujan (D-03)
http://lujan.house.gov/

New York

Sen. Kirsten E. Gillibrand (D)
http://www.gillibrand.senate.gov/

Sen. Charles E. Schumer (D)
http://www.schumer.senate.gov/

Rep. Lee Zeldin (R-01)
http://zeldin.house.gov/

Rep. Pete King (R-02)
http://peteking.house.gov/

Rep. Steve Israel (D-03)
http://israel.house.gov/

Rep. Kathleen Rice (D-04)
http://kathleenrice.house.gov/

Rep. Gregory W. Meeks (D-05)
http://meeks.house.gov/

Rep. Grace Meng (D-06)
http://meng.house.gov/

Rep. Nydia M. Velásquez (D-07)
http://velazquez.house.gov/index.
shtml

Rep. Hakeem Jeffries (D-08)
http://jeffries.house.gov/

Rep. Yvette D. Clarke (D-09)
http://clarke.house.gov/

Rep. Jerrold Nadler (D-10)
http://nadler.house.gov/

Vacant, District 11

Rep. Carolyn Maloney (D-12)
http://maloney.house.gov/

Rep. Charles B. Rangel (D-13)
http://rangel.house.gov/

Rep. Joseph Crowley (D-14)
http://crowley.house.gov/

Rep. José E. Serrano (D-15)
http://serrano.house.gov/

Rep. Eliot Engel (D-16)
http://engel.house.gov/

Rep. Nita Lowey (D-17)
http://lowey.house.gov/

Rep. Sean Patrick Maloney (D-18)
http://seanmaloney.house.gov/

Rep. Chris Gibson (R-19)
http://gibson.house.gov/

Rep. Paul D. Tonko (D-20)
http://tonko.house.gov/

Rep. Elise Stefanik (R-21)
http://stefanik.house.gov/

Rep. Richard Hanna (R-22)
http://hanna.house.gov/

Rep. Tom Reed (R-23)
http://reed.house.gov/

Rep. John Katko (R-24)
http://katko.house.gov/

Rep. Louise Slaughter (D-25)
http://www.louise.house.gov/

Rep. Brian Higgins (D-26)
http://higgins.house.gov/

Rep. Chris Collins (R-27)
http://chriscollins.house.gov/

North Carolina

Sen. Richard Burr (R)
http://www.burr.senate.gov/

Sen. Thom Tillis (R)
http://www.tillis.senate.gov/

Rep. G.K. Butterfield (D-01)
http://butterfield.house.gov/

Rep. Renee Ellmers (R-02)
http://ellmers.house.gov/

Rep. Walter B. Jones (R-03)
http://jones.house.gov/

Rep. David Price (D-04)
http://price.house.gov/

Rep. Virginia Foxx (R-05)
http://foxx.house.gov/

Rep. Mark Walker (R-06)
http://walker.house.gov/

Rep. David Rouzer (R-07)
http://rouzer.house.gov/

Rep. Richard Hudson (R-08)
http://hudson.house.gov/

Rep. Robert Pittenger (R-09)
http://pittenger.house.gov/

Rep. Patrick T. McHenry (R-10)
http://mchenry.house.gov/

Rep. Mark Meadows (R-11)
http://meadows.house.gov/

Rep. Alma Adams (D-12)
http://adams.house.gov/

Rep. George Holding (R-13)
http://holding.house.gov/

North Dakota

Sen. Heidi Heitkamp (D)
http://www.heitkamp.senate.gov/

Sen. John Hoeven (R)
http://www.hoeven.senate.gov/

Rep. Kevin Cramer (R-At Large)
http://cramer.house.gov/

Northern Mariana Islands

Del. Gregorio Sablan (D-At Large)
http://sablan.house.gov/

Ohio

Sen. Sherrod Brown (D)
http://www.brown.senate.gov/

Sen. Rob Portman (R)
http://www.portman.senate.gov/

Rep. Steve Chabot (R-01)
http://chabot.house.gov/

Rep. Brad Wenstrup (R-02)
http://wenstrup.house.gov/

Rep. Joyce Beatty (D-03)
http://beatty.house.gov/

Rep. Jim Jordan (R-04)
http://jordan.house.gov/

Rep. Robert E. Latta (R-05)
http://latta.house.gov/

Rep. Bill Johnson (R-06)
http://billjohnson.house.gov/

Rep. Bob Gibbs (R-07)
http://gibbs.house.gov/

Rep. John A. Boehner (R-08)
http://johnboehner.house.gov/

Rep. Marcy Kaptur (D-09)
http://www.kaptur.house.gov/

Rep. Michael Turner (R-10)
http://turner.house.gov/

Rep. Marcia L. Fudge (D-11)
http://fudge.house.gov/

Rep. Pat Tiberi (R-12)
http://tiberi.house.gov/

Rep. Tim Ryan (D-13)
http://timryan.house.gov/

Rep. David Joyce (R-14)
http://joyce.house.gov/

Rep. Steve Stivers (R-15)
http://stivers.house.gov/

Rep. Jim Renacci (R-16)
http://renacci.house.gov/

Oklahoma

Sen. James Lankford (R)
http://www.lankford.senate.gov/

Sen. James M. Inhofe (R)
http://www.inhofe.senate.gov/

Rep. Jim Bridenstine (R-01)
http://bridenstine.house.gov/

Rep. Markwayne Mullin (R-02)

http://mullin.house.gov/

Rep. Frank Lucas (R-03)
http://lucas.house.gov/

Rep. Tom Cole (R-04)
http://cole.house.gov/

Rep. Steve Russell (R-05)
http://russell.house.gov/

Oregon

Sen. Jeff Merkley (D)
http://www.merkley.senate.gov/

Sen. Ron Wyden (D)
http://www.wyden.senate.gov/

Suzanne Bonamici (D-01)
http://bonamici.house.gov/

Rep. Greg Walden (R-02)
http://walden.house.gov/

Rep. Earl Blumenauer (D-03)
http://blumenauer.house.gov/

Rep. Peter DeFazio (D-04)
http://defazio.house.gov/

Rep. Kurt Schrader (D-05)
http://schrader.house.gov/

Pennsylvania

Sen. Robert P. Casey, Jr. (D)
http://www.casey.senate.gov/

Sen. Patrick J. Toomey (R)
http://www.toomey.senate.gov/

Rep. Robert Brady (D-01)
http://brady.house.gov/

Rep. Chaka Fattah (D-02)
http://fattah.house.gov/

Rep. Mike Kelly (R-03)
http://kelly.house.gov/

Rep. Scott Perry (R-04)
http://perry.house.gov/

Rep. Glenn W. Thompson (R-05)
http://thompson.house.gov/

Rep. Ryan Costello (R-06)
http://costello.house.gov/

Rep. Pat Meehan (R-07)
http://meehan.house.gov/

Rep. Michael G. Fitzpatrick (R-08)
http://fitzpatrick.house.gov/

Rep. Bill Shuster (R-09)
http://shuster.house.gov/

Rep. Tom Marino (R-10)
http://marino.house.gov/

Rep. Lou Barletta (R-11)
http://barletta.house.gov/

Rep. Keith Rothfus (R-12)
http://rothfus.house.gov/

Rep. Brendan Boyle (D-13)
http://boyle.house.gov/

Rep. Mike Doyle (D-14)
http://doyle.house.gov/

Rep. Charles W. Dent (R-15)
http://dent.house.gov/

Rep. Joseph R. Pitts (R-16)
http://pitts.house.gov/

Rep. Matthew Cartwright (D-17)
http://cartwright.house.gov/

Rep. Tim Murphy (R-18)
http://murphy.house.gov/

Puerto Rico

Del. Pedro Pierluisi (D-At Large)
http://pierluisi.house.gov/

Rhode Island

Sen. Jack Reed (D)
http://www.reed.senate.gov/

Sen. Sheldon Whitehouse (D)
http://www.whitehouse.senate.
gov/

Rep. David Cicilline (D-01)
http://cicilline.house.gov/

Rep. Jim Langevin (D-02)
http://langevin.house.gov/

South Carolina

Sen. Lindsey Graham (R)
http://www.lgraham.senate.gov/

Sen. Tim Scott (R)
http://www.scott.senate.gov/

Rep. Mark Sanford (R-01)
http://sanford.house.gov/

Rep. Joe Wilson (R-02)
http://joewilson.house.gov/

Rep. Jeff Duncan (R-03)
http://jeffduncan.house.gov/

Rep. Trey Gowdy (R-04)
http://gowdy.house.gov/

Rep. Mick Mulvaney (R-05)
http://mulvaney.house.gov/

Rep. James E. Clyburn (D-06)
http://clyburn.house.gov/

Rep. Tom Rice (R-07)
http://rice.house.gov/

South Dakota

Sen. Mike Rounds (R)
http://www.rounds.senate.gov/

Sen. John Thune (R)
http://www.thune.senate.gov/

Rep. Kristi Noem (R-At Large)
http://noem.house.gov/

Tennessee

Sen. Lamar Alexander (R)
http://www.alexander.senate.gov/

Sen. Bob Corker (R)
http://www.corker.senate.gov/

Rep. Phil Roe (R-01)
http://roe.house.gov/

Rep. John J. Duncan, Jr. (R-02)
http://duncan.house.gov/

Rep. Chuck Fleischmann (R-03)
http://fleischmann.house.gov/

Rep. Scott DesJarlias (R-04)
http://desjarlais.house.gov/

Rep. Jim Cooper (D-05)
http://cooper.house.gov/

Rep. Diane Black (R-06)
http://black.house.gov/

Rep. Marsha Blackburn (R-07)
http://blackburn.house.gov/

Rep. Stephen Fincher (R-08)
http://fincher.house.gov/

Rep. Steve Cohen (D-09)
http://cohen.house.gov/

Texas

Sen. John Cornyn (R)
http://www.cornyn.senate.gov/

Sen. Ted Cruz (R)
http://www.cruz.senate.gov/

Rep. Louie Gohmert (R-01)
http://gohmert.house.gov/

Rep. Ted Poe (R-02)
http://poe.house.gov/

Rep. Sam Johnson (R-03)
http://samjohnson.house.gov/

Rep. John Ratcliffe (R-04)
http://ratcliffe.house.gov/

Rep. Jeb Hensarling (R-05)
http://hensarling.house.gov/

Rep. Joe Barton (R-06)
http://joebarton.house.gov/

Rep. John Culberson (R-07)
http://culberson.house.gov/

Rep. Kevin Brady (R-08)
http://kevinbrady.house.gov/

Rep. Al Green (D-09)
http://algreen.house.gov/

Rep. Michael T. McCaul (R-10)
http://mccaul.house.gov/

Rep. K. Michael Conaway (R-11)
http://conaway.house.gov/

Rep. Kay Granger (R-12)
http://kaygranger.house.gov/

Rep. Mac Thornberry (R-13)
http://thornberry.house.gov/

Rep. Randy Weber (R-14)
http://weber.house.gov/

Rep. Rubén Hinojosa (D-15)
http://hinojosa.house.gov/

Rep. Beto O'Rourke (D-16)
http://orourke.house.gov/

Rep. Bill Flores (R-17)
http://flores.house.gov/

Rep. Sheila Jackson Lee (D-18)
http://jacksonlee.house.gov/

Rep. Randy Neugebauer (R-19)
http://randy.house.gov/

Rep. Joaquin Castro (D-20)
http://castro.house.gov/

Rep. Lamar Smith (R-21)
http://lamarsmith.house.gov/

Rep. Pete Olson (R-22)
http://olson.house.gov/

Rep. Will Hurd (R-23)
http://hurd.house.gov/

Rep. Kenny Marchant (R-24)
http://marchant.house.gov/

Rep. Roger Williams (D-25)
http://williams.house.gov/

Rep. Michael Burgess (R-26)
http://burgess.house.gov/

Rep. Blake Farenthold (R-27)
http://farenthold.house.gov/

Rep. Henry Cuellar (D-28)
http://cuellar.house.gov/

Rep. Gene Green (D-29)
http://green.house.gov/

Rep. Eddie Bernice Johnson (D-30)
http://ebjohnson.house.gov/

Rep. John Carter (R-31)
http://carter.house.gov/

Rep. Pete Sessions (R-32)
http://sessions.house.gov/

Rep. Marc Veasey (D-33)
http://veasey.house.gov/

Rep. Filemon Vela (D-34)
http://vela.house.gov/

Rep. Lloyd Doggett (D-35)
http://doggett.house.gov/

Rep. Brian Babin (R-36)
http://babin.house.gov/

Utah

Sen. Orrin G. Hatch (R)
http://www.hatch.senate.gov/

Sen. Mike Lee (R)
http://www.lee.senate.gov

Rep. Rob Bishop (R-01)
http://robbishop.house.gov/

Rep. Chris Stewart (R-02)
http://stewart.house.gov/

Rep. Jason Chaffetz (R-03)
http://chaffetz.house.gov/

Rep. Mia Love (R-04)
http://love.house.gov/

Vermont

Sen. Patrick J. Leahy (D)
http://www.leahy.senate.gov/

Sen. Bernard Sanders (I)
http://www.sanders.senate.gov/

Rep. Peter Welch (D-At Large)
http://www.welch.house.gov/

Virgin Islands

Rep. Stacey Plaskett (D-At Large)
http://plaskett.house.gov/

Virginia

Sen. Tim Kaine (D)
http://www.kaine.senate.gov/

Sen. Mark R. Warner (D)
http://www.warner.senate.gov/

Rep. Robert J. Wittman (R-01)
http://www.wittman.house.gov/

Rep. Scott Rigell (R-02)
http://rigell.house.gov/

Rep. Robert C. Scott (D-03)
http://www.bobbyscott.house.gov/

Rep. J. Randy Forbes (R-04)
http://forbes.house.gov/

Rep. Robert Hurt (R-05)
http://hurt.house.gov/

Rep. Bob Goodlatte (R-06)
http://goodlatte.house.gov/

Rep. Dave Brat (R-07)
http://brat.house.gov/

Rep. Don Beyer (D-08)
http://beyer.house.gov/

Rep. Morgan Griffith (R-09)
http://morgangriffith.house.gov/

Rep. Barbara Comstock (R-10)
http://comstock.house.gov/

Rep. Gerald E. "Gerry" Connolly
(D-11)
http://connolly.house.gov/

Washington

Sen. Maria Cantwell (D)
http://www.cantwell.senate.gov/

Sen. Patty Murray (D)
http://www.murray.senate.gov/

Rep. Suzan DelBene (D-01)
http://delbene.house.gov/

Rep. Rick Larsen (D-02)
http://larsen.house.gov/

Rep. Jaime Herrera Beutler (R-03)
http://herrerabeutler.house.gov/

Rep. Dan Newhouse (R-04)
http://newhouse.house.gov/

Rep. Cathy McMorris Rodgers (R-05)
http://mcmorris.house.gov/

Rep. Derek Kilmer (D-06)
http://kilmer.house.gov/

Rep. Jim McDermott (D-07)
http://mcdermott.house.gov/

Rep. David G. Reichert (R-08)
http://reichert.house.gov/

Rep. Adam Smith (D-09)
http://adamsmith.house.gov/

Rep. Denny Heck (D-10)
http://dennyheck.house.gov/

West Virginia

Sen. Joe Manchin III (D)
http://www.manchin.senate.gov/

Sen. Shelley Moore Capito (R)
http://www.capito.senate.gov/

Rep. David McKinley (R-01)
http://mckinley.house.gov/

Rep. Alex Mooney (R-02)
http://mooney.house.gov/

Rep. Evan Jenkins (D-03)
http://evanjenkins.house.gov/

Wisconsin

Sen. Tammy Baldwin (D)
http://www.baldwin.senate.gov/

Sen. Ron Johnson (R)
http://www.ronjohnson.senate.gov/

Rep. Paul Ryan (R-01)
http://paulryan.house.gov/

Rep. Mark Pocan (D-02)
http://pocan.house.gov/

Rep. Ron Kind (D-03)
http://kind.house.gov/

Rep. Gwen Moore (D-04)
http://gwenmoore.house.gov/

Rep. F. James Sensenbrenner (R-05)
http://sensenbrenner.house.gov/

Rep. Glenn Grothman (R-06)
http://grothman.house.gov/

Rep. Sean P. Duffy (R-07)
http://duffy.house.gov/

Rep. Reid Ribble (R-08)
http://ribble.house.gov/

Wyoming

Sen. John Barrasso (R)
http://www.barrasso.senate.gov/

Sen. Michael B. Enzi (R)
http://www.enzi.senate.gov/

Rep. Cynthia M. Lummis
(R-At Large)
http://lummis.house.gov/

Appendix B

Congressional Committees

This appendix lists the committees and related Web sites for the 114th Congress's House, Senate, and Joint committees.

United States House of Representatives
    http://www.house.gov/

Standing Committees

Committee on Agriculture
    http://agriculture.house.gov/
    Chairman: K. Michael Conway (R), Texas
    Ranking Member: Collin C. Peterson (D), Minnesota

Committee on Appropriations
    http://appropriations.house.gov/
    Chairman: Harold Rogers (R), Kentucky
    Ranking Member: Nita Lowey (D), New York

Committee on Armed Services
    http://armedservices.house.gov/
    Chairman: Mac Thornberry (R), Texas
    Ranking Member: Adam Smith (D), Washington

Committee on the Budget
    http://budget.house.gov/
    Chairman: Tom Price (R), Georgia
    Ranking Member: Chris Van Hollen (D), Maryland

Committee on Education and the Workforce
    http://edworkforce.house.gov/
    Chairman: John Kline (R), Minnesota
    Ranking Member: Robert "Bobby" Scott (D), Virginia

Committee on Energy and Commerce
  http://energycommerce.house.gov/
  Chairman: Fred Upton (R), Michigan
  Ranking Member: Frank Pallone, Jr. (D), New Jersey

Committee on Ethics
  http://ethics.house.gov/
  Chairman: Charles W. Dent (R), Pennsylvania
  Ranking Member: Linda T. Sánchez (D), California

Committee on Financial Services
  http://financialservices.house.gov/
  Chairman: Jeb Hensarling (R), Texas
  Ranking Member: Maxine Waters (D), California

Committee on Foreign Affairs
  http://foreignaffairs.house.gov/
  Chairman: Edward R. Royce (R), California
  Ranking Member: Eliot Engel (D), New York

Committee on Homeland Security
  http://homeland.house.gov/
  Chairman: Michael McCaul (R), Texas
  Ranking Member: Bennie G. Thompson (D), Mississippi

Committee on House Administration
  http://cha.house.gov/
  Chairman: Candice Miller (R), Michigan
  Ranking Member: Robert Brady (D), Pennsylvania

Committee on the Judiciary
  http://judiciary.house.gov/
  Chairman: Bob Goodlatte (R), Virginia
  Ranking Member: John Conyers, Jr., (D), Michigan

Committee on Natural Resources
  http://naturalresources.house.gov/
  Chairman: Rob Bishop (R), Utah
  Ranking Member: Raul Grijalva (D), Arizona

Committee on Oversight and Government Reform
  http://oversight.house.gov/
  Chairman: Jason Chaffetz (R), Utah
  Ranking Member: Elijah Cummings (D), Maryland

Committee on Rules
http://www.rules.house.gov/
Chairman: Pete Sessions (R), Texas
Ranking Member: Louise Slaughter (D), New York

Committee on Science, Space, and Technology
http://science.house.gov/
Chairman: Lamar Smith (R), Texas
Ranking Member: Eddie Bernice Johnson (D), Texas

Committee on Small Business
http://smallbusiness.house.gov/
Chairman: Steve Chabot (R), Ohio
Ranking Member: Nydia M. Velázquez (D), New York

Committee on Transportation and Infrastructure
http://transportation.house.gov/
Chairman: Bill Shuster (R), Pennsylvania
Ranking Member: Peter A. DeFazio (D), Oregon

Committee on Veterans' Affairs
http://veterans.house.gov/
Chairman: Jeff Miller (R), Florida
Ranking Member: Corinne Brown (D), Florida

Committee on Ways and Means
http://waysandmeans.house.gov/
Chairman: Paul Ryan (R), Wisconsin
Ranking Member: Sander Levin (D), Michigan

Select and Special Committees

House Permanent Select Committee on Intelligence
http://intelligence.house.gov/
Chairman: Devin Nunes (R), California
Ranking Member: Adam Schiff (D), California

United States Senate
http://www.senate.gov/

Standing Committees

Committee on Agriculture, Nutrition, and Forestry
http://www.agriculture.senate.gov/
Chairman: Pat Roberts (R), Kansas

Vice Chairman: Debbie Stabenow (D), Michigan

Committee on Appropriations
http://appropriations.senate.gov/
Chairman: Thad Cochran (R), Mississippi
Vice Chairman: Barbara Mikulski (D), Maryland

Committee on Armed Services
http://armed-services.senate.gov/
Chairman: John McCain (R), Arizona
Vice Chairman: Jack Reed (D), Rhode Island

Committee on Banking, Housing, and Urban Affairs
http://banking.senate.gov/public/
Chairman: Richard Shelby (R), Alabama
Vice Chairman: Sherrod Brown (D), Ohio

Committee on the Budget
http://budget.senate.gov/
Chairman: Mike Enzi (R), Wyoming
Vice Chairman: Bernie Sanders (I), Vermont

Committee on Commerce, Science, and Transportation
http://commerce.senate.gov/public/
Chairman: John Thune (R), South Dakota
Vice Chairman: Bill Nelson (D), Florida

Committee on Energy and Natural Resources
http://energy.senate.gov/public/
Chairman: Lisa Murkowski (R), Alaska
Vice Chairman: Maria Cantwell (D), Washington

Committee on Environment and Public Works
http://epw.senate.gov/
Chairman: Jim Inhofe (R), Oklahoma
Vice Chairman: Barbara Boxer (D), California

Committee on Finance
http://finance.senate.gov/
Chairman: Orrin G. Hatch (R), Utah
Vice Chairman: Ron Wyden (D), Oregon

Committee on Foreign Relations
  http://foreign.senate.gov/
  Chairman: Bob Corker (R), Tennessee
  Vice Chairman: Ben Cardin (D), Maryland

Committee on Health, Education, Labor, and Pensions
  http://help.senate.gov/
  Chairman: Lamar Alexander (R), Tennessee
  Vice Chairman: Patty Murray, (D), Washington

Committee on Homeland Security and Governmental Affairs
  http://www.hsgac.senate.gov/
  Chairman: Ron Johnson (R), Wisconsin
  Vice Chairman: Thomas Carper (D), Delaware

Committee on the Judiciary
  http://judiciary.senate.gov/
  Chairman: Chuck Grassley (R), Iowa
  Vice Chairman: Patrick J. Leahy, (D) Vermont

Committee on Rules and Administration
  http://rules.senate.gov/public/
  Chairman: Roy Blunt (R), Missouri
  Vice Chairman: Charles E. Schumer (D), New York

Committee on Small Business and Entrepreneurship
  http://sbc.senate.gov/public/
  Chairman: David Vitter (R), Louisiana
  Vice Chairman: Jeanne Shaheen (D), New Hampshire

Committee on Veterans' Affairs
  http://veterans.senate.gov/
  Chairman: Johnny Isakson (R), Georgia
  Vice Chairman: Richard Blumenthal (D), Connecticut

Special, Select, and Other Committees

Committee on Indian Affairs
  http://indian.senate.gov/
  Chairman: John Barrasso (R), Wyoming
  Vice Chairman: Jon Tester (D), Montana

Select Committee on Ethics
http://ethics.senate.gov/public/
Chairman: Johnny Isakson (R), Georgia
Vice Chairman: Barbara Boxer (D), California

Select Committee on Intelligence
http://intelligence.senate.gov/
Chairman: Richard Burr (R), North Carolina
Vice Chairman: Dianne Feinstein (D), California

Special Committee on Aging
http://aging.senate.gov/
Chairman: Susan Collins (R), Maine
Vice Chairman: Claire McCaskill (D), Missouri

Joint Committees

Joint Committee on Printing
http://cha.house.gov/jointcommittees/joint-committee-on-printing
Chairman: Charles Schumer (D), New York
Vice Chairman: Gregg Harper (R), Mississippi

Joint Committee on Taxation
https://www.jct.gov/
Chairman: Paul Ryan (R), Wisconsin
Vice Chairman: Orrin G. Hatch (R), Utah

Joint Committee on the Library
http://cha.house.gov/jointcommittees/joint-committee-library
Chairman: Gregg Harper (R), Mississippi
Vice Chairman: Charles E. Schumer (D), New York

Joint Economic Committee
http://jec.senate.gov/public/
Chairman: Daniel Coats (R), Indiana
Vice Chairman: Carolyn B. Maloney (D), New York

Appendix C

U.S. Embassies Abroad

NOTE: Countries with which the United States does not have diplomatic relations are noted. Consulate offices are not included. Countries that share an embassy have the embassy country location clearly marked. Information is from http://www.usembassy.gov/, a State Department Web site.

A

Afghanistan (Kabul)
http://kabul.usembassy.gov/
Ambassador: P. Michael McKinley

Albania (Tirana)
http://tirana.usembassy.gov/
Ambassador: Donald Lu

Algeria (Algiers)
http://algiers.usembassy.gov/
Ambassador: Joan A. Polaschik

Angola (Luanda)
http://angola.usembassy.gov/
Ambassador: Helen Meagher La Lime

Antigua and Barbuda
(Bridgetown, Barbados)
http://barbados.usembassy.gov/
Ambassador: Larry L. Palmer

Argentina (Buenos Aires)
http://argentina.usembassy.gov/
Ambassador: Noah B. Mamet

Armenia (Yerevan)
http://armenia.usembassy.gov/
Ambassador: Richard M. Mills, Jr.

Australia (Canberra)
http://canberra.usembassy.gov/
Ambassador: John Berry

Austria (Vienna)
http://austria.usembassy.gov/
Ambassador: Alexa Wesner

Azerbaijan (Baku)
http://azerbaijan.usembassy.gov/
Ambassador: Robert F. Cekuta

B

Bahamas, The (Nassau)
http://nassau.usembassy.gov/
Ambassador: Lisa A. Johnson
(chargé d'affaires, a.i.)

Bahrain (Manama)
http://bahrain.usembassy.gov/
Ambassador: William V. Roebuck

Bangladesh (Dhaka)
http://dhaka.usembassy.gov/

Ambassador: Marcia Stephens Bloom Bernicat

Barbados (Bridgetown)
http://barbados.usembassy.gov/
Ambassador: Larry L. Palmer

Belarus (Minsk)
http://minsk.usembassy.gov/
Ambassador: Scott Rauland
(chargé d'affaires, a.i.)

Belgium (Brussels)
http://belgium.usembassy.gov/
Ambassador: Denise Campbell Bauer

Belize (Belmopan)
http://belize.usembassy.gov/
Ambassador: Carlos R. Moreno

Benin (Cotonou)
http://cotonou.usembassy.gov/
Ambassador: Michael Raynor

Bhutan (New Delhi, India)
http://newdelhi.usembassy.gov/
Ambassador: Richard R. Verma

Bolivia (La Paz)
http://bolivia.usembassy.gov/
Ambassador: Peter M. Brennan
(chargé d'affaires, a.i.)

Bosnia and Herzegovina (Sarajevo)
http://sarajevo.usembassy.gov/
Ambassador: Maureen Cormack

Botswana (Gaborone)
http://botswana.usembassy.gov/
Ambassador: Michelle Gavin

Brazil (Brasilia)
http://brazil.usembassy.gov/
Ambassador: Liliana Ayalde

Brunei (Bandar Seri Begawan)
http://brunei.usembassy.gov/
Ambassador: Craig Allen

Bulgaria (Sofia)
http://bulgaria.usembassy.gov/
Ambassador: Marcie Ries

Burkina Faso (Ouagadougou)
http://ouagadougou.usembassy.gov/
Ambassador: Tulinabo S. Mushingi

Burma (Rangoon)
http://burma.usembassy.gov/
Ambassador: Derek J. Mitchell

Burundi (Bujumbura)
http://burundi.usembassy.gov/
Ambassador: Dawn M. Liberi

C

Cambodia (Phnom Penh)
http://cambodia.usembassy.gov/
Ambassador: William E. Todd

Cameroon (Yaounde)
http://yaounde.usembassy.gov/
Ambassador: Michael S. Hoza

Canada (Ottawa)
http://canada.usembassy.gov/
Ambassador: Bruce Heyman

Cape Verde (Praia)
http://praia.usembassy.gov/
Ambassador: Donald L. Heflin

Central African Republic (Bangui)
http://bangui.usembassy.gov/
Ambassador: David Brown (chargé d'affaires, a.i.)

Chad (N'Djamena)
http://ndjamena.usembassy.gov/
Ambassador: James Knight

Chile (Santiago)
http://chile.usembassy.gov/
Ambassador: Michael A. Hammer

China (Beijing)
http://beijing.usembassy-china.org.
cn/
Ambassador: Max Sieben Baucus

Colombia (Bogota)
http://bogota.usembassy.gov/
Ambassador: Kevin Whitaker

Congo, Democratic Republic of the
(Kinshasa)
http://kinshasa.usembassy.gov/
Ambassador: James C. Swan

Congo, Republic of the
(Brazzaville)
http://brazzaville.usembassy.gov/
Ambassador: Stephanie S. Sullivan

Costa Rica (San Jose)
http://costarica.usembassy.gov/
Ambassador: Roy Perrin (chargé
d'affaires, a.i.)

Cote d'Ivoire (Abidjan)
http://abidjan.usembassy.gov/
Ambassador: Terence P. McCulley

Croatia (Zagreb)
http://zagreb.usembassy.gov/
Ambassador: Kenneth Merten

Cuba (United States Interest Page)
http://havana.usint.gov/
Chief of Mission: Jeffrey DeLau-
rentis

Please note: According to the Web
site, "The functions of USINT are
similar to those of any U.S. government presence abroad: Consular
Services, a Political and Economic
Section, a Public Diplomacy Program, and Refugee Processing
unique to Cuba. The objectives of
USINT in Cuba are for rule of law,
individual human rights and open
economic and communication systems. Bilateral relations are based
upon the Migration Accords designed to promote safe, legal and
orderly migration, the Interests
Section Agreement, and efforts to
reduce global threats from crime
and narcotics."

Curacao (Mission to the Dutch
Caribbean)
http://curacao.usconsulate.gov/
Consul General: James R. Moore

Cyprus (Nicosia)
http://cyprus.usembassy.gov/
Ambassador: John M. Koenig

Czech Republic (Prague)
http://prague.usembassy.gov/
Ambassador: Andrew H. Schapiro

D
Denmark (Copenhagen)
http://denmark.usembassy.gov/
Ambassador: Rufus Gifford

Djibouti (Djibouti)
http://djibouti.usembassy.gov/
Ambassador: Tom Kelly

Dominica (Bridgetown, Barbados)
http://barbados.usembassy.gov/
Ambassador: Larry L. Palmer

Dominican Republic
(Santo Domingo)
http://santodomingo.usembassy.
gov/
Ambassador: James (Wally)
Brewster

E
Ecuador (Quito)
http://ecuador.usembassy.gov/
Ambassador: Adam E. Namm

Egypt (Cairo)
http://egypt.usembassy.gov/
Ambassador: R. Steven Beecroft

El Salvador (San Salvador)
http://sansalvador.usembassy.gov/
Ambassador: Mari Carmen Aponte

Equatorial Guinea (Malabo)
http://malabo.usembassy.gov/
Ambassador: Mark L. Asquino

Eritrea (Asmara)
http://eritrea.usembassy.gov/
Ambassador: Louis Mazel (chargé
d'affaires, a.i.)

Estonia (Tallinn)
http://estonia.usembassy.gov/
Ambassador: Jeff Levine

Ethiopia (Addis Ababa)
http://ethiopia.usembassy.gov/
Ambassador: Patricia M. Haslach

F
Fiji (Suva)
http://suva.usembassy.gov/
Ambassador: Judith Beth Cefkin

Finland (Helsinki)
http://finland.usembassy.gov/
Ambassador: Bruce J. Oreck

France (Paris)
http://france.usembassy.gov/
Ambassador: Jane D. Hartley

G
Gabon (Libreville)
http://libreville.usembassy.gov/
Ambassador: Cynthia Akuetteh

Gambia, The (Banjul)
http://banjul.usembassy.gov/
Ambassador: George Staples (chargé d'affaires, a.i.)

Georgia (Tbilisi)
http://georgia.usembassy.gov/
Ambassador: Richard Norland

Germany (Berlin)
http://germany.usembassy.gov/
Ambassador: John B. Emerson

Ghana (Accra)
http://ghana.usembassy.gov/
Ambassador: Gene A. Cretz

Greece (Athens)
http://athens.usembassy.gov/
Ambassador: David D. Pearce

Grenada (Bridgetown, Barbados)
http://barbados.usembassy.gov/
Ambassador: Larry L. Palmer

Guatemala (Guatemala City)
http://guatemala.usembassy.gov/
Ambassador: Todd D. Robinson

Guinea (Conakry)
http://conakry.usembassy.gov/
Ambassador: Mark Laskaris

Guinea-Bissau (Virtual Presence
Post)
http://guinea-bissau.usvpp.gov/

Ambassador: James P. Zumwalt (also Ambassador to Senegal)

Guyana (Georgetown)
http://georgetown.usembassy.gov/
Ambassador: Bryan D. Hunt (chargé d'affaires, a.i.)

H

Haiti (Port-au-Prince)
http://haiti.usembassy.gov/
Ambassador: Pamela A. White

Honduras (Tegucigalpa)
http://honduras.usembassy.gov/
Ambassador: James D. Nealon

Hong Kong
http://hongkong.usconsulate.gov/
Consul General: Clifford A. Hart, Jr.

Hungary (Budapest)
http://hungary.usembassy.gov/
Ambassador: Colleen Bradley Bell

I

Iceland (Reykjavik)
http://iceland.usembassy.gov/
Ambassador: Robert C. Barber

India (New Delhi)
http://newdelhi.usembassy.gov/
Ambassador: Richard R. Verma

Indonesia (Jakarta)
http://jakarta.usembassy.gov/
Ambassador: Robert O. Blake, Jr.

Iran (Virtual Embassy)
http://iran.usembassy.gov/
Please note: The United States does not currently have diplomatic relations with Iran.

Iraq
http://iraq.usembassy.gov/
Ambassador: Stuart E. Jones

Ireland (Dublin)
http://dublin.usembassy.gov/
Ambassador: Kevin F. O'Malley

Israel (Tel Aviv)
http://israel.usembassy.gov/
Ambassador: Daniel B. Shapiro

Italy (Rome)
http://italy.usembassy.gov/
Ambassador: John Phillips

J

Jamaica (Kingston)
http://kingston.usembassy.gov/
Ambassador: Luis G. Moreno

Japan (Tokyo)
http://japan.usembassy.gov/
Ambassador: Caroline Bouvier Kennedy

Jordan (Amman)
http://jordan.usembassy.gov/
Ambassador: Alice G. Wells

K

Kazakhstan (Astana)
http://kazakhstan.usembassy.gov/
Ambassador: George A. Krol

Kenya (Nairobi)
http://nairobi.usembassy.gov/
Ambassador: Robert F. Godec

Korea, North
Please note: The United States does not have diplomatic relations with North Korea.

Korea, South
http://seoul.usembassy.gov/
Ambassador: Mark Lippert

Kosovo (Pristina)
http://pristina.usembassy.gov/
Ambassador: Tracey Ann Jacobson

Kuwait (Kuwait City)
http://kuwait.usembassy.gov/
Ambassador: Douglas A. Silliman

Kyrgyz Republic (Bishkek)
http://bishkek.usembassy.gov/
Ambassador: Richard M. Miles
(chargé d'affaires, a.i.)

L
Laos (Vientiane)
http://laos.usembassy.gov/
Ambassador: Daniel A. Clune

Latvia (Riga)
http://riga.usembassy.gov/
Ambassador: Sharon Hudson-Dean (chargé d'affaires, a.i.)

Lebanon (Beirut)
http://lebanon.usembassy.gov/
Ambassador: David Hale

Lesotho (Maseru)
http://maseru.usembassy.gov/
Ambassador: Matthew T. Harrington

Liberia (Monrovia)
http://monrovia.usembassy.gov/
Ambassador: Deborah R. Malac

Libya (Tripoli)
http://libya.usembassy.gov/
Ambassador: Deborah K. Jones

Lithuania (Vilnius)
http://vilnius.usembassy.gov/
Ambassador: Deborah A. McCarthy

Luxembourg (Luxembourg)
http://luxembourg.usembassy.gov/
Ambassador: Alison Shorter-Lawrence (chargé d'affaires, a.i.)

M
Macau
http://hongkong.usconsulate.gov/
Consul General: Clifford A. Hart, Jr.

Macedonia (Skopje)
http://macedonia.usembassy.gov/
Ambassador: Jess L. Bailey

Madagascar (Antananarivo)
http://www.antananarivo.usembassy.gov/
Ambassador: Robert T. Yamate

Malawi (Lilongwe)
http://lilongwe.usembassy.gov/
Ambassador: Virginia Palmer

Malaysia (Kuala Lumpur)
http://malaysia.usembassy.gov/
Ambassador: Joseph Y. Yun

Maldives (included in Sri Lanka)
http://srilanka.usembassy.gov/
Ambassador: Andrew (Drew) C. Mann (chargé d'affaires, a.i.)

Mali (Bamako)
http://mali.usembassy.gov/
Ambassador: Andrew Young (chargé d'affaires, a.i.)

Malta (Valletta)
http://malta.usembassy.gov/

Ambassador: Gina Abercrombie-Winstanley

Marshall Islands (Majuro)
http://majuro.usembassy.gov/
Ambassador: Thomas Hart Armbruster

Mauritania (Nouakchott)
http://mauritania.usembassy.gov/
Ambassador: Larry E. André, Jr.

Mauritius (Port Louis)
http://mauritius.usembassy.gov/
Ambassador: Shari Villarosa

Mexico (Mexico City)
http://mexico.usembassy.gov/
Ambassador: Earl Anthony "Tony" Wayne

Micronesia, Federated States of (Kolonia)
http://kolonia.usembassy.gov/
Ambassador: Dorothea-Maria (Doria) Rosen

Moldova (Chisinau)
http://moldova.usembassy.gov/
Ambassador: James D. Pettit

Mongolia (Ulaanbaatar)
http://mongolia.usembassy.gov/
Ambassador: Piper Anne Wind Campbell

Montenegro (Podgorica)
http://podgorica.usembassy.gov/
Ambassador: Margaret Ann Uyehara
Morocco (Rabat)

http://morocco.usembassy.gov/
Ambassador: Dwight L. Bush, Sr.

Mozambique (Maputo)
http://maputo.usembassy.gov/
Ambassador: Douglas M. Griffiths

N
Namibia (Windhoek)
http://windhoek.usembassy.gov/
Ambassador: Thomas F. Daughton

Nepal (Kathmandu)
http://nepal.usembassy.gov/
Ambassador: Peter W. Bodde

Netherlands, The (The Hague)
http://thehague.usembassy.gov/
Ambassador: Timothy Broas

New Zealand (Wellington)
http://newzealand.usembassy.gov/
Ambassador: Mark Gilbert

Nicaragua (Managua)
http://nicaragua.usembassy.gov/
Ambassador: Phyllis M. Powers

Niger (Niamey)
http://niamey.usembassy.gov/
Ambassador: Eunice S. Reddick

Nigeria (Abuja)
http://nigeria.usembassy.gov/
Ambassador: James F. Entwistle

Norway (Oslo)
http://norway.usembassy.gov/
Ambassador: Julie   Furuta-Toy
(chargé d'affaires, a.i.)

O

Oman (Muscat)
http://oman.usembassy.gov/
Ambassador: Greta C. Holtz

P

Pakistan (Islamabad)
http://islamabad.usembassy.gov/
Ambassador: Richard Olson

Palau, Republic of
http://palau.usembassy.gov/
Ambassador: Amy J. Hyatt

Panama (Panama City)
http://panama.usembassy.gov/
Ambassador: Jonathan D. Farrar

Papua New Guinea (Port Moresby)
http://portmoresby.usembassy.
gov/
Ambassador: Walter North

Paraguay (Asuncion)
http://paraguay.usembassy.gov/
Ambassador: James H. Thessin

Peru (Lima)
http://lima.usembassy.gov/
Ambassador: Brian A. Nichols

Philippines (Manila)
http://manila.usembassy.gov/
Ambassador: Philip S. Goldberg

Poland (Warsaw)
http://poland.usembassy.gov/
Ambassador: Stephen Mull

Portugal (Lisbon)
http://portugal.usembassy.gov/
Ambassador: Robert A. Sherman

Q

Qatar (Doha)
http://qatar.usembassy.gov/
Ambassador: Dana Shell Smith

R

Romania (Bucharest)
http://romania.usembassy.gov/
Ambassador: Dean   Thompson
(chargé d'affaires, a.i.)

Russia (Moscow)
http://moscow.usembassy.gov/
Ambassador: John F. Tefft

Rwanda (Kigali)
http://rwanda.usembassy.gov/
Ambassador: Erica J. Barks-Ruggles

S

Saint Kitts and Nevis(Bridgetown, Barbados)
http://barbados.usembassy.gov/
Ambassador: Larry L. Palmer

Saint Lucia (Bridgetown, Barbados)
http://barbados.usembassy.gov/
Ambassador: Larry L. Palmer

Saint Vincent and the Grenadines (Bridgetown, Barbados)
http://barbados.usembassy.gov/
Ambassador: Larry L. Palmer

Samoa (Apia)
http://samoa.usembassy.gov/
Ambassador: Mark Gilbert

Saudi Arabia (Riyadh)
http://riyadh.usembassy.gov/
Ambassador: Joseph Westphal

Senegal (Dakar)
http://dakar.usembassy.gov/
Ambassador: James P. Zumwalt

Serbia (Belgrade)
http://serbia.usembassy.gov/
Ambassador: Michael D. Kirby

Seychelles (Virtual Presence Post)
http://seychelles.usvpp.gov/
Ambassador: Shari Villarosa

Sierra Leone (Freetown)
http://freetown.usembassy.gov/
Ambassador: John Hoover

Singapore (Singapore)
http://singapore.usembassy.gov/
Ambassador: Kirk Wagar

Slovakia (Bratislava)
http://slovakia.usembassy.gov/
Ambassador: Theodore Sedgwick

Slovenia (Ljubljana)
http://slovenia.usembassy.gov/
Ambassador: Brent R. Hartley

Solomon Islands (Port Moresby, Papua New Guinea)
http://portmoresby.usembassy.gov/
Ambassador: Walter North

Somalia (Virtual Presence Post)
http://somalia.usvpp.gov/
U.S. Special Representative for Somalia: James P. McAnulty

South Africa (Pretoria)
http://southafrica.usembassy.gov/
Ambassador: Patrick H. Gaspard

South Sudan (Juba)
http://southsudan.usembassy.gov/

Ambassador: Charles Twining (chargé d'affaires, a.i.)

Spain(Madrid)
http://madrid.usembassy.gov/
Ambassador: James Costos

Sri Lanka (Colombo)
http://srilanka.usembassy.gov/
Ambassador: Andrew (Drew) C. Mann (chargé d'affaires, a.i.)

Sudan (Khartoum)
http://sudan.usembassy.gov/
Deputy Chief of Mission: Jerry P. Lanier (chargé d'affaires, a.i.)

Suriname (Paramaribo)
http://suriname.usembassy.gov/
Ambassador: Jay N. Anania

Swaziland(Mbabane)
http://swaziland.usembassy.gov/
Ambassador: Makila James

Sweden (Stockholm)
http://sweden.usembassy.gov/
Ambassador: Mark F. Brzezinski

Switzerland (Bern)
http://bern.usembassy.gov/
Ambassador: Suzan G. LeVine

Syria (Damascus)
http://damascus.usembassy.gov/
Ambassador: Daniel Rubinstein (special envoy)

T
Taiwan
Please note: According to the Web site, "The U.S. maintains unofficial relations with the people of Taiwan through the American Institute in Taiwan (AIT), a private nonprofit

corporation, which performs citizen and consular services similar to those at diplomatic posts. See AIT's website www.ait.org.tw/en/ for details."

Tajikistan (Dushanbe)
http://dushanbe.usembassy.gov/
Ambassador: Susan M. Elliott

Tanzania (Dar es Salaam)
http://tanzania.usembassy.gov/
Deputy Chief of Mission: Mark Childress

Thailand (Bangkok)
http://bangkok.usembassy.gov/
Ambassador: W. Patrick Murphy (chargé d'affaires, a.i.)

Timor-Leste (Dili)
http://timor-leste.usembassy.gov/
Ambassador: Karen Stanton

Togo (Lome)
http://togo.usembassy.gov/
Ambassador: Robert E. Whitehead

Trinidad and Tobago (Port of Spain)
http://trinidad.usembassy.gov/
Ambassador: Margaret B. Diop (chargé d'affaires, a.i.)

Tunisia (Tunis)
http://tunisia.usembassy.gov/
Ambassador: Jake Walles

Turkey (Ankara)
http://turkey.usembassy.gov/
Ambassador: John Bass

Turkmenistan (Ashgabat)
http://turkmenistan.usembassy.gov/

Ambassador: Allan Phillip Mustard

U
Uganda (Kampala)
http://kampala.usembassy.gov/
Ambassador: Scott DeLisi

Ukraine (Kyiv)
http://ukraine.usembassy.gov/
Ambassador: Geoffrey R. Pyatt

United Arab Emirates (Abu Dhabi)
http://abudhabi.usembassy.gov/
Ambassador: Barbara A. Leaf

United Kingdom (London)
http://london.usembassy.gov/
Ambassador: Matthew W. Barzun

Uruguay (Montevideo)
http://uruguay.usembassy.gov/
Ambassador: Brad Freden (chargé d'affaires, a.i.)

U.S. Mission to the African Union
http://www.usau.usmission.gov/
Ambassador: Reuben Brigety

U.S. Mission to ASEAN
http://asean.usmission.gov/
Ambassador: Nina Hachigian

U.S. Mission to the ICAO
http://icao.usmission.gov/
Ambassador: Michael A. Lawson

U.S. Mission to International Organization in Vienna
http://vienna.usmission.gov/
Ambassador: Laura E. Kennedy (chargé d'affaires, a.i)

U.S. Mission to the EU
http://useu.usmission.gov/

Ambassador: Anthony L. Gardner

U.S. Mission to the NATO
http://nato.usmission.gov/
Ambassador: Douglas Lute

U.S. Mission to the the OAS
http://www.usoas.usmission.gov/
Ambassador: Michael J. Fitzpatrick
(interim U.S. Permanent Representative)

U.S. Mission to the OECD
http://usoecd.usmission.gov/
Ambassador: Daniel W. Yohannes

U.S. Mission to the OSCE
http://osce.usmission.gov/
Ambassador: Daniel Baer

U.S. Mission to the U.N.: Geneva
http://geneva.usmission.gov/
Ambassador: Pamela Hamamoto

U.S. Mission to the U.N.: New York
http://www.usunnewyork.usmission.gov/
Ambassador: Samantha Power

U.S. Mission to the U.N.: Rome
http://usunrome.usmission.gov/
Ambassador: David Lane

U.S. Mission to UNESCO
http://unesco.usmission.gov/
Ambassador: Crystal Nix-Hines

Uzbekistan (Tashkent)
http://uzbekistan.usembassy.gov/
Ambassador: Pamela L. Spratlen

V
Vanuatu (Port Moresby, Papua New Guinea)
http://portmoresby.usembassy.gov/
Ambassador: Walter North

Vatican, The (Holy See)
http://vatican.usembassy.gov/
Ambassador: Kenneth F. Hackett

Venezuela (Caracas)
http://caracas.usembassy.gov/
Ambassador: Lee McClenny
(chargé d'affaires, a.i.)

Vietnam (Hanoi)
http://vietnam.usembassy.gov/
Ambassador: Ted Osius

Y
Yemen (Sana'a)
http://yemen.usembassy.gov/
Ambassador: Matthew H. Tueller

Z
Zambia (Lusaka)
http://zambia.usembassy.gov/
Ambassador: Eric T. Schultz

Zimbabwe(Harare)
http://harare.usembassy.gov/
Ambassador: David Bruce Wharton

Appendix D

Foreign Embassies in the United States

Web sites are from http://www.state.gov/s/cpr/rls/dpl/32122.htm. List of ambassadors is from http://www.state.gov/s/cpr/rls/dpl/101885.htm.

A

Afghanistan
http://www.
embassyofafghanistan.org/
Ambassador: Eklil Ahmad Hakimi

African Union:
Ambassador: Amina Salum Ali

Albania
http://www.embassyofalbania.org
Ambassador: Mamica Toska

Algeria
http://www.algerianembassy.org/
Ambassador: Mohamed Yazid Boudiz

Andorra
Ambassador: Narcis Casal de Fonsdeviela

Angola
http://www.angola.org/
Ambassador: Agostinho Tavares da Silva Neto

Antigua and Barbuda
Ambassador: Joy Dee Samantha Davis (chargé d'affaires, a.i.)

Argentina
http://www.embajadaargentina-usa.org
Ambassador: Maria Cecilia Nahon

Armenia
http://www.usa.mfa.am
Ambassador: Tigran Sargsyan

Australia
http://www.usa.embassy.gov.au/
Ambassador: Kim Christian Beazley

Austria
http://www.austria.org
Ambassador: Hans Peter Manz

Azerbaijan
http://www.azembassy.us/
Ambassador: Elin Emin Oglu Suleymanov

B

Bahamas, The
Ambassador: Eugene Glenwood Newry

Bahrain
http://www.bahrainembassy.org/

621

Ambassador: Abudlla Mohamed Alkhalifa

Bangladesh
http://www.bdembassyusa.org/
Ambassador: Mohammad Ziauddin

Barbados
Ambassador: John Ernest Beale

Belarus
http://www.belarusembassy.org/
Ambassador: Pavel Shidlovsky

Belgium
http://www.diplobel.us/
Ambassador: Johan Cecilia Verbeke

Belize
http://www.embassyofbelize.org/
Ambassador: Nestor Enrique Mendez

Benin
http://www.beninembassy.us/
Ambassador: Omar Arouna

Bolivia
http://www.bolivia-usa.org/
Ambassador: Freddy Bersatti Tudela

Bosnia and Herzegovina
http://www.bhembassy.org/
Ambassador: Jadranka Negodic

Botswana
http://www.botswanaembassy.org/
Ambassador: Emolemo Morake

Brazil
http://www.brasilemb.org/
Ambassador: Ernesto Henrique Fraga Araujo

Brunei
http://www.bruneiembassy.org/
Ambassador: DK Nor Hashimah PG MD Hassan

Bulgaria
http://www.bulgaria-embassy.org/
Ambassador: Elena B. Poptodorova Petrova

Burkina Faso
http://www.burkina-usa.org/
Ambassador: Seydou Sinka

Burma
Ambassador: Kyaw Myo Htut

Burundi
http://www.burundiembassy-usa.org/
Counselor: Ernest Ndabashinze

C
Cambodia
http://www.embassyofcambodia.org/
Ambassador: Heng Hem

Cameroon
http://www.ambacam-usa.org/
Ambassador: Bienvenu Joseph C. Foe Atangana

Canada
http://www.canadianembassy.org
http://www.ambassadeducanada.org
Ambassador: Gary Albert Doer

Cape Verde
http://www.
capeverdeusaembassy.org
Ambassador: Jose Luis Fialho Rocha

Central African Republic
Ambassador: Stanislas Moussa Kembe

Chad
Ambassador: Hassane Mahamat Nasser

Chile
http://www.chile-usa.org/
Ambassador: Juan Gabriel Valdes Soublette

China
http://www.china-embassy.org/eng/
Ambassador: Tiankai Cui

Colombia
http://www.colombiaemb.org/
Ambassador: Luis Carlos Villegas Echeverri

Comoros
Ambassador: Mohamed Soilihi Soilih

Congo, Democratic Republic of the
Ambassador: Faida Maramuke Mitifu

Congo, Republic of the
Ambassador: Serge Mombouli

Costa Rica
http://www.costarica-embassy.org/
Ambassador: Roman Macaya Hayes

Cote d'Ivoire
Ambassador: Daouda Diabate

Croatia
http://us.mvep.hr/en/
Ambassador: Josip Paro

Cyprus
http://www.cyprusembassy.net/home/
Ambassador: Georgios Chacalli

Czech Republic
http://www.mzv.cz/washington/
Ambassador: Petr Gandalovic

D
Denmark
http://www.ambwashington.um.dk
Ambassador: Peter Taskoe Jensen

Djibouti
Ambassador: Roble Olhaye

Dominica
embdomdc@aol.com
Ambassador: Hubert John Charles

Dominican Republic
http://www.domrep.org/
Ambassador: Jose Thomas Perez Vasquez

E
Ecuador
http://www.ecuador.org
Ambassador: Saskia Nathalie Cely Suarez

Egypt
http://www.egyptembassy.net/
Ambassador: Mohamed Mostafa Mohamed Tawfik

El Salvador
http://www.elsalvador.org/
Ambassador: Francisco R. Altschul
Fuentes

Equatorial Guinea
Ambassador: Roman Obama Ekua

Eritrea
Ambassador: Berhane Gebrehiwet
Solomon

Estonia
http://www.estemb.org/
Ambassador: Eerik Marmei

Ethiopia
http://www.ethiopianembassy.org/
index.shtml
Ambassador: Girma Birru Geda

European Union
http://www.eurunion.org
Ambassador: David O. Sullivan

F
Fiji
http://www.fijiembassydc.com/
Ambassador: Winston Thompson

Finland
http://www.finland.org
Ambassador: Ritva Inkeri Koukku
Ronde

France
http://www.info-france-usa.org
Ambassador: Gerard Roger Araud

G
Gabon
http://www.gabonembassyusa.org
Ambassador: Michael   Moussa
Adamo

Gambia, The
http://www.gambiaembassy.us/
Ambassador: Sheikh Omar Faye

Georgia
http://usa.mfa.gov.ge
Ambassador: Archil Gegeshidze

Germany
http://www.germany.info/
Ambassador: Niels Peter Georg
Ammon

Ghana
http://www.ghanaembassy.org/
Ambassador: Joseph Henry Smith

Greece
http://www.mfa.gr/usa/en/
Ambassador: Christos Panagopou-
los

Grenada
http://www.grenadaembassyusa.
org/
Ambassador: Ethelstan Angus
Friday

Guatemala
http://www.guatemala-embassy.
org
Ambassador: Julio Ligorria Carbal-
lido

Guinea
http://www.pngembassy.org/
Ambassador: Mamady Conde

Guinea-Bissau
Ambassador: Vacant

Guyana
http://www.guyana.org
Ambassador: Bayney Ram Karran

H

Haiti
http://www.haiti.org/
Ambassador: Paul Getty Altidor

Holy See
http://www.holyseemission.org/
Ambassador: Carlo Maria Vigano

Honduras
http://www.hondurasemb.org/
Ambassador: Jorge Alberto Milla Reyes

Hungary
http://washington.kormany.hu/
Ambassador: Peter Kalotai

I

Iceland
http://www.iceland.org/us
Ambassador: Geir Hilmar Haarde

India
http://www.indianembassy.org
Ambassador: Subrahmanyam Jaishankar

Indonesia
http://www.embassyofindonesia.org/
Ambassador: Budi Bowolesksono

Iraq
http://www.iraqiembassy.org/
Ambassador: Lukman Abdulraheem A. Al Faily

Ireland
http://www.irelandemb.org/
Ambassador: Anne Anderson

Israel
http://www.israelemb.org/
Ambassador: Ron Dermer

Italy
http://www.ambwashingtondc.esteri.it/ambasciata_washington
Ambassador: Claudio Bisogniero

J

Jamaica
http://www.jamaicanconsulatechicago.org/
Ambassador: Stephen Charles Vasciannie

Japan
http://www.embjapan.org
Ambassador: Kenichiro Sasae

Jordan
http://www.jordanembassyus.org
Ambassador: Alia Mohamad Ali Hatough Bouran

K

Kazakhstan
http://www.kazakhembus.com /
Ambassador: Kairat Umarov

Kenya
http://www.kenyaembassy.com/
Ambassador: Robinson Njeru Githae

Kiribati
Ambassador: Makurita Baaro

Korea, South
http://usa.mofa.go.kr/english/am/usa/main/
Ambassador: Ho Young Ahn

Kosovo
http://ambasada-ks.net/us/
Ambassador: Akan Ismaili

Kuwait
Ambassador: Sheikh Salem Abdullah Al Jaber Alsabah

Kyrgyz Republic
http://www.kyrgyzembassy.org/
Ambassador: Mukhamed Lou

L
Laos
http://www.laoembassy.com/
Ambassador: Seng Soukhathivong

Latvia
http://www.mfa.gov.lv/en/usa
Ambassador: Andris Razans

Lebanon
http://www.lebanonembassyus.org/
Ambassador: Antoine Chedid

Lesotho
http://www.lesothoemb-usa.gov.ls/
Ambassador: Eliachim Molapi Sebatane

Liberia
http://www.embassyofliberia.org/
Ambassador: Jeremiah Conbegh Sulunteh

Libya
Ambassador: Wafa M. T. Bughaighis (chargé d'affaires, a.i.)

Liechtenstein
http://www.liechtensteinusa.org/
Ambassador: Claudia Fritsche

Lithuania
http://usa.mfa.lt/usa/en/
Ambassador: Zygmantas Pavilionis

Luxembourg
http://washington.mae.lu/en
Ambassador: Jean Louis Wolzfeld

M
Macedonia
http://www.missions.gov.mk/
Ambassador: Vasko Naumovski

Madagascar
Malagasy@embassy.org
Ambassador: Velotiana Rakotoanosy Raobelina

Malawi
http://www.malawiembassy-dc.org/
Ambassador: Stephen Dick Tennyson Matenje

Malaysia
malwashdc@kln.gov.my
Ambassador: Awang Adek Bin Hussin

Maldives
http://www.maldivesembassy.us
Ambassador: Ahmed Sareer

Mali
http://www.maliembassy.us/
Ambassador: Tiena Coulibaly

Malta
http://www.magnet.mt
First Secretary and Consul: Marisa Maria Louis Micallef

Marshall Islands
http://www.rmiembassyus.org/
Ambassador: Charles Rudolph Paul

Mauritania
Ambassador: Mohamed Lemine El Haycen

Mauritius
http://www.maurinet.com
Ambassador: Hans Irvin Antish Bhugun

Mexico
http://embamex.sre.gob.mx/eua/index.php/es
Ambassador: Eduardo Tomas Medina Mora Icaza

Micronesia, Federated States of
http://www.fsmembassydc.org/
Ambassador: Asterio R. Takesy

Moldova
http://www.sua.mfa.md
Ambassador: Igor Munteanu

Monaco
http://www.monaco-usa.org
Ambassador: Maguy Maccario Doyle

Mongolia
http://www.mongolianembassy.us/default.php
Ambassador: Altangerel Bulgaa

Montenegro
Ambassador: Srdan Darmanovic

Morocco
http://www.embassyofmorocco.us/
Ambassador: Mohammed Rachad Bouhlal

Mozambique
http://www.embamoc-usa.org/
Ambassador: Amelia Narciso Matos Sumbana

N

Namibia
http://www.namibianembassyusa.org/
Ambassador: Martin Andjaba

Nauru
Ambassador: Marlene Inemwin Moses

Nepal
http://www.nepalembassyusa.org/
Ambassador: Rishi Ram Ghmire

Netherlands
http://www.netherlands-embassy.org
Ambassador: Rudolf Simon Bekink

New Zealand
http://www.nzembassy.com/
Ambassador: Michael Kenneth Moore

Nicaragua
Ambassador: Francisco Obadiah Campbell Hooker

Niger
http://www.embassyofniger.org/
Ambassador: Moussa Rilla Boubacar

Nigeria
http://www.nigeriaembassyusa.org/
Ambassador: Adebowale Ibidapo Adefuye

Norway
http://www.norway.org/
Ambassador: Kaare Reidar Aas

O

Oman
Ambassador: Hunaina Sultan Ahmed Al Mughairy

P

Pakistan
Ambassador: Jalil Abbas Jilani

Palau
Ambassador: Hersey Kyota

Panama
http://www.embassyofpanama.org/
Ambassador: Emanuel A. Gonzalez Revilla Lince

Papua New Guinea
http://www.pngembassy.org/
Ambassador: Rupa Abraham Mulina

Paraguay
Ambassador: Igor Alberto Pangrazio Vera

Peru
http://www.peruvianembassy.us
Ambassador: Luis Miguel Castilla Rubio

Philippines
http://www.philippineembassy-usa.org/
Ambassador: Jose Jr Lampe Cuisia

Poland
http://www.polandembassy.org/
Ambassador: Ryszard Marian Schnepf

Portugal
http://www.embassyportugal-us.org/

Ambassador: Nuno F. Alves Salvador E Brito

Q

Qatar
http://www.qatarembassy.net/
Ambassador: Mohamed Jamin Al Kuwari

R

Romania
http://www.roembus.org/
Ambassador: Iulian Buga

Russia
http://www.russianembassy.org/
Ambassador: Sergey Ivanovich Kislyak

Rwanda
http://www.rwandemb.org/rwanda/
Ambassador: Mathilde Mukantabana

S

Saint Kitts and Nevis
Ambassador: Jacinth Lorna Henry Martin

Saint Lucia
Ambassador: Elizabeth Darius Clarke

Saint Vincent and the Grenadines
http://www.embsvg.com/
Ambassador: La Celia Aritha Prince

Samoa
Ambassador: Aliioaiga Feturi Elisaia

San Marino
http://www.embassypages.com/
sanmarino
Ambassador: Paolo Rondelli

Saudi Arabia
http://www.saudiembassy.net/
Ambassador: Adel A.M. Al Jubeir

Senegal
Ambassador: Babcar Diagne

Serbia
http://www.serbiaembusa.org/
Ambassador: Derd Matkovic

Seychelles
seychelles@un.int
Ambassador: Marie Louise Cecile
Potter

Sierra Leone
http://embassyofsierraleone.net/
Ambassador: Bockari Kortu Stevens

Singapore
http://www.mfa.gov.sg/
washington/
Ambassador: Ashok Kumar

Slovakia
http://www.mzv.sk
Ambassador: Peter Kmec

Slovenia
Ambassador: Bozo Cerar

Solomon Islands
Ambassador: Collin David Beck

South Africa
http://www.saembassy.org
Ambassador: Mninwa Johannes
Mahlangu

South Sudan
Ambassador: Baak Valentino Akol
Wol

Spain
www.spainemb.org
Ambassador: Ramon Gil Casares
Satrustegui

Sri Lanka
http://www.slembassyusa.org/
Ambassador: Prasad Kariywasam

Sudan
Minister: Maowia Osman Khalid
Mohammed (chargé d'affaires, a.i.)

Suriname
http://www.surinameembassy.org/
Ambassador: Subhas Chandra
Mungra

Swaziland
http://www.gov.sz/
Ambassador: Abednego Mandla
Ntshangase

Sweden
http://www.swedenabroad.com
Ambassador: Bjoern Olof Lyrvall

Switzerland
http://www.swissemb.org
Ambassador: Martin Werner Dahinden

Syria
http://www.syrianembassy.us
Ambassador: Vacant

T

Taiwan
Please note: According to the Web
site http://www.usembassy.gov/,
"The U.S. maintains unofficial rela-

tions with the people of Taiwan through the American Institute in Taiwan (AIT), a private nonprofit corporation, which performs citizen and consular services similar to those at diplomatic posts. See AIT's website www.ait.org.tw/en/ for details."

Tajikistan
http://www.tjus.org/
Ambassador: Farhod Salim

Tanzania
http://www.tanzaniaembassy-us.org/
Ambassador: Liberata Rutageruka Mulamula

Thailand
http://www.thaiembdc.org/
Ambassador: Vijavat Isarabhakdi

Timor-Leste
http://www.timorlesteembassy.org/
Ambassador: Domingos Sarmento Alves

Togo
Ambassador: Edawe Limbiye Kadangha Bariki

Tonga
Ambassador: Mahe Uliuli Sandhurst Tupouniua

Trinidad and Tobago
Ambassador: Neil Nadesh Parsan

Tunisia
http://tunisia.usembassy.gov/
Ambassador: Mhamed Ezzine Chelaifa

Turkey
http://www.turkey.org
Ambassador: Serdar Kilic

Turkmenistan
http://www.turkmenistanembassy.org/
Ambassador: Meret Bairamovich Orazov

Tuvalu
Ambassador: Aunese Makoi Simati

U
Uganda
http://www.ugandaembassy.com/
Ambassador: Oliver Wonekha

Ukraine
http://www.usa.mfa.gov.ua
Ambassador: Olexander Motsyk

United Arab Emirates
http://uae-embassy.org/
Ambassador: Yousif Mana Saeed Alotaiba

United Kingdom
http://www.gov.uk/
Ambassador: Peter John Westmacott

Uruguay
http://www.uruwashi.org/
Ambassador: Juan Carlos Pita Alvariza

Uzbekistan
http://www.uzbekistan.org/
Ambassador: Baktiya Turadjanovich Gulyamov

V

Venezuela
http://www.embavenez-us.org
Ambassador: Maximilien Sanchez
Arvelaiz

Vietnam
http://www.vietnamembassy-usa.
org/
Ambassador: Vinh Quang Pham

Y

Yemen
http://www.yemenembassy.org/
Counselor: Adel Ali Ahmed Alsu-
naini

Z

Zambia
http://www.zambiaembassy.org/
Ambassador: Palan Mulonda

Zimbabwe
http://www.zimbabwe-embassy.
us/
Ambassador: Ammon Mutembwa

Index